W. H. AUDEN

PROSE

VOLUME VI: 1969–1973

THE COMPLETE
WORKS OF

W. H. AUDEN

POEMS

PLAYS (WITH CHRISTOPHER ISHERWOOD)

LIBRETTI (WITH CHESTER KALLMAN)

PROSE

W. H. AUDEN

PROSE

VOLUME VI

□

1969–1973

EDITED BY

Edward Mendelson

PRINCETON UNIVERSITY
PRESS

Published by Princeton University Press, 41 William Street,
Princeton, New Jersey, 08540

In the United Kingdom: Princeton University Press, 6 Oxford Street,
Woodstock, Oxfordshire OX20 1TW

Library of Congress Catalog Card Number 2007920515
ISBN-13: 978-0-691-16458-8
This book has been composed in New Baskerville

Printed on acid-free paper.
press.princeton.edu

Printed in the United States of America
2 4 6 8 10 9 7 5 3 1

CONTENTS

FOREWORDS AND AFTERWORDS

ADDENDA TO PREVIOUS VOLUMES

APPENDICES

TEXTUAL NOTES

PREFACE

THIS volume, the eighth to be published in a complete edition of Auden's works, includes the essays, reviews, and other prose that he published or prepared for publication from 1969 until his death in 1973. It is published simultaneously with *Prose, Volume V: 1963–1968*, because Auden's work in prose from 1963 through 1973, although too large for a single volume, is best understood as a single body of work. The remaining volumes in the edition will contain his complete poems. The volumes published earlier in this edition contain his complete plays, libretti, and other dramatic writings, and his prose works and travel books written from 1926 through 1962. The texts throughout this edition are, wherever possible, newly edited from Auden's manuscripts, and the notes report variant readings from all published editions.

An introduction to both Volume V and the present volume appears in Volume V.

ACKNOWLEDGEMENTS

THE TEXT and notes in this volume have benefitted from the learning and intelligence of John Fuller, Nicholas Jenkins, and many other colleagues and friends. The entire edition continues to be based ultimately on years of research by B. C. Bloomfield, followed by many more years of his advice. For help with major and minor problems I am grateful to the late Alan Ansen, R. Sherman Beattie, the late John Bodley, Thekla Clark, the late Valerie Eliot, Alan Jacobs, Samuel Hynes, the late Sir Frank Kermode, the late Charles Monteith, Elisabeth Sifton, Alexander McCall Smith, and Robert Wilson.

Much of my work on this volume was conducted in the generous company of librarians and curators. I am indebted above all to Isaac Gewirtz, Stephen Crook, and Philip Milito at the Henry W. and Albert A. Berg Collection of the New York Public Library; the curators and staff of all the many departments of the Columbia University Library; Stephen Enniss, David Faulds, and David Young at the Emory University Library; and the expert staff of the BBC Written Archives Centre. I am grateful for courtesies received from librarians and curators at the American Academy of Arts and Letters, the British Library Sound Archive, Edinburgh University Library, Harvard College Library, the Library of Congress, the New York Public Library Manuscripts and Archives Division, the Paley Center for Media, Princeton University Library, Sussex University Library, Syracuse University Library, and the Yale University Library.

Auden's readers will share my continuing gratitude to Jan Lilly for the clarity and elegance of her design for this edition and to Princeton University Press for the intelligence and care with which it has published this and all previous volumes.

THE TEXT OF THIS EDITION

THIS VOLUME includes the prose that Auden wrote for publication from 1969 until his death in 1973. Auden compiled *A Certain World* mostly in 1968, revised it in 1969, and published it in 1970. My excuse for including it in this volume is that it was not finished until 1969, but the more compelling reason is that it would have made Volume V impossibly large.

Two prose pieces written by Auden and Chester Kallman for the première of their opera *Love's Labour's Lost* may be found in this edition in the volume titled *Libretti*. These pieces are "Love's Labour's Lost as a Libretto" and "Labour of Love".

An essay that appeared in 1969, "The Greatest of the Monsters", was written earlier and may be found in *Prose V*. An essay that appeared in 1970, "L'Homme d'Esprit" (Auden's introduction to *Analects*, by Paul Valéry), was written in 1955 and may be found in *Prose III*.

Some of Auden's prose pieces were originally printed exactly as he wrote them; others were cut and reshaped by editors; and it is often impossible to say how closely a printed text represents what Auden wrote. In the few instances where a manuscript exists, and where the printed version closely resembles it, the text in this edition has been newly edited from the manuscript. In all other cases, the printed text has been reprinted with a minimum of regularization, and I have not tried to impose consistency on spelling or punctuation. With the exception of a bracketed editorial reconstruction in a previously unpublished piece (p. 645), all footnotes and square brackets in the main text are Auden's own. Auden's manuscripts generally indicate footnotes with asterisks, and these have been used in place of the numbers added by some editors and publishers.

Many of the reviews and some of the essays in this volume were almost certainly given their titles by the editors of the magazines and books in which they appeared. Subtitles and breaks that were obviously inserted by newspaper and magazine subeditors in order to break up long columns of type have been omitted; such subtitles and breaks appeared in almost all of Auden's work that first appeared in newspapers or in *Encounter* and some other magazines. At the head of each book review is a listing in a consistent format of the title, author, publisher, and price of the book reviewed. The format of these headings in the original publications varied according to the style sheets of the magazines and newspapers where the reviews appeared; some magazines used footnotes instead of headings.

The essays and reviews are arranged as closely as possible in chronological order of composition. In most cases, however, no direct evidence of the date of composition survives, and chronological order of publication has been used instead. The original date and place of publication is printed at the end of each work, together with the date of composition when this is known to have been much earlier than the publication date. The dates in the running heads are dates of composition, if known.

Auden almost invariably made minor errors when copying extracts from other authors. The text in this volume corrects the obvious misspellings that the original editors could reasonably be expected to have caught, but in all other instances I have preferred to print the text that Auden wrote instead of the text that he perhaps ought to have written. The text that Auden wrote includes the words that he thought he found on the page from which he was copying, which was not always the text that was in fact printed there. I have, however, corrected errors that are clearly the work of a typist or compositor working from Auden's hand. The textual notes indicate all significant deviations from the originals.

Auden subdivided many of his essays by using headings and outline levels. The indents and spacing in this edition have been very slightly regularized. In some instances, the punctuation of outline numbers has been changed from a style evidently introduced by a publisher to a style that more closely represents the typical punctuation in Auden's prose manuscripts. Auden generally circled the numbers and letters of his outline headings; these circles are represented here by pairs of parentheses, thus: (1). Where a surviving typescript has only a closing parenthesis after a number in a heading, an opening parenthesis has been added.

Some of the daily newspapers and weekly magazines to which Auden contributed were edited hurriedly, and I have in rare instances silently supplied a comma where the original has an incomplete pair of commas around a subordinate clause, and have made other similarly trivial corrections. In some of his manuscripts Auden inconsistently used double quotation marks to set off quoted extracts and single quotation marks to set off concepts and abstractions; every competent editor normalized the inconsistency by using the same style of quotation marks for both extracts and concepts. I have normalized the rare instances where Auden's practice slipped through to the printed text, but have indicated these instances in the notes. Substantial emendations are listed in the textual notes.

The textual notes also explain some references that would have been familiar to Auden's contemporaries but are now obscure, and provide brief accounts of the magazines to which Auden contributed; more detail is provided for lesser-known publications than for familiar ones, and little or no description is provided for magazines described in notes to earlier volumes.

A CERTAIN WORLD

A Certain World
A Commonplace Book

[*1970*]

FOR
GEOFFREY GRIGSON

FOREWORD

Biographies of writers, whether written by others or themselves, are always superfluous and usually in bad taste. A writer is a maker, not a man of action. To be sure, some, in a sense all, of his works are transmutations of his personal experiences, but no knowledge of the raw ingredients will explain the peculiar flavor of the verbal dishes he invites the public to taste: his private life is, or should be, of no concern to anybody except himself, his family and his friends.

I realize, however, that this compilation is a sort of autobiography. As Chesterton wrote:

> There is at the back of every artist's mind something like a pattern or a type of architecture. The original quality in any man of imagination is imagery. It is a thing like the landscape of his dreams; the sort of world he would like to make or in which he would wish to wander; the strange flora and fauna of his own secret planet; the sort of thing he likes to think about. This general atmosphere, and pattern or structure of growth, governs all his creations, however varied.

Here, then, is a map of my planet. Certain features are, deliberately or necessarily, missing. There are, for example, hardly any references to music, which is very important to me. Aside from purely technical analysis, nothing can be *said* about music, except when it is bad; when good, one can only listen and be grateful.

Then, much as we should all like to, none of us can preserve our personal planet as an unsullied Eden. According to our time and place, unpleasant facts from the world we all share in common keep intruding, matters about which either we are compelled, against our will, to think or we feel it our duty to think, though in such matters nobody can tell another what his duty is. The bulk of this book will, I hope, make pleasant reading, but there are some entries which will, I trust, disturb a reader as much as they disturb me.

I have tried to keep my own reflections (the unsigned entries) to a minimum, and let others, more learned, intelligent, imaginative, and witty than I, speak for me.

W. H. A.

ACCIDIE

Our sixth contending is with that which the Greeks called ακηδία and which we may describe as tedium or perturbation of heart. It is akin to dejection and especially felt by wandering monks and solitaries, a persistent and obnoxious enemy to such as dwell in the desert, disturbing the monk especially about midday, like a fever mounting at a regular time, and bringing its highest tide of inflammation at definite accustomed hours to the sick soul. And so some of the Fathers declare it to be the demon of noontide which is spoken of in the Ninety-first Psalm.

When this besieges the unhappy mind, it begets aversion from the place, boredom with one's cell, and scorn and contempt for one's brethren, whether they be dwelling with one or some way off, as careless and unspiritually minded persons. Also, towards any work that may be done within the enclosure of our own lair, we become listless and inert. It will not suffer us to stay in our cell, or to attend to our reading: we lament that in all this while, living in the same spot, we have made no progress, we sigh and complain that bereft of sympathetic fellowship we have no spiritual fruit; and bewail ourselves as empty of all spiritual profit, abiding vacant and useless in this place; and we that could guide others and be of value to multitudes have edified no man, enriched no man with our precept and example. We praise other and far distant monasteries, describing them as more helpful to one's progress, more congenial to one's soul's health. . . . Towards eleven o'clock or midday it induces such lassitude of body and craving for food as one might feel after the exhaustion of a long journey and hard toil, or the postponing of a meal throughout a two or three days' fast. Finally one gazes anxiously here and there, and sighs that no brother of any description is to be seen approaching: one is for ever in and out of one's cell, gazing at the sun as though it were tarrying to its setting: one's mind is an irrational confusion, like the earth befogged in a mist, one is slothful and vacant in every spiritual activity, and no remedy, it seems, can be found for this state of siege than a visit from some brother, or the solace of sleep.

—*The Desert Fathers* (trans. Helen Waddell)

ACRONYMS

The Oxford English Dictionary does not recognize this term for a typical modern horror. As the author of the following poem says:

Anyone who reads the newspapers these days has to have a basic vocabulary of spare-part words like UNO and NATO (though the French, with characteristic awkwardness, of course, spell them backwards—ONU, OTAN), plus their specialized cousins like UNESCO, WHO, and GATT.

The massive congestion of linguistic traffic by these spare-part vehicles called acronyms is an entirely modern development, a product of our technological age that the developing nations have readily adopted, even though they are still short of more tangible forms of communication like telephones.

Intercom in Nasakom

"Euratom!" cried the Oiccu, sly and nasa,
"I'll wftu in the iscus with my gatt."
"No! No!" the Eldo pleaded, pale with asa.
"My unctad strictly nato on comsat."

The Oiccu gave a wacy little intuc,
He raft and waved his anzac oldefo.
"Bea imf!" he eec, a smirk upon his aituc,
And smote the Eldo on his ganefo.

The Eldo drew his udi from its cern,
He tact his unicet with fearless fao.
The Oiccu swerved but could not comintern;
He fell afpro, and dying moaned, "Icao!"

The moon came up above the gasbiindo,
The air no longer vip with intercom.
A creeping icftu stirred the maphilindo
And kami was restored to Nasakom.

"O kappi gum!" the fifa sang in cento,
"O cantat till the neddy unficyp."
The laser song re-echoed through the seato,
As the Eldo radar home to unmogip.

—Towyn Mason

Aging

I was both the youngest child and the youngest grandchild in my family. Being a fairly bright boy, I was generally the youngest in my school class. The result of this was that, until quite recently, I have always assumed that, in any gathering, I was the youngest person present. It was not that I imagined myself to be younger in years than I actually was, a fatal delusion in a writer: I simply thought of others as older. It is only in the last two or three years that I have begun to notice, to my surprise, that most of the people I see on the streets are younger than I. For the first time, too, though still in good health, I am almost able to believe that I shall die.

After a certain age, the more one becomes oneself, the more obvious one's family traits become.

—M. Proust

. . . As the time of rest, or of departure, approaches me, not only do many of the evils I had heard of, and prepared for, present themselves in more grievous shapes than I had expected; but one which I had scarcely ever heard of, torments me increasingly every hour.

I had understood it to be in the order of things that the aged should lament their vanishing life as an instrument they had never used, now to be taken from them; but not as an instrument, only then perfectly tempered and sharpened, and snatched out of their hands at the instant they could have done some real service with it. Whereas, my own feeling, now, is that everything which has hitherto happened to me, or been done by me, whether well or ill, has been fitting me to take greater fortune more prudently, and do better work more thoroughly. And just when I seem to be coming out of school—very sorry to have been such a foolish boy, yet having taken a prize or two, and expecting to enter now upon some more serious business than cricket,—I am dismissed by the Master I hoped to serve, with a—"That's all I want of you, sir."

—Ruskin

The young man is deliberately odd and prides himself on it; the old man is unintentionally so, and it mortifies him.

Nothing is more beautiful than cheerfulness in an old face.

—J. P. Richter

Old age lives minutes slowly, hours quickly; childhood chews hours and swallows minutes.

—Malcolm de Chazal

It does not become a man of years to follow the fashion, either in his thinking or his dress.

—Goethe

After the age of eighty, all contemporaries are friends.

—Mme De Nino

Twenty Years Ago

O, the rain, the weary, dreary rain,
How it plashes on the window sill!
Night, I guess too, must be on the wane,
Strass and Gass around are grown so still,
Here I sit, with coffee in my cup—
Ah, 'twas rarely I beheld it flow
In the taverns where I used to sup
Twenty golden years ago.

Twenty years ago, alas!—but stay,
  On my life, 'tis half-past twelve o'clock!
After all, the hours do slip away—
  Come, here goes to burn another block!
For the night, or morn, is wet and cold,
  And my fire is dwindling rather low:—
I had fire enough, when young and bold,
  Twenty golden years ago!

Dear! I don't feel well at all, somehow:
  Few in Weimar dream how bad I am;
Floods of tears grow common with me now,
  High-Dutch floods that Reason cannot dam.
Doctors think I'll neither live nor thrive
  If I mope at home so—I don't know—
Am I living *now*? I *was* alive
  Twenty golden years ago.

Wifeless, friendless, flagonless, alone,
  Not quite bookless, though, unless I chuse,
Left with nought to do, except to groan,
  Not a soul to woo, except the Muse—
O! this, this is hard for *me* to bear,
  Me, who whilome lived so much *en haut*,
Me, who broke all hearts like chinaware
  Twenty golden years ago.

. . .

Tick-tick, tick-tick!—Not a sound save Time's,
  And the windgust, as it drives the rain—
Tortured torturer of reluctant rhymes,
  Go to bed, and rest thine aching brain!
Sleep! no more the dupe of hopes or schemes;
  Soon thou sleepest where the thistles blow—
Curious anticlimax to thy dreams
  Twenty golden years ago.

—J. C. Mangan

Venus and John Gower

Halvinge of scorn, sche seide thus:
"Thou wost wel that I am Venus,
Which al only my lustes seche;
And wel I wot, thogh thou beseche
My love, lustes ben ther none,

Whiche I may take in thy persone;
For loves lust and lockes hore
In chambre acorden nevermore,
And thogh thou feigne a yong corage,
It scheweth wel be the visage
That olde grisel is no fole;
Ther ben ful manye yeeres stole
With thee and with suche othre mo,
That outward feignen youthe so
And ben withinne of pore assay
'Min herte wolde and I ne may'
Is noght beloved nowadayes;
Er thou make eny such assayes
To love, and faile upon the fet,
Betre is to make a beau retret;
For thogh thou mightest love atteigne,
Yit were it bot an idel peine,
Whan that thou art noght sufficant
To holde love his covenant.
Forthy tak hom thin herte ayein,
That thou travaile noght in vein,
Whereof my Court may be deceived.
I wot and have it wel conceived,
How that thy will is good ynough;
Bot more behoveth to the plough,
Wherof thee lacketh, as I trowe:
So sitte it wel that thou beknowe
Thy fieble astat, er thou beginne
Thing wher thou might non ende winne.
What bargain scholde a man assaye,
Whan that him lacketh forto paye?
My sone, if thou be wel bethoght,
This toucheth thee; foryet it noght:
The thing is torned into was;
That which was whilom grene gras,
Is weiked hey at time now.
Forthy my conseil is that thou
Remembre wel how thou art old."
 Whan Venus hath hir tale told,
And I bethoght was al aboute,
Tho wiste I wel without doute
That ther was no recoverir;

And as a man the blase of fir
With water quencheth, so ferd I;
A cold me caughte sodeinly,
For sorwe that min herte made,
My dedly face pale and fade
Becam, and swoune I fell to grounde. . . .

Bot Venus wente noghte therfore,
Ne Genius, whiche thilke time
Abiden bothe faste by me
And sche which may the hertes binde
In loves cause and ek unbinde,
Er I out of my trance aros,
Venus, which hield a boiste clos,
And wolde noght I scholde deye,
Tok out—more cold than eny keye—
An oignement, and in such point
Sche hath my wounded herte enoignt,
My temples and my reins also.
And forth withal sche tok me tho
A wonder mirour forto holde,
In whiche sche bad me to beholde
And taken hiede of that I sighe;
Wherinne anon min hertes yghe
I caste, and sigh my colour fade,
Min yghen dimme and al unglade,
My chiekes thinne, and al my face
With elde I mighte se deface,
So riveled and so wo-besein,
That ther was nothing full ne plein;
I sigh also min heres hore.
My will was tho to se no more. . . .

Venus behield me than and lough,
And axeth as it were in game,
What love was: and I for schame
Ne wiste what I scholde answere;
And natheles I gan to swere
That be my trouthe I knew him noght;
So ferr it was out of my thoght,
Right as it hadde nevere be.
"My goode sone," thou quod sche,
"Now at this time I lieve it wel,

So goth the fortune of my whiel;
Forthy my conseil is thou leve."

"Ma dame," I seide, "be your leve,
Ye witen wel, and so wot I,
That I am unbehovely
Your Court fro this day forth to serve:
And for I may no thonk deserve,
And also for I am refused,
I preye you to ben excused
And natheles as for the laste,
Whil that my wittes with me laste,
Touchende my confession
I axe an absolucioun
Of Genius, er that I go."
The prest anon was redy tho,
And seide, "Sone, as of thy schrifte
Thou hast ful pardoun and foryifte;
Foryet it thou, and so wol I."
"Min holy fader, grant mercy,"
Quod I to him, and to the queene
I fell on knes upon the grene,
And tok my leve forto wende.
Bot sche, that wolde make an ende,
As therto which I was most able,
A peire of bedes blak as sable
Sche tok and heng my necke aboute;
Upon the gaudes al without
Was write of gold, *Por Reposer.*
"Lo," thus sche seide, "John Gower,
Now thou art ate laste cast,
This have I for thin ese cast,
That thou no more of love sieche.
Bot my will is that thou besieche
And prey hierafter for thee pes,
And that thou make a plein reles
To love, which taketh litel hiede
Of olde men upon the nede,
Whan that the lustes ben aweye:
Forthy to thee nis bot o weye,
In which let reson be thy guide;
For he may sone himself misguide
That seth noght the peril tofore.
My sone, be wel war therfore,

And kep the sentence of my lore,
And tarye thou my Court no more. . . .

For in the lawe of my commune
We be noght schape to comune,
Thyselfe and I, nevere after this.
Now have I said al that ther is
Of love as for thy final ende:
Adieu, for I mot fro thee wende."
And with that word al sodeinly,
Enclosed in a sterred sky,
Venus, which is the queene of love,
Was take into hire place above,
More wist I noght where sche becam.
And thus my leve of hire I nam,
And forth withal the same tide
Hire prest, which wolde noght abide,
Or be me lief or be me loth,
Out of my sighte forth he goth,
And I was left withouten helpe.
So wiste I noght whereof to yelpe,
Bot only that I hadde lore
My time, and was sory therfore,
And thus bewhaped in my thoght.
Whan al was turned into noght,
I stod amased for a while,
And in myself I gan to smile
Thenkende upon the bedes blake,
And how they weren me betake,
For that I schulde bidde and preye.
And whanne I sigh no othre weye,
Bot only that I was refused,
Unto the lif which I hadde used
I thoghte never torne ayein:
And in this wise, soth to sein,
Homward a softe pas I wente.

—John Gower

Algebra

Algebra reverses the relative importance of the factors in ordinary language. It is essentially a written language, and it endeavors to exemplify in its written structures the patterns which it is its purpose to convey. The pattern of the marks on paper is a particular instance of the pattern to be conveyed to thought. The algebraic method is our best approach to the expression of necessity, by reason of its reduction of accident to the ghostlike character of the real variable.

—A. N. Whitehead

Strictly speaking, the nought ought to be eliminated from algebra. Algebra and money are essentially levellers; the first intellectually, the second effectively.

—Simone Weil

David Hartley offered a vest-pocket edition of his moral and religious philosophy in the formula $W = F^2/L$, where W is the love of the world, F is the fear of God, and L is the love of God. It is necessary to add only this. Hartley said that as one grows older L increases and indeed becomes infinite. It follows then that W, the love of the world, decreases and approaches zero.

Alps, The

September 22, 1816

Left Thoun in a boat which carried us the length of the lake in three hours. The lake small; but the banks fine. Rocks down to the water's edge. Landed at Newhause; passed Interlachen; entered upon a range of scenes beyond all description or previous conception. Passed a rock; inscription—2 brothers—one murdered the other; just the place for it. After a variety of windings came to an enormous rock. Girl with fruit—very pretty; blue eyes, good teeth, very fair: long but good features—reminded me rather of Fanny. Bought some of her pears, and patted her upon the cheek; the expression of her face very mild, but good, and not at all coquettish. Arrived at the foot of the Mountain (the *Yung frau*, i.e., the Maiden); Glaciers; torrents; one of these torrents *nine hundred* feet in height of visible descent. Lodge at the Curate's. Set out to see the Valley; heard an Avalanche fall, like thunder; saw Glacier—enormous. Storm came on, thunder, lightning, hail; all in perfection and beautiful. I was on horseback; Guide wanted to carry my cane; I was going to give it him, when I recollected that it was a Swordstick, and I thought the lightning might be attracted toward him; kept it myself; a good deal encumbered with it, and my cloak, as it was too heavy for a whip, and the horse was stupid, and stood still with every other peal. Got in, not very wet; the Cloak being staunch. Hobhouse wet through; H. took refuge in cottage; sent man, umbrella, and cloak (from the Curate's when I arrived) after him. Swiss Curate's house very good indeed—much better than most English Vicarages. It is immediately opposite the torrent I spoke of. The torrent is in shape curving over the rock, like the *tail* of a white horse streaming in the wind, such as it might be conceived would be that of the "*pale* horse" on which *Death* is mounted in the Apocalypse. It is neither mist nor water, but a something between both; its immense height (nine hundred feet) gives it a wave, a curve, a spreading here, a condensation there, wonderful and indescribable. Think, upon the whole, that this day has been better than any of this present excursion.

September 23

Before ascending the mountain, went to the torrent (7 in the morning) again; the Sun upon it forming a *rainbow* of the lower part of all colors, but principally purple and gold; the bow moving as you move; I never saw anything like this; it is only in the Sunshine. Ascended the Wengen Mountain; at noon reached a valley on the summit; left the horses, took off my coat, and went to the summit, 7000 feet (English feet) above the level of the *sea,* and about 5000 above the valley we left in the morning. On one side, our view comprised the *Yung frau* with all her glaciers; then the *Dent d'Argent,* shining like truth; then the Little Giant (the Kleiner Eigher), and last, but not least, the Wetterhorn. The height of Jungfrau is 13,000 feet above the sea, 11,000 above the valley; she is the highest of this range. Heard the Avalanches falling every five minutes nearly—as if God was pelting the Devil down from Heaven with snowballs. From where we stood, on the Wengen Alp, we had all these in view on one side: on the other, the clouds rose from the opposite valley, curling up perpendicular precipices like the foam of the Ocean of Hell, during a Springtide—it was white and sulphury, and immeasurably deep in appearance. The side we ascended was (of course) not of so precipitous a nature; but on arriving at the summit, we looked down the other side upon a boiling sea of cloud, dashing against the crags on which we stood (these crags on one side quite perpendicular). Stayed a quarter of an hour; began to descend; quite clear from cloud on that side of the mountain. In passing the masses of snow, I made a snowball and pelted H. with it.

Got down to our horses again, ate something; remounted; heard the Avalanches still; came to a morass; H. dismounted; H. got over well: I tried to pass my horse over; the horse sank up to the chin, and of course he and I were in the mud together; bemired all over but not hurt; laughed and rode on. Arrived at the Grindenwald; dined, mounted again, and rode to the higher Glacier—, twilight but distinct—very fine Glacier, like a *frozen hurricane.* Starlight, beautiful, but the devil of a path! Never mind, got safe in; a little lightning; but the whole of the day as fine in point of weather as the day on which Paradise was made. Passed *whole woods of withered pines, all withered*; trunks stripped and barkless, branches lifeless; done by a single winter—their appearance reminded me of me and my family.

—Lord Byron

There are many spots among the inferior ridges of the Alps, such as the Col de Ferret, the Col d'Anterne, and the associated ranges of the Buet, which, though commanding prospects of great nobleness, are themselves very nearly types of all that is most painful to the human mind. Vast wastes of mountain ground, covered here and there with dull grey grass or moss, but breaking continually into black banks of shattered slate, all glistening and sodden with slow tricklings of clogged, incapable streams; the snow water oozing through them in a cold sweat, and spreading itself in creeping stains among their dust; ever and anon a shaking here and there, and a handful or two of their particles or flakes trembling down, one sees not why, into more total dissolution; leaving a few jagged teeth, like the edges of knives eaten away by vinegar, projecting through the half-dislodged mass from the inner rock, keen enough to cut the hand or foot that rests on them, yet crumbling as they wound, and soon sinking again into the smooth, slippery, glutinous heap, looking like a beach of black scales of dead fish, cast ashore from a poisonous sea; and sloping away into foul ravines, branched down immeasurable slopes of barrenness, where the winds howl and wander continually, and the snow lies in wasted and sorrowful fields, covered with sooty dust, that collects in streaks and stains at the bottom of all its thawing ripples.

—Ruskin

Anagrams

Almost any name with a good distribution of alphabetic letters can be turned into either a flattering or an unflattering anagram of itself. Thus the full name of the author of this book, DMITRI ALFRED BORGMANN, lends itself to the flattering anagram, GRAND MIND, MORTAL FIBRE!, as well as the negative anagram, DAMN MAD BORING TRIFLER!

—D. A. Borgmann

WHY SHUN A NUDE TAG?

In 1610 Galileo published his observations of the planet Saturn in the form of an anagram:

SMAISMRMILMEPOETALEVMIBVNENVGTTAVIRAS

The solution:

ALTISSIMVM PLANETAM TERGEMINVM OBSERVAVI (I have observed that the farthest planet is a triplet.)

In 1656, using a much stronger telescope, Christian Huygens corrected this observation, and he, too, published his correction in the form of an anagram:

> AAAAAAA CCCCC D EEEEE G H IIIIII LLLL MM NNNNNNNNN OOOO Q RR S TTTTT UUUUU

The solution:

> ANNULO CINGITUR, TENUI, PLANO, NUSQUAM COHAERENTE, AD ECLIPTICAM INCLINATO. (A thin ring, plane, without adherence, inclined to the ecliptic.)

To read a mystical significance into anagrams is asking for trouble. When Lady Eleanor Davis (1590–1652) discovered that the letters of her maiden name, ELEANOR AUDLEY, could make the anagram REVEALE O DANIEL, she became convinced that she possessed the gift of prophecy, and from then on there was no stopping her. Her two husbands tried; one dropped dead, the other went mad. In 1628 she prophesied that the Duke of Buckingham would die in August; he did. Emboldened by her success, she then foretold that King Charles the First would come to a bad end like Belshazzar. This was too much, and she was arrested. At her trial she was momentarily disconcerted when one of the judges, taking her married name, DAME ELEANOR DAVIS, produced the anagram NEVER SO MAD A LADIE, but not for long. Her two persecutors, Archbishop Laud and King Charles, both ended on the scaffold, and she hailed Cromwell as the deliverer of his people. By this time, however, her crossword skill seems to have deteriorated. O. CROMWEL: what could that mean but HOWL ROME? It was the last and also the worst of her anagrams, for she had added an H and forgotten the C.

ANESTHESIA

> Anesthesia may be characterized by the fact that a variety of medical problems requiring *immediate solution* meet very dramatically at the anesthesiologist's end of the table; (general physiology, neurology, cardiology, etc., etc.). These multiple disciplines converge suddenly, occupying, as it were, the same space at the same time. This *simultaneity* constitutes a definite, specific trait of anesthesia, its distinctive stamp. How to deal with it is not only a technical challenge and a demand on scientific knowledge but also a philosophical problem: time acquires a new meaning, which must be explored.
>
> Another inherent trait of anesthesia which again, and in an even more pointed way, brings up the problem of time, is its *reversibility*. The abolition of the defense reflexes and all possible complications such as apnea, tachycardia, bradycardia or anoxia are expected to disappear without leaving any traces. This means that reversibility is a conditio

sine qua non. But what is reversibility, philosophically speaking, if not a negation of time? "What has happened—can it unhappen?" (Kierkegaard). Generalized and applied to the whole of human life, reversibility can mean only one thing: the complete overcoming and negation of time and history. . . .

Whatever its ultimate aim and reason, administration of anesthesia means intoxicating the patient. Anesthesia, in fact, is always evil, and the art is of choosing between lesser and greater evil, not between good and evil. This puts anesthesia on a par with other crucial problems of our contemporary life.

What first strikes the student of anesthesia and what is, later, ignored or taken for granted, is his complete, unmitigated loneliness. We may, of course, consider that the people in the operating room are working on the patient as a team. However, this must be further defined: the surgeon has an assistant, even two or three if need be; the scrub nurse has a second scrub nurse and a circulating nurse and a bell to ring for help with; they are all working in the same operating field and in apparent communion! Only the anesthesiologist is on his own. The surgeon may ask him whether everything is going well, the exceptionally kind circulating nurse may fetch him a larger airway, but those are minor, external contacts. Intellectually and spiritually the anesthesiologist is alone, facing that lesser evil.

The pathologist is in the lab with the specimen. He may know that cancer begins long before the cells show "atypical deviations," but discussions of this kind do not enter into his day's work. He prepares the slides in a friendly atmosphere, can make a telephone call to a colleague, and give an answer such as "frozen section not clear," "suspicious" (whatever that means) or "we need a paraffin preparation"; he can even send the slide by special delivery to Illinois or Massachusetts, can correspond, deliberate, and then come up with the answer: "I don't know what it is, I once had a similar case, the patient died, apparently from a lymphosarcoma. . . ."

The anesthetist, for obvious reasons, cannot do his work in such a fashion. He must always deliver the goods, here and now, by himself, in the presence of the impatient, often hostile, surgeon, and regardless of whether it "looks suspicious" or not, or whether he has already had such a case or not.

Considering that the time element does not exist for him in the usual sense, the anesthetist really cannot be assisted from without. Least of all in so-called private, i.e. commercial, institutions, where there are only competitors around. It is like in a Greek tragedy where the hero struggles against fate; or like a world series game with the pitcher throwing the ball while the classic chorus, the stadium audience, roars mercilessly: "Let's go, let's go—what's the matter!" This is also the voice of the surgeon—for the contemporary surgeon who races from one hospital to another, from a hernia to a pilonidal cyst and on to a stomach, cannot afford to lose ten minutes for induction and preparation of his case, or so it seems to him. He cannot understand why one induction takes five minutes and the next perhaps five times as long.

If this surgeon were asked how he would like the ideal anesthesiologist to behave, he would probably answer somewhat along these lines: "As a matter of fact I prefer a nurse anesthetist. But if I have to work with an anesthesiologist he ought not to be seen or heard and, in general, not be noticeable."

It is, indeed, ideal if the anesthetist's performance does not attract anybody's attention. In the easy, good-risk cases this is often achieved. But it so happens that sometimes, like the surgeon who cannot find the common duct because of anatomical anomalies, the anesthesiologist, too, encounters difficulties. Of course, he does the best he can—with the anatomical and physiological material furnished by the patient. If the cards you are dealt include aces and kings you easily win the rubber; if there are no honors you go down. In the latter case, the art consists in losing as little as possible.

After an easy, uneventful case, the surgeon may compliment the anesthesiologist; after a difficult case with ups and downs, in which the patient was still pulled through, the surgeon complains. And yet it is in the latter instance that the anesthetist demonstrates to the full his experience, judgment, knowledge and skill. So it is in retreat that a general demonstrates his talents and endurance. But the general has help—subordinates, assistants, chiefs of staff—while the anesthesiologist is alone: between him and the failing patient there is no one (perhaps only a prayer). . . .

It is the nature of anesthesia to strip the patient biologically and to put him through different antecedent stages of evolution. First, in the classic case, the spinal cord is affected, and reflexes are exaggerated before they are cut down; then, the cortex is irritated (hallucinations) prior to being completely switched off (unconsciousness); finally, cardiac and respiratory centers are approached. Thus the patient reverses as it were his phylogenetic stages—from human back to vertebrate and ameba. During this process, he may manifest himself in primitive forms, resembling in succession an anthropoid, a rodent, a fish, a mollusc, a vegetation. This is when racial, constitutional, genetic factors come to the fore, checked only, perhaps, by acquired and firmly established cultural and educational patterns. Lacking these, we have before us on the operating table what is, in great part, a result of physiological and phylogenetic factors. This crude material reacts differently in varying races, nations, and social stratas. . . .

While the patient is undergoing changes due to narcosis, the surgeon and the anesthesiologist too may demonstrate new, surprising aspects: under situations of specific stress this occurs frequently! The anesthesiologist suddenly discloses his other, underlying, constitution; the same may be true for the surgeon: the great contemporary hero, the bully, the primadonna, suddenly loses his head and calls for a doctor in the house. There is in surgical procedure the moment of truth exactly as in the corridas. An anesthesiologist or a surgeon who has once lost a child on the operating table can be recognized, like the previously gored toreador. During the preliminaries he does everything as he used to, as custom and accepted technique ordain. But at the decisive moment, when the "kill" must be performed, the man is frightened, frozen, paralyzed, and the arena understands: he is through, he must quit or he will be killed. And he either quits or gets killed. So it is with the toreador.

The case of the anesthetist or the surgeon is different: next morning you see them again. At this stage of the game they never voluntarily quit. As it is usually not the physician who expires in the operating room, they continue for several years their inadequate and disturbing activity. We all have seen such "wounded" specialists: they manifest an exaggerated reaction during a sudden complication—something similar to combat fatigue.

The patient in his turn, when brought into the operating room, may control himself in a civilized way, with dignity, or go completely to pieces, in panic and hysteria, despite premedication.

Thus, in the operating room we can always distinguish the worthy man from the pseudo-hero, the bully, the hum-bug. This holds true—in differing degrees and for different reasons—for patient, surgeon and anesthesiologist.

—Basile Yanovsky

Angelology

Surely, one of the oddest pastimes of the human mind. I owe the following information to Gustav Davidson's *A Dictionary of Angels.*

According to the fourteenth-century Cabalists, the total number of angels is 301,655,722.

Angels of the Months (January–December): Gabriel, Barchiel, Malchidiel, Asmodel, Ambriel or Amriel, Muriel, Verchiel, Hamaliel, Zuriel or Uriel, Barbiel, Adnachiel or Advachiel, Hanael or Anael.

Angels of the Seasons (Winter–Autumn): Farlas, Telvi, Casmaran, Andarcel.

Angels of the Week (Sunday–Saturday): Michael, Gabriel, Samael, Raphael, Sachiel, Anael, Cassiel.

Angels of the Elements: Fire: Seraph or Nathaniel. Air: Cherub. Water: Tharsis or Tharsus. Earth: Ariel.

Miscellaneous: Wild beasts: Thegri. Tame beasts: Behemiel. Birds: Arael. Fish: Gagiel. Wild fowl: Trgiaob. Water insects: Shakziel.

Anglo-Saxon Poetry

In the small extant corpus of Anglo-Saxon poetry, there is nothing as good as the best poems in the Elder Edda, but it was my first introduction to the "barbaric" poetry of the North, and I was immediately fascinated both by its metric and its rhetorical devices, so different from the post-Chaucerian poetry with which I was familiar.

The following example is more lyrical than is typical of Anglo-Saxon verse, but it is one of my favorites.

Deor

Wayland knew the wanderer's fate:
that single-willed earl suffered agonies,
sorrow and longing the sole companions
of his ice-cold exile. Anxieties bit
when Nithhad put a knife to his hamstrings,
laid cunning bonds on a better man.
    That changed; this may too.

Beadohild mourned her murdered brothers:
but her own plight pained her more
—her womb grew great with child.
When she knew that, she could never hold
steady before her wit what was to happen.
    That has gone; this may too.

All have heard of Hild's ravishing:
the Geat's lust was ungovernable,
their bitter love banished sleep.
    That passed over; this may too.

Thirty winters Theodric ruled
the Maering city: and many knew it
    That went by; this may too.

We all know that Eormanric
had a wolf's wit. Wide Gothland
lay in the grasp of that grim king,
and through it many sat, by sorrows environed,
foreseeing only sorrow; sighed for the downfall
and thorough overthrow of the thrall-maker.
    That blew by; this may too.

When each gladness has gone, gathering sorrow
may cloud the brain; and in his breast a man

can not then see how his sorrows shall end.
But he may think how throughout this world
it is the way of God, who is wise, to deal
to the most part of men much favour
and a flourishing fame; to a few the sorrow-share.

Of myself in this regard I shall say this only:
that in the hall of the Heodenings I held long the makarship,
lived dear to my prince, Deor my name;
many winters I held this happy place
and my lord was kind. Then came Heorrenda,
whose lays were skilful; the lord of fighting-men
settled on him the estate bestowed once on me.
That has gone; this may too.

—(trans. Michael Alexander)

A few years ago I was amazed to find that the standard verse line of northern poetry, consisting of two half lines, separated by a strong caesura and linked by alliteration, also occurs in Somali poetry. In it, however, every line of a poem must contain the same alliterative sound. In the original of the following poem, the alliterating consonant in every line is *k*, e.g.:

Sida *k*oorta yucub oo La suray *k*orommo buubaal ah
Ama geel *k*a reeb ah oo nirgaha Laga *k*achaynaayo

The Poet's Lament on the Death of His Wife

Like the yu'ub wood bell tied to gelded camels that are running away,
Or like camels which are being separated from their young,
Or like people journeying while moving camp,
Or like a well which has broken its sides or a river which has overflowed its banks,
Or like an old woman whose only son was killed,
Or like the poor, dividing the scraps for their frugal meal,
Or like the bees entering their hive, or food cracking in the frying,
Yesterday my lamentations drove sleep from all the camps.
Have I been bereft in my house and shelter?
Has the envy of others been miraculously fulfilled?
Have I been deprived of the fried meat and reserves for lean times which were so plentiful for me?
Have I to-day been taken from the chessboard?
Have I been borne on a saddle to a distant and desolate place?
Have I broken my shin, a bone which cannot be mended?

—Raage Ugaas (trans. B. W. Andrzejewski and I. M. Lewis)

Ants

Jan. 21, 1852

One day, when I went out to my wood-pile, or rather my pile of stumps, I observed two large ants, the one red, the other much larger and black, fiercely contending with one another, and rolling over on the chips. It was evidently a struggle for life and death which had grown out of a serious feud. Having once got hold, they never let go of each other, but struggled and wrestled and rolled on the chips, each retaining his hold with mastiff-like pertinacity. Looking further, I found to my astonishment that the chips were covered with such combatants, that it was not a *duellum* but a *bellum*, a war between two races of ants, the red always pitted against the black, and frequently two red ones to one black. They covered all the hills and vales of my wood-yard, and, indeed, the ground was already strewn with the dead, both red and black. It was the only war I had ever witnessed, the only battle-field I ever trod while the battle was raging; internecine war; the red republicans and the black despots or imperialists. On every side they were engaged in deadly combat, yet without any noise that I could hear, and never human soldiers fought so resolutely. I watched a couple, in a little sunny valley amid the chips, that were fast locked in each other's embraces, now at noonday prepared to fight till the sun went down. The smaller red champion had fastened himself like a vice to his adversary's front, and through all the tumblings on that field never for an instant ceased to gnaw at one of his feelers near the root, having already caused the other to go by the board, while the stronger black one dashed him from side to side, and, as I saw on looking nearer, had divested him of several of his members. None manifested a disposition to retreat from the combat equal or unequal. It was evident that their battle-cry was conquer or die. They fought like mastiffs or bulldogs, who will not let go though all their legs are cut off. In the meanwhile there came along a single red ant on the side hill of this valley, evidently full of excitement, who either had dispatched his foe or had not yet taken part in the battle; probably the latter, for he had lost none of his limbs. He saw this unequal combat from afar—for the blacks were nearly twice the size of the reds—he drew near with rapid pace till he stood his guard within half an inch of the combatants, then, watching his opportunity, he sprang upon the black warrior and commenced his operations near the root of his right fore-leg, leaving the other to select among his own members, and so there were three united for life until death—as if a new kind of attraction had been invented, which put all other locks and cements to shame. . . .

I took up the chip on which the three I have particularly described were struggling, carried it into my house, and placed it under a tumbler on my window-sill, wishing to see the issue. Holding a microscope to the first-mentioned red ant, I saw that though he was assiduously gnawing at the near foreleg of his enemy, having severed his remaining feeler, his own breast was all torn away, exposing what vitals he had there to the jaws of the black warrior, whose own breastplate was apparently too thick for him; and the dark carbuncles of his eyes shone with ferocity such as wars only could excite. They struggled for half an hour longer under the tumbler, and when I looked again, the black soldier had severed the heads of his foes from their bodies, and the former were hanging on either side of him still apparently as firmly fastened as ever, and he was endeavouring with feeble struggles, being without feelers and with only one or two legs, and I know not how many other wounds, to divest himself of them; which at length, after half an hour more, he had accomplished. I raised the tumbler, and he went off over the window-sill in that crippled state. Whether he finally survived that combat and had a pension settled on him, I do not know. But I thought that his industry would not be worth much thereafter.

Which part was victorious I never learned, nor the cause of the war. But I felt for the rest of that day as if I had had my feelings harrowed and excited by witnessing the struggle, the ferocity and carnage, of a human battle before my door.

—H. D. Thoreau

Arborvitae

With honeysuckle, over-sweet, festooned;
With bitter ivy bound;
Terraced with funguses unsound;
Deformed with many a boss
And closèd scar, o'ercushioned deep with moss;
Bunched all about with pagan mistletoe;
And thick with nests of the hoarse bird
That talks, but understands not his own word;
Stands, and so stood a thousand years ago,
A single tree.
Thunder has done its worst among its twigs,
Where the great crest yet blackens, never pruned,
But in its heart, always
Ready to push new verdurous boughs, whene'er
The rotting saplings near it fall and leave it air,
Is all antiquity and no decay.
Rich, though rejected by the forest pigs,
Its fruit, beneath whose rough compelling rind

Those that will it break find
Heart-succouring savor of each several meat,
And kernelled drink of brain-renewing power,
With bitter condiment and sour,
And sweet economy of sweet,
And odors that remind
Of haunts of childhood and a different day.
Beside this tree,
Praising no Gods nor blaming, sans a wish,
Sits, Tartar-like, the Time's civility,
And eats its dead-dog off a golden dish.

—Coventry Patmore

Articles, the Thirty-Nine

Scene from A Play, Acted at Oxford,
Called "Matriculation"

[*Boy discovered at a table, with the Thirty-Nine Articles before him.—Enter the Rt. Rev. Doctor Philpots.*]

Doctor P. There, my lad, lie the Articles—[*boy begins to count them*] just thirty-nine—
No occasion to count—you've now only to sign.
At Cambridge where folks are less High-church than we,
The whole Nine-and-Thirty are lumped into Three.
Let's run o'er the items;—there's Justification,
Predestination and Supererogation,—
Not forgetting Salvation and Creed Athanasian,
Till we reach, at last, Queen Bess's Ratification.
That's sufficient—now, sign—having read quite enough,
You "believe in the full and true meaning thereof."
[*Boy stares*]
Oh, a mere form of words, to make things smooth and brief,—
A commodious and short make-believe of belief,
Which our Church has drawn up, in a form thus articular,
To keep out, in general, all who're particular.
But what's the boy doing? what! reading all through,
And my luncheon fast cooling!—this never will do.

Boy [*poring over the Articles*]. Here are points which—pray, Doctor, what's "Grace of Congruity"?

Doctor P. [*sharply*]. You'll find out, young sir, when you've more ingenuity.
At present, by signing, you pledge yourself merely,

Whate'er it may be, to believe it sincerely.
Both in dining and signing we take the same plan—
First, swallow all down, then digest—as we can.
BOY [*still reading*]. I've to gulp, I see, St Athanasius's Creed,
Which, I'm told, is a very tough morsel indeed;
As he damns—
DOCTOR P. [*aside*]. Ay, and so would *I*, willingly, too,
All confounded particular young boobies, like you.
This comes of Reforming! all's o'er with our land,
When people won't stand what they can't *under*stand;
Nor perceive that our ever-revered Thirty-Nine
Were made, not for men to *believe*, but to *sign*.
[*Exit Doctor P. in a passion*]

—Thomas Moore

BANDS, BRASS

When I was young, brass-band concerts were a regular attraction in the public parks of cities. Am I mistaken in thinking that they have become rarities? All I know is that this poem fills me with nostalgia.

Park Concert

Astounding the bucolic grass,
The bandsmen sweat in golds and reds
And put their zeal into the brass.
A glorious flustered major heads

Their sort of stationary charge.
Their lips are pursed, their cheeks get pink;
The instruments are very large
Through which they render Humperdinck.

The sailors and the parlourmaids
Both vote the music jolly good,
But do not worry if it fades
As they stroll deeper in the wood,

Where twenty French horns wouldn't stir
A leaf. The intrepid band try not
To mind the applause (as though it were
A testing fusillade of shot),

Polish their mouthpieces and cough,
Then throw their shoulders back to play
A Pomeranian march. They're off!
And Sousa scares the tits away.

—James Michie

Baroque

Of all architectural styles, Baroque is the most this-worldly, a visible hymn to earthly pomp and power. At the same time, by its excessive theatricality, it reveals, perhaps unintentionally, the essential "camp" of all worldly greatness. It is, therefore, the ideal style for princely palaces. But as ecclesiastical architecture it simply will not do, for nothing could be further removed from the Christian view of God and Man. The same is true of the baroque literature, of *Paradise Lost*, or Bossuet's sermons, or the following example, which I found in Friedrich Heer's *The Intellectual History of Europe.*

> In his *Délices de l'Esprit*, Desmarets has given us a perfect statement of this baroque view of the world. Man's inner life was, Desmarets wrote, a palace, and the great house of the Duc de Richelieu would seem to have been the model for it. In it, the hero, Philedon, was received in the apartment of Faith, visited the loge of humility and the prison of nothingness (*cachet du Néant*). Next he saw the balcony of hope, the thirty-three caverns of obedience, the grotto of patience, the halls of prayer, of meditation and of union with God. There was even a marine museum in Desmaret's heavenly palace in which various vehicles for missionary journeys were displayed. The staff of the palace consisted of Mary, the patriarchs, prophets and the Christian virtues who received and guided the visitors. An exceedingly ingenious system of mechanical staircases, on which Philedon ascended when he wanted to rise, led the way to different floors. The great architect, master mechanic, magician and mystic ruler of the palace was Christ himself. From the "great salon of God's love," the walls glittering with marble, gold and precious stones, Philedon passed through several arcades into the "chamber of love of the extension of the Faith" (*chambre de l'amour de l'extension de la Foi*).
>
> Desmarets published the book in 1654, and went on to realise these "delights" as the leader of the secret police of State and Church.
>
> —Friedrich Heer

When Westward, like the Sun, you took your Way,
And from benighted *Britain* bore the Day,
Blue *Triton* gave the Signal from the Shore,
The ready *Nereids* heard, and swam before,
To smooth the Seas; a soft *Etesian* Gale
But just inspir'd, and gently swell'd the Sail;
Portunus took his Turn, whose ample Hand
Heav'd up the lighten'd Keel, and sunk the Sand,
And steer'd the sacred Vessel safe to Land.
The Land, if not restrain'd, had met Your Way,
Projected out a Neck, and jutted to the Sea.
Hibernia, prostrate at your Feet, ador'd,
In You the Pledge of her expected Lord,

Due to her Isle; a venerable Name;
His Father and his Grandsire known to Fame;
Aw'd by that House, accustom'd to command,
The sturdy *Kerns* in due subjection stand,
Nor fear the Reins in any Foreign Hand.
At your approach, they crowded to the Port;
And scarcely landed, You create a Court:
As *Ormond*'s Harbinger, to you they run;
For *Venus* is the Promise of the *Sun*.
The Waste of Civil Wars, their Towns destroy'd,
Pales unhonor'd, Ceres unemployed,
Were all forgot; and one Triumphant Day
Wip'd all the Tears of three Campaigns away.
Blood, Rapines, Massacres, were cheaply bought,
So mighty Recompense Your Beauty brought.
As when the Dove returning bore the Mark
Of Earth restor'd to the long-lab'ring Ark,
The Relicks of Mankind, secure of Rest,
Op'd ev'ry Window to receive the Guest,
And the fair Bearer of the Message bless'd;
So, when You came, with loud repeated Cries,
The Nation took an Omen from your Eyes,
And God advanc'd his Rainbow in the Skies,
To sign inviolable Peace restor'd;
The Saints, with solemn Shouts, proclaim'd the new accord.

—John Dryden

Bath, The Cold

As cultural habits go, short-lived. I don't know precisely when it was first introduced (1840?), but I know more or less when it came to an end. When I was young, not only was every boy at a boarding school compelled to take a cold bath every morning, a rule based on the entirely erroneous theory that cold water subdued the carnal passions, but also most adult males of the upper and middle classes took one of their own free will. I believe I belong to the first generation which resolved, once we left school and got to the university, that we would never take a cold bath in our lives again. Today, inquiries lead me to think that there are few schools now where cold baths are obligatory, and I am sure no adult ever takes one except during a heat wave. Upon my sufferings in early youth, Ogden Nash has said the last word:

I test my bath before I sit,
And I am always moved to wonderment
That what chills the finger not a bit
Is so frigid upon the fundament.

BEAUTY, FEMININE

Shee was brighter of her blee
  then was the bright sonn:
Her rudd redder than the rose
  that on the rise hangeth:
Meekly smiling with her mouth,
  and merry in her lookes.
Ever laughing for love,
  as she like would.
And as shee came by the bankes,
  the boughes eche one
They louted to that ladye,
  and layd forth their branches;
Blossomes, and burgens
  breathed full sweete;
Flowers flourished in the frith,
  where shee forth stepped;
And the grasse, that was gray,
  greened belive.

—Anon.

Perfectioni Hymnus

What should I call this creature,
  Which now is grown unto maturity?
How should I blaze this feature
  As firm and constant as Eternity?
Call it Perfection? Fie!
  'Tis perfecter than brightest names can light it:
Call it Heaven's mirror? Aye.
  Alas, best attributes can never right it.
Beauty's resistless thunder?
  All nomination is too straight of sense:
Deep contemplation's wonder?
  That appellation give this excellence.
Within all best confined
  (Now feebler Genius end thy slighter rhyming)
No suburbs, all is *Mind*,
  As far from spots, as possible defining.

—John Marston

He saw coming from her bee-hives
Many centuries of beauty
In a few years of age.

—Góngora (trans. Gerald Brenan)

Virginal exquisite queen, of long gentle thinking,
the colour of breaking day on a deserted sea.
—Cynddelw (trans. Glwn Williams)

Behaviorism

Of course, Behaviorism "works." So does torture. Give me a no-nonsense, down-to-earth behaviorist, a few drugs, and simple electrical appliances, and in six months I will have him reciting the Athanasian Creed in public.

Some phobias persist as habits long after the emotional conflict or trauma which gave origin to them has disappeared. One case, for example, was that of a professional man who suffered from an intense fear of thunderstorms. Since thunderstorms are not uncommon in Britain, he was often in a state of considerable tension, fearing that he would incur the ridicule of his colleagues if he suddenly felt obliged to seek refuge from thunder by hiding under the table or retiring to a lavatory. His symptom took origin from a traumatic experience in early childhood in which he had nearly been struck by a flash of lightning which was accompanied by a deafening clap of thunder. In other respects, a more or less superficial enquiry indicated that this man was both happy and successful. This isolated phobia of thunderstorms had little obvious connection with the rest of his character structure; but, like a diseased appendix, was a pathological appendage of which he would have been thankful to be rid, and the removal of which was likely to cause small disturbance to the rest of his personality. In such a case, a behavior therapist would probably expose the patient gradually to increasing intensities of the noise of thunder and electrical flashes; at first, perhaps, combining this with sedation or other methods of extinguishing responses. When the patient had become sufficiently accustomed to reacting without fear to artificial thunder and lightning in the laboratory, it would be hoped that he could finally be exposed to a real thunderstorm and discover that his response of fear had been abolished.

If behavior therapy had been available at the time that this patient was seen, the author would undoubtedly have advised it: but such cases, unfortunately, are the exception rather than the rule in psychiatric practice. The majority of phobias do not spring from isolated traumatic incidents, but are intimately connected with the patient's style of life and his whole development from childhood onwards.

—Anthony Storr

BELIEF

To all human experience, with the possible exception of physical pain, the maxim *Credo ut intelligam* applies. It is impossible for a man to separate a fact of experience from his interpretation of it, an interpretation which, except in the case of the insane, is not peculiar to himself but has been learned from others.

It is true, as Pascal says, that "to believe, to doubt, and to deny well are to the man what the race is to the horse," but only in that order. We must believe before we can doubt, and doubt before we can deny. And, with the exception of autistic children, we all do begin by believing what we are told.

> Man is what he believes.
>
> —A. Chekhov

> If there were a verb meaning "to believe falsely," it would not have any sigificant first person, present indicative.
>
> —Ludwig Wittgenstein

"By their fruits you shall know them" is a test which is, no doubt, true in the long run. In the short run, however, it seems ineffective. Out of erroneous beliefs, men have done the most absurd and wicked things, but how are they to recognise that their behavior is absurd and wicked until they have replaced their beliefs by truer ones?

> Some like to understand what they believe in. Others like to believe in what they understand.
>
> —Stanislaus Lec

> He who believes in nothing still needs a girl to believe in him.
>
> —Eugen Rosenstock-Huessy

> There is a great difference between *still* believing something and believing it *again*.
>
> —G. C. Lichtenberg

Doubts, unlike denials, should always be humorous.

It is fatal to repress doubt; it turns the doubter into a humorless bigot.

> To deny A is to put A behind bars.
>
> —Paul Valéry

BIRDS

Surcharged with discontent,
To Sylvane's bower I went
To ease my heavy grief-oppressed heart,

And try what comfort winged creatures
Could yield unto my inward troubled smart,
By modulating their delightful measures
To my ears pleasing ever.
Of strains so sweet, sweet birds deprive us never.

The thrush did pipe full clear,
And eke with merry cheer
The linnet lifted up her pleasant voice.
The goldfinch chirped and the pie did chatter,
The blackbird whistled and bade me rejoice,
The stockdove mumured with solemn flatter.
The little daw, ka-ka he cried;
The hic-quale he beside
Tickled his part in a parti-coloured coat.
The jay did blow his hautboy gallantly.
The wren did treble many a pretty note.
The woodpecker did hammer melody.
The kite, tiw-whiw, full oft
Cried, soaring up aloft,
And down again returned presently.
To whom the herald of cornutus sung cuckoo
Ever, whilst poor Margery cried: "Who
Did ring nights 'larum bell?"
Withal all did do well.
O might I hear them ever.
Of strains so sweet, sweet birds deprive us never.

Then Hesperus on high
Brought cloudy night in sky,
When lo, the thicket-keeping company
Of feathered singers left their madrigals,
Sonnets and elegies, and presently
Shut them within their mossy severals,
And I came home and vowed to love them ever.
Of strains so sweet, sweet birds deprive us never.

—Anon. (set by John Bartlet)

When I awoke, dimly aware of some commotion and outcry in the clearing, the light was slanting down through the pines in such a way that the glade was lit like some vast cathedral. I could see the dust motes of wood pollen in the long shaft of light, and there on the extended branch sat an enormous raven with a red and squirming nestling in its beak.

The sound that awoke me was the outraged cries of the nestling's parents, who flew helplessly in circles about the clearing. The sleek black monster was indifferent to them. He gulped, whetted his beak on the dead branch a moment and sat still. Up to that point the little tragedy had followed the usual pattern. But suddenly, out of all that area of woodland, a soft sound of complaint began to rise. Into the glade fluttered small birds of half a dozen varieties drawn by the anguished cries of the tiny parents.

No one dared to attack the raven. But they cried there in some instinctive common misery, the bereaved and the unbereaved. The glade filled with their soft rustling and their cries. They fluttered as though to point their wings at the murderer. There was a dim intangible ethic he had violated, that they knew. He was a bird of death.

And he, the murderer, the black bird at the heart of life, sat on there, glistening in the common light, formidable, unperturbed, untouchable.

The sighing died. It was then I saw the judgment. It was the judgment of life against death. I will never see it again so forcefully presented. I will never hear it again in notes so tragically prolonged. For in the midst of protest, they forgot the violence. There, in that clearing, the crystal note of a song sparrow lifted hesitantly in the hush. And, finally, after painful fluttering, another took the song, and then another, the song passing from one bird to another, doubtfully at first, as though some evil thing was being slowly forgotten. Till suddenly they took heart and sang from many throats joyously together as birds are known to sing. They sang because life is sweet and sunlight beautiful. They sang under the brooding shadow of the raven. In simple truth they had forgotten the raven, for they were the singers of life, and not of death.

—Loren Eiseley

Bishops

It is an idle but entertaining pastime to imagine an alternative career to that which one has actually chosen, but in which one believes one possesses the talent and temperament which could have made one successful.

In my own case, I like to fancy that, had I taken Anglican Holy Orders, I might by now be a bishop, politically liberal I hope, theologically and liturgically conservative I know. I should like to believe that I would be long-suffering with those of my clergy who held different views, but I rather fear that I might be as intolerant as the dean of whom Sydney Smith said, "He deserves to be preached to death by wild curates."

In literature, bishops are usually presented as either unsympathetic or slightly comic characters, a price they pay for their worldly eminence and their odd clothes. A comic presentation is, in their case, particularly easy because they can be referred to, not by their own names, but by the place-names of their sees.

> Frequently did Lord John meet the destroying Bishops; much did he commend their daily heap of ruins; sweetly did they smile on each other, and much charming talk there was of meteorology and catarrh and the particular cathedral they were pulling down at the time; till one fine morning the Home Secretary, with a voice more bland, and a look more ardently affectionate, than that which the masculine mouse bestows on his nibbling female, informed them that the Government meant to take all the Church property into their own hands, to pay the rates out of it, and deliver the residue to the rightful possessors. Such an effect, they say, was never before produced by a *coup de théâtre.* The Commission was separated in an instant: London clenched his fist; Canterbury was hurried out by his chaplains and put into a warm bed; a solemn vacancy spread itself over the face of Gloucester; Lincoln was taken out in strong hysterics.
>
> —Sydney Smith

Black

In my opinion, the most heroic living American is Mr John Howard Griffin. He comes from an old Texas family, is a Roman Catholic and a musicologist. There is now, it seems, a substance which, when injected into the body, so darkens the pigmentation of the skin that a white man can pass for a Negro. The effect, however, is temporary, so that, when the injections are discontinued, he regains his natural color. These injections Mr Griffin took, and in his book *Black Like Me* he has described his experiences in the Deep South as a pseudo-Negro. When the book came out his parents were forced to leave their home town, and Mr Griffin himself, while traveling in Mississippi, was hauled out of his car and beaten over the kidneys with chains, so that his health is now permanently impaired. Here are three extracts.

> Behind the custard stand stood an old unpainted privy leaning badly to one side. I returned to the dispensing window of the stand.
>
> "Yes, sir," the white man said congenially. "You want something else?"
>
> "Where's the nearest rest room I could use?" I asked.
>
> He brushed his white, brimless cook's cap back and rubbed his forefinger against his sweaty forehead. "Let's see. You can go on up there to the bridge and then cut down the road to the left . . . and just follow that road. You'll come to a little settlement—there's some stores and gas stations there."

"How far is it?" I asked, pretending to be in greater discomfort than I actually was.

"Not far—thirteen, maybe fourteen blocks." . . .

"Isn't there anyplace closer?" I said, determined to see if he would not offer me the use of the dilapidated outhouse, which certainly no human could degrade more than time and the elements had.

His seamed face showed the concern and sympathy of one human being for another in a predicament every man understands. "I can't think of any . . .", he said slowly.

I glanced around the side toward the outhouse. "Any chance of me running in there for a minute?"

"Nope," he said—clipped, final, soft, as though he regretted it but could never permit such a thing. "I'm sorry." . . .

By dark I was away from the beach area and out in the country. Strangely, I began getting rides. Men would pass you in daylight but pick you up after dark.

I must have had a dozen rides that evening. They blear into a nightmare, the one scarcely distinguishable from the other.

It quickly became obvious why they picked me up. All but two picked me up the way they would pick up a pornographic photograph or book—except that this was verbal pornography. With a Negro, they assumed they need give no semblance of self-respect or respectability. The visual element entered into it. In a car at night visibility is reduced. A man will reveal himself in the dark, which gives an illusion of anonymity more than he will in the bright light. Some were shamelessly open, some shamelessly subtle. All showed morbid curiosity about the sexual life of the Negro, and all had, at base, the same stereotyped image of the Negro as an inexhaustible sex-machine with oversized genitals and a vast store of experiences, immensely varied. . . .

. . . Each time one of them let me out of his car, I hoped the next would spare me his pantings. I remained mute and pleaded my exhaustion and lack of sleep.

"I'm so tired, I just can't think," I would say.

Like men who had promised themselves pleasure, they would not be denied. It became a strange sort of hounding as they nudged my skull for my sexual reminiscences.

"Well, did you ever do such-and-such?"

"I don't know . . ." I moaned.

"What's the matter—haven't you got any manhood? My old man told me you wasn't a man till you'd done such-and-such."

Or the older ones, hardened, cynical in their lechery. "Now, don't try to kid me. I wasn't born yesterday. You know you've done such-and-such, just like I have. Hell, it's good that way. Tell me, did you ever get a white woman?"

"Do you think I'm crazy?" . . .

"I didn't ask if you was crazy," he said. "I asked if you ever had one—or ever wanted one." Then, conniving, sweet-toned, "There's plenty white women would like to have a good buck Negro."

"A Negro'd be asking for the rope to get himself mixed up with white women."

"You're just telling me that, but I'll bet inside you think differently. . . ."

"This is sure beautiful country through here. What's the main crop?"

"*Don't* you? You can tell me. Hell, I don't care."

"No, sir," I sighed.

"You're lying in your teeth and you know it."

Silence. Soon after, almost abruptly he halted the car and said, "Okay, this is as far as I go." He spoke as though he resented my uncooperative attitude, my refusal to give him this strange verbal sexual pleasure.

I thanked him for the ride and stepped down onto the highway. He drove on in the same direction. . . .

The policeman nodded affably to me and I knew then that I had successfully passed back into white society, that I was once more a first-class citizen, that all doors into cafés, rest rooms, libraries, movies, concerts, schools and churches were suddenly open to me. After so long I could not adjust to it. A sense of exultant liberation flooded through me. I crossed over to a restaurant and entered. I took a seat beside white men at the counter and the waitress smiled at me. It was a miracle. . . .

I ate the white meal, drank the white water, received the white smiles and wondered how it could be. What sense could a man make of it?

I left the café and walked to the elegant Whitney Hotel. A Negro rushed to take my knapsacks. He gave me the smiles, the "yes, sir—yes, sir."

I felt like saying, "You're not fooling me," but now I was back on the other side of the wall. There was no longer communication between us, no longer the glance that said everything.

—John Howard Griffin

Book Reviews, Imaginary

Brittle Galaxy. By Barbara Snorte.

A colorful and courageous attempt to put the point of view of the artist misunderstood in a world of wars and rumors of wars. Dalton Sparleigh is the eternal figure of the hero who is the center of his world, and regards his own personality as the most important thing in life. 1,578 pages of undiluted enthrallment.

Groaning Carcase. By Frederick Duddle.

A very delicate and tactfully written plea for old horses, against a background of country-house life. It is fiction made more compelling than fact by one who seems to be right inside the horse's mind.

Splendid Sorrow. By Walter Fallow.

Was Ernst Hörenwurst, adventurer and rake, the Margrave Friedrich Meiningen of Hohefurstenau-Lebensbletter? Mr Fallow, in his new historical romance, has no hesitation in leaving the question unanswered.

Tricks with Cheese. By "Cheesophile" (of *Cheese World*).

The author appears to be able to make everything, from a model of the Palace of Justice in Brussels to a bust of his aunt, out of cheese. A good book for the fireside.

Fain Had I Thus Loved. By Freda Trowte.

Miss Trowte has been called by the *Outcry* the Anatole France of Herefordshire. There is an indescribable quality of something evocative yet elusively incomprehensible about her work. The character of Nydda is burningly etched by as corrosive a pen as is now being wielded anywhere.

No Second Churning. By Arthur Clawes.

An almost unbearably vital study of a gas-inspector who puts gas-inspecting before love. Awarded the Prix de Seattle, this book should enhance the author's growing reputation as an interpreter of life's passionate bypaths.

Pursuant To What Shame. By Goola Drain.

All those who enjoyed Miss Drain's romantic handling of a love-story in *Better Thine Endeavor* and *Immediate Beasts* will welcome this trenchant tale of an irresponsible girl who poisons her uncle. A famous tennis player said, before he had even seen the book, "In my opinion Miss Drain is unique and unchallengeable. Her command of words is a delight."

—J. B. Morton

Bores

Who on earth invented the silly convention that it is boring or impolite to talk shop? Nothing is more interesting to listen to, especially if the shop is not one's own.

We are almost always bored by just those whom we must not find boring.

—La Rochefoucauld

What is more enchanting than the voices of young people when you can't hear what they say?

—L. P. Smith

The most intolerable people are provincial celebrities.

—A. Chekhov

'Twas when fleet Snowball's head was waxen gray,
A luckless leveret met him on his way,—
Who knows not Snowball—he whose race renowned
Is still victorious on each coursing ground?
Swaffham, Newmarket, and the Roman Camp
Have seen them victors o'er each meaner stamp.—
In vain the youngling sought with doubling wile
The hedge, the hill, the thicket, or the stile.
Experience sage the lack of speed supplied,
And in the gap he sought, the victim died.
So was I once, in thy fair street, Saint James,
Through walking cavaliers, and car-borne dames,
Descried, pursued, turned o'er again and o'er,
Coursed, coted, mouthed by an unfeeling bore.

—Walter Scott

Calvin

. . . It ought to be easier for us than for the nineteenth century to understand his attraction. He was a man born to be the idol of revolutionary intellectuals; an unhesitating doctrinaire, ruthless and efficient in putting his doctrine into practice. Though bred as a lawyer, he found the time before he was thirty to produce the first text of the *Institutio* (1536) and never made any serious modification of its theory. By 1537 he was already at Geneva and the citizens were being paraded before him in bodies of ten to swear to a system of doctrine. Sumptuary legislation and the banishment of the dissentient Caroli made it plain that here was the man of the new order who really meant business. . . . The moral severity of his rule laid the foundations of the meaning which the word "puritan" has since acquired. But this severity did not mean that his theology was, in the last resort, more ascetic than that of Rome. It sprang from his refusal to allow the Roman distinction between the life of "religion" and the life of the world, between the Counsels and the Commandments. Calvin's picture of the fully Christian life was less hostile to pleasure and to the body than Fisher's; but then Calvin demanded that every man should be made to live the fully Christian life. In academic jargon, he lowered the honours standard and abolished the pass degree.

Modern parallels are always to some extent misleading. Yet . . . it may be useful to compare the influence of Calvin on that age with the influence of Marx on our own; or even of Marx and Lenin in one, for Calvin had both expounded the new system in theory and set it going in practice. This will at least serve to eliminate the absurd idea that Elizabethan Calvinists were somehow grotesque, elderly people, standing outside the main forward current of life. In their own day they were, of course, the very latest thing. Unless we can imagine the freshness, the audacity, and (soon) the fashionableness of Calvinism, we shall get our whole picture wrong. It was the creed of progressives, even of revolutionaries. It appealed strongly to those tempers that would have been Marxist in the nineteen-thirties. The fierce young don, the learned lady, the courtier with intellectual leanings, were likely to be Calvinists. When hard rocks of Predestination outcrop in the flowery soil of the *Arcadia* or the *Faerie Queene*, we are apt to think them anomalous, but we are wrong. The Calvinism is as modish as the shepherds and goddesses. . . . Youth is the taunt commonly brought against the puritan leaders by their opponents: youth and cocksureness. As we recognize the type we begin, perhaps, to wonder less that such a work as the *Institutio* should have been so eagerly welcomed. In it Calvin goes on from the original Protestant experience to build a system, to extrapolate, to raise all the dark questions and give without flinching the dark answers. It is, however, a masterpiece of literary form; and we may suspect that those who read it with most approval were troubled by the fate of predestined vessels of wrath just about as much as young Marxists in our own age are troubled by the approaching liquidation of the *bourgeoisie.* Had the word "sentimentality" been known to them, Elizabethan Calvinists would certainly have used it of any who attacked the *Institutio* as morally repulsive.

—C. S. Lewis

Camps, Concentration

. . . The decision to remain alive or die is probably a supreme example of self-determination. Therefore the SS attitude toward suicide may be mentioned.

The stated principle was: the more prisoners to commit suicide, the better. But even there, the decision must not be the prisoner's. An SS man might provoke a prisoner to commit suicide by running against the electrically charged wire fence, and that was all right. But for those who took the initiative in killing themselves, the SS issued (in Dachau in 1933) a special order: prisoners who attempted suicide but did not succeed were to receive twenty-five lashes and prolonged solitary confinement. Supposedly this was to punish them for their failure to do away with themselves; but I am convinced it was much more to punish them for the act of self-determination. . . .

The layers of courtesy and kindness which made even negative attitudes sufferable outside the camp were nearly always absent. There was rarely a "No, thank you" either in tone or words; responses were always in their harshest forms. One heard nothing but, "Idiot!" "Go to hell!" "Shit!" or worse; and no provoking was needed to get this in answer to a neutral question. Men lay in wait for any opening to spit out their pent-up frustration and anger. Also, the chance to express vehemence was an added relief. . . . Even hurting someone's feelings was a satisfaction. It proved there was still somebody or something one mattered to, had an effect on, even if it was a painful effect. But in the process one came a step closer to the SS way of meeting life and its problems. . . .

Slowly most prisoners accepted terms of verbal aggression that definitely did not originate in their previous vocabulary, but were taken over from the very different vocabulary of the SS. . . . From copying SS verbal aggressions to copying their form of bodily aggression was one more step, but it took several years to reach that. It was not unusual, when prisoners were in charge of others, to find old prisoners (and not only former criminals) behaving worse than the SS. Sometimes they were trying to find favor with the guards, but more often it was because they considered it the best way to treat prisoners in the camp.

Old prisoners tended to identify with the SS not only in their goals and values, but even in appearance. They tried to arrogate to themselves old pieces of SS uniforms, and when that was not possible they tried to sew and mend their prison garb until it resembled the uniforms. . . . When asked why they did it, they said it was because they wanted to look smart. To them looking smart meant to look like their enemies.

Old prisoners felt great satisfaction if, during the twice daily counting of prisoners, they really had stood well at attention or given a snappy salute. They prided themselves on being as tough, or tougher, than the SS. In their identification they went so far as to copy SS leisure time activities. One of the games played by the guards was to find out who could stand being hit the longest without uttering a complaint. This game was copied by old prisoners, as if they were not hit often enough without repeating the experience as a game. . . .

Prisoners who came to believe the repeated statements of the guards—that there was no hope for them, and they would never leave the camp except as a corpse—who came to feel that their environment was one over which they could exercise no influence whatsoever, these prisoners were, in a literal sense, walking corpses. In the camp they were called "moslems" (*Muselmänner*). . . . It began when they stopped acting on their own. And that was the moment when other prisoners recognized what was happening and separated themselves from these now "marked" men, because any further association with them could lead only to one's own destruction. At this point such men still obeyed orders, but only blindly or automatically; no longer selectively or with any inner reservation or any hatred at being so abused. They still looked about, or at least moved their eyes around. The looking stopped much later, though even then they still moved their bodies when ordered, but never did anything on their own any more. Typically, this stopping of action began when they no longer lifted their legs as they walked, but only shuffled them. When finally even the looking about on their own stopped, they soon died. . . .

As long as they still asked for food, followed someone to get it, stretched out a hand for it and ate what was given eagerly, they could still, with great effort, have been returned to "normal" prisoner status, deteriorated as they were. In the next stage of disintegration, receiving food unexpectedly still led to a momentary lighting up of the face and a grateful hangdog look, though hardly any verbal response. But when they no longer reached out for it spontaneously, no longer responded with thanks, an effort to smile, or a look at the giver, they were nearly always beyond help. Later they took food, sometimes ate it, sometimes not, but no longer had a feeling response. In the last, just before the terminal stage, they no longer ate it. . . .

To survive as a man, not a walking corpse, as a debased and degraded but still human being, one had first and foremost to remain informed and aware of what made up one's personal point of no return beyond which one would never, under any circumstances, give in to the oppressor, even if it meant risking and losing one's life. It meant being aware that if one survived at the price of overreaching this point one would be holding on to a life that had lost all meaning. It would mean surviving —not with lowered self-respect, but without any. . . .

Second in importance was keeping oneself informed of how one felt about complying when the ultimate decision as to where to stand firm was not called into question. . . . One had to comply with debasing and amoral commands if one wished to survive; but one had to remain cognizant that one's reason for complying was "to remain alive and unchanged as a person." Therefore, one had to decide, for any given action, whether it was truly necessary for one's safety or that of others, and whether committing it was good, neutral or bad. This keeping informed and aware of one's actions—though it could not alter the required act, save in extremities—this minimal distance from one's own behavior, and the freedom to feel differently about it depending on its character, this too was what permitted the prisoner to remain a human being. . . .

Prisoners who understood this fully came to know that this, and only this, formed the crucial difference between retaining one's humanity (and often life itself) and accepting death as a human being (or perhaps physical death): whether one retained the freedom to choose autonomously one's attitude to extreme conditions even when they seemed totally beyond one's ability to influence them.

—Bruno Bettelheim

Affliction stamps the soul to its very depths with the scorn, the disgust and even the self-hatred and sense of guilt that crime logically should produce but actually does not.

—Simone Weil

A Commandant Reminisces

Even those petty incidents that others might not notice I found hard to forget. In Auschwitz I truly had no reason to complain that I was bored.

If I was deeply affected by some incident, I found it impossible to go back to my home and family. I would mount my horse and ride, until I had chased the terrible picture away. Often, at night, I would walk through the stables and seek relief among my beloved animals.

It would often happen, when at home, that my thoughts suddenly turned to incidents that had occurred during the extermination. I then had to go out. I could no longer bear to be in my homely family circle. When I saw my children happily playing, or observed my wife's delight over our youngest, the thought would often come to me: how long will our happiness last? My wife could never understand these gloomy moods of mine, and ascribed them to some annoyance connected with my work.

When at night I stood out there beside the transports or by the gas-chambers or the fires, I was often compelled to think of my wife and children, without, however, allowing myself to connect them closely with all that was happening.

It was the same with the married men who worked in the crematoriums or at the fire pits.

When they saw the women and children going into the gas chambers, their thoughts instinctively turned to their own families.

I was no longer happy in Auschwitz once the mass exterminations had begun.

I had become dissatisfied with myself. To this must be added that I was worried because of anxiety about my principal task, the never-ending work, and the untrustworthiness of my colleagues.

Then the refusal to understand, or even to listen to me, on the part of my superiors. It was in truth not a happy or desirable state of affairs.

Yet everyone in Auschwitz believed that the commandant lived a wonderful life.

My family, to be sure, were well provided for in Auschwitz. Every wish that my wife or children expressed was granted them. The children could lead a free and untrammeled life. My wife's garden was a paradise of flowers. The prisoners never missed an opportunity for doing some little act of kindness to my wife or children and thus attracting their attention.

No former prisoner can ever say that he was in any way or at any time badly treated in our house. My wife's greatest pleasure would have been to give a present to every prisoner who was in any way connected with our household.

The children were perpetually begging me for cigarettes for the prisoners. They were particularly fond of the ones who worked in the garden.

My whole family displayed an intense love of agriculture and particularly for animals of all sorts. Every Sunday I had to walk them across the fields, and visit the stables, and we might never miss the kennels where the dogs were kept. Our two horses and the foal were especially beloved.

The children always kept animals in the garden, creatures the prisoners were forever bringing them. Tortoises, martens, cats, lizards: there was always something new and interesting to be seen there. In summer they splashed in the wading pool in the garden, or in the Sola. But their greatest joy was when Daddy bathed with them. He had, however, so little time for all these childish pleasures. Today I deeply regret that I did not devote more time to my family. I always felt that I had to be on duty the whole time. This exaggerated sense of duty has always made life more difficult for me than it need have been. Again and again my wife reproached me and said: "You must think not only of the service always, but of your family too."

Yet what did my wife know about all that lay so heavily on my mind? She has never been told.

When, on Pohl's suggestion, Auschwitz was divided up, he gave me the choice of being commandant of Sachsenhausen or head of DK.

It was something quite exceptional for Pohl to allow any officer a choice of jobs. He gave me twenty-four hours in which to decide. It was really a kindly gesture in good will, a recompence, as he saw it, for the task I had been given at Auschwitz.

At first I felt unhappy at the prospect of uprooting myself, for I had become deeply involved with Auschwitz as a result of all the difficulties and troubles and the many heavy tasks that had been assigned to me there.

But then I was glad to be free from it all.

—Rudolf Hoess

Castration Complex

As a child, one of my favorite books was an English translation of Dr Hoffmann's *Struwwelpeter*, and my favorite poem in the book was "The Story of Little Suck-a-Thumb."

One day, Mamma said: "Conrad dear,
I must go out and leave you here.
But mind now, Conrad, what I say,
Don't suck your thumb while I'm away.
The great tall tailor always comes
To little boys that suck their thumbs;
And ere they dream what he's about,
He takes his great sharp scissors out
And cuts their thumbs clean off—and then,
You know, they never grow again.

Mamma had scarcely turn'd her back,
The thumb was in, Alack! Alack!

The door flew open, in he ran,
The great, long, red-legged scissor-man.
Oh! children, see! the tailor's come
And caught out little Suck-a-Thumb.
Snip! Snap! Snip! the scissors go;
And Conrad cries out—Oh! Oh! Oh!
Snip! Snap! Snip! They go so fast,
That both his thumbs are off at last.

Mamma comes home; there Conrad stands,
And looks quite sad, and shows his hands;
"Ah!" said Mamma, "I knew he'd come
To naughty little Suck-a-Thumb."

Reading this poem today, I say to myself, "Of course, it's not about thumb-sucking at all, but about masturbation, which is punished by castration." But if so, why did I enjoy the poem as a child? Why was I not frightened? In so far as it did arouse fear, it was a wholly pleasing fictional fear. It so happened that I was a nail-biter, but I knew perfectly well that Suck-a-Thumb's fate would not be mine, because the scissor-man was a figure in a poem, not a real person.

Very different is the fear aroused in me by spiders, crabs, and octopi, which are, I suspect, symbols to me for the castrating *Vagina Dentata.*

Cats

The Monk and His Pet Cat

I and my white pangur
Have each his special art:
His mind is set on hunting mice,
Mine is upon my special craft.

I love to rest—better than any fame!—
With close study at my little book;
White Pangur does not envy me:
He loves his childish play.

When in our house we two are all alone—
A tale without tedium!
We have sport never-ending!
Something to exercise our wit.

At times by feats of derring-do
A mouse sticks in his net,
While into my net there drops
A difficult problem of hard meaning.

He points his full shining eye
Against the fence of the wall:
I point my clear though feeble eye
Against the keenness of science.

He rejoices with quick leaps
When in his sharp claw sticks a mouse:
I too rejoice when I have grasped
A problem difficult and dearly loved.

Though we are thus at all times,
Neither hinders the other,
Each of us pleased with his own art
Amuses himself alone.

He is a master of the work
Which every day he does:
While I am at my own work
To bring difficulty to clearness.

—Anon. Irish (trans. Kuno Meyer)

Peter

Strong and slippery, built for the midnight grass-party confronted by
four cats,
he sleeps his time away—the detached first claw on the foreleg,
which corresponds
to the thumb, retracted to its tip; the small tuft of fronds
or katydid-legs above each eye, still numbering the unit in each
group;
the shadbones regularly set about the mouth, to droop or rise

in unison like the porcupine's quills—motionless. He lets
himself be flat-
tened out by gravity, as it were a piece of seaweed
tamed and weakened by
exposure to the sun; compelled when extended, to lie
stationary. Sleep is the result of his delusion that one must do as
well as one can for oneself; sleep—epitome of what is to

him as to the average person, the end of life. Demonstrate on him how
the lady caught the dangerous southern snake, placing
a forked stick on either
side of its innocuous neck; one need not try to stir
him up; his prune-shaped head and alligator eyes are not a
party to the
joke. Lifted and handled, he may be dangled like an eel or set

up on the forearm like a mouse; his eyes bisected by pupils of a pin's
width, are flickeringly exhibited, then covered up. May
be? I should say
might have been; when he has been got the better of in a
dream—as in a fight with nature or with cats—we all know it.
Profound sleep is
not with him a fixed illusion. Springing about with frog-like accuracy, emitting jerky cries when taken in the hand, he is himself
again; to sit caged by the rungs of a domestic
chair would be unprofit-
able—human. What is the good of hypocrisy? It
is permissible to choose one's employment, to abandon
the wire nail, the
roly-poly, when it shows signs of being no longer a pleas-

ure, to score the adjacent magazine with a double line of strokes. He
can

talk, but insolently says nothing. What of it?
When one is frank, one's very
presence is a compliment. It is clear that he can see
the virtue of naturalness, that he is one of those who
do not regard
the published fact as a surrender. As for the disposition

invariably to affront, an animal with claws wants to have to use
them; that eel-like extension of trunk into tail is not an
accident. To
leap, to lengthen out, divide the air—to purloin, to pursue.
To tell the hen: fly over the fence, go in the wrong way in your
perturba-
tion—this is life; to do less would be nothing but dishonesty.

—Marianne Moore

The Long Cat

A short-haired black cat always looks longer than any other cat. But this particular one, Babou, nicknamed the Long-cat, really did measure, stretched right out flat, well over a yard. I used to measure him sometimes.

"He's stopped growing longer," I said one day to my mother. "Isn't it a pity?"

"Why a pity? He's too long as it is. I can't understand why you want everything to grow bigger. It's bad to grow too much, very bad indeed!"

It's true that it always worried her when she thought her children were growing too fast, and she had good cause to be anxious about my elder half-brother, who went on growing until he was twenty-four.

"But I'd love to grow a bit taller."

"D'you mean you'd like to be like that Brisedoux girl, five-feet-seven tall at twelve years old? A midget can always make herself liked. But what can you do with a gigantic beauty? Who would want to marry her?"

"Couldn't Babou get married then?"

"Oh, a cat's a cat. Babou's only too long when he really wants to be. Are we even sure he's black? He's probably white in snowy weather, dark blue at night, and red when he goes to steal strawberries. He's very light when he lies on your knees, and very heavy when I carry him into the kitchen in the evenings to prevent him from sleeping on my bed. I think he's too much of a vegetarian to be a real cat."

For the Long-cat really did steal strawberries, picking out the ripest of the variety called Docteur-Morere which are so sweet, and of the Hautboys which taste faintly of nuts. According to the season he would also go for the tender tips of the asparagus, and when it came to melons his choice was not so much for cantaloups as for the kind called Noir-des-Carmes whose rind, marbled light and dark like the skin of a salamander, he knew how to rip open. In all this he was not exceptional. I once had a she-cat who used to crunch rings of raw onion, provided they were the sweet onions of the South. There are cats who set great store by oysters, snails, and clams . . .

By virtue of his serpent-like build, the Long-cat excelled in strange leaps in which he nearly twisted himself into a figure of eight. In full sunlight his winter coat, which was longer and more satiny than in summer, revealed the waterings and markings of his far-off tabby ancestor. A tom will remain playful until he is quite old; but even in play his face never loses the gravity that is stamped on it. The Long-cat's expression softened only when he looked at my mother. Then his white whiskers would bristle powerfully, while into his eyes crept the smile of an innocent little boy. He used to follow her when she went to pick violets along the wall that separated M. de Fourolles' garden from ours. The close-set border provided every day a big bunch which mother let fade, either pinned to her bodice or in an empty glass, because violets in water lose all their scent. Step by step the Long-cat followed his stooping mistress, sometimes imitating with his paw the gesture of her hand groping among the leaves, and imitating her discoveries also. "Ha, ha!" he would cry, "me too!" and thereupon show his prize: a bombardier beetle, a pink worm, or a shrivelled cockchafer.

—Colette (trans. Enid McLeod)

Chamber Music

Of the audience at a chamber-music concert, an Oxford Don once remarked, "They look like the sort of people who go to the English Church abroad."

Chamber music is essentially an intimate affair, to be played in private houses by friends for friends. In the anonymous atmosphere of a public concert hall, it becomes "arty."

Chamber Music

First Violin. I, in love with the beauty of this world, endow it with my own beauty. The world has no abyss. Streaming out, my heart spends itself. I am only song: I sound.

Second Violin. For me, beside your more ethereal being, it is forbidden to have an I. Not the world—but more firmly and substantially: the earth has taught me. There it is growing dark. Let me accompany you, sister!

VIOLA. My grey hair makes it my duty to name the abyss for you. As you two childlike kindred spirits skim along, even the quarrel about nothing becomes attractive. But I suffer.

CELLO. I know in my heart of hearts, that all is fate, the finely done and the unrelieved. I am true to the whole: enjoy life and repent! I do not warn. I weep with you. I console.

—Josef Weinheber (trans. Patrick Bridgewater)

CHEF, LIFE OF A

CARÊME, Marie-Antoine: Like Theseus and Romulus, like all founders of empires, Carême was a sort of lost child. He was born in Paris in 1784, in a woodyard where his father was employed. There were fifteen children, and the father did not know how to feed them all.

One day, when Marie-Antoine was eleven years old, his father took him to the town gate for dinner. Then, leaving him in the middle of the street, he said to him: "Go, little one. There are good trades in this world. Let the rest of us languish in the misery in which we are doomed to die. This is a time when fortunes are made by those who have the wit, and that you have. Tonight or tomorrow, find a good house that may open its doors to you. Go with what God has given you and what I may add to that." And the good man gave him his blessing.

From that time on, Marie-Antoine never again saw his father and mother, who died young, nor his brothers and sisters, who were scattered over the world.

Night fell. The boy saw a lighted window and knocked on it. It was a cookshop whose proprietor's name has not been preserved in history. He took the boy and put him to work next day.

At sixteen, he quit this dingy tavern and went to work as an assistant to a restaurateur. His progress was rapid, and he already knew what he wanted to be. He went to work for Bailly, a famous pastrycook on the Rue Vivienne, who excelled in cream tarts and catered to the Prince de Talleyrand. From that moment he saw his future clearly. He had discovered his vocation.

"At seventeen," he says in his *Mémoires,* "I was chief pastrycook at Bailly's. He was a good master and took an interest in me. He gave me time off to study designs from prints. He put me in charge of preparing several set pieces for the table of the First Consul. I used my designs and my nights in his service, and he repaid me with kindness. In his establishment I began to innovate. The illustrious pastrycook Avice was then flourishing. His work aroused my enthusiasm, and knowledge of his methods gave me courage. I sought to follow without imitating him.

I learned to execute every trick of the trade, and made unique, extraordinary pieces by myself. But to get there, young people, how many sleepless nights! I could not work on my designs and calculations until after nine or ten o'clock, and I worked three quarters of the night.

"I left M. Bailly with tears in my eyes and went to work for the successor of M. Gendron. I made it a condition that if I had the opportunity to make an 'extra' I could have someone replace me. A few months later, I left the great pastryshops behind altogether, and devoted myself to preparing great dinners. It was enough to do. I rose higher and higher and earned a lot of money. Others became jealous of me, a poor child of labor, and I have often been the butt of attacks from little pastrycooks who will have far to climb to where I am now."

During the prodigality of the Directoire, Carême refined cooking into the delicate luxury and exquisite sensuality of the Empire. The Talleyrand household was served with wisdom and grandeur, Carême says. It gave an example to others and kept them in mind of his basic principles.

The culinary director in this household was Bouché, or Bouchésèche, who came from the Condé household, famous for its fine fare. So Talleyrand's cuisine was simply a continuation of the cuisine of the Condé household. Carême dedicated his *Pâtissier royal* to Bouché. It was there that he made the acquaintance of Laguipière, the Emperor's cook, who died in the retreat from Moscow. Until that time, Carême had followed his art. After Laguipière, he learned to improvise. But practice did not satisfy him any longer. He wanted to go more profoundly into theory, to copy designs, to read and analyze scientific works and follow through with studies parallel to his profession. He wrote and illustrated a *History of the Roman Table*, but, unfortunately, both manuscript and drawings have been lost. Carême was a poet. He placed his art on the same level as all the others. And he was right to do so.

"From behind my stoves," he says, "I contemplated the cuisines of India, China, Egypt, Greece, Turkey, Italy, Germany, and Switzerland. I felt the unworthy methods of routine crumble under my blows."

Carême had grown up under the Empire, and you can imagine his distress when he saw it crash. He had to be forced to execute the gigantic royal banquet in the Plaine des Vertus in 1814. The following year the Prince Regent called him to Brighton as his chef. He stayed with the English Regent two years. Every morning he prepared his menu with His Highness, who was a blasé gourmand. During these discussions he went through a course in gastronomic hygiene that, if printed, would be one of the classic books of cookery.

Bored with the gray skies of England, Carême returned to Paris but went back when the Prince Regent became King. From London he went to St Petersburg as one of the Emperor Alexander's chefs, then to Vienna to direct a few great dinners for the Austrian Emperor. He returned to London with Lord Stuart, the English ambassador, but soon quit to return to Paris to write and publish. He was constantly torn from his study of theory by calls from monarchs and congresses. His work shortened his life. "The charcoal is killing us," he said, "but what does it matter? The fewer the years, the greater the glory." He died before reaching the age of fifty, on January 12, 1833.

—Alexandre Dumas (trans. Louis Colman)

Chiasmus

Ev'ry Swain shall pay his Duty
Grateful every Nymph shall prove;
And as these Excell in Beauty,
Those shall be Renown'd for Love.

—John Dryden

Childhood

Gradually I came to know where I was, and I tried to express my wants to those who could gratify them, yet could not, because my wants were inside me, and they were outside, nor had they any power of getting into my soul. And so I made movements and sounds, signs like my wants, the few I could, the best I could; for they were not really like my meaning. And when I was not obeyed, because people did not understand me, or because they would not do me harm, I was angry, because elders did not submit to me, because freemen would not slave for me, and I avenged myself on them by tears.

—St Augustine

De Puero Balbutiente

Methinks 'tis pretty sport to hear a child,
Rocking a word in mouth yet undefiled;
The tender racquet rudely plays the sound,
Which, weakly bandied, cannot back rebound;
And the soft air the softer roof doth kiss,
With a sweet dying and a pretty miss,
Which hears no answer yet from the white rank
Of teeth, not risen from their coral bank.
The alphabet is searched for letters soft,
To try a word before it can be wrought,

And when it slideth forth, it goes as nice
As when a man does walk upon the ice.

—Thomas Bastard

To think that physical comfort makes for human relations is an error we make because the absence of all comfort interferes with good relations. But we base it on the correct observation that when a parent takes pleasure in going out of his way to provide comfort for his child, the child takes it as a proof that he is loveable and deserves care and respect. This feeling enables him to trust—we can trust our well-being to persons who find us so important. Out of such trust in their intentions toward us, and our importance to them, develop first fleeting and then permanent relations.

This is where a society of plenty can make it harder for a child to relate. If comfort for the child can only be gained, by the parent, with a certain amount of trouble, he will very likely feel pleasure when he offers it to his child. It is this, the parent's pleasure, that gives the child a sense of worth and sets going the process of relating. (Of course, there are many pitfalls, such as when the parent feels his effort is too great, and creates guilt in the child as the comfort is offered.) But if comfort is so readily available that the parent feels no particular pleasure in being able to provide it, then the child cannot develop self-esteem around the giving and receiving of comfort.

Many children, four to six years of age, communicate mainly in terms of their favorite shows and relate much better to the TV screen than to their parents. Some of them seem unable to respond any more to the simple and direct language of their parents because it sounds unimpressive compared to the suave diction and emotionally loaded idiom of TV professionals. . . . Children who have been taught, or conditioned, to listen passively most of the day to the warm verbal communications coming from the TV screen, to the deep emotional appeal of the so-called TV personality, are often unable to respond to real persons because they arouse so much less feeling than the skilled actor. Worse, they lose the ability to learn from reality because life experiences are more complicated than the ones they see on the screen, and there is no one who comes in at the end to explain it all. . . . Conditioned to being given explanations, the "TV Child" has not learned to puzzle for one on his own; he gets discouraged when he cannot grasp the meaning of what happens to him and is thrown back once more to find comfort in predictable stories on the screen. . . . This being seduced into passivity and discouraged about facing life actively, on one's own, is the real danger of TV, much more than the often asinine or gruesome content of the shows.

—Bruno Bettelheim

It is not that the child lives in a world of imagination, but that the child within us survives and starts into life only at rare moments of recollection, which makes us believe, and it is not true, that, as children, we were imaginative.

—Cesare Pavese

Buildings as Drawn by Girls and by Boys

The girl's scene is a house *interior*, represented either as a configuration of furniture without any surrounding walls or by a simple *enclosure* built with blocks. In the girl's scene, people and animals are mostly *within* such an interior or enclosure, and they are primarily people or animals in a *static* (sitting or standing) position. Girls' enclosures consist of low walls, i.e. only one block high, except for an occasional *elaborate doorway*. These interiors of houses with or without walls were, for the most part, expressly *peaceful*. Often, a little girl was playing the piano. In a number of cases, the interior was *intruded* by animals or dangerous men. Yet the idea of an intruding creature did not necessarily lead to the defensive erection of walls or the closing of doors. Rather, the majority of these intrusions have an element of humor and pleasurable excitement.

Boys' scenes are either houses with elaborate walls or façades with *protrusions* such as cones or cylinders representing ornaments or cannons. There are *high towers*, and there are entirely exterior scenes. In boys' constructions more people and animals are *outside* enclosures or buildings, and there are more automotive objects and animals *moving* along streets and intersections. There are elaborate automotive *accidents*, but there is also traffic channelled or arrested by the policeman. While *high structures* are prevalent in the configurations of the boys, there is also much play with the danger of *collapse* or downfall; *ruins* were exclusively boys' constructions.

—Erik Erikson

My parents were—in a sort—visible powers of nature to me, no more loved than the sun and the moon: only I should have been annoyed and puzzled if either of them had gone out . . . still less did I love God; not that I had any quarrel with Him, or fear of Him; but simply found, what people told me was His service, disagreeable; and what people told me was His book, not entertaining. I had no companions to quarrel with, either; nobody to assist, and nobody to thank. Not a servant was ever allowed to do anything for me, but what it was their duty to do; and why should I have to be grateful to the cook for cooking, or the gardener for gardening,—when the one dared not give me a baked potato without asking leave, and the other would not let my ants' nests alone, because they made the walks untidy.

My times of happiness had always been when *nobody* was thinking of me; and the main discomfort and drawback to all proceedings and designs, the attention and interference of the public—represented by my mother and the gardener. The garden was no waste place for me, because I did not suppose myself an object of interest either to the ants or the butterflies; and the only qualification of the entire delight of my evening walk at Champagnole or St Laurent was the sense that my father and mother *were* thinking of me, and would be frightened if I was five minutes late for tea.

—Ruskin

Childhood

III

In the woods there is a bird, his song stops you and makes you blush.
There is a clock that never strikes.
There is a hollow with a nest full of white beasts.
There is a little carriage left in the copse, or which runs down the lane with ribbons on it.
There is a troupe of little actors in costume, glimpsed on the road through the edge of the woods.
There is, lastly, when you are hungry and thirsty, someone who chases you away.

IV

I am the saint, praying on the terrace—as the peaceful beasts gaze down to the sea of Palestine.
I am the scholar in the dark armchair. Branches and rain hurl themselves at the library windows.
I am the traveller on the high road through the stunted woods; the roar of the sluices drowns my steps. For a long time I watch the melancholy golden wash of the sunset.
I might be the child left on the jetty washed out to sea, the little farm boy following the lane whose crest touches the sky.
The paths are rough. The hillocks are covered with broom. The air is motionless. How far away the birds and springs are! It can only be the end of the world, ahead.

And if, having surprised him at unclean compassions, his mother took fright, the deep signs of the child's affection would throw themselves, in defence, upon her astonishment. Everything was all right. She had received that blue gaze—which lies!

—Arthur Rimbaud
(trans. Oliver Bernard, slightly modified by W. H. A.)

Aha, Wanton is my name!
I can many a quaynte game.
Lo, my toppe I dryve in same,
Se, it torneth rounde!
I can with my scorge-stycke
My felowe upon the heed hytte,
And lyghtly from hym make a skyppe;
And blere on hym my tonge.
If brother or syster do me chide
I wyll scratche and also byte.
I can crye, and also kyke,
And mock them all berewe.
If fader or mother wyll me smyte,
I wyll wrynge with my lyppe;
And lyghtly from hym make a skyppe;
And call my dame shrewe.
Aha, a newe game have I founde:
Se this gynne it renneth rounde;
And here another have I founde,
And yet mo can I fynde.
I can mowe on a man;
And make a lesynge well I can,
And mayntayne it ryght well than.
This connynge came me of kynde.
Ye, syrs, I can well gelde a snayle;
And catche a coew by the tayle;
This is a fayre connynge!
I can daunce, and also skyppe;
I can playe at the chery pytte;
And I can wystell you a fytte,
Syres, in a whylowe ryne.
Ye, syrs, and every daye
Whan I to scole shall take the waye
Some good mannes gardyn I wyll assaye,
Perys and plommes to plucke.
I can spye a sparowes nest.
I wyll not go to scole but whan me lest,
For there begynneth a sory fest
Whan the mayster sholde lyfte my docke.
But syrs, what I was seven yere of age,
I was sent to the Worlde to take wage.
And this seven yere I have been his page
And kept his commaundment . . .

—Anon.

From infancy through childhood's giddy maze,
Froward at school, and fretful in his plays,
The puny tyrant burns to subjugate
The free republic of the whip-gig state.
If one, his equal in athletic frame,
Or, more provoking still, of nobler name,
Dare step across his arbitrary views,
An Iliad, only not in verse, ensues:
The little Greeks look trembling at the scales,
Till the best tongue, or heaviest hand prevails.

—W. Cowper

False Security

. . . I ran to the ironwork gateway of number seven
Secure at last on the lamplit fringe of Heaven.
Oh who can say how subtle and safe one feels
Shod in one's children's sandals from Daniel Neal's,
Clad in one's party clothes made of stuff from Heal's?
And who can still one's thrill at the candle shine
On cakes and ices and jelly and blackcurrant wine,
And the warm little feel of my hostess's hand in mine?
Can I forget my delight at the conjuring show?
And wasn't I proud that I was the last to go?
Too overexcited and pleased with myself to know
That the words I heard my hostess's mother employ
To a guest departing, would ever diminish my joy,
I WONDER WHERE JULIA FOUND THAT STRANGE, RATHER COMMON LITTLE BOY?

—John Betjeman

The Gate

We sat, two children, warm against the wall
Outside the towering stronghold of our fathers
That frowned its stern security down upon us.
We could not enter there. That fortress, life,
Our safe protection, was too gross and strong
For our unpractised palates. Yet our guardians
Cherished our innocence with gentle hands,
(They, who had long since lost their innocence,)
And in grave play put on a childish mask
Over their tell-tale faces, as in shame
For the fine food that plumped their lusty bodies
And made them strange as gods. We sat that day

With the great parapet behind us, safe
As every day, yet outcast, safe and outcast
As castaways thrown upon an empty shore.
Before us lay our well-worn scene, a hillock
So small and smooth and green, it seemed intended
For us alone and childhood, a still pond
That opened upon no sight a quiet eye,
A little stream that tinkled down the slope.
But suddenly all seemed old
And dull and shrunken, shut within itself
In a sullen dream. We were outside, alone.
And then behind us the huge gate swung open.

—Edwin Muir

A child of seven is excited by being told that Tommy opened a door and saw a dragon. But a child of three is excited by being told that Tommy opened a door. Boys like romantic tales; but babies like realistic tales—because they find them romantic. In fact, a baby is about the only person, I should think, to whom a modern realistic novel could be read without boring him.

The child does not know that men are not only bad from good motives, but also often good from bad motives. Therefore the child has a hearty, healthy, unspoiled, and unsatiable appetite for mere morality, for the mere difference between a good little girl and a bad little girl.

In turning the pages of one of the papers my eye catches the following sentence: "By the light of modern science and thought, we are in a position to see that each normal human being in some way repeats historically the life of the human race." This is a very typical modern assertion; that is, it is an assertion for which there is not and never has been a single spot or speck of proof. We know precious little about what the life of the human race has been; and none of our scientific conjectures about it bear the remotest resemblance to the actual growth of a child. According to this theory, a baby begins by chipping flints and rubbing sticks together to find fire. One so often sees babies doing this. About the age of five the child, before the delighted eyes of his parents, founds a village community. By the time he is eleven it has become a small city state, replica of ancient Athens. Encouraged by this, the boy proceeds, and before he is fourteen has founded the Roman Empire. But now his parents have a serious set-back. Having watched him so far, not only with pleasure, but with a very natural surprise, they must strengthen themselves to endure the spectacle of decay. They have now to watch their child going through the decline of the Western Empire and the

Dark Ages. They see the invasion of the Huns and that of the Norsemen chasing each other across his expressive face. He seems a little happier after he has "repeated" the Battle of Chalons and the unsuccessful Siege of Paris; and by the time he comes to the twelfth century, his boyish face is as bright as it was of old when he was "repeating" Pericles or Camillus. I have no space to follow this remarkable demonstration of how history repeats itself in the youth; how he grows dismal at twenty-three to represent the end of Medievalism, brightens because the Renaissance is coming, darkens again with the disputes of the later Reformation, broadens placidly through the thirties as the rational eighteenth century, till at last, about forty-three, he gives a great yell and begins to burn the house down, as a symbol of the French Revolution. Such (we shall all agree) is the ordinary development of a boy.

—G. K. Chesterton

In every man there lies hidden a child between five and eight years old, the age at which naïveté comes to an end. It is this child whom one must detect in that intimidating man with his long beard, bristling eyebrows, heavy moustache, and weighty look—a captain. Even he conceals, and not at all deep down, the youngster, the booby, the little rascal, out of whom age has made this powerful monster.

—Paul Valéry

Children, Autistic

According to Dr Bruno Bettelheim, who seems to have an unusual gift for handling autistic children, the cause of "autism" is that the child is convinced, rightly or wrongly, that its parents wish it did not exist. Consequently the world an autistic child creates is based upon total doubt. (*See* Belief.)

Many who have reflected on the autistic child's desire for sameness recognize that its purpose is to reduce anxiety. What is not stressed as much is that it stands for an ordering of things, an effort to establish laws by which things must happen.

With us, too, scientific law signifies that, given the same conditions, the same events will take place. If the search for natural laws has a purpose, it is to predict events and master nature so as to make our lives more secure. Social law, too, has no purpose except to safeguard our common existence. This—their intrinsic purpose—all our laws have in common with the laws the autistic child creates. He is firmly convinced that those he lives by are essential to his security. They must be observed or his life will fall apart, just as society would decay if no one accepted the law of the land. To prevent this, he must arrange his toys in the same way and with the same enunciation. What distinguishes his laws from ours is that his are non-adaptive and universal. One and the same law governs everything.

All autistic children demand that time must stop still. Time is the destroyer of sameness. If sameness is to be preserved, time must stop in its tracks. Therefore the autistic child's world consists only of space. Neither time nor causality exist there, because causality involves a sequence in time where events have to follow one another. In the autistic child's world the chain of events is not conditioned by the causality we know. But since one event does follow another, it must be because of some timeless cosmic law that ordains it. An eternal law. Things happen because they must, not because they are caused.

Time also implies hope. Without time there is no hope but also no disappointment nor the fear that things might get even worse. Hence infantile autism and the cosmic law. Once and for all, and absolutely, it ordains how things must be ordered. Sensible laws can be subjected to sensible revision and hence permit hope to arise. Thus it must be an insensible law that never changes. And the essential content of this law is "You must never hope that anything can change."

—Bruno Bettelheim

For anybody interested in language, the linguistic behavior of autistic children is of the greatest interest and significance.

Joey's language, step by step, became abstract, depersonalised, detached. He lost the ability to use personal pronouns correctly, later lost the use of them entirely.

While at first Joey named foods correctly, calling them, "butter", "sugar", "water", and so forth, he later gave this up. He then called sugar "sand", butter "grease", water "liquid" and so on. Thus he deprived food of taste and smell, and these qualities he replaced by the way they feel to the touch. Clearly he had the ability to engage in abstract thinking. It is also clear that in his transposing of names, as much as his giving up of pronouns, the autistic child creates a language to fit his emotional experience of the world. Far from not knowing how to use language correctly, there is a spontaneous decision to create a language which will match how he experiences things—and things only, not people.

(After a period of therapy Joey began to use personal pronouns again, but in reverse, as do most autistic children. He referred to himself as "you" and to the adult he was speaking to as "I".) Shortly after his treatment there was ended, he was able to use the "I" correctly and to name some of the children in addition to his therapist. But he never used names or personal pronouns in direct address, only in the indirect third person when referring to them. He never referred to anyone by name; other than simply "That person"; later, with some differentiation, "the small person" or "the big person".

By not permitting himself to be an "I", by not permitting himself to say "yes" to anything, the autistic child is complying with what he considers a parental wish that he should not exist. This is why the "you"—those others who are permitted to exist—and the "no" which is essentially a denial of existence, are so much more readily available to him.

—Bruno Bettelheim

Choirboys

As a boy, both before and after it broke, I had the luck to possess a voice which, though certainly not of solo quality, was good enough for a choir.

As a choirboy, I had to learn, not only to sight-read music, but also to enunciate words clearly—there is a famous tongue twister in the *Jubilate*—"For why, it is He that hath made us and not we ourselves"—and to notice the difference between their metrical values when spoken and when sung, so that, long before I took a conscious interest in poetry I had acquired a certain sensitivity to language which I could not have acquired in any other way.

The Choir Boy

And when he sang in choruses
His voice o'ertopped the rest,
Which is very inartistic,
But the public like that best.

—Anon.

Like luxurious cygnets in their cloudy lawn, a score of young singing-boys were awaiting their cue: Low-masses, cheapness and economy, how they despised them, and how they would laugh at "Old Ends" who snuffed out the candles.

"Why should the Church charge higher for a short *Magnificat* than for a long *Miserere*?"

The question had just been put by the owner of a dawning moustache and a snub, though expressive, nose.

"Because happiness makes people generous, stupid, and often as not they'll squander, boom, but unhappiness makes them calculate. People grudge spending much on a snivel—even if it lasts an hour."

"It's the choir that suffers."

"This profiteering . . ." there was a confusion of voices.

"Order!" A slim lad, of an ambered paleness, raised a protesting hand. Indulged and made-much-of by the hierarchy, he was Felix Ganay, known as Chief-dancing-choir-boy to the cathedral of Clemenza.

"Aren't they awful?" he addressed a child with a very finished small head. Fingering a score of music he had been taking the lead in a mass of Palestrina; and had the vaguely distraught air of a kitten that had seen visions.

—Ronald Firbank

Christmas

Love is plonte of pees, most precious of vertues,
For hevene holde hit ne mighte, so hevy hit semede,
Til hit hadde of erthe y-yoten hitselve.
Was nevere lef upon linde lighter therafter
As whanne hit hadde of the folde flesch and blode ytake.
Tho was hit portatif and persaunt as the pointe of a nelde:
May none armure hit lette, ne none hye walles.

—William Langland

Of the Nativity of Christ

Rorate celi desuper!
Hevins, distill your balmy schouris,
For now is rissin the bricht day ster,
Fro the ros Mary, flour of flouris:
The cleir Sone, quhome no clud devouris,
Surminting Phebus in the est,
Is cumin of his hevinly touris:
Et nobis Puer natus est.

Archangellis, angellis, and dompnationis,
Tronis, potestatis, and marteiris seir,
And all ye hevinly operationis,
Ster, planeit, firmament, and speir,
Fyre, erd, air, and watter cleir,
To him gife loving, most and lest,
That come in to so meik maneir;
Et nobis Puer natus est.

Synnaris be glaid, and pennance do,
And thank your Makar hairtfully;
For he that ye mycht nocht cum to,
To yow is cummin full humly,
Your saulis with his blud to by,
And lous yow of the feind is arrest,
And only of his awin mercy;
Pro nobis Puer natus est.

All clergy do to him inclyne,
And bow unto that barne benyng,
And do your observance devyne
To him that is of kingis King;
Ensence his altar, reid and sing
In haly kirk, with mynd degest,
Him honouring attour all thing,
Qui nobis Puer natus est.

Celestiall fowlies in the are
Sing with your jottis upoun hicht;
In firthis and in forrestis fair
Be myrthful now, at all your mycht,
For passit is your dully nycht,
Aurora hes the cluddis perst,
The son is rissin with glaidsum lycht,
Et nobis Puer natus est.

Now spring up flouris fra the rute,
Revert yow upwart naturaly,
In honour of the blessit frute
That rais up fro the rose Mary;
Lay out your levis lustely,
Fro dei tak lyfe now at the lest
In weirschip of that Prince wirthy,
Qui nobis Puer natus est.

Syng hevin imperiall, most of hicht,
Regions of air mak harmony;
All fishe in flud and foull of licht
Be mirthful and mak melody:
All *Gloria in excelsis* cry,
Hevin, erd, se, man, bird, and best,
He that is crownit abone the sky
Pro nobis Puer natus est.

—William Dunbar

The Nativity of Our Lord and Saviour Jesus Christ

Where is this stupendous stranger,
    Swains of Solyma, advise,
Lead me to my Master's manger,
    Shew me where my Saviour lies? . . .

Nature's decorations glisten
Far above their usual trim;
Birds on box and laurel listen,
As so near the cherubs hymn.

Boreas now no longer winters
On the desolated coast;
Oaks no more are riv'n in splinters
By the whirlwind and his host.

Spinks and ouzels sing sublimely,
"We too have a Saviour born";
Whiter blossoms burst untimely
On the blest Mosaic thorn.

God all-bounteous, all-creative,
Whom no ills from good dissuade,
Is incarnate, and a native
Of the very world he made.

—Christopher Smart

Cities, Modern

Some cities are really successful, and present the solid and definite achievement of the thing at which their builders aimed; and when they do this, they present, just as a fine statue presents, something of the direct divinity of man, something immeasurably superior to mere nature, to mere common mountains, to mere vulgar seas. . . . The modern city is ugly, not because it is a city, but because it is not enough of a city, because it is a jungle, because it is confused and anarchic, and surging with selfish and materialistic energies. In short, the modern town is offensive because it is a great deal too like nature, a great deal too like the country.

—G. K. Chesterton

Noise is manufactured in the city, just as goods are manufactured. The city is the place where noise is kept in stock, completely detached from the object from which it came.

—Max Picard

The official acropolis outdoes the most colossal conceptions of modern barbarity. It is impossible to describe the dull light produced by the unchanging grey sky, the imperial brightness of the masonry, and the eternal snow on the ground. They have reproduced, in singularly outrageous taste, all the classical marvels of architecture. I go to exhibitions of painting in places twenty times vaster than Hampton Court. What painting! A Norwegian Nebuchadnezzar designed the staircases of the ministries; the minor officials I did see are prouder than Brahmins as it is, and the looks of the guardians of colossi and of the building foremen made me tremble. By their grouping of the buildings, in closed squares, terraces, and courtyards, they have squeezed out the bell-towers. The parks present primeval nature cultivated with marvellous art. There are parts of the better district which are inexplicable: an arm of the sea, without boats, rolls its sheet of blue ground glass between quays covered with giant candelabra. A short bridge leads to a postern immediately below the dome of the Holy Chapel. This dome is an artistic framework of steel about fifteen thousand feet in diameter.

From certain points on the copper foot-bridges, the platforms, the stairways which wind round the covered markets and the pillars, I thought I could judge the depth of the city. This was the marvel I was unable to verify: what are the levels of the other districts above and below the acropolis? For the foreigner in our times exploration is impossible. The commercial district is a circus all in the same style, with galleries of arcades. One can see no shops, but the snow on the roadway is trampled; a few nabobs, as rare as walkers on a Sunday morning in London, move towards a stage-coach made of diamonds. There are a few red velvet divans: polar drinks are served, whose prices range from eight hundred to eight thousand rupees. To my idea of looking for theatres in this circus, I reply that the shops must contain some pretty gloomy dramas. I think there is a police force; but the laws must be so strange that I give up trying to imagine what the adventurers of this place are like.

The outlying part, as elegant as a fine street in Paris, is favoured with the appearance of light; the democratic element numbers a few hundred souls. Here again, the houses are not in rows; the suburb loses itself oddly in the country, the "County" which fills the endless west of forests and huge plantations where misanthropic gentlemen hunt for news by artificial light.

—Arthur Rimbaud
(trans. Oliver Bernard, slightly modified by W. H. A.)

Here malice, rapine, accident conspire,
And now a rabble rages, now a fire;
Their ambush here relentless ruffians lay,
And here the fell attorney prowls for prey;
Here falling houses thunder on your head,
And here a female atheist talks you dead.

—Dr Johnson

A Nocturnal Sketch

Even is come; and from the dark Park, hark,
The signal of the setting sun—one gun!
And six is sounding from the chime, prime time
To go and see the Drury-Lane Dane slain,—
Or hear Othello's jealous doubt spout out,—
Or Macbeth raving at that shade-made blade,
Denying to his frantic clutch much touch;—
Or else to see Ducrow with wide stride ride
Four horses as no other man can span;
Or in the small Olympic Pit, sit split
Laughing at Liston, while you quiz his phiz.

Anon Night comes, and with her wings brings things
Such as, with his poetic tongue, Young sung;
The gas up-blazes with its bright white light,
And paralytic watchmen prowl, howl, growl,
About the streets and take up Pall-Mall Sal,
Who, hasting to her nightly jobs, robs fobs.

Now thieves to enter for your cash, smash, crash,
Past drowsy Charley in a deep sleep, creep,
But frightened by Policeman B.3, flee,
And while they're going, whisper low, "No go!"

Now puss, while folks are in their beds, treads leads,
And sleepers waking, grumble—, "Drat that cat!"
Who in the gutter caterwauls, squalls, mauls
Some feline foe, and screams in shrill ill-will.

Now Bulls of Bashan, and of prize size, rise
In childish dreams, and a roar, gore, poor
Georgy, or Charley, or Billy, willy-nilly;—
But Nursemaid in a nightmare rest, chest-pressed,
Dreameth of one of her old flames, James Games,
And that she hears—what faith is man's—Ann's banns
And his, from Reverend Mr Rice, twice, thrice:
White ribbons flourish, and a stout shout out
That upward goes, shows Rose knows those bows' woes.

—Thomas Hood

Climber, An Amateur

Eskdale, Friday, Augt 6th (1802) at an Estate House called Toes.

There is one sort of Gambling, to which I am much addicted; and that not of the least criminal kind for a man who has children & a

Concern.—It is this. When I find it convenient to descend from a mountain, I am too confident & too indolent to round about & wind about 'till I find a track or other symptom of safety; but I wander on, & where it is first possible to descend, there I go—relying upon fortune for how far down this possibility will continue. So it was yesterday afternoon. I passed down from Broadcrag, skirted the Precipices, and found myself cut off from a most sublime Crag-summit, that seemed to rival Sca'Fell Man in height, & to outdo it in fierceness. A Ridge of Hill lay low down, & divided this Crag (called Doe-crag) & Broad-crag—even as the Hyphen divides the words broad & crag. I determined to go thither; the first place I came to, that was not Direct Rock, I slipped down, & went on for a while with tolerable ease—but now I came (it was midway down) to a smooth perpendicular Rock about 7 feet high—this was nothing—I put my hands on the Ledge, & dropped down / in a few yards came just such another / I dropped that too / and yet another, seemed not higher—I would not stand for a trifle / so I dropped that too / but the stretching of the muscle(s) of my hand & arms, & the jolt of the Fall on my Feet, put my whole Limbs in a Tremble, and I paused, & looking down, saw that I had little else to encounter but a succession of these little Precipices—it was in truth a Path that in a very hard Rain is, no doubt, the channel of a most splendid Waterfall. / So I began to suspect that I ought not to go on / but then unfortunately tho' I could with ease drop down a smooth Rock 7 feet high, I could not climb it / so go on I must / and on I went / the next 3 drops were not half a Foot, at least not a foot more than my own height / but every Drop increased the Palsy of my Limbs—I shook all over, Heaven knows without the least influence of Fear / and now I had only two more to drop down / to return was impossible—but of these two the first was tremendous / it was twice my own height, & the Ledge at the bottome was (so) exceedingly narrow, that if I dropt down upon it I must of necessity have fallen backwards & of course killed myself. My Limbs were all in a tremble—I lay upon my Back to rest myself, & I was beginning according to my Custom to laugh at myself for a Madman, when the sight of the Crags above me on each side, & the impetuous Clouds just over them, posting so luridly & so rapidly northward, overawed me / I lay in a state of almost prophetic Trance & Delight—& blessed God aloud, for the powers of Reason & the Will, which remaining no Danger can overpower us! O God, I exclaimed aloud—how calm, how blessed am I now / I know not how to proceed, how to return / but I am calm & fearless & confident / if this reality were a Dream, if I were asleep, what agonies had I suffered! what screams!—When the Reason & the Will are away, what remains to us but Darkness & Dimness & a bewildering Shame, and Pain that is utterly Lord over us, or fantastic Pleasure, that draws the Soul along swimming through the air in man shapes, even as Flight of Starlings in a Wind.—I arose, and looking down saw at the bottom a heap of stones—which had fallen abroad—and rendered the narrow Ledge on which they had been piled, double dangerous / at the bottom of the third Rock that I dropt from, I met a dead Sheep quite rotten—This heap of Stones, I guessed, & have since found that I guessed aright, had been piled up by the Shepherd to enable him to climb & free the poor creature whom he had observed to be crag-fast—but seeing nothing but rock over rock, he had desisted & gone for help—& in the mean time the poor creature had fallen down & killed itself.—As I was looking at these I glanced my eye to my left & observed that the Rock was rent from top to bottom—I measured the breadth of the Rent, and found that there was no danger of my being wedged in / so I put my Knap-sack round to my side, & slipped down as between two walls, without any danger or difficulty—the next Drop brought me down on the Ridge called the How / I hunted out my Besom Stick, which I had flung before me when I first came to the Rocks—and wisely gave over all thoughts of ascending Doe-Crag—for the Clouds were again coming in most tumultuously—so I began to descend / when I felt an odd sensation across my whole Breast—not pain nor itching—& putting my hand on it I found it all bumpy—and on looking saw the whole of my Breast from my Neck (to my Navel)—& exactly all that my Kamell-hair Breast-shield covers, filled with great red heatbumps, so thick that no hair could lie between them. They still remain / but are evidently less—& I have no doubt will wholly disappear in a few Days. It was however a startling proof to me of the violent exertions which I had made.—I descended this low Hill which was all hollow beneath me—and was like the rough green Quilt of a Bed of waters—at length two streams burst out & took their way down, one on (one) side a high Ground upon this Ridge, the other on the other—I took that to my right (having on my left this high Ground, & the other Stream, & beyond that Doe-crag, on the other side of which is Esk Halse, where the head-spring of the Esk rises, & running down the Hill & in upon the Vale looks and actually deceived me, as a great Turnpike Road—in which, as in many other respects the Head of Eskdale much resembles Langdale) & soon the channel sank all at once, at least 40 yards, & formed a magnificent Waterfall—and close under this a succession of Waterfalls 7 in number, the third of which is nearly as high as the first. When I had almost reached the bottom of the Hill, I stood so as to command the whole 8 Waterfalls, with the great triangle-Crag looking in above them, & on the one side of them the enormous more than perpendicular Precipices & Bull's-Brows, of Sc'Fell! And now the Thunder-storm was coming on, again & again!—Just at the bottom of the Hill I saw on before me in the Vale, lying just above the River on the side of a

Hill, one, two, three, four Objects, I could not distinguish whether Peat-hovels, or hovel-shaped Stones—I thought in my mind, that 3 of them would turn out to be stones—but that the fourth was certainly a Hovel. I went on toward them, crossing & recrossing the Becks & the River & found that they were all huge Stones—the one nearest the Beck which I had determined to be really a Hovel, retained It's likeness when I was close beside / in size it is nearly equal to the famous Bowder stone, but in every other respect greatly superior to it—it has a complete Roof, & that perfectly thatched with weeds, & Heath, & Mountain-Ash Bushes—I now was obliged to ascend again, as the River ran greatly to the Left, & the Vale was nothing more than the Channel of the River, all the rest of the interspace between the mountains was a tossing up and down of Hills of all sizes—and the place at which I am now writing is called—Te-as, & spelt, Toes—as the Toes of Sc'Fell—. It is not possible that any name can be more descriptive of the Head of Eskdale—I ascended close under Sca'Fell, & came to a little Village of Sheep-folds / there were 5 together / & the redding Stuff, & the Shears, & an old Pot, was in the Passage of the first of them. Here I found an imperfect Shelter from a Thunder-shower—accompanied with such Echoes! O God! what thoughts were mine! O how I wished for Health & Strength that I might wander about for a Month together in the stormiest month of the year, among these Places, so lonely & savage & full of sounds!

After the Thunder-storm I shouted out all your names in the Sheep-fold —when Echo came upon Echo / and then Hartley & Derwent & then I laughed and shouted Joanna / it leaves all the Echoes I ever heard far far behind, in number, distinctness & humanness of Voice—& then not to forget an old Friend I made them all say Dr Dodd & c.—

—S. T. Coleridge

Climber, A Professional

The Summit

There was no one to tell about it. There was, perhaps, nothing to tell. All the world we could see lay motionless in the muted splendor of the sunrise. Nothing stirred, only we lived; even the wind had forgotten us. Had we been able to hear a bird calling from some pine-tree, or sheep bleating in some valley, the summit stillness would have been familiar; now it was different, perfect. It was as if the world had held its breath for us. Yet we were so tired . . . the summit meant first of all a place to rest. We sat down just beneath the top, ate a little of our lunch, and had a few sips of water. Ed had brought a couple of firecrackers all the way up; now he wanted to set one off, but we were afraid it would knock the cornices loose. There was so little to do, nothing we really had the energy for, no gesture appropriate to what we felt we had accomplished: only a numb happiness, almost a languor. We photographed each other and the views, trying even as we took the pictures to impress the sight on our memories more indelibly than the cameras could on the film. . . . I thought then, much as I had when Matt and I sat on the glacier just after flying in, that I wanted to know how the others felt and couldn't. Trying to talk about it now would have seemed profane; if there was anything we shared, it was the sudden sense of quiet and rest. For each of us, the high place we had finally reached culminated ambitions and secret desires we could scarcely have articulated had we wanted to. And the chances are our various dreams were different. If we had been able to know each other's, perhaps we could not have worked so well together. Perhaps we would have recognised, even in our partnership, the vague threats of ambition, like boats through a fog: the unrealisable desires that drove us beyond anything we could achieve, that drove us in the face of danger; our unanswerable complaints against the universe—that we die, that we have so little power, that we are locked apart, that we do not know. So perhaps the best things that happened on the summit were what we could see happening, not anything beneath. Perhaps it was important for Don to watch me walk across the top of the east ridge; for Matt to see Ed stand with a cigarette in his mouth, staring at the sun; for me to notice how Matt sat, eating only half of his candy bar; for Ed to hear Don insist on changing to black-and-white film. No one else could see these things; no one else could even ask whether or not they were important. Perhaps they were all that happened.

—David Roberts

Commitment

The "great" commitment is so much easier than the ordinary everyday one—and can all too easily shut our hearts to the latter. A willingness to make the ultimate sacrifice can be associated with, and even produce, a great hardness of heart.

—Dag Hammarskjöld

Those who serve a cause are not those who love that cause. They are those who love the life which has to be led in order to serve it—except in the case of the very purest, and they are rare. For the idea of a cause doesn't supply the necessary energy for serving it.

—Simone Weil

The scrupulous and the just, the noble, humane and devoted natures, the unselfish and the intelligent, may begin a movement—but it passes away from them. They are not the leaders of a revolution. They are its victims.

—Joseph Conrad

The young man plays at busying himself with problems of the collective type, and at times with such passion and heroism that anyone ignorant of the secrets of human life would be led to believe that his preoccupation was genuine. But, in truth, all this is a pretext for concerning himself with himself, and so that he may be occupied with self.

During periods of crisis, positions which are false or feigned are very common. Entire generations falsify themselves to themselves; that is to say, they wrap themselves up in artistic styles, in doctrines, in political movements which are insincere and which fill the lack of genuine conviction. When they get to be about forty years old, those generations become null and void, because at that age one can no longer live on fictions.

—Ortega y Gasset

By all means let a poet, if he wants to, write *engagé* poems, protesting against this or that political evil or social injustice. But let him remember this. The only person who will benefit from them is himself; they will enhance his literary reputation among those who feel as he does. The evil or injustice, however, will remain exactly what it would have been if he had kept his mouth shut.

Conception, The Immaculate

Behind this ingenious doctrine lies, I cannot help suspecting, a not very savory wish to make the Mother of God an Honorary Gentile. As if we didn't all know perfectly well that the Holy Ghost and Our Lady both speak British English, He with an Oxford, She with a Yiddish, accent.

Conscience

Freud recognized that there was a profound difference between the Voice of Conscience, i.e. the Voice of the Holy Spirit, and the Voice of the Superego, but was too inclined, in my opinion, to identify the former with the Voice of Reason. The superego speaks loudly and either in imperatives or interjections—"Do this! Don't do that! Bravo! You son of a bitch!" Conscience speaks softly and in the interrogative—"Do you really think so? Is that really true?"

To say that their voices are different does not mean, of course, that they never coincide; indeed in a perfect society they always would coincide. The Pharisee with his strong superego is a very lucky fellow; the Publican, whose superego is weak, a very unlucky one. The former, for example, cannot be said to be "tempted" to steal, for, should the idea of stealing occur to him, he will immediately dismiss it from his mind as something which is "not done"; every time the idea of stealing occurs to the Publican, it requires a moral effort to resist for which he may not have the strength. What is wrong with the Pharisee is his refusal to recognize his good fortune; he takes to himself the credit which is properly due to his parents and teachers.

The limitation of the superego as a guide to conduct is that, since it is a social creation, it is only effective so long as social conditions remain unchanged; if they change, it doesn't know what to say. At home the Spartans did not use money; consequently, when they traveled to countries that did they were helpless to resist the temptations of money, and it was said in the ancient world that a Spartan could always be bribed.

Cosmos, The Medieval

. . . Go out on a starry night and walk about for half an hour trying to see the sky in terms of the old cosmology. Remember that now you have an absolute Up and Down. The Earth is really the centre, really the lowest place; movement to it from whatever direction is downward movement. As a modern you located the stars at a great distance. For distance you must now substitute that very special, and far less abstract, sort of distance which we call height; height which speaks immediately to our muscles and nerves. The Medieval Model is vertiginous. And the fact that the height of the stars in the medieval astronomy is very small compared with their distance in the modern, will turn out not to have the kind of importance you anticipated. For thought and imagination, ten million miles and a thousand million are much the same. Both can be conceived (that is, we can do sums with both) and neither can be imagined; and the more imagination we have the better we shall know this. The really important difference is that the medieval universe, while unimaginably large, was also unambiguously finite. And one unexpected result of this is to make the smallness of Earth more vividly felt. In our universe she is small, no doubt; but so are the galaxies, so is everything—and so what? But in theirs there was an absolute standard of comparison. The furthest sphere, Dante's *maggior corpo*, is, quite simply and finally, the largest object in existence. The word "small" as applied to Earth thus takes on a far more absolute significance. Again, because the medieval universe is finite, it has a shape, the perfect spherical shape, containing within itself an ordered variety. Hence to look out on the night sky with modern eyes is like looking out over a sea that fades away into mist, or looking about one in a trackless forest—trees forever and no horizon. To look up at the towering medieval universe is much more like looking at a great building. The "space" of modern astronomy may arouse terror, or bewilderment or vague reverie; the spheres of the old present us with an object in which the mind can rest, overwhelming in its greatness but satisfying in its harmony. That is the sense in which our universe is romantic, and theirs was classical.

—C. S. Lewis

Cuckoo, The

Before the cuckoo lays her egg she picks up an egg from the host's nest, holds it in her bill as she sits and flies off some distance to eat it. Country rhymes show that something of this was known long before British ornithologists studied the bird's behavior.

In Northamptonshire the cuckoo is called "Suck-egg". According to the Scots song,

> The cuckoo's a fine bird, he sings as he flies;
> He brings us good tidings, he tells us no lies.
> He sucks little birds' eggs to make his voice clear,
> And when he sings "cuckoo" the summer is near.

The Sussex version ends with,

> She picks up the dirt in the spring of the year,
> And eats little birds' eggs to make her voice clear.

In Devon it is said that the cuckoo "comes to eat up the dirt," and continental sayings of a similar nature show that the meaning is that the bird arrives when the land is drying up after the winter. Germans say that the cuckoo cannot call until he has eaten a bird's egg and a Spanish proverb declares, "I am like the cuckoo which cannot sing until I have my stomach full." Another continental tradition is that the cuckoo stammers late in the year because of an egg in its throat. . . .

All over the world the calling of various species of cuckoo is associated with rain and the birds are often called "rain-crow" or its equivalent—due, no doubt, to their loud, reiterative notes coinciding with the rainy season. . . .

From being associated with changes in the weather the cuckoo acquired a reputation as forecaster of the weather and other events. Hesiod advised the farmer to plough when the cuckoo called from the oaks, but more recent tradition attributes to it foresight concerning the whole season:

> When the cuckoo comes to the bare thorn,
> Sell your cow and buy your corn;
> But when she comes to the full bit,
> Sell your corn and buy your sheep.

There are Irish and Welsh rhymes to the same effect.

The next step in the chain of association was to assume that a bird so knowledgeable about future events was able to forecast tides in the affairs of men. . . . Practically throughout western Europe the bird is more or less playfully consulted concerning future events. Yorkshire and Guernsey children recite a rhyme asking the cuckoo to foretell by the number of its calls how long they have to live. This belief goes back at least to the 13th century, for it is mentioned in *Le Roman du Renart*, and is, or was, widespread in Europe. In England and on the continent, as, for example, in Portugal, it was believed that a girl could discover how long she would remain unmarried by counting the calls of the first cuckoo. No wonder the Danes say that the cuckoo does not build a nest because it is kept too busy answering the questions of young and old.

So percipient a bird may predict evil as well as blessedness; and in the magical world of portents your luck may turn on what might seem a trivial detail. In Scotland and Norway it is unlucky to hear the cuckoo before breakfast, but the Scots say that good fortune awaits you if you hear it while walking. . . . In the Hebrides it bodes ill to hear the cuckoo while hungry. Welshfolk used to say that a child born the first day the cuckoo calls would be lucky all his life, but in the Principality and also in Somerset, a cuckoo heard after midsummer may be a portent of death. To be gazing on the ground on hearing the first cuckoo was believed in Midlothian, Berwickshire and Cornwall to be a warning of an untimely fate. . . .

The point of the compass at which the cuckoo calls may be considered fraught with significance. In Cornwall a cuckoo heard on one's right was lucky, and in Ireland a cuckoo on one's left was unlucky. Irish folk thought that the direction in which you heard the first cuckoo indicated where you would live during the year. . . . According to a German tradition, if the first cuckoo were heard in the north, the year would be disastrous, if in the south, it would be a good butter year.

—Edward A. Armstrong

Cultures, The Two

Of course, there is only one. Of course, the natural sciences are just as "humane" as letters. There are, however, two languages, the spoken verbal language of literature, and the written sign language of mathematics, which is the language of science. This puts the scientist at a great advantage, for, since like all of us he has learned to read and write, he can understand a poem or a novel, whereas there are very few men of letters who can understand a scientific paper once they come to the mathematical parts.

When I was a boy, we were taught the literary languages, like Latin and Greek, extremely well, but mathematics atrociously badly. Beginning with the multiplication table, we learned a series of operations by rote which, if remembered correctly, gave the "right" answer, but about any basic principles, like the concept of number, we were told nothing. Typical of the teaching methods then in vogue is this mnemonic which I had to learn.

> Minus times Minus equals Plus:
> The reason for this we need not discuss.

Curtain Lines

The best actual curtain line I know of is the end of Cocteau's *Les Chevaliers de la Table Ronde.* Merlin, the villain, has been defeated, the Waste Land blooms again, and the birds once more start to sing. One of the Knights, Sagramour, used to understand the language of the birds. The others excitedly ask him to tell them what the birds are saying. After listening for a short while, he makes out their message: "*Paie, paie, paie. Il faut payer, payer, payer. Paie, paie, paie, paie.*"

The best imaginary line, suggested to his brother by Max Beerbohm: "I'm leaving for the Thirty Years' War."

The most impossible line for an actor to say, the end of Drinkwater's *Abraham Lincoln*: "He's with the ages now." (Which word shall he accent?)

Probably apocryphal. Mrs Fiske, who had the reputation for always demanding the last word, was to play Mrs Alving in Ibsen's *Ghosts.* In rehearsals she was faithful to the text, but on opening night the finale went thus:

Oswald. Give me the sun, Mother.
Mrs Alving. No!

Cygnet

A cygnet is born. He thinks himself a king, the restless lord of the sluggish marsh. He sits on his mother's back, comes and goes, an object of public solicitude.

He feeds on scraps and on boys' gifts thrown from the bridge. He wastes the time of the servants who hurry along the crowded road bringing articles for the kitchens;

For just born things please everyone; beauty reigns as a goddess on earth; what has the charm of being fresh and young captivates the eyes of the crowd.

Yet the parents of the young cygnet swim round their offspring in mistrust. They hiss, they scream, they stir the pool in threatening flight.

Let not our love be like that. The gods who rule over men forbid the muses to know what the nymphs teach their voiceless companions.

—Poem in Latin by William Johnson Cory
(trans. Frederick Brittain)

DARK AGES, THANK GOD FOR THE

Theodosianism betrays a fatal confusion of ideas. For to envisage the faith as a political principle was not so much to christianize civilization as to "civilize" Christianity; it was not to consecrate human institutions to the service of God but rather to identify God with the maintenance of human institutions, i.e., with that of the *pax terrena.* And, in this case, the *pax terrena* was represented by the tawdry and meretricious empire, a system which, originating in the pursuit of human and terrestrial aims, had so far degenerated as to deny to men the very values which had given it birth; and was now held together only by sheer and unmitigated force. By so doing, it rendered the principle purely formal while, at the same time, it suggested the application of conventional "political" methods for its realization. While, therefore, under governmental pressure, the empire rapidly shed the trappings of secularism to assume those of Christianity, it remained at heart profoundly pagan and was, to that extent, transformed merely into a whited sepulchre.

—C. N. Cochrane

A. "*Dum has exitiorum communium clades suscitat turba feralis, urbem aeternam Leontius regens, multa spectati judicis documenta praebebat, in audiendo celer, in disceptando justissimus, natura benevolus, licet autoritatis causa servandae acer quibusdam videbatur, et inclinatior ad amandum.*" (While that carrion crew was causing these catastrophes of general destruction, Leontius, governor of the Eternal City, gave many evidences of being an excellent judge—speedy in hearings, most just in decisions, by nature benevolent, though he seemed to some to be severe in the matter of maintaining his authority and over-inclined toward sensual love.)—Ammianus

B. "*Gravia tunc inter Toronicos bella civilia surrexerunt.*" (Serious local fighting arose at that time between the inhabitants of the region of Tours.)—Gregory of Tours

A complete change has taken place since the days of Ammianus and Augustine. Of course, as has often been observed, it is a decadence, a decline in culture and verbal disposition; but it is not only that. It is a reawakening of the directly sensible. Both style and treatment of content had become rigid in late antiquity. An excess of rhetorical devices, and the somber atmosphere which enveloped the events of the time, gave the authors of late antiquity, from Tacitus and Seneca to Ammianus, a something that is labored, artificial, overstrained. With Gregory the rigidity is dissolved. He has many horrible things to relate; treason, violence, manslaughter are everyday occurrences; but the simple and practical vivacity with which he reports them prevents the formation of that oppressive atmosphere which we find in the late Roman writers and which even the Christian writers can hardly escape. When Gregory writes, the catastrophe has occurred, the Empire has fallen, its organization has collapsed, the culture of antiquity has been destroyed. But the tension is over. And it is more freely and directly, no longer haunted by insoluble tasks, no longer burdened by unrealizable pretensions, that Gregory's soul faces living reality, ready to apprehend it as such and to work in it practically. . . . [The sentence by Ammianus] surveys and masters a many-faceted situation, as well as supplying in addition a clear connection between what came first and what followed. But how labored it is and how rigid! Is it not a relief to turn from it to Gregory's . . . ? To be sure, his *tunc* is only a loose and vague connective, and the language as a whole is unpolished, for *bella civilia* is certainly not the proper term for the disorderly brawls and thefts and killings which he has in mind. But things come to Gregory directly; he no longer needs to force them into the straitjacket of the elevated style; they grow or even run wild, no longer laced into the apparatus of the Diocletian-Constantinian reform, which brought only a new rule, being too late to bring a new life. Sensory reality, which, in Ammianus, where it was burdened by the fetters of tyrannical rules and the periodic style, could show itself only spectrally and metaphorically, can unfold freely in Gregory.

—Erich Auerbach

Day, Times of

Daybreak

Dyonea, nycht hyrd, and wach of day,
The starnis chasit of the hevin away,
Dame Cynthea doun rolling in the see,
And Venus lost the bewte of hir E,
Fleand eschamyt within Cylenyus cave;
Mars onbydrew, for all his grundin glave,
Nor frawart Saturn, from his mortall speyr,
Durst langar in the firmament appeir,
Bot stall abak yond in his regioun far
Behynd the circulat warld of Jupiter;
Nycthemyne, affrayit of the lycht,
Went undir covert, for gone was the nycht;
As fresch Aurora, to mychty Tythone spous,
Ischit of hir safron bed and evir hous,
In crammysin cled and granit violat,
With sanguyne cape, the selvage purpurat,

Onschot the windois of hyr large hall,
Spred all wyth rosys, and full of balm ryall,
And eik the hevinly portis crystallyne
Upwarpis braid, the warld to illumyn.
The twinkling stremowris of the orient
Sched purpour sprangis with gold and asure ment,
Persand the sabill barmkyn nocturnall,
Bet doun the skyis clowdy mantill wall:
Eous the steid, with ruby hamis reid,
Abuf the seyis lyftis furth his heid,
Of cullour soyr, and sum deill broun as berry,
For to alichtyn and glaid our emyspery,
The flambe owtbrastyng at his neys thyrlys;
Sa fast Phaeton wyth the quhip him quhirlys,
To roll Apollo his faderis goldin chair,
That schrowdyth all the hevynnis and the ayr;
Quhill schortly, with the blesand torch of day,
Abilyeit in his lemand fresch array,
Furth of hys palyce ryall ischyt Phebus,
Wyth goldin croun and vissage gloryus,
Crysp haris, brycht as chrysolite or topace,
For quhais hew mycht nane behald his face,
The fyry sparkis brastyng fra his ene,
To purge the ayr, and gylt the tendyr grene,
Defundand from hys sege etheriall
Glaid influent aspectis celicall.
Before his regale hie magnificens
Mysty vapour upspringand, sweit as sens,
In smoky soppis of donk dewis wak,
Moich hailsum stovis ourheildand the slak;
The aureat fanys of hys trone soverane
With glytrand glans ourspred the occiane,
The large fludis lemand all of lycht
Bot with a blenk of his supernale sycht.
For to behald, it was a gloir to se
The stabillit wyndis and the cawmyt see,
The soft sessoun, the firmament serene,
The lowne illumynat air, and fyrth amene;
The sylver scalyt fyschis on the greit
Ourthwort cleir stremis sprynkland for the heyt,
Wyth fynnis schynand broun as synopar,
And chyssell talis, stowrand hery and thar;

The new cullour alychtyng all the landis,
Forgane thir stannyris schane the beryall strandis,
Quhill the reflex of the diurnal bemis
The bene bonkis kest ful of variant glemis,
And lusty Flora did hyr blomis spreid
Under the feit of Phebus sulyart steid;
The swardit soyll enbroud wyth selcouth hewis
Wod and forest obumbrat with thar bewis,
Quhois blissfull branchis, porturat on the grund,
With schaddois schene schew rochis rubycund:
Towris, turattis, kyrnellis, pynnaclis hie
Of kirkis, castellis, and ilke fair cite,
Stude payntit, every fyall, fane, and stage,
Apon the plane grund, by thar awin umbrage.

—Gavin Douglas

Morning

'Tis the hour when white-horsed Day
Chases Night her mares away,
When the Gates of Dawn (they say)
  Phoebus opes:
And I gather that the Queen
May be uniformly seen,
Should the weather be serene,
  On the slopes.

When the ploughman, as he goes
Leathern-gaitered o'er the snows,
From his hat and from his nose
  Knocks the ice;
And the panes are frosted o'er
And the lawn is crisp and hoar,
As has been observed before
  Once or twice.

When arrayed in breastplate red
Sings the robin, for his bread,
On the elmtree that hath shed
  Every leaf;
While, within, the frost benumbs
The still sleepy schoolboy's thumbs,
And in consequence his sums
  Come to grief.

But when breakfast-time hath come,
And he's crunching crust and crumb,
He'll no longer look a glum
   Little dunce;
But be as brisk as bees that settle
On a summer rose's petal:
Wherefore, Polly, put the kettle
   On at once.

—C. S. Calverley

Afternoon

When down from heaven more radiant gladness pours, a joy approaches for human kind, so that they marvel at much that is visible, higher, agreeable:

How beautifully with it does sacred song combine! How laughingly in hymns does the heart dwell upon the truth that in an image is rejoicing—over the pathway sheep set out on

Their track, that takes them almost to glimmering woods. The meadows, however, which are covered with flawless green, are like that heath which habitually is to be found

Near the dark wood. There, on the meadows too these sheep remain. The peaks that are round about, bare heights, are covered with oaks and with rare pine-trees.

There, where the river's lively wavelets are, so that someone passing there on his way looks at them happily, there the gentle shape of the mountains and the vineyard rises high.

True, amidst the grape-vines the steps steeply ascend, where the fruit-tree stands above it in blossom, and fragrance lingers upon wild hedges, where the hidden violets burgeon;

But waters come trickling down, and a rustling is faintly audible there all day long; the villages in that region, however, rest and are silent throughout the afternoon.

—Hölderlin (trans. Michael Hamburger)

Evening

The Day's grown old, the fainting Sun
Has but a little way to run,
And yet his Steeds, with all his skill,
Scarce lug the Chariot down the Hill.

With Labour spent, and Thirst opprest,
While they strain hard to gain the West,

From Fetlocks hot drops melted light,
Which turn to Meteors in the Night.

The Shadows now so long do grow,
That Brambles like tall Cedars show,
Mole-hills seem Mountains, and the Ant
Appears a monstrous Elephant.

A very little little Flock
Shades thrice the Ground that it would stock;
Whilst the small Stripling following them,
Appears a mighty *Polypheme.*

These being brought into the Fold,
And by the thrifty Master told,
He thinks his Wages are well paid,
Since none are either lost, or stray'd.

Now lowing Herds are each-where heard,
Chains rattle in the Villains Yard,
The Cart's on Tayl set down to rest,
Bearing on high the Cuckolds Crest.

The Hedge is stript, the Clothes brought in,
Nought's left without should be within,
The Bees are hiv'd, and hum their Charm,
Whilst every House does seem a Swarm.

The Cock now to the Roost is prest:
For he must call up all the rest;
The Sow's fast pegg'd within the Sty,
To still her squeaking Progeny.

Each one has had his Supping Mess,
The Cheese is put into the Press,
The Pans and Bowls clean scalded all,
Rear'd up against the Milk-house Wall.

And now on Benches all are sat
In the cool Air to sit and chat,
Till *Phœbus,* dipping in the West,
Shall lead the World the Way to Rest.

—Charles Cotton

Night

Every star its diamond, every cloud its white plume, sadly the moon marches on.

Onward marches while it lights up fields, hills, meadows, rivers, where the day is failing.
Fails the day, the dark night falls, falls, little by little, over the green mountains.
Green and leafy, sprinkled with rivulets, beneath the shade of the branches.
Branches where sing the twittering birds that rise with the first light.
Which all night sleep that the crickets may come out and trill among the shadows.

—Rosalía Castro (trans. Gerald Brenan)

Death

Yonder he is through the stream, a man without a coat, a man without a belt, a man of hard slender legs, it is my woe that I cannot run.

—Irish riddle

Madam Life's a piece in bloom
Death goes dogging everywhere:
She's the tenant of the room
He's the ruffian on the stair.

You shall see her as a friend,
You shall bilk him once or twice;
But he'll trap you in the end,
And he'll stick you for her price.

With his kneebones at your chest,
And his knuckles in your throat,
You would reason—plead—protest!
Clutching at her petticoat.

But she's heard it all before,
Well she knows you've had your fun,
Gingerly she gains the door,
And your little job is done.

—W. E. Henley

De Profundis

The metallic weight of iron;
The glaze of glass;
The inflammability of wood . . .

You will not be cold there;
You will not wish to see your face in a mirror;
There will be no heaviness,
Since you will not be able to lift a finger.

There will be company, but they will not heed you;
Yours will be a journey only of two paces
Into view of the stars again; but you will not make it.

There will be no recognition;
No one, who should see you, will say—
Throughout the uncountable hours—

"Why . . . the last time we met, I brought you some flowers!"

—Walter de la Mare

"Are you in pain, dear mother?"

"I think there's a pain somewhere in the room," said Mrs Gradgrind, but I couldn't positively say that I have got it."

After this strange speech, she lay silent for some time. Louisa holding her hand, could feel no pulse; but kissing it, could see a slight thin shred of life in fluttering motion.

"You very seldom see your sister," said Mrs Gradgrind. "She grows like you. I wish you would look at her. Sissy, bring her here."

She was brought, and stood with her hand in her sister's. Louisa had observed her with her arm round Sissy's neck, and she felt the difference of this approach.

"Do you see the likeness, Louisa?"

"Yes, mother, I should think her like me. But"—

"Eh? Yes, I always say so," Mrs Gradgrind cried, with unexpected quickness, "and that reminds me. I—I want to speak to you, my dear. Sissy, my good girl, leave us alone a minute."

Louisa had relinquished the hand: had thought that her sister's was a better and brighter face than hers had ever been: had seen in it, not without a rising feeling of resentment, even in that place and at that time, something of the gentleness of the other face in the room: the sweet face with the trusting eyes, made paler than watching and sympathy made it, by the rich dark hair.

Left alone with her mother, Louisa saw her lying with an awful lull upon her face, like one who was floating away upon some great water, all resistance over, content to be carried down the stream. She put the shadow of a hand to her lips again, and recalled her.

"You were going to speak to me, mother."

"Eh? Yes, to be sure, my dear. You know your father is almost always away now, and therefore I must write to him about it."

"About what, mother? Don't be troubled. About what?"

"You must remember, my dear, that whenever I have said anything, on any subject, I have never heard the last of it, and consequently, that I have long left off saying anything."

"I can hear you, mother." But, it was only by dint of bending down to her ear, and at the same time attentively watching the lips as they moved, that she could link such faint and broken sounds into any chain of connection.

"You learnt a great deal, Louisa, and so did your brother. Ologies of all kinds, from morning to night, If there is any Ology left, of any description, that has not been worn to rags in this house, all I can say is, I hope I shall never hear its name."

"I can hear you, mother, when you have strength to go on." This, to keep her from floating away.

"But there is something—not an Ology at all—that your father has missed, or forgotten, Louisa. I don't know what it is. I have often sat with Sissy near me, and thought about it. I shall never get its name now. But your father may. It makes me restless. I want to write to him, to find out for God's sake, what it is. Give me a pen, give me a pen."

Even the power of restlessness was gone, except from the poor head, which could just turn from side to side.

She fancied, however, that her request had been complied with, and that the pen she could not have held was in her hand. It matters little what figures of wonderful no-meaning she began to trace upon her wrappers. The hand soon stopped in the midst of them; the light that had always been feeble and dim behind the weak transparency went out; and even Mrs Gradgrind, emerged from the shadow in which man walketh and disquieteth himself in vain, took upon her the dread solemnity of the sages and patriarchs.

—Charles Dickens

And smart as little Tommie be, one man kill the whole world—Mr Debt.

—Jamaican riddle

Death, Dance of

It is a commonplace of literary historians that, because of linguistic changes, the English poets between Chaucer and Wyatt were metrically all at sea. I can only say that if the rhythms of these stanzas are an accident it is a very lucky accident.

Death. O thou minstral, that cannest so note and pipe
Unto folkes for to do pleasaunce,
By the right honde anoone I shal thee gripe,
With these other to go upon my daunce.
Ther is no scape nouther avoidaunce,
On no side to contrarye my sentence,

For in music be crafte and accordaunce
Who maister is shall shew his science.

MINSTREL. This newe daunce is to me so straunge,
Wonder diverse and passingly contrarye;
The dredful foting dothe so ofte chaunge,
And the mesures so ofte sithes varye,
Whiche now to me is no thing necessarye
Yif hit were so that I might asterte:
But many a man, yif I shal not tarye,
Ofte daunceth, but no thinge of herte.

—Lydgate

DEJECTION

March 22, 1782

I spent the time idly. *Mens turbata.* In the afternoon it snowed.

—Dr Johnson

December 3, 1854

A very dark day. Mary Hales suffered torments from tooth-extraction, very unsuccessfully done, and was crying with pain at intervals throughout the day; my wife's voice had gone through a severe cold; my elder daughter was suffering from a boil, and I with rheumatism; the weather was dreadful, and it was becoming dark at three. All these things tried the tempers of the party so that I was not sorry to solace myself with the *Guardian* and a pipe after they had all gone to bed.

—Benjamin John Armstrong

The deadliest of all things to me is my loss of faith in nature. No spring—no summer. Fog always, and the snow faded from the Alps.

—Ruskin

August 16, 1873

We hurried too fast and it knocked me up. We went to the College, the seminary being wanted for the secular priests' retreat: almost no gas, the retorts were being mended; therefore candles in bottles, things not ready, darkness and despair. In fact, being unwell, I was quite downcast: nature in all her parcels and faculties gaped and fell apart, *fatiscebat,* like a clod cleaving and holding only by strings of root.

—Gerard Manley Hopkins

The high hills have a bitterness
Now they are not known,
And memory is poor enough consolation

For the soul hopeless gone.
Up in the air there beech tangles wildly in the wind—
That I can imagine.
But the speed, the swiftness, walking into clarity,
Like last year's briony, are gone.

—Ivor Gurney

Wednesday, May 25, 1932

. . . since we came back, I'm screwed up into a ball; can't get into step; can't make things dance; feel awfully detached; see youth; feel old; no, that's not quite it: wonder how a year or so perhaps is to be endured. Think, yet people do live; can't imagine what goes on behind faces. All is surface hard; myself only an organ that takes blows, one after another; the horror of the hard raddled faces in the flower show yesterday: the inane pointlessness of all this existence: hatred of my own brainlessness and indecision; the old treadmill feeling, of going on and on and on, for no reason: Lytton's death; Carrington's; a longing to speak to him; all that cut away, gone: . . . women: my book on professions: shall I write another novel; contempt for my lack of intellectual power; reading Wells without understanding; . . . society; buying clothes; Rodmell spoilt; all England spoilt: terror at night of things generally wrong in the universe; buying clothes; how I hate Bond Street and spending money on clothes: worst of all is this dejected barrenness. And my eyes hurt: and my hand trembles.

—Virginia Woolf

When the bells jussle in the tower,
The hollow night amid,
Then on my tongue the taste is sour
Of all I ever did.

—A. E. Housman

Departure, Prose and Poetry of

The world, we think, makes a great mistake on the subject of saying, or acting, farewell. The word or deed should partake of the suddenness of electricity; but we all drawl through it at a snail's pace. We are supposed to tear ourselves from our friends; but tearing is a process which should be done quickly. What is so wretched as lingering over a last kiss, giving the hand for the third time, saying over and over again, "Goodbye, John, God bless you; and mind you write!" Who has not seen his dearest friends standing round the window of a railway carriage, while the train would not start, and has not longed to say to them, "Stand not upon the order of your going, but go at once!" And of all such farewells, the ship's farewell is the longest and most dreary. One sits on a damp bench, snuffling up the odour of oil and ropes, cudgelling one's brains to think what further word of increased tenderness can be spoken. One returns again and again to the weather, to coats and cloaks, perhaps even to sandwiches and the sherry flask. All effect is thus destroyed, and a trespass is made even upon the domain of feeling.

I remember a line of poetry, learnt in my earliest youth, and which I believe to have emanated from a sentimental Frenchman, a man of genius, with whom my parents were acquainted. It was as follows:—

Are you go? Is you gone? And I left? Ver vell!

Now the whole business of a farewell is contained in that line. When the moment comes, let that be said; let that be said and felt, and then let the dear ones depart.

—A. Trollope

Sufficiently seen. The vision has been encountered under all skies.
Sufficiently experienced. The sounds of cities, in the evening, and in the sunlight, and always.
Sufficiently known. The limits of life. O Sounds and Visions!
Departure into the new affection and the new noise.

—Arthur Rimbaud
(trans. Oliver Bernard, modified by W. H. A.)

At that moment Elrond came out with Gandalf, and he called the Company to him. "This is my last word," he said in a low voice. "The Ring-Bearer is setting out on the Quest of Mount Doom. On him alone is any charge laid: neither to cast away the Ring, nor to deliver it to any servant of the Enemy nor indeed to let any handle it, save members of the Company and the Council, and only then in gravest need. The others go with him as free companions, to help him on his way. You may tarry, or come back, or turn aside into other paths, as chance allows. The further you go, the less easy will it be to withdraw; yet no oath or bond is laid on you to go further than you will. For you do not yet know the strength of your hearts, and you cannot foresee what each may meet upon the road."

"Faithless is he that says farewell when the road darkens," said Gimli.

"Maybe," said Elrond, "but let him not vow to walk in the dark, who has not seen the nightfall."

"Yet sworn word may strengthen the quaking heart," said Gimli.

"Or break it," said Elrond. "Look not too far ahead! But go now with good hearts! Farewell, and may the blessing of Elves and Men and all Free Folk go with you. May the stars shine upon your faces!"

—J. R. R. Tolkien

Diaries, Fate of the Obscure in

The historical reputation of a public figure is based upon a large number of known data, some favorable, some unfavorable. Consequently, a single derogatory remark in a contemporary memoir affects his reputation, for better or worse, very little.

In the case of an obscure private individual, however, the single derogatory remark may damn him forever, because it is all we shall ever hear about him.

> *January 3, 1854*
>
> In the evening went to a party at Mr Anfrere's. Very slow—small rooms, piano out of tune, bad wine, and stupid people.
>
> —Benjamin John Armstrong

Poor Mr Anfrere! No doubt he had many virtues, but to posterity he is simply an incompetent host.

Dogs

> *Lupus and Aureus*
>
> The reticent exclusiveness and the mutual defence at any price are properties of the wolf which influence favorably the character of all strongly wolf-blooded dog breeds and distinguish them to their advantage from Aureus dogs, which are mostly "hail-fellow-well-met" with every man and will follow anyone who holds the other end of the lead in his hand. A Lupus dog, on the contrary, who has once sworn allegiance to a certain man is forever a one-man dog, and no stranger can win from him so much as a single wag of his bushy tail. Nobody who has once possessed the one-man love of a Lupus dog will ever be content with one of pure Aureus blood. Unfortunately, this fine characteristic of the Lupus dog has against it various disadvantages which are indeed the immediate results of the one-man loyalty. That a mature Lupus dog can never become *your* dog is a matter of course. But worse, if he is already yours and you are forced to leave him, the animal becomes literally mentally unbalanced, obeys neither your wife nor children, sinks morally, in his grief, to the level of an ownerless street cur, loses his restraint from killing and, committing misdeed upon misdeed, ravages the surrounding district.
>
> Besides this, a predominantly Lupus-blooded dog is, in spite of his boundless loyalty and affection, never quite sufficiently submissive. He is ready to die for you, but not to obey you. . . . If you walk with a Lupus dog in the woods you can never make him stay near you. All he will do is to keep in very loose contact with you and honor you with his companionship only now and again.

Not so the Aureus dog; in him, as a result of his age-old domestication, that infantile affection has persisted which makes him a manageable and tractable companion. (Instead of the proud manly loyalty of the Lupus dog which is far removed from obedience, the Aureus dog will grant you that servitude which, day and night, by the hour and by the minute, awaits your command and even your slightest wish.) When you take him for a walk, an Aureus dog of a more highly domesticated breed will, without previous training, always run with you, keeping the same radius whether he runs before, behind or beside you, and adapting his speed to yours. He is naturally obedient—that is to say, he answers to his name not only when he wishes to and when you cajole him, but also because he knows he *must* come. The harder you shout, the more surely he will come, whereas a Lupus dog, in this case, comes not at all but seeks to appease you from a distance with a friendly gesture.

Opposed to these good and congenial properties of the Aureus dog are unfortunately some others which also arise from the permanent infantility of these animals and are less agreeable for an owner. . . . Like many spoilt human children who call every grown-up "uncle", they pester people and animals alike with overtures to play. . . . The worst part of it lies in the literally "dog-like" submission that these animals, who see in every man an "uncle", show towards anyone who treats them with the least sign of severity; the playful storm of affection is immediately transformed into a cringing state of humility. Everyone is acquainted with this kind of dog which knows no happy medium between perpetual exasperating "jumping up", and fawningly turning upon its back, its paws waving in supplication.

—Konrad Lorenz

Bibbles

. . . Oh Bibbles, oh Pips, oh Pipsey,
You little black love-bird!
Don't you love *everybody*!
Just everybody.
You love 'em all.
Believe in the One Identity, don't you,
You little Walt-Whitmanesque bitch?
First time I lost you in Taos plaza,
And found you after endless chasing,
Came upon you prancing round the corner in exuberant, bibbling affection
After the black-green skirts of a yellow-green old Mexican woman
Who hated you, and kept looking round at you and cursing you in a mutter,

While you pranced and bounced with love of her, you indiscriminating
animal,
All your wrinkled *miserere* Chinese black little face beaming
And your black little body bouncing and wriggling
With indiscriminate love, Bibbles;
I had a moment's pure detestation of you . . .

. . .

Yet you're so nice,
So quick, like a little black dragon.
So fierce, when the coyotes howl, barking like a whole little lion, and
rumbling,
And starting forward in the dusk, with your little black fur all bristling
like plush
Against those coyotes, who would swallow you like an oyster.

And in the morning, when the bedroom door is opened,
Rushing in like a little black whirlwind, leaping straight as an arrow on
the bed at the pillow
And turning the day suddenly into a black tornado of *joie de vivre*,
Chinese dragon.

So funny
Lobbing wildly through deep snow like a rabbit,
Hurtling like a black ball through the snow,
Champing it, tossing a mouthful,
Little black spot in the landscape!

So absurd
Pelting behind on the dusty trail when the horse sets off home at a
gallop:
Left in the dust behind like a dust-ball tearing along,
Coming up on fierce little legs, tearing fast to catch up, a real little
dust-pig, ears almost blown away,
And black eyes bulging bright in a dust-mask
Chinese-dragon-wrinkled, with a pink mouth grinning, under jaw
shoved out
And white teeth showing in your dragon-grin as you race, you split-
face,
Like a trundling projectile swiftly whirling up.

. . .

Plenty of conceit in you.
Unblemished belief in your own perfection

And utter lovableness, you ugly-mug;
Chinese puzzle-face,
Wrinkled underhung physiog that looks as if it had done with
  everything,
Through with everything.

Instead of which you sit there and roll your head like a canary
And show a tiny bunch of white teeth in your underhung blackness,
Self-conscious little bitch,
Aiming again at being loved. . . .

—D. H. Lawrence

Tulip

She has two kinds of urination, Necessity and Social. Different stances are usually, though not invariably, adopted for each. In necessity she squats squarely and abruptly, right down on her shins, her hind legs forming a kind of dam against the stream that gushes out from behind; her tail curves up like a scimitar; her expression is complacent. For social urination, which is mostly preceded by the act of smelling, she seldom squats, but balances herself on one hind leg, the other being withdrawn or cocked up in the air. The reason for this seems obvious; she is watering some special thing and wishes to avoid touching it. It may also be that in this attitude she can more accurately bestow her drops. Often they are merely drops, a single token drop will do, for the social flow is less copious. The expression on her face is business-like, as though she were signing a cheque.

She attends socially to a wide range of objects. The commonest group are the droppings, both liquid and solid, of other animals. Fresh horse dung has a special attraction for her and is always liberally sprayed. Then she sprinkles any food that has been thrown about—buns, bones, fish, bread, vomit—unless it is food she wishes to eat. Dead and decaying animals are carefully attended to. There are advanced stages of decay, when flesh turns into a kind of tallow, which affect her so deeply that urination appears to be an inadequate expression of her feelings. Try as she may she cannot lift her leg, and tottering round the object in a swooning way would prostrate herself upon it if the meddling voice of authority did not intervene. . . .

She drips also upon drains, disinfectants and detergents (in a street of doorsteps it is generally the one most recently scoured which she selects), and pieces of newspaper. Once she spared a few drops for a heap of socks and shoes left on the foreshore of the river by some rowing men who had gone sculling. Following her antics with the utmost curiosity I used to wonder what on earth she was up to. I saw that, excepting perhaps for the newspapers, unless she was moved by printers' ink, all these objects had a quality in common, smell; even so, why did she pee on them? It could not be because other dogs had done so before her, for that only pushed the question further back: who began, and why? Nor did I think she was staking a kind of personal claim; nothing in her subsequent behaviour suggested appropriation. I came to the conclusion that she was simply expressing an appreciative interest; she was endorsing these delectable things with her signature, much as we underline a book we are reading. . . .

. . . Some people believe they [dogs] hate sex; others regard it as unnecessary, or odious, or positively dangerous. Some, hugging to themselves all the love, which dogs feel only for the human race, will not allow that there is a sexual instinct also. To this large category belong those nervous women who, far from being sympathetic to intimate canine relationships, prevent their creatures, male or female, even from speaking to their own kind. Never off the lead, they are twitched away from all communication with other dogs, in case of fights, contagion, or "nasty" behaviour, they are so greatly loved. Men, too, frequently exhibit the deepest aversion to such poor sexual satisfactions as are left to their beasts. I meet it constantly, the intolerant reaction to the natural conduct of a dog and a bitch. No sooner does some canine admirer begin to pay Tulip court than the master's stick will stir, the reproof will be uttered: "Come off it, Rex! Now stop it, I say! How often must I tell you?" Nor can "the feelings of others", though they may occasionally be the modest motive, always be advanced in excuse, for the same thing happens when there is no-one else about. "Do let them be!" I sometimes expostulate. "They're doing no harm." But the stick stirs. One gentleman, fidgeting from foot to foot in the solitude of Putney Common, exclaimed: "I hate to see dogs do that!"

When Tulip is actually in the canine news—that is to say when she is on the verge of heat or just coming out of it—incidents are more frequent and more serious. The little dog approaches her and begins to flatter her. This she graciously permits. The master, who is stationary ten paces away watching the rowing crews on the river, notices and calls his dog. Both animals are safely on the pavement, they are clearly on the best of terms, the master is in no hurry. But the amount of totally unnecessary interference in canine lives, the exercise of authority for its own sake, has to be seen to be believed. The little creature cannot tear himself away. The master calls more harshly. The dog wags his tail but cannot go. Sensing trouble I summon Tulip and put her on the lead.

"It's not his fault," I say mildly. "I'm afraid my bitch is just coming into heat."

The master gives me a brief look but no reply. He calls a third time, and now that Tulip has been withdrawn, the little dog rejoins him, wagging his tail. . . .

"Come here!" says the master, upright in his aquascutum.

The little dog creeps forward to his very feet. The master lashes out. With a yelp the little dog shrinks away.

"Come here!" says the master.

Inch by inch, on his stomach, the little dog crawls once more up to his master's boots. The lash descends. Now the master is satisfied. A lesson has been taught. Two lessons, one lash for each: obedience, propriety. He squares his shoulders and their interrupted walk is resumed.

—J. R. Ackerley

Sled Dogs

A dog has a wonderful mind of its kind but it lives on incident, and monotony is death to it. Yet monotony is an ever-present feature of the Barrier, where for 200 miles one is out of sight of land; where on a bright day there is nothing to see but the shadows of snow furrows or the painful glint of light reflected from ice crystals in the air or on the surface.

On a clouded day there is nothing but a blank whiteness from underfoot to overhead, not even a horizon to steady oneself. To a man this monotony is infinitely wearisome, to a dog it is almost insupportable, and he just longs for something, anything, however trivial, to claim his attention.

After a night sleeping on the snow still in his harness there is the men's tent to watch, their preparation for the start, the yelping of his companions, the general eagerness to be off, and there is the glorious gallop for the first half-mile when the sledge seems to weigh nothing and the driver has to mount it or be left behind. But after that first zest of movement things begin to pall. The place where the harness rubs begins to ache, the jerking of the sledge is annoying, the stumbles of his yoke-mate yank him viciously to the side, the caked snow on his belly-band feels rougher every minute. He could endure all these things if only there were something to see or to smell, but there is nothing in air or snow which can raise a single spark of interest for him.

When the going is really heavy the driver can walk ahead of the team and raise the dogs' spirits by giving them something to look at, but usually the only features in a day's march were the cairns every five miles raised by the pony-party ahead or the occasional pony droppings, black on the white snow, which, miraged up, would look like a penguin or a seal and cause ears to cock and footsteps to quicken. Captain Scott always said that the Barrier is no place for a Christian, and we may add that it is even worse for a dog.

—Frank Debenham

Rover

The dog that lives with his master constantly, sleeping before his fire, instead of in the kennel, and hearing and seeing all that passes, learns if at all quick-witted to understand not only the meaning of what he sees going on, but also, frequently in the most wonderful manner, all that is talked of. I have a favourite retriever, a black water-spaniel, who for many years has lived in the house and been constantly with me; he understands and notices everything that is said, if it at all relates to himself or to the sporting plans for the day: if at breakfast time I say, without addressing the dog himself, "Rover must stop at home to-day, I cannot take him out," he never attempts to follow me; if, on the contrary, I say, however quietly, "I shall take Rover with me today," the moment that breakfast is over he is all on the *qui vive*, following me wherever I go, evidently aware that he is to be allowed to accompany me. When left at home, he sits on the step of the front door, looking out for my return, occasionally howling and barking in an ill-tempered kind of voice; his great delight is going with me when I hunt the woods for roe and deer. I had some covers about five miles from the house, where we were accustomed to look for roe: we frequently made our plans over night while the dog was in the room. One day, for some reason, I did not take him: in consequence of this, invariably when he heard us at night, forming our plan to beat the woods, Rover started alone very early in the morning, and met us up there. He always went to the cottage where we assembled, and sitting on a hillock in front of it, which commanded a view of the road by which we came, waited for us; when he saw us coming, he met us with a peculiar kind of grin on his face, expressing, as well as words could, his half doubt of being well received, in consequence of his having come without permission: the moment he saw that I was not angry with him, he threw off all his affectation of shyness, and barked and jumped upon me with the most grateful delight.

As he was very clever at finding deer, I often sent him with the beaters or hounds to assist, and he always plainly asked me on starting, whether he was to go with me to the pass, or to accompany the men. In the latter case, though a very exclusive dog in his company at other times, he would go with any one of the beaters, although a stranger to him, whom I told him to accompany, and he would look to that one man for orders as long as he was with him. I never lost a wounded roe when he was out, for once on the track he would stick to it, the whole day if necessary, not fatiguing himself uselessly, but quietly and determinedly following it up. If the roe fell and he found it, he would return to me, and then lead me up to the animal, whatever the distance might be. With red-deer he was also most useful. The first time that he saw me kill a deer he was very much surprised; I was walking alone with him through some woods in Ross-shire, looking for woodcocks; I had killed two or three, when I saw such recent signs of deer, that I drew the shot from one barrel, and replaced it with ball. Then I continued my walk. Before I had gone far, a fine barren hind sprung out of a thicket, and as she crossed a small hollow, going directly away from me, I fired at her, breaking her backbone with the bullet; of course she dropped immediately, and Rover, who was a short distance behind me, rushed forward in the direction of the shot, expecting to have to pick up a woodcock; but on coming up to the hind, who was struggling on the ground, he ran round her with a look of astonishment, and then came back to me with an expression in his face plainly saying, "What have you done now?—you have shot a cow or something." But on my explaining to him that the hind was fair game, he ran up to her and seized her by the throat like a bulldog. Ever afterwards he was peculiarly fond of deerhunting, and became a great adept, and of great use. When I sent him to assist two or three hounds to start a roe—as soon as the hounds were on the scent, Rover always came back to me and waited at the pass: I could enumerate endless anecdotes of his clever feats in this way.

Though a most aristocratic dog in his usual habits, when staying with me in England once, he struck up an acquaintance with a ratcatcher and his curs, and used to assist in their business when he thought that nothing else was to be done, entering into their way of going on, watching motionless at the rats' holes when the ferrets were in, and as the ratcatcher told me, he was the best dog of them all, and always to be depended on for showing if a rat was in a hole, corn-stack, or elsewhere; never giving a false alarm, or failing to give a true one. The moment, however, that he saw me, he instantly cut his humble friends, and denied all acquaintance with them in the most comical manner.

—C. G. W. St John

Wanted: a dog that neither barks nor bites, eats broken glass and shits diamonds.

—Goethe

To be sure, the dog is loyal. But why, on that account, should we take him as an example? He is loyal to men, not to other dogs.

—Karl Kraus

Donkey, The

A horse translated into Dutch.

—G. C. Lichtenberg

Dons, Humor of

Dr Spooner, who could still be seen in the streets of Oxford when I was an undergraduate, did not himself, it seems, make many spoonerisms (q.v.). His conversation, however, could be very odd. In his *Memories* Sir Maurice Bowra reports the following snatch of dialogue.

> Dr Spooner. I want you to come to tea next Thursday to meet Mr Casson.
>
> Mr Casson. But I am Mr Casson.
>
> Dr Spooner. Come all the same.

And here are three more anecdotes from the same source.

> It was told that once, when he [Joseph Wells] heard a fearful row in the back quad, he walked up in the dark and said, "If you don't stop at once, I shall light a match." They stopped.
>
> Symons never admitted that he was wrong. An undergraduate was found drunk, and Symons abused another, quite innocent man for it, who said that his name was not that by which Symons had called him, but Symons would not admit it. "You're drunk still. You don't even know your own name. Go to your room at once."
>
> Brabant kept a car and drove it badly, even by academic standards, which, from myopia, or self-righteousness, or loquacity, or absorption in other matters, are notoriously low. Once when I was with him, he drove straight into a cow and knocked it down, fortunately without damage. When the man in charge of it said quite mildly, "Look out where you are going," Brabant said fiercely, "Mind your own business," and drove on.
>
> —Maurice Bowra

In Memoriam Examinatoris Cuisdam

Lo, where yon undistinguished grave
Erects its grassy pile on
One who to all Experience gave
An Alpha or Epsilon.

The world and eke the world's content,
And all therein that passes,
With marks numerical (per cent)
He did dispose in classes:

Not his to ape the critic crew
Which vulgarly appraises
The Good, the Beautiful, the True
In literary phrases:

He did his estimate express
  In terms precise and weighty,—
And Vice got 25 (or less),
  While Virtue rose to 80.

Now hath he closed his earthly lot
  All in his final haven,—
(And be the stone that marks the spot
  On one side only graven);

Bring papers on his grave to strew
  Amid the grass and clover,
And plant thereby that pencil blue
  Wherewith he looked them over!

There freed from every human ill
  And fleshly trammels gross, he
Lies in his resting place until
  The final Viva Voce:

So let him rest till crack of doom,
  Of mortal tasks aweary,—
And nothing write upon his tomb
  Save β–?

—A. D. Godley

An Election Address
(To Cambridge University, 1882)

I venture to suggest that I
  Am rather noticeably fit
To hold the seat illumined by
  The names of Palmerston and Pitt.

My principles are such as you
  Have often heard expressed before:
They are, without exception, true;
  And who can say, with candor, more?

My views concerning Church and State
  Are such as bishops have professed:
I need not recapitulate
  The arguments on which they rest.

Respecting Ireland, I opine
  That Ministers are in a mess,
That Landlords rule by Right Divine,
  That Firmness will relieve Distress.

I see with horror undisguised
   That freedom of debate is dead:
The Liberals are organised;
   The Caucus rears its hideous head.

Yet need'st thou, England, not despair
   At Chamberlain's or Gladstone's pride,
While Henry Cecil Raikes is there
   To organise the other side.

I never quit, as others do,
   Political intrigue to seek
The dingy literary crew,
   Or hear the voice of science speak.

But I have fostered, guided, planned
   Commercial enterprise: in me
Some ten or twelve directors and
   Six worthy chairmen you may see.

My academical career
   Was free from any sort of blot:
I challenge anybody here
   To demonstrate that it was not.

At classics, too, I worked amain,
   Whereby I did not only pass,
But even managed to obtain
   A very decent second class.

And since those early days, the same
   Success has crowned the self-same plan:
Profundity I cannot claim;
   Respectability I can.

—J. K. Stephen

Double-Entendre, Unconscious

It is possible to make one through sheer inattention. While translating *Die Zauberflöte,* I wrote a stage direction which sent my collaborator, Mr Chester Kallman, into fits of laughter. It ran: "Pamina's Chamber. Two Slaves are cleaning it." It must have been sheer inattention, too, that permitted Laurence Binyon to write: "Why hurt so hard by little pricks?"

Usually, however, the double-entendre is caused by an historical change in the meaning of a word. The most obvious example of this is the change, which has taken place during my lifetime, in the meaning of the word *fairy*.

It is still possible to speak of fairy stories, but if one wishes to speak of fairies one must now refer to them as elves.

At a dinner party I once was seated next to Miss Rose Fyleman, author of "There Are Fairies at the Bottom of My Garden," and it was clear that nobody had told her what Beatrice Lillie had done with her song. Among her poems there are much more extraordinary examples.

There are no wolves in England any more;
The fairies have driven them all away.

and

My fairy muff is made of pussy-willow

and

The best thing the fairies do, the best thing of all
Is sliding down steeples—you know they're very tall.
Climb up the weather-cock and, when you hear it crow,
Fold your wings, and clutch your things, and then—Let go!

They've lots of other games: cloud-catching's one,
And mud-mixing after rain is lots and lots of fun.
But when you go to stay with them, then never mind the rest:
Take my advice—they're very nice—but steeple-sliding's best.

The most (unconsciously) obscene poem in English that I know of I ran across in Quiller-Couch's *Oxford Book of Victorian Verse.*

When love meets love, breast urged to breast,
God interposes
An unacknowledged guest,
And leaves a little child among our roses.

We love, God makes: in our sweet mirth
God spies occasion for a birth.
Then is it His, or ours?
I know not—He is fond of flowers.

—T. E. Brown

Dreams

There are four distinguishable stages of sleep, each with characteristic brainwave patterns. The first stage usually lasts a few minutes; the sleeper is easily awakened, the electric waves from the brain are low voltage and irregular. Stage II is characterised by "spindles"—sudden bursts of electrical activity—with a slow rolling of the eyes. Then Stage III gradually supervenes: large slow brainwaves emerge, about one per second, with five times the voltage of the waking rhythms. The heart rate slows, temperature and blood pressure drop, the muscles relax somewhat.

Finally, the sleeper enters Stage IV, the deepest sleep of all, when he is most impervious to noise and disturbance. A large portion of the first part of the night tends to be spent in this deep sleep. Curiously, it is also the phase in which sleepwalking starts.

The most dramatic events begin usually some 90 minutes after going to sleep. The sleeper begins to surface again, back through Stages III, II and I. But instead of entering into a light Stage I sleep, there appears what is virtually a new state of experience. It is signalled by rapid eye movements ("REMs"), quite distinct from the slow rolling of the eyes during deeper sleep. Perhaps the central discovery of sleep research was made in the early 1950's when Nathaniel Kleitman and Eugene Aserinsky, at the University of Chicago, discovered that people woken in this phase of sleep almost always reported a vivid dream.

The whole REM state has proved, on investigation, to be quite extraordinary. For instance, some muscles of the dreamer are, to begin with, completely flaccid. Yet a host of other physiological symptoms suggest that the REM state is one of intense emotional experience and inner concentration: hormones pour into the blood, the heartbeat becomes irregular, blood pressure varies considerably. Breathing may be shallow and rapid, oxygen consumption rises and so does the temperature deep within the brain (as it does on waking).

Luce and Segal call it an "internal storm", and there are usually four to five REM periods each night. They come at roughly 90 minute intervals, and last longer as the night proceeds. Most people thus spend about an hour and a half each night in this strange turmoil.

The peculiar muscular limpness which accompanies the REM state may account for a familiar type of nightmare in which the dreamer struggles to flee from some terror or to cry out, but finds himself paralysed.

But the most astonishing feature of these episodes began to emerge through a now-famous series of experiments by a former student of Kleitman, William Dement. He set out to discover what would happen if people were deprived of dreams by waking them as soon as the REM periods began. Some volunteers subjected to this treatment for a few nights became irritable and forgetful, began to concentrate poorly, reported obscure feelings of uneasiness. Tests with flickering lights produced grotesque hallucinations. Personality changes began to show. The striking thing, though, was that on falling asleep subjects made increasingly frequent "attempts" to dream: they would move almost instantly into the REM state.

On the first night of undisturbed sleep they were allowed, subjects spent an excessive amount of time in the REM state: they appeared to be catching up, not on sleep, but on dream. Control experiments with subjects awakened just as often, but from deep sleep rather than REM periods, showed far less ill effect: although here, too, there was a "rebound", and the subjects took more deep sleep than usual in the first undisturbed night.

Since then, a great deal of evidence has accumulated to show the functional but still obscure importance of the REM state. Even relatively primitive warm-blooded animals like the opossum show REM sleep and suffer if deprived of it. Young animals and human infants spend far more time in the REM state than adults (about half their sleep time in new-born babies). Premature infants take even more.

The day's events are often woven into REM dreams, although sometimes in disguised forms. As the night proceeds, the dreams seem to concern themselves with an increasingly distant past, as though the sleeper were moving back in time. Simultaneously, the dream content tends to become more vivid and laden with imagery.

Recently, workers at Mount Sinai Hospital in New York found that in men almost all REM periods are accompanied by an erection. The erections occur even when a dream appears to have no erotic content. . . . However, it has also been found that if the REM state is prevented, the erections will still occur at the time the REM periods are due, suggesting that some physiological clock is also involved. Indeed, there is the classical hen-and-egg problem here concerning the links between bodily and mental phenomena.

—John Davy

Is sleep a mating with oneself?

—Novalis

In dreams I do not recollect that state of feeling so common when awake, of thinking of one subject and looking at another.

—S. T. Coleridge

I cannot say I was hostile to him, nor friendly either: I have never dreamed of him.

—G. C. Lichtenberg

If all the dreams which men had dreamed during a particular period were written down, they would give an accurate notion of the spirit which prevailed at that time.

—G. W. F. Hegel

"Dreaming permits each and every one of us to be quietly and safely insane every night of our lives." (Charles Fisher) Precisely. So far as my own experience goes, my dreams, however physiologically and psychologically necessary, seem to me, on waking, to be boring in exactly the same way that lunatics are, that is to say, repetitious, devoid of any sense of humor, and insanely egocentric. Only once in my life have I had a dream which, on conscious consideration, seemed interesting enough to write down.

A Nightmare—August 1936

I was in hospital for an appendectomy. There was somebody there with green eyes and a terrifying affection for me. He cut off the arm of an old lady who was going to do me an injury. I explained to the doctors about him, but they were inattentive, though, presently, I realized that they were very concerned about his bad influence over me. I decide to escape from the hospital, and do so, after looking in a cupboard for something, I don't know what. I get to a station, squeeze between the carriages of a train, down a corkscrew staircase and out under the legs of some boys and girls. Now my companion has turned up with his three brothers (there may have been only two). One, a smooth-faced, fine-fingernailed blond, is more reassuring. They tell me that they never leave anyone they like and that they often choose the timid. The name of the frightening one is Giga (in Icelandic *Gigur* is a crater), which I associate with the name Marigold and have a vision of pursuit like a book illustration and, I think, related to the long red-legged Scissor Man in *Schockheaded Peter.* The scene changes to a derelict factory by moonlight. The brothers are there, and my father. There is a great banging going on which, they tell me, is caused by the ghost of an old aunt who lives in a tin in the factory. Sure enough, the tin, which resembles my mess tin, comes bouncing along and stops at our feet, falling open. It is full of hard-boiled eggs. The brothers are very selfish and seize them, and only my father gives me half his.

> I dreamed that I had landed from a fairly large boat on the shore of a fertile island with a luxuriant vegetation, where I had been told one could get the most beautiful pheasants. I immediately started bargaining for these birds with the natives, who killed them and brought them to me in great numbers. I knew they were pheasants, although, since dreams usually transform things, they had long tails covered with iridescent eyelike spots similar to those of peacocks or rare birds of paradise. The natives brought them on board and neatly arranged them so that their heads were inside the boat and the long gaily-colored feather tails hung outside. In the brilliant sunshine, they made the most splendid pile imaginable, and there were so many of them that there was hardly room for the steersman and the rowers. Then we glided over calm waters and I was already making a mental list of the names of friends with whom I meant to share these treasures. At last we reached a great port. I lost my way among huge masted ships, and climbed from one deck

to another, looking for some place where I could safely moor my little boat.

—Goethe (trans. W. H. A. with Elizabeth Mayer)

I

Weary birds, large weary birds, perched upon a tremendous cliff that rises out of dark waters, await the fall of night. Weary birds turn their heads towards the blaze in the west. The glow turns to blood, the blood is mixed with soot. We look across the waters towards the west and upwards into the soaring arch of the sunset. Stillness—Our lives are one with that of this huge far-off world, as it makes its entry into the night.—Our few words, spoken or unspoken (My words? His words?), die away: now it is too dark for us to find the way back.

II

Night. The road stretches ahead. Behind me it winds up in curves towards the house, a gleam in the darkness under the dense trees of the park. I know that, shrouded in the dark out there, people are moving, that all around me, hidden by the night, life is a-quiver. I know that something is waiting for me in the house. Out of the darkness of the park comes the call of a solitary bird: and I go—up there.

III

Light without a visible source, the pale gold of a new day. Low bushes, their silk-grey leaves silvered with dew. All over the hills, the cool red of the cat's foot in flower. Emerging from the ravine where a brook runs under a canopy of leaves, I walk out onto a wide open slope. Drops, sprinkled by swaying branches, glitter on my hands, cool my forehead, and evaporate in the gentle morning breeze.

—Dag Hammarskjöld (trans. W. H. A. with Leif Sjöberg)

She told me about a dream she had had a few nights before and as I listened I couldn't help feel that perhaps everything would work out alright.

"It was such a lovely warm dream," she said. "I dreamed that Errol and I were married and that we had such a lovely home. Everything in the house was white. There was a white marble stairway and a completely white bedroom with white chiffon bedspreads. And I know this will please you, Mother. I also dreamed that I had a gold pipe organ to play, just like the one you always wanted me to have. But the best part of all was the baby I was going to have. Errol's baby. I wore this gorgeous black velvet top and gold trousers and gold shoes with the toes turned up. And I was so happy to have Errol's baby that I danced all through the halls of our lovely house."

—Florence Aadland

Drinking Songs

Since the dawn of history alcoholic beverages have been among the greatest blessings of life, but there is not, to my knowledge, a single drinking song of first-rate poetic quality. About even the best of them there is an air of false *bonhomie*, characteristic of an all-male company, of "the boys" whooping it up. About the drinking song in *Antony and Cleopatra*, act II, scene vii, it is worth noting, firstly, that it is the worst lyric Shakespeare ever wrote, and, secondly, that in the context (Pompey's Galley) a good poem would have been dramatically wrong.

The only tolerable English example I can find seems to celebrate solitary drinking.

I have no pain, dear Mother, now,
But, Oh, I am so dry;
So connect me to a brewery,
And leave me there to die.

Oddly enough, there is a very good poem about drug taking.

Cocaine Lil and Morphine Sue

Did you ever hear tell about Cocaine Lil?
She lived in Cocaine town on Cocaine hill,
She had a cocaine dog and a cocaine cat,
They fought all night with a cocaine rat.

She had cocaine hair on her cocaine head.
She had a cocaine dress that was poppy red:
She wore a snowbird hat and sleigh-riding clothes,
On her coat she wore a crimson, cocaine rose.

Big gold chariots on the Milky Way,
Snakes and elephants silver and gray.
Oh the cocaine blues they make me sad,
Oh the cocaine blues make me feel bad.

Lil went to a snow party one cold night,
And the way she sniffed was sure a fright.
There was Hophead Mag with Dopey Slim,
Kankakee Liz and Yen Shee Jim.

There was Morphine Sue and the Poppy Face Kid,
Climbed up snow ladders and down they skid;
There was the Stepladder Kit, a good six feet,
And the Sleigh-riding Sister who were hard to beat.

Along in the morning about half past three
They were all lit up like a Christmas tree;

Lil got home and started for bed,
Took another sniff and it knocked her dead.

They laid her out in her cocaine clothes:
She wore a snowbird hat with a crimson rose;
On her headstone you'll find this refrain:
"She died as she lived, sniffing cocaine."

Easter

Easter Day, April 17, 1870

The happiest, brightest, most beautiful Easter I have ever spent. As I had hoped, the day was cloudless, a glorious morning. My first thought was "Christ is Risen". It is not well to lie in bed on Easter morning, indeed it is thought very unlucky. I got up between five and six and was out soon after six. There had been a frost and the air was rimy with a heavy thick white dew on hedge, bank and turf, but the morning was not cold. Last night poor Mrs Chalmers was in trouble because she had not been able to get any flowers to dress her husband's grave and Miss Chalmers was in deep distress about it. Some boys who had promised to bring them some primroses had disappointed them. So I thought I would go and gather some primroses this morning and flower the grave for them. I strolled down the lane till I came in sight of the full mill pond shining between the willow trunks like a lake of indefinite size. Here and there the banks and road sides were spangled with primroses and they shone like stars among the little brakes and bramble thickets overhanging the brook. A sheep and lamb having broken bonds were wandering about the lane by themselves and kept on fording and refording the brook where it crosses the road to get out of my way. The mill was silent except for the plash of the water from "the dark round of the dripping wheel". The mill pond was full, but I forgot to look at the sun to see if he was dancing as he is said to do on Easter morning. There was a heavy white dew with a touch of hoar frost on the meadows, and as I leaned over the wicket gate by the mill pond looking to see if there were any primroses in the banks but not liking to venture into the dripping grass suddenly I heard the cuckoo for the first time this year. He was near Peter's Pool and he called three times quickly one after another. It is very well to hear the cuckoo for the first time on Easter Sunday morning. I loitered up the lane again gathering primroses where I could from among the thorn and bramble thickets and along the brook banks, not without a good many scratches. Some few grew by the mill pond edge and there was one plant growing on the trunk of a willow some way from the ground. The children have almost swept the lane clear of primroses for the same purpose for which I wanted them. However I got a good handful with plenty of green leaves and brought them home.

The village lay quiet and peaceful in the morning sunshine, but by the time I came back from primrosing there was some little stir and people were beginning to open their doors and look out into the fresh fragrant splendid morning. Hannah Whitney's door was open. I tied my primroses up in five bunches, borrowed an old knife etc. and a can of water from Mary and went to Mrs Powell's for the primroses Annie had tied for me last night, but no one in the house was up and the door was locked. Anthony and Richard Brooks were standing in the road by the churchyard wall and I asked them if they could show me Mr Chalmers' grave. Richard Brooks came along with me and showed me where he believed it to be, and it proved to be the right grave. So I made a simple cross upon it with my five primrose bunches. There were a good many people about in the churchyard by this time finishing flowering the graves and looking at last night's work. John Davies and a girl seeing me at work came and dressed the rest of the four Chalmers graves. By this time Mrs Powell was just opening her door so I went to the house with Charlie Powell and got the primroses which had been in water all night and were exquisitely fresh and fragrant. With these five bunches I made a primrose cross on the turf at the foot of the white marble cross which marks Mr Henry Venables' grave. Then I went to the school.

It was now 8 o'clock and Mrs Evans was down and just ready to set about finishing the moss crosses. She and Mary Jane went out to gather fresh primroses in the Castle Clump as last night's were rather withered. The moss had greatly improved and freshened into green during the night's soaking and when the crosses were pointed each with five small bunches of primroses they looked very nice and pretty because so simple. Directly they were finished I carried them to the churchyard and placed them standing, leaning against the stone tombs of the two Mr Venables. People came up to look at the crosses and they were much admired. Then I ran home to dress and snatched a mouthful of breakfast.

There was a very large congregation at morning church, the largest I have seen for some time, attracted by Easter and the splendour of the day, for they have an immense reverence for Easter Sunday. The anthem went very well and Mr Baskerville complimented Mr Evans after church about it, saying that it was sung in good tune and time and had been a great treat. Mr V read prayers and I preached from I. John III.2, 3 about the Risen Body and Life. There were more communicants than usual: 29. This is the fifth time I have received the Sacrament within four days. After morning service I took Mr V round the churchyard and showed him the crosses on his mother's, wife's, and brother's graves. He was quite taken by surprise and very much gratified. I am glad to see that our primrose crosses seem to be having some effect for I think I notice this Easter some attempt to copy them and an advance towards the form of the cross in some of the decorations of the graves. I wish we could get the people to adopt some little design in the disposition of the flowers upon the graves instead of sticking sprigs into the turf aimlessly anywhere, anyhow and with no meaning at all. But one does not like to interfere too much with their artless, natural way of showing their respect and love for the dead. I am thankful to find this beautiful custom on the increase, and observed more and more every year. Some years ago it was on the decline and nearly discontinued. On Easter Day all the young people come out in something new and bright like butterflies. It is almost part of their religion to wear something new on this day. It was an old saying that if you don't wear something new on Easter Day, the crows will spoil everything you have on. Mrs Chalmers tells me that if it is fine on Easter Day it is counted in Yorkshire a sign of a good harvest. If it rains before morning church is over it is a sign of a bad harvest.

Between the services a great many people were in the churchyard looking at the graves. I went to Bettws Chapel in the afternoon. It was burning hot and as I climbed the hill the perspiration rolled off my forehead from under my hat and fell in drops on the dusty road. Lucretia Wall was in chapel looking pale and pretty after her illness. I went into the farmhouse after Chapel and when I came away Lucretia and Eliza both looking very pretty were leading little Eleanor about the farmyard between them, a charming home picture. Coming down the hill it was delightful, cool and pleasant. The sweet suspicion of spring strengthens, deepens, and grows more sweet every day. Mrs Prig gave us lamb and asparagus at dinner.

—Francis Kilvert

Eating

The significance of the Mass. As biological organisms, we must all, irrespective of sex, age, intelligence, character, creed, assimilate other lives in order to live. As conscious beings, the same holds true on the intellectual level: all learning is assimilation. As children of God, made in His image, we are required in turn voluntarily to surrender ourselves to being assimilated by our neighbors according to their needs.

The slogan of Hell: Eat *or* be eaten.
The slogan of Heaven: Eat *and* be eaten.

Grub first: then ethics.

—Bertolt Brecht

Eating is touch carried to the bitter end.

—Samuel Butler II

Soup and fish explain half the emotions of life.

—Sydney Smith

What is patriotism but the love of the good things we ate in our childhood?

—Lin Yutang

The discovery of a new dish does more for human happiness than the discovery of a new star.

—Brillat-Savarin

There is more simplicity in the man who eats caviare on impulse than in the man who eats grapenuts on principle.

—G. K. Chesterton

Dinnertime is the most wonderful period of the day and perhaps its goal—the blossoming of the day. Breakfast is the bud. The dinner itself, like life, is a curve: it starts off with the lightest courses, then rises to the heavier, and concludes with light courses again.

—Novalis

. . . gastronomical perfection can be reached in these combinations: one person dining alone, usually upon a couch or a hillside; two people, of no matter what sex or age, dining in a good restaurant; six people, of no matter what sex or age, dining in a good home. . . .

The six should be capable of decent social behaviour: that is, no two of them should be so much in love as to bore the others, nor at the opposite extreme should they be carrying on any sexual or professional feud which could put poison on the plates all must eat from. A good combination would be one married couple, for warm composure; one less firmly established, to add a note of investigation to the talk; and two strangers of either sex, upon whom the better-acquainted could sharpen their questioning wits. . . .

Hunger and fair-to-good health are basic requirements, for no man stayed by a heavy midafternoon snack or gnawed by a gastric ulcer can add much to the general well-being.

—M. F. K. Fisher

. . . A certain esteem for each other is clearly evident in all who eat together. This is already expressed by the fact of their *sharing*. The food in the common dish before them belongs to all of them together. Everyone takes some of it and sees that others take some too. Everyone tries to be fair and not to take advantage of anyone else. The bond between the eaters is strongest when it is *one* animal they partake of, one body which they knew as a living unit, or one loaf of bread. . . .

Modern man likes eating in restaurants, at separate tables, with his own little group, for which *he* pays. Since everyone else in the place is doing the same thing, he eats his meal under the pleasing illusion that everyone everywhere has enough to eat.

—Elias Canetti

When one despairs of the human race ever learning anything, it is some small comfort to recall that certain patriotic absurdities, common in the First World War, had disappeared in the Second. In the latter, for example, no restaurant proprietor on either side felt it necessary to Anglicize or Germanize the names of dishes. In the former, they did. Karl Kraus gives the following examples from Viennese menus:

Potage à la Colbert	*Suppe mit Wurzelwerk und verlorenem Ei*
Irish stew	*Hammelfleisch im Topf auf bürgerliche Art*
Ragout	*Mischgericht*
Vol-au-vent	*Blätterteighohlpastete*
Mixed pickles	*Scharfes Allerlei*
Sauce mayonnaise	*Eieröltunke*
Pommes à la maître d'hôtel	*Erdäpfel nach Haushofmeister-Art*
Rumpsteak	*Beiried-Doppelstück*
Macaroni	*Treubruchnudeln*
Romadour	*Hofratskäschen*

How much depends upon the way things are presented in this world can be seen from the very fact that coffee drunk out of wine-glasses is really miserable stuff, as is meat cut at the table with a pair of scissors. Worst of all, as I once actually saw, is butter spread on a piece of bread with an old though very clean razor.

—G. C. Lichtenberg

In 1855, George Musgrave, author of *A Ramble through Normandy*, watched a honeymoon couple on a river steamer at Rouen consume the following meal:

Soup, fried mackerel, beefsteak, French beans and fried potatoes, an omelette *fines herbes*, a fricandeau of veal with sorrel, a roast chicken, garnished with mushrooms, a hock of pork served upon spinach, an apricot tart, three custards, an endive salad, a small roast leg of lamb, with chopped onion and nutmeg sprinkled upon it, coffee, two glasses of absinthe, *eau dorée*, a Mignon cheese, pears, plums, grapes and cakes. With the meal two bottles of Burgundy and one of Chablis.

(Quoted by Elizabeth David in *French Provincial Cooking*)

Once Archchancellor Cambacérès received two enormous sturgeons, one weighing 324 pounds, the other 374, the same day. There was to be a grand dinner that day, and the maître d'hôtel closeted himself with His Highness to resolve the difficulty that arose. If both were served at the same dinner, one would evidently belittle the other. On the other hand, it was unthinkable to serve two fish of the same variety on succeeding days. He emerged beaming from the conference. Here is how the problem was solved.

The smaller sturgeon was bedded on flowers and foliage. A concert of violins and flutes announced it. The flutist and the two violinists, dressed like chefs, preceded the fish, which was flanked by four footmen, bearing torches, and two kitchen assistants, bearing knives. The chef, halberd in hand, marched at the fish's head.

The procession paraded around the table, arousing such admiration that the guests, forgetting their respect for Monseigneur, stood on their chairs to see the monster. But just as the tour was completed, as the fish was about to be taken out for carving, one of the bearers made a false step, fell on one knee, and the fish slid to the floor.

A cry of despair rose from every heart, or rather from every stomach. There was a moment when everyone was talking, giving advice on how to save the situation. But the voice of Cambacérès dominated the tumult.

"Serve the other," he cried.

And the other, larger fish appeared, but with two flutists, four violinists, and four footmen. Applause succeeded cries of anguish as the first fish, weighing fifty pounds less, was taken away.

—Alexandre Dumas (trans. Louis Colman)

When a poor man eats a chicken, one of them is sick.

—Yiddish proverb

Elizabeth found nothing to complain of in starvation corner as far as soup went: indeed Figgis's rationing had been so severe that she got a positive lake of it. She was pleased at having a man on each side of her, her host on her right, and Georgie on her left, whereas Lucia had quaint Irene on her right. Turbot came next; about that Figgis was not to blame, for people helped themselves, and they were all so inconsiderate that, when it came to Elizabeth's turn, there was little left but spine and a quantity of shining black mackintosh, and as for her first glass of champagne, it was merely foam. By this time, too, she was beginning to get uneasy about Benjy. He was talking in a fat contented voice, which she seldom heard at home, and neither by leaning back nor by leaning forward could she get any really informatory glimpse of him or his wine-glasses. She heard his gobbling laugh at the end of one of his own stories, and Susan said, "Oh fie, Major, I shall tell on you." This was not reassuring.

Elizabeth stifled her uneasiness and turned to her host.

"Delicious turbot, Mr Wyse," she said. "So good. And did you see the *Hastings Chronicle* this morning about the great Roman discoveries of the *châtelaine* of Mallards. Made me feel quite a Dowager."

Mr Wyse had clearly foreseen the deadly feelings that might be aroused by that article, and had made up his mind to be extremely polite to everybody, whatever they were to each other. He held up a deprecating hand.

"You will not be able to persuade your friends of that," he said. "I protest against your applying the word Dowager to yourself. It has the taint of age about it. The ladies of Tilling remain young for ever, as my sister Amelia so constantly writes to me."

Elizabeth tipped up her champagne-glass, so that he could scarcely help observing that there was nothing in it.

"Sweet of the dear Contessa," she said. "But in my humble little Grebe, I feel quite a country mouse, so far away from all that's going on. Hardly Tilling at all: my Benjy-boy tells me I must call the house 'Mouse-trap'."

Irene was still alert for attacks on Lucia.

"How about calling it Cat and Mouse trap, Mapp?" she enquired across the table.

"Why, dear?" said Elizabeth with terrifying suavity.

Lucia instantly engaged quaint Irene's attention, or something even more quaint might have followed, and Mr Wyse made signals to Figgis and pointed towards Elizabeth's glass. Figgis thinking that he was only calling his notice to wine-glasses in general filled up Major Benjy's which happened to be empty, and began carving the chicken. The maid handed round the plates and Lucia got some nice slices off the breast. Elizabeth, receiving no answer from Irene, wheeled round to Georgie.

"What a day it will be when we are all allowed to see the great Roman remains," she said.

A dead silence fell on the table except for Benjy's jovial voice.

"A saucy little customer she was. They used to call her the Pride of Poona. I've still got her photograph somewhere, by Jove."

Rockets of conversation, a regular bouquet of them, shot up all round the table.

"And was Poona where you killed those lovely tigers, Major?" asked Susan. "What a pretty costume Elizabeth made of the best bits. So ingenious. Figgis, the champagne."

"Irene dear," said Lucia in her most earnest voice.

"I think you must manage your summer picture-exhibition this year. My hands are so full. Do persuade her to, Mr Wyse."

"I see on all sides of me such brilliant artists and such competent managers—" he began.

"Oh, pray not me!" said Elizabeth. "I'm quite out of touch with modern art."

"Well, there's room for old masters and mistresses, Mapp," said Irene encouragingly. "Never say die."

Lucia had just finished her nice slice of breast when a well-developed drumstick, probably from the leg on which the chicken habitually roosted, was placed before Elizabeth. Black roots of plucked feathers were dotted about in the yellow skin.

"Oh, far too much for me," she said. "Just a teeny slice after my lovely turbot."

Her plate was brought back to her with a piece of the drumstick cut off. Chestnut ice with brandy followed, and the famous oyster savoury, and then dessert, with a compôte of figs and honey.

"A little Easter gift from my sister Amelia," explained Mr Wyse to Elizabeth. "A domestic product of which the recipe is an heirloom of the Mistress of Castello Faraglione. I think Amelia had the privilege of sending you a spoonful or two of the Faraglione honey not so long ago."

The most malicious brain could not have devised two more appalling *gaffes* than this pretty speech contained. There was that unfortunate mention of the word "recipe" again, and everyone thought of lobster, and who could help recalling the reason why Countess Amelia had sent Elizabeth the jar of nutritious honey? The pause of stupefaction was succeeded by a fresh gabble of conversation, and a spurt of irresistible laughter from quaint Irene.

—E. F. Benson

I know a large, greedy, and basically unthinking man who spent all the middle years of his life working hard in a small town and eating in waffle shops and now and then gorging himself at friends' houses on Christmas Day. Quite late he married a large, greedy, and unthinking woman who introduced him to the dubious joys of whatever she heard about on the radio: Miracle Sponge Delight, Aunt Martha's Whipped Cheese Surprise, and all the homogenized, pasteurized, vitalized, dehydratized products intrinsic to the preparation of the Delights and the Surprises. My friend was happy.

He worked hard in the shop and his wife worked hard at the stove, her sink-side portable going full blast in order not to miss a single culinary hint. Each night they wedged themselves into their breakfast-bar-dinette and ate and ate and ate. They always meant to take up Canfield, but somehow they felt too sleepy. About a year ago he brought home a little set of dominoes, thinking it would be fun to shove the pieces around in a couple of games of Fives before she cleared the table. But she looked hard at him, gave a great belch, and died.

He was desperately lonely. We all thought he would go back to living in the rooming-house near the shop, or take up straight rye whisky, or at least start raising tropical fish.

Instead he stayed home more and more, sitting across from the inadequate little chromiumed chair his wife had died in, eating an almost ceaseless meal. He cooked it himself, very carefully. He listened without pause to her radio, which had literally not been turned off since her death. He wrote down every cooking tip he heard, and "enclosed twenty-five cents in stamps" for countless packages of Whipperoo, Jellerino, and Vita-glugg. He wore her tentlike aprons as he bent over the stove and sink and solitary table, and friends told me never, never, *never* to let him invite me to a meal.

But I liked him. And one day when I met him in the Pep Brothers' Shopping Basket—occasionally I fought back my claustrophobia-among-the-cans long enough to go there for the best frozen fruit in town—he asked me so nicely and straightforwardly to come to supper with him that I said I'd love to. He lumbered off, a look of happy purpose wiping the misery from his big face; it was like sunlight breaking through smog. I felt a shudder of self-protective worry, which shamed me.

The night came, and I did something I very seldom do when I am to be a guest: I drank a sturdy shot of dry vermouth and gin, which I figured from long experience would give me an appetite immune to almost any gastronomical shocks. I was agreeably mellow and uncaring by the time I sat down in the chair across from my great, wallowing, bewildered friend and heard him subside with a fat man's alarming *puff!* into his own seat.

I noticed that he was larger than ever. You like your own cooking, I teased. He said gravely to me that gastronomy had saved his life and reason, and before I could recover from the shock of such fancy words on his strictly one-to-two syllable tongue, he had jumped up lightly, as only a fat man can, and started opening oven doors.

We had a tinned "fruit cup," predominantly gooseberries and obviously a sop to current health hints on station JWRB. Once having disposed of this bit of medical hugger-muggery, we surged on happily through one of the ghastliest meals I ever ate in my life. On second thought I can safely say, *the* ghastliest. There is no point in describing it, and to tell the truth a merciful mist has blurred its high points. There was too much spice where there should be none; there was sogginess where crispness was all-important; there was an artificially whipped and heavily sweetened canned-milk dessert where nothing at all was wanted.

And all through the dinner, in the small, hot, crowded room, we drank lukewarm Muscatel, a fortified dessert wine sold locally in gallon jugs, mixed in cheese-spread glasses with equal parts of a popular bottled lemon soda. It is incredible, but it happened.

I am glad it did. I know now what I may only have surmised theoretically before: there is indeed a gastronomic innocence, more admirable and more enviable than any cunning cognizance of menus and vintages and kitchen subtleties. My gross friend, untroubled by affectations of knowledge, served forth to me a meal that I was proud to partake of. If I felt myself at times a kind of sacrificial lamb, stretched on the altar of devotion, I was glad to be that lamb, for never was nectar poured for any goddess with more innocent and trusting enjoyment than was my hideous glass filled with a mixture of citric acid, carbon dioxide, and pure vinous hell for me. I looked into the little gray eyes of my friend and drank deep and felt the better for it.

—M. F. K. Fisher

Echoes

In a district as diversified as this, so full of hollow vales and hanging woods, it is no wonder that echoes should abound. Many we have discovered, that return the cry of a pack of dogs, the notes of a hunting horn, a tunable ring of bells, or the melody of birds very agreeably; but we were still at a loss for a polysyllabical articulate echo, till a young gentleman, who had parted from his company in a summer evening walk, and was calling after them, stumbled upon a very curious one in a spot where it might least be expected. At first he was very much surprised, and could not be persuaded but that he was mocked by some boys; but, repeating his trials in several languages, and finding his respondent to be a very adroit polyglot, he then discerned the deception.

This echo, in an evening before rural noises cease, would repeat ten syllables most articulately and distinctly, especially if quick dactyls were chosen. The last syllable of

> Tityre, tu patulae recubans—

were as audibly and intelligibly returned as the first; and there is no doubt, could trial have been made, but that at midnight, when the air is very elastic, and a dead stillness prevails, one or two syllables more might have been obtained; but the distance rendered so late an experiment very inconvenient.

Quick dactyls, we observed, succeeded best; for when we came to try its powers in slow, heavy, embarrassed spondees of the same number of syllables

> Monstrum horrendum, informe, ingens—

we could perceive a return of but four or five.

—Gilbert White

Eclipses

March 15, 1858

First-rate congregations yesterday. I question whether the solar eclipse to-day had not something to do with it. The days have gone when such a phenomenon would have brought a whole nation to its knees. But, notwithstanding the advancement of science, the generality know as little as ever.

—Benjamin John Armstrong

June 30, 1927

We got out and found ourselves very high, on a moor, boggy, heathery, with butts for grouse shooting. There were grass tracks here and there and people had already taken up positions. So we joined them, walking out to what seemed the highest point overlooking Richmond. One light burned down there. Vales and moors stretched, slope after slope, round us. It was like the Haworth country. But over Richmond, where the sun was rising, was a soft grey cloud. We could see by a gold spot where the sun was. But it was early yet. We had to wait, stamping to keep warm. Ray had wrapped herself in the blue striped blanket off a double bed. She looked incredibly vast and bedroomish. Saxon looked very old. Leonard kept looking at his watch. Four great red setters came leaping over the moor. There were sheep feeding behind us. Vita had tried to buy a guinea pig—Quentin advised a savage—so she observed the animals from time to time. There were thin places in the clouds and some complete holes. The question was whether the sun would show through a cloud or through one of these hollow places when the time came. We began to get anxious. We saw rays coming through the bottom of the clouds. Then, for a moment, we saw the sun, sweeping—it seemed to be sailing at a great pace and clear in a gap; we had out our smoked glasses; we saw it crescent, burning red; next moment it had sailed fast into the cloud again; only the red streamers came from it; then only a golden haze, such as one has often seen. The moments were passing. We thought we were cheated; we looked at the sheep; they showed no fear; the setters were racing round; everyone was standing in long lines, rather dignified, looking out. I thought how we were like very old people, in the birth of the world—druids on Stonehenge; (this idea came more vividly in the first pale light though). At the back of us were great blue spaces in the cloud. These were still blue. But now the colour was going out. The clouds were turning pale; a reddish black colour. Down in the valley it was an extraordinary scrumble of red and black; there was the one light burning; all was cloud down there, and very beautiful, so delicately tinted. Nothing could be seen through the cloud. The 24 seconds were passing. Then one looked back again at the blue; and rapidly, very very quickly, all the colours faded; it became darker and darker as at the beginning of a violent storm; the light sank and sank; we kept saying this is the shadow; and we thought now it is over—this is the shadow; when suddenly the light went out. We had fallen. It was extinct. There was no colour. The earth was dead. That was the astonishing moment; and the next when as if a ball had rebounded the cloud took colour on itself again, only a sparky ethereal colour and so the light came back. I had very strongly the feeling as the light went out of some vast obeisance; something kneeling down and suddenly raised up when the colours came. They came back astonishingly lightly and quickly and beautifully in the valley and over the hills—at first with a miraculous glittering and ethereality, later normally almost, but with a great sense of relief. It was like recovery. We had been much worse than we had expected. We had seen the world dead. This was within the power of nature. Our greatness had been apparent too. Now we became Ray in a blanket, Saxon in a cap etc. We were bitterly cold. I should say that the cold had increased as the light went down. One felt very livid. Then—it was over till 1999. What remained was the sense of the comfort which we get used to, of plenty of light, and colour. This for some time seemed a definitely welcome thing. Yet when it became established all over the country, one rather missed the sense of its being a relief and a respite, which one had had when it came back after the darkness. How can I express the darkness? It was a sudden plunge, when one did not expect it; being at the mercy of the sky; our own nobility; the druids; Stonehenge; and the racing red dogs; all that was in one's mind.

—Virginia Woolf

Education, Classical

The modern revolt against centering the school curriculum around the study of Latin and Greek is understandable enough, but deplorably mistaken.

In the Middle Ages Latin was the international language for all topics, so that it was as obvious why a "clerk" must learn it as it is obvious why a surgeon must learn anatomy. Then came the sixteenth-century humanists, who turned Latin into a dead, purely literary, language, incapable of dealing with any matters which could not be expressed in the Ciceronian vocabulary. The study of Latin and, later, of Greek continued to have a vocational value, but in a special, limited sense; a classical education was thought of as providing a common cultural background for a leisured ruling class.

Today, gentlemen are no longer in demand, but specialists are, so that a classical education no longer appears to have an obvious utility value. It has a great one, nevertheless. It is, no doubt, a pleasure to be able to read the Greek and Latin poets, philosophers, and historians in the original, but very few persons so educated in the past "kept up" their Greek and Latin after leaving school. Its real value was something quite different. Anybody who has spent many hours of his youth translating into and out of two languages so syntactically and rhetorically different from his own, learns something about his mother tongue which I do not think can be learned so well in any other way. For instance, it inculcates the habit, whenever one uses a word, of automatically asking, "What is its exact meaning?"

The people who have really suffered since a classical education became "undemocratic" are not the novelists and poets—their natural love of language sees them through—but all those, like politicians, journalists, lawyers, the man-in-the-street, etc., who use language for everyday and nonliterary purposes. Among such one observes an appalling deterioration in precision and conciseness.

Nobody, for example, who had had a classical education could have perpetrated this sentence by a film critic, quoted by Penelope Gilliatt in *The New Yorker.* "He [a film director] expresses the dichotomy between man and woman in the images of the bra and Dachau."

Elegies

Poets seem to be more generally successful at writing elegies than at any other literary genre. Indeed, the only elegy I know of which seems to me a failure is "Adonais."

The Last Signal
(Oct. 11, 1886)
A Memory of William Barnes

Silently I footed by an uphill road
That led from my abode to a spot yew-boughed;
Yellowly the sun sloped low down to westward,
And dark was the east with cloud.

Then, amid the shadow of that livid sad east,
Where the light was least, and a gate stood wide,
Something flashed the fire of the sun that was facing it,
Like a brief blaze on that side.

Looking hard and harder I knew what it meant—
The sudden shine sent from the livid east scene;

It meant the west mirrored by the coffin of my friend there,
    Turning to the road from his green,

  To take his last journey forth—he who in his prime
  Trudged so many a time from that gate athwart the land!
Thus a farewell to me he signalled on his grave-way,
    As with a wave of his hand.

—Thomas Hardy

I. M.
Walter Ramsden
ob. March 26th, 1947
Pembroke College, Oxford.

Dr Ramsden cannot read *The Times* obituary to-day.
    He's dead.
Let monographs on silk worms by other people be
    Thrown away
    Unread
For he who best could understand and criticize them, he
    Lies clay
    In bed.

The body waits in Pembroke College where the ivy taps the panes
    All night;
That old head so full of knowledge, that good heart that kept the brains
    All right,
Those old cheeks that faintly flushed as the port suffused the veins,
    Drain'd white.

Crocus in the Fellows' Garden, winter jasmine up the wall
    Gleam gold.
Shadows of Victorian chimneys on the sunny grassplot fall
    Long, cold.
Master, Bursar, Senior Tutor, these, his three survivors, all
    Feel old.

They remember, as the coffin to its final obsequations
    Leaves the gates,
Buzz of bees in window boxes on their summer ministrations,
    Kitchen din,
    Cups and plates,
And the getting of bump suppers for the long-dead generations
    Coming in,
    From Eights.

—John Betjeman

Enchantment

> Where is your Self to be found? Always in the deepest enchantment that you have experienced.
>
> —Hugo Von Hofmannsthal

The state of enchantment is one of certainty. When enchanted, we neither believe nor doubt nor deny: we *know*, even if, as in the case of a false enchantment, our knowledge is self-deception.

All folk tales recognize that there are false enchantments as well as true ones. When we are truly enchanted we desire nothing for ourselves, only that the enchanting object or person shall continue to exist. When we are falsely enchanted, we desire either to possess the enchanting being or be possessed by it.

We are not free to choose by what we shall be enchanted, truly or falsely. In the case of a false enchantment, all we can do is take immediate flight before the spell really takes hold.

Recognizing idols for what they are does not break their enchantment.

All true enchantments fade in time. Sooner or later we must walk alone in faith. When this happens, we are tempted, either to deny our vision, to say that it must have been an illusion and, in consequence, grow hardhearted and cynical, or to make futile attempts to recover our vision by force, i.e. by alcohol or drugs.

A false enchantment can all too easily last a lifetime.

Christ did not enchant men; He demanded that they believe in Him. Except on one occasion, the Transfiguration. For a brief while, Peter, James, and John were permitted to see Him in His glory. For that brief while they had no need of faith. The vision vanished, and the memory of it did not prevent them from all forsaking Him when He was arrested, or Peter from denying that he had ever known Him.

God loves all men but is enchanted by none.

My neighbor: someone who needs me but by whom I am not enchanted.

Enclosure

> By far the most conspicuous element in the new landscape were the small hedged fields—small, that is, by comparison with the vast open fields that had preceded them, which usually ran to several hundred acres unbroken by a single hedge. As far as possible the enclosure com-

missioners formed square or squarish fields. Where we find long narrow fields they are nearly always adjacent to the village, lying behind or beside the "ancient homesteads," as they are called in the awards. These represent in most instances the crofts or separate paddocks of half an acre to an acre in size which have been hedged around since medieval times.

The new enclosures varied in size according to the size of the farms. On small farms of which there were great numbers in the Midlands and East Anglia—the holdings of the free peasantry—the new fields were usually five to ten acres in size. On large farms they ran up to fifty or sixty acres. But in grazing country these larger fields were soon reduced to a number of smaller fields of round about ten acres apiece. . . .

The conversion of the former arable fields to small enclosed fields of pasture had therefore two visible effects on the landscape. It tended to produce a monotonous field-pattern and it also produced "a continuous sheet of greensward," as William Marshall observed of Leicestershire in 1790, instead of the multi-coloured patchwork of the old arable strips. . . .

The new fields were hedged around with quickset, whitethorn, or hawthorn, to give its alternative names, with a shallow ditch on one side or both sides of the fence. In the upland stone country, dry-walling took the place of hedges. . . . Ash and elm were planted in the hedgerows, and the flashing grey-green willow along the banks of the streams.

The thousands of miles of new hedgerows in the Midland countryside, when they came to full growth after a generation, added enormously to the bird population, especially with the extermination of the larger hawks and kites, a process that is abundantly recorded in the churchwardens' accounts or the field-reeves' books of Midland villages. Millions of small birds now sing in the hedges and spinneys. But it was not all gain. The heathland birds have disappeared over large areas, and become rarer altogether. . . .

A great number of new by-roads came into existence as a result of the enclosure movement. They are immediately recognizable on the one-inch map by the manner in which they run from village to village practically straight across the country, with perhaps an occasional sudden right-angled bend and then on again. More significantly still, these straight roads sometimes do not run to the nearest village but continue for some miles through open country, reaching the villages by means of side-roads. There is none of that apparently aimless wandering in short stretches, punctuated by frequent bends, going halfway round the compass to reach the next hamlet or village, which characterizes the by-roads in country that has never been in open field or left it several centuries ago. . . .

There is, too, another feature of this piece of country which is characteristic of all country enclosed from open fields or common of any kind. It is the complete absence of any *lanes*. . . . Lanes—true lanes that is, deep and winding—are characteristic of country fabricated piecemeal with small medieval implements. In recently enclosed country we have instead an open regular mesh of by-roads, and a few field-paths and bridle-roads to fill in the larger spaces between the villages. In Leicestershire, the man who wishes to forget income-tax, hydrogen bombs, and the relentless onward march of science, walks the field-paths, to which special maps and guides are provided; in Devon he takes to the deep lanes between the farms. It is a fundamental difference in landscape-history.

—W. G. Hoskins

Eclogue: Two Farms in Woone

ROBERT. You'll lose your meäster soon, then, I do vind;
He's gwaï'n to leäve his farm, as I do larn,
At Miëlmas; an' I be sorry vor'n.
What, is he then a little bit behind?
THOMAS. Oh no! at Miëlmas his time is up,
An' thik there sly wold fellow, Farmer Tup,
A-fearen that he'd get a bit o'bread,
'V a-been an' took his farm here over's head.
ROBERT. How come the Squire to treat your meäster zoo?
THOMAS. Why, he an' meäster had a word or two.
ROBERT. Is Farmer Tup a-gwaï'n to leäve his farm?
He han't a-got noo young woones vor to zwarm.
Poor over-reachen man! why to be sure
He don't want all the farms in parish, do er?
THOMAS. Why ees, all ever he can come across.
Last year, you know, he got away the eäcre
Or two o' ground a-rented by the beäker,
An' what the butcher had to keep his hoss;
An' vo'k do beä'nhan' now, that meäster's lot
Will be a-drow'd along wi' what he got.
ROBERT. That's it. In theäse here pleäce there used to be
Eight farms avore they were a-drow'd together,
An' eight farm-housen. Now how many be there?
Why after this, you know, there'll be but dree.
THOMAS. An' now they din't imploy so many men
Upon the land as work'd upon it then,
Vor all they midden crop it worse, nor stock it.
The lan'lord, to be sure, is into pocket;
Vor half the housen be-en down, 'tis clear,

Don't cost so much to keep em up, a-near.
But then the jobs o' work in wood an' mortar
Do come I 'spose, you know, a little shorter;
An' many that were little farmers then,
Be now a-come all down to leäb'ren men;
An' many leäb'ren men, wi' empty hands,
Do live lik drones upon the workers' lands.
ROBERT. Aye, if a young chap, woonce, had any wit
To try an' screäpe together zome vew pound,
To buy some cows an' teäke a bit o' ground,
He mid become a farmer, bit by bit.
But, hang it! now the farms be all so big,
An' bits o' groun' so skeä'ce, woone got no scope;
If woone could seäve a poun', woone coudden hope
To keep noo live stock but a little pig.
THOMAS. Why here wer vourteen men, zome years agoo,
A-kept a-drashen half the winter drough;
An' now, woone's drashels be'n't a bit o' good.
They got machines to drashy wi', plague teäke em!
An' he that vu'st vound out the way to meäke em,
I'd drash his busy zides vor'n if I could!
Avore they took away our work, they ought
To meäke us up the bread our leäbour bought.
ROBERT. They hadden need meäke poor men's leäbour less,
Vor work a'ready is uncommon skeä'ce.
THOMAS. Ah! Robert! times be badish vor the poor;
Ah' worse will come, I be afeärd, if Moore
In theäse year's almanick do tell us right.
ROBERT. Why then we sartainly must starve. Good night!

—William Barnes

Enclosure

By Langley Bush I roam, but the bush hath left its hill,
On Cowper Green I stray, 'tis a desert strange and chill,
And the spreading Lea Close Oak, ere decay had penned its will,
To the axe of the spoiler and self-interest fell a prey,
And Crossberry Way and old Round Oak's narrow lane
With its hollow trees like pulpits I shall never see again,
Enclosure like a Buonaparte let not a thing remain,
It levelled every bush and tree and levelled every hill
And hung the moles for traitors—though the brook is running still
It runs a naked stream, cold and chill.

—John Clare

Eruptions

Eruption of the Öraefajökull

In the year 1727, on the 7th of August, which was the tenth Sunday after Trinity, after the commencement of divine service in the church of Sandfell, as I stood before the altar, I was sensible of a gentle concussion under my feet, which I did not mind at first; but, during the delivery of the sermon, the rocking continued to increase, so as to alarm the whole congregation; yet they remarked that the like had often happened before. One of them, a very aged man, repaired to a spring, a little below the house, where he prostrated himself on the ground, and was laughed at by the rest for his pains; but, on his return, I asked him what it was he wished to ascertain, to which he replied, "Be on your guard, Sir; the earth is on fire!" Turning, at the same moment, towards the church door, it appeared to me, and all who were present, as if the house contracted and drew itself together. I now left the church, necessarily ruminating on what the old man had said; and as I came opposite to Mount Flega, and looked upwards, towards the summit, it appeared alternately to expand and be heaved up, and fall again to its former state. Nor was I mistaken in this, as the event shewed; for on the morning of the 8th, we not only felt frequent and violent earthquakes, but also heard dreadful reports, in no respect inferior to thunder. Everything that was standing in the houses was thrown down by these shocks; and there was reason to apprehend that mountains as well as houses would be overturned in the catastrophe. What most augmented the terror of the people was that nobody could divine in what place the disaster would originate, or where it would end.

After nine o'clock, three particularly loud reports were heard, which were almost instantaneously followed by several eruptions of water that gushed out, the last of which was the greatest, and completely carried away the horses and other animals that it overtook in its course. When these exudations were over, the ice mountain itself ran down into the plain, just like melted metal poured out of a crucible; and on settling, filled it to such a height, that I could not discover more of the well-known mountain Lounagrupr than about the size of a bird. The water now rushed down the east side without intermission, and totally destroyed what little of the pasture-grounds remained. It was a most pitiable sight to behold females crying, and my neighbours destitute both of counsel and courage: however, as I observed that the current directed itself towards my house, I removed my family up to the top of a high rock on the side of the mountain, called Dalskardstorfa, where I caused a tent to be pitched, and all the church utensils, together with our food, clothes and other things that were most necessary, to be conveyed thither; drawing the conclusion that, should the eruption break forth at some other place, this height would escape the longest, if it were the will of God, to whom we committed ourselves, and remained there.

Things now assumed quite a different appearance. The Jökull itself exploded, and precipitated masses of ice, many of which were hurled out to the sea; but the thickest remained on the plain at a short distance from the foot of the mountain. The noise and reports continuing, the atmosphere was so completely filled with fire and ashes, that day could scarcely be distinguished from night, by reason of the darkness that followed, and which was barely rendered visible by the light of the fire that had broken through five or six cracks in the mountain. In this manner the parish of Öraefa was tormented for three days together; yet it is not easy to describe the disaster as it was in reality; for the surface of the ground was entirely covered with pumice-sand, and it was impossible to go out in the open air with safety, on account of the red-hot stones that fell from the atmosphere. Any who did venture out, had to cover their heads with buckets, and such other wooden utensils as could afford them some protection.

On the 11th it cleared up a little in the neighbourhood; but the ice-mountain still continued to send forth smoke and flames. The same day I rode, in company with three others, to see how matters stood with the parsonage, as it was the most exposed, but we could only proceed with the utmost danger, as there was no other way except between the ice-mountain and the Jökull which had been precipitated into the plain, where the water was so hot that the horses almost got unmanageable: and, just as we entertained the hope of getting through by this passage, I happened to look behind me, when I descried a fresh deluge of hot water directly above me which, had it reached us, must inevitably have swept us before it. Contriving, of a sudden, to get on the ice, I called to my companions to make the utmost expedition in following me and, by this means, we reached Sandfell in safety.

The whole of the farm, together with the cottages of the tenants, had been destroyed; only the dwelling houses remained, and a few spots of the tuns. The people stood crying in the church. The cows which, contrary to all expectation, both here and elsewhere, had escaped the disaster, were lowing beside a few haystacks that had been damaged during the eruption. At the time the exudation of the Jökull broke forth, the half of the people belonging to the parsonage were in four nearly-constructed sheepcotes, where two women and a boy took refuge on the roof of the highest; but they had hardly reached it when, being unable to resist the force of the thick mud that was borne against it, it was carried away by the deluge of hot water and, as far as the eye could reach, the three unfortunate persons were seen clinging to the roof. One of the women was afterwards found among the substances that had proceeded from the Jökull, but burnt and, as it were, parboiled; her body was so soft that it could scarcely be touched. Everything was in the most deplorable condition. The sheep were lost; some of which were washed up dead from the sea in the third parish from Öraefa. The hay that was saved was found insufficient for the cows so that a fifth part of them had to be killed; and most of the horses which had not been swept into the ocean were afterwards found completely mangled. The eastern part of the parish of Sida was also destroyed by the pumice and sand; and the inhabitants were on that account obliged to kill many of their cattle.

The mountain continued to burn night and day from the 8th of August, as already mentioned, till the beginning of Summer in the month of April the following year, at which time the stones were still so hot that they could not be touched; and it did not cease to emit smoke till near the end of the Summer. Some of them had been completely calcined; some were black and full of holes; and others were so loose in their contexture that one could blow through them. On the first day of Summer 1728, I went in company with a person of quality to examine the cracks in the mountain, most of which were so large that we could creep into them. I found there a quantity of salpetre and could have collected it, but did not choose to stay long in the excessive heat. At one place a heavy calcined stone lay across a large aperture; and, as it rested on a small basis, we easily dislodged it into the chasm but could not observe the least sign of its having reached the bottom. These are the more remarkable particulars that have occurred to me with respect to this mountain; and thus God hath led me through fire and water, and brought me through much trouble and adversity to my eightieth year. To Him be the honour, the praise, and glory for ever.

—Jon Thorlaksson
(quoted by Sir George MacKenzie in *Travels in Iceland*)

March 6, 1787

Reluctantly, but out of loyal comradeship, Tischbein accompanied me today on my ascent of Vesuvius. To a cultured artist like him, who occupies himself only with the most beautiful human and animal forms and even humanizes the formless—rocks and landscapes—with feeling and taste, such a formidable, shapeless heap as Vesuvius, which again and again destroys itself and declares war on any sense of beauty, must appear loathsome.

We took two cabriolets, since we didn't trust ourselves to find our own way through the turmoil of the city. The driver shouted incessantly, "Make way! Make way!" as a warning to donkeys, burdened with wood or refuse, carriages going in the opposite direction, people walking bent down under their loads or just strolling, children and aged persons, to move aside so that he could keep up a sharp trot.

The outer suburbs and gardens already gave sign that we had entered the realm of Pluto. Since it had not rained for a long time, the leaves of the evergreens were coated with a thick layer of ash-grey dust; roofs, fascias and every flat surface were equally grey; only the beautiful blue sky and the powerful sun overhead gave witness that we were still among the living.

At the foot of the steep slope we were met by two guides, one elderly, one youngish, but both competent men. The first took me in charge, the second Tischbein, and they hauled us up the mountain. I say "hauled," because each guide wears a stout leather thong around his waist; the traveller grabs on to this and is hauled up, at the same time guiding his own feet with the help of a stick.

In this manner we reached the flat base from which the cone rises. Facing us in the north was the debris of the Somma. One glance westward over the landscape was like a refreshing bath, and the physical pains and fatigue of our climb were forgotten. We then walked round the cone, which was still smoking and ejecting stones and ashes. So long as there was space enough to remain at a safe distance, it was a grand, uplifting spectacle. After a tremendous, thundering roar which came out of the depth of the cauldron, thousands of stones, large and small, and enveloped in clouds of dust, were hurled into the air. Most of them fell back into the abyss, but the others made an extraordinary noise as they hit the outer wall of the cone. First came the heavier ones, struck with a dull thud and hopped down the slope, then the lighter rattled down after them and, last, a rain of ash descended. This all took place at regular intervals, which we could calculate exactly by counting slowly.

However, the space between the cone and the Somma gradually narrowed till we were surrounded by fallen stones which made walking uncomfortable. Tischbein grew more depressed than ever when he saw that the monster, not content with being ugly, was now threatening to become dangerous as well.

But there is something about an imminent danger which challenges Man's spirit of contradiction to defy it, so I thought to myself that it might be possible to climb the cone, reach the mouth of the crater and return, all in the interval between two eruptions. While we rested safely under the shelter of a projecting rock and refreshed ourselves with the provisions we had brought with us, I consulted our guides. The younger one felt confident that we could risk it; we lined our hats with linen and silk handkerchiefs, I grabbed his belt, and, sticks in hand, we set off.

The smaller stones were still clattering, the ashes still falling about us as the vigorous youth hauled me up the glowing screes. There we stood on the lip of the enormous mouth; a light breeze blew the smoke away from us but also veiled the interior of the crater; steam rose all around us from thousands of fissures; now and then we could glimpse the cracked rock walls. The sight was neither instructive nor pleasing, but this was only because we could not see anything, so we delayed in the hope of seeing more. We had forgotten our slow count and were standing on a sharp edge of the monstrous abyss when, all of a sudden, thunder shook the mountain and a terrific charge flew past us. We ducked instinctively, as if that would save us when the shower of stones began. The smaller stones had already finished clattering down when, having forgotten that another interval had begun, and happy to have survived, we reached the foot of the cone under a rain of ashes which thickly coated our hats and shoulders. . . .

March 20

The news that another emission of lava had just occurred, invisible to Naples since it was flowing towards Ottaiano, tempted me to make a third visit to Vesuvius. On reaching the foot of the mountain, I had hardly jumped down from my two-wheeled, one-horse vehicle before the two guides who had accompanied us the last time appeared on the scene and I hired them both.

When we reached the cone, the elder stayed with our coats and provisions while the younger followed me. We bravely made our way towards the enormous cloud of steam, which was issuing from a point halfway below the mouth of the cone. Having reached it, we descended carefully along its edge. The sky was clear and at last, through the turbulent clouds of steam, we saw the lava stream.

It was only about ten feet wide, but the manner in which it flowed down the very gentle slope was most surprising. The lava on both sides of the stream cools as it moves, forming a channel. The lava on its bottom also cools, so that this channel is constantly being raised. The stream keeps steadily throwing off to right and left the scoria floating on its surface. Gradually, two levels of considerable height are formed, between which the fiery stream continues to flow quietly like a mill brook. We walked along the foot of this embankment while the scoria kept steadily rolling down its sides. Occasionally there were gaps through which we could see the glowing mass from below. Further down, we were also able to observe it from above.

Because of the bright sunshine, the glow of the lava was dulled. Only a little smoke rose into the pure air. I felt a great desire to get near the place where the lava was issuing from the mountain. My guide assured me that this was safe, because the moment it comes forth, a flow forms a vault of cooled lava over itself, which he had often stood on.

To have this experience, we again climbed up the mountain in order to approach the spot from the rear. Luckily, a gust of wind had cleared the air, though not entirely, for all around us puffs of hot vapour were emerging from thousands of fissures. By now we were actually standing on the lava crust, which lay twisted in coils like a soft mush, but it projected so far out that we could not see the lava gushing forth.

We tried to go half a dozen steps further, but the ground under our feet became hotter and hotter and a whirl of dense fumes darkened the sun and almost suffocated us. The guide who was walking in front turned back, grabbed me, and we stole away from the hellish cauldron.

After refreshing our eyes with the view and our throats with wine, we wandered about observing other features of this peak of hell which towers up in the middle of paradise. I inspected some more volcanic flues and saw that they were lined up to the rim with pendent, tapering formations of some stalactitic matter. Thanks to the irregular shape of the flues, some of these deposits were in easy reach, and with the help of our sticks and some hooked appliances we managed to break off some pieces. At the lava dealer's, I had already seen similar ones, listed as true lavas, so I felt happy at having made a discovery. They were a volcanic soot, precipitated from the hot vapours; the condensed minerals they contained were clearly visible.

A magnificent sunset and evening lent their delight to the return journey. However, I could feel how confusing such a tremendous contrast must be. The Terrible beside the Beautiful, the Beautiful beside the Terrible, cancel one another out and produce a feeling of indifference. The Neapolitan would certainly be a different creature if he did not feel himself wedged between God and the Devil.

—Goethe (trans. W. H. Auden with Elizabeth Mayer)

Eskimos

When a child is born it comes into the world with a soul of its own (*nappan*), but this soul is as inexperienced, foolish, and feeble as a child is and looks. It is evident, therefore, that the child needs a more experienced and wiser soul than its own to do the thinking for it and take care of it. Accordingly the mother, so soon as she can after the birth of the child, pronounces a magic formula to summon from the grave the waiting soul of the dead to become the guardian soul of the new-born child, or its *atka*, as they express it.

Let us suppose that the dead person was an old wise man by the name of *John*. The mother then pronounces the formula which may be roughly translated as follows: "Soul of John, come here, come here, be my child's guardian! Soul of John, come here, come here, be my child's guardian!" (Most magic formulae among the Eskimo must be repeated twice.)

When the soul of John, waiting at the grave, hears the summons of the mother, it comes and enters the child. . . . The spirit of John not only teaches the child to talk, but after the child learns to talk it is really the soul of John which talks to you and not the inborn soul of the child. The child, therefore, speaks with all the acquired wisdom which John accumulated in the long lifetime, plus the higher wisdom which only comes after death. Evidently, therefore, the child is the wisest person in the family or in the community, and its opinions should be listened to accordingly. What it says and does may seem foolish to you, but that is mere seeming and in reality the child is wise beyond your comprehension. . . . If it cries for a knife or a pair of scissors, it is not a foolish child that wants the knife, but the soul of the wise old man John that wants it, and it would be presumptuous of a young mother to suppose that she knows better than John what is good for the child, and so she gives it the knife. If she refused the knife (and this is the main point), she would not only be preferring her own foolishness to the wisdom of John, but also she would thereby give offense to the spirit of John, and in his anger John would abandon the child. Upon the withdrawal of his protection the child would become the prey to disease and would probably die, and if it did not die, it would become stupid or hump-backed or otherwise deformed or unfortunate. John must, therefore, be propitiated at every cost. . . .

As the child grows up, the soul with which he was born (the *nappan*) gradually develops in strength, experience, and wisdom, so that after the age of ten or twelve years it is fairly competent to look after the child and begins to do so; at that age it therefore becomes of less vital moment to please the guardian spirit (*atka*), and accordingly it is customary to begin forbidding children and punishing them when they come to the age of eleven or twelve years.

—Vilhjalmur Stefansson

My husband and I were on a journey from Igdlulik to Ponds Inlet. On the way he had a dream, in which it seemed that a friend of his was being eaten by his own kin. Two days after, we came to a spot where strange sounds hovered in the air. At first we could not make out what it was, but coming nearer it was like the ghost of words; as if it were one trying to speak without a voice. And at last it said:

"I am one who can no longer live among human kind, for I have eaten my own kin."

We could hear now that it was a woman. Then searching round, we found a little shelter built of snow and a fragment of caribou skin. Close by was a thing standing up; we thought at first it was a human being, but saw it was only a rifle stuck in the snow. But all this time the voice was muttering. And going nearer again we found a human head, with the flesh gnawed away. And at last, entering into the shelter, we found the woman seated on the floor. Her face was turned towards us and we saw that blood was trickling from the corners of her eyes, so greatly had she wept.

"Kikaq," (a gnawed bone) she said, "I have eaten my husband and my children!"

She was but skin and bone herself, and seemed to have no life in her. And she was almost naked, having eaten most of her clothing. My husband bent down over her, and she said:

"I have eaten him who was your comrade when he lived."

And my husband answered: "You had the will to live, and you are still alive." Then we put up our tent close by, cutting off a piece of the fore-curtain to make a shelter for the woman; for she was unclean, and might not be in the tent with us. And we gave her frozen caribou meat to eat, but when she had eaten a mouthful or so, she fell to trembling all over, and could eat no more.

We ceased from our journey then and turned back to Igdlulik, taking her with us, for she had a brother there. She is still alive to this day and married to a great hunter, named Igtussarssua, and she is his favorite wife, though he had one before.

—Knud Rasmussen

Face, The Human

The countenances of children, like those of animals, are masks, not faces, for they have not yet developed a significant profile of their own.

Our notion of symmetry is derived from the human face. Hence, we demand symmetry horizontally and in breadth only, not vertically nor in depth.

—B. Pascal

Chins are exclusively a human feature, not to be found among the beasts. If they had chins, most animals would look like each other. Man was given a chin to prevent the personality of his mouth and eyes from overwhelming the rest of his face, to prevent each individual from becoming a species unto himself.

The ears are the last feature to age.

—Malcolm de Chazal

Jack on one side, Tom on the other; and yet Jack cannot see Tom.

—Bermudan riddle

Hair a-top, hair a-bottom; only a dance in the middle.

—Jamaican riddle

If the eyes are often the organ through which the intelligence shines, the nose is generally the organ which most readily publishes stupidity.

—M. Proust

The noses of fat men do not follow suit with the rest of them as they age. The noses become, if anything, sharper, thinner.

—Max Beerbohm

The glance embroiders in joy, knits in pain, and sews in boredom.

When indifferent, the eye takes stills, when interested, movies.

Laughter is regional: a smile extends over the whole face.

—Malcolm de Chazal

The wink was not our best invention.

—Ralph Hodgson

A man is always as good as the good which appears in his face, but he need not be as evil as the evil which appears in it, because evil does not always realize itself immediately; indeed, sometimes it never realizes itself at all.

—Max Picard

Fatigue

I observed that, in proportion as our strength decayed, our minds exhibited symptoms of weakness, evinced by a kind of unreasonable pettishness with each other. Each of us thought the other weaker in intellect than himself, and more in need of advice and assistance. So trifling a circumstance as a change of place, recommended by one as being warmer and more comfortable, and refused by the other from a dread of motion, frequently called forth fretful expressions which were no sooner uttered than atoned for, to be repeated perhaps in the course of a few minutes. The same thing often occurred when we endeavoured to assist each other in carrying wood to the fire; none of us were willing to receive assistance, although the task was disproportionate to our strength.

—John Franklin

Fish

Man's life is warm, glad, sad, 'twixt loves and graves,
  Boundless in hope, honoured with pangs austere,

Heaven-gazing, and his angel-wings he craves:—
   The fish is swift, small-needing, vague yet clear,
A cold, sweet, silver life, wrapped in round waves,
   Quickened with touches of transporting fear.

—Leigh Hunt

FORGIVENESS

In contrast to revenge, which is the natural, automatic reaction to transgression and which, because of the irreversibility of the action process, can be expected and even calculated, the act of forgiving can never be predicted; it is the only reaction that acts in an unexpected way and thus retains, though being a reaction, something of the original character of action.

—Hannah Arendt

Many promising reconciliations have broken down because, while both parties came prepared to forgive, neither party came prepared to be forgiven.

—Charles Williams

No one ever forgets where he buried the hatchet.

—Kin Hubbard

PRIEST: "Do you forgive your enemies?"
A DYING SPANIARD: "I have no enemies. I have shot them all."

Tout comprendre, c'est tout pardonner. No commonplace is more untrue. Behavior, whether conditioned by an individual neurosis or by society, can be understood; that is to say, one knows exactly why such and such an individual behaves as he does. But a personal action or deed is always mysterious. When we really act, precisely because it is a matter of free choice, we can never say exactly why we do this rather than that. But it is only deeds that we are required to forgive. If someone does me an injury, the question of forgiveness only arises if I am convinced (*a*) that the injury he did me was a free act on his part and therefore no less mysterious to him than to me, and (*b*) that it was me personally whom he meant to injure. Christ does not forgive the soldiers who are nailing him to the Cross; he asks the Father to forgive them. He knows as well as they do *why* they are doing this—they are a squad, detailed to execute a criminal. They do not know *what* they are doing, because it is not their business, as executioners, to know *whom* they are crucifying.

If the person who does me an injury does not know *what* he is doing, then it is as ridiculous for me to talk about forgiving him as it would be for me to "forgive" a tile which falls on my head in a gale.

Friday, Good

Our crucifixes exhibit the pain, but they veil, perhaps necessarily, the obscenity: but the death of the God-Man was both.

—Charles Williams

Christmas and Easter can be subjects for poetry, but Good Friday, like Auschwitz, cannot. The reality is so horrible, it is not surprising that people should have found it a stumbling block to faith. The Manicheans of the third century argued: "Jesus was the Christ, the Son of God. Therefore, he cannot have been really crucified. The body on the cross was either a phantom body or Judas Iscariot." The liberal humanists of the eighteenth century argued: "Jesus was crucified. Therefore, he cannot have been the Son of God."

Poems about Good Friday have, of course, been written, but none of them will do. "The Dream of the Rood" turns Christ into an epic hero, but no epic hero would say "I thirst" or "My God, my God, why hast Thou forsaken me?" The "*Stabat Mater*," which sentimentalizes the event, is the first poem in medieval literature which can be called vulgar and "camp" in a pejorative sense.

Just as we were all, potentially, in Adam when he fell, so we were all, potentially, in Jerusalem on that first Good Friday before there was an Easter, a Pentecost, a Christian, or a Church. It seems to me worth while asking ourselves who we should have been and what we should have been doing. None of us, I'm certain, will imagine ourselves as one of the Disciples, cowering in agony of spiritual despair and physical terror. Very few of us are big wheels enough to see ourselves as Pilate, or good churchmen enough to see ourselves as a member of the Sanhedrin. In my most optimistic mood I see myself as a Hellenized Jew from Alexandria visiting an intellectual friend. We are walking along, engaged in philosophical argument. Our path takes us past the base of Golgotha. Looking up, we see an all too familiar sight—three crosses surrounded by a jeering crowd. Frowning with prim distaste, I say, "It's disgusting the way the mob enjoy such things. Why can't the authorities execute criminals humanely and in private by giving them hemlock to drink, as they did with Socrates?" Then, averting my eyes from the disagreeable spectacle, I resume our fascinating discussion about the nature of the True, the Good, and the Beautiful.

Friendship

What friends really mean to each other can be demonstrated better by the exchange of a magic ring or a horn than by psychology.

—Hugo von Hofmannsthal

In friendship, nobody has a double.

—F. Schiller

Our friends show us what we can do; our enemies teach us what we must do.

—Goethe

Glossolalia

It is extraordinary that sects of religious enthusiasts, from the Montanists down to the Catholic Apostolics, should have imagined that to make verbal noises which nobody else could understand was evidence of Divine Inspiration, a repetition of the miracle of Pentecost. What happened at Pentecost was exactly the opposite, the miracle of instantaneous translation—everybody could understand what everybody else was saying.

In his great book *Enthusiasm*, Father Ronald Knox gives us two examples of "speaking with tongues": "*Hippo gerosto niparos boorasti farini O fastor sungor boorinos epoongos menati,*" and "*Hey amei hassan alla do hoc alors lovre has heo massan amor ho ti prov hir aso me.*" Of these, he says, "The philology of another world does not abide our question, but if we are to judge these results by merely human standards, we must admit that a child prattles no less convincingly."

Goat, Nanny

There she is, perched on her manger, looking over the boards into the day
Like a belle at her window.
And immediately she sees me she blinks, stares, doesn't know me, turns her head and ignores me vulgarly with a wooden blank on her face.

What do I care for her, the ugly female, standing up there with her long-tangled sides like an old rug thrown over a fence?
But she puts her nose down shrewdly enough when the knot is untied,
And jumps staccato to earth, a sharp, dry jump, still ignoring me,
Pretending to look round the stall.

Come on, you, crapa! I'm not your servant!

She turns her head away with an obtuse, female sort of deafness, bête.
And then invariably she crouches her rear and makes water.
That being her way of answer, if I speak to her.—Self-conscious!
Le bestie non parlano, poverine! . . .

—D. H. Lawrence

God

Speculations over God and the World are almost always idle, the thoughts of idlers, spectators of the theatre of life. "Is there a God?"

"Has Man a soul?" "Why must we die?" "How many hairs has the Devil's Grandmother?" "When is the Day of Judgment?"—all these are idle questions, and one fool can ask more of them than a hundred wise men can answer. Nevertheless, teachers, parents, bishops, must give answers to such questions because, otherwise, the idlers will spread their corruption. Every idle question can ensnare at least one innocent heart. The Church Councils found themselves in the position of parents whose daughters are on the point of being seduced by young louts. The dogmas of the Church have to deal with blasphemous scoundrels, and therefore they have to speak their language, the language of shamelessness.

—Eugen Rosenstock-Huessy

Nicea then was a double climax. The spectacle of magnificence was accompanied by an intellectual ostentation of dogma. "The great and sacred Synod" exhibited itself in the two worlds. Christ was throned in heaven and in Constantinople. Yet at times, as the jewels seem only jewels, so the words seem only words. "Father," "Son," "Holy Spirit," "person," "essence and nature," "like and unlike"—what has such a pattern of definition to do with a Being that must exist always in its incomprehensibility? It is not surprising that the human mind should revolt against the jewels and words. It is, of course, a revolt of immature sensibility, an ignorant, a young-romantic revolt, but it is natural. "The great and sacred Synod" looms sublimely anti-pathetic. From such revolts there have sprung the equally immature and romantic devotions to the simple Jesus, the spiritual genius, the broad-minded international Jewish working-man, the falling-sparrow and grass-of-the-field Jesus. They will not serve. The Christian idea from the beginning had believed that his Nature reconciled earth and heaven, and all things met in him, God and Man. A Confucian Wordsworth does not help there. Jewels and words are but images, but then so are grass and sparrows. And jewels and words are no less and no more necessary than cotton and silence.

—Charles Williams

Theologians are in the difficult position of having to use language, which by its nature is anthropomorphic, to deny anthropomorphic conceptions of God. Dogmatic theological statements are neither logical propositions nor poetic utterances. They are "shaggy dog" stories; they have a point, but he who tries too hard to get it will miss it.

From a Christian point of view the whole of learned theology is really a corollary; and is declined like *mensa.*

—Søren Kierkegaard

> Among medieval and modern philosophers anxious to establish the religious significance of God, an unfortunate habit has prevailed of paying him metaphysical compliments.
>
> —A. N. Whitehead

It is generally agreed among theologians that in giving men freedom of will, freedom to reject His love and defy His commandments, God has, in a sense, chosen to limit His omnipotence. But unless, at the same time, He has chosen to limit His omniscience, the Calvinist doctrine of predestination is an inevitable conclusion. May it not be that, just as we have to have faith in Him, God has to have faith in us and, considering the history of the human race so far, may it not be that "faith" is even more difficult for Him than it is for us?

> To talk *about* God, except in the context of prayer, is to take His name in vain.
>
> One may, indeed, talk to a child about God, but this is on a par with telling him that he was brought to his mother by a stork.
>
> —Ferdinand Ebner

> It is as difficult to be quite orthodox as it is to be quite healthy. Yet the need for orthodoxy, like the need for health, is imperative.
>
> There is a great deal of scepticism in believers, and a good deal of belief in non-believers; the only question is where we decide to give our better energy. "Lord, I believe; help thou mine unbelief" may, and should, be prayed both ways.
>
> —Charles Williams

> An atheist may be simply one whose faith and love are concentrated on the impersonal aspects of God.
>
> —Simone Weil

> God does not die on the day when we cease to believe in a personal deity, but we die on the day when our lives cease to be illuminated by the steady radiance, renewed daily, of a wonder, the source of which is beyond all reason.
>
> —Dag Hammarskjöld

> You can change your faith without changing gods, and vice versa.
>
> —Stanislaus Lec

> It always strikes me, and it is very peculiar, that, whenever we see the image of indescribable and unutterable desolation—of loneliness, poverty, and misery, the end and extreme of things—the thought of God comes into one's mind.
>
> —Van Gogh

> We have to believe in a God who is like the true God in everything except that he does not exist, since we have not reached the point where God exists.
>
> —Simone Weil

"God is Love," we are taught as children to believe. But when we first begin to get some inkling of how He loves us, we are repelled; it seems so cold, indeed, not love at all as we understand the word.

> All the passions produce prodigies. A gambler is capable of watching and fasting almost like a saint; he has premonitions, etc. There is a great danger of loving God as the gambler loves his game.
>
> —Simone Weil

> Every time a priest adds his *personal fervor* to the "canons" something terrible results (a hypocrite, a Torquemada); only when the priest is "slack" is it right. Why is this so? Why so *here?*
>
> —V. Rozanov

> There is always a danger of intense love destroying what I might call the "polyphony" of life. What I mean is that we should love God eternally with our whole hearts, but not so as to compromise or diminish our earthly affections, but as a kind of *cantus firmus* to which the other melodies of life provide the counterpoint. Earthly affection is one of these contrapuntal themes, a theme which enjoys an autonomy of its own.
>
> —Dietrich Bonhoeffer

> The word of him who wishes to speak with men without speaking to God is not fulfilled; but the word of him who wishes to speak with God without speaking with men goes astray.
>
> —Martin Buber

In this world, so long as we are vigorous enough to be capable of action, God, surely, does not intend us to sit around thinking of and loving Him like anything. Aside from rites of public worship in which we bring our bodies to God, we should direct our mental attention towards Him only for so long as it takes us to learn what He wills us to do here and now. This may take only a moment if the task he sets us is easy; if hard, a little longer. But once we know what it is, we should forget all about Him and concentrate our mental and physical energies upon our task.

The "dead" God: a god Who never existed but in Whom, undoubtedly, many people who thought of themselves as Christians believed—a Zeus without Zeus's vices. Science has certainly killed Him.

The Christian God is not *both* transcendent and immanent. He is a reality other than being Who is present to being, by which presence He makes being to be.

—Leslie Dewart

In German the word *sein* signifies both things: to be and to belong to Him.

—Kafka

Hands

The fingers must be educated; the thumb is born knowing.

The thumb takes the responsibility, the index finger the initiative.

The little finger looks through a magnifying glass, the index finger through a lorgnette.

The gestures of an adult are those of a carpenter, the gestures of an infant those of a mason.

—Malcolm de Chazal

Hangman, The

The story of Edward Dennis (in *Barnaby Rudge*) is not an invention. There was such a man, and he did take part in the Gordon riots. He said himself that his profession was known to the other rioters; and when he was arrested, the Brideswell in Tothill Fields would not take him in because (said the keeper, who recognized him) the other prisoners would cut him up as soon as he got inside. Dennis was tried and sentenced to death, but naturally he was pardoned, and went back to work hanging the rioters.

Nor is Dennis alone at the dark intersection of crime and punishment. At least three other hangmen in England in the eighteenth century were found guilty of hanging crimes, and one of them was actually hanged. To bring the bizarre register up to date, let me match these with contemporary cases. In 1948 the busy public executioner in East Berlin was found to have organized gangs of young delinquents who stole, robbed, and (at a pinch) murdered. Shortly after this, a prisoner in gaol in Brunswick with time on his hands applied for the job of executioner there, and under the heading of "Previous Experience" claimed that he had murdered thirty-three people. He had overstated his qualifications, as applicants will: it turned out that he had really murdered only twelve.

More characteristically, perhaps, and more modestly (he was after all an Englishman), the assistant hangman in Nottingham in 1954 was sentenced for running a sideline in sadistic books and obscene photographs.

—J. Bronowski

HARE, HUNTING A

Hunting a hare. Our dogs are raising a racket;
Racing, barking, eager to kill, they go,
And each of us in a yellow jacket
Like oranges against the snow.

One for the road. Then, off to hound a hare,
My cab-driver friend who hates a cop, I,
Buggins' brother and his boy, away we tear.
Our jalopy,

That technological marvel goes bounding,
Scuttling along on its snow-chains. Tallyho!
After a hare we go.
Or is it ourselves we're hounding?

I'm all dressed up for the chase
In boots and jacket: the snow is ablaze.
But why, Yuri, why
Do my gun-sights dance? Something is wrong, I know,
When a glassful of living blood has to fly
In terror across the snow.

The urge to kill, like the urge to beget,
Is blind and sinister. Its craving is set
Today on the flesh of a hare: tomorrow it can
Howl the same way for the flesh of a man.

Out in the open the hare
Lay quivering there
Like the gray heart of an immense
Forest or the heart of silence:

Lay there, still breathing,
Its blue flanks heaving,
Its tormented eye a woe,
Blinking there on the cheek of the snow.

Then, suddenly, it got up,
Stood upright: suddenly,
Over the forest, over the dark river,

The air was shivered
By a human cry.

Pure, ultrasonic, wild,
Like the cry of a child.
I knew that hares moan, but not like this:
This was the note of life, the wail
Of a woman in travail,

The cry of leafless copses
And bushes hitherto dumb,
The unearthly cry of a life
Which death was about to succumb.

Nature is all wonder, all silence:
Forest and lake and field and hill
Are permitted to listen and feel,
But denied utterance.

Alpha and Omega, the first and last
Word of Life as it ebbs away fast,
As, escaping the snare, it flies
Up to the skies.

For a second only, but while
It lasted we were turned to stone
Like actors in a movie-still.

The boot of the running cab-driver hung in mid-air,
And four black pellets halted, it seemed,
Just short of their target:
Above the horizontal muscles, the blood-clotted fur of the neck,
A face flashed out.

With slanting eyes, set wide apart, a face
As in frescoes of Dionysus,
Staring at us in astonishment and anger,
It hovered there, made one with its cry,
Suspended in space,
The contorted transfigured face
Of an angel or a singer.

Like a long-legged archangel a golden mist
Swam through the forest.
"Shit!" spat the cab-driver. "The little faking freak!"
A tear rolled down the boy's cheek.

Late at night we returned,
The wind scouring our faces: they burned
Like the traffic lights as, without remark,
We hurtled through the dark.

—Andrei Voznesensky (trans. W. H. A.)

Hell

Ethics does not treat of the world. Ethics must be a condition of the world, like logic.

—Ludwig Wittgenstein

Men are not punished for their sins, but by them.

—E. Hubbard

All theological language is necessarily analogical, but it was singularly unfortunate that the Church, in speaking of sin and punishment for sin, should have chosen the analogy of criminal law, for the analogy is incompatible with the Christian belief in God as the creator of Man.

Criminal laws are *laws-for*, imposed on men, who are already in existence, with or without their consent, and, with the possible exception of capital punishment for murder, there is no logical relation between the nature of a crime and the penalty inflicted for committing it.

If God created man, then the laws of man's spiritual nature must, like the laws of his physical nature, be *laws-of*, laws, that is to say, which he is free to *defy* but no more free to *break* than he can break the law of gravity by jumping out of the window, or the laws of biochemistry by getting drunk, and the consequences for defying them must be as inevitable and as intrinsically related to their nature as a broken leg or a hangover.

To state spiritual laws in the imperative—Thou *shalt* love God with all thy being, Thou *shalt* love thy neighbor as thyself—is simply a pedagogical technique, as when a mother says to her small son, "Stay away from the window!" because the child does not yet know what will happen if he falls out of it.

In the case of physical laws, we learn very soon the painful consequences of defying them, though even this certain knowledge does not prevent some of us from destroying ourselves with alcohol or drugs. But in the case of spiritual laws, where the consequences of defiance are not perceptible to the senses and take effect only gradually, we are all too inclined to behave, either like madmen who imagine they are magicians who can fly, or like suicides who smash themselves up out of despair or, more often, out of spite.

All sin tends to be addictive, and the terminal point of addiction is what is called damnation.

Since God has given us the freedom either to accept His love and obey the laws of our created nature or to reject it and defy them, He cannot prevent us from going to Hell and staying there if that is what we insist upon.

Origen, sensing the horror of the idea of Hell as a criminal prison and torture chamber, but failing to realize that the analogy was false, tried to mitigate the horror by saying that Hell would not be eternal, that in the end God's love would prove too strong and the devils and the damned would repent and be saved. If, however, it were ever possible for God's love to be compulsive, then He would be a monster for ever letting things get so far; He should never have allowed Eve to taste of the Tree in the first place.

History, Political

To read History is to run the risk of asking, "Which is more honorable? To rule over people, or to be hanged?"

—J. G. Seume

Politics is what a man does in order to conceal what he is and what he himself does not know.

—Karl Kraus

Political history is far too criminal and pathological to be a fit subject of study for the young. All teachers know this. In consequence, they bowdlerize, but to bowdlerize political history is not to simplify but to falsify it. Children should acquire their heroes and villains from fiction. I have read somewhere that Hitler's boyhood hero was Sulla.

Hitler

I have the gift of reducing all problems to their simplest foundations.

Why babble about brutality and be indignant about tortures? The masses want that. They need something that will give them a thrill of horror.

The day of individual happiness has passed.

Don't waste your time over "intellectual" meetings and groups drawn together by mutual interests. Anything you may achieve with such folk to-day by means of reasonable explanation may be erased tomorrow by an opposite explanation. But what you tell the people in the mass, in a receptive state of fanatic devotion, will remain words received under an hypnotic influence, ineradicable, and impervious to every reasonable explanation.

A new age of magic interpretation of the world is coming, of interpretation in terms of the will and not of the intelligence. There is no such thing as truth, either in the moral or in the scientific sense.

I am restoring to force its original dignity, that of the source of all greatness and the creatrix of order.

—Quoted by H. Rauschning

August 31, 1944

I think it's pretty obvious that this war is no pleasure for me. For five years I have been separated from the rest of the world. I haven't been to the theatre, I haven't heard a concert, and I haven't seen a movie.

—Quoted by Felix Gilbert

We have forged with fire a sword of steel out of ice.

—(From a speech)

When I come to power, I promise you, every German girl shall get a German husband.

—(From a speech)

HOLMES, SHERLOCK

"He appears to have a passion for definite and exact knowledge."

"Very right too."

"Yes, but it may be pushed to excess. When it comes to beating the subjects in the dissecting-rooms with a stick, it is certainly taking rather a bizarre shape."

"Beating the subjects!"

"Yes, to verify how far bruises may be produced after death. I saw him at it with my own eyes."

"And yet you say he is not a medical student?"

Among these unfinished tales is that of Mr James Phillimore, who, stepping back into his own house to get his umbrella, was never more seen in this world. No less remarkable is that of the cutter *Alicia*, which sailed one spring morning into a small patch of mist from where she never again emerged, nor was anything further ever heard of herself and her crew. A third case worthy of note is that of Isadore Persana, the well-known journalist and duellist, who was found stark staring mad with a match box in front of him which contained a remarkable worm said to be unknown to science.

I deprecate, however, in the strongest way the attempts which have been made lately to get at and destroy these papers. The source of these outrages is known, and if they are repeated I have Mr Holmes's authority for saying that the whole story concerning the politician, the lighthouse, and the trained cormorant will be given to the public. There is at least one reader who will understand.

—Arthur Conan Doyle

Home

Home is the only place where you can go out and in. There are places you can go into, and places you can go out of, but the one place, if you do but find it, where you may go out and in both, is home.

—George Macdonald

. . . "How quick," to someone's lip
The words came, "will the beaten horse run home!"

The word "home" raised a smile in us all three,
And one repeated it, smiling just so
That all knew what he meant and none would say.
Between three counties far apart that lay
We were divided and looked strangely each
At the other, and we knew we were not friends
But fellows in a union that ends
With the necessity for it, as it ought.

Never a word was spoken, not a thought
Was thought, of what the look meant with the word
"Home" as we walked and watched the sunset blurred.
And then to me the word, only the word,
"Homesick," as it were playfully occurred:
No more.

If I should ever more admit
Than the mere word I could not endure it
For a day longer: this captivity
Must somehow come to an end, else I should be
Another man, as often now I seem,
Or this life be only an evil dream.

—Edward Thomas

Homer and the Definite Article

In Greece, the verbal—and that is to say: the intellectual—seeds of scientific language are of a very ancient date. To take one example: we could scarcely imagine the existence of Greek science or Greek philosophy if there had been no definite article. For how could scientific thought get along without such phrases as *to hydro* (water), *to psychron* (the cold), *to noein* (thought)? If the definite article had not permitted the forming of these "abstractions" as we call them, it would have been impossible to develop an abstract concept from an adjective or a verb, or to formulate the universal as a particular. As far as the use of the definite article is concerned, Homer's speech is already more advanced than the classical Latin of Cicero. Cicero finds it very difficult to reproduce the simplest philosophical concepts, for no other reason than the lack of an article. To express ideas which to a Greek come easily and naturally, he has to fall back upon circumlocutions: his translation of *to agathon* (the good) is: *id quod* (*re vera*) *bonum est.*

Its [the definite article's] evolution from the demonstrative pronoun, via the specific article, into the generic article was slow and halting. *The* horse, in Homer, is never the concept of a horse, but always a particular horse. This demonstrative use of the article enables Homer to promote an adjective to the status of a noun, as in the case of the superlative: *ton ariston Achaion,* "the best of the Achaeans". In the same way Homer is free to say: *ta t' eonta ta t' essomena pro t' eonta,* "the present, the future, the past". The plural number shows that Homer does not yet "abstract" permanent being, but merely draws together the sum total of all that is now, and distinguishes it from all that will be.

—Bruno Snell

Homer and Seeing

. . . Homer uses a great variety of verbs to denote the operation of sight. . . . Of these several have gone out of use in later Greek, at any rate in prose literature and living speech: *derkesthai, leussein, ossesthai, paptainein.* Only two words make their appearance after the times of Homer: *blepein* and *theorin.* The words which were discarded tell us that the older language recognized certain needs which were no longer felt by its successor. *Derkesthai* means: to have a particular look in one's eye. *Drakon,* the snake, whose name is derived from *derkesthai,* owes this designation to the uncanny glint in his eye. He is called "the seeing one", not because he can see particularly well, but because his stare commands attention. By the same token Homer's *derkesthai* refers not so much to the function of the eye as to its gleam noticed by someone else. The verb is used of the Gorgon whose glance incites terror, and of the raging boar whose eyes radiate fire. . . . Many a passage in Homer reveals its proper beauty only if this meaning is taken into consideration: e.g. [Odysseus]: *ponton ep' atrugeton derkesketo dakrua leibon. Derkesthai* means "to look with a specific expression," and the context suggests that the word here refers to the nostalgic glance which Odysseus, an exile from his homeland, sends across the seas. . . . Of the eagle it may be said that *ozutaton derketai,* he looks very sharply; but whereas in English thc adjective would characterize the function and capacity of the visual organ, Homer has in mind the beams of the eagle's eye, beams which are as penetrating as the rays of the sun which are also called "sharp" by Homer; like a pointed weapon they cut through everything in their path. *Derkesthai* is also used with an external object; in such a case the present would mean: "his glance rests upon something," and the aorist: "his glance falls upon an object," "it turns toward something," "he casts his glance on someone." . . .

The same is true of another of the verbs which we have mentioned as having disappeared in later speech. *Paptainein* is also a mode of looking, namely a "looking about" inquisitively, carefully, or with fear. Like *derkesthai,* therefore, it denotes a visual attitude, and does not hinge upon the function of sight as such. Characteristically enough neither word is found in the first person. . . . A man would notice such attitudes in others rather than ascribing them to himself. *Leusso* behaves quite differently. Etymologically it is connected with *leukos,* "gleaming," "white"; three of the four cases in the *Iliad* where the verb is followed by an accusative object pertain to fire and shining weapons. The meaning clearly is: to see something bright. It also means: to let one's eyes travel. . . . Pride, joy, and a feeling of freedom are expressed in it. Frequently *leusso* appears in the first person, which distinguishes it from *derkesthai* and *paptainein,* those visual attitudes which are mostly noticed in others. . . . It is never used in situations of sorrow or anxiety.

It goes without saying that even in Homer men used their eyes "to see," i.e. to receive optical impressions. But apparently they took no decisive interest in what we justly regard as the basic function, the objective essence, of sight. . . .

—Bruno Snell

Honor, Sense of

Christos Milionis

Three little birds are perched on the ridge by the klephts stronghold,
One looks on Armyro, the other on to Valto;
The third, the fairest, sings a dirge and says:
"Lord, what has become of Christos Milionis?
At Valto he is not seen, nor in Kryavrisi.
They told us he had gone away and entered into Arta,
And taken captive the kadi, and two agas as well."
The Musselim heard of it, and sorely was he troubled;

He called Mavromati and Mukhtar Klisura:
"If you wish for bread, and if you would have captaincies,
First do you kill Christos, kill Captain Milionis:
So does our Sultan order it, and he has sent me a firman."
Friday dawned,—would it had dawned never!—
And Suleiman was sent to go to find him.
At Armyro he overtook him and as friends they greeted each other;
And all night they drank, until dawn.
And as the dawn began to shine, they went up to the *limeria*,
And Suleiman shouted to Captain Milionis:
"Christos, the Sultan wants you, the Agas too want you."
"While life is in Christos, to Turks he does not do homage."
With gun in hand they ran to meet, as one would eat the other;
Fire answered fire and they fell dead on the spot.

Note: Mukhtar had entrusted the task of killing Christos Milionis to the Albanian Suleiman, a former brother in arms of Milionis.

—*The Klephtic Ballads* (trans. John Baggally)

Horse, Evolution of the

The evolution of the horse must have involved organic changes of many kinds, but naturally we can know only those that show themselves in the fossilized skeleton, and of these, four are outstanding. They are: an increase in size, a reduction of toes or digits on all four feet, an elongation of the facial region, and finally a marked change in the teeth. The earliest horse, *Eohippus*, was about the size of a fox-terrier, had four digits on each foot, and low-crowned teeth adapted to browsing off comparatively succulent vegetation. Subsequent development, culminating in the horse we know and protracted over some fifty million years, was towards a progressively larger animal with a more highly developed brain. Accompanying these changes there arose a tendency towards supporting the weight more and more on the tips of the toes, in such a way as to make the lateral digits less and less necessary. This gave the creature enhanced speed, and it ended with the single-toed horse of today with vestigial splint-bones, invisible externally, as the sole remnants of the lateral digits. As for the teeth, they underwent a change from the low-crowned sort with a simple surface-pattern, to a new type longer in proportion to their width and with an intricate surface-pattern suitable for the mastication of harder and drier grasses. All these changes were adaptive, for the later horses were grazing as opposed to browsing creatures, and their development can be correlated with a changing habitat during the Miocene Period when forests were tending to disappear and drier, open, grassy plains, admirable for galloping over, were taking their place. Life on these plains set a premium on speed and on the ability to chew tough-stemmed grasses. But it must not be supposed that there was this one line of development only. On the contrary there were many lines, but none persisted for as long as that which gave rise to the large, one-toed, grazing horses. One line continued from the original forest-living browsers, which remained as such. They too developed, but differently and less rapidly, reaching a sort of culmination, with three toes instead of four, at about the time when the future grazers were beginning to take to the plains. Finally they became extinct.

Where then does pre-adaptation figure in this story? Very notably. One example of it has already been referred to, namely that the forest-dwelling browsers, while they could still so be described, had undergone a reduction in the number of digits from four to three. But that is by no means all, for the interesting and highly significant conclusion emerging from study of the skeletons of the many kinds of horse destined in time to develop into the animal that we know to-day, is that their evolution was materially assisted by organic changes that had already begun to manifest themselves while they yet lived in forests and browsed off leaves. In other words those structural changes fitting them so admirably for life on the plains—increase in size and reduction of digits; the transition from low- to high-crowned, grinding teeth; elongation of the facial region, giving space for more teeth—began to develop before the conditions responsible for their final perfection had begun to appear.

—Leslie Reid

Hospital Talk

"My name's Butler, Captain Ernest Butler. Been in here six weeks—you going to be long? Now take my case," and before I had time to accept or reject "his case," Captain Butler was in full swing again; "now take my case, four years ago they said it was hopeless, absolutely hopeless, not a chance in a thousand. Not a chance in a thousand. Then I was sent to see Mr Carver, really through my uncle's wife's daughter, she was a nurse . . . well, it was her who first mentioned Mr Carver; and Mr Carver says, 'Captain Butler, I'm interested in your case, very interested. I should like to do an . . .'"; at this point Captain Butler flashed a medical word of some six syllables, two of which rang with accentuated diphthongs, "I'd like to do it on Monday, that was four weeks ago yesterday, I beg your pardon, tomorrow; you get so confused with days in hospital after all this time." This last remark faded into the ward, attempting self-pity, but in fact swollen with pride for his four weeks' seniority and suffering. "So there I was for the 'chopper,' not a bit nervous, but first of all, two days before the op, they did a lot of X-rays." At this moment his face lit up with an enthusiasm rarely expressed by X-ray plates. "They've got a smashing set-up there; they first of all pump in a lot of blue stuff, well, you might say it was purple, I've always been a little colour blind, they first of all pump in a lot of this blue stuff into your arteries—only the ones they're going to X-ray of course—then they blow them up." At this last remark he seemed to grow larger and more important. "They did fourteen, that was in the afternoon, and six more next morning, which doesn't include the ones they'd done the first day I arrived."

At this point Captain Butler paused to allow his point, and the blue-cum-purple injections, to be fully injected. "You could tell they knew their job," again Captain Butler managed to effect the feeling that they had learnt this special knowledge for his benefit alone, "Oh they knew their job all right. It's a smashing set-up over there; of course it's a long journey but they take you by ambulance." Captain Butler was filled with delighted remembrance of that ambulance ride when he had been helped down the three steps by a fair, pretty nurse on arrival. "Now my boy's good at photography and all that sort of thing; you may think I'm boasting if I tell you he won the Tech. College prize for his colour photos —his Spanish holiday and all that—but it's a fact. Well, when I told him about the set-up over there, in the X-ray department, you should have seen his face . . ."

Captain Butler's eyes misted over and he was back in that world of egocentrical, X-ray seclusion, where his whole history of suffering was exposed, and permanently fixed by chemicals, on twenty semi-matt dark sheets of negative, and which, now that his Captain's rank was one of name and not authority, was his sole link with the world of importance; for a short time everything had revolved round him in a way that it had only done during the war. Consequently he treasured his disease most preciously and nursed it indulgently. His eyes unmisted a little and he continued, "Mind you, they can't do this op on everyone, it just doesn't work." The last four words were uttered as if he had watched all the cases on which it had not worked. I saw body after body expiring, with blue-cum-purple-blood spurting, which no doctor could stem.

"But I was lucky; it was a risk, mind you, but I took it," he added hastily, "now look at my legs; of course they'll never be the same . . . still . . ." and his voice faded.

—Anthony Rossiter

Hosts

The men and women who make the best boon companions seem to have given up hope of doing something else. They have, perhaps, tried to be poets or painters; they have tried to be actors, scientists, and musicians. But some defect of talent or opportunity has cut them off from their pet ambition and has thus left them with leisure to take an interest in the lives of others. Your ambitious man is selfish. No matter how secret his ambition may be, it makes him keep his thoughts at home. But the heartbroken people—if I may use the word in a mild benevolent sense—the people whose wills are subdued to fate, give us consideration, recognition and welcome.

—John Jay Chapman

HUMANISTS, THE

. . . It is largely to the humanists that we owe the curious conception of the "classical" period in a language, the correct or normative period before which all was immature or archaic and after which all was decadent. Thus Scalinger tells us that Latin was "rude" in Plautus, "ripe" from Terence to Virgil, decadent in Martial and Juvenal, senile in Ausonius. . . . When once this superstition was established it led naturally to the belief that good writing in the fifteenth or sixteenth century meant writing which aped as closely as possible that of the chosen period in the past. All real development of Latin to meet the changing needs of new talent and new subject-matter was thus precluded; with one blow of "his Mace petrific" the classical spirit ended the history of the Latin tongue. This was not what the humanists intended. They had hoped to retain Latin as the living esperanto of Europe while putting back the great clock of linguistic change to the age of Cicero. From that point of view, humanism is a great archaizing movement parallel to that which Latin had already undergone at the hands of authors like Apuleius and Fronto. But this time it was too thorough. They succeeded in killing the medieval Latin: but not in keeping alive the schoolroom severities of their restored Augustanism. Before they had ceased talking of a rebirth it became evident that they had really built a tomb. . . . A negative conception of excellence arose: it was better to omit a beauty than to leave in anything that might have the shadow of an offence. . . . Men vied with one another in smelling out and condemning "unclassical" words, so that the permitted language grew steadily poorer. . . .

Gravity, prudence, the well ordered *civitas*; on the other hand boorishness and rusticity—these are the clues. Whatever else humanism is, it is emphatically not a movement towards freedom and expansion. It is the impulse of men who feel themselves simple, rustic, and immature, towards sophistication, urbanity, and ripeness. In a word, it is the most complete opposite we can find to the Romantic desire for the primitive and the spontaneous. . . .

The humanists' revolt against medieval philosophy was not a philosophical revolt. What it really was can best be gauged by the language it used. Your philosophers, says Vives . . . are straw-splitters, makers of unnecessary difficulties, and if you call their jargon Latin, why then we must find some other name for the speech of Cicero. "The more filthie barbarisme they haue in their style . . . the greater theologians they doe account themselues," says Erasmus. . . . "Calle ye Thomas Aquinas a doctor?" said Johan Wessel. "He knew no tongue but the Latin and barely that!" . . . These are not the terms in which a new philosophy attacks an old one: they are, unmistakably, the terms in which at all times the merely literary man, the bellettrist, attacks philosophy itself. No humanist is now remembered as a philosopher. They jeer and do not refute. The schoolman advanced, and supported, propositions about things: the humanist replied that his words were inelegant. Of the scholastic terminology as an instrument of thought—that instrument which, according to Condorcet, has created *une précision d'idées inconnue aux anciens*—no reasoned criticism was usually vouchsafed. Words like *realitas* and *identificatio* were condemned not because they had no use but because Cicero had not used them.

. . . The medieval philosophy is still read as philosophy, the history as history, the songs as songs: the hymns are still in use. The "barbarous" books have survived in the only sense that really matters: they are used as their authors meant them to be used. It would be hard to think of one single text in humanists' Latin, except the *Utopia*, of which we can say the same. Petrarch's Latin poetry, Politian, Buchanan, even sweet Sannazarus, even Erasmus himself, are hardly ever opened except for an historical purpose. We read the humanists, in fact, only to learn about humanism; we read the "barbarous" authors in order to be instructed or delighted about any theme they choose to handle.

—C. S. Lewis

The men of the Renaissance discovered suddenly that the world for ten centuries had been living in an ungrammatical manner, and they made it forthwith the end of human existence to be grammatical. And it mattered thenceforth nothing what was said, or what was done, so only that it was said with scholarship, and done with system. Falsehood in a Ciceronian dialect had no opposers; truth in patois no listeners. A Roman phrase was thought worth any number of Gothic facts.

—Ruskin

Humility

A brother asked the abbot Alonius, "What is contempt?" And the old man said, "To be below the creatures that have no reason, and to know that they are not condemned."

—*The Desert Fathers* (trans. Helen Waddell)

We do not have to acquire humility. There is humility in us—only we humiliate ourselves before false gods.

—Simone Weil

Humor, Scatological

Most of it is only for children, but this verse, which so delighted myself and my brothers when we were little, still seems to me funny.

While shepherds watched their flocks by night,
  All shitting on the ground,
An angel of the Lord came down
  And handed paper round.

And this anonymous Neapolitan lyric is, surely, beautiful.

Strunz'...
Nel sole fumante
Come un incenso
A Dio...
Una mosca
Ti canta
Una ninna-nanna...
Zzz... Zzz...
Ma... tu non ascolti...
Strunz'....

(Turd, smoking in the sun to God like a thurifer . . . A fly sings you a hush-a-bye . . . Zzz . . . Zzzz . . . but . . . you don't listen . . . Turd! . . .)

Hurdy-Gurdy

When I was a child the streets of any city were full of street vendors and street entertainers of every kind, and of the latter the Italian organ-grinder with his monkey was one of the most endearing. Today, officialdom seems to have banished them all, and the only persons who still earn their living on the streets are prostitutes and dope peddlers.

Over there, beyond the village, a hurdy-gurdy man stands,
Grinding away with numbed fingers as best he can.
He staggers barefoot on the ice
And his little plate remains ever empty.
No one wants to hear him, no one looks at him,

And the dogs snarl about the old man.
But he lets the world go by,
He turns the handle, and his hurdy-gurdy is never still.
Strange old man—shall I go with you?
Will you grind your music to my songs?

—Wilhelm Müller (trans. S. S. Prawer)

Hygiene, Personal

Errol was exceptionally tidy in his personal habits. Sometimes he shaved twice a day and he took constant showers. But one day Beverly said to me: "Mama, isn't it strange? He doesn't use anything under his arms. You'd think a man who's been around would know about a little thing like that, wouldn't you?"

I certainly agreed. He wasn't offensive—far from it. But it proved to me once again that those women he'd run around with for years—all those top sex charmers—were a bunch of dummies in some departments. You'd think one of them might have gotten around to giving Errol the message. But not one of them knew how to tell him.

With Beverly herself it was simply no problem. She was such a sweet person she didn't need an under-arm deodorant, but she used one just to be safe.

One night when she and Errol were preparing to go some where in New York, she suddenly brought up the subject. It was always her way to be quite frank with him.

"Errol," she said, "why don't you use Mennen's under the arms, or something like that?"

He took it as quite an insult. He had been shaving and he turned away from the washbowl and gave her a hurt look.

"Well," he said sarcastically, "I've always considered myself a fairly clean man."

"But why not use one," said Beverly.

Her persistence made him a little angry.

"Damn it," he said. "Who uses that stuff anyway? Besides, how come you know so much about what men are supposed to put on?" He looked at her half-suspiciously, half-jokingly. "I thought you were supposed to be a virgin before you met me. So how come you know all about this? Who told you?"

"My *father*!" snapped Beverly. "That's who! He's the cleanest man that ever was. He always asks me to give him Mennen toilet water for Christmas!"

—Florence Aadland

ICEBERGS

The Berg
A Dream

I saw a ship of martial build
(Her standards set, her brave apparel on)
Directed as by madness mere
Against a stolid iceberg steer,
Nor budge it, though the infatuate ship went down.
The impact made huge ice-cubes fall
Sullen, in tons that crashed the deck;
But that one avalanche was all—
No other movement save the foundering wreck.

Along the spurs of ridges pale,
Not any slenderest shaft and frail,
A prism over glass-green gorges lone,
Toppled; nor lace of traceries fine,
Nor pendant drops in grot or mine
Were jarred, when the stunned ship went down.
Nor sole the gulls in cloud that wheeled
Circling one snow-flanked peak afar,
But nearer fowl the floes that skimmed
And crystal beaches, felt no jar.
No thrill transmitted stirred the lock
Of jack-straw needle-ice at base;
Towers undermined by waves—the block
Atilt impending—kept their place.
Seals, dozing sleek on sliddery ledges
Slipt never, when by loftier edges
Through very inertia overthrown,
The impetuous ship in bafflement went down.

Hard Berg (methought), so cold, so vast,
With mortal damps self-overcast;
Exhaling still thy dankish breath—
Adrift dissolving, bound for death;
Though lumpish thou, a lumbering one—
A lumbering lubbard, loitering slow,
Impingers rue thee and go down,
Sounding thy precipice below,
Nor stir the slimy slug that sprawls
Along thy dead indifference of walls.

—Herman Melville

Imagination

I will not refrain from setting among these precepts a new device for consideration which, although it may appear trivial and almost ludicrous, is nevertheless of great utility in arousing the mind to various inventions.

And this is that if you look at any walls spotted with various stains or with a mixture of different kinds of stones, if you are about to invent some scene you will be able to see in it a resemblance to various different landscapes adorned with mountains, rivers, rocks, trees, plains, with valleys and various groups of hills. You will also be able to see divers combats and figures in quick movement, and strange expressions of faces, and outlandish costumes and an infinite number of things which you can then reduce into separate and well-conceived forms. With such walls and blends of different stones, it comes about as it does with the sound of bells in whose clanging you may discover every name and word you can imagine.

—Leonardo Da Vinci

He hath consumed a whole night in lying looking at his great toe, about which he hath seen Tartars and Turks, Romans and Carthaginians, fight in his imagination.

—Ben Jonson

A nurse was having difficulty in measuring two quantities against each other on a scales. The left dish insisted upon outweighing the other, and I saw it as the bully in life, the one with "the whip hand"; the right dish, uncomfortably aloft, seemed to stand small chance, as does the "little man" in life, of exerting its influence. Then, quite suddenly, a small miracle occurred. The nurse equated the scales more nearly to a perfect balance, there was a tremor of delight as the two opposing dishes made a final frictional effort to disagree, and then there was perfection as the dual forces married in harmony. Even in my drowsy state, my heart stirred with joy at this revelation and perfection.

—Anthony Rossiter

Think of a white cloud as being holy, you cannot love it; but think of a holy man within the cloud, love springs up in your thoughts, for to think of holiness distinct from man is impossible to the affections. Thought alone can make monsters, but the affections cannot.

—William Blake

While we were enjoying the unlimited vistas, we noticed a commotion on the water at some distance to our left and, somewhat nearer on our right, a rock rising out of the sea; one was Charybdis, the other Scylla.

Because of the considerable distance in nature between these two objects which the poet has placed so close together, people have accused poets of fibbing. What they fail to take into account is that the human imagination always pictures the objects it considers significant as taller and narrower than they really are, for this gives them more character, importance and dignity. A thousand times I have heard people complain that some object they had known only from a description was disappointing when seen in reality, and the reason was always the same. Imagination is to reality what poetry is to prose: the former will always think of objects as massive and vertical, the latter will always try to extend them horizontally.

—Goethe

I hear that someone is painting a picture "Beethoven writing the Ninth Symphony". I could easily imagine the kind of thing such a picture would show me. But suppose someone wanted to represent what Goethe would have looked like writing the Ninth Symphony? Here I could imagine nothing that would not be embarrassing and ridiculous.

—Ludwig Wittgenstein

It is better to say, "I'm suffering," than to say, "This landscape is ugly."

Imaginary evil is romantic and varied; real evil is gloomy, monotonous, barren, boring. Imaginary good is boring, real good is always new, marvellous, intoxicating. "Imaginative literature," therefore, is either boring or immoral or a mixture of both.

—Simone Weil

Good can imagine Evil, but Evil cannot imagine Good.

Inverted Commas, Transformation by

As the editors of the anthology *The Stuffed Owl* were the first to realize, there is a certain kind of bad poetry which, had it been written with the conscious satiric intention of being bad, instead of in all earnestness, would be very good.

When I was twenty, I wrote a line which, had I intended it to be a caption for a Thurber cartoon, I should today be very proud of; alas, I did not, so that I now blush when I recall it: "And Isobel who with her leaping breasts pursued me through a summer."

Again, anyone wishing to write a satire on the "socially conscious" poetry of the thirties, could hardly do better than the final line of Miss Genevieve Taggard's poem "On Planting a Tree in Vermont": "Bloom for the People. Don't be a family shrub."

With inverted commas round his verses, William McGonagall (1830–?) becomes one of the greatest comic poets in English. For example:

Then as for Leith Fort, it was erected in 1779, which was really grand,
And which is now the artillery headquarters in Bonnie Scotland;
And as for the Docks, they are magnificent to see,
They comprise five docks, two piers, 1,141 yards long respectively . . .

Besides, there are sugar refineries and distilleries,
Also engineer works, saw-mills, rope-works, and breweries
Where many of the inhabitants are daily employed,
And the wages they receive make their hearts feel overjoyed

or

Friends of humanity, of high and low degree,
I pray ye all come listen to me;
And truly I will relate to ye
The tragic fate of the Rev. Alexander Heriot Mackonochie.

Who was on a visit to the Bishop of Argyle
For the good of his health, for a short while;
Because for the last three years his memory had been affected,
Which prevented him from getting his thoughts collected.

INSCAPE

Rings

A veäiry ring so round's the zun
In summer leäze did show his rim,
An' near, at hand, the weäves did run
Athirt the pond wi' rounded brim:
An' there by round built ricks ov haÿ,
By het a-burn'd, by zuns a-brown'd,
We all in merry ring did plaÿ,
A-springen on, a-wheelen round.

As there a stwone that we did fling
Did zweep, in flight, a lofty bow,
An' vell in water, ring by ring
O' weäves bespread the pool below,
Bezide the bridge's arch, that sprung
Between the banks, within the brims,
Where swung the lowly benden swing,
On elem boughs, on mossy limbs.

—William Barnes

JACKDAWS

Once the social order of rank amongst the members of a colony has been established, it is most conscientiously observed by jackdaws, much more so than by hens, dogs or monkeys. A spontaneous reshuffling, without outside influence, and due only to the discontent of one of the lower orders, has never come to my notice. Only once, in my colony, did I witness the dethroning of the hitherto ruling tyrant, Goldgreen. It was a returned wanderer, who, having lost in his long absence his former deeply imbued respect for his ruler, succeeded in defeating him in their first encounter. In the autumn of 1931 the conqueror "Double Aluminum" —he derived this strange name from the rings on his feet—came back, after having been away the whole summer. He returned home strong in heart and stimulated by his travels, and at once subdued the former autocrat. . . .

The way in which my attention was drawn to this revolution was quite unusual. Suddenly, at the feeding-tray, I saw, to my astonishment, how a little, very fragile, and, in order of rank, low-standing lady sidled ever closer to the quietly feeding Goldgreen, and finally, as though inspired by some unseen power, assumed an attitude of self-display, whereupon the large male quietly and without opposition vacated his place. Then I noticed the newly returned hero, Double-Aluminum,—and saw that he had usurped the position of Goldgreen, and I thought at first that the deposed despot, under the influence of his recent defeat, was so subdued that he had allowed himself to be intimidated by the other members of the colony, including the aforesaid young female. But the assumption was false: Goldgreen had been conquered by Double-Aluminum only, and remained forever second in command. But Double-Aluminum, on his return, had fallen in love with the young female and within the course of two days was publicly engaged to her. Since the partners in a jackdaw marriage support each other loyally and bravely in every conflict, and as no pecking order exists between them, they automatically rank as of equal status in their disputes with all other members of the colony; a wife is therefore, of necessity, raised to her husband's position. But the contrary does not hold good—an inviolable law dictates that no male may marry a female that ranks above him. The extraordinary part of the business is not the promotion as such, but the amazing speed with which the news spreads that such a little jackdaw lady, who hitherto had been maltreated by eighty per cent of the colony, is, from to-day, the "wife of the president" and may no longer receive so much as a black look from any other jackdaw. But, more curious still—the promoted bird knows of its promotion . . . that little jackdaw knew within forty-eight hours exactly what she could allow herself, and I'm sorry to say that she made the fullest use of it. She lacked entirely that noble or even blasé tolerance which jackdaws of high rank should exhibit towards their inferiors. She used every opportunity to snub former superiors, and she did not stop at gestures of self-importance, as high-rankers of long standing nearly always do. No—she always had an active and malicious plan of attack ready at hand. In short, she conducted herself with the utmost vulgarity.

—Konrad Lorenz

JOURNALISM

THWAITES. Then, before leaving you—since you are so reluctant to leave me—let me make a very necessary apology. (*The reporters get their notebooks and pencils ready.*) I thought, while you were questioning me, how much better the world would be if you and your employers were utterly abolished. But I am sorry to have thought that. Without you, we should have no way of knowing what we are like—no mirror in which to study the diseases of our skins. You are our spite, our greed, our pleasure in the pains of others, our love of lies, our perfect emptiness.

3RD REPORTER. Sir Augustus! Statements of that sort are of no interest to our readers.

THWAITES. In you, our fear of taking any decisive steps finds its perfect illustration. We know that you are too disgusting to live, but we are so afraid that your suppression might lead to something just a shade *more* disgusting that we have not the courage to do away with you. Thus, the liberty which you enjoy is the reflection of our own cowardice, and until we are brave enough to trample you down, you will always be present to reflect the yellowness of our hearts, the corruption of our manliness, and the collapse of our powers of decision.

3RD R (*good-humouredly*). We are grateful for all that information, Sir Augustus. But we have heard it many times before.

LADY R. Very many times before. (*She takes her mirror from her handbag, studies her face, then applies lipstick.*)

THWAITES. It is not dramatic? It is not interesting? It is not personal?

3RD R (*still good-humouredly*). I'm afraid not.

THWAITES. Then may I draw your attention to something that is?

3RD R. I'm sure we'd all be much obliged.

THWAITES (*moving to the 3rd R and pointing*). There is something the matter with your left arm. Has it been withered from birth?

(*There is an astonished gasp from the others.*)

3RD R (*after a pause*). Yes.

THWAITES. But how dramatic! How interesting! How personal! I wish *my* readers could hear about it. They love stories about cripples.

May I photograph it? And perhaps you will tell me the influence it has had on your life? A story of shame, suffering and courage—always such a pleasure to others. (*The 3rd R turns sharply and goes out.*) Oh! He is gone! (*He turns to the Lady R.*) Madam. Did you see the pain in his face? Where was your camera? He is degraded! He is humiliated! He feels the whole world knows. How will he recover, now? (*He crosses to the Lady R.*) Answer me that, madam—you with your poor, tired, stretched face. Ah, Madam, yours was an unhappy marriage, was it not? And the child? Never born? Ah, so sad—but to read about at breakfast time—*your* kidneys on *my* toast.

LADY R (*clenching her fists, furiously*). It's not true!

THWAITES (*shrugging*). Pooh, pooh, pooh! Who cares what's true?

—Nigel Dennis

Journalists write because they have nothing to say, and they have something to say because they write.

A journalist is stimulated by a dead-line: he writes worse when he has time.

The public doesn't understand German; and in Journalese I can't tell them so.

—Karl Kraus

With all that can be said, justly, against journalists, there is one kind of journalist to whom civilization owes a very great debt, namely, the brave and honest reporter who unearths and makes public unpleasant facts, cases of injustice, cruelty, corruption, which the authorities would like to keep hidden, and which even the average reader would prefer not to be compelled to think about.

JUSTICE AND INJUSTICE

Whoever suffers from the malady of being unable to endure any injustice, must never look out of the window, but stay in his room with the door shut. He would also do well, perhaps, to throw away his mirror.

—J. G. Seume

Justice: to be ever ready to admit that another person is something quite different from what we read when he is there, or when we think about him. Or rather, to read in him that he is certainly something different, perhaps something completely different, from what we read in him.

Justice consists in seeing that no harm is done to men. Whenever a man cries inwardly, "Why am I being hurt?", harm is being done to him. He is often mistaken when he tries to define the harm, and why and by whom it is being inflicted upon him. But the cry itself is infallible.

—Simone Weil

To commit violent and unjust acts, it is not enough for a government to have the will or even the power; the habits, ideas, and passions of the time must lend themselves to their committal.

—Alexis de Tocqueville

Injustice cannot reign if the community does not furnish a due supply of unjust agents.

—Herbert Spencer

The dispensing of injustice is always in the right hands.

—Stanislaus Lec

A Review only continues to have life in it so long as each issue annoys at least one fifth of its subscribers. Justice lies in seeing that this fifth is not always the same one.

—Charles Péguy

Kilns

Severn has kilns set all along her banks
Where the thin reeds grow and rushes in ranks;
And the carts tip rubbish there from the town;
It thunders and raises white smoke and goes down.
I think some of those kilns are very old,
An age is on those small meres, and could unfold
Tales of the many tenders of kilns, and tales
Of the diggers and earth-delvers of those square weals
Or oblong of Severn bank. And all the flowers
June ever imagined stand and fulfil June's hours.
I think of the countless slabs gone out from all of them;
Farm house, cottage, loved of generations of men,
Fronting day as equal, or in dusk shining dim;
Of the Dane-folk curious of the sticky worthy stuff;
Kneading, and crumbling till the whim wearied enough.
Of the queer bricks unlearned hands must have made;
Spoiling clay, wasting wood, working out the war's trade;
With one hand the clear eyes fending, keeping in shade
Fierce Fire that grazes and melts with its regardings rough.
Or the plays children had of Dane-Saxon breed,
Chasing round the square kilns with devil-may-care
Headlong roughness of heedless body-reckless speed;
Grazing knees and knuckles to disaster there,
Of the creeping close to parents when November azure
Melancholy made company, and stillness, a new pleasure,
And the wonder of fire kept the small boys to stay sure.

And the helping of fathers build well of the new brick,
The delight in handling over thin and thick—the youthful critic.

Of the Normans, how they liked kilns, that thrust to endure
Endless abbeys and strong chapels up in the air,
And Domesday questioners who worried the too evasive
Owner as to tales and day's work to a story unplausive,
As to the fuels used, and the men there and the hours, the wage hours.

—Ivor Gurney

Landscape: Basalt

Far and wide through the moors of the northern counties run the dykes and sills of hard black basaltic rock called whinstone. Nature has forced it between softer layers of rock much as cement is driven between the crumbling stones of a cathedral wall. But this volcanic grouting is so much harder than sedimentary rock, and the operation was carried out so many hundreds of thousands of years ago, that the basaltic bonds have outlasted the layers which they compact, and now project beyond them. Dykes are vertical layers of whinstone, which out-top the moor's surface by 20 or 40 feet, like a wall. Sills show where the molten greenstone was forced between horizontal beds; where it emerges, the sill's edge so stubbornly resists erosion that it forms a hard black cliff-face. Sometimes the whinstone is roughly columnar, and suggests the more perfect basaltic architecture of the Giant's Causeway. Often the sill forms only part of the cliff, but has protected by its durability the softer limestone beneath it, and to a less extent above. Sometimes the heat of the rock has turned the limestone next it, not merely into marble—for marble is baked limestone—but into a crumbling layer like white sugar. Where moorland streams meet these cliffs or sills, they form waterfalls. In a few miles of Upper Teesdale, the Tees plunging over two whinstone cliffs forms the two grandest waterfalls in England—Caldron Snout and High Force. Beside these two falls, voluminous and naked, Lodore, or Scale Force, in the Lake Country is but an exquisite wild toy.

It gives a fresh attraction to rambles through all that wide, wild country from Eden Valley, near Applesby, over the Pennine backbone, and away to the coast of Northumberland, to pencil down from a geological map the course of the great outcrops of whinstone. When we meet them again it is pleasant to feel that they are old friends, and impressive, in the light of day, to think of that vast sheet of hard volcanic rock which probably underlies hundreds of square miles of the moorlands between the unknown point at which the earth's fiery stomach disgorged it, and the outcrops by which we stand. The Tees at High Force pours over a line of crag which runs far eastward through County Durham.

Northumberland has the Acklington Dyke, about thirty-five miles long, from the Cheviot to the coast near the mining village of Acklington. But the most famous of all these basaltic bands is the Great Whin Sill. Its outcrop begins in the moors between Middleton-in-Teesdale and Appleby, and is leaped by the Tees at Caldron Snout. Soon a descending beck carves the narrow gap of High Cup Nick, which gives access across the moors from High Force to Appleby, and forms the finest of the longer approaches to the Lake Mountains. Turning east, the Sill runs for nearly fifty miles through Northumberland, carrying the Roman Wall on its crest. It rears up on the brink of salt water into the splendid and storied rock of Bamburgh, and sinks at last beneath the North Sea, after throwing up the Castle Rock on Holy Island, like a Bamburgh in miniature, and the seafowl-haunted pinnacles of the Farnes.

—Anthony Collett

Landscape: Cultivated

From Swindon we came up into the *down-country*; and these downs rise *higher* even than the Cotswold. . . . My companion, though he had been to London, and even to France, had never seen *downs* before; and it was amusing to me to witness his surprise at seeing the immense flocks of sheep, which were now (ten o'clock) just going out from their several folds to the downs for the day, each having its shepherd, and shepherd his dog. We passed the homestead of a farmer Woodman, with *sixteen* banging wheat-ricks in the rick-yard, two of which were old ones; and rick-yard, farm-yard, waste-yard, horse-paddock, and all round about, seemed to be swarming with fowls, ducks and turkeys, and on the whole of them, *not one feather but was white*! Turning our eyes from the sight, we saw, just going out from the folds of this farm, three separate and numerous flocks of sheep, one which (the *lamb*-flock) we passed close by the side of. The shepherd told us, that his flock consisted of *thirteen score and five*; but, apparently; he could not, if it had been to save his soul, tell us how many *hundreds* he had: and, if you reflect a little, you will find that his way of counting is much the easiest and best. This was a most beautiful flock of lambs; short-legged, and, in every respect, what they ought to be. George, though born and bred among sheep-farms, had never before seen sheep with dark-colored faces and legs; but his surprise, at this sight, was not nearly so great as the surprise of both of us, at seeing numerous and very large pieces (sometimes 50 acres together) of very good early turnips, *Swedish* as well as *White*! All the three counties of Worcester, Hereford and Gloucester (except on the Cotswold) do not, I am convinced, contain as great a weight of turnip bulbs, as we here saw in one single *piece*; for here there are, for miles and miles, no hedges, and no fences of any sort.

Doubtless they must have had *rain* here in the months of June and July; but, as I once before observed, (though I forget when), a *chalk bottom* does not suffer the surface to *burn,* however shallow the top soil may be. It seems to me to absorb and to *retain* the water, and to keep it ready to be drawn up by the heat of the sun. At any rate, the fact is, that the surface above it *does not burn*; for, there never yet was a summer, not even this last, when the downs did not *retain their greenness to a certain degree,* while the rich pastures, and even the meadows (except actually watered) were burnt so as to be *as brown as the bare earth.*

This is a most pleasing circumstance attending the *down-countries*; and there are no *downs* without a chalk bottom.

Along here, the country is rather *too bare*; here, until you come to AUBURN or ALDBOURNE, there are *no meadows* in the valleys, and *no trees,* even round the homesteads. This, therefore, is too naked to please me; but I love the *downs* so much, that, if I had *to choose,* I would live even here, and especially I would *farm* here, rather than on the banks of the WYE in Herefordshire, in the vale of Gloucester, or Worcester, or of Evesham, or, even in what the Kentish men call their "*garden of Eden.*" I have now seen (for I have, years back, seen the vales of Taunton, Glastonbury, Honiton, Dorchester and Sherborne) what are deemed the richest and most beautiful parts of England; and, if called upon to name the spot, which I deem the brightest and most beautiful and, of its extent, *best* of all, I should say, the villages of *North Bovant and Bishops-strow,* between Heytesbury and Warminster in Wiltshire; for there is, as appertaining to rural objects, *every thing* that I delight in. Smooth and verdant down in hills and valleys of endless variety as to proportion, and these watered at pleasure; and, lastly, the homesteads and villages, sheltered in winter and shaded in summer by lofty and beautiful trees; to which may be added, roads never dirty and a stream never dry.

—William Cobbett

Caltanissetta, April 28, 1787

At last we can say we have seen with our own eyes the reason why Sicily earned the title of "The Granary of Italy." Soon after Girgenti, the fertility began. There are no great level areas, but the gently rolling uplands were completely covered with wheat and barley in one great unbroken mass. Wherever the soil is suitable to their growth, it is so well tended and exploited that not a tree is to be seen. Even the small hamlets and other dwellings are confined to the ridges, where the limestone rocks make the ground untillable. The women live in these hamlets all the year round, spinning and weaving, but during the season of field labour, the men spend only Saturdays and Sundays with them; the rest of the week they spend in the valleys and sleep at night in reed huts. . . .

A few more geological observations. As one descends from Girgenti, the soil turns whitish; the older type of limestone appears to be followed immediately by gypsum. Then comes a new type of limestone, more friable, slightly decomposed and, as one can see from the tilled fields, varying in colour from a light yellow to a darker, almost violet tint. Halfway between Girgenti and Caltanissetta, gypsum reappears. This favours the growth of a beautiful purple, almost rose-red sedum, while the limestone harbours a bright yellow moss. . . .

The valleys are beautiful in shape. Even though their bottoms are not completely level, there is no sign of heavy rain, for it immediately runs off into the sea; only a few little brooks, which one hardly notices, trickle along.

The dwarf-palms and all the flowers and shrubs of the southwestern zone had disappeared and I did not see much red clover. Thistles are allowed to take possession only of the roads, but all the rest is Ceres' domain. . . . They plough with oxen and it is forbidden to slaughter cows or calves. We have met many goats, donkeys and mules on our trip, but few horses. Most of these were dapple greys with black feet and black manes. They have magnificent stables with built-in stone mangers.

Manure is only used in growing beans and lentils; the other crops are grown after they have been harvested. Red clover and sheaves of barley, in the ear but still green, are offered for sale to passing riders.

—Goethe

Landscape: Fens

A certain sadness is pardonable to one who watches the destruction of a grand natural phenomenon, even though its destruction brings blessings to the human race. Reason and conscience tell us that it is right and good that the Great Fen should have become, instead of a waste and howling wilderness, a garden of the Lord, where

> All the land in flowery squares
> Beneath a broad and equal-blowing wind,
> Smells of the coming summer.

And yet the fancy may linger, without blame, over the shining meres, the golden reed-beds, the countless waterfowl, the strange and gaudy insects, the wild nature, the mystery, the majesty—for mystery and majesty there were—which haunted the deep fens for many a hundred years. Little thinks the Scotsman, whirled down by the Great Northern

Railway from Peterborough to Huntingdon, what a grand place, even twenty years ago, was that Holme and Whittlesea, which is now but a black, unsightly, steaming flat, from which the meres and reed-beds of the old world are gone, while the corn and roots of the new world have not as yet taken their place.

But grand enough it was, that black ugly place, when backed by Caistor Hanglands and Holme Wood, and the patches of the primaeval forest; while dark-green alders, and pale-green reeds, stretched for miles round the broad lagoon, where the coot clanked, and the bittern boomed, and the sedge-bird, not content with its own sweet song, mocked the notes of all the birds around; while high overhead hung, motionless, hawk beyond hawk, buzzard beyond buzzard, kite beyond kite, as far as eye could see. Far off, upon the silver mere, would rise a puff of smoke from a punt, invisible from its flatness and its white paint. Then down the wind came the boom of the great stanchion-gun; and after that sound another sound, louder as it neared; a cry as of all the bells of Cambridge, and all the hounds of Cottesmore; and overhead rushed and whirled the skein of terrified wild-fowl, screaming, piping, clacking, croaking, filling the air with the hoarse rattle of their wings, while clear above all sounded the wild whistle of the curlew, and the trumpet note of the great wild swan.

They are all gone now. No longer do the ruffs trample the sedge into a hard floor in their fighting-rings, while the sober reeves stand round, admiring the tournament of their lovers, gay with ears and tippets, no two of them alike. Gone are ruffs and reeves, spoonbills, bitterns, avosets; the very snipe, one hears, disdains to breed. Gone too, not only from Whittlesea but from the whole world is that most exquisite of English butterflies, Lycaena dispar—the great copper; and many a curious insect more. Ah, well, at least we shall have wheat and mutton instead, and no more typhus and ague; and, it is to be hoped, no more brandy-drinking and opium-eating; and children will live and not die. For it was a hard place to live in, the old Fen; a place wherein one heard of "unexampled instances of longevity," for the same reason that one hears of them in savage tribes—that few lived to old age at all, save those iron constitutions which nothing could break down.

—Charles Kingsley

Landscape: Industrial

It was a town of red brick, or of brick that would have been red if the smoke and ashes had allowed it; but, as matters stood, it was a town of machinery and tall chimneys, out of which interminable serpents of smoke trailed themselves for ever and ever, and never got uncoiled. It had a black canal in it, and a river that ran purple with ill-smelling dye, and vast piles of buildings full of windows where there was a rattling and a trembling all day long, and where the piston of the steam-engine worked monotonously up and down, like the head of an elephant in a state of melancholy madness. It contained several large streets all very like one another, and many small streets still more like one another, inhabited by people equally like one another, who all went in and out at the same hours, with the same sound upon the same pavements, to do the same work, and to whom every day was the same as yesterday and tomorrow, and every year the counterpart of the last and the next. . . .

You saw nothing in Coketown but what was severely workful. If the members of a religious persuasion built a chapel there—as the members of eighteen religious persuasions had done—they made it a pious warehouse of red brick, with sometimes (but this only in highly ornamented examples) a bell in a bird-cage on the top of it. The solitary exception was the New Church; a stuccoed edifice with a square steeple over the door, terminating in four short pinnacles like florid wooden legs. All the public inscriptions in the town were painted alike, in severe characters of black and white. The jail might have been the infirmary, the infirmary might have been the jail, the town-hall might have been either, or both, or anything else, for anything that appeared to the contrary in the graces of their construction. Fact, fact, fact, everywhere in the material aspect of the town; fact, fact, fact, everywhere in the immaterial. The M'Choakum-child school was all fact, and the school of design was all fact, and the relations between master and man were all fact, and everything was fact between the lying-in hospital and the cemetery, and what you couldn't state in figures, or show to be purchaseable in the cheapest market and saleable in the dearest, was not, and never should be, world without end. Amen.

—Charles Dickens

Landscape: Limestone

. . . Mountain limestone has almost as much scenery within it as without. There is stranger and more fantastic climbing within the portals of Gaping Gill in the West Riding than anywhere on the sunny side of the caverns' dome. Exploration of limestone caverns is often interrupted by the stream which has formed them, plunging suddenly through a widened joint in the rock to new halls at unknown depths. When every peak on earth has been mapped, and climbed, there are still likely to be strands that no foot has trodden in caves beneath the peaceful surface of a Mendip or Craven sheepwalk.

The fuller the channels beneath the limestone surface, the drier they run above, and the chief limestone districts are full of streams that dive into swillets or swallow-holes, to emerge again, in putative identity, miles away and many fathoms lower. Buttertubs Pass, between Wensleydale and Swaledale, gains its racy name from swallow-holes of this kind. In wet weather one of these leaky stream-beds may make a fair show of holding water; the natural sinks cannot take all that comes, and it is not until the stranger returns to slake his thirst on a hot day that he discovers it has vanished. Elsewhere streams make their dive where the trap in the rock is concealed by a substantial layer of surface soil, and forms a conspicuous funnel. Elms and ashes spring luxuriant on the sides of the pit, with ivied trunks that mark by a muddy stain the highest recent freshet. Months may pass without the surface-water seeking this singular exit; then bursts the autumn rain, and the brown flood eddying round the trunks forms a restless whirlpool. Great limestone gorges, like that at Cheddar, may be the channels of ancient subterranean rivers, of which the roofs have fallen in. Through all the mountain limestone country the interest of its surface moulding and the attraction of its plant and insect life is heightened by the sense of the unknown sculpture in the roots of the rocks—the unpolluted rivers running, through caverns measureless, to sunless seas.

Thin though moist is the turf of the grey limestone hills, and it is characteristic of their scenery for the live rock to break out freely at the surface. Sometimes its slabs and bands assume a dreary largeness, and, reducing the turf and herbage to narrow terraced strips, look like misshapen masonry. The long white tilted layers of the limestone hills near Carnforth have a touch of that power first to repel and at last to fascinate which is possessed by all barren and thirsty places. Elsewhere the rock juts through its cloak of turf in warm lichened bosses. Beside them the sheep couch, for dryness, and upon them the tawny wall butterflies, which delight in a limestone country, fan and shift in the rays of the sun. Limestone and chalk are close enough akin to have nurtured the same delicate flora, though some of the rarest that love lime are confined to the sunnier slopes of the southern chalk. Both on limestone hills and chalk downs the thyme fills the turf with its delicate summer scent that floats even in January among the withered tufts when the sun shines warm on the hillside. Many orchids love both soils—the bee, the butterfly, the pyramidal and the fragrant, among the commoner kinds. The limestones of the west and north were the last haunts of the almost extinct lady's slipper, and the chalk still guards the lizard and the military orchids, now almost equally rare. Equally common on both these warm and porous rocks, and of a finer growth than when we find it straggling among coarser gravels, the delicate golden cistus, or rock-rose, shakes out, morning by morning, its crumpled petals to the midsummer sunshine. When limestone rises among red rocks, or chalk from blue clay, the change of soil is instantly signaled by these yellow blossoms. On one side of a brook the turf may be sprinkled by the almost universal flowers —buttercups, milfoil, knapweed, clover—undistinguished either in number or kind; but immediately beyond the thread of mint-tinged water the grey rock shows its side, and the hill turf is variegated with rock-roses, and scented with the wandering prostrate thyme-threads.

—Anthony Collett

Landscape: West of England

Larches

Larches are most fitting to small red hills
That rise like swollen ant-heaps likeably
And modest before big things like near Malvern
Or Cotswold's farther early Italian
Blue arrangement, unassuming as the
Cowslip, celandines, buglewort and daisies
That trinket out the green swerves like a child's game.
O, never so careless or lavish as here . . .

—Ivor Gurney

Landscape: Wild

The Precipice

Such precipices are among the most impressive as well as the most dangerous of mountain ranges; in many spots inaccessible with safety either from below or from above; dark in colour robed with everlasting mourning, for ever tottering like a great fortress shaken by war, fearful as much in their weakness as in their strength, and yet gathered after every fall into darker frowns and unhumiliated threatening; for ever incapable of comfort or healing from herb or flower, nourishing no root in their crevices, touched by no hue of life on buttress or ledge, but, to the utmost, desolate, knowing no shaking of leaves in the wind, nor of grass beside the stream,—no motion but their own mortal shivering, the dreadful crumbling of atom from atom in their corrupting stones; knowing no sound of living voice or living tread, cheered neither by the kid's bleat nor the marmot's cry; haunted only by uninterrupted echoes from far off, wandering hither and thither, among their walls, unable to escape, and by the hiss of angry torrents, and sometimes the shriek of a bird that flits near the face of them, and sweeps frightened back from under their shadow into the gulph of air; and, sometimes, when the echo has fainted, and the wind has carried the sound of the torrent away, and the bird has vanished, and the mouldering stones are still for a little time,—a brown moth, opening and shutting its wings upon a grain of dust, may be the only thing that moves, or feels, in all that waste of weary precipice, darkening five thousand feet of the blue depth of heaven.

—Ruskin

Lead Mine, Visit to a

Parties of ladies and gentlemen desirous of visiting the mines, can have suitable dresses provided by the landlord of the inn. A coat, pair of trowsers, and hat suffice for a gentleman, while the softer sex are often indebted to the landlady's wardrobe. Old shawls, hats, aprons, and even bedgowns, are taken to the mining shop, and the fair form of beauty and fashion is there disguised in such heterogeneous garments as to create no small share of amusement. The grotesque and novel appearance, both of ladies and gentlemen, frequently contributes not a little to the mirth of the company, and also tends to dissipate any timorous feeling. As mines, like states and empires, "have their periods of declension, and feel in their turn what distress and poverty are," it is thought better not to limit this sketch of a subterranean visit to any particular mine, but rather to describe such features as are generally presented in the Alston Mines. Permission to view the mines is in the most instances readily obtained.

The author ventures from his own observation to premise, that visitors will generally be gratified with the rustic but kind civility and attention of the miners, and in some instances also with their intelligence, due allowance being made for local dialect and limited education. Their readiness to afford information and to render assistance greatly contributes to the interest and comfort of the excursion, by imparting knowledge to the inquirer, and confidence to the timorous.

Arrived at the mine, the visitor has a full view of the various apparatus used in washing the ore. A lofty heap of stones, clay, and other earthy substances, called *the dead heap*, forms a promminent feature at the entrance of all extensively wrought mines. A railway carried on a frame-work gallery over several deposits of *bouse*, or mixed stone and ore, forms the *bouse teams*, and the work of the separate partnerships of miners is divided by partitions. From these *bouse teams* the contents are carried away to undergo the various and, it may be said, amusing processes of washing; for strangers who have leisure to examine them are usually much entertained with the ingenious and cunning devices to obtain every particle of ore. In stone recesses called *bing steads*, sundry heaps of shining ore are laid, some in broken lumps, and others in fine powder. These are ready to be conveyed to the smelt-mills, there to be converted into lead and silver, provided the latter exists in sufficient proportion to repay expense of refining.

The party being suitably arrayed, have sometimes to wait a little until the waggons come out, and in the mean time are each furnished with a candle, round which a piece of clay is fixed to hold it by. At length the rumbling noise of the approaching waggons rapidly increases, and their contents having been deposited, they are prepared for the visitors, the inside being cleaned, and a board placed at each end for a seat. The entrance to the mine, or *the level mouth,* resembles an open arched doorway, into which the waggons are driven at a moderate pace, and the visitors experience the novel sensations which so unusual a conveyance is apt to create. The jolting, tottering motion of the waggon, the splashing of the water, and the dark and narrow passage, all concur to produce a strange effect, which, however, soon wears off, and the subterranean traveller finds leisure to observe the rugged roof and walls of the level, or to listen to the guide urging forward his horse, in tones which the echoes of the mine often render musical. Even the fragment of a song from the driver sometimes enlivens the journey, but, on no account, is whistling allowed to be heard in a mine. The same prejudice exists among seamen, but whence its origin is probably unknown.

After advancing some distance into the interior, the visitor passes the rise foots, in some of which a store of *bouse* is laid ready to be taken away, and at length the waggons stop, and the company get out at one of these openings. A powerful vociferation of "*put nought down,*" is sent forth as a warning to those above to throw no work down, and a further summons brings a few miners to render their assistance. When a signal is to be made to some distance, it is done by beating on the rails or posts, five beats, the first two slow, and other three quick, and this is repeated several times. The same signal is used in the Newcastle coal-mines, where it is denominated "jowling."

The ascent of a rise is frequently attended with some difficulty, especially to ladies; but the gallantry of the gentlemen and the effective civility of the miners soon overcome the apparent dangers, and, one by one, they are raised into the workings of the vein. Hence the party are conducted along the mine drift of the vein, and this part of the expedition must of course greatly vary in different mines; in all, however, the stranger is apt to be impressed with feelings of awe at the idea of being so far underground. The contemplative mind cannot but find many interesting subjects of reflection on the distribution of so much wealth in a country otherwise so barren—the various uncertainties which are the means of so extensive employment—the fluctuations of fortune so often resulting from mining adventures, and the ingenuity displayed in prosecuting them, are all circumstances which may engage the attention of a reflecting mind. To the mineralogist, the interior of a mine, especially if it contain any spar-encrusted caverns, is a sort of "home, sweet home," where the lovers of that science and of geology may derive copious stores of intellectual enjoyment.

Blende and calamine, the ores of zinc, are sometimes found spreading their glossy sparkling blackness in the veins; and fluor spar and quartz are the principal, almost the only, sparry ornaments that abound. The traveller at Alston is not gratified by the sight of such beautiful caverns as are found in the Coalcleugh and Allendale mines. The latter, however, being private property, and worked by the proprietor, cannot be considered as generally accessible to public curiosity, though intelligent strangers of scientific pursuits will doubtless receive every attention from the hospitality and liberal-minded feeling of the resident agents.

The progress along vein workings is often "with cautious steps and slow," especially among the intricacies of flat workings. The friendly caution of "take care ye dinna *fall* down the *rise*," sometimes calling the visitor's attention (absorbed perhaps in other thoughts) to a yawning gulf not to be passed over without some caution. Sometimes an almost perfect stillness is suddenly broken by a noise like distant thunder, the report of a blast, which, rolling through the workings of the mine, at length, after many reverberations, dies away. The noise of work "*falling down a rise*," and the rumblings of waggons occasionally salute the ear; the sound of the latter, gradually increasing and lessening, resembles the solemn effect of distant thunder.

The process of blasting has been already described. The miners usually describe this and other modes of entertainment of the visitor; but, when near at hand, the effect is by no means so striking as when distance softens the noise and adds repeated echoes to it. At length arrived at the far end or *forehead* of the vein, the party usually rest, and a pleasant company is occasionally formed by the accession of two or three partnerships. Spirits or other refreshments are sometimes taken by the visitors; and those who choose to spend half an hour in the company of miners may frequently derive both information and amusement. Most of the miners are well acquainted with practical mining, and with this is necessarily blended a knowledge of many facts in geology and mineralogy. But many of them are also tolerably well informed on other subjects, and a friend of the author's was much surprised in one of these forehead meetings, to hear Blackstone's Commentaries quoted by a miner both with accuracy and direct reference to the subject of discussion.

The miners work by what is often in other trades called piece-work, so that the time spent with strangers is taken from their own labour, and the prodigal expenditure of light is also at their own cost. By the latter is meant the custom of miners of not putting out their candles, however numerous the company may be, and a forehead assemblage presents a brilliant illumination, twenty or thirty candles being sometimes placed against the wall. If any partners of the mine are present, many are the speculations on the goodness and improving of the *grove.* The *bonny donk* and *excellent rider,* as well as the ore, come in for a share of gratulation, and are often considered harbingers of the vein being still more productive. Many a lively song and joke are often added to the entertainment of such an assemblage as we are now describing. One example, spoken by a miner, may suffice as a specimen of dialect and humor. "An folk wad nobbit let folk like folk as weel as folk wad like to like folk, folk wad like folk as weel as folk ever liked folk sin folk was folk!" It may here be remarked, that the conversation of miners sometimes has a curious effect from their assuming, as it were, a sort of volition in the mineral world. Thus they speak of a vein being *frightened* to climb the hill, and that she therefore *swings away* to the sun side, (a feminine appellation being generally used). The throw of the strata is attributed, as it were, to an *act* of the vein,—"*she throws* the north cheek up." These are homely but they are also expressive modes of describing what they have frequent occasion to speak of, and they save a world of words.

Ladies seldom pursue a subterranean excursion further than the main workings, or such others as are easily accessible, while their more adventurous companions frequently accompany the guides into other parts of the mine. In so doing, obstacles present themselves more difficult of accomplishment than those already described. Lofty rises with rude and slippery *stemples* are sometimes found extremely awkward to climb, and still more so to descend. It sometimes happens that the *stemples* are covered over with boards to prevent their being injured by falling ore, etc. thrown from the workings above, and the only footholds then to be had are the spaces between these boards. The attention of the miners, however, who climb and descend with perfect confidence, prevents any real danger, though to a stranger the idea of climbing fifty or a hundred feet on so perilous a footing is seldom unattended with some sense of fearful apprehension.

Journeying through the drifts of a narrow vein is a less dangerous but often equally fatiguing task, especially if, by reason of accumulated work, the hands and knees are to be put in requisition for several fathoms over sharp angular blocks of rock, which all but fill the narrow passage. At the end or forehead of such drifts, buried as it were in a deep and lonely cavern, a single miner is often found pursuing his solitary labours at a string or thin vein of ore, which, like a bright silvery stream, is seen traversing the rock. It is considered that in general a solid rib of ore two or three inches wide, will pay for working, and as a much greater space is required for *vein room*, the procuring of this slender thread of ore is attended with a great proportion of unprofitable labour, hence the inconvenient but economical narrowness of the drift. The persevering visitor, who would explore every part of a mine, after *descending the rise* to the level, is probably next taken to a sump head, where he is required to trust his person to a substantial rope hung on the axle of a hand whimsey, often of seemingly frail construction, and is thus lowered down into the deeper workings of the mine, the aspect of which is similar to those above.

The subterranean researches of our visitors being at length completed, the waggons are again entered, and the eye accustomed to such scenery surveys with greater clearness the strata of the roof and sides,—pendent drops are seen hanging from above, and the wooden posts, which in some places support the level roof, are covered with woolly snow-like fungi. The timorous sensations felt on entering are now dissipated, and the party can fearlessly look at these and other swiftly passing objects, on which at length a faint white gleam of light is seen to blend with the yellower rays of the candles. The rocky prominences become more and more illuminated, and the solar light, together with the sparkling drops of water impart so bright and silvery an aspect as to excite the greatest admiration. This rapidly increases until, amid the splashing of water and the noisy rattling of their rugged cars, the party emerge from the dark chambers of the earth to the magnificent and almost overpowering brightness of "THE DAY."

—T. Sopwith

Liturgy, Reform of

I don't know if it is any better with the Anglican Church in England, but the Episcopalian Church in America seems to have gone stark raving mad. Here are some features of a proposed reformed Holy Communion service.

(I) The Prayer of Humble Access and the General Confession have been cut. Roman Catholics have to go to auricular confession before taking communion. We do not. Surely, some verbal act of contrition is required.

(II) The Prayer for the Church Militant has become an interminable and boring attempt to pray for all sorts and conditions of men, a futile attempt, since if we were really to pray for them *all*, we should never get away. Thus, we pray for farmers, but not for barbers.

(III) Presumably out of ecumenical good will, the *Filioque* clause is omitted from the Creed. How often does a member of the Greek Orthodox Church turn up in a parish church?

(IV) Worst of all, the Epistle and Gospel are read in some appalling "modern" translation. In one such, the Greek word which St Paul uses in Romans VIII and which the Authorized Version translates as *flesh* turns into *our lower nature*, a concept which is not Christian, but Manichean.

And why? The poor Roman Catholics have had to start from scratch, and, as any of them with a feeling for language will admit, they have made a cacophonous horror of the Mass. We had the extraordinary good fortune in that our Book of Common Prayer was composed at exactly the right historical moment. The English language had already become more or less what it is today, so that the Prayer Book is no more difficult to follow than Shakespeare, but the ecclesiastics of the sixteenth century still possessed a feeling for the ritual and ceremonious which today we have almost entirely lost. Why should we spit on our luck?

Logic

If language had been the creation, not of poetry, but of logic, we should only have one.

—Hebbel

Grammar and logic free language from being at the mercy of the tone of voice. Grammar protects us against misunderstanding the sound of an uttered name; logic protects us against what we say having a double meaning.

—Eugen Rosenstock-Huessy

In logic (mathematics) process and result are equivalent. Hence no surprises.

—Ludwig Wittgenstein

It is always easy to be on the negative side. If a man were not to deny that there is salt on the table, you could not reduce him to an absurdity.

—Dr Johnson

Logic is the art of going wrong with confidence.

—Anon.

A proof tells us where to concentrate our doubts.

—Anon.

Sufficient unto the day is the rigor thereof.

—E. H. Moore

Logic is like the sword—those who appeal to it shall perish by it. Faith is appealing to the living God, and one may perish by that too, but somehow one would rather perish that way than the other, and one has got to perish sooner or later.

—Samuel Butler II

Four Logical Exercises

(1) Everything, not absolutely ugly, may be kept in a drawing-room;
(2) Nothing, that is encrusted with salt, is ever quite dry;
(3) Nothing should be kept in a drawing-room, unless it is free from damp;
(4) Bathing machines are always kept near the sea;
(5) Nothing that is made of mother-of-pearl can be absolutely ugly;
(6) Whatever is kept near the sea gets encrusted with salt.

(1) I call no day "unlucky" when Robinson is civil to me;
(2) Wednesdays are always cloudy;
(3) When people take umbrellas, the day never turns out fine;
(4) The only days when Robinson is uncivil to me are Wednesdays;
(5) Everybody takes his umbrella with him when it is raining;
(6) My lucky days always turn out fine.

(1) No shark ever doubts that it is well fitted out;
(2) No fish, that cannot dance a minuet, is contemptible;
(3) No fish is quite certain it is well fitted out, unless it has three rows of teeth;
(4) All fishes, except sharks, are kind to children;
(5) No heavy fish can dance a minuet;
(6) A fish with three rows of teeth is not to be despised.

(1) All the human race, except my footmen, have a certain amount of common-sense;
(2) No one, who lives on barley-sugar, can be anything but a mere baby;
(3) None but a hop-scotch player knows what real happiness is;
(4) No mere baby has a grain of common-sense;
(5) No engine-driver ever plays hop-scotch;
(6) No footman of mine is ignorant of what true happiness is.

—Lewis Carroll

Love, Romantic

No notion of our Western culture has been responsible for more human misery and more bad poetry than the supposition, initiated by the Provençal poets, though not fully vulgarized by them, that a certain mystical experience called falling or being "in love" is one which every normal man and woman can expect to have. As a result, thousands and thousands of unfortunate young persons have persuaded themselves they were "in love" when their real feelings could be more accurately described in much cruder terms, while others, more honest, knowing that they have never been "in love," have tormented themselves with the thought that there must be something wrong with them.

The experience certainly does occur, but only, I should guess, to those with a livelier imagination than the average. In the case of a man, its proper effect should be to stimulate all his powers, physical and intellectual. The warrior who is "in love" should, like Troilus, become a better warrior, the scientist a better scientist. Under its influence, the poet, too, should write better poetry—about something else. Alas, he all too often tries to write about the experience itself, and the results are seldom satisfactory, even if he is a great poet. I must confess that I find the personal love poems of Dante, Shakespeare, Donne, for all their verbal felicities, embarrassing. I find the romantic vocabulary only tolerable in allegorical poems where the "Lady" is not a real human being. For instance:

She commaunded her minstrelles right anone to play
Mamours, the swete and the gentill daunce;
With La Bell Pucell that was faire and gaye
She me recommaunded with all pleasaunce
To daunce true mesures without variaunce.
O Lorde God, how glad than was I,
So for to daunce with my swete lady.

By her propre hande soft as ony silke
With due obeisaunce I dide her than take.
Her skinne was white as whalles bone or milke;
My thought was ravisshed; I might not aslake
My brenninge hert: she the fire dide make.
These daunces truely Musicke hath me tought:
To lute or daunce but it availed nought.

For the fire kindled and waxed more and more;
The dauncinge blewe it with her beaute clere;
My hert sekened and began waxe sore:
A minute six houres, and six houres a yere,
I thought it was, so hevy was my chere;
But yet for to cover my great love aright,
The outwarde countenance I made gladde and light.

—Stephen Hawes

Simple, or elaborate, praise of physical beauty is always charming, but when it comes to writing about the emotional relation between the sexes, whether in verse or prose, I prefer the comic or the coarse note to the hot-and-bothered or the whining-pathetic.

Wulf and Edwacer

The men of my tribe would treat him as game:
if he comes to the camp: they will kill him outright.
  Our fate is forked.

Wulf is on one island, I on another.
Mine is a fastness: the fens girdle it
and it is defended by the fiercest men.
If he comes to the camp they will kill him for sure.
  Our fate is forked.

It was rainy weather, and I wept by the hearth,
thinking of my Wulf's far wanderings;
one of the captains caught me in his arms.
It gladdened me then; but it grieved me too.

Wulf, my Wulf, it was wanting you
that made me sick, your seldom coming,
the hollowness at heart; not the hunger I spoke of.

Do you hear, Edwacer? Our whelp
  Wulf shall take to the wood.
What was never bound is broken easily,
  our song together.

—Anon. Anglo-Saxon (trans. Michael Alexander)

In Secreit Place This Hyndir Nycht

In secreit place this hyndir nycht,
I hard ane beyrne say till ane bricht,
"My huny, my hart, my hoip, my heill,
I have bene lang your luifar leill,
And can of yow get confort nane;
How lang will ye with danger deill?
Ye brek my hart, my bony ane!"

His bony beird was kemmit and croppit
Bot all wit cale it was bedroppit,
And he wes townysche, peirt, and gukit;
He clappit fast, he kist, and chukkit,
As with the glaikis he wer ouirgane;
Yit be his feirris he wald have fukkit;
"Ye brek my hart, my bony ane!"

Quod he, "My hairt, sweit as the hunye,
Sen that I borne wes of my mynnye,

I nevir wowit weycht bot yow;
My wambe is of your lufe sa fow,
That as ane gaist I glour and grane,
I trymble sa, ye will not trow;
Ye brek my hart, my bony ane!"

"Tehe!" quod scho, and gaif ane gawfe,
"Be still my tuchan and my calfe,
My new spanit howffing fra the sowk,
And all the blythnes of my bowk;
My sweit swanking, saif yow allane
Na leyd I luiffit all this owk;
Fow leis me that graceless gane."

Quod he, "My claver, and my curldodie,
My huny soppis, my sweit possodie,
Be not oure bosteous to your billie,
Ne warme hairtit and not evill willie;
Your heylis, quhyt as quhalis bane,
Garris ryis on loft my quhillelillie;
Ye brek my hart, my bony ane!"

Quod scho, "My clype, my unspaynit gyane,
With moderis mylk yit in your mychane,
My belly huddrun, my swete hurle bawsy,
My huny gukkis, my slawsy gawsy,
Your musing waild perse ane harte of stane,
Tak gud confort, my grit heidit slawsy,
Fow leifis me that graceless gane."

Quod he, "My kid, my capirculyoun,
My bony baib with the ruch brylyoun,
My tendir gurle, my wallie gowdye,
My tirlie myrlie, my crowdie mowdie;
Quhone that oure mouthis dois meit at ane,
My stang dois storkyn with your towdie;
Ye brek my hairt, my bony ane!"

Quo scho, "Now tak me be the hand,
Welcum! my golk of Marie land,
My chirrie and my maikles munyoun,
My sowklar sweit as ony unyoun,
My strumill stirk, yit new to spane,
I am applyit to your opunyoun;
I luif rycht weill your graceless gane."

He gaiff to hir ane apill rubye;
Quod scho, "Gramercye! my sweit cowhubye."
And thai twa to ane play began,
Quhilk men dois call the dery dan;
Quhill that thair myrthis met baythe in ane.
"Wo is me!" quod scho, "quhair will ye, man?
Bot now I luif that graceless gane."

—William Dunbar

La Bella Bona Roba

I cannot tell who loves the Skeleton
Of a poor Marmoset, nought but boan, boan.
Give me a nakedness with her cloath's on.

Such whose white-sattin upper coat of skin,
Cuts upon Velvet rich Incarnadin,
Ha's yet a Body (and of Flesh) within.

Sure it is meant good Husbandry in men,
Who do incorporate with Aëry leane,
T' repair their sides, and get their Ribb agen.

Hard hap unto that Huntsman that Decrees
Fat joys for all his swet, when as he sees,
After his Say, nought but his Keepers Fees.

Then Love I beg, when next thou tak'st thy Bow,
Thy angry shafts, and dost Heart-chasing go,
Passe *Rascall Deare*, strike me the largest Doe.

—Richard Lovelace

Language has not the power to speak what love indites:
The soul lies buried in the ink that writes.

—John Clare

The Cranes

See there two cranes veer by one with another,
The clouds they pierce have been their lot together,
Since from their nest and by their lot escorted
From one life to a new life they departed
At equal speed with equal miles below them,
And at each other's side alone we see them,
That so the crane and cloud may share the lovely,
The lonely sky their passage heightens briefly;
That neither one may tarry back nor either

Mark but the ceaseless lolling of the other
Upon the wind that goads them imprecisely
As on their bed of air they lie more closely.
What though the wind into the void should lead them,
While they live and let nothing yet divide them:
So for that while no harm can touch their heaven,
So for that while they may be from all places driven,
Where storms are lashing or the hunt beginning:
In one another lost, they find their power
And fly from?
Everyone.
And bound for where?
For nowhere.
So all true lovers are.
Do you know what time
They have spent together?
A short time.
And when will they veer asunder?
Soon.
So love to lovers keeps eternal noon.

—Bertolt Brecht (trans. Chester Kallman)

As I walked out one night, it being dark all over,
The moon did show no light I could discover,
Down by a river-side where ships were sailing,
A lonely maid I spied, weeping and bewailing.

I boldly stept up to her, and asked what grieved her,
She made this reply, "None could relieve her,
For my love is pressed," she cried, "to cross the ocean,
My mind is like the Sea, always in motion."

He said, "My pretty fair maid, mark well my story,
For your true love and I fought for England's glory,
By one unlucky shot we both got parted,
And by the wounds he got, I'm broken hearted.

"He told me before he died, his heart was broken,
He gave me this gold ring, take it for a token,—
'Take this unto my dear, there is no one fairer,
Tell her to be kind and love the bearer.'"

Soon as these words he spoke she ran distracted,
Not knowing what she did, nor how she acted,
She run ashore, her hair showing her anger,
"Young man, you've come too late, for I'll wed no stranger."

Soon as these words she spoke, his love grew stronger,
He flew into her arms, he could wait no longer,
They both sat down and sung, but she sung clearest,
Like a nightingale in spring, "Welcome home, my dearest."

He sang, "God bless the wind that blew him over."
She sang, "God bless the ship that brought him over."
They both sat down and sung but she sung clearest,
Like a nightingale in spring, "Welcome home, my dearest."

—Anon.

Take Him

LINDA. Take him, you don't have to pay for him,
Take him, he's free.
Take him, I won't make a play for him,
He's not for me.
True that his head is like lumber,
True that his heart is like ice:
You'll find this little number
Cheap at half the price.

Take him, and just for the lure of it
Marry him too.
Keep him for you can be sure of it,
He can't keep you.
So take my old jalopy,
Keep him from falling apart.
Take him, but don't ever take him to heart.

VERA. Thanks, little Mousie,
For the present and all that,
But in this housie
I would rather keep a rat.
Only a wizard
Could reform that class of male:
They say a lizard
Cannot change his scale.

LINDA. Take him, I won't put a price on him,
Take him, he's yours.
Take him, pyjamas look nice on him,
But how he snores.
Though he is well-adjusted,
Certain things make him a wreck:
Last year his arm was busted,
Reaching from a check.

His thoughts are seldom consecutive,
He just can't write.
I know a movie executive
Who's twice as bright.
Lots of good luck, you'll need it,
And you'll need aspirin too.
Take him, but don't ever let him take you.

DUET. I hope that things will go well with him,
I bear no hate.
All I can say is:—"To hell with him,
He gets the gate."
So take my benediction,
Take my old Benedict too.
Take him away, he's too good to be true.

—Lorenz Hart

. . . "Give me my diamond anemones," the Queen commanded, and motioning to her Maid: "Pray conclude, mademoiselle, those lofty lines."

With a slight sigh, the lectress took up the posture of a Dying Intellectual.

"*Live with an aim, and let that aim be high!*" she reiterated in tones tinged perceptibly with emotion.

"But not *too* high, remember, Mademoiselle de Nazianzi . . ."

There was a short pause. And then—

"Ah, Madam. What a dearest he is!"

"I think you forget yourself," the Queen murmured with a quelling glance. "You had better withdraw."

"He has such strength! One could niche an idol in his dear, dinted chin."

"Enough!"

And a moment later the enflamed girl left the room warbling softly: *Depuis le Jour.*

A Fragment of Sappho

"I'm not going to inflict upon you a speech," the Professor said, breaking in like a piccolo to Miss Compostella's harp.

"Hear, hear!" Mr Sophax approved.

"You have heard, of course, how, while surveying the ruins of Crocodileopolis Arsinoë, my donkey, having—"

And then, after what may have been an anguishing obbligato, the Professor declaimed impressively the imperishable lines.

"Oh, delicious!" Lady Listless exclaimed, looking quite perplexed. "Very charming indeed!"

"Will anyone tell me what it means," Mrs Thumbler queried, "in plain English? Unfortunately, my Greek—"

"In plain English," the Professor said, with some reluctance, "it means: 'Could not' (he wagged a finger) 'Could not, for the fury of her feet!'"

"Do you mean she ran away?"

"Apparently!"

"O-h!" Mrs Thumbler seemed inclined to faint.

—Ronald Firbank

The maxim for any love affair is: "Play and pray; but on the whole do not pray when you are playing and do not play when you are praying." We cannot yet manage such simultaneities.

—Charles Williams

Machines

Machines are beneficial to the degree that they eliminate the need for labor, harmful to the degree that they eliminate the need for skill.

I cannot imagine a housewife not being glad to come by a dishwashing machine. But for some couples the electric dish-washer eliminated the one thing they did together every day; one of them washed while the other dried. As one woman put it, she now enjoys not only less fatigue but a pure gift of time. Yet she added wistfully, "But it *was* cozy, just the two of us together for that little while every night after we got the kids to bed. . . ." The comfortable intimacy that went with the chore was hardly noticed until it vanished. But just as obviously, the arrival of the machine in the home meant the couple would have to find some other occasion for spending their brief while together. Only then would the machine truly add, and not detract from their lives with each other. This, as I say, is obvious. But in how many families does this "obvious" become an actuality?

Just as modern machines can no longer be recognized as obvious extensions of our bodily organs, or as performing bodily functions more efficiently—though that may have been their origin—so in modern delusions we find more and more non-human projections. For example, a characteristic feature of modern insanity is the "influencing machine", a device that supposedly puts thoughts into a person's head as if they were his own, or forces him to act against his conscious will. . . .

It can be shown that the influencing machine, too, began as a projection of the human body, but the essential point is that it does not retain this image; it becomes ever more complex and the psychotic person ends up feeling controlled by mechanical devices that no longer resemble anything human or even animal-like. Thus modern man, when he is haunted, whether sane or profoundly disturbed, is no longer haunted by other men or by grandiose projections of man, but by machines.

—Bruno Bettelheim

Machines are better than people. People go further than they should.

—An autistic child

Madness

The last thing that can be said of a lunatic is that his actions are causeless. If any human acts may loosely be called causeless, they are the minor acts of a healthy man; whistling as he walks; slashing the grass with a stick; kicking his heels or rubbing his hands. It is the happy man who does the useless things; the sick man is not strong enough to be idle. It is exactly such careless and causeless actions that the madman could never understand; for the madman (like the determinist) generally sees too much cause in everything. The madman would read a conspiratorial significance into these empty activities. He would think that the lopping of the grass was an attack on private property. He would think that the kicking of the heels was a signal to an accomplice. If the madman could for an instant become careless, he would become sane. Every one, who has had the misfortune to talk with people in the heart or on the edge of mental disorder, knows that their most sinister quality is a horrible clarity of detail; a connecting of one thing with another in a map more elaborate than a maze. If you argue with a madman, it is extremely probable that you will get the worst of it; for in many ways his mind moves all the quicker for not being delayed by the things that go with good judgment. He is not hampered by a sense of humor or by charity, or by the dumb certainties of experience. He is more logical for losing certain sane affections. Indeed, the common phrase for insanity is in this respect a misleading one. The madman is not the man who has lost his reason. The madman is the man who has lost everything except his reason.

The madman's explanation of a thing is always complete, and often in a purely rational sense satisfactory. Or, to speak more strictly, the insane explanation, if not conclusive, is at least unanswerable; this may be observed specially in the two or three commonest kinds of madness. If a man says (for instance) that men have a conspiracy against him, you cannot dispute it except by saying that all the men deny that they are conspirators; which is exactly what conspirators would do. His explanation covers the facts as much as yours. Or if a man says that he is the rightful King of England, it is no complete answer to say that the existing authorities call him mad; for if he were King of England, that might be the wisest thing for the existing authorities to do. Or if a man says that he is Jesus Christ, it is no answer to tell him that the world denies his divinity; for the world denied Christ's.

—G. K. Chesterton

It was utterly wonderful to me to find that I could go so heartily and headily mad; for you know I had been priding myself on my peculiar sanity! And it was more wonderful yet to find the madness made up into things so dreadful out of things so trivial. One of the most provoking and disagreeable of the spectres was developed out of the fire-light on my mahogany bed-post; and my fate, for all futurity, seemed continually to turn on the humour of dark personages who were materially nothing but the stains of damp on the ceiling. But the sorrowfullest part of the matter was, and is, that while my illness at Matlock encouraged me by all its dreams in after work, this one has done nothing but humiliate and terrify me; and leaves me nearly unable to speak any more except of the natures of stones and flowers.

—Ruskin (*Letter to Carlyle, June 23, 1878*)

I seemed to read messages in chairs, stoves, tables, pots, pans, flowers, in anything. It is the way in which you act upon this revelation which determines your sanity. If you see these messages as contacts with deeper realities, you are using them correctly, as symbols expressing something greater than themselves. If you kneel down in front of a dressing-gown crucifixion, you are very near insanity.

—Anthony Rossiter

Sanity is perhaps the ability to punctuate.

—Idris Parry

Asylum Dialogue

JONES (*Laughs loudly, then pauses*). I'm McDougal myself.

SMITH. What do you do for a living, little fellow? Work on a ranch or something?

J. No, I'm a civilian seaman. Supposed to be high muckamuck society.

S. A singing recording machine, huh? I guess a recording machine sings sometimes. If they're adjusted right. Mm-hm. I thought that was it. My towel, mm-hm. We'll be going back to sea in about—eight or nine months though. Soon as we get our—destroyed parts repaired. (*Pause*)

J. I've got lovesickness, secret love.

S. Secret love, huh? (*Laughs*)

J. Yeah.

S. I ain't got any secret love.

J. I fell in love, but I don't feed any woo—that sits over—looks something like me—walking around over there.

S. My, oh, my only one, my only one is the shark. Keep out of the way of him.

J. Don't they know I have a life to live. (*Long pause*)

S. Do you work at the air base? Hm?

J. You know what I think of work. I'm thirty-three in June, do you mind?

S. June?

J. Thirty-three years old in June. This stuff goes out of the window after I live this, uh—leave the hospital. So I lay off cigarettes. I'm a spatial condition, from outer space, myself, no shit.

S (*Laughs*). I'm a real space ship from across.

J. A lot of people talk, uh—that way like crazy, but Believe It or Not by Ripley, take it or leave it—alone it's in the *Examiner*, it's in the comic section, Believe It or Not by Ripley, Robert E. Ripley, Believe It or Not, but we don't have to believe anything unless I feel like it. (*Pause*) Every little rosette—too much alone.

(*Pause*)

S. Could be possible. (*Phrase inaudible because of aeroplane noise*)

J. I'm a civilian seaman.

S. Could be possible. (*Sighs*) I take my bath in the ocean.

J. Bathing stinks. You know why? Cause you can't quit when you feel like it. You're in the service.

S. I can quit whenever I feel like quitting. I can get out when I feel like getting out.

J. (*Talking at the same time*). Take me, I'm a civilian. I can quit.

S. Civilian?

J. Go my—my way.

S. I guess we have, in port, civilian. (*Long pause*)

J. What do they want with us?

S. Hm?

J. What do they want with you and me?

S. What do they want with you and me? How do I know what they want with you? I know what they want with me. I broke the law, so I have to pay for it. (*Silence*)

—Quoted by J. Haley

'Tis very difficult to write like a madman, but 'tis a very easy matter to write like a fool.

—Nathaniel Lee

I have observed that poets on the verge of madness are often easier to translate into another tongue than sane ones, since, even in their own language, much of their poetic effect comes from their odd associations of ideas and images, which are equally odd in any language. The following poem by

Hölderlin, for example, even in a prose translation, "comes across" in a way that Goethe very rarely does.

> Heavenly Love, you the tender! If I should forget you, if ever I should, O you fateful ones, you fiery ones that are full of ashes and even before were deserted and lonely,
>
> Beloved islands, eyes of the world of marvels! For you have become my one and only concern, your shores where the idolatrous, where Love does penance, but to the Heavenly alone.
>
> For, all too thankful, there the holy ones served in the days of beauty, and the wrathful heroes; and many trees, and the cities, stood in that place,
>
> Visible, like a pondering man; now the heroes are dead, the islands of Love are almost disfigured, Thus everywhere must Love be tricked and exploited, silly. . . .
>
> —Hölderlin (trans. Michael Hamburger)

MAN

One log has nine holes.

—Turkish riddle

Man was created in order that a beginning might be made.

—St Augustine

Man is an exception, whatever he is. If it is not true that a divine being fell, then we can only say that one of the animals went entirely off its head.

Men are men, but Man is a woman.

—G. K. Chesterton

To breed an animal with the right to make promises—is not this the paradoxical problem nature has set herself with regard to man?

—Nietzsche

Man only plays when, in the full meaning of the word, he is a man, and he is only completely a man when he plays.

—F. Schiller

Man is the only animal that laughs and weeps; for he is the only animal that is struck by the difference between what things are and what they might have been.

—William Hazlitt

Man is only man at the surface. Remove his skin, dissect, and immediately you come to machinery.

—Paul Valéry

. . . Bedizened or stark
naked, man, the self, the being we call human, writing-
master to this world, griffons a dark
"Like does not like like that is obnoxious"; and writes error with four
r's. Among animals, *one* has a sense of humor.
Humor saves a few steps, it saves years. Unignorant,
modest and unemotional, and all emotion,
he has everlasting vigor,
power to grow,
though there are few creatures who can make one
breathe faster and make one erecter.

Not afraid of anything is he,
and then goes cowering forth, tread paced to meet an obstacle
at every step. Consistent with the
formula—warm blood, no gills, two pairs of hands and a few hairs—that
is a mammal; there he sits in his own habitat,
serge-clad, strong-shod. The prey of fear, he, always
curtailed, extinguished, thwarted by the dusk, work partly done,
says to the alternating blaze,
"Again the sun!
anew each day; and new and new and new,
that comes into and steadies my soul."

—Marianne Moore

In the Beginning

When is Tellus
to give her dear fosterling
her adaptable, rational, elect
and plucked-out otherling
a reasonable chance?
Not yet—but soon, very soon
as lithic phases go.
So before then?
Did the fathers of those
who forefathered them
(if by genital or ideate begetting)
set apart, make other, oblate?

By what rote, if at all
had they the suffrage:
Ascribe to, ratify, approve
in the humid paradises
of the Third Age?

But who or what, before these?
Had they so far to reach the ground?
and what of the pelvic inclination of their co-laterals, whose far cognates went—on how many feet? —in the old time before *them*?
For all WHOSE WORKS FOLLOW THEM
among any of these or them
dona eis requiem.
(He would lose, not any one
from among them.
Of all those given him
he would lose none.)

By the uteral marks
that make the covering stone an artefact.
By the penile ivory
and by the viatic meats.
Dona ei requiem.
Who was he? Who?
Himself at the cave-mouth
the last of the father-figures
to take the diriment stroke
of the last gigantic leader of thick-felled cave-fauna?
Whoever he was
Dona ei requiem
sempiternam.
(He would not lose him
. . . *non perdidi*
ex eis quemquam.)

Before the melt-waters
had drumlin-dammed a high hill-water for the water-maid to lave her maiden hair.

Before they morained Tal-y-llyn, cirqued a high hollow for Idwal, brimmed a deep-dark basin for Peris the Hinge and for old Paternus.

Long ages since they'd troughed, in solid Ordovician
his Bala bed for Tacitus.
Long, long ago they'd turned the flow about.
But had they as yet morained
where holy Deva's entry is?
Or pebbled his mere, where
still the Parthenos
she makes her devious exit?

Before the Irish sea-borne sheet lay tattered on the gestatorial
couch of Camber the eponym
        lifted to every extremity of the sky by pre-Cambrian oreos-heavers
        for him to dream
the Combroges' epode.
In his high *sêt* there.
        Higher than any of 'em
south of the Antonine limits.
Above the sealed hypogéum
    where the contest was
over the great *mundus* of sepulture (there the *ver-tigérnus* was)
here lie dragons and old Pendragons
            very bleached.
His unconforming bed, as yet
    is by the muses kept.

And shall be, so these Welshmen say, till the thick rotundities
give, and the bent flanks of space itself give way
    and the whitest of the Wanderers
falters in her transit
    at the Sibyl's *in favilla*-day.

Before the drift
        was over the lime-face.
Sometime between the final and the penultimate débâcle.
    (Already Arcturus deploys his reconnoitering chills in greater
strength: soon his last *Putsch* on any scale.)
Before this all but proto-historic transmogrification of the land-face.
Just before they rigged the half-lit stage for dim-eyed Clio to step with
some small confidence the measures of her brief and lachrymal pavan.

—David Jones

The life of mankind could very well be conceived as a speech in which different men represented the various parts of speech (that might also be applied to the nations in their relations to one another). How many people are merely adjectives, interjections, conjunctions, adverbs; and how few are substantives, verbs, etc.; how many are copula?

In relation to each other men are like irregular verbs in different languages; nearly all verbs are slightly irregular.

There are people whose position in life is like that of the interjection, without influence on the sentence— They are the hermits of life, and at the very most take a case, e.g. *O me miserum.*

Our politicians are like Greek reciprocals (alleeloin) which are wanting in the nominative singular and all subjective cases. They can only be thought of in the plural and possessive cases.

The sad thing about me is that my life (the condition of my soul) changes according to declensions where not only the endings change but the whole word is altered.

—Søren Kierkegaard (trans. A. Dru)

Marriage

Like everything which is not the involuntary result of fleeting emotion but the creation of time and will, any marriage, happy or unhappy, is infinitely more interesting and significant than any romance, however passionate.

Love is an ideal thing, marriage a real thing; a confusion of the real with the ideal never goes unpunished.

It is a mistake for a taciturn, serious-minded woman to marry a jovial man, but not for a serious-minded man to marry a lighthearted woman.

—Goethe

If you are afraid of loneliness, don't marry.

—A. Chekhov

No trap so mischievous to the field preacher as wedlock, and it is laid for him at every hedge corner. Matrimony has quite maimed poor Charles [Wesley], and might have spoiled John [Wesley] and George [Whitefield], if a wise Maker had not graciously sent them a pair of ferrets. Dear George has now got his liberty again, and he will 'scape well if he is not caught by another tenter-hook. Eight or nine years ago, having been grievously tormented with housekeepers, I truly had thought about looking out for a Jezebel myself. But it seemed highly needful to ask advice of the Lord. So falling down on my knees beside a table, with a Bible between my hands, I besought the Lord to give me direction . . . This method of procuring divine intelligence is much flouted by flimsy professors who walk at large, and desire not that sweet and secret access to the mercy-seat which babes of the Kingdom do find.

—Berridge of Everton

What did I get married for?
That's what I want to know:
I was led to the altar
Like a lamb to the slaughter.
We met on a Friday;
My luck was out, I'm sure:
I took her for better or worse, but she
Was worse than I took her for.

—Anon.

Wenn der Rabbi trennt,
Schocklen sich die Wend,
Und alle Hassidim
Kleppen mit die Hend.

(When the Rabbi has marital intercourse, the walls shake, and all the Hassidim clap their hands.)

—Anon.

They went quietly down into the roaring streets, inseparable and blessed; and as they passed along in sunshine and in shade, the noisy and the eager, and the arrogant and the forward and the vain, fretted and chafed, and made their usual uproar.

—Charles Dickens

In England a few years ago, during a suit for damages involving the proprietor of a circus and a midget, whose midget wife had been injured by an elephant, a witness said it was a well-known fact among circus people that midget married couples are so devoted that if one of them is sick, the other cannot be expected to work.

When asked about "the quiet affection" which is supposed to replace passion in marriage, Charles Williams said, "Well, it certainly isn't quiet, and it isn't exactly affection, but the phrase will have to do."

When I hear that "Possession is the grave of love," I remember that a religion may begin with the resurrection.

—F. H. Bradley

When the husband drinks to the wife, all would be well; when the wife drinks to the husband, all is.

—English proverb

The wife carries the husband on her face; the husband carries the wife on his linen.

—Bulgarian proverb

With all her experience, every woman expects to do better when she marries a second time, and some do.

—William Feather

Remarried widowers, it has been observed, tend to confound the persons of their wives. The reason, I suppose, is that they identify the substance.

—F. H. Bradley

Arnold Bennett says that the horror of marriage lies in its "dailiness." All acuteness of relationship is rubbed away by this. The truth is more like this: life—say 4 days out of 7—becomes automatic; but on the 5th day a bead of sensation (between husband and wife) forms which is all the fuller and more sensitive because of the automatic customary unconscious days on either side. That is to say the year is marked by moments of great intensity. Hardy's "moments of vision." How can a relationship endure for any length of time except under these conditions?

—Virginia Woolf

Charlotte played the piano extremely well. Eduard performed not quite so well on the flute; for, although he practiced diligently from time to time, he was by nature not patient or persevering enough to train such a talent successfully. Therefore he played his part unevenly—some passages well but perhaps too quickly; in others he had to slow down because he was not familiar enough with the music; and it would have been difficult for any one but Charlotte to go through an entire duet with him. But Charlotte knew how to cope with it; she slowed down, and then allowed him to run away with her, fulfilling in this way the double duty of a good conductor and an intelligent house-wife, both of whom always know how to preserve a general moderate measure, even if single passages may not always be in the right tempo.

—Goethe (trans. Elizabeth Mayer and Louise Bogan)

She Revisits Alone the Church of Her Marriage

I have come to the church and chancel,
Where all's the same!
—Brighter and larger in my dreams
Truly it shaped than now, meseems,
Is its substantial frame.
But, anyhow, I made my vow,
Whether for praise or blame,
Here in this church and chancel
Where all's the same.

Where touched the check-floored chancel
My knees and his?
The step looks shyly at the sun,
And says, "'Twas here the thing was done,
For bale or else for bliss!"
Of all those there I least was ware
Would it be that or this
When touched the check-floored chancel
My knees and his!

Here in this fateful chancel
Where all's the same,
I thought the culminant crest of life
Was reached when I went forth the wife
I was not when I came.
Each commonplace one of my race,
Some say, has such an aim—
To go from a fateful chancel
As not the same.

Here, through this hoary chancel
Where all's the same,
A thrill, a gaiety even, ranged
That morning when it seemed I changed
My nature with my name.
Though now not fair, though gray my hair,
He loved me, past proclaim,
Here in this hoary chancel,
Where all's the same.

—Thomas Hardy

Tokens

Green mwold on zummer bars do show
That they've a-dripp'd in winter wet;
The hoof-worn ring o' groun' below
The tree, do tell o' storms or het;
The trees in rank along a ledge
Do show where woonce did bloom a hedge;
An' where the vurrow-marks do stripe
The down, the wheat woonce rustled ripe.
Each mark ov things a-gone vrom view—
To eyezight's woone, to soulzight two.

The grass ageän the mwoldren door
'S a token sad o' vo'k a-gone,
An' where the house, bwoth wall an' vloor.
'S a-lost, the well mid linger on.
What tokens, then, could Meäry gi'e
That she'd a-liv'd an' liv'd for me,
But things a-done vor thought an' view?
Good things that nwone ageän can do,
An' every work her love ha' wrought
To eyezight's woone, but two to thought.

—William Barnes

Asphodel, That Greeny Flower

. . . All women are not Helen,
I know that,
but have Helen in their hearts.
My sweet,
you have it also, therefore
I love you
and could not love you otherwise.
Imagine you saw
a field made up of women
all silver-white.
What should you do
but love them?
The storm bursts
or fades! it is not
the end of the world.
Love is something else,
or so I thought it,
a garden which expands,
though I knew you as a woman
and never thought otherwise,
until the whole sea
has been taken up
and all its gardens.
It was the love of love,
the love that swallows up all else,
a grateful love,
a love of nature, of people,
animals,
a love engendering
gentleness and goodness
that moved me
and *that* I saw in you.
I should have known,
though I did not,
that the lily-of-the-valley
is a flower that makes many ill
who whiff it.
We had our children,
rivals in the general onslaught.
I put them aside
though I cared for them
as well as any man

could care for his children
according to my lights.
You understand
I had to meet you
after the event
and have still to meet you.
Love
to which you too shall bow
along with me—
a flower
a weakest flower
shall be our trust
and not because
we are too feeble
to do otherwise
but because
at the height of my power
I risked what I had to do,
therefore to prove
that we love each other
while my very bones sweated
that I could not cry to you
in the act.
Of asphodel, that greeny flower,
I come, my sweet
to sing to you!
My heart rouses
thinking to bring you news
of something
that concerns you
and concerns many men. Look at
what passes for the new.
You will not find it there but in
despised poems.
It is difficult
to get the news from poems
yet men die miserably every day
for lack
of what is found there.
Hear me out
for I too am concerned
and every man

who wants to die at peace in his bed
besides.

—William Carlos Williams

My dear Heart,—My sad parting was so far from making me forget you, that I scarce thought upon myself since, but wholly upon you. Those dear embraces which I yet feel, and shall never lose, being the faithful testimonies of an indulgent husband, have charmed my soul to such a reverence of your remembrance, that were it possible, I would, with my own blood, cement your dead limbs to live again, and (with reverence) think it no sin to rob Heaven a little longer of a martyr. Oh! my dear, you must now pardon my passion, this being my last (oh fatal word!) that ever you will receive from me; and know, that until the last minute that I can imagine you shall live, I shall sacrifice the prayers of a Christian, and the groans of an afflicted wife. And when you are not (which sure by sympathy I shall know), I shall wish my own dissolution with you, so that we may go hand in hand to Heaven. 'Tis too late to tell you what I have, or rather have not done for you; how being turned out of doors because I came to beg for mercy; the Lord lay not your blood to their charge.

I would fain discourse longer with you, but dare not; passion begins to drown my reason, and will rob me of my devoirs, which is all I have left to serve you. Adieu, therefore, ten thousand times, my dearest dear; and since I must never see you more, take this prayer—May your faith be so strengthened that your constancy may continue; and then I know Heaven will receive you; whither grief and love will in a short time (I hope) translate,

My dear,

Your sad, but constant wife, even to love your ashes when dead,

—Arundel Penruddock

May the 3rd, 1655, eleven o'clock at night. Your children beg your blessing and present their duties to you.

[*Her husband, John Penruddock, a Royalist who joined the insurrection of 1655, was taken at South Molton, and beheaded at Exeter.*]

MEDICINE

I can remember my father, who was a physician, quoting to me when I was a young boy an aphorism by Sir William Osler: "Care more for the individual patient than for the special features of his disease." In other words, a doctor, like anyone else who has to deal with human beings, each of them unique, cannot be a scientist; he is either, like the surgeon, a craftsman, or, like the physician and the psychologist, an artist. As Novalis wrote, "Every sickness is a musical problem; every cure a musical solution. . . ." This means that in order to be a good doctor a man must also have a good character, that is to say, whatever weaknesses and foibles he may have, he must love his fellow human beings in the concrete and desire their good before his own. A doctor, like a politician, who loves other men only in the abstract or regards them simply as a source of income can, however clever, do nothing but harm.

It is precisely those members of the medical profession who make the bogus claim that they are "scientific" who are most likely to refuse to consider new evidence. To its shame, the profession has always had its unacknowledged "Holy Office," which has dealt with the heterodox, like Kaspar Wolff and Semmelweis, every bit as unscrupulously and ruthlessly as the Inquisition ever dealt with heretics.

PRIEST: "Croyez-vous?"
A DYING 18TH-CENTURY PHYSICIAN: *"Je crois à tout, sauf le médecin."*

MEMORY

When Hoare was a young man of about five-and-twenty, he one day tore the quick of his finger-nail—I mean, he separated the fleshly part of the finger from the nail—and this reminded him that many years previously while quite a child he had done the same thing. Thereon he fell to thinking of that time, which was impressed upon his memory partly because there was a great disturbance in the house about a missing five-pound note, and partly because it was while he had the scarlet fever.

Having nothing to do he followed the train of thought aroused by his torn finger, and asked himself how he tore it. After a while it came back to him that he had been lying ill in bed as a child of about seven years old at the house of an aunt who lived in Hertfordshire. His arms often hung out of the bed and as his hands wandered over the wooden frame of the bed he felt there was a place where a nut had come off so that he could stuff his fingers in; one day, in trying to stuff a piece of paper into this hole, he stuffed it so far and so tightly that he tore the quick of his nail. The whole thing came back so vividly, though he had not thought of it for twenty years, that he could see the room in his aunt's house, and remembered how his aunt used to sit by his bedside writing at a little table from which he had got the piece of paper which he had stuffed into the hole.

So far so good; but then there flashed upon him an idea that was not so pleasant. I mean it came upon him with irresistible force that the piece of paper he had stuffed into the hole in the bedstead was the missing five-pound note about which there had been so much disturbance. At that time he was so young that a five-pound note was to him only a piece of paper; when he heard that five pounds were missing he had thought it was five sovereigns; or perhaps he was too ill to know anything, or to be questioned. I forget what I was told about this—at any rate he had no idea of the value of the piece of paper he was stuffing into the hole but now that the matter had recurred to him at all he felt so sure it was the note that he immediately went down to Hertfordshire where his aunt was living, and asked to the surprise of everyone to be allowed to wash his hands in the room he had occupied as a child. He was told there were friends staying with them who had the room at present, but, on his saying he had a reason, and particularly begging to be allowed to remain alone a little while in this room, he was taken upstairs and left there.

He immediately went to the bed, lifted up the chintz which then covered the frame, and found his old friend the hole.

A nut had been supplied and he could no longer get his fingers into it.

He rang the bell and, when the servant came, asked for a bedkey. All this time he was rapidly acquiring the reputation of being a lunatic throughout the whole house, but the key was brought, and by the help of it Hoare got the nut off. When he had done so, there sure enough, by dint of picking with his pocket-knife, he found the missing five-pound note.

—Samuel Butler II

Middle-Class, English

In spite of Belloc's description of Lord Heygate as "The sort of peer who well might pass / For someone of the Middle-Class," the label does not, thank God, carry with it the pejorative associations of the label *bourgeois.* Both in France and England, until very recently, nearly all the writers, painters, composers, scientists, and philosophers came from this class, but we do not, like our unfortunate French colleagues, have to apologize for the fact.

One may sneer as one will at its narrow-mindedness, its repressions, its dullness, but let it be remembered that it was the middle-class who first practiced, if it did not invent, the virtue of financial honesty, the first class to be scrupulous about paying bills and taxes. The aristocracy paid its gambling debts but not its tailors' bills; the poor stole.

We even have our martyr, Sir Walter Scott, who, when made bankrupt through no fault of his own, worked himself to death to pay off his creditors. In our modern economy it seems unlikely that the middle-class morality about money will be able to survive. I, for example, was brought up never to buy anything until I had the cash to pay for it. If everyone did the same, i.e. bought nothing on credit, our economy would go smash.

Mind, The Human

Over the water,
Under the water,
Round the world it ranges,
Never been seen by the eye of man,
But oftentimes it changes.

—Nova Scotian riddle

Mind is rather a little bourgeois, yet you can't dispense with the *tiers état.*

—V. Rozanov

A man is infinitely more complicated than his thoughts.

Consciousness reigns but doesn't govern.

Cogito, ergo sum. This is not a piece of reasoning. It's a fist coming down on the table, to corroborate the words in the mind.

A *thinker* is a *talker* before the fact.

—Paul Valéry

Speech is the Mother, not the handmaid, of Thought.

—Karl Kraus

When we think a thing, the thing we think is not the thing we think we think, but only the thing we think we think we think.

—Anon.

The highest and deepest thoughts do not "voluntarily move harmonious numbers," but run rather to grotesque epigram and doggerel.

—Coventry Patmore

The proper, unique, and perpetual object of thought: that which does not exist, that which is not before me, that which was, that which will be, that which is possible, that which is impossible.

—Paul Valéry

In the study of ideas, it is necessary to remember that insistence on hard-headed clarity issues from sentimental feeling, as it were a mist, cloaking the perplexities of fact. Insistence on clarity at all costs is based on sheer superstition as to the mode in which human intelligence functions.

It is a profoundly erroneous truism, repeated by all copy-books and by eminent people when they are making speeches, that we should cultivate the habit of thinking what we are doing. The precise opposite is the case. Civilization advances by extending the number of important operations which we can perform without thinking about them.

—A. N. Whitehead

Thinking is more interesting than knowing, but less interesting than looking.

—Goethe

The Climate of Thought

The climate of thought has seldom been described.
It is no terror of Caucasian frost,
Nor yet that brooding Hindu heat
For which a loin-rag and a dish of rice
Suffice until the pestilent monsoon.
But, without winter, blood would run too thin;
Or, without summer, fires would burn too long.
In thought the seasons run concurrently.

Thought has a sea to gaze, not voyage on;
And hills, to rough the edge of the bland sky,
Not to be climbed in search of blander prospect;
Few birds, sufficient for such caterpillars
As are not fated to turn butterflies;
Few butterflies, sufficient for such flowers
As are the luxury of a full orchard;
Wind, sometimes, in the evening chimneys, rain
On the early morning roof, on sleepy sight;
Snow streaked upon the hilltop, feeding
The fond brook at the valley-head
That greens the valley and that parts the lips;
The sun, simple, like a country neighbour;
The moon, grand, not fanciful with clouds.

—Robert Graves

It seems to me that the soul, when alone with itself and speaking to itself, uses only a small number of words, none of them extraordinary. This is how one recognizes that there *is* a soul at that moment, if at the same time one experiences the sensation that everything else—everything that would require a larger vocabulary—is mere possibility.

—Paul Valéry

Whenever I hear people talking about "liberal" ideas, I am always astounded that men should so love to fool themselves with empty sounds. An idea should never be liberal: it must be vigorous, positive, and without loose ends so that it may fulfill its divine mission and be productive. The proper place for liberality is in the realm of emotions.

—Goethe

The Jansenists put a rigor into the *heart* that belongs to the mind.
—Paul Valéry

Every abstract thinker tears love and time asunder.

The primary questions for an adult are not *why* or *how*, but *when* and *where*.
—Eugen Rosenstock-Huessy

I have drawn from the well of language many a thought which I do not have and which I could not put into words.
—Karl Kraus

In mathematical analysis we call *x* the undetermined part of line *a*; the rest we don't call *y*, as we do in common life, but *a–x*. Hence mathematical language has great advantages over the common language.
—G. C. Lichtenberg

We are all capable of evil thoughts, but only very rarely of evil deeds: we can all do good deeds, but very few of us can think good thoughts.
—Cesare Pavese

Thou hast commanded that an ill-regulated mind should be its own punishment.
—St Augustine

Mnemonics

Mnemonics, or aids to memory, should be quoted from memory, which means that I cannot vouch for the accuracy of any of my examples.

Some of the earliest poetry I can remember are the mnemonic rhymes in Kennedy's *Shorter Latin Primer.* For example, the list of prepositions taking the ablative:

A, ab, absque, coram, de,
Palam, clam, cum, ex, and e.
Sine, tenus, pro and prae,
Add super, subter, sub and in
When State not Motion 'tis they mean.

or

Nouns denoting males in *a*
Are by meaning Mascula,
And masculine is found to be
Hadria, the Adriatic Sea.

I can also recall a prose, somewhat surrealistic, mnemonic I made up myself when studying Chemistry in order to remember the metals in Group II.

Are (arsenic) any (antimony) taxis (tin) made (manganese) like (lead) corpulent (copper) business (bismuth) charlatans (cadmium)?

The oddest mnemonics I have come across are in Sigmund Spaeth's *Great Symphonies and How to Recognize Them,* intended, apparently, to help schoolchildren taking classes in musical appreciation.

On the chord we are starting,
And once more we're Mozarting.

Beethoven still is great
In the symphony he numbers Eight.

This music is real, and not just a dream:
'Tis Schubert, not Mozart, who composed this theme.

This music has a less pathetic strain,
It sounds more sane and not so full of pain,
Sorrow is ended, grief may be mended,
It seems Tchaikovsky will be calm again.

I am a little puzzled by his words for Tchaikovsky's Fifth Symphony. Admirable as the sentiments may be, I cannot see how they can help a student to remember either the name of the composer or the number of the Symphony.

Tell every nation, all of creation,
That it is time we should end all warfare:
Utter it loudly, utter it proudly,
Ye who are wise, may ye bring your powers to bear,
No more inciting madmen to fighting . . .

—Sigmund Spaeth

Mole, The

A Dead Mole

Strong-shouldered mole,
That so much lived below the ground,
Dug, fought and loved, hunted and fed,
For you to raise a mound
Was as for us to make a hole;
What wonder now that being dead
Your body lies here stout and square
Buried within the blue vault of the air?

—Andrew Young

Money

The King's Coins

They laid the coins before the council.
Kay, the king's steward, wise in economics, said:
"Good; these cover the years and the miles
and talk one style's dialects to London and Omsk.
Traffic can hold now and treasure be held,
streams are bridged and mountains of ridged space
tunnelled; gold dances deftly over frontiers.
The poor have choice of purchase, the rich of rents,
and events move now in a smoother control
than the swords of lords or the orisons of nuns.
Money is the medium of exchange."

Taliessin's look darkened; his hand shook
while he touched the dragons; he said, "We had a good thought.
Sir, if you made verse, you would doubt symbols.
I am afraid of the little loosed dragons.
When the means are autonomous, they are deadly; when words
escape from verse they hurry to rape souls;
when sensation slips from intellect, expect the tyrant;
the brood of carriers levels the good they carry.
We have taught our images to be free; are ye glad?
are we glad to have brought convenient heresy to Logres?"

The Archbishop answered the lords;
his words went up through a slope of calm air:
"Might may take symbols and folly make treasure,
and greed bid God, who hides himself for man's pleasure
by occasion, hide himself essentially: this abides—
that the everlasting house the soul discovers
is always another's; we must lose our own ends;
we must always live in the habitation of our lovers,
my friend's shelter for me, mine for him.
This is the way of this world in the day of that other's;
make yourselves friends by means of the riches of iniquity,
for the wealth of the self is the health of the self exchanged.
What saith Heraclitus?—and what is the City's breath?—
dying each other's life, living each other's death.
Money is a medium of exchange."

—Charles Williams

Money is human happiness in the abstract: he, then, who is no longer capable of enjoying human happiness in the concrete devotes himself utterly to money.

—Schopenhauer

Everyone, even the richest and most munificent of men, pays much by cheque more lightheartedly than he pays little in specie.

—Max Beerbohm

Nothing knits man to man like the frequent passage from hand to hand of cash.

—W. Sickert

I am not sure just what the unpardonable sin is, but I believe it is a disposition to evade the payment of small bills.

—E. Hubbard

Many priceless things can be bought.

—Maria von Ebner-Eschenbach

You will never find people laboring to convince you that you may live very happily upon a plentiful fortune.

—Dr Johnson

Two evenings spent at *La Scala*, Milan, one of them standing up, the other sitting down. On the first evening, I was continuously conscious of the existence of the spectators who were seated. On the second evening, I was completely unconscious of the existence of the spectators who were standing up (and of those who were seated also).

—Simone Weil

If the rich could hire other people to die for them, the poor could make a wonderful living.

—Yiddish proverb

Names, Proper

Proper names are poetry in the raw. Like all poetry they are untranslatable. Someone who is translating into English a German novel, the hero of which is named *Heinrich*, will leave the name as it is; he will not Anglicize it into *Henry*.

The early epic poets, composing for an audience with the same mythology, heroic legends, topography as themselves, had half their poetic work done for them. Later, when the poet's audience became a cultured elite, their cultural background was still the same as his own: Milton, for example, could assume that any name taken from Greek and Roman mythology or from the Bible would be familiar to his readers. A modern poet, on the other hand, can hardly use a single proper name without wondering whether he ought not to footnote it. In 1933 I wrote a poem in which the name *Garbo* appeared, assuming, I think rightly, that at that time her name was a household word. When, after the War, Mr Richard Hoggart included the poem in a selection he had made from my work, he felt it necessary to gloss the name.

> "I" is not the name of a person, nor "here" of a place, and "this" is not a name. But they are connected with names. Names are explained by means of them. It is also true that it is characteristic of physics not to use these words.
>
> —Ludwig Wittgenstein

> With knowledge of the name comes a distincter recognition and knowledge of the thing.
>
> —H. D. Thoreau

> Words do not change their meaning so drastically in the course of centuries as, in our minds, names do in the course of a year or two.
>
> —M. Proust

> The first book of Moses cites as one of the distinctive marks of man: to give animals names. Now it is characteristic of the ordinary man, the man of the people, to have that gift. If the ordinary man sees a bird for some years, which is not normally seen, he immediately gives it a name, and a characteristic name. But take ten learned men and how incapable they are of finding a name. What a satire on them when one reads scientific works and sees the names which come from the people, and then the silly miserable names when once in a while a learned man has to think of a name. Usually they can think of nothing better than calling the animal or the plant after their own names.
>
> —Søren Kierkegaard (trans. A. Dru)

NAMES FOR THE GREEN WOODPECKER

Sprite
Hickway
Woodspite
Popinjay
Yaffle
Highoe
Rindtabberer
Yaffingale
Green Peck
Yuckel
Cutbill
Rain Pie
Nickerpecker
Woodweele

NAMES FOR THE CUCKOO-PINT

Aaron
Adam-and-Eve
Adders Meat
Bloody-Man's-Finger
Bobbin-Joan
Bulls-and-Cows
Calf's-Foot
Friar's-Cowl
Lamb-in-a-Pulpit
Lily Grass
Nightingales
Wake-Robin

Names of Veins in the Lead-Mining District of Tideswell, Derbyshire

Dirtland Rake
Bacchus Pipe
Kettle-End Vein
Moss Rake
Chapmaiden Rake
Tideslaw
Pearson's Venture
Hubnub
Pyenest
Old Nestor's Pipe

Dinah's Rake
Hunt's Coldberry
Barbara Load
Friarfold Hush
Reformer's
Legrim's Palfrey
Horse-buttock
Blobber
Flappy
Modesty Flat

Names for the Genitals

Male

Bald-headed Hermit
Dr Johnson
Fiddle-bow
Silent (one-eyed) Flute
Goose's Neck
Hampton Wick
Jack-in-the-Cellar
Ladyweave
Nimrod
Stargazer
Tackle
Titmouse
Donkey
Giggle-Stick
Impudence
Power
Rector

Female

Ace of Spades
Almanack
Cabbage
Fart-Daniel
Fig
Front-Attic (Garden)
Fumbler's Hall
Garden Gate
Goldfinch's Nest
Grotto
Gyvel
Jacob's Ladder
Leather Lane
Lobster Pot
Mother of St Patrick
Milliner's Shop
Jack Nasty-Face
Oyster
Pen wiper
Purse
Receipt of Custom
Regulator
Hans Carvel's Ring
Saddle
Sportsman's Gap
Sugar Basin
Teazle
Growler

Trench Nomenclature

Genius named them, as I live! What but genius could compress
In a title what man's humour said to man's supreme distress?
Jacob's Ladder ran reversed, from earth to a fiery pit extending,
With not angels but poor Angles, those for the most part descending.
Thence *Brocks Benefit* commanded endless fireworks by two nations,
Yet some voices there were raised against the rival coruscations.
Picturedome peeped out upon a dream, not Turner could surpass,
And presently the picture moved, and greyed with corpses and morass.
So down south; and if remembrance travel north, she marvels yet
At the sharp Shakespearean names, and with sad mirth her eyes are
wet.
The Great Wall of China rose, a four-foot breastwork, fronting guns
That, when the word dropped, beat at once its silly ounces with brute
tons;
Odd *Krab Krawl* on paper looks, and odd the foul-breathed alley
twisted,
As one feared to twist there too, if *Minnie*, forward quean, insisted.
Where the Yser at *Dead End* floated on its bloody waters
Dead and rotten monstrous fish, note (east) *The Pike and Eel*
headquarters.
Ah, such names and apparitions! name on name! what's in a name?
From the fable's vase the genie in his shattering horror came.

—Edmund Blunden

Naming Animals

Birds are given human christian names in accordance with the species to which they belong more easily than are other zoological classes, because they can be permitted to resemble men for the very reason that they are so different. They are feathered, winged, oviparous, and they are also physically separated from human society by the element in which it is their privilege to move. As a result of this fact, they form a community which is independent of our own but, precisely because of this independence, appears to us like another society, homologous to that in which we live: birds love freedom; they build themselves homes in which they live a family life and nurture their young; they often engage in social relations with other members of their species; and they communicate with them by acoustic means recalling articulate language.

Consequently everything objective conspires to make us think of the bird world as a metaphorical human society. . . . Now, this metaphorical relation which is imagined between the society of birds and the society of men, is accompanied by a procedure of naming, itself of a metonymical order . . . when species of birds are christened "Pierrot," "Margot," or "Jacquot," these names are drawn from a portion which is the preserve of human beings and the relation of bird names to human names is thus that of part to whole.

The position is exactly the reverse in the case of dogs. Not only do they not form an independent society; as "domestic" animals they are part of human society, although with so low a place in it that we should not dream of following the example of some Australians and Amerindians in designating them in the same way as human beings—whether what is in question are proper names or kinship terms. On the contrary, we allot them a special series: "Azor," "Medor," "Sultan," "Fido," "Diane" (the last of these is of course a human christian name but in the first instance conceived as mythological). Nearly all these are like stage names, forming a series parallel to the names people bear in ordinary life or, in other words, metaphorical names. Consequently, when the relation between (human and animal) species is socially conceived as metaphorical, the relation between the respective systems of naming takes on a metonymical character; and when the relation between species is conceived as metonymical, the system of naming assumes a metaphorical character.

Let us now consider another case, that of cattle, the social position of which is metonymical (they form part of our technical and economic system) but different from that of dogs in that cattle are more overtly treated as "objects" and dogs as "subjects". . . . Now, the names given to cattle . . . are generally descriptive terms, referring to the colour of their coats, their bearing or temperament: "Rustaud," "Rousset," "Blanchette," "Douce," etc. These names often have a metaphorical character but they differ from the names given to dogs in that they are epithets coming from the syntagmatic chain, while the latter come from a paradigmatic series; the former thus tend to derive from speech, the latter from language.

Finally, let us consider the names given to horses—not ordinary horses whose place approximates more or less closely to that of cattle or that of dogs according to the class and occupation of their owner, and is made even more uncertain by the rapid technological changes of recent times, but racehorses, whose sociological position is clearly distinguishable from the cases already examined. The first question is how to define their position. They cannot be said to constitute an independent society after the manner of birds, for they are products of human industry and they are born and live as isolated individuals juxtaposed in stud farms devised for their sake. On the other hand, they do not form part of human society either as subjects or as objects. Rather, they constitute the desocialized condition of a private society: that which lives off racecourses or frequents them. Another difference, in the system of naming, corresponds to these, although two reservations must be made in drawing this comparison: the names given to racehorses are chosen in accordance with particular rules which differ for thoroughbreds and half-breds and they display an eclecticism which draws on learned literature rather than oral tradition. This said, there is no doubt that there is a significant contrast between the names of racehorses and those of birds, dogs or cattle. They are rigorously individualized since . . . two individuals cannot have the same name; and, although they share with the names given to cattle the feature of being formed by drawing upon the syntagmatic chain: "Ocean," "Azimuth," "Opera," "Belle-de-Nuit," "Telegraphe," "Luciole," "Orvietan," "Weekend," "Lapis-Lazuli," etc., they are distinguished from them by the absence of descriptive connotation.

Their creation is entirely unrestricted so long as they satisfy the requirement of unambiguous individuation and adhere to the particular rules referred to above. Thus, while cattle are given descriptive names formed out of words of discourse, the names assigned to racehorses are words from discourse which rarely, if ever, describe them. The former type of name perhaps resembles a nickname [*surnom*] and these latter perhaps merit the title of sub-names [*sous-nom*] as it is in this second domain that the most extreme arbitrariness reigns.

To sum up: birds and dogs are relevant in connection with human society either because they suggest it by their own social life (which men look on as an imitation of theirs), or alternatively because, having no social life of their own, they form part of ours.

Cattle, like dogs, form part of human society, but as it were, asocially, since they verge on objects. Finally racehorses, like birds, form a series disjoined from human society, but like cattle, lacking in intrinsic sociability. If, therefore, birds are *metaphorical human beings* and dogs, *metonymical human beings*, cattle may be thought of as *metonymical inhuman beings* and race-horses as *metaphorical inhuman beings*. . . .

—Lévi-Strauss

Star Names

For the names of the group of the Hyades the following explanations have been offered.

(1) The Hyades are so called because they were the sisters of Hyas, whose untimely end—of which there is more than one account—they are ever lamenting; whence their association with a season of moisture. This is a possible explanation of the name Hyades, but does not help us to find one for the name Hyas.

(2) The shape of the Hyades reminds us of a capital V, and must have reminded the ancient Greek of their letter Upsilon. The name of Hyades, therefore, must originally mean simply the "the V stars".

This explanation has found a modern supporter in the great scholar Buttmann, whose argument, however, seems to lead decidedly rather towards its rejection than its acceptance.

He points out that the bright stars of Cassiopeia, if viewed the right way up, form a conspicuous capital W. Is it not certain, he asks, that if we had now for the first time to name the constellations, unbiassed, as we are now, by the tales of our grandfathers, we should call this bright and unmistakeable group, "the W"?

Perhaps we might, but as a matter of fact we do not. And that our ancestors under similar conditions would have done so seems much less probable. For on the one hand, whereas nowadays we can all read—even alas! in these days base advertisements scrawled upon the sky itself—it is exceedingly doubtful whether in pre-Homeric times, from which the name of the Hyades certainly descends, the vast majority of the people who used the name had any familiarity at all with written characters. And on the other hand, it is a pure assumption that the first people to notice that the Hyades were like a V were not already provided with a name for the group.

(3) The word Hyades (Ὑάδες) is connected with ὕειν, "to rain". It means therefore "the rainy stars", just as the Pleiades, connected with πλεῖν, "to sail", means "the stars of the sailing season". It may seem strange that two groups, so near each other in the sky, should have such different meteorological characters, but whereas it is the morning rising of the Pleiades that may have inaugurated the sailing season, it is the morning setting of the Hyades which may have been taken to announce, or even to cause, the rains. This took place in November.

There can, I think, be no doubt that such meteorological explanation is far more satisfactory as applied to the Hyades than it is in the case of the Pleiades. For one thing, there is evidence that the Hyades were actually regarded by plain men as bringers of rain: in the *Ion* of Euripides we find them described as the surest of all such signs possessed by the seaman. And for another, the reasons for this surety are apparent: the opening of a rainy season is a much more definite and observable thing than that of good boating weather, and moreover the Hyades are not, like the Pleiades, a close swarm of faint stars, but contain one conspicuous member, the bright star now known as Aldebaran, remarkable to the ancients, as to us, not only for its magnitude but for its color. The date on which such a star could for the last time be seen to go down, before the light of dawn made it invisible, could be fixed with comparative precision.

But for all that, I cannot believe that the rainy Hyades had no name before they were found to be rainy, and greatly prefer the next explanation, namely:

(4) The word Ὑάδες is connected, not with ὕειν, "to rain", but with ὗς, "a swine". The Hyades were originally seen as a litter of pigs, or perhaps rather as a "sounder" of wild swine.

Perhaps the reluctance of critics, ancient and modern, to accept this explanation may have been partly caused by a feeling that there is nothing at all celestial about the pig as he is usually regarded by civilised man. This feeling must certainly go back as far as the time of Circe. But the domestic pig is degenerate. No one who has seen the wild boar in freedom has ever thought of him as an ignoble animal, and no one has expressed admiration of him more warmly than it is expressed in Homer. Why is it more unlikely that the Greeks should have seen Aldebaran and his companions as swine than that the Arabs, according to Al Sufi, should have seen them as camels? And that they did so is strongly suggested by the curious fact that the old Roman name for the group seems to have been *suculae*, "little pigs". It is true that Cicero disdains this piece of evidence, apparently considering that *suculae* is merely a mistranslation of the Greek ὑάζες. But this seems very improbable. The natural meaning of Cicero's words and those of Pliny after him is that *nostri*, the Romans of their day, did really call the Hyades *suculae*, and that *suculae* did really mean "little pigs".

The object of this chapter has been to show, not merely that it is untrue to say, with the old scholiast, that most star-names have been given for purposes of instruction, but that it is actually the reverse of the truth. Even if we rank among instructors such rude folk as Kepler's sailors and husbandmen, we shall find that the names they used have for the most part no connection with the functions which the stars bearing these names have been found to discharge. The vast majority of star-names, it is here contended, are of popular origin and have usually a descriptive meaning.

—E. J. Webb

Napoleon

Now that all the facts about Napoleon's life, including his table conversation, have been unearthed and published, it seems a thousand pities that, when he surrendered to them, the British did not immediately hang him from the yardarm and sink his body in the sea, as an enemy of civilization.

Just how appalling political and social conditions in England at the time must have been is indicated by the fact that many liberal-minded young Englishmen could think of him as a liberator. How would one feel if, in the following poem, the refrain ran, *Since Hitler killed himself in Berlin*?

Song

When working blackguards come to blows,
And give or take a bloody nose,
Shall injuries try such gods as those,
  Now Nap lies at Saint Helena?

No, let the Great Unpaid decide,
Without appeal, on tame bull's hide,
Ash-planted well, or fistified,
  Now Nap died at Saint Helena.

When Sabbath stills the dizzy mill,
Shall Cutler Tom, or Grinder Bill,
On footpaths wander where they will,
  Now Nap lies at Saint Helena?

No, let them curse, but *feel* our power;
Dogs! let them spend their idle hour
Where burns the highways' dusty shower;
  For Nap died at Saint Helena.

Huzza! the rascal Whiglings work
For better man than Hare and Burke,
And envy Algerine and Turk,
  Since Nap died at Saint Helena.

Then close each path that sweetly climbs
Suburban hills, where village chimes
Remind the rogues of other times,
  Ere Nap died at Saint Helena.

We tax their bread, restrict their trade;
To toil for us, their hands are made;
Their doom is sealed, their prayer is prayed;
  Nap perished at Saint Helena.

Dogs! would they toil and fatten too?
They grumble still, as dogs will do:
We conquered *them* at Waterloo;
  And Nap lies at Saint Helena.

But shall the villains meet and prate
In crowds about affairs of state?
Ride, yeomen, ride! Act, magistrate!
  Nap perished at Saint Helena.

—Ebenezer Elliott

Narcissus

A mirror has no heart but plenty of ideas.

—Malcolm de Chazal

Narcissus leant over the spring, enthralled by the only man in whose eyes he had ever dared—or been given the chance—to forget himself.

Narcissus leant over the spring, enchanted by his own ugliness which he prided himself upon having the courage to admit.

—Dag Hammarskjöld

Egoism puts the feelings in Indian file.

—Malcolm de Chazal

Every man likes the smell of his own farts.

—Icelandic proverb

Every stink that fights the ventilator thinks it is Don Quixote.

—Stanislaus Lec

Nature

Many years ago, as now, my mind strove with eager delight to study and discover the creative life of Nature. It is eternal unity in manifold manifestation; the great is little, the little is great, and everything after its kind; ever changing and yet preserving itself, near and far, and far and near, and so shaping and re-shaping itself—to marvel at it is what I am here for.

The reason why I prefer the society of nature to any other is that nature is always right and the error, if any, can only be on my side. But if I hold converse with men, they will err, then I will, and so on forever, and we never get to see matters clearly.

Everything factual is, in a sense, theory. The blue of the sky exhibits the basic laws of chromatics. There is no sense in looking for something behind phenomena: they *are* theory.

—Goethe

There is no nature at an instant.

—A. N. Whitehead

Repetition is the only form of permanence that nature can achieve.

—G. Santayana

In the physical world, one cannot increase the size or quantity of anything without changing its quality. Similar figures exist only in pure geometry.

—Paul Valéry

Nature has wit, humor, fantasy, etc. Among animals and plants one finds natural caricatures. Nature is at her wittiest in the animal kingdom; there she is humorous throughout. The mineral and vegetable kingdoms bear more the stamp of fantasy; in the world of man, rational nature is bejeweled with fantasy and wit.

Are not plants, perhaps, the product of a feminine nature and a masculine spirit, animals the product of a masculine nature and a feminine spirit? Are not plants, as it were, the girls, animals the boys, of nature?

—Novalis

How do we distinguish the oak from the beech, the horse from the ox, but by the bounding outline? How do we distinguish one face or countenance from another, but by the bounding line and its infinite inflections and movements. Leave out the line, and you leave out life itself; all is chaos again, and the line of the Almighty must be drawn out upon it before man or beast can exist.

—William Blake

The one who loves and understands a thing best will incline to use the personal pronouns in speaking of it. To him there is no neuter gender.

—H. D. Thoreau

All colors are the friends of their neighbors and the lovers of their opposites.

No scent is a virgin.

—Malcolm de Chazal

The extrahuman in the experience of the greatness of Nature. This does not allow itself to be reduced to an expression of our human reactions, nor can we share in it by expressing them. Unless we each find a way to chime in as one note in the organic whole, we shall only observe ourselves observing the interplay of its thousand components in a harmony outside our experience of it as harmony.

—Dag Hammarskjöld

And ich bowede my body · by-holdynge al a-boute,
And seih the sonne and the see · and the sand after,
Wher that briddes and bestes · by here makes yeden,
Wilde wormes in wodes · and wonderful foules
With fleckede fetheres · and of fele colours; . . .
Briddes ich by-helde · in bosshes maden nestes,
Hadde neuere weye wit · to worche the leste.
Ich hadde wonder at wham · and wher that the pye
Lernede legge styckes · that leyen in here neste;

Ther is no wryght, as ich wene · sholde worche here nest to paye.
Yf eny mason therto · makede a molde
With all here wyse castes · wonder me thynketh!
  And yut ich meruaillede more · menye of tho bryddes
Hudden and heleden · durneliche here egges,
For no foul sholde hem funde · bote hus fere and hym-self.
And some treden, ich tok kepe · and on trees bredden,
And brouhten forth here bryddes · al aboue the grounde.
In maries and in mores · in myres and in wateres
Dompynges dyueden · "deere god," ich sayde,
"Where hadden these wilde suche witt · and at what scole?"
And when the pocok caukede · ther-of ich took kepe,
How vn-corteisliche the cok · hus kynde forth strenede,
And ferliche hadde of hus fairnesse · and of hus foule ledene.
  And siththe ich loked on the see · and so forth on the sterres,
Meny selcouth ich seih · aren nouht to seggen nouthe;
Ne what on floures in feldes · and of hure faire coloures,
How out of greot and of gras · grewe so meny huwes,
Somme soure and somme swete · selcouth me thouhte;
Of here kynde and of here colours · to carpen hit were to longe.

—William Langland

If nature be regarded as the teacher and we poor human beings as her pupils, the human race presents a very curious picture. We all sit together at a lecture and possess the necessary principles for understanding it, yet we always pay more attention to the chatter of our fellow students than to the lecturer's discourse. Or, if our neighbor copies something down, we sneak it from him, stealing what he himself may have heard imperfectly, and add to it our own errors of spelling and opinion.

—G. C. Lichtenberg

In relation to nature, early man was so weak and nature so strong as to make man almost her slave. It was natural, therefore, that he should have dreamed of a future in which their relative positions would be reversed, a time when he would be the master and nature the slave.

We have already reached the point where there is almost nothing we cannot compel nature to do, but we are finding to our cost that nature cannot be enslaved without enslaving ourselves. If nobody or nothing in the universe is responsible for man, then we must conclude that man is responsible, to God, for the universe, just as Adam was made responsible for the Garden of Eden. This means that it is our task to discover what everything in the universe, from electrons upwards, could, to its betterment, become, but cannot become without our help. This means reintroducing into science the notion of teleology, long a dirty word. For our proper relation to nonliving things, the right analogy might be that of the sculptor. Every sculptor thinks of himself, not as someone who forcibly imposes a form on stone, but as someone who reveals a form already latent in it. For our relation to living creatures, the analogy might be that of the good trainer of animals. A well-trained, well-treated sheep dog is more of a dog than a wild one, just as a stray, terrified by ill-usage, or a spoilt lap dog has had its "dogginess" debased. We have to realize that every time we make an ugly lampstand, we are torturing helpless metal, every time we make a nuclear bomb we are corrupting the morals of a host of innocent neutrons below the age of consent.

Rhea

On her shut lids the lightning flickers,
Thunder explodes above her bed,
An inch from her lax arm the rain hisses;
Discrete she lies,

Not dead but entranced, dreamlessly
With slow breathing, her lips curved
In a half-smile archaic, her breast bare,
Hair astream.

The house rocks, a flood suddenly rising
Bears away bridges: oak and ash
Are shivered to the roots—royal green timber.
She nothing cares.

(Divine Augustus, trembling at the storm,
Wrapped sealskin on his thumb; divine Gaius
Made haste to hide himself in a deep cellar,
Distraught by fear.)

Rain, thunder, lightning: pretty children.
"Let them play," her mother-mind repeats;
"They do no harm, unless from high spirits
Or by mishap."

—Robert Graves

Neighbor, Love of One's

Belief in the existence of other human beings as such is love.

To love our neighbor as ourselves does not mean that we should love all people equally, for I do not have an equal love for all the modes of existence of myself. Nor does it mean that we should never make them suffer, for I do not refuse to make myself suffer. But we should have with each person the relationship of one conception of the universe to another conception of the universe, and not to a part of it.

> Standing in front of a human being, whoever it may be—not to wish him either immortal or dead.
>
> —Simone Weil

We are not commanded (or forbidden) to love our mates, our children, our friends, our country because such affections come naturally to us and are good in themselves, although we may corrupt them. We are commanded to love our neighbor because our "natural" attitude toward the "other" is one of either indifference or hostility.

> Most people really believe that the Christian commandments (e.g. to love one's neighbor as oneself) are intentionally a little too severe—like putting the clock ahead half an hour to make sure of not being late in the morning.
>
> —Søren Kierkegaard

> Two brethren made their way to the city to sell their handiwork: and when, in the city, they went different ways, divided one from the other, one of them fell into fornication. After a while came his brother, saying, "Brother, let us go back to our cell." But he made answer, "I am not coming." And the other questioned him, saying, "Wherefore, brother?" And he answered, "Because when thou didst go from me, I ran into temptation, and I sinned in the flesh." But the other, anxious to help him, began to tell him, saying, "But so it happened with me: when I was separated from thee, I too ran into fornication. But let us go, and do penance together with all our might: and God will forgive us that are sinful men." And they came back to the monastery and told the old men what had befallen them, and they enjoined on them the penance they must do. But the one began his penance, not for himself but for his brother, as if he himself had sinned. And God, seeing his love and labor, after a few days revealed to one of the old men that for the great love of this brother who had not sinned He had forgiven the brother who had.
>
> —*The Desert Fathers* (trans. Helen Waddell)

> We found ourselves on the track with several car-loads of Japanese wounded. These unfortunates were on their own and without medical care.
>
> No longer fit for action in Burma, they had been packed into railway cars which were being returned to Bangkok. They had been packed up and dropped off according to the make-up of the trains. Whenever one of them died en route he was thrown off into the jungle. The ones who survived to reach Bangkok presumably would receive some kind of medical treatment. But they were given none on the way.
>
> They were in a shocking state. I have never seen men filthier. Uniforms were encrusted with mud, blood and excrement. Their wounds,

sorely inflamed and full of pus, crawled with maggots. The maggots, however, in eating the putrefying flesh, probably prevented gangrene.

It was apparent why the Japanese were so cruel to their prisoners. If they didn't care a tinker's damn for their own, why should they care for us?

The wounded men looked at us forlornly as they sat with their heads against the carriages, waiting for death. They had been discarded as expendable, the refuse of war. These were the enemy. They were more cowed and defeated than we had ever been.

Without a word most of the officers in my section unbuckled their packs, took out part of their ration and a rag or two, and, with water canteens in their hands, went over to the Japanese train.

Our guards tried to prevent us, bawling, "No goodka! No goodka!" But we ignored them and knelt down by the enemy to give water and food, to clean and bind up their wounds. Grateful cries of "Aragotto!" ("Thank you!") followed us when we left.

An allied officer from another section of the train had been taking it all in.

"What bloody fools you are!" he said to me.

"Have you never heard the story of the man who was going from Jerusalem to Jericho?" I asked him. . . .

"But that's different," the officer protested angrily. "That's in the Bible. These are the swine who have starved us and beaten us. These are our enemies." . . . He gave me a scornful glance and, turning his back, left me. . . .

I regarded my comrades with wonder. Eighteen months ago they would have joined readily in the destruction of our captors had they fallen into their hands. Now these same officers were dressing the enemy's wounds.

—Ernest Gordon

Non-Sequitur, A

Because I am wild about women
I'm mad about the hills.

—W. B. Yeats

Numbers

Numbers, Friendly and Perfect

Pythagoras, when asked what a friend was, replied: "One who is the other I, such are 220 and 284." Expressed in modern terminology this meant: the divisors of 284 are 1, 2, 4, 71, and 142, and these add up to 220; while the divisors of 220 are 1, 2, 4, 5, 10, 11, 20, 22, 44, 55, and

110, and these in turn add up to 284. Such numbers the Pythagoreans called *amicable* numbers.

. . . The general question whether there exists an infinity of such couples has not been settled to this day, although almost a hundred are known. . . .

Then there were the *perfect* numbers. Consider first a number such as 14; add up its divisors which are 1, 2, and 7; we get 10. The number 14 therefore is greater than the sum of its divisors, and is for this reason called *excessive.* On the other hand the sum of the divisors of 12 is 16—greater than 12, and for this reason 12 is said to be *defective.* But in a *perfect* number there is neither excess nor deficiency; the number equals the sum of its own divisors.

The smallest perfect numbers are 6 and 28, and were known to the Hindus as well as to the Hebrews. Some commentators of the Bible regard 6 and 28 as the basic numbers of the Supreme Architect. They point to the 6 days of creation and the 28 days of the lunar cycle. Others go so far as to explain the imperfection of the second creation by the fact that eight souls, not six, were rescued in Noah's ark.

Said St Augustine:

> Six is a number perfect in itself, and not because God created all things in six days; rather the converse is true; God created all things in six days because this number is perfect, and it would have been perfect even if the work of the six days did not exist.

The next two perfect numbers seem to have been the discovery of Nicomachus. We quote from his *Arithmetica.*

> . . . the perfect are both easily counted and drawn up in a fitting order: for only one is found in the units, 6; and only one in the tens, 28; and a third in the depth of the hundreds, 496; as a fourth the one, on the border of the thousands, that is short of the ten thousand, 8128. It is their uniform attribute to end in 6 or 8, and they are invariably even.

If Nicomachus meant to imply that there was a perfect number in every decimal class, he was wrong, for the fifth perfect number is 33,550,336. But his guess was excellent in every other respect. While the impossibility of an odd perfect number was never proved, no example of such a number is known. Furthermore it is true that an even perfect number must end in either 6 or 8. . . .

Numbers, Irrational

. . . From Egypt the Pythagoreans imported the "golden" triangle, the sides of which were in the ratio 3:4:5. Soon other "Pythagorean" triangles, such as 5:12:13 and 8:15:17, were discovered. The conviction that all triangles were *rational* had evidence to feed on. . . .

The contemplation of such triangles led to a capital discovery, which to this day bears the name of Pythagoras and which is one of the basic theorems of classical geometry. It reads: *In any right triangle the sum of the squares built on the legs is equal to the square built on the hypothenuse.* . . .

[Pythagoras] and his disciples attached the greatest importance to it; for *therein they saw the inherent union between geometry and arithmetic*, a new confirmation of their dictum: "Number rules the universe."

But the triumph was short-lived. Indeed, one of the immediate consequences of the theorem was another discovery: *the diagonal of the square is incommensurable with its side.* Who it was that first established this, and how it was done, will probably remain a mystery forever. . . . But . . . there is little doubt that it caused great consternation in the ranks of the Pythagoreans. . . . *Alogon*, the *unutterable*, these incommensurables were called, and the members of the order were sworn not to divulge their existence to outsiders. . . .

Says Proclus:

> It is told that those who first brought out the irrationals from concealment into the open perished in shipwreck, to a man. For the unutterable and the formless must needs be concealed. . . .

Zero

. . . Any attempt to make a permanent record of a counting-board operation would meet the obstacle that such an entry as ≡ = may represent any one of several numbers: 32, 302, 320, 3002, and 3020 among others. In order to avoid this ambiguity it is essential to have some method of representing the gaps, i.e. what is needed is a *symbol for an empty column.*

We see therefore that no progress was possible until a symbol was invented for an *empty* class, a symbol for *nothing*, our modern *zero*. The concrete mind of the ancient Greeks could not conceive the void as a number, let alone endow the void with a symbol.

And neither did the unknown Hindu see in zero the symbol of nothing. The Indian term for zero was *sunya*, which meant *empty* or *blank*, but had no connotation of "void" or "nothing." And so, from all appearances, the discovery of zero was an accident brought about by an attempt to make an unambiguous permanent record of a counting-board operation. . . .

. . . When the Arabs of the tenth century adopted the Indian numeration, they translated the Indian *sunya* by their own *sifr*, which meant empty in Arabic. When the Indo-Arabic numeration was first introduced into Italy, *sifr* was latinized into *zephirum*. This happened at the beginning of the thirteenth century, and in the course of the next hundred years the word underwent a series of changes which culminated in the Italian *zero.*

About the same time Jordanus Nemerarius was introducing the Arabic system into Germany. He kept the Arabic word, changing it slightly to *cifra.* That for some time in the learned circles of Europe the word *cifra* and its derivatives denoted zero is shown by the fact that the great Gauss, the last of the mathematicians of the nineteenth century who wrote in Latin, still used *cifra* in this sense. In the English language the word *cifra* has become *cipher* and has retained its original meaning of zero.

The attitude of the common people toward this new numeration is reflected by the fact that soon after its introduction into Europe, the word *cifra* was used as a secret sign. . . . The verb *decipher* remains as a monument of these early days.

. . . the essential part played by zero in this new system [of reckoning] did not escape the notice of the masses. Indeed, they identified the whole system with its most striking feature, the *cifra,* and this explains how this word in its different forms, *ziffer, chiffre,* etc., came to receive the meaning of numeral, which it has in Europe today.

This double meaning, the popular *cifra* standing for numeral and the *cifra* of the learned signifying zero, caused considerable confusion . . . the matter was eventually settled by adopting the Italian zero in the sense in which it is used today.

The same interest attaches to the word *algorithm.* As the term is used today, it applies to any mathematical procedure consisting of an indefinite number of steps, each step applying to the result of the one preceding it. But between the tenth and fifteenth centuries *algorithm* was synonymous with positional numeration. We now know that the word is merely a corruption of Al Kworesmi, the name of the Arabian mathematician of the ninth century whose book (in Latin translation) was the first work on this subject to reach Western Europe.

Today, when positional numeration has become a part of our daily life, it seems that the superiority of this method, the compactness of its notation, the ease and elegance it introduced into calculations, should have assured the rapid and sweeping acceptance of it. In reality, the transition, far from being immediate, extended over long centuries. The struggle between the *Abacists,* who defended the old traditions, and the *Algorists,* who advocated the reform, lasted from the eleventh to the fifteenth century. . . . In some places Arabic numerals were banned from official documents; in others, the art was prohibited altogether. And, as usual, *prohibition* did not succeed in abolishing, but merely served to spread *bootlegging,* ample evidence of which is found in the thirteenth century archives of Italy, where, it appears, merchants were using the Arabic numerals as a sort of secret code.

Binary System (Torres Straits)

1 urapun
2 okosa
3 okosa-urapun
4 okosa-okosa
5 okosa-okosa-urapun
6 okosa-okosa-okosa

Quinary System (Api Language of the New Hebrides)

tâi
lua
tolu
vari
luna (hand)
otai (other hand)
olua
otolu
oviar
lua luna (hands)

Vigesimal System (Maya Language)

1	hun
20	kal
400	bak
8000	pic
160,000	calab
3,200,000	kinchel
64,000,000	alce

—Tobias Dantzig

Counting Rhymes

Eena, deena, deina, duss,
Catala, weena, weina, wuss,
Spit, spot, must be done,
Twiddlum, twaddlum, twenty-one.

Un, deux, trois, j'irai dans le bois,
Quatre, cinq, six, chercher des cerises,
Sept, huit, neuf, dans mon panier neuf;
Dix, onze, douze, elles seront toutes rouges;
Treize, quatorze, quinze, pour mon petit Prince;
Seize, dix-sept, dix-huit, je les apporterai tout de suite.
Dix-neuf, vingt, pour qu'elles prennent leurs bains.

Eine kleine weisse Bohne wollte gern nach Engelland,
Engelland war zugeschlossen, und der Schlüssel war zerbrochen.
Bauer bind den Pudel an,
Dass er mich nicht beissen kann.
Beisst er mich, so kost es dich
Tausend Thaler sicherlich.

Nursery Library, My

As readers, we remain in the nursery stage so long as we cannot distinguish between Taste and Judgment, so long, that is, as the only possible verdicts we can pass on a book are two: this I like; this I don't like.

For an adult reader, the possible verdicts are five: I can see this is good and I like it; I can see this is good but I don't like it; I can see this is good and, though at present I don't like it, I believe that with perseverance I shall come to like it; I can see that this is trash but I like it; I can see that this is trash and I don't like it.

Nonfictional Prose

T. Sopwith	*A Visit to Alston Moor*
?	*Underground Life*
?	*Machinery for Metalliferous Mines*
His Majesty's Stationery Office	*Lead and Zinc Ores of Northumberland and Alston Moor*
?	*The Edinburgh School of Surgery*
?	*Dangers to Health* (a Victorian treatise, illustrated, on plumbing, good and bad)

Fiction

Beatrix Potter	All her books
Hans Andersen	*The Snow Queen*
Morris and Magnusson	*Icelandic Stories*
Lewis Carroll	The two *Alice* books
George Macdonald	*The Princess and the Goblin*
Jules Verne	*The Child of the Cavern, Journey to the Centre of the Earth*
Rider Haggard	*King Solomon's Mines, She*
Dean Farrar	*Eric, or Little by Little*
Ballantyne	*The Cruise of the Cachelot*
Conan Doyle	The *Sherlock Holmes* stories

Poetry

Hoffmann	*Shock-headed Peter*
Hilaire Belloc	*Cautionary Tales*
Harry Graham	*Ruthless Rhymes for Heartless Homes*

Opera, Soap

While it flourished, it seemed awful, but now that television has killed it, one remembers it with a nostalgic regret.

Diseases of

The people of Soapland are subject to a set of special ills. Temporary blindness, preceded by dizzy spells and headaches, is a common affliction of Soapland people. The condition usually clears up in six or eight weeks, but once in a while it develops into brain tumor and the patient dies. One script writer, apparently forgetting that General Mills was the sponsor of his serial, had one of his women characters go temporarily blind because of an allergy to chocolate cake. There was hell to pay, and the writer had to make the doctor in charge of the patient hastily change his diagnosis. Amnesia strikes almost as often in Soapland as the common cold in our world. There have been as many as eight or nine amnesia cases on the air at one time. The hero of *Rosemary* stumbled around in a daze for months last year. When he regained his memory, he found that in his wanderings he had been lucky enough to marry a true-blue sweetie. The third major disease is paralysis of the legs. This scourge usually attacks the good males. Like mysterious blindness, loss of the use of the legs may be either temporary or permanent. The hero of *Life Can Be Beautiful* was confined to a wheel chair until his death last March, but young Dr Malone, who was stricken with paralysis a year ago, is up and around again. I came upon only one crippled villain in 1947: Spencer Hart rolled through a three-month sequence of *Just Plain Bill* in a wheel chair. When their men are stricken, the good women become nobler than ever. A disabled hero is likely to lament his fate and indulge in self-pity now and then, but his wife or sweetheart never complains. She is capable of twice as much work, sacrifice, fortitude, endurance, ingenuity, and love as before. Joyce Jordan, M.D., had no interest in a certain male until he lost the use of both legs and took to a wheel chair. Then love began to bloom in her heart. . . .

The children of the soap towns are subject to pneumonia and strange fevers, during which their temperatures run to 105 or 106. Several youngsters are killed every year in automobile accidents or die of mysterious illnesses. Infantile paralysis and cancer are never mentioned in serials, but Starr, the fretful and errant wife in *Ma Perkins,* died of tuberculosis in March as punishment for her sins. There are a number of Soapland ailments that are never named or are vaguely identified by the doctors as "island fever" or "mountain rash." A variety of special maladies affect the glands in curious ways. At least three Ivorytown and Rinsoville doctors are baffled for several months every year by strange seizures and unique symptoms.

Next to physical ills, the commonest misfortune in the world of soap is false accusation of murder. . . .

Time in

Compared to the swift flow of time in the real world, it is a glacier movement. It took one male character in a soap opera three days to get an answer to the simple question, "Where have you been?" If, in *When a Girl Marries*, you missed an automobile accident that occurred on a Monday broadcast, you could pick it up the following Thursday and find the leading woman character still unconscious and her husband still moaning over her beside the wrecked car. In one sequence of *Just Plain Bill*, the barber of Hartville said, "It doesn't seem possible to me that Ralph Wilde arrived here only yesterday." It didn't seem possible to me, either, since Ralph Wilde had arrived, as mortal time goes, thirteen days before. Bill recently required four days to shave a man in the living room of the man's house. A basin of hot water Bill had placed on a table Monday (our time) was still hot on Thursday when his customer stopped talking and the barber went to work.

—James Thurber

Owls, Barn

Up to the year 1813, the barn owl had a sad time of it at Walton Hall. Its supposed mournful notes alarmed the aged housekeeper. She knew full well what sorrow it had brought into other houses when she was a young woman; and there was enough of mischief in the midnight wintry blast, without having it increased by the dismal screams of something which people knew very little about, and which everybody said was far too busy in the churchyard at night-time. Nay, it was a well-known fact, that if any person were sick in the neighbourhood, it would be for ever looking in at the window, and holding a conversation outside with somebody, they did not know whom. The gamekeeper agreed with her in everything she said on this important subject; and he always stood better in her books, when he had managed to shoot a bird of this bad and mischievous family. However, in 1813, on my return from the wilds of Guiana, having suffered myself and learned mercy, I broke in pieces the code of penal laws which the knavery of the gamekeeper and the lamentable ignorance of the other servants had hitherto put in force, far too successfully, to thin the numbers of this poor, harmless, unsuspecting tribe. On the ruin of the old gateway, against which, tradition says, the waves of the lake have dashed for the better part of a thousand years, I made a place with stone and mortar about four feet square, and affixed a thick oaken stick firmly into it. Huge masses of ivy now quite cover it. In about a month or so after it was finished, a pair of barn owls came and took up their abode in it. I threatened to strangle the keeper if ever, after this, he molested either the old birds or their young ones; and I assured the housekeeper that I would take upon myself the whole responsibility of all the sickness, woe, and sorrow that the new tenants might bring into the Hall. She made a low curtsy, as much as to say, "Sir, I fall into your will and pleasure." But I saw in her eye, that she had made up her mind to have to do with things of fearful and portentous shape, and to hear many a midnight wailing in the surrounding woods. I do not think that, up to the day of this old lady's death, which took place in her eighty-fourth year, she ever looked with pleasure or contentment on the barn owl, as it flew round the large sycamore trees which grew near the old ruined gateway.

—Charles Waterton

Paradise, The Earthly

There is an island far away, around which the sea-horses glisten, flowing on their white course against its shining shore; four pillars support it.

It is a delight to the eye, the plain which the hosts frequent in triumphant ranks; coracle races against chariot in the plain south of Findargad.

Pillars of white bronze are under it, shining through aeons of beauty, a lovely land through the ages of the world, on which many flowers rain down.

There is a huge tree there with blossom, on which the birds call at all hours; it is their custom that they all call together in concert every hour.

Colours of every hue gleam throughout the soft familiar fields; ranged round the music, they are ever joyful in the plain south of Argadnél.

Weeping and treachery are unknown in the pleasant familiar land; there is no fierce harsh sound there, but sweet music striking the ear.

Without sorrow, without grief, without death, without any sickness, without weakness, that is the character of Emhaim; such a marvel is rare.

Loveliness of a wondrous land, whose aspects are beautiful, whose view is fair, excellent; incomparable is its haze.

Then if one sees Airgthech, on which dragon-stones and crystals rain down, the sea makes the wave foam against the land, with crystal tresses from its mane.

Riches, treasures of every colour are in Cíuin, have they not been found? Listening to sweet music, drinking choice wine.

Golden chariots race across the plain of the sea rising with the tide to the sun; chariots of silver in Magh Mon, and of bronze without blemish.

Horses of golden yellow there on the meadow, other horses of purple colour; other noble horses beyond them, of the colour of the all-blue sky.

There comes at sunrise a fair man who lights up the level lands, he strides over the bright plain which the sea washes so that it becomes blood.

There comes a host across the clear sea, to the land they display their rowing; then they row to the bright stone from which a hundred songs arise.

Through the long ages it sings a melody which is not sad; the music swells up in choruses of hundreds, they do not expect decay nor death.

Emhnae of many shapes, beside the sea, whether it is near or whether it is far, where there are many thousands of motley-dressed women; the pure sea surrounds it.

If one has heard the sound of the music, the song of little birds from Imchíuin, a troop of women comes from the hill to the playing-field where it is.

Holiday-making and health come to the land around which laughter echoes; in Imchíuin with its purity come immortality and joy.

Through the perpetual good weather silver rains on the lands; a very white cliff under the glare of the sea, over which its heat spreads from the sun.

The host rides across Magh Mon, a lovely sport which is not weakly; in the many-coloured land with great splendour they do not expect decay nor death.

Listening to music in the night, and going to Ildathach the many-coloured land, a brilliance with clear splendour from which the white cloud glistens.

—Anon. seventh–eighth-century Irish (trans. K. H. Jackson)

Ambition not in thee
Do we expect to find,
Hydroptic of the wind;
Nor Envy with her food,

The Egyptian serpent brood;
Nor her, who though a human face surmounts,
Is a wild beast below,
A Sphinx persuasive, who
Makes the Narcissus new
Solicit echoes and disdain the founts;
Nor her who wastes, impertinent, in show
All the essential powder of her age.
O foolish Courtesy!
At whom the villagers sincere may laugh
Over their crooked staff.
O well found hermitage,
Whatever hour it be.

—Góngora (trans. E. M. Wilson)

PARROT, A

I saw it all, Polly, how when you call'd for sop
and your good friend the cook came and fill'd up your pan
you yerk'd it out deftly by beakfuls scattering it
away far as you might upon the sunny lawn
then summon'd with loud cry the little garden birds
to take their feast. Quickly came they flustering around
Ruddock and Merle and Finch squabbling among themselves
nor gave you thanks nor heed while you sat silently
watching, and I beside you in perplexity
lost in the maze of all mystery and all knowledge
felt how deep lieth the fount of man's benevolence
if a bird can share it and take pleasure in it.
If you, my bird, I thought, had a philosophy
it might be a sounder scheme than what our moralists
propound: because thou, Poll, livest in the darkness
which human Reason searching from outside would pierce,
but, being of so feeble a candle-power, can only
show up to view the cloud that it illuminates.
Thus reason'd I: then marvell'd how you can adapt
your wild bird-mood to endure your tame environment
the domesticities of English household life
and your small brass-wire cabin, who sh'dst live on wing
harrying the tropical branch-flowering wilderness:
Yet Nature gave you a gift of easy mimicry
whereby you have come to win uncanny sympathies
and morsell'd utterance of our Germanic talk

as schoolmasters in Greek will flaunt their hackey'd tags
φωνᾶντα συνετοῖσιν and κτῆμα ἐς ἀεί,
ἡ γλῶσσ' ὀμώμοχ', ἡ δὲ φρὴν ἀνώμοτος
tho' you with a better ear copy us more perfectly
nor without connotation as when you call'd for sop
all with that stumpy wooden tongue and vicious beak
that dry whistling shrieking tearing cutting pincer
now eagerly subservient to your cautious claws
exploring all varieties of attitude
in irrepressible blind groping for escape
—a very figure and image of man's soul on earth
the almighty cosmic Will fidgeting in a trap—
in your quenchless unknown desire for the unknown life
of which some homely British sailor robb'd you, alas!
'Tis all that doth your silly thoughts so busy keep
the while you sit moping like Patience on a perch
—*Wie viele Tag' und Nächte bist du geblieben!*
La possa delle gambe posta in tregue—
the impeccable spruceness of your grey-feather'd poll
a model in hairdressing for the dandiest old Duke
enough to qualify you for the House of Lords
or the Athenaeum Club, to poke among the nobs
great intellectual nobs and literary nobs
scientific nobs and Bishops *ex officio*:
nor lack you simulation of profoundest wisdom
such as men's features oft acquire in very old age
by mere cooling of passion and decay of muscle
by faint renunciation even of untold regrets;
who seeing themselves a picture of that which man should be
learn almost what it were to be what they are—not.
But you can never have cherish'd a determined hope
consciously to renounce or lose it, you will live
your three score years and ten idle and puzzle-headed
as any mumping monk in his unfurnish'd cell
in peace that, poor Polly, passeth Understanding—
merely because you lack what we men understand
by Understanding. Well! well! that's the difference
C'est la seule différence, mais c'est important.
Ah! your pale sedentary life! but would you change?
exchange it for one crowded hour of glorious life,
one blind furious tussle with a madden'd monkey
who would throttle you and throw your crude fragments away
shreds unintelligible of an unmeaning act

dans la profonde horreur de l'éternelle nuit?
Why ask? You cannot know. 'Twas by no choice of yours
that you mischanged for monkey's man's society,
'twas that British sailor drove you from Paradise—
Εἴθ ὤφελ' Ἀργους μὴ δ ιαπτάσθαι σκάφος!
I'd hold embargoes on such a ghastly traffic.
I am writing verses to you and grieve that you sh'd be
absolument incapable de les comprendre,
Tu, Polle, nescis ista nec potes scire:—
Alas! Iambic, scazon and alexandrine,
spondee or choriamb, all is alike to you—
my well-continued fanciful experiment
wherein so many strange verses amalgamate
on the secure bedrock of Milton's prosody:
not but that when I speak you will incline an ear
in critical attention lest by chance I might
possibly say something that was worth repeating:
I am adding (do you think?) pages to literature
that gouty excrement of human intellect
accumulating slowly and everlastingly
depositing, like guano on the Peruvian shore,
to be perhaps exhumed in some remotest age
(*piis secunda, vate me, detur fuga*)
to fertilize the scanty dwarf'd intelligence
of a new race of beings the unhallow'd offspring
of them who shall have quite dismember'd and destroy'd
our temple of Christian faith and fair Hellenic art
just as that monkey would, poor Polly, have done for you.

—Robert Bridges

Penis Rivalry

Whether, as some psychologists believe, some women suffer from penis envy, I am not sure. I am quite certain, however, that all males without exception, whatever their age, suffer from penis rivalry, and that this trait has now become a threat to the future existence of the human race.

Behind every quarrel between men, whether individually or collectively, one can hear the taunt of a little urchin: "My prick (or my father's) is bigger than yours (or your father's), and can pee further."

Nearly all weapons, from the early spear and sword down to the modern revolver and rocket, are phallic symbols. Men, to be sure, also fashion traps, most forms of which are vaginal symbols, but they never take a pride in them as they do in their weapons. The epic poets frequently give a loving and detailed description of some weapon, and, when heroes exchange gifts in earnest of friendship, weapons figure predominantly. But where in literature can one find a loving description of a trap, or hear of one as a precious gift?

Today our phallic toys have become too dangerous to be tolerated. I see little hope for a peaceful world until men are excluded from the realm of foreign policy altogether and all decisions concerning international relations are reserved for women, preferably married ones.

I would go further and say that, while men should still as in the past be permitted to construct machines, it should be for women to decide what kinds of machines shall be constructed.

Phrase Books, Foreign

Compared with the compilers of phrase books for tourists traveling abroad, the so-called surrealist poets are amateurs. For example:

At the Doctor's

Is your digestion all right?
The medicine was no good.
Shake the bottle.
For external use only.
You have broken your arm.
He has fractured his skull.
I have had a bad concussion.
I am injured.
Have you sprained your ankle?
I must bandage your foot.
You are badly bruised.
He has an internal ulcer.
The illness gets better (worse).
Are you feeling better?
The cut is healed but you can see the scar.
I must bandage your wounds.
I can't hear.
I am deaf.
She is deaf and dumb.
You must go to an ear specialist.
Your middle-ear is inflamed.
Where does the oculist live?
I am shortsighted.
He is longsighted.
She is blind.

I need spectacles.
He squints a little.

—Viola Ellis, *Serbo-Croatian Phrase Book*

In 1945 an Italian-English phrase book was hastily compiled in Florence to promote a better understanding between the Florentines and British and American troops. It contained the following entry:

Italian	English
Posso presentare il conte.	Meet the cunt.

Plants

Most poems about plants are even more indifferent to their natural properties than poems about animals. (In both cases D. H. Lawrence is a happy exception.)

The Fear of Flowers

The nodding oxeye bends before the wind,
The woodbine quakes lest boys their flowers should find,
And prickly dog-rose, spite of its array,
Can't dare the blossom-seeking hand away,
While thistles wear their heavy knobs of bloom
Proud as a war-horse wears its haughty plume,
And by the roadside danger's self defy;
On commons where pined sheep and oxen lie,
In ruddy pomp and ever thronging mood
It stands and spreads like danger in a wood,
And in the village street, where meanest weeds
Can't stand untouched to fill their husks with seeds,
The haughty thistle o'er all danger towers,
In every place the very wasp of flowers.

—John Clare

The Lettuce

People have included this among your praises—that once upon a time you are said to have cured Augustus when he was ill. I certainly would not have wished you to heal that man, infamous from having banished Ovid and slain Cicero. But I imagine that you knew neither of them, and I do not wonder that you were willing to confer a favour on the tyrant of the world. You are indeed a useful medicine to all tyrants, and madness flees when touched with your divine coolness. Gird, I pray you, their heads with a better crown; and, if you can, bring succour through them to this world. At your command, love, the greatest of tyrants, sometimes abandons inflamed hearts. It is a false love, for you do not attempt to expel true love, which has the title of a just king and deserves to be loved. That dog-star lust which slays green things with its fire and gives birth to monsters is rightly hated by you.

—Abraham Cowley (trans. from Latin by Frederick Brittain)

The ageing of a plant is quite different from that of an animal. In an animal the processes of growth occur all over the body until maturity, and the animal may then continue to live a long time even though growth has stopped. In a plant the processes of growth are localised at the growing tips of the stems. In a corn plant, for example, cells at the tip are continually dividing to form new leaves. Above the youngest leaves there always remains a zone of newly formed cells, called the meristem, from which subsequent growth will come. The manner of growth of a corn plant from its tip is, to use a far-fetched analogy, rather like the growth of a knitted woolen sock from the needles at one end. It follows, therefore, that a plant is not the same age all over; its lower leaves may be three or four months old while the uppermost leaf is only a few hours old. So long as the plant is growing, new meristem cells are being formed at the tip of the stem.

Thus in time-age the tip is perpetually young. But it is certainly not perpetually young in physiological age. In a young plant the meristem cells give rise to juvenile leaves; in an older plant they give rise to adult leaves and eventually to flowers. And it appears that this inexorable process of ageing goes on even when the plant has a constant supply of nutrients and constant conditions of light.

. . . Recently at the University of Manchester we have begun to study the ageing of a plant under constant environmental conditions. The plant we use is the common floating duckweed, which can be found in almost any stagnant pond. Each leaflike frond produces a "daughter" frond from a pocket to its side; when this "daughter" is fully grown, a second daughter is produced from a similar pocket on the other side of the parent. By the time the second daughter is grown the first daughter frond has broken away and become a separate plant, and out of the empty pocket a third daughter appears. This is followed by a fourth daughter in the pocket formerly occupied by the second daughter. In this way a mother frond may bring forth up to five daughter fronds, after which the mother frond dies. The life expectation of a mother frond is about 45 days. The five daughter fronds produced in this time are similar to five leaves on a normal plant.

The remarkable fact is that even in the most carefully controlled artificial environment each of the daughter fronds is smaller than the one before, so that the fourth and fifth daughters are less than half the size of the first daughter. To put it another way, the meristem cells of the mother frond are, as it were, "running down".

. . . But that is not the entire story. If it were, then successive generations in a colony of duckweed plants would become smaller and smaller and ultimately disappear. This does not happen; indeed the average size of fronds in a colony remains about the same. The reason is that the impoverished fourth or fifth daughter fronds reverse the trend and produce "granddaughter" fronds that are larger than themselves. The process of ageing during the life of a frond is followed by a process of rejuvenation. Each new frond in a duckweed colony is in fact part of a cycle of ageing and rejuvenation. Physiological age, unlike time-age, can be put in reverse.

—Eric Ashby

Pleasure

It is nonsense to speak of "higher" and "lower" pleasures. To a hungry man it is, rightly, more important that he eat than that he philosophize. All pleasures are equally good, but there is no pleasure which the Evil One cannot, according to our natures, use to tempt us into evil. If we yield, no matter what the particular pleasure be, the same thing always happens: what at first was a pleasurable activity becomes an addiction which gives us no pleasure but from which we cannot break loose. Compulsive eaters, drinkers, and smokers no longer enjoy food, alcohol, tobacco; compulsive seducers, like Don Giovanni, no longer enjoy sexual pleasure. But it is usually by the bait of pleasure that the Evil One first leads us astray. There is a certain kind of Catholic novelist who would rewrite the fall of Eve like this:

> And when the woman saw that the tree was poisonous and that it was hideous to look at, she took of the fruit thereof and did eat.

We are not born quite so corrupt as that.

All pleasures are good; but there is an antithesis between "holy" and "unholy" joy.

Praise, Epithets of

All peoples in the cultural phase which one might call "epic" give praise-epithets to any being they regard as numinous. In Greek and Norse epic poetry, praise-epithets are reserved for gods and heroic warriors. But to the cattle-raising tribe of the Bahima in Uganda, cattle are just as numinous as heroes, and therefore accorded praise-epithets.

Abatangaaza

(by Kagarame, son of Buzoora, chief herdsman of the Omugabe Kahaya. c. 1918)

1 At Katunguru near Rurangizi, She Who Teases lay back on her horns and so did She Who Approaches The Fighters;
2 At Kahama near Kambarango, we deceived The One Who Drives Back The Others with the calf of The One Whose Horns Are Well Spread pretending it was hers.
3 At Rwenfukuzi near Ndeego, the lazy ones of Migina marvelled at the white patch on the daughter of The One With The Blaze On Her Forehead as she gambolled;
4 At Kabura and Nyansheko, they marvelled at the horns of the strawberry beast of Rwaktungu, She Whose Horns Are Not Stunted,
5 At Kiyegayega near Migina, the varied herd made a noise as they went to Rusheesha;
6 At Rwekubo near Kinanga, the herd walked proudly having killed a loaned beast,
7 She Whose Horns Stand Out Above The Herd gave birth and so did She Who Has Straightened Our Her Horns.
8 She Who Prevents Others' Approaching became friendly with The One Whose Horns Are As Straight As Planks.
9 At Akkabare at Nyamukondo's, they prepared their camps;
10 At Igwanjura and Wabinyonyi, they had slim bodies.
11 At Byembogo, they played with the antelopes;
12 At Ntarama, they borrowed the dress of the sorcerers,
13 At Kakona near Rubaya, we gave them another bell when they refused to increase.
14 At Shagama and Rwabigyemana, they displayed the tips of their horns;
15 At Bunonko in Rwanda, they danced about and played in the light rain;
16 At Nsikizi in Rwanda, they prevented the bell of The Leader from ringing.
17 At Burunga at the home of The One Who Is Not Dissuaded From Fighting,*
18 At Rwoma and Ihondaniro, they returned facing Kaaro;
19 At Nyumba and Rwemiganda, they were patient in death;
20 At Obukomago and Nyambindo, they died as the princes died in Buganda;
21 Alas! I am heartbroken by the groaning of The One Who Returns Home with Pride. . . .

—H. F. Morris, *The Heroic Recitations of the Bahima of Ankole (Uganda)*

*The name of a person, not a cow.

Prayer, Nature of

To pray is to pay attention to something or someone other than oneself. Whenever a man so concentrates his attention—on a landscape, a poem, a geometrical problem, an idol, or the True God—that he completely forgets his own ego and desires, he is praying. Choice of attention—to pay attention to *this* and ignore *that*—is to the inner life what choice of action is to the outer. In both cases, a man is responsible for his choice and must accept the consequences, whatever they may be. The primary task of the schoolteacher is to teach children, in a secular context, the technique of prayer.

> Intellectual adherence is never owed to anything whatsoever, for it is never in any degree a voluntary thing. Attention alone is voluntary. It alone forms the subject of an obligation.
>
> —Simone Weil

> Tell me to what you pay attention and I will tell you who you are.
>
> —Ortega y Gasset

> To pray is to think about the meaning of life.
>
> —Ludwig Wittgenstein

Prayers, Petitionary

Our wishes and desires—to pass an exam, to marry the person we love, to sell our house at a good price—are involuntary and, therefore, not in themselves prayers. They only become prayers when addressed to a God whom we believe to know better than ourselves whether we should be granted or denied what we ask. A petition does not become a prayer unless it ends with the words, spoken or unspoken, "nevertheless not as I will but as Thou wilt."

> Your cravings as a human animal do not become a prayer just because it is God whom you ask to attend to them.
>
> —Dag Hammarskjöld

> The Father will never give the child a stone that asks for bread; but I am not sure that He will never give a child a stone who asks for a stone. If the Father say, "My child, that is a stone; it is no bread," and the child answer, "I am sure it is bread; I want it," may it not be well that he should try his "bread"?
>
> —George Macdonald

> He took his hands from his head, and clasping them together, said a little prayer. It may be doubted whether he quite knew for what he was praying. The idea of praying for her soul, now that she was dead, would have scandalized him. He certainly was not praying for his own soul. I

think he was praying that God might save him from being glad that his wife was dead.

—A. Trollope

Make me chaste and continent, but not just yet.

—St Augustine

"Heaven help me," she prayed, "to be decorative and to do right."

—Ronald Firbank

The Lord's Prayer

Doctor Thornton's Tory Translation, Translated out of its disguise in the Classical & Scotch languages into the vulgar English.

Our Father Augustus Caesar, who art in these thy Substantial Astronomical Telescopic Heavens, Holiness to Thy Name or Title, & reverence to thy Shadow. Thy Kingship come upon Earth first & then in Heaven. Give us day by day our Real Taxed Substantial Money bought Bread; deliver from the Holy Ghost whatever cannot be Taxed; for all is debts & Taxes between Caesar & us & one another; lead us not to read the Bible, but let our Bible be Virgil & Shakespeare; & deliver us from Poverty in Jesus, that Evil One. For thine is the Kingship or Allegoric Godship, & the Power, or War, & the Glory, or Law, Ages after Ages in thy descendants; for God is only an Allegory of Kings & nothing Else. Amen.

—William Blake

Almighty God, Father of all mercies, we pray Thee to be gracious with those who fly this night. Guard and protect those of us who venture out into the darkness of Thy heaven. Uphold them on Thy wings. Keep them safe both in body and soul and bring them back to us. Give to us all the courage and strength for the hours that are ahead; give to them rewards according to their efforts. Above all else, our Father, bring peace to Thy world. May we go forward trusting in Thee and knowing we are in Thy presence now and forever. Amen.

—Prayer by Chaplain Downey, ending the briefing session preliminary to the bombing of Nagasaki

Prose, Annihilating

To be real, it must be written in response to some specific event or person that has aroused the author's anger and scorn. This I think, disqualifies Housman's savage remarks, funny though they are, because it seems that he wrote them *in vacuo* before he had found the victim to whom they would apply.

Mr James Macpherson,—I received your foolish and impudent letter. Any violence offered me I shall do my best to repel; and what I cannot do for myself, the law shall do for me. I hope I shall never be deterred from detecting what I think a cheat, by the menaces of a ruffian.

What would you have me retract? I thought your book an imposture; I think it an imposture still. For this opinion I have given my reasons to the public, which I here dare you to refute. Your rage I defy. Your abilities, since your Homer, have not been so formidable; and what I hear of your morals, inclines me to pay regard not to what you shall say, but to what you shall prove. You may print this if you will.

—Dr Johnson

We do not suppose all preservers of game to be so bloodily inclined that they would prefer the death of a poacher to his staying away. Their object is to preserve game; they have no objection to preserving the lives of their fellow-creatures also, if both can exist at the same time; if not, the least worthy of God's creatures must fall—the rustic without a soul—not the Christian partridge—not the immortal pheasant—not the rational woodcock, or the accountable hare.

—Sydney Smith

The freedoms of the young three—who were, by-the-way, not in their earliest bloom either—were thus bandied about in the void of the gorgeous valley without even a consciousness of its shrill, its recording echoes. . . . The immodesty was too colossal to be anything but inane. And they were alive, the slightly stale three: they talked, they laughed, they sang, they shrieked, they romped, they scaled the pinnacle of publicity and perched on it, flapping their wings, whereby they were shown in possession of many of the movements of life.

—Henry James

Prose, Impressionistic

Dined *versus* six o' the clock. Forgot that there was a plum-pudding (I have added, lately, *eating* to my "family of vices") and had dined before I knew it. Drank half of a bottle of some sort of spirits—probably spirits of wine; for what they call brandy, rum, etc., etc., here is nothing but spirits of wine, colored accordingly. Did *not* eat two apples, which were placed by way of dessert. Fed the two cats, the hawk, and the tame (but not tamed) crow. Read Mitford's *History of Greece*—Xenophon's *Retreat of the Ten Thousand.* Up to this present moment writing, 6 minutes before 8 o' the clock—French hours, not Italian.

Hear the carriage—order pistols and great coat—necessary articles. Weather cold—carriage open, and inhabitants rather savage—rather treacherous and highly inflamed by politics. Fine fellows though—good materials for a nation. Out of chaos God made a world, and out of high passions come a people.

Clock strikes—going out to make love. Somewhat perilous but not disagreeable. Memorandum—a new screen put up today. It is rather antique but will do with a little repair.

—Lord Byron

Prose, Judges'

Mr Gluckstein can take an action at law if he likes. If he hesitates to take that course, or takes it and fails, then his only recourse lies in an appeal to that sense of honour which is popularly supposed to reside among robbers of a humbler type.

—Mr Justice Macnaughten

If the defendant is to be believed, he combined the forbearance of a Christian Martyr with the dignity of a Grandee of Spain. The defendant, it will be remembered, is a company promoter.

—Another Judge

Prose, Purple

Oh, young boys, if your eyes ever read these pages, pause and beware. The knowledge of evil is ruin, and the continuance in it hell. That little matter—that beginning of evil—it will be like the snow-flake detached by the breath of air from the mountain-top, which, as it rushes down, gains size and strength and impetus, till it has swollen to the mighty and irresistible avalanche that overwhelms garden and field and village in a chaos of undistinguishable death.

Kibbroth-Hattavah! Many and many a young Englishman has perished there. Many and many a happy English boy, the jewel of his mother's heart—brave, and beautiful, and strong—lies buried there. Very pale their shadows rise before us—the shadows of our young brothers who have sinned and suffered. From the sea and the sod, from foreign graves and English churchyards, they start up and throng around us in the paleness of their fall. May every schoolboy who reads this page be warned by the waving of their wasted hands, from that burning marl of passion where they found nothing but shame and ruin, polluted affections, and an early grave.

—F. W. Farrar

Prose, Woozy

No St George any more to be heard of; no more dragon-slaying possible: this child,* born on St George's Day, can only make manifest the dragon,

*This child: Turner.

not slay him, sea-serpent as he is; whom the English Andromeda, not fearing, takes for her lord. The fairy English Queen once thought to command the waves, but it is the sea-dragon now who commands her valleys; of old the Angel of the Sea ministered to them, but now the Serpent of the Sea; where once flowed clear springs now spreads the black Cocytus pool; and the fair blooming of the Hesperid meadows fades into ashes beneath the Nereid's Guard.

Yes, Albert of Nuremberg; the time has at last come. Another nation has arisen in the strength of its Black anger; another hand has portrayed the spirit of its toil. Crowned with fire, and with the wings of the bat.

—Ruskin

Puns

M. Denis de Rougemont told me of this dedication by a French authoress to her publisher. I have, unfortunately, forgotten her name.

Je méditerai,
Tu m'éditeras.

I would have said that a pathetic pun was impossible, until I came across this verse by Praed:

Tom Mill was used to blacken eyes
  Without the fear of sessions;
Charles Medlar loathed false quantities
  As much as false professions;
Now Mill keeps order in the land,
  A magistrate pedantic;
And Medlar's feet repose unscanned
  Beneath the wide Atlantic.

Puritanism

. . . Theologically, Protestantism was either a recovery, or a development, or an exaggeration (it is not for the literary historian to say which) of Pauline theology. . . . In the mind of a Tyndale or Luther, as in the mind of St Paul himself, this theology was by no means an intellectual construction made in the interests of speculative thought. It springs directly out of a highly specialized religious experience; and all its affirmations, when separated from that context, become meaningless or else mean the opposite of what was intended. . . . The experience is that of catastrophic conversion. The man who has passed through it feels like one who has waked from nightmare into ecstasy. Like an accepted lover, he feels that he has done nothing, and never could have done anything, to deserve such astonishing happiness. Never again can he "crow from the dunghill of desert". All the initiative has been on God's side; all has been free, unbounded grace. . . . His own puny and ridiculous efforts would be as helpless to retain the joy as they would have been to achieve it in the first place. Fortunately they need not. Bliss is not for sale, cannot be earned. "Works" have no "merit", though, of course faith, inevitably, even unconsciously, flows out into works of love at once. He is not saved because he does works of love: he does works of love because he is saved. It is faith alone that has saved him: faith bestowed by sheer gift. From this buoyant humility, this farewell to the self with all its good resolutions, anxiety, scruples, and motive-scratchings, all the Protestant doctrines originally sprang. . . .

It follows that nearly every association which now clings to the word *puritan* has to be eliminated when we are thinking of the early Protestants. Whatever they were, they were not sour, gloomy, or severe; nor did their enemies bring any such charge against them. On the contrary, Harpsfield (in his *Life of More*) describes their doctrines as "easie, short, pleasant lessons" which lulled their unwary victim in "so sweete a sleepe as he was euer after loth to wake from it". For More, a Protestant was one "dronke of the new must of lewd lightnes of minde and vayne gladnesse of harte". . . . Luther, he said, had made converts precisely because "he spiced al the poison" with "libertee". . . . Protestantism was not too grim, but too glad, to be true; "I could for my part be verie wel content that sin and pain all were as shortlye gone as Tyndale telleth us."

—C. S. Lewis

Reformation, Vocabulary of the

The Reformation seems, with its insistence on the *inwardness* of all true grace, to have been but another manifestation of that steady shifting inwards of the centre of gravity of human consciousness which we have already observed in the scientific outlook. That shift is, in a larger sense, the story told by the whole history of the Aryan languages. Thus *religion* itself, which had formerly been used only of external observances or of monastic orders, took on at about this time its modern, subjective meaning. Now it was that *piety*, differentiating itself from *pity*, began to acquire its present sense. *Godly*, *godlinesss*, and *godless* are first found in Tyndale's writings, and *evangelical* and *sincere* are words which have been noted by a modern writer as being new at this time and very popular among the Protestants. The great word *Protestant* itself was applied formerly to the German Princes who had dissented from the decision of the Diet of Spires in 1529, and together with *Reformation* it now acquired its new and special meaning, while the old words, *dissent* and *disagree*, were transferred at about the same time from material objects to matters of opinion. . . .

Very soon after the Reformation we find alongside the syllables of tenderness and devotion a very pretty little vocabulary of abuse. *Bigoted, faction, factious, malignant, monkish, papistical, pernicious, popery* are among the products of the struggle between Catholic and Protestant; and the terms *Roman, Romanist,* and *Romish* soon acquired such a vituperative sense that it became necessary to evolve *Roman Catholic* in order to describe the adherents of that faith without giving offence to them. The later internecine struggles among the Protestants themselves gave us *Puritan, precise, libertine*—reminiscent of a time when "liberty" of thought was assumed as a matter of course to include licence of behaviour—*credulous, superstitious, selfish, selfishness* and the awful Calvinistic word *reprobate.* It was towards the end of the Puritan ascendancy that *atone* and *atonement* (at-one-ment) acquired their present strong suggestion of legal expiation, and it may not be without significance that the odious epithet *vindictive* was then for the first time applied approvingly to the activities of the Almighty Himself.

—Owen Barfield

Renaissance, The

The Middle Ages paid their normal attention to the ordinary affairs of men, as all normal attention must be paid, *semper, ubique, ab omnibus.* When, however, they thought about those affairs, they imagined them in terms of God and grace. And eventually their energy could not live up to the dazzling circle of dogma within which it operated. God was everywhere the circumstance of all lives. Men had been over-nourished on such metaphysics, and the Renascence abandoned the idea of that universal Circumstance to attend to lesser circumstances. Change, sin, and intelligent delight in the creation had been at work, and now they did not so much break bounds as withdraw from the bounds. The thought of the Middle Ages was not limited, but perhaps its philosophical vocabulary was. Persistently and universally the stress changed. The Lord Alexander VI was not worse than some of the medieval Popes but he was—ever so little—different. He and Julius II and Leo X all accepted the Mass. But it is difficult to think of any of them as being primarily and profoundly concerned with the Mass. They were probably—even Julius—more humane than Urban VI but they were also more human. . . . Erasmus was as Christian as—and much less anti-Papal (so to call it) than—Dante. But the monks, the heavy and certainly stupid monks, who denounced Erasmus were, in a sense, right. There was a good deal to be said from their point of view, though (as so often happens) they themselves were precisely the wrong people to say it. Erasmus can be studied and admired as a devout scholar. He can hardly be ranked as a scholarly devotee. Leonardo was probably a pious, if sceptical, scientist. But he could hardly be said, except in a highly mathematical manner, to exalt piety by science. The opponents of either were no more pious or devout than scholarly or scientific. The habitual and rather worn religious intelligence of the time was not so high that it could afford to abuse Leonardo or Erasmus, as those periods might have done, with a better chance, to which grace was still a dreadful reality. . . . The Middle Ages had desired greatness and glory and gold as much as their children; virtue after them was not so very much impaired. But the metaphysical vision which had illuminated those otherwise base things was passing; they were no longer mythological beyond themselves. Man was left to take glory in, and to glorify, himself and his works. Had chances been different, there might have been a revival of the old wisdom of Christ as *anthropos*; the secrets of Christendom might have enriched with new significance the material world. It was not to be; the *anthropos* had been forgotten for the *theos*, and now the other *anthropos*, the Adam of Augustine, the *homo sapiens* of science, preoccupied European attention.

—Charles Williams

The Renaissance was, as much as anything, a revolt from the logic of the Middle Ages. We speak of the Renaissance as the birth of rationalism; it was in many ways the birth of irrationalism. It is true that the medieval Schoolmen, who had produced the finest logic that the world has ever seen, had in later years produced more logic than the world can ever be expected to stand. They had loaded and lumbered up the world with libraries of mere logic; and some effort was bound to be made to free it from such endless chains of deduction. Therefore, there was in the Renaissance a wild touch of revolt, not against religion but against reason. . . . When all is said, there is something a little sinister in the number of mad people there are in Shakespeare. We say that he uses his fools to brighten the dark background of tragedy; I think he sometimes uses them to darken it. . . . What is felt faintly even in Shakespeare is felt far more intensely in the other Elizabethan and Jacobean dramatists; they seem to go in for dancing ballets of lunatics and choruses of idiots, until sanity is the exception rather than the rule. . . .

The Elizabethan epoch was of intense interest, of intensive intelligence; of piercing sharpness and delicacy in certain forms of diplomacy and domestic policy, and the arts of the ambassador and the courtier; and especially in one or two great men, of vivid and concentrated genius in the study of certain particular problems of character. But it was not spacious. . . . Its special and specialist studies involved men in almost everything except fresh air. In literature it was the age of conceits. In politics it was the age of conspiracies. . . . It is almost in a double sense that we talk of Shakespeare's plots. In almost every case, it is a plot about a plot.

—G. K. Chesterton

Revenge

. . . The lord of Chateau-roux in France maintained in the castle a man whose eyes he had formerly put out, but who, by long habit, recollected the ways of the castle, and the steps leading to the towers. Seizing an opportunity of revenge, and meditating the destruction of the youth, he fastened the inward doors of the castle, and took the only son and heir of the governor of the castle to the summit of a high tower, from whence he was seen with the utmost concern by the people beneath. The father of the boy hastened thither, and, struck with terror, attempted by every possible means to procure the ransom of his son, but received for answer, that this could not be effected, but by the same mutilation of those lower parts, which he had likewise inflicted on him. The father, having in vain entreated mercy, at length assented, and caused a violent blow to be struck on his body; and the people around him cried out lamentably, as if he had suffered mutilation. The blind man asked him where he felt the greatest pain? When he replied in his reins, he declared it was false and prepared to precipitate the boy. A second blow was given, and the lord of the castle asserting that the greatest pain was at his heart, the blind man expressing his disbelief, again carried the boy to the summit of the tower. The third time, however, the father, to save his son, really mutilated himself; and when he exclaimed that the greatest pain was in his teeth; "It is true," said he, "as a man who has had experience should be believed, and thou hast in part revenged my injuries. I shall meet death with more satisfaction, and thou shalt neither beget any other son, nor receive comfort from this." Then, precipitating himself and the boy from the summit of the tower, their limbs were broken, and both instantly expired. The knight ordered a monastery built on the spot for the soul of the boy, which is still extant, and called De Doloribus. . . .

—Giraldus Cambrensis

Roads

Up hill, down hill,
Stands still, but goes to mill every day.

—Ozarks riddle

Tracing the Remains of the Roman Roads

Evidence of the alignment is of course the fundamental characteristic, and it is the rigidly straight length of modern road ending suddenly for no apparent reason and continuing only as a winding road that directs attention upon the map to many a Roman line. A word of caution is necessary, however, for straight lengths of roads across commons, or the enclosed land of former commons, often show very similar features, the straight length terminating at the end of the area with which the enclosure surveyors were dealing, but a little experience will soon enable such roads to be easily recognised.

Where substantial remains of the *agger* still exist, even if derelict, overgrown or under plough, the road can generally be recognised fairly easily, but in many cases the typical indications are very inconspicuous, although really very definite, and call for some observational experience in recognising them. Most often the *agger* will then appear as a very slight broad ridge, hardly more than a gentle swelling in the ground; there may be indications of metalling if ploughing has scattered it, and the hard surface may be felt on probing just below the tilth. Or the road may have been removed, either for the sake of the stone which could be usefully employed elsewhere, or to clear the land for better cultivation; in these cases a wide shallow hollow may mark its course, especially on a hill where water action would tend to deepen the original slight excavation. If the road is running along a hillside a slight terracing may remain even if it is crossing a field long under plough, but the break in the slope may be so slight that it will perhaps only be apparent when viewed in certain lights and from a favourable angle. The ditches of the road frequently disappear by silting, and the resultant increase in the top-soil depth may result in excessive growth of the crop at that point, with consequent "lodging" in wet weather. These are the kinds of signs which necessarily show most clearly from the air and so can best be studied on air photographs when these are available. It must be emphasized, however, that many such signs are seasonal in character, owing to the growth of the crops, whilst the time of day may also be important in its effect upon the lighting of the picture: thus it does not follow that such photographs, taken at any time not suitably chosen, will show the details required.

The road when derelict is nearly always covered with soil, owing to the accumulation of fallen leaves and weed growth, and when it is under grass this may become parched in dry weather, owing to the stony layer beneath, and appear as a brown or light-coloured strip, recognizable as one walks over it and showing very plainly indeed from the air.

Hedgerow lines, sometimes of considerable length, and lanes or minor roads, with footpaths and tracks, often mark parts of the course and are very significant if a long line of them can be traced across country, even when in discontinuous lengths upon the same alignment. Parish boundaries, often of very early Saxon origin, follow Roman roads very frequently and are sometimes a useful indication that the line is really old.

In some places however, especially in forest areas upon soft soil, the road will be entirely invisible, not even a hedgerow marking its course, but it does not follow that the road is not there. Experience has shown that it may have survived with its metalled surface quite intact but entirely buried below the level of cultivation. Such roads are necessarily hard to trace, and indeed this can only be done when some other parts of the route are more normally visible so that the alignment can be established. Probing along the line may then enable the invisible portions to be recovered. In some areas it seems probable that routes at present incompletely known will eventually be proved in this way.

When the roads have remained in use there is usually much less of interest to be found. The alignment will be clearly shown by the course of the road, and probably the most distinctive sign of its Roman origin will be the abrupt changes of direction, always taking place at a high point from which the sighting could be done. Often the road can be seen to be well raised, especially if it is a minor road which has not suffered greatly from wear, but if the soil is soft, and especially in hilly regions, the road may have greatly worn down during the centuries of neglect and far from being raised, will now be found in a deep hollow. Sometimes the hollow has become too waterlogged for use and a new road has taken its place alongside, in which case the hollow will be so overgrown that its existence may hardly be suspected as one passes it. Another indication of Roman origin in a road still in use is its behaviour when an obstacle is encountered; the road will negotiate this by short straight lengths, resuming the original line upon the far side, and if a steep hill has to be climbed the road may do so in a distinct zig-zag course which will very likely have been modified in later times to ease the gradient and hairpin bends, but it may still be traceable in its original form, now partly abandoned, as terraces upon the hillside. Narrow enclosed plots along the side of a road are nearly always evidence that the road is old, and they may mask its original straightness considerably.

Place names are, of course, very useful evidence for the existence of a Roman road. To the Saxon a "street" was a road with a paved or metalled surface, and since the only examples of these he could meet were Roman it follows that his Streathams, Stratfords, Strattons, Strettons, Old Streets, and so on, indicate Roman roads with much certainty. Similar names derived from "Stone" or "Stane" such as Stanford, Stanstead,

Stone Street, Stane Street, are also significant. The name High Street where it occurs in open country and does not mean the village street is another, referring probably to the raised roadway, as do also such names as Ridgeway, The Ridge, Causeway, Long Causeway, Devil's Causeway, etc., while a derelict length of road may bear the name Green Street. Names such as Street Farm and Street Field in country areas are very significant, as the name almost certainly refers to such a road, and in the case of a field may establish its like position very closely.

—Ivan D. Margary

Roads

I love roads:
The goddesses that dwell
Far along invisible
Are my favourite gods.

Roads go on
While we forget, and are
Forgotten like a star
That shoots and is gone.

On this earth 'tis sure
We men have not made
Anything that doth fade
So soon, so long endure.

The hill road wet with rain
In the sun would not gleam
Like a winding stream
If we trod it not again.

They are lonely
While we sleep, lonelier
For lack of the traveller
Who is now a dream only.

From dawn's twilight
And all the clouds like sheep
On the mountains of sleep
They wind into the night.

The next turn may reveal
Heaven: upon the crest
The close pine clump, at rest
And black, may Hell conceal.

Often footsore, never
Yet of the road I weary,
Though long and steep and dreary,
As it winds on for ever.

Helen of the roads,
The mountain ways of Wales
And the Mabinogian tales,
Is one of the true gods,

Abiding in the trees,
The threes and fours so wise,
The larger companies,
That by the roadside be,

And beneath the rafter
Else uninhabited
Excepting by the dead;
And it is her laughter

At morn and night I hear,
When the thrush cock sings
Bright irrelevant things,
And then the chanticleer

Calls back to their own night
Troops that make loneliness
With their light footsteps' press,
As Helen's own are light.

Now all roads lead to France*
And heavy is the tread
Of the living; but the dead
Returning lightly dance:

Whatever the road bring
To me or take from me,
They keep me company
With their pattering,

Crowding the solitude
Of the loops over the downs,
Hushing the roar of towns
And their brief multitude.

—Edward Thomas

*The poem was written during World War I.

The Middleness of The Road

The road at the top of the rise
Seems to come to an end
And take off into the skies.
So at the distant bend

It seems to go into a wood,
The place of standing still
As long the trees have stood.
But say what Fancy will,

The mineral drops that explode
To drive my ton of car
Are limited to the road.
They deal with near and far,

But have almost nothing to do
With the absolute flight and rest
The universal blue
And local green suggest.

—Robert Frost

Sometimes a new road will follow an old one for miles together, ignoring the crossing tracks, and sometimes, turning suddenly where four roads meet, it leaves its own prolongation to the traffic of rare farm carts and lurching gipsy vans. If we follow the obsolete routes at such a crossing, between their high banks full of flowers and birds' nests, we often see how they lead to some feature of vanished importance—some dry common where we still trace the pit-dwellings, some deep and easily accessible spring, or some sly passage between the hills which a new road strides over. The old tracks have almost died out of use with the gradual shifting of the population. But it is by following their covert windings, and not by rushing along new coach-roads, or still newer motor-roads, that we often discover the finest specimens of old local architecture, and the seats of legend. This is true of the by-lanes in most English counties, but doubly true in Wales. Of old dwellings, indeed, we shall not here find many, except of the humblest kind. In Wales, the houses of ancient kings and chiefs, or of the later squires who inherited their lands and their leadership, are often shrunken and insignificant. But if we care for the ancient traditions, this farmhouse was the summer palace of an extinguished dynasty, that cottage with white walls beneath the sycamores, was the birthplace of a famous bard; and we can still see the stream of rustic life flowing persistently through the old hollow lanes. Here the fine new road that runs down the middle of the valley only dates from the coaching days, though English traffic began to be wrested into new and directer channels by the Romans some sixteen hundred years earlier.

Let us fly westward on the wings of the imagination into the heart of the Mid-Welsh kingdom of Powys, or else take train or car to Welshpool and on to Llanfair Caereinion, and push thence from railhead towards the sea. Boldly above the Banwy river looms the great hill called Moel Bentych, with its legend of a dull-witted dragon or "gwyber" (i.e. wyvern), which was befooled and slain by a cunning blacksmith with a spiky tar-baby. Our road cuts over a low pass behind it to a substantial stone bridge at Llanerfyl, and another at Garthbeibio, three miles beyond. But do not think that it was by this fine high road, or by any road on the site of it, that in the days when the kings of Powys held the fat lands of Shropshire they came riding in the spring weather from Pengwern, which we call Shrewsbury, to their "hafod" of Llyssun, halfway down that sunny bank sprinkled with red Hereford oxen. If they had occasion to call at Llanfair, they did not cross the shining Banwy by Neuadd Bridge, as we do today, because there was no bridge then, but joined the track from Meifod, and then followed the steep and delightful lane which winds at the dry feet of the hills round all the crooks and crannies of the rocky river until it reaches Llyssun. Thenceforward the old road and the new coincide as far as the hamlet called the Foel, that is, the bare hill-top; for beyond Llangadfan the river runs through marshy meadows, and the new road no more tries to cut straight across them than the old did. Between the Foel and Garthbeibio church, high on the hillside, the peat-stained Twrch (not the same Twrch which we met at Llanuwchllyn) comes marching like a highlander into the vale. But before we reach Foel Bridge the old road has left us; it creeps to the right, up the Twrch stream, and crosses it where its bounding rocks meet closest, by a pack-bridge of a single span. Then we know why Garthbeibio church is perched so high on the hill. Though inconveniently placed for most of its modern congregation, it stands on the direct route from the old bridge, up the opposite side of the valley, over the moors that lead to the Dovey and the Dee. And the strange thing is that though the new road has invited them for more than a hundred years, the tramps and vagrants who form more of a separate caste in Wales than in England have never learnt to use it. On the high road, you would almost think that vagrancy had ceased. Follow the hill-trails between the little ancient bridges, high over the curlew-haunted moors among the roots of the mountains, and there, twice or thrice in a week, you will meet that shuffling, half-savage figure, red-haired and sullen of visage, following the trails that his fathers followed before the Romans came, and scowling still at the stranger.

To-day all hollow lanes form rivulets after rain, but it is clear from the lie of the land that some were traced by human feet before the water followed. They prick down the crests of narrow bridges, with a view over the valleys on each side. These were tracks before they were streams; but it is also likely that other watery lanes in the hill-countries were streams before they were tracks. There are advantages in the continuity and the hard bottom of a rivulet descending from the moor to the valley which more than compensate for a little additional water. Follow the bank above the wet lane, in the fields or on the moor above it, and see how much more tiresome is the going. The soil turns to mud after every storm of rain, and there are bogs on the moor in which we stumble from rush-clump to rush-clump. We return gladly to the rocky floor of the track, where the water has cut through the soft earth down to firm rock and gravel. In the shelter of the hollow lane there is comfort against keen north wind and driving rain-storms; and the wild life of the valleys and dingles spreads up the lanes to the very shoulder of the moor. Sheltered banks and running water make many of these lanes a wild garden, and they are sought out by the beasts and the birds. Here on spring mornings we meet the hare and the hedgehog—the hare daintily tripping to us among the wet pebbles with that strange incapacity of her sidelong vision to see danger in front, and the hedgehog just emerged from its leafy winter lair, and too eager to search the turf for beetles, or for brother hedgehogs, to wait for night. Weasels wind along the banks on their blood-quests; and from behind the curtains of dry bracken we hear the needle-sharp ejaculations of the shrew.

—Anthony Collett

Royalty

The Queen had a passion for motoring. She would motor for hours and hours with her crown on; it was quite impossible to mistake her. . . .

"Just hark to the crowds!" the Prince evasively said. And never too weary to receive an ovation, he skipped across the room towards the nearest window, where he began blowing kisses to the throng.

"Give them the Smile Extending, darling," his mother beseeched.

"Won't you rise and place your arm about him, Madam?" the Countess suggested.

"I'm not feeling at all up to the mark," her Dreaminess demurred, passing her fingers over her hair.

"There is sunshine, ma'am . . . and you have your *anemones* on . . ." the Countess cajoled, "and to please the people, you ought indeed to squeeze him." And she was begging and persuading the Queen to rise as the King entered the room preceded by a shapely page (of sixteen) with cheeks fresher than milk.

"Go to the window, Willie," the Queen exhorted her Consort, fixing an eye on the last trouser button that adorned his long, straggling legs. The King, who had the air of a tired pastry-cook, sat down.

"We feel," he said, "to-day, we've had our fill of stares!"

"One little bow, Willie," the Queen entreated, "that wouldn't kill you."

"We'd give perfect worlds," the King went on, "to go, by Ourselves, to bed."

". . . and now, let me hear your lessons: I should like," Mrs Montgomery murmured, her eyes set in detachment upon the floor, "the present-indicative tense of the Verb *To be*! Adding the words, Political H-Hostess; —more for the sake of the pronunciation than for anything else."

And after considerable persuasion, prompting, and "bribing" with various sorts of sweets:

"I am a Political Hostess,
Thou art a Political Hostess,
He is a Political Hostess,
We are Political Hostesses,
Ye are Political Hostesses,
They are Political Hostesses."

"Very good, dear, and only one mistake. *He* is a Political H-Hostess: can you correct yourself? the error is so slight. . . ."

But alas the Prince was in no mood for study; and Mrs Montgomery very soon afterwards was obliged to let him go.

—Ronald Firbank

For some reason he [Edward VII] spoke English with a heavy German accent, very guttural. . . . When he was still Prince of Wales and living at Marlborough House, Sir Sidney Lee, the Shakespearean scholar, came to the Prince with a proposal. It was on the eve of the publication of the *Dictionary of National Biography*. It was Sir Sidney's idea that the Prince ought to give a dinner to those responsible for the completion of this monumental work. The monumental work had escaped the Prince's attention, don't you know, and Sir Sidney had painfully to explain to him what it was. The Prince, you know, was not an omnivorous reader. Sir Sidney managed to obtain his grudging consent. "How many?" asked the Prince. "Forty," said Sir Sidney. The Prince was appalled. "For-r-ty!" he gasped. "For-r-ty wr-ri-ter-rs! I can't have for-r-ty wr-ri-ter-rs in Marlborough House! Giff me the list!" Sir Sidney gave it him, and the Prince, with a heavy black pencil, started slashing off names. Sir Sidney's heart sank when he saw that the first name the Prince had slashed was that of Sir Leslie Stephen. He conveyed, as tactfully as he could, that this was a bad cut, since Stephen was the animating genius of the whole enterprise. Reluctantly, the Prince allowed Sir Leslie to come. Eventually, Sir Sidney put over his entire list. The dinner took place. Among the contributors present was Canon Ainger, a distinguished cleric whose passion was Charles Lamb, on whom he was considered a very great authority indeed. He had written the articles on Charles and Mary Lamb for the *Dictionary*. Sir Sidney sat at the Prince's right and found it heavy weather, don't you know. The Prince must have found it heavy going also; to be having dinner with forty writers was not his idea of a cultivated way to spend an evening. His eye roamed the table morosely, in self-objurgation for having let himself in for a thing like this. Finally, his eye settled on Canon Ainger. "Who's the little parson?" he asked Lee. "Vy is *he* here? He's not a wr-ri-ter!" "He is a very great authority", said Lee, apologetically, "on Lamb." This was too much for the Prince. He put down his knife and fork in stupefaction; a pained outcry of protest heaved from him: "on *lamb!*"

—Max Beerbohm (as reported by S. N. Behrman)

Here is an incident which may make some of you smile. It happened shortly after the death of Prince Henry of Battenberg, the husband of Queen Victoria's daughter, Princess Beatrice. His death had greatly upset the Queen, for she had grown very fond of her son-in-law. He had brought a great deal of interest and life into the rather mournful atmosphere which still prevailed at Court.

On this particular afternoon to which I refer—a dark, dank afternoon in February—the Queen was at Osborne, and she went for her customary drive with Lady Errol, who was then in waiting. These dear, elderly ladies, swathed in crêpe, drove in an open carriage, called a sociable. The Queen was very silent, and Leila (Lady Errol) thought it time to make a little conversation. So she said, "Oh, Your Majesty, think of when we shall see our dear ones again in Heaven!"

"Yes," said the Queen.

"We will all meet in Abraham's bosom," said Leila.

"I will *not* meet Abraham," said the Queen.

An entry in Queen Victoria's diary for this day runs: "Dear Leila, not at all consolatory in moments of trouble!"

—Princess Marie Louise

We were unaware, Sir, that the corridors of our palace were damp.

—(Attributed to George V, on contemplating a visitor at a time when turned-up trousers had just become fashionable)

Abroad is bloody.

—(Attributed to George VI)

Saints

Health is the state about which Medicine has nothing to say; Sanctity is the state about which Theology has nothing to say.

I have met in my life two persons, one a man, the other a woman, who convinced me that they were persons of sanctity. Utterly different in character, upbringing and interests as they were, their effect on me was the same. In their presence I felt myself to be ten times as nice, ten times as intelligent, ten times as good-looking as I really am.

Reading *The Penguin Book of Saints*, I am sorry to learn that St Catherine of the Catherine wheel never existed. Another nonexistent saint is St Uncumber, who, according to legend, miraculously grew a beard in order to avoid marriage. Whom now are wives to invoke when their husbands are too sexually importunate?

Of my own saint, St Wystan, all that appears to be known is that he objected to the uncanonical marriage of his widowed mother to his godfather, whereupon they bumped him off. A rather Hamlet-like story.

Catholicism baptized polytheism by substituting for the old pagan cults the cults of local and patron saints. Such cults can and have led to abuses, but they are infinitely more healthy than the cult of the fashionable film star or pop singer, which is all that Protestantism has to offer in their stead.

> In our era, the road to holiness necessarily passes through the world of action.
>
> —Dag Hammarskjöld

Science

> Art is I; Science is We.
>
> —Claude Bernard

> Science is spectrum analysis: Art is photosynthesis.
>
> —Karl Kraus

> Someone remarked to me once: "Physicians shouldn't say, I have cured this man, but, this man didn't die under my care." In physics too, instead of saying, I have explained such and such a phenomenon, one might say, I have determined causes for it the absurdity of which cannot be conclusively proved.
>
> —G. C. Lichtenberg

> Many scientific theories have, for very long periods of time, stood the test of experience until they had to be discarded owing to man's decision, not merely to make other experiments, but to have different experiences.
>
> —Erich Heller

The hunger of the Eighteenth Century to believe in the power of reason, to wish to throw off authority, to wish to secularise, to take an optimistic view of man's condition, seized on Newton and his discoveries as an illustration of something which was already deeply believed in quite apart from the law of gravity and the laws of motion. The hunger with which the Nineteenth Century seized on Darwin had very much to do with the increasing awareness of history and change, with the great desire to naturalise man, to put him into the world of nature, which preexisted long before Darwin and which made him welcome. I have seen an example in this century where the great Danish physicist Niels Bohr found in the quantum theory when it was developed thirty years ago this remarkable trait: it is consistent with describing an atomic system, only much less completely than we can describe large-scale objects. We have a certain choice as to which traits of the atomic system we wish to study and measure and which to let go; but we have not the option of doing them all. This situation, which we all recognize, sustained in Bohr his long-held view of the human condition: that there are mutually exclusive ways of using our words, our minds, our souls, any one of which is open to us, but which cannot be combined: ways as different, for example, as preparing to act and entering into an introspective search for the reasons for action. This discovery has not, I think, penetrated into general cultural life. I wish it had; it is a good example of something that would be relevant, if only it could be understood.

—J. Robert Oppenheimer

Although this may seem a paradox, all exact science is dominated by the idea of approximation.

—Bertrand Russell

Scientific reasoning is completely dominated by the pre-supposition that mental functionings are not properly part of nature.

—A. N. Whitehead

When we speak of the picture of nature in the exact science of our age, we do not mean a picture of nature so much as a picture of our relationship with nature. Science no longer confronts nature as an objective observer, but sees himself as an actor in this interplay between man and nature. The scientific method of analysing, explaining and classifying has become conscious of its human limitations, which arise out of the fact that by its intervention science alters and refashions the object of its investigation. In other words, method and object can no longer be separated. *The scientific world view has ceased to be a scientific view in the true sense of the word.*

—Werner Heisenberg

Without my work in natural science I should never have known human beings as they really are. In no other activity can one come so close to direct perception and clear thought, or realize so fully the errors of the senses, the mistakes of the intellect, the weaknesses and greatnesses of human character.

—Goethe

It just so happens that during the 1950's, the first great age of molecular biology, the English Schools of Oxford and particularly of Cambridge produced more than a score of graduates of quite outstanding ability—much more brilliant, inventive, articulate, and dialectically skillful than most young scientists; right up in the [James D.] Watson class. But Watson had one towering advantage over all of them: in addition to being extremely clever he had something important to be clever *about.* This is an advantage which scientists enjoy over most people engaged in intellectual pursuits.

—P. B. Medawar

Freeman Dyson, in an article, *Innovation in Physics,* recalled that in 1958 the German physicist Werner Heisenberg and Pauli put forward an unorthodox theory of particles which would explain the violations of parity in weak interactions. Pauli was lecturing in New York on these new ideas to a group of scientists that included Niels Bohr. In the discussion that followed the talk, younger scientists were sharply critical of Pauli.

Bohr rose to speak. "We are all agreed," he said to Pauli, "that your theory is crazy. The question which divides us is whether it is crazy enough to have a chance of being correct. My own feeling is that it is not crazy enough."

Dyson commented in his article:

"The objection that they are not crazy enough applies to all the attempts which have so far been launched at a radically new theory of elementary particles. It applies especially to the crackpots. Most of the papers which are submitted to *The Physical Review* are rejected, not because it is impossible to understand them, but because it is possible. Those which are impossible to understand are usually published."

—Martin Gardner

Generally speaking and to a varying extent, scientists follow their temperaments in their choice of problems.

—Charles Hermite

Experimental typhus of the guinea-pig is a very minimal disease. It is reduced to small changes in the temperature curve, and could not be diagnosed without a thermometer, since the animal does not seem to suffer or have any other symptoms.

Now it happened occasionally that we discovered amongst our guinea-pigs, inoculated with the same virus, some who had no fever at all. The first time we discovered this, we thought it was due to an accident in the inoculation or to the particular resistance of the inoculated animal. These were the two hypotheses by which all bacteriologists of that era would have explained this phenomenon.

When the phenomenon kept recurring, we felt that our explanations had been too superficial, and that it must be due to another specific reason. We kept in mind the table of sensitivity to typhus of various races and species that we had observed or infected. At the top of the scale was the European adult who had immigrated to regions where typhus is endemic, and in whom the disease is most severe and often fatal. Below him appeared the aboriginal adult who is seriously infected but who, when there are no complications, generally escapes death. Then there comes the indigenous child for whom typhus, with few exceptions, is only a mild disease. Below our species there figures the chimpanzee, less sensitive still than the child, followed by even less sensitive small monkeys, and finally the guinea-pig whose infection is reduced to a thermometer curve. Could there not be below this hardly recognizable disease an even smaller degree of sensitivity, where, in the absence of fever, the only means of diagnosing typhus would be the positive results of an inoculation of blood into an animal of definite sensitivity? That this was the case was soon proved by experiment. Other experiments very soon proved to us that latent typhus, exceptional as it was in the case of guinea-pigs, was the only form of typhus in some other species.

This latent typhus which we were the first to discover is a typhus of first infection. We were able to demonstrate the existence of the same sub-clinical type in other guinea-pigs, that had had primary typhus and were then reinoculated. The natural recurrence in man can also be of the sub-clinical type.

Subsequently we, and others after us, extended the notion of latent infection to a number of bacterial infections. The list increases daily.

Thus there exists a whole pathology that cannot be reached by clinical methods. If we add that it is in these unrecognizable forms that contagious and epidemic diseases are preserved, the practical importance of this new information is obvious. Now the starting-point of our discovery had been the simple absence of a temperature rise in some examples of a species which commonly becomes feverish after being inoculated with a virus.

—Charles Nicolle

The scientific method cannot lead mankind because it is based upon experiment, and every experiment postpones the present moment until one knows the result. We always come to each other and even to ourselves too late so soon as we wish to know in advance what to do.

—Eugen Rosenstock-Huessy

That's an old besetting sin; they think calculating is inventing. And that because they have been right so often, their wrong-headedness is right-minded. And that because their science is exact, none of them can be crazy.

We need a categorical imperative in the natural sciences just as much as we need one in ethics.

—Goethe

Science alone, and only in its purest rigor, can give a precise content to the notion of providence, and in the domain of knowledge, it can do nothing else.

—Simone Weil

Seasons, The Four

Explore deep mountain chasms, soar high in the air in the wake of clouds; to brook and valley the Muse calls—a thousand and a thousand times.

When a fresh calyx newly blooms, it calls for new songs; and though streaming time flees from us, the seasons come again.

—Goethe (trans. David Luke)

Winter to Spring: the west wind melts the frozen rancour,
The windlass drags to sea the thirsty hull;
Byre is no longer welcome to beast or fire to ploughman,
The field removes the frost-cap from his skull.

Venus of Cythera leads the dances under the hanging
Moon and the linked line of Nymphs and Graces
Beat the ground with measured feet while the busy Fire-God
Stokes his red-hot mills in volcanic places.

Now is the time to twine the spruce and shining head with myrtle,
Now with flowers escaped the earthly fetter,
And sacrifice to the woodland god in shady copses
A lamb or a kid, whichever he likes better.

Equally heavy is the heel of white-faced Death on the pauper's
Shack and the towers of kings, and O my dear,
The little sum of life forbids the ravelling of lengthy
Hopes. Night and the fabled dead are near

And the narrow house of nothing, past whose lintel
  You will meet no wine like this, no boy to admire
Like Lycidas, who today makes all young men a furnace
  And whom tomorrow girls will find a fire.

—Horace (trans. Louis MacNeice)

The Objects of The Summer Scene

The objects of the summer scene entone
  Or image present peace or dear regrets;
Something that life to be content must own,
  Smiles near, though restless grief remotely frets;
Green sycamores brooding in the quiet sun;
  And on gray hills beyond the golden sheaves,
Lone poplars, sisters of fallen Phaeton,
  Quivering innumerate inconsolable leaves.

In wintry evening walks I turn where rest
  Within one tomb affection's first, and last;
As in a wind, of some dead wind in quest,
  I homeward pace companioned by the past.
For earth's great grave far ocean seems to moan;
  And the sad mind but marks anear, afar,
The tinkle of the dead leaf by the lone
  Sea road, the sad look of the setting star.

—W. C. Irwin

Summer

    Winter is cold-hearted,
    Spring is yea and nay,
Autumn is a weathercock
    Blown every way.
    Summer days for me
When every leaf is on its tree;

    When Robin's not a beggar,
    And Jenny Wren's a bride,
And larks hang singing, singing, singing
    Over the wheat-fields wide,
    And anchored lilies ride,
    And the pendulum spider
    Swings from side to side.

And blue-black beetles transact business,
    And gnats fly in a host,

And furry caterpillars hasten
    That no time be lost,
    And moths grow fat and thrive,
    And ladybirds arrive.

    Before green apples blush,
    Before green nuts embrown,
    Why, one day in the country
    Is worth one month in town;
    Is worth a day and a year
Of the dusty, musty, lag-last fashion
    That days drone elsewhere.

—Christina Rossetti

The Fall

The length o' days ageän do shrink
  An' flowers be thin in meäd, among
  The eegrass, a-sheenèn bright, along
Brook upon brook, an' brink by brink.

Noo starlens do rise in vlock on wing—
  Noo goocoo in nest-green leaves do sound—
  Noo swallows be now a-wheelèn round—
Dip after dip, an' swing by swing.

The wheat that did leätely rustle thick
  Is now up in mows that still be new,
  An' yollow bevore the sky o' blue—
Tip after tip, an' rick by rick.

While shooters do rove bezide the knoll
  Where leaves be a-rolled on quivren grass;
  Or down where the sky-blue stream do pass,
Vall after vall, an' shoal by shoal;

Their brown-dappled dogs do briskly trot
  By russet-brown boughs, while gun smoke grey
  Do melt in the aïr o' sunny day,
Reef after reef, an' shot by shot.

While now I can walk a dusty mile
  I'll teäke me a day, while days be clear,
  To vind a vew friends that still be dear,
Feäce after feäce, an' smile by smile.

—William Barnes

Look how the snow lies deeply on glittering
Soracte. White woods groan and protestingly
  Let fall their branch-loads. Bitter frost has
    Paralysed rivers: the ice is solid.

Unfreeze the cold! Pile plenty of logs in the
Fireplace! And you, dear friend Thaliarchus, come
  Bring out the Sabine wine-jar four years
    Old and be generous. Let the good gods

Take care of all else. Later, as soon as they've
Calmed down this contestation of winds upon
  Churned seas, the old ash-trees can rest in
    Peace and the cypresses stand unshaken.

Try not to guess what lies in the future, but
As Fortune deals days enter them into your
  Life's book as windfalls, credit items,
    Gratefully. Now that you are young, and peevish

Grey hairs are still far distant, attend to the
Dance-floor, the heart's sweet business; for now is the
  Right time for midnight assignations,
    Whispers and murmurs in Rome's piazzas

And fields, and soft, low laughter that gives away
The girl who plays love's games in a hiding-place—
  Off comes a ring coaxed down an arm or
    Pulled from a faintly resisting finger.

—Horace (trans. James Michie)

Winter Cold

Cold, cold, chill to-night is wide Moylurg; the snow is higher than a mountain, the deer cannot get at its food.

Eternal cold! The storm has spread on every side; each sloping furrow is a river and every ford is a full mere.

Each full lake is a great sea and each mere is a full lake; horses cannot get across the ford of Ross, no more can two feet get there.

The fishes of Ireland are roving, there is not a strand where the wave does not dash, there is not a town left in the land, not a bell is heard, no crane calls.

The wolves of Cuan Wood do not get repose or sleep in the lair of wolves; the little wren does not find shelter for her nest on the slope of Lon.

The keen wind and the cold ice have burst out upon the company of little birds; the blackbird does not find a bank it would like, shelter for its side in the Woods of Cuan.

Snug is our cauldron on its hook, ramshackle the hut on the slope of Lon: snow has crushed the wood here, it is difficult to climb up Benn Bó.

The eagle of brown Glen Rye gets affliction from the bitter wind; great is its misery and its suffering, the ice will get in its beak.

It is foolish for you—take heed of it—to rise from quilt and featherbed; there is much ice on every ford; that is why I say "Cold!"

—Anon. tenth-century (trans. K. H. Jackson)

Serpent, The

There are myriads lower than this, and more loathsome, in the scale of being; the links between dead matter and animation drift everywhere unseen. But it is the strength of the base element that is so dreadful in the serpent; it is the very omnipotence of the earth. That rivulet of smooth silver—how does it flow, think you? It literally rows the earth, with every scale for an oar; it bites the dust with the ridges of its body. Watch it, when it moves slowly:—A wave, but without wind! a current, but with no fall! all the body moving at the same instant, yet some of it to one side, some to another, or some forward, and the rest of the coil backwards; but all with the same calm will and equal way—no contraction, no extension; one soundless, causeless march of sequent rings, and spectral procession of spotted dust, with dissolution in its fangs, dislocation in its coils. Startle it;—the winding stream will become a twisted arrow;—the wave of poisoned life will lash through the grass like a cast lance. It scarcely breathes with its one lung (the other shrivelled and abortive); it is passive to the sun and shade, and is cold or hot like a stone; yet, "it can outclimb the monkey, outswim the fish, outleap the jerboa, outwrestle the athlete, and crush the tiger." It is a divine hieroglyph of the demoniac power of the earth,—of the entire earthly nature. As the bird is the clothed power of the air, so this is the clothed power of the dust; as the bird is the symbol of the spirit of life, so this of the grasp and sting of death.

—Ruskin

Shakespeare and the Computers

I read in a newspaper that a certain Mrs Winifred Venton, with the help of the Enfield College of Technology computer, has at last cracked the cipher of the *Sonnets.*

The Message: Shakespeare was really King Edward VI, who did not die, as the history books say, when he was sixteen, but at the age of 125. In addition to writing "Shakespeare," he wrote not only all of Ben Jonson and Bacon, but *Don Quixote* as well.

Sin

We can reach the point where it becomes possible for us to recognise and understand Original Sin, that dark counter-centre of evil in our nature—that is to say, though it *is* not our nature, it is *of* it—that something within us which rejoices when disaster befalls the very cause we are trying to serve, or misfortune overtakes even those we love.

Life in God is not an escape from this, but a way to gain full insight concerning it. It is not our depravity which forces a fictitious religious explanation upon us, but the experience of religious reality which forces the "Night Side" out into the light.

It is when we stand in the righteous all-seeing light of love that we can dare to look at, admit, and *consciously* suffer under this something in us which wills disaster, misfortune, defeat to everything outside the sphere of our narrowest self-interest.

—Dag Hammarskjöld

You talk of Gayety and Innocence!
The moment when the fatal fruit was eaten,
They parted ne'er to meet again; and Malice
Has ever since been playmate to light Gayety,
From the first moment when the smiling infant
Destroys the flower or butterfly he toys with,
To the last chuckle of the dying miser,
Who on his deathbed laughs his last to hear
His wealthy neighbor has become a bankrupt.

—Walter Scott

Sin is nothing else but the refusal to recognise human misery: It is unconscious misery, and for that very reason guilty misery.

All sins are attempts to fill voids.

Evil is to love what mystery is to intelligence.

—Simone Weil

Certain sins can manifest themselves as their mirror opposites which the sinner is able to persuade himself are virtues. Thus Gluttony can manifest itself as Daintiness, Lust as Prudery, Sloth as Senseless Industry, Envy as Hero Worship.

My senses tell me that the world is inhabited by a number of human individuals whom I can count and compare with each other, and I do not doubt the evidence of my senses. It requires, however, an act of faith on my part to believe that they enjoy a unique personal existence as I do, that when they say "I" they mean what I mean when I say it, for this my senses cannot tell me. Vice versa, my own personal existence is to me self-evident; what, where I am concerned, calls for an act of faith, is to believe that I, too, am a human individual like the others, brought into the world by an act of sexual intercourse and exhibiting socially conditioned behavior. The refusal to make this double act of faith constitutes the Primal Sin, the Sin of Pride.

Society, High

The Challenge
A Court Ballad
To the tune of "To All You Ladies Now at Land"

To *one* fair Lady out of Court,
And *two* fair Ladies in,
We think the *Turk* and *Pope* a Sport,
And Wit and Love no Sin;
Come, these soft Lines, with nothing stiff in,
To *Bellenden, Lepell,* and *Griffin.*
    With a fa, la, la.

What passes in the dark third Row,
And what behind the Scene,
Couches and crippled Chairs I know,
And Garrets hung with Green;
I know the Swing of sinful Hack,
Where many Damsels cry Alack.
    With a fa, la, la.

Then why to Court should I repair,
Where's such ado with *Townshend,*
To hear each Mortal stamp and swear,
And every speech with *Zowns* end;
To hear 'em rail at honest *Sunderland,*
And rashly blame the Realm of *Blunderland.*
    With a fa, la, la.

Alas! like *Schutz*, I cannot pun,
Like *Grafton* court the *Germans*;
Tell *Pickenbourg* how Slim she's grown,
Like *Meadowes* run to Sermons;

To Court ambitious Men may roam,
But I and *Marlbro'* stay at Home.
With a fa, la, la.

In Truth, by what I can discern,
Of Courtiers 'twixt you *Three,*
Some Wit you have, and more to learn
From Court, than *Gay* or *Me*:
Perhaps, in Time, you'll leave high Diet,
To sup with us on Milk and Quiet.
With a fa, la, la.

At *Leicester-Fields,* a House full high,
With door all painted green,
Where Ribbons wave upon the Tye,
(A *Milliner* I mean);
There may you meet us *Three* to *Three,*
For *Gay* can well make *Two* of Me.
With a fa, la, la.

But shou'd you catch the Prudish Itch,
And each become a Coward,
Bring sometimes with you Lady *Rich,*
And sometimes Mistress *Howard*;
For Virgins to keep Chaste, must go
Abroad with such as are not so.
With a fa, la, la.

And thus, fair Maids, my Ballad ends;
God send the King safe Landing;
And make all honest Ladies friends
To Armies that are Standing;
Preserve the Limits of these Nations,
And take off Ladies Limitations.
With a fa, la, la.

—Alexander Pope

Solitude and Loneliness

He who does not enjoy solitude will not love freedom.

—Schopenhauer

Man is a gregarious animal, and much more so in his mind than in his body. He may like to go alone for a walk, but he hates to stand alone in his opinions.

—G. Santayana

Solitude. In what does its value actually consist? For we are in the presence of ordinary matter (even the sky, the stars, the moon, trees in flower), things of lesser value perhaps than a human spirit. Its value consists in the superior possibility of attention. If one could be attentive to the same degree in the presence of a human being . . . (?)

—Simone Weil

In natural objects we feel ourselves, or think of ourselves, only by *likenesses*—among men too often by *differences.* Hence the soothing love-kindling effect of rural nature and the bad passions of human societies.

—S. T. Coleridge

Letting rip a fart—
It doesn't make you laugh
When you live alone.

—Anon. Japanese (trans. Geoffrey Bownas)

Where I could think of no thoroughfare,
Away on the mountain up far too high,
A blinding headlight shifted glare
And began to bounce down a granite stair
Like a star fresh fallen out of the sky.
And I away in my opposite wood
Am touched by that unintimate light
And made feel less alone than I rightly should,
For traveler there could do me no good
Were I in trouble with night tonight.

—Robert Frost

A lonely man always deduces one thing from the other and thinks everything to the worst.

—Martin Luther

Loneliness is not the sickness-unto-death. No, but can it be cured except by death? And does it not become the harder to bear the closer one comes to death?

—Dag Hammarskjöld

Songs

The French *Symbolistes* asserted that poetry should be as like music as possible. Some of them, however, made the mistake of writing about music itself, thereby showing that they had no understanding whatever of that art. To them, music was not an organized structure of sound, but a stimulus to vague erotic reverie. By *la poésie pure,* I take it that they meant the kind of poetry we enjoy, not because of anything it tells us about the world we live in, but as a purely verbal experience, a paradise of language. The best examples, in English poetry at least, are songs, poems written with the intention that they be set to music, either by the poet himself, if, like Campion, he be also a composer, or by another musician. The song writer has to be much more conscious of the metrical values of words and the sounds of syllables than the writer of a lyric which is intended to be spoken or read.

A New Year Carol

Here we bring new water
from the well so clear,
For to worship God with,
this happy New Year,
Sing levy dew, sing levy dew,
the water and the wine;
The seven bright gold wires
and the bugles that do shine.

Sing reign of Fair Maid,
with gold upon her toe,—
Open you the West Door,
and turn the Old Year go.

Sing reign of Fair Maid
with gold upon her chin,—
Open you the East Door,
and let the New Year in.
Sing levy dew, sing levy dew,
the water and the wine;
The seven bright gold wires
and the bugles they do shine.

—Anon.

Bethsabe's Song

Hot sun, cool fire, tempered with sweet air,
Black shade, fair nurse, shadow my white hair:
Shine, sun; burn, fire; breathe, air, and ease me;
Black shade, fair nurse, shroud me, and please me:
Shadow, my sweet nurse, keep me from burning,
Make not my glad cause cause of my mourning.
    Let not my beauty's fire
    Inflame unstaid desire,
    Nor pierce any bright eye
    That wandereth lightly.

—George Peele

Weep, O mine eyes, and cease not,
These your spring tides, alas, methinks increase not:
O when, O when begin you
To swell so high that I may drown me in you.

—Anon. (set by John Bennet)

About the maypole new, with glee and merriment,
While as the bagpipe tooted it,
Thyrsis and Cloris fine together footed it.
And to the wanton instrument
Still they went to and fro and finely flaunted it,
And then both met again, and thus they chaunted it:
Fa la la!

The shepherds and the nymphs them round enclosed had,
Wondring with what facility
About they turned them in such strange agility.
And still, when they unloosed had,
With words full of delight they gently kissed them,
And thus sweetly to sing they never missed them:
Fa la la!

—Anon. (set by Thomas Morley)

Dance, dance, and visit the shadows of our joy,
All in height, and pleasing state, your changed forms employ.
And as the bird of Jove salutes, with lofty wings, the morn,
So mount, so fly, these trophies to adorn.
Grace them with all the sounds and motions of delight,
Since all the earth cannot express a lovelier sight.
View them with triumph, and in shades the truth adore:
No pomp or sacrifice can please Jove's greatness more.
Turn, turn, and honor now the life these figures bear:
Lo, how heavenly natures far above all art appear:
Let their aspects revive in you the fire that shined so late,
Still mount and still retain your heavenly state.
Gods were with dance and with music served of old,
Those happy days derived their glorious style from gold:
This pair, by Hymen joined, grace you with measures then,
Since they are both divine and you are more than men.

—T. Campion

To Musick, to Becalme a Sweet-Sick-Youth

Charms, that call down the moon from out her sphere,
On this sick youth work your enchantment here:

Bind up his senses with your numbers, so,
As to entrance his paine, or cure his woe.
Fall gently, gently, and a while him keep
Lost in the civill Wildernesse of sleep:
That done, then let him, dispossest of paine,
Like to a slumbring Bride, awake againe.

—Robert Herrick

Hunter's Song

The toils are pitched, and the stakes are set,
Ever sing merrily, merrily;
The bows they bend, and the knives they whet,
Hunters live so cheerily.

It was a stag, a stag of ten,
Bearing its branches sturdily;
He came stately down the glen,
Ever sing hardily, hardily.

It was there he met with a wounded doe,
She was bleeding dreadfully;
She warned him of the toils below,
O so faithfully, faithfully!

He had an eye, and he could heed,
Ever sing warily, warily;
He had a foot, and he could speed—
Hunters watch so narrowly.

—Walter Scott

The Meeting of The Waters

There is not in this wide world a valley so sweet
As that vale in whose bosom the bright waters meet;
Oh! the last rays of feeling and life must depart,
Ere the bloom of that valley shall fade from my heart.

Yet it *was* not that Nature had shed o'er the scene
Her purest of crystal and brightest of green;
'Twas *not* her soft magic of streamlet or hill,
Oh! No—it was something more exquisite still.

'Twas that friends, the beloved of my bosom were near,
Who made every scene of enchantment more dear,
And who felt how the best charms of nature improve,
When we see them reflected from looks that we love.

Sweet vale of Avoca! how calm could I rest
In thy bosom of shade, with the friends I love best,
Where the storms that we feel in this cold world should cease,
And our hearts, like thy waters, be mingled in peace.

—Thomas Moore

Time's Song

O'er the level plains, where mountains greet me as I go,
O'er the desert waste, where fountains at my bidding flow,
On the boundless beam by day, on the cloud by night,
I am riding hence away! Who will chain my flight?

War his weary watch was keeping;—I have crushed his spear:
Grief within her bower was weeping;—I have dried her tear:
Pleasure caught a minute's hold;—then I hurried by,
Leaving all her banquet cold, and her goblet dry.

Power had won a throne of glory;—where is now his fame?
Genius said,—"I live in story";—who hath heard his name?
Love, beneath a myrtle bough, whispered,—"Why so fast?"
And the roses on his brow withered as I past.

I have heard the heifer lowing o'er the wild wave's bed;
I have seen the billow flowing where the cattle fed;
Where began my wanderings?—Memory will not say!
Where will rest my weary wings?—Science turns away!

—W. M. Praed

Mandrake's Song

Folly hath now turned out of door
Mankind and Fate, who were before
  Jove's Harlequin and clown;
The World's no stage, no tavern more—
  Its sign the Fool ta'en down.

  With poppy rain and cypress dew
  Weep all, for all, who laughed for you,
For goose-grass is no medicine more,
  But the owl's brown eye's the sky's new blue.
    Heigho! Foolscap!

—T. L. Beddoes

During Wind and Rain

They sing their dearest songs—
He, she, all of them—yea,
Treble and tenor and bass,

And one to play;
With the candles mooning each face. . . .
Ah, no; the years O!
How the sick leaves reel down in throngs!

They clear the creeping moss—
Elders and juniors—aye,
Making the pathways neat
And the garden gay;
And they build a shady seat. . . .
Ah, no; the years, the years;
See the white storm-birds wing across!

They are blithely breakfasting all—
Men and maidens—yea,
Under the summer tree,
With a glimpse of the bay,
While pet fowl come to the knee. . . .
Ah, no; the years O!
And the rotten rose is ript from the wall.

They change to a high new house,
He, she, all of them—aye,
Clocks and carpets and chairs
On the lawn all day,
And brightest things that are theirs. . . .
Ah, no; the years, the years;
Down their carved names the rain-drop ploughs.

—Thomas Hardy

Spa

The Warwickshire Avon falls into the Severn here, and on the sides of both, for many miles back, there are the finest meadows that ever were seen. In looking over them, one wonders *what can become of all the meat?* By riding on about eight or nine miles further, however, this wonder is a little diminished; for here we come to one of the devouring WENS; namely CHELTENHAM, which is what they call a "watering place"; that is to say, a place to which East India plunderers, West India floggers, English tax-gorgers, together with gluttons, drunkards, and debauchees of all descriptions, *female* as well as male, resort, at the suggestion of silently laughing quacks, in the hope of getting rid of the bodily consequences of their manifold sins and iniquities. When I enter a place like this, I always feel disposed to squeeze up my nose with my fingers. It is nonsense, to be sure; but I conceit that every two-legged creature, that I see coming near me, is about to cover me with the poisonous proceeds of its impurities. To places like these come all that is knavish and all that is foolish and all that is base; gamesters, pick-pockets, and harlots; young wife-hunters in search of rich and ugly and old women, and young husband-hunters in search of rich and wrinkled or half-rotten men, the former resolutely bent, be the means what they may, to give the latter heirs to their lands and tenements. These things are notorious; and, Sir William Scott, in his speech of 1802, *in favour of the non-residence of the Clergy*, expressly said, that they and their families ought to appear at *watering places*, and that this was amongst the means of *making them respected by their flocks*! Memorandum: he was a member for Oxford when he said this!

—William Cobbett

Sparrows

3 sorts The common house Sparrow The Hedge Sparrow & Reed Sparrow often calld the fen sparrow The common sparrow is well known but not so much in a domesticated state as few people think it worth while bringing up a sparrow When I was a boy I kept a tamed cock sparrow 3 years it was so tame that it would come when calld & flew where it pleasd when I first had the sparrow I was fearful of the cat killing it so I usd to hold the bird in my hand toward her & when she attempted to smell of it I beat her she at last woud take no notice of it & I ventured to let it loose in the house they were both very shy at each other at first & when the sparrow venturd to chirp the cat woud brighten up as if she intended to seize it but she went no further than a look or smell at length she had kittens & when they were taken away she grew so fond of the sparrow as to attempt to caress it the sparrow was startld at first but came to by degrees & ventured so far at last as to perch upon her back puss would call for it when out of sight like a kitten & woud lay mice before it the same as she woud for her own young & they always livd in harmony so much the sparrow woud often take away bits of bread from under the cat's nose & even put itself in a posture of resistence when offended as if it reckoned her no more than one of its kind. In winter when we coud not bear the door open to let the sparrow come out & in I was alowd to take a pane out of the window but in the spring of the third year my poor tom Sparrow for that was the name he was calld by went out & never returnd I went day after day calling out for tom & eagerly eying every sparrow on the house but none answerd the name for he woud come down in a moment to the call & perch upon my hand to be fed I gave it out that some cat which it mistook for its old favourite betrayed its confidence & destroyed it

—John Clare

Spider, The

Little City

Spider, from his flaming sleep,
staggers out into the window frame;
swings out from the red den where he slept
to nest in the gnarled glass.
Fat hero, burnished cannibal
lets down a frail ladder and ties a knot,
sways down to a landing with furry grace.

By noon this corner is a bullet-colored city
and the exhausted architect
sleeps in his pale wheel,
waits without pity for a gold visitor
or coppery captive, his aerial enemies
spinning headlong down the window to the trap.

The street of string shakes now and announces
a surprised angel in the tunnel of thread,
Spider dances down his wiry heaven to taste the moth.
A little battle begins and the prison trembles.
The round spider hunches like a judge.
The wheel glistens.
But this transparent town that caves in at a breath
is paved with perfect steel.
The victim hangs by his feet, and the spider
circles invisible avenues, weaving a grave.

By evening the web is heavy with monsters,
bright constellations of wasps and bees,
breathless, surrendered.
Bronze skeletons dangle on the wires
and a thin wing flutters.
The medieval city hangs in its stars.

Spider lumbers down the web
and the city stretches with the weight of his walking.
By night we cannot see the flies' faces
and the spider, rocking.

—Robert Horan

Spoonerisms

Winter Eve

Drear fiend: How shall this spay be dent?
I jell you no toque—I do not know.
What can I do but snatch the woe
that falls beyond my pane, and blench
my crows and ted my briny shears?
Now galls another class. I'll sit
and eye the corm that's fought in it.
Maces will I fake, and heart my pare.
Is this that sold elf that once I was
with lapped chips and tolling lung?
I hollow sward and tight my bung
for very shame, and yet no cause—
save that the beery witchery
of Life stows grail. Shall I abroad?
Track up my punks? Oh gray to pod
for him who sanders on the wee!
I'll buff a stag with shiny torts
and soulful hocks, a truthbush too,
perhaps a rook to bead—but no!
my wishes must be dashed. Reports
of danger shake the reaming scare.
Whack against blight! Again that tune,
"A gritty pearl is just like a titty prune"
blows from the fox. I cannot bear
this sweetness. Silence is best. I mat
my mistress and my sleazy lumber.
I'll shake off my toes, for they encumber.
What if I tub my stow? The newt
goes better fakèd to the cot.
I'll hash my wands or shake a tower,
(a rug of slum? a whiskey sour?)
water my pants in all their plots,
slob a male hairy before I seep—
and dropping each Id on heavy lie,
with none to sing me lullaby,
slop off to dreep, slop off to dreep.

—Robert Morse

Sunday

Sunday should be different from another day. People may walk, but not throw stones at birds.

—Dr Johnson

Swallow, The

It is an owl that has been trained by the Graces. It is a bat that loves the morning light. It is the aerial reflection of a dolphin. It is the tender domestication of a trout.

—Ruskin

Time

Among primitive peoples, the notion that the year has any particular length or duration is generally lacking. The seasons recur, and there may be a word for the cycle of recurring seasons which we can translate as "year," but it cannot be defined as a period of so many moons or days. Nevertheless the counting of moons (lunar months) is quite common, even among primitive peoples. . . .

Any seasonal cycle reckoned in moons must clearly be calibrated by some natural event which, from our point of view, appears to occur at a fixed time in the sidereal year. . . . It is important to realize that such corrections can be made without any awareness of the existence of a solar or sidereal year. . . . The Yami of Botel-Tobago Island near Formosa have an economy greatly influenced by the seasonal arrival of large shoals of flying-fish, which appear in these waters around March. A further seasonal fact is that, from about mid-June, typhoons are so frequent that deep-sea fishing is impracticable in the small craft of the Yami. They reckon time by moons, and all their festivals occur at a particular new or full moon. The check-point for their year is a festival in the dark phase between months nine and ten of their cycle; that is, about March. At this festival, the Yami go out to summon the flying-fish with lighted flares. Before this event, flare-fishing is taboo. Provided the flying-fish turn up to the summons, the flare-fishing continues for three moons until the end of the twelfth month, and this is then deemed the end of the yearly cycle. From the beginning of the first month, flare-fishing is taboo again. If no flying-fish turn up to the summons, the Yami do not blame themselves for miscalculating the time—they blame the fish for being late for the appointment. In such years, they extend the flare-fishing season an extra moon, and the year-cycle continues for 13 months instead of 12. In this way, over a period of years the Yami calendar will keep in step with the sidereal year, although the

Yami themselves have no notion of such a year and make no astronomical observations.

In ancient centralized states, such as Egypt and Mesopotamia, the common man was still concerned only with the present; his year was a recurring cycle of activities. The official, on the other hand, looked at the past, and was concerned with maintaining precedents and ordering activities into categories. The year and its divisions became instruments of organisation. For the priest, the names and numbers associated with these divisions provided an acrostic which led ultimately to astrology.

In almost all early societies, there were priests or priest-magicians whose status and authority depended upon their secret knowledge. In primitive societies these secrets are techniques of ritual and verbal spells, but, as writing develops, such formulae tend to become associated with geometrical shapes and magic numbers. Arithmetic and number theory may later be developed for their own sake without reference to practical utility. For example, the sexagesimal system of enumeration of ancient Mesopotamia and China was the invention of learned men who must have pursued complexity for the sake of complexity. For the peasant with ten fingers, there is no convenience in having 60 minutes to an hour, 24 hours to a day, and 360 degrees in a circle, but these numbers have exceptionally numerous simple factors, and so have fascination for arithmeticians interested more in magical combinations than in practical calculation. Thus, the administrative official, and the priest, are both interested—for different reasons—in devising time-systems which are neat, symmetrical, and arithmetically attractive. There are two ways of doing this. One is to devise and operate a pure number-system, ignoring the facts of astronomy. The other is to devise a pure number-system, but from time to time to introduce supplementary rules—also of a formal kind—which will gradually bring the number-system into relation with astronomical fact.

The ancient Egyptians, the Chinese, the Maya, and the Greeks each tackled this problem in a slightly different way. The Egyptians produced a number-system which ignored seasons. The Chinese maintained two separate official calendars, one for the peasant, which followed the seasons, and one for the scribe, which was a pure number-system. The Maya devised a pure number-system, and became obsessed by the marvellous intricacy of numbers. They took note of astronomical facts, but only to provide themselves with more and more complex number series which might be built into their magical system. The Greeks pursued a system of magical geometry, and in the process developed a time self-conscious science.

The important dates, from the Maya point of view, were those which completed a cycle, since, in Maya theory, the good or ill fortune of a particular period could be divined from a knowledge of its date of completion. A date which completed several different cycles all at once was correspondingly more important. Thus, by analogy to our system, Saturday would be important as being the last day of a week; a Saturday falling on the 31st day of December would be more important; Saturday, 31st December falling on the last day of a century would be yet more important.

The Maya had 20 basic digits instead of our ten, and they developed positional notation. Thus, a number we should write 861 (i.e. 8×10×10+6×10+1) was written by the Maya as 2.3.1 (i.e. 2×20×20+3×20+1). Each of the first 13 digits had special magical associations.

There were 20 day-names comparable to our days of the week, following on perpetually in continuous sequence. These days were, however, also numbered in series of 13, likewise in continuous sequence. Thus, each day had both a name and number. If we denote the names by capital letter down to the twentieth letter, which is T, a series might run,

1A; 2B; 3C; 4D; 5E; 6F; 7G; 8H; 9I; 10J; 11K; 12L; 13M;
1N; 2O; 3P; 4Q; 5R; 6S; 7T; 8A; 9B; 10C; 11D; 12E; 13F.

In a period of 260 days, no two days will have both the same name and the same number, but after 260 days the cycle will repeat itself.

—E. R. Reach

Dogged morn till bed-time by its dull demands,
The veriest numskull *clock*-cluck understands,
Eked out by solemn gestures of its hands:
A subtler language stirs in whispering sands:

That double ovoid of translucent glass;
The tiny corridor through which they pass,
Shaping a crescent cone where nothing was,

Which mounts in exquisite quiet as the eye
Watches its myriad molecules slip by;
While, not an inch above, as stealthily,

A tiny shallowing on the surface seen
Sinks to a crater where a plane has been.
Could mutability be more serene?

Invert the fragile frame; and yet again
Daydream will rear a castle built in Spain.
"Time" measured thus is dewfall to the brain. . . .

And clepsydra—the clock that Plato knew,
Tolling the varying hours each season through;

Oozing on, drop by drop, in liquid flow,
Its voice scarce audible, bell-like and low
As Juliet's communings with her Romeo.

More silent yet; pure solace to the sight—
The dwindling candle with her pensive light
Metes out the leaden watches of the night.
And, in that service, from herself takes flight.

—Walter de la Mare

THE MARSCHALLIN. Time is a very strange thing.
So long as one takes it for granted, it is nothing at all.
But then, all of a sudden, one is aware of nothing else.
It is all about us, it is within us also,
In our faces it is there, trickling,
In the mirror it is there, trickling,
In my sleep it is there, flowing,
And between me and you,
There, too, it flows, soundless, like an hour-glass.
Oh, Quinquin, sometimes I hear it flowing
Irresistibly on.
Sometimes I get up in the middle of the night
And stop the clocks, all, all of them.
Nevertheless, we are not to shrink from it,
For it, too, is a creature of the Father who created us all.

—Hugo von Hofmannsthal

TORTOISE, THE

Tortoise Family Connections

On he goes, the little one,
Bud of the universe,
Pediment of life.

Setting off somewhere, apparently.
Whither away, brisk egg?
His mother deposited him on the soil as if he were no more than droppings,
And now he scuffles tinily past her as if she were an old rusty tin.

A mere obstacle,
He veers round the slow great mound of her—
Tortoises always foresee obstacles.

It's no use my saying to him in an emotional voice:
"This is your mother, she laid you when you were an egg."

He does not even trouble to answer: "Woman, what have I to do with thee?"
He wearily looks the other way,
And she even more wearily looks another way still,
Each with the utmost apathy,
Incognisant,
Unaware,
No thing.

As for papa
He snaps when I offer him his offspring,
Just as he snaps when I poke a bit of stick at him,
Because he is irascible this morning, an irascible tortoise
Being touched with love, and devoid of fatherliness.

Father and mother,
And three little brothers,
And all rambling aimless, like little perambulating pebbles scattered in the garden,
Not knowing each other from bits of earth or old tins.

Except that papa and mama are old acquaintances, of course.
Though family feeling there is none, not even the beginnings.
Fatherless, motherless, brotherless, sisterless
Little tortoise.

Row on then, small pebble,
Over the clods of the autumn, wind-chilled sunshine,
Young gaiety.

Does he look for a companion?

No, no, don't think it.
He doesn't know he is alone;
Isolation is his birthright,
This atom.

To row forward, and reach himself tall on spiney toes,
To travel, to burrow into a little loose earth, afraid of the night,
To crop a little substance,
To move, and be quite sure that he is moving:
Basta!
To be a tortoise!
Think of it, in a garden of inert clods,
A brisk, brindled little tortoise, all to himself—
Adam!

In a garden of pebbles and insects
To roam, and feel the slow heart beat
Tortoise-wise, the first bell sounding
From the warm blood, in the dark-creation morning.

Moving, and being himself,
Slow, and unquestioned,
And inordinately there, O stoic!
Wandering in the slow triumph of his own existence,
Ringing the soundless bell of his presence in chaos,
And biting the frail grass arrogantly,
Decidedly arrogantly.

—D. H. Lawrence

Tradition

Tradition means giving votes to the most obscure of all classes—our ancestors. It is the democracy of the dead. Tradition refuses to submit to the small and arrogant oligarchy of those who merely happen to be walking around.

—G. K. Chesterton

I should be glad to break free of tradition, and be original right through, but that is a big undertaking and leads to much vexation of spirit. As a genuine earth-native, I should regard it as a supreme point of honor, if I were not so strangely a tradition myself.

—Goethe (trans. David Luke)

Respect for the past must be pious, but not mad.

—V. Rozanov

What is it sacrilege to destroy? The *metaxu.* No human being should be deprived of his *metaxu*, that is to say, of those relative and mixed blessings (home, country, traditions, culture, etc.) which warm and nourish the soul and without which, short of sainthood, a *human* life is impossible.

—Simone Weil

Translation

To translate means to serve two masters—something nobody can do. Hence, as is true of all things that in theory no one can do—it becomes in practice everybody's job. Everyone must translate and everyone does translate. Whoever speaks is translating his thought for the comprehension he expects from the other, not for an imaginary general "other" but for this particular other in front of him, whose eyes widen with eagerness or close with boredom. . . . The listener translates the words that strike his ear . . . into the language he himself uses. . . . The theoretical impossibility of translating can mean to us only . . . that in the course of the "impossible" and necessary compromises which in their sequence make the stuff of life, this theoretical impossibility will give us the courage of a modesty which will then demand of the translation not anything impossible but simply whatever must be done. Thus, in speaking or listening, the "other" need not have my ears or my mouth—this would render unnecessary not only translation but also speaking and listening. . . . What is needed is neither a translation that is so far from being a translation as to be the original—this would eliminate the listening nation—nor one that is in effect a new original—this would eliminate the speaking nation.

—Franz Rosenzweig

Ever since his own day Tyndale's translation has been blamed for being tendentious. If we are thinking of his violent marginal glosses, this is fair enough; if of his peculiar renderings (*congregation* for *ecclesia*, *senior* or *elder* for *presbuteros*, *favour* for *charis*, and the like), a little explanation seems to be needed. The business of a translator is to write down what he thinks the original meant. And Tyndale sincerely believed that the mighty theocracy with its cardinals, abbeys, pardons, inquisition, and treasury of grace which the word *Church* would undoubtedly have suggested to his readers was in its very essence not only distinct from, but antagonistic to, the thing that St Paul had in mind whenever he used the word *ecclesia*. You may of course disagree with his premises; but his conclusion (that *Church* is a false rendering of *ecclesia*) follows from it of necessity. Thomas More, on the other hand, believed with equal sincerity that the "Church" of his own day was in essence the very same mystical body which St Paul addressed; from his premise it followed of course that *Church* was the only correct translation. Both renderings are equally tendentious in the sense that each presupposes a belief. In that sense all translations of scripture are tendentious; translation, by its very nature, is a continuous implicit commentary. It can become less tendentious only by becoming less of a translation.

—C. S. Lewis

An interesting example of a "translation," in which the original is deliberately altered for satirical purposes, is Matthew Prior's treatment of Boileau Despréaux.

Contemplez dans la tempeste,
Qui sort de ces Boulevars,
La Plume qui sur sa teste
Attire tous les regards.

A cet Astre redoutable
Toujours un sort favorable
S'attache dans les Combats:
Et toûjours ave la Gloire
Mars amenant la Victoire
Vôle, & le suit à grands pas.

—*Ode sur la Prise de Namur,*
Par les Armes du Roy, L'Année 1692

Now let us look for *Louis*' Feather,
That us'd to shine so like a Star:
The Gen'rals could not get together
Wanting that Influence, great in War.
O Poet! Thou had'st been discreeter,
Hanging the Monarch's Hat so high;
If Thou had'st dubbed thy Star, a Meteor,
That did but blaze, and rove, and die.

—*An English Ballad, on the Taking of*
Namur by the King of Great Britain, 1695

Tyranny

Tyranny over a man is not tyranny: it is rebellion, for man is royal.

—G. K. Chesterton

Tyranny is always better organized than freedom.

—Charles Péguy

Under conditions of tyranny it is far easier to act than to think.

—Hannah Arendt

It is always observable that the physical and exact sciences are the last to suffer under despotisms.

—Richard Henry Dana

How lucky it is for tyrants that one half of mankind doesn't think, and the other half doesn't feel.

—J. G. Seume

Tyrants are always assassinated too late; that is their great excuse.

—E. M. Cioran

Despotism or unlimited sovereignty is the same in a majority of a popular assembly, an aristocratical council, an oligarchical junta, and a single emperor.

—J. Q. Adams

Every class is unfit to govern.

—Lord Acton

The belief that politics can be scientific must inevitably produce tyrannies. Politics cannot be a science, because in politics theory and practice cannot be separated, and the sciences depend upon their separation. The scientist frames a hypothesis and devises an experiment to test it; if the experiment gives a negative result, he must abandon it. Only when the experiment has confirmed his hypothesis will he begin to consider any practical applications. He can afford to wait for the truth. Since the subjects of his experiments have no will of their own, he does not have to take any subjective factors into consideration. The situation of the politician is utterly different. He cannot try out an hypothesis under laboratory conditions, but must immediately apply it to an historical situation and upon human beings, who not only have wills and opinions of their own but can change them. Consequently, no result at any moment can prove beyond doubt that he is mistaken. I hold the theory, let us say, that farmers will be happier and food production increased if agriculture is collectivized. I collectivize it. The farmers are obviously rebellious and food production drops. Does this prove me mistaken? Not necessarily. I can always argue that the failure is due to the malice and stupidity of the farmers and that, if I continue with the experiment long enough, they will come to see that I am right. Empirical politics must be kept in bounds by democratic institutions, which leave it up to the subjects of the experiment to say whether it shall be tried, and to stop it if they dislike it, because, in politics, there is a distinction, unknown to science, between Truth and Justice.

A Modern Nightmare

When Satan finds a rebel in his realm,
He laces round the head of the poor fool
A frightful mask, a sort of visored helm
That has a lining soaked in vitriol.
The renegade begins to scream with pain.
(The mask is not designed to gag the sound,
Which propagates the terror of his reign.)
The screams come through the visor, but are drowned
By the great shouting of the overlord,
Who, in relaying them, distorts the sense
So that the cringing listeners record
Mere cries of villainy or penitence . . .
Yet Satan has a stronger hold: the fear
That, if his rule is threatened, he will tear
The mask from that pain-crazed automaton
And show his vassals just what he has done.

—Norman Cameron

For the entourage of a modern tyrant, life must be pretty much the same as it was for those in attendance on Henry VIII.

> Stond who so list upon the Slipper toppe
> Of courtes estates, and lett me heare rejoyce;
> And use me quyet without lett or stoppe,
> Unknowen in courte, that hath suche brackishe joyes:
> In hidden place, so lett my dayes forthe passe,
> That when my yeares be done, withouten noyse,
> I may dye aged after the common trace.
> For hym death greep' the right hard by the croppe
> That is moche knowen of other; and of him self alas,
> Doth dye unknowen, dazed with dreadfull face.
>
> —T. Wyatt

Unfavorites and Favorites

Like everyone else, I have my black list of unfavorite authors and critics, and among intimate friends I sometimes say exactly what I think of them, but I have the feeling that to express my opinions publicly would be in bad taste, that, to people whom one does not know personally, one should speak only of the authors and critics one is fond of.

I find reading savage reviews like reading pornography; though I often enjoy them, I feel a bit ashamed of myself for doing so. Still, I must admit that I find Nietzsche's list of his "impracticals" great fun.

> *Seneca*, or the toreador of virtue.
> *Schiller*, or the moral trumpeter of Sackingen.
> *Rousseau*, or return to nature in impuris naturabilis.
> *Dante*, or the hyena *poetizing* among the tombs.
> *Kant*, or cant as an intelligible character.
> *Victor Hugo*, or Pharos in the sea of absurdity.
> *Liszt*, or the school of running after women.
> *George Sand*, or *lactea ubertas*; i.e. the milch-cow with the "fine style."
> *Michelet*, or enthusiasm which strips off the coat.
> *Carlyle*, or pessimism as an undigested dinner.
> *John Stuart Mill*, or offensive transparency.
> *Les frères de Goncourt*, or the two Ajaxes struggling with Homer. Music by Offenbach.
> *Zola*, or "the delight to stink."

To list my own "underbreds," with apt descriptions of the various kennels that sired them—how tempting! But I must stick to my principles and list my "pets" instead. The list is not, of course, exhaustive—there are many, many others I enjoy and admire, and I excluded comic poets because it is impossible to dislike them—but it does name those elder modern poets and modern critics from whom I have learned most.

Arranged in alphabetical order, they run thus:

Poets: Berthold Brecht (the lyric poet), Robert Bridges, Constantine Cavafy, Robert Frost, Robert Graves, Thomas Hardy, David Jones, D. H. Lawrence (of *Birds, Beasts and Flowers*), Walter de la Mare, Marianne Moore, Wilfred Owen, Laura Riding, Edward Thomas, William Carlos Williams (in his last period).

Critics: Erich Auerbach, G. K. Chesterton, T. S. Eliot (the quoter), Rudolf Kassner, W. P. Ker, Karl Kraus, C. S. Lewis, Eugen Rosenstock-Huessy, Leo Spitzer, Paul Valéry, Charles Williams.

Two Plugs:

The greatest long poem written in English in this century: *The Anathemata* by David Jones.

The only first-rate volume of poems specifically about World War II: *Rhymes of a Pfc* by Lincoln Kirstein.

Unitarians

A Unitarian is a person who believes there is, at most, one God.

—A. N. Whitehead

Verse, Quantitative English

When, under the influence of the Humanists, English poets of the sixteenth century tried to write English verse in classical meters, they found themselves in difficulties. Firstly, they ran up against the problem of the relation between vowel length and stress. I certainly don't know myself, and I doubt if the scholars can say with absolute certainty, whether when the Greek and Latin poets recited their verses, long vowels and stresses always coincided, but it is clear that in English they do not. For example, the first syllable of *merry* is short but stressed, the first syllable of *proceed* unstressed but long. Secondly, they found that in a language like English, which has lost most of its inflexional endings, vowels which are in themselves short are constantly becoming long by position, that is to say, followed by more than one consonant. For example, in the line "Of man's first disobedience and the fruit" there is, when scanned quantitatively, only one short syllable, *dis.*

In the following poem, by Campion, the metrical base consists of one spondee, two choriambs and an iambus, but Campion cannot make up his mind as to whether it is more important that the vowel quantities conform to the pattern or that the stresses should. Some lines conform in both respects, some in quantity, some in stress, and some in neither.

Canto Secundo

What faire pompe have I spide of glittering Ladies;
With locks sparckled abroad, and rosie Coronet

On their yvorie browes, trackt to the daintie thies
With roabs like *Amazons*, blew as Violet,
With gold Aiglets adornd, some in a changeable
Pale; with spangs wavering taught to be moveable.

Then those Knights that a farre off with dolorous viewing
Cast their eyes hetherward; loe, in an agonie,
All unbrac'd, crie aloud, their heavie state ruing:
Moyst cheekes with blubbering, painted as *Ebonie*
Blacke; their feltred haire torne with wrathful hand:
And whiles astonied, starke in a maze they stand.

But hearke! what merry sound! what sodaine harmonie!
Looke looke neere the grove where the Ladies doe tread
With their Knights the measures waide by the melodie.
Wantons! whose travesing make men enamoured;
Now they faine an honor, now by the slender wast
He must lift hir aloft, and seale a kisse in hast.

Straight downe under a shadow for weariness they lie
With pleasant daliance, hand knit with arme in arme,
Now close, now set aloof, they gaze with an equall eie,
Changing kisses alike; streight with a false alarme,
Mocking kisses alike, powt with a lovely lip.
Thus drownd with jollities, their merry daies doe slip.

But stay! now I discerne they goe on a Pilgrimage
Towards Loves holy land, faire *Paphos* or *Cyprus*.
Such devotion is meete for a blithesome age;
With sweet youth, it agrees well to be amorous.
Let olde angrie fathers lurke in an Hermitage:
Come, weele associate this jolly Pilgrimage!

In the nineteenth century one or two poets like Tennyson experimented with quantitative verse, but the majority, when they wished to imitate classical poetry, scanned by accent and ignored quantity. The meter they generally chose to imitate was the hexameter. Unfortunately, the English language does not fall naturally into hexameters; in English the meter sounds eccentric. Clough was the first poet to discover that if the accentual hexameter can be used in English at all it is better suited to a low, conversational style than to a high, epic one.

DEAR MISS ROPER,—It seems, George Vernon, before we left Rome, said
Something to Mr Claude about what they call his intentions.
Susan, two nights ago, for the first time, heard this from Georgina.
It is *so* disagreeable and *so* annoying to think of!
If it could only be known, though we may never meet him again, that

It was all George's doing, and we were entirely unconscious,
It would extremely relieve—Your ever affectionate Mary.

—Arthur Hugh Clough

So far as I know, Bridges was the first to write quantitative verse in English which ignores stress altogether.

Thus the following extract is written in hexameters, but no ear that listens for stresses will hear them as such.

What was Alexander's subduing of Asia, or that
Sheep-worry of Europe, when pigmy Napoleon enter'd
Her sovereign chambers, and her kings with terror eclips'd?
His footsore soldiers inciting across the ravag'd plains,
Thro' bloody fields of death tramping to an ugly disaster?
Shows any crown, set above the promise (so rudely accomplisht)
Of their fair godlike young faces, a glory to compare
With the immortal olive that circles bold Galileo's
Brows, the laurel'd halo of Newton's unwithering fame,
Or what a child's surmise, how trifling a journey Columbus
Adventur'd, to a land like that which he sailed from arriving,
If compar'd to Bessel's magic divination, awarding
Magnificent Sirius his dark and invisible bride.

—Robert Bridges

Voyages

May 14, 1787

The afternoon passed without our having entered the Gulf of Naples. On the contrary, we were steadily drawn in a westerly direction; the boat moved further and further away from Cape Minerva and nearer and nearer to Capri.

Everybody was glum and impatient, except Kniep and myself. Looking at the world with the eyes of painters, we were perfectly content to enjoy the sunset, which was the most magnificent spectacle we had seen during the whole voyage. Cape Minerva and its adjoining ranges lay before us in a display of brilliant colours. The cliffs stretching to the south had already taken on a bluish tint. From the Cape to Sorrento the whole coast was lit up. Above Vesuvius towered an enormous smoke cloud, from which a long streak trailed away to the east, suggesting that a violent eruption was in progress. Capri rose abruptly on our left and, through the haze, we could see the outlines of its precipices.

The wind had dropped completely, and the glittering sea, showing scarcely a ripple, lay before us like a limpid pond under the cloudless sky. Kniep said what a pity it was that no skill with colours, however great, could reproduce this harmony and that not even the finest English pencils, wielded by the most practised hand, could draw these contours. I was convinced, on the contrary, that even a much poorer memento than this able artist would produce would be very valuable in the future, and urged him to make an attempt at it. He followed my advice and produced a most accurate drawing which he later coloured, which shows that pictorial representation can achieve the impossible.

With equally rapt attention we watched the transition from evening to night. Ahead of us Capri was now in total darkness. The cloud above Vesuvius and its trail began to glow, and the longer we looked the brighter it grew, till a considerable part of the sky was lit up as if by summer lightning.

We had been so absorbed in enjoying these sights that we had not noticed that we were threatened with a serious disaster; but the commotion among the passengers did not leave us long in doubt. Those who had more experience of happenings at sea than we bitterly blamed the captain and his helmsman, saying that, thanks to their incompetence, they had not only missed the entrance to the straits but were now endangering the lives of the passengers, the cargo and everything else confided to their care. We asked why they were so anxious, for we did not see why there could be any cause to be afraid when the sea was so calm. But it was precisely the calm that worried them: they saw we had already entered the current which encircles Capri and by the peculiar wash of the waves draws everything slowly and irresistibly towards the sheer rock face, where there is no ledge to offer the slightest foothold and no bay to promise safety.

The news appalled us. Though the darkness prevented us from seeing the approaching danger, we could see that the boat, rolling and pitching, was moving nearer to the rocks, which loomed ever darker ahead. A faint afterglow was still spread over the sea. Not the least breath of wind was stirring. Everyone held up handkerchiefs and ribbons, but there was no sign of the longed-for breeze. The tumult among the passengers grew louder and louder. The women and children knelt on the deck or lay huddled together, not in order to pray, but because the deck space was too cramped to let them move about. The men, with their thoughts ever on help and rescue, raved and stormed against the captain. They now attacked him for everything they had silently criticized during the whole voyage—the miserable accommodation, the outrageous charges, the wretched food and his behaviour. Actually, he had not been unkind, but very reserved; he had never explained his actions to anyone and even last night he had maintained a stubborn silence about his manoeuvres. Now they called him and his helmsman mercenary adventurers who knew nothing about navigation, but had got hold of a boat out of sheer greed, and were now by their incompetent bungling about to bring to grief the lives of all those in their care. The captain remained silent and still seemed to be preoccupied with saving the boat. But I, who all my life have hated anarchy worse than death, could keep silent no longer. I stepped forward and addressed the crowd, with almost the same equanimity I had shown in facing the "Birds" of Malcesine. I pointed out to them that, at such a moment, their shouting would only confuse the ears and minds of those upon whom our safety depended, and make it impossible for them to think or communicate with one another. "As for you," I exclaimed, "examine your hearts and then say your prayers to the Mother of God, for she alone can decide whether she will intercede with her Son, that he may do for you what He once did for His apostles on the storm-swept sea of Tiberias. Our Lord was sleeping, the waves were already breaking into the boat, but when the desperate and helpless men woke Him, He immediately commanded the wind to rest, and now, if it should be His will, He can command the wind to stir."

These words had an excellent effect. One woman, with whom I had had some conversation about moral and spiritual matters, exclaimed: "*Ah, il barlamè. Benedetto il barlamè,*" and as they were all on their knees anyway, they actually began to say their litanies with more than usual fervour. They could do this with greater peace of mind, because the crew were now trying another expedient, which could at least be seen and understood by all. They lowered the pinnace, which could hold from six to eight men, fastened it to the ship by a long rope, and tried, by rowing hard, to tow the ship after them. But their very efforts seemed to increase the counter-pull of the current. For some reason or other, the pinnace was suddenly dragged backwards towards the ship and the long towing rope described a bow like a whiplash when the driver cracks it. So this hope vanished.

Prayers alternated with lamentations and the situation grew more desperate, when some goatherds on the rocks above us whose fires we had seen for some time shouted with hollow voices that there was a ship below about to founder. Much that they cried was unintelligible, but some passengers, familiar with their dialect, took these cries to mean that they were gleefully looking forward to the booty they would fish out of the sea the next morning. Any consoling doubt as to whether our ship was really dangerously near the rocks was soon banished when we saw the sailors taking up long poles with which, if the worst came to the worst, they could keep fending the ship off the rocks. Of course, if the poles broke, all would be lost. The violence of the surf seemed to be increasing, the ship tossed and rolled more than ever; as a result, my seasickness returned and I had to retire to the cabin below. I lay down half dazed but with a certain feeling of contentment, due, perhaps, to the sea of Tiberias; for in my mind's eye, I saw clearly before me the etching from the Merian Bible. It gave me proof that all impressions of a sensory-moral nature are strongest when a man is thrown completely on his own resources.

How long I had been lying in this kind of half-sleep I could not tell, but I was roused out of it by a tremendous noise over my head. My ears told me that it came from dragging heavy ropes about the deck, and this gave me some hope that the sails were being hoisted. Shortly afterwards Kniep came down in a hurry to tell me we were safe. A very gentle breeze had sprung up; they had just been struggling to hoist the sails, and he himself had not neglected to lend a hand. We had, he said, visibly moved away from the cliff, and, though we were not yet completely out of the current, there was hope now of escaping from it. On deck everything was quiet again. Presently, several other passengers came to tell me about the lucky turn of events and to lie down themselves.

—Goethe

April 9, 1868

The night voyage, though far from pleasant, has not been as bad as might have been anticipated. He is fortunate, who, after ten hours of sea passage can reckon up no worse memories than those of a passive condition of suffering—of that dislocation of mind and body, or inability to think straightforward, so to speak, when the outer man is twisted, and rolled, and jerked, and the movements of thought seem more or less to correspond with those of the body. Wearily go by

"The slow sad hours that bring us all things ill,"

and vain is the effort to enliven them as every fresh lurch of the vessel tangles practical or pictorial suggestions with untimely scraps of poetry, indistinct regrets and predictions, couplets for a new *Book of Nonsense*, and all kinds of inconsequent imbecilities—after this sort—

Would it not have been better to have remained at Cannes, where I had not yet visited Theoule, the Saut de Loup, and other places?

Had I not said, scores of times, such and such a voyage was the last I would make?

To-morrow, when "morn broadens on the borders of the dark," shall I see Corsica's "snowy mountain-tops fringing the (Eastern) sky"?

Did the sentinels of lordly Volaterra see, as Lord Macaulay says they did, "Sardinia's snowy mountain-tops," and not rather these same Corsican tops, "fringing the southern sky"?

Did they see any tops at all, or if any, which tops?

Will the daybreak ever happen?

Will 2 o'clock ever arrive?

Will the two poodles above stairs ever cease to run about the deck?

Is it not disagreeable to look forward to two or three months of travelling quite alone?

Would it not be delightful to travel, as J. A. S. is about to do, in company with a wife and child?

Does it not, as years advance, become clearer that it is very odious to be alone?

Have not many very distinguished persons, Œnone among others, arrived at this conclusion?

Did she not say, with evident displeasure—

> "And from that time to this I am alone,
> And I shall be alone until I die"?—

Will those poodles ever cease from trotting up and down the deck?

Is it not unpleasant, at fifty-six years of age, to feel that it is increasingly probable that a man can never hope to be otherwise than alone, never, no, never more?

Did not Edgar Poe's raven distinctly say, "Nevermore"?

Will those poodles be quiet? "Quoth the raven, nevermore."

Will there be anything worth seeing in Corsica?

Is there any romance left in that island? Is there any sublimity or beauty in its scenery?

Have I taken too much baggage?

Have I not rather taken too little?

Am I not an idiot for coming at all?—

Thus, and in such a groove, did the machinery of thought go on, gradually refusing to move otherwise than by jerky spasms, after the fashion of mechanical Ollendorff exercises, or verb-catechisms of familiar phrases—

Are there not Banditti?
Had there not been Vendetta?
Were there not Corsican brothers?
  Should I not carry clothes for all sorts of weather?
  Must THOU not have taken a dress coat?
  Had HE not many letters of introduction?
    Might WE not have taken extra pairs of spectacles?
    Could YOU not have provided numerous walking boots?
    Should THEY not have forgotten boxes of quinine pills?
      Shall WE possess flea-powder?
      Could YOU not procure copper money?
      May THEY not find cream cheeses?
        Should there not be innumerable moufflons?
        Ought not the cabin lamps and glasses to cease jingling?
        Might not the poodles stop worrying?—

thus and thus, till by reason of long hours and monotonous rolling and shaking, a sort of comatose insensibility, miscalled sleep, takes the place of all thought, and so the night passes.

—Edward Lear

War

There have been few more radical changes in the history of Western culture than the change in attitude towards war and the military profession brought about by World War I. Western literature began as the literature of a warrior aristocracy, and until 1914 it took the warrior ethic for granted; it assumed that war was glorious, and the words *hero* and *warrior* were almost synonymous. Conscription and "sophisticated" weapons have changed all that. We may still believe that in certain circumstances a war is just and necessary, but nobody imagines any longer that it will be fun; today we know that war is an atrocious and corrupting business. We can no longer read an epic like the *Iliad* in the same way that even our grandfathers read it; to us, the passages in which Homer describes combat are painful reading, and we turn with relief to the Chinese poets, for whom the soldier was an object of pity, not admiration.

The symbol of the change was the construction after 1918 in all the belligerent countries of monuments to the Unknown Soldier. Previously, monuments had always been erected to known individuals, victorious generals and admirals. About the Unknown Soldier nothing is known whatever except that he lost his life. For all we know, he may, personally, have been a coward. In his monument, that is to say, we pay homage to the warrior, not as a hero but as a martyr.

The story goes that during World War I a Guards officer was on leave. "Do tell us," said his clubmates, "what is war like?" "Awful!" he replied. "The noise! And the *people!*"

Three-quarters of a soldier's life is spent in aimlessly waiting about.

—Eugen Rosenstock-Huessy

Soldiers who don't know what they are fighting for, know, nevertheless, what they're not fighting for.

—Karl Kraus

I hate war: it ruins conversation.

—Fontenelle

After a lost war one should only write comedies.

—Novalis

A nation which lives a pastoral and innocent life never decorates the shepherd's staff or the plough-handle; but races who live by depredation and slaughter nearly always bestow exquisite ornaments on the quiver, the helmet and the spear.

You talk of the scythe of Time, and the tooth of Time: I tell you, Time is scytheless and toothless; it is we who gnaw like the worm—we who smite like the scythe. It is ourselves who abolish—ourselves who consume: we are the mildew, and the flame; and the soul of man is to its own work as the moth that frets when it cannot fly, and as the hidden flame that blasts where it cannot illuminate. All these lost treasures of human intellect have been wholly destroyed by human industry of destruction; the marble would have stood its two thousand years as well in the polished statue as in the Parian cliff; but we men have ground it to powder, and mixed it with our own ashes. The walls and the ways would have stood—it is we who have left but one stone upon another, and restored its pathlessness to the desert; the great cathedrals of the old religion would have stood—it is we who have dashed down the carved work with axes and hammers, and bid the mountain-grass bloom upon the pavement, and the sea-winds chant in the galleries.

—Ruskin

All living beings have received their weapons through the same process of evolution that moulded their impulses and inhibitions; for the structural plan of the body and the system of behaviour of a species are parts of the same whole. There is only one being in possession of weapons which do not grow on his body and of whose working plan, therefore, the instincts of his species know nothing and in the usage of which he has no corresponding inhibition.

—Konrad Lorenz

What a country calls its vital economic interests are not the things which enable its citizens to live, but the things which enable it to make war. Gasoline is much more likely than wheat to be a cause of international conflict.

—Simone Weil

The Night Watch

Here they stand watch in an ambush of moonshadow
cast by the sloping mountains where night is born

and soars up bearing its stars like bright eagles.

Some rest—those who trust courage—sword-guarded,
mute, safe from fear's grip in their sheltering long shields.

What hour does night's round-shield say it is?
The Big Dipper keeps ladling out stars.

Over there the mercenaries start bragging of luck,
yesterday's, to-morrow's, to hurry the festive day.

Kill legions . . . strip the fat fields, take towns
. . . or a woman, what luck's truer than a woman?

And over there others try to muzzle their gut-gripes:

When will there be a lull in the fighting, when
will hard war end? Our plows, our fields wait.

The sky slowly changes its huge guard of stars.

And there's the young lieutenant, sword buckled
over his heart and his soul on his smooth face:

Soon it's to be life or death . . . either one
means someone's harvest or old age shall ripen.
Live, die, I'm not afraid. Father, fatherland . . .
life-giving earth . . . be safe.

The night marches on, armored in burning stars.

The freedom they shall fight for, may it last forever.

—Ennius (assembled from fragments
and trans. by Janet Lembke)

The War-Song of Dinas Vawr

The mountain sheep are sweeter,
But the valley sheep are fatter;
We therefore deemed it meeter
To carry off the latter;
We made an expedition,
We met a host and quelled it;
We forced a strong position,
And killed the men who held it.

On Dyfed's richest valley,
Where herds of kine were browsing,
We made a mighty sally,
To finish our carousing.
Fierce warriors rushed to meet us;
We met them and o'erthrew them:
They struggled hard to beat us;
But we conquered them and slew them.

As we drove our prize at leisure,
The king marched forth to catch us;

His rage surpassed all measure,
But his people could not match us.
He fled to his hall-pillars;
And, ere our force we led off,
Some sacked his house and cellars,
While others cut his head off.

We there, in strife bewild'ring,
Spilt blood enough to swim in:
We orphaned many children,
And widowed many women.
The eagles and the ravens
We glutted with our foemen;
The heroes and the cravens,
The spearmen and the bowmen.

We brought away from battle,
And much their land bemoaned them,
Two thousand head of cattle,
And the head of him who owned them:
Ednyfed, King of Dyfed,
His head was borne before us;
His wine and beasts supplied our feasts,
And his overthrow, our chorus.

—T. L. Peacock

War Song

In anguish we uplift
A new unhallowed song:
The race is to the swift,
The battle to the strong.

Of old it was ordained
That we in packs like curs,
Some thirty million trained
And licensed murderers,
In crime should live and act,
If cunning folk say sooth
Who flay the naked fact
And carve the heart of truth.

The rulers cry aloud,
"We cannot cancel war,
The end and bloody shroud
Of wrongs the worst abhor,
And order's swaddling band:
Know that relentless strife

Remains by sea and land
The holiest law of life.
From fear in every guise,
From sloth, from lust of pelf,
By war's great sacrifice
The world redeems itself.
War is the source, the theme
Of art, the goal, the bent
And brilliant academe
Of noble sentiment;
The augury, the dawn
Of golden times of grace;
The true catholicon
And blood-bath of the race."

We thirty million trained
And licensed murderers,
Like zanies rigged, and chained
By drill and scourge and curse
In shackles of despair
We know not how to break—
What do we victims care
For art, what interest take
In things unseen, unheard?
Some diplomat no doubt
Will launch a heedless word,
And lurking war leap out.

We spell-bound armies then,
Huge brutes in dumb distress,
Machines compact of men
Who once had consciences,
Must trample harvests down—
Vineyard and corn and oil;
Dismantle town by town,
Hamlet and homestead spoil
On each appointed path,
Till lust of havoc light
A blood-red blaze of wrath
In every frenzied sight.

In many a mountain pass,
Or meadow green and fresh,
Mass shall encounter mass
Of shuddering human flesh;
Opposing ordnance roar

Across the swathes of slain,
And blood in torrents pour
In vain—always in vain.
For war breeds war again.

The shameful dream is past,
The subtle maze untrod;
We recognize at last
That war is not of God.
Wherefore we now uplift
Our new unhallowed song:
The race is to the swift,
The battle to the strong.

—John Davidson

Walcheren
Dumb Show

A vast army is encamped here, and in the open spaces are infantry on parade—skeletoned men, some flushed, some shivering, who are kept moving because it is dangerous to stay still. Every now and then one falls down, and is carried away to a hospital with no roof, where he is laid, bedless, on the ground.

In the distance soldiers are digging graves for the funerals which are to take place after dark, delayed till then that the sight of so many may not drive the living melancholy-mad. Faint noises are heard in the air.

SHADE OF THE EARTH. What storm is this of souls dissolved in sighs,
And what the dingy doom it signifies?

SPIRIT OF THE PITIES. We catch a lamentation shaped thuswise:

CHORUS OF PITIES (*aerial music*). "We who withstood the blasting blaze of war
When marshalled by the gallant Moore awhile,
Beheld the grazing death-bolt with a smile,
Closed combat edge to edge and bore to bore,
Now rot upon this Isle!

"The ever wan morass, the dune, the blear
Sandweed, and tepid pool, and putrid smell,
Emaciate purpose to a fractious fear,
Beckon the body to its last low cell—
A chink no chart will tell.

"O ancient Delta, where the fen-lights flit!
Ignoble sediment of loftier lands,
Thy humour clings about our hearts and hands

And solves us to its softness, till we sit
As we were part of it.

"Such force as fever leaves is maddened now,
With tidings trickling in from day to day
Of others' differing fortunes, wording how
They yield their lives to baulk a tyrant's sway—
Yielded not vainly, they!

"In champaigns green and purple, far and near,
In town and thorpe where quiet spire-cocks turn,
Through vales, by rocks, beside the brooding burn
Echoes the aggressor's arrogant career;
And we pent pithless here!

"Here where each creeping day the creeping file
Draws past with shouldered comrades score on score,
Bearing them to their lightless last asile,
Where weary wave-wails from the clammy shore
Will reach their ears no more.

"We might have fought, and had we died, died well,
Even if in dynasts' discords not our own;
Our death-spot some sad haunter might have shown,
Some tongue have asked our sires or sons to tell
The tale of how we fell.

"But such bechanced not. Like the mist we fade,
No lustrous lines engrave in story we,
Our country's chiefs, for their own fames afraid,
Will leave our names and fates by this pale sea
To perish silently!"

SPIRIT OF THE YEARS. Why must ye echo as mechanic mimes
These mortal minions' bootless cadences,
Played on the stops of their anatomy
As is the mewling music on the strings
Of yonder ship-masts by the unweeting wind,
Or the frail tune upon this withering sedge
That holds its papery blades against the gale?
—Men pass to dark corruption, at the best,
Ere I can count five score: these why not now?—
The Immanent Shaper builds Its beings so,
Whether ye sigh their sighs with them or no!

The night fog enwraps the isle and the dying English army.

—Thomas Hardy

Journey to the North

From hump-backed paths I gaze on the temple of Fu;
Valleys and precipices appear and disappear in turn.
Already my path has reached the water's edge.
My serving man is still among the trees.
The horned owl hoots amid yellow mulberries.
The field mice run from their scattered holes.
In the depth of night we cross a battlefield;
A cold moon shines on white bones.
I ponder the fate of a myriad soldiers speedily defeated
In days gone by on the fields of Tung-kuan,
When half the people of the province of Ch'ing
Fell dead, were wounded, were injured and slain.

Chariots Go Forth to War

Chariots rumble and roll; horses whinney and neigh;
Men are marching with bows and arrows at their hips.
Their parents and wives hurry to bid farewell,
Raising clouds of dust over Hsien-yang Bridge.
They pull at the soldiers' clothes, stamp their feet and cry out.
The sound of their crying soars to the clouds.

Some passers-by speak to the soldiers;
They shake their heads dumbly and say:
"Since the age of fifteen we have defended the northern rivers.
Till we are forty we shall serve on the western front.
We leave our homes as youths and return as gray-haired men.
Along the frontiers there flows the sea of our blood.
The King hungers for territory—therefore we fight.

"Have you not heard, sir,
How through two hundred countries east of the Tai-yeng Mountains
Through thousands of villages and tens of thousands of hamlets
Thorns and nettles run wild?
Sturdy peasant women swing the hoes and drive the plow,
But neither in the east nor west is anything raised or sown.
The soldiers of Sh'and will fight to the end,
But they cannot be slain like dogs or like hens.

"Oh, sir, it is kind of you to ask me,
But how dare we express our resentment?
Winter has come and the year is passing away;
The war on the western passes is still going on.
The magistrates are pressing us to pay our taxes,
But where shall we get the money?
If only I had known the fate in store for boys,

I would have had my children all girls,
For girls may be married to the neighbors,
But boys are born only to be cut down and buried beneath the grass.

"Do you not see, sir,
The long dead ancient bones near the Blue Sea bleached by the sun?
And now the lament of those who have just died
Mingles with the voices of those who died long ago,
And darkness falls, and the rain, and the ghostly whimpering of voices."
—Tu Fu (trans. Pu Chiang-hsing)

Song of Fraternization

I remember when I was just seventeen
When the foe invaded our land:
With a smile he laid aside his sabre,
And with a smile he gave me his hand.
That May the days were bright,
And starry every night.
The regiment stood on parade:
They gave their drums the usual thwack,
They led us then behind a stack,
Where they fraternized with us.

Our foes were strong and many,
An army-cook was mine:
I hated my foe by daylight,
But, O, I loved him by moonshine.
Now all the days are bright,
And starry every night.
The regiment stands on parade:
They give their drums the usual thwack,
Again, again, behind a stack,
There they fraternize with us.

Such a love must come from Heaven,
It was the will of Fate:
The others could never understand me,
How could I love where I should date.
Then came a rainy morn,
A day of grief and scorn.
The regiment stood on parade:
They drums beat as they always do.
There stood my foe, my darling too:
Then they marched away from us.
—Bertolt Brecht (trans. W. H. Auden)

Bed-Wetting in Barracks

Various writers have observed that enuresis seems to be unduly common among soldiers. Discounting the not inconsiderable number of cases of malingering, where bed-wetting is deliberately resorted to in an attempt to obtain a disability discharge or at least to escape active service, veritable epidemics of real enuresis occur from time to time. If these outbreaks were reported only among men who are actively engaged in combat or who are training for imminent service, the logical assumption would be that anxiety is here the prime etiological factor. The fact that enuresis may also be recurrent or more or less chronic in barracks during times of prolonged peace suggests a different explanation, namely, that the discipline and arbitrary treatment which form so large a part of military training may reinstate in young men attitudes of hostility and resentment which they felt as children toward parental authority. . . .

—O. H. Mowrer

4th Armored

. . . That Colonel Abrams. He sure saved a lotta lives.
Abrams love his ole radio. He git him inta town;
What a lotta bullshit that man throw;
"Now hear this. Now hear this. We have you surrouned."
Surrouned? My ass, but that's Abrams.

"Hear this, you-all.
We have you poor sonsa bitches completely surrouned.
If you-all doan come out an surrener esatly ten minutes,
Our artillery, which have your town already pinpoint,
Will commence."

In esatly ten minute everyone come out. An surrener.
Like usually they do; sometime, not.
One time we lose four tanks in fifteen minute to some of them
Goddam Hitler youth with panzer fists.
They burn our tanks. Flame-throwers. Cooked. We didn have
A chance. Them Hitler-youth kids. Was they fierce!

"We see one stand up with his girl, her about twelve, maybe thirteen,
Both of them with their type bazooka.
Charlie have his Heinie P.38. Wasn use to it then neither.
One hunerd yards, a long shot fera pistol. Hell, long fera carbeen.
Hot damn. That kid drop like a hammer hit him.
Later, went over fera look. Charlie plug him jus unner the left eye.

He was going to pot sister too. I guess it was his sister.
I say: "Charlie, doan do that."

Then this door. I open up, easy-like. Tavern sorta bar;
They sell beer an santwitches?
Inside?
I'm a son of a bitch if weren twenty-eight Heinie officers,
Two machine-gun tripods, mounted low, on tables—
Swing roun angle one huner eighty degree;
Twenty-eight men, all officers. I count three womin too.
I tell you, mac. I had a lotta things go through my head.

I riz my hand jus like to say:
"Not one peep outa you bastids. You-all jus come on out."
I do this cause I know damn well we have evrythin set up, outside.
Atually, this town was very well covered.

Them Krauts come out. They lef their weapons heap on a table.
This here P.38, the one Charlie got; he got it here.
Another time, a bluff like this mightn work.
Atually, these Krauts almos didn believe me or somethin
Some silly son of a bitch start to open up.

We had 75's, 88's, 101's, evry fuckin gun you kin think of
In hills back of this town, listenin fer one shot.
They hear this one shot.
Christ: we start to fire, just at roof level:
One, two, three.
Then we hit a leetle lower, a leetle lower—an lower.
Special, we pick out any tall tower, like a church steeple.
One, two, three.
Man, was this cute! Like a typewriter:
One, two,
Three.

—Lincoln Kirstein

A Wartime Baby

Anna's life began in a dugout under a farmer's house in Poland, where her Jewish parents were in hiding to escape extermination by the Germans. Her parents were ill-mated. The mother found the father utterly unattractive and had rejected his courtship for years. Both parents felt they were of opposite temperaments and background. By the time World War II broke out, the father had given up hope of winning the mother, but the invasion of Poland suddenly changed things.

Foreseeing what would happen once Germany had occupied Poland, the father collected a large amount of wool and made arrangements with a gentile peasant friend to staple it in a dugout under his farm-house, together with a loom. When the Germans began to exterminate all Jews, Anna's father took permanent refuge in his small earthen cellar. But first he tried once more to persuade the woman he loved to join him. This proposal she again firmly rejected. She had no use for him, she said, and would sooner be killed by the Germans than be his wife.

Soon things worsened and most of her family was killed. The father, who could no longer leave his hiding place, sent word to her again through his peasant friend, asking her to join him. By this time she was homeless and alone. So very much against her will she took refuge with the father . . . Her condition for accepting was that they would have no sexual relations.

The father managed to support himself and her, and in part also the peasant who hid them during the whole of the German occupation, by weaving in his underground hole. The peasant sold the sweaters that were woven, and by spending what he got for them (clothing being at a premium) he and the couple in hiding were able to live. But the dugout was so small there was not enough space for the parents to so much as stretch out at night unless the loom was taken down. Only then could they bed themselves for the night, using the wool for both cover and bed. . . .

About what then happened, the parents' stories differ. According to the father, they had to tremble for their lives every day, but he at least had his work to keep him going, while his wife was beginning to lose her will to live. In desperation he decided that if she had a child, it would restore her interest in living and might even make her accept him. So he convinced her to have a child, and she agreed to have sex relations for this purpose alone. These were the circumstances in which his wife became pregnant.

According to the mother, the father had never ceased his sexual pursuit. After a year of this, he was no longer willing or able to stand the presence of a woman whom he wanted so much and who rejected him, so he threatened to drive her out of the refuge. Either she slept with him as his wife, or she had to leave—which was tantamount to a death warrant. Under such duress she gave in.

As one can imagine, both before and after Anna was born, there were many fights—the mother screaming how she hated him, couldn't be his wife, had no use for him, and he fighting back in bitterness. To make matters worse, the peasant feared for his life if they should be heard, and threatened to kick them out unless they remained absolutely still and kept the peace. . . .

When Anna, the child of this relation, was born, she did occupy the mother and give her some interest in life, but it made life still more difficult in their narrow confinement. When Anna tried to cry, as infants do, one of the parents had to hold a hand over her mouth since any noise, particularly a baby's crying, would have given them all away. . . .

As long as the mother could nurse Anna, the infant had at least enough food. But her milk gave out before Anna was a year and a half old. Then all the parents could feed her were raw vegetables or such like, since they could not cook in their dugout. Only in 1945, when the Russian occupation had replaced that of the Germans, did things improve a bit. But by that time Anna was unmanageable.

—Bruno Bettelheim

Water, Running

Though much a little map unfolds, more still—
Far more—is that which now dissolving mists
The sun confounds and distances deny;
Dumb Wonder speaks by silence, her blind eye
Allows the river, son of that same hill,
    Whose prolix discourse twists
Benevolent to tyrannise the plain.
Its borders lined with many an orchard lawn,
If not with flowers stolen from the Dawn,
The stream flows straight while it does not aspire
The heights with its own crystals to attain;
Flees from itself to find itself again,
Is lost, and searching for its wanderings.
Both errors sweet and sweet meanderings
The waters make with their lascivious fire;
And, linking buildings in its silver force.
With bowers crowned, majestically flows
Into abundant branches, there to wind
'Mid isles that green parentheses provide
In the main period of the current's course;
From the high cavern where it first arose,
Until the liquid jasper, there to find
All memory lost and forfeited all pride.

—Góngora (trans. E. M. Wilson)

Springs

There is attraction in every spring or source, but the birthplace of great rivers, as of great men, is sometimes comparatively uninspiring and obscure. Neither Thames Head, near Coberley, nor the Seven Springs, near Kemble—rival sources of the Thames—is to-day very impressive, while the bright Test rises in a dull little Pond by a Hampshire farm, and both Severn and Wye trickle from trifling basins on the boggy slopes of Plinlimmon. Peaty hills and alluvial lowlands alike confuse the sources of their rivers, though they sustain their flow. The fascination of a clear and quivering well-head is redoubled by its comparative rarity among the soft soils and gently moulded hillocks of most English landscapes. Water is the prime necessity of life, and there is a magic in its mysterious upwelling; from the earliest days springs were centres of Nature-worship—natural shrines—and when we play at wishing our wish by the well at Upwey, it is the shadow of an ancient prayer. Their purity is symbolic, and saints and hermits dwelt beside them for their spiritual suggestiveness as well as for the satisfaction of physical need. Beside churches in Wales we can still see the spring, though often sapped and shrunken, that sustained the missionary saint. New settlers clustered thickest where springs were most frequent. Follow the road from Dunstable to Wallingford beneath the Chiltern Hills, or from Helmsley nearly to Scarborough in Yorkshire, and see how closely the villages follow. Often the church, and the mill, and some old cottages, gather close around the spring, forming an unspoilt village picture. The spring called Broadwell, close beside the church at Dursley, in Gloucestershire, preserves in a small town of reviving manufactures the freshness of its older life; and at Swangge the millpond still hangs by the church on the hillside, as if the watering-place was still a quarrymen's village.

Deep springs welling from a shaft in soft soil rise with unearthly colours. The blueness of complete purity mingles with the faint green of the slightest vegetable contamination into a confusion of wavering lights like the flames over a snapdragon dish. Beneath the blue and the green dance the sand-clouds in a moonlit glimmer. The unearthliness of these colours is heightened by the apparent suspension of the laws of gravity, for the sand seems to rise in defiance of any known principle—so quietly, except for this one sign, gushes the spring. Smaller springs reveal their mechanics more clearly. On the shallow floor we can trace by the small sand-eddies the vents in the angled unworn gravel from which the water is rising. However closely the cresses and blue water-speedwell press upon it, the restlessness of these sand-spirts keeps a clear space of grit and gravel for the issue of the spring. Minnows flick past the spinning sand-towers, like whales between waterspouts; and that broad-headed brookfish, called miller's thumb, or bullhead, lurks, spotted, among the pebbles on the spring's floor. In many of the chalk counties the outlet of the spring has been widened to make a watercress-bed, and is verdant and full of life at all seasons. Wagtails, pied and gold-washed, run and clamber among the cresses to seize small water-snails and water-flies; as frost seals the crust of the fields, and coats the ponds with ice, the cottage child filling the morning bucket sees a snipe dart from the unfrozen edge where it has fed. Kingfishers perch on the holly boughs stretched from the bank above the spring, and splash in the stillness as they dive for miller's thumb or minnow. Yet fair as are these limpid risings, still more radiant, and in England much rarer, are the fountains which stream from gashes in live rock. They plunge with a flash and babble which has the gaiety of a town fountain in a setting of rustic freshness; and though they half reveal no such mysterious depths as a deep chalk spring, they restore for us, among our own scenes of flag and fern, the pictured charm of Italian spouting marbles, and of the stream which Moses struck from the Rock.

—Anthony Collett

A Mill

Two leaps the water from its race
Made to the brook below,
The first leap it was curving glass,
The second bounding snow.

—William Allingham

Weather, The

I would give part of my lifetime for the sake of knowing what is the average barometer reading in Paradise.

—G. C. Lichtenberg

No man, I suspect, ever lived long in the country without being bitten by . . . meteorological ambitions. He likes to be hotter and colder, to have been more deeply snowed up, to have more trees and larger blown down than his neighbors.

—James Russell Lowell

Rain

Rain, midnight rain, nothing but the wild rain
On this bleak hut, and solitude, and me
Remembering again that I shall die
And neither hear the rain nor give it thanks
For washing me cleaner than I have been
Since I was born into this solitude.
Blessed are the dead that the rain rains upon:
But here I pray that none whom I once loved
Is dying to-night or lying still awake
Solitary, listening to the rain,
Either in pain or thus in sympathy
Helpless among the living and the dead,

Like a cold water among broken reeds,
Myriads of broken reeds all still and stiff,
Like me who have no love which this wild rain
Has not dissolved except the love of death,
If love it be towards what is perfect and
Cannot, the tempest tells me, disappoint.

—Edward Thomas

I look out of the window; there walks long Anthony.

—Russian riddle

Clouds

I must here relate something that appears very interesting to me, and something, which, though it must have been seen by every man that has lived in the country, or at least, in any hilly country, has never been particularly mentioned by anybody as far as I can recollect. We frequently talk of clouds coming from dews; and we actually see the heavy fogs become clouds. We see them go up to the tops of hills, and, taking a swim round, actually come, and drop down upon us, and wet us through. But, I am now going to speak of clouds, coming out of the sides of hills in exactly the same manner that you see smoke come out of a tobacco pipe, and, rising up, with a wider and wider head, like the smoke from a tobacco-pipe, go to the top of the hill or over the hill, or very much above it, and then come over the valleys in rain. At about a mile's distance from Mr Palmer's house at Bollitree, in Herefordshire, there is a large, long beautiful wood, covering the side of a lofty hill, winding round in the form of a crescent, the bend of the crescent being toward Mr Palmer's house. It was here, that I first observed this mode of forming clouds. The first time I noticed it, I pointed it out to Mr Palmer. We stood and observed cloud after cloud, come from different parts of the side of the hill, and tower up and go over the hill out of sight. He told me that that was a certain sign that it would rain that day, for that these clouds would come back again, and would fall in rain. It rained sure enough; and I found that the country people, all round about, held this mode of the forming of the clouds as a sign of rain. The hill is called Penyard, and this forming of the clouds, they call Old Penyard's smoking his pipe; and it is a rule that it is sure to rain during the day, if Old Penyard smokes his pipe in the morning. These appearances take place, especially in warm and sultry weather. It was very warm yesterday morning: it had thundered violently the evening before: we felt it hot even while the rain fell upon us at Butser-hill. Petersfield lies in a pretty broad and very beautiful valley. On three sides of it are very lofty hills, partly downs and partly covered with trees: and, as we proceeded on our way from the bottom of Butser-hill to Petersfield, we saw thousands upon thousands of clouds, continually coming puffing out from different parts of these hills and towering up to the top of them. I stopped George several times to make him look at them; to see them come puffing out of the chalk downs as well as out of the woodland hills; and bade him remember to tell his father of it, when he should go home, to convince him that the hills of Hampshire, could smoke their pipes, as well as those of Herefordshire. This is a really curious matter. I have never read, in any book, anything to lead me to suppose that the observation has ever found its ways into print before. Sometimes you will see only one or two clouds during a whole morning, come out of the side of a hill; but we saw thousands upon thousands, bursting out, one after another, in all parts of these immense hills. The first time that I have leisure, when I am in the high countries again, I will have a conversation with some old shepherd about this matter: if he cannot enlighten me upon the subject, I am sure that no philosopher can. . . .

—William Cobbett

Winter of 1784

The first week in December was very wet, with the barometer very low. On the 7th, with the barometer at 28, five-tenths, came on a vast snow, which continued all that day and the next, and most part of the following night; so that by the morning of the 9th the works of men were quite overwhelmed, the lanes filled so as to be impassable, and the ground covered twelve or fifteen inches without any drifting. In the evening of the 9th, the air began to be so very sharp that we thought it would be curious to attend to the motions of a thermometer: we therefore hung out two; one made by Martin and one by Dolland, which soon began to show us what we were to expect; for, by ten o'clock, they fell to 21, and at eleven to 4, when we went to bed. On the 10th, in the morning, the quicksilver of Dolland's glass was down to half a degree below zero; and that of Martin's, which was absurdly graduated only to four degrees above zero, sunk quite into the brass guard of the ball; so that when the weather became most interesting this was useless. On the 10th, at eleven at night, though the air was perfectly still, Dolland's glass went down to one degree below zero! This strange severity of the weather made me very desirous to know what degree of cold there might be in such an exalted and near situation as Newton. We had therefore, on the morning of the 10th, written to Mr ——, and entreated him to hang out his thermometer, made by Adams; and to pay some attention to it morning and evening; expecting wonderful phænomena, in so elevated a region, at two hundred feet or more above my house. But, behold! on the 10th, at eleven at night, it was down only to 17, and the next morning at 22, when mine was at 10! . . .

I must not omit to tell you that, during those two Siberian days, my parlour-cat was so electric, that had a person stroked her, and been properly insulated, the shock might have been given to a whole circle of people.

—Gilbert White

The Thunderstorm

Suddenly there was a brief glimmer all around us, reddening the rocks. It was the first flash of lightning, but it had been silent, and no thunder followed it.

We walked on. Presently there was more lightning, and as the evening had already darkened appreciably, and the light was diffused by the opaque cloud layer, the limestone turned rose-red before our eyes at every flash.

When we reached the point at which our ways parted, the priest stopped and looked at me. I conceded that the storm was breaking, and said that I would go home with him.

So we took the road leading to the Kar, and walked down the gentle rocky slope into the meadow.

On reaching the presbytery, we sat down for a little on the wooden bench in front of the house. The storm was now in full development and was standing from end to end of the sky like a dark rampart. Presently, against this unbroken darkness, across the foot of the storm wall, we saw long puffed-up streaks of drifting white vapor. So over there the storm had perhaps already begun, although where we were there was still not a leaf or a blade of grass stirring. Those drifting swollen clouds are often bad omens in stormy weather; they always presage violent gales and often hail and flooding. And the flashes of lightning were now being followed by clearly audible thunder.

Finally we went into the house.

The priest said that when there was a storm at night, it was his habit to place a lighted candle on his table and to sit quietly in front of it until the storm was over. During the day, he said, he sat at the table without a candle. He asked me if I had any objection to his observing this custom on the present occasion too. I reminded him of his promise not to put himself out in the slightest degree on my account. So he accompanied me through the entrance hall into the familiar little room, and invited me to take off my things.

I usually carried with me on a leather strap over my shoulder a case containing drawing materials, and also some surveying instruments. Fastened next to the case was a satchel where I kept my cold food, my wine, my drinking glass, and my wine cooler. I took these things off and hung them over the back of a chair in a corner of the room. I stood my long measuring rod against one of the yellow cupboards.

Meanwhile the priest had left the room, and he now entered carrying a candle. It was a tallow candle in a brass candlestick. He placed the candlestick on the table and laid a pair of brass snuffers beside it. Then we both sat down at the table and remained seated, waiting for the storm.

It now seemed imminent. When the priest had brought the candle, the small remnant of daylight that was still coming through the windows had vanished. The windows stood like black panels, and night had fallen completely. The lightning was more vivid, and in spite of the candle each flash lit up every corner of the room. The thunder became more solemn and menacing. Thus things continued for some time. Then at last came the first blast of the storm wind. The tree in front of the house trembled softly for a moment, as if stricken by a fleeting breeze, then it was still again. A little while later there was another tremor, more prolonged and profound. Shortly afterwards came a violent blast, all the leaves rustled, the branches seemed to be shuddering, to judge by the noise we heard from indoors; and now the roar continued unabated. The tree by the house, the hedges surrounding it, and all the bushes and trees of the neighborhood were caught up in one great rushing howl that merely waxed and waned by turns. Through it came the peals of thunder. They grew more and more frequent and penetrating. But the storm had still not reached us. There was still an interval between lightning and thunder, and the lightning, brilliant though it was, came in sheets and not in forked flashes.

At last the first raindrops struck the windows. They hammered singly against the glass but soon there were more of them, and before long, the rain was streaming down in torrents. It increased rapidly, with a hissing, rushing sound, until in the end it was as if whole continuous massive volumes of water were pouring down onto the house, as if the house were throbbing under the weight of it and one could feel the throbbing and groaning from inside. Even the rolling thunder was scarcely audible through the roar of the water; the roaring water became a second thunder. Finally the storm was immediately overhead. The lightning fell like lanyards of fire, the flashes were followed instantly by the hoarse thunderclaps which now triumphed over all the rest of the uproar, and the windowpanes shuddered and rattled under their deep reverberating echoes.

I was glad now that I had followed the priest's advice. I had seldom experienced such a storm. The priest was sitting quietly and simply by the table in his little room, with the light of the tallow candle shining on him.

At last there came a crash of thunder that seemed to try to lift the whole house up out of its foundations and hurl it down, and a second crash followed at once. Then there was a short pause, as often happens in the course of such phenomena; the rain broke off for a moment as if in alarm; even the wind stopped. But soon everything was as before; and yet the main onslaught had been broken, and everything continued more steadily. Little by little the storm abated. The gale fell to no more than a steady wind, the rain weakened, the lightning paled, and the thunder became a dull mutter that seemed to be retreating across-country.

At last, when the rain had died down to a mere continuous drizzle and the lightning to a flicker, the priest stood up and said: "It is over."

—Adalbert Stifter (trans. David Luke)

Windmill, A

. . . At eve thou loomest like a one-eyed giant
To some poor crazy knight, who pricks along
And sees thee wave in haze thy arms defiant,
And growl the burden of thy grinding song.

Against thy russet sail-sheet slowly turning,
The raven beats belated in the blast:
Behind thee ghastly, blood-red Eve is burning,
Above, rose-feathered drifts are racking fast.

The curlews pipe around their plaintive dirges,
Thou art a Pharos to the sea-mews hoar,
Set sheer above the tumult of the surges,
As sea-mark on some spacious ocean floor.

My heart is sick with gazing on thy feature,
Old blackened sugar-loaf with fourfold wings,
Thou seemest as some monstrous insect creature,
Some mighty chafer armed with iron stings.

Emblem of man who, after all his moaning,
And strain of dire immeasurable strife,
Has yet this consolation, all atoning—
Life, as a windmill grinds the bread of Life.

—Lord de Tabley

Words, Last

In these days when it has become the medical convention, firstly, to keep the dying in ignorance of their condition and, secondly, to keep them under sedation, how are any of us to utter what could be legitimately called our "last" words? Still, it is fun to imagine what one would like them to be. The best proposed comment I know of is that of my friend Chester Kallman: "I've never done this before."

Among those last words which are reputedly historical, some seem too much in character to be credible as really "last." For instance:

"But the peasants—how do the *peasants* die?"

—Tolstoy

"What's the use? She would only want me to take a message to dear Albert."

—Disraeli (on hearing that Queen Victoria would like to visit him)

"Let us go in; the fog is rising."

—Emily Dickinson

For stylishness, it would be difficult to do better than the French eighteenth-century aristocratic lady (whose name I've forgotten):

"*Un instant, Monsieur le Curé; nous partirons ensemble.*"

Words, Long

Longest word in Shakespeare: HONORIFICABILITUDINITATIBUS (*Love's Labour's Lost*). 27 letters.

Longest word in Scott: FLOCCINAUCINIHILIPILIFICATION (*Journals*). 29 letters. Meaning: "The action of estimating something as worthless."

Longest word in Peacock: OSSEOCARNISANGUINEOVISCERICARTILAGINONERVOMEDULLARY (*Headlong Hall*). A description of the structure of the human body. 51 letters.

Word coined by Dr Edward Strother, to describe the waters at Bristol: AEQUEOSALINOCALCALINOSETACEOALUMINOSOCUPREOVITRIOLIC. 52 letters.

—Dmitri A. Borgmann

Work, Labor, and Play

So far as I know, Miss Hannah Arendt was the first person to define the essential difference between Work and Labor. To be happy, a man must feel, firstly, free and, secondly, important. He cannot be really happy if he is compelled by society to do what he does not enjoy doing, or if what he enjoys doing is ignored by society as of no value or importance. In a society where slavery in the strict sense has been abolished, the sign that what a man does is of social value is that he is paid money to do it, but a laborer today can rightly be called a wage slave. A man is a laborer if the job society offers him is of no interest to himself but he is compelled to take it by the necessity of earning a living and supporting his family.

The antithesis to Labor is Play. When we play a game, we enjoy what we are doing, otherwise we should not play it, but it is a purely private activity; society could not care less whether we play it or not.

Between Labor and Play stands Work. A man is a worker if he is personally interested in the job which society pays him to do; what from the point of view of society is necessary labor is from his own point of view voluntary play. Whether a job is to be classified as Labor or Work depends, not on the job itself, but on the tastes of the individual who undertakes it. The difference does not, for example, coincide with the difference between a manual and a mental job; a gardener or a cobbler may be a worker, a bank clerk a laborer. Which a man is can be seen from his attitude towards leisure. To a worker, leisure means simply the hours he needs to relax and rest in order to work efficiently. He is therefore more likely to take too little leisure than too much; workers die of coronaries and forget their wives' birthdays. To the laborer, on the other hand, leisure means freedom from compulsion, so that it is natural for him to imagine that the fewer hours he has to spend laboring, and the more hours he is free to play, the better.

What percentage of the population in a modern technological society are, like myself, in the fortunate position of being workers? At a guess I would say sixteen per cent, and I do not think that figure is likely to get bigger in the future.

Technology and the Division of Labor have done two things: by eliminating in many fields the need for special strength or skill, they have made a very large number of paid occupations which formerly were enjoyable work into boring labor, and by increasing productivity they have reduced the number of necessary laboring hours. It is already possible to imagine a society in which the majority of the population, that is to say, its laborers, will have almost as much leisure as in earlier times was enjoyed by the aristocracy. When one recalls how aristocracies in the past actually behaved, the prospect is not cheerful. Indeed, the problem of dealing with boredom may be even more difficult for such a future mass society than it was for aristocracies. The latter, for example, ritualized their time; there was a season to shoot grouse, a season to spend in town, etc. The masses are more likely to replace an unchanging ritual by fashion which it will be in the economic interest of certain people to change as often as possible. Again, the masses cannot go in for hunting, for very soon there would be no animals left to hunt. For other aristocratic amusements like gambling, dueling, and warfare, it may be only too easy to find equivalents in dangerous driving, drug-taking, and senseless acts of violence. Workers seldom commit acts of violence, because they can put their aggression into their work, be it physical like the work of a smith, or mental like the work of a scientist or an artist. The role of aggression in mental work is aptly expressed by the phrase "getting one's teeth into a problem."

> It may be proved, with much certainty, that God intends no man to live in this world without working: but it seems to me no less evident that He intends every man to be happy in his work. . . . Now in order that people may be happy in their work, these three things are needed: They must be fit for it: they must not do too much of it: and they must have a sense of success in it—not a doubtful sense, such as needs some testimony of others for its confirmation, but a sure sense, or rather knowledge, that so much work has been done well, and fruitfully done, whatever the world may say or think about it. So that in order that a man may be happy, it is necessary that he should not only be capable of his work, but a good judge of his work.
>
> —Ruskin

World, Creation of the

I tell of Giants from times forgotten,
Those who fed me in former days:
Nine worlds I can reckon, nine roots of the Tree,
The wonderful Ash, way under the ground.

When Ymir lived long ago
Was no sand or sea, no surging waves,
Nowhere was there earth nor heaven above,
But a grinning gap and grass nowhere.

The Sons of Bur then built up the lands,
Moulded in magnificence Middle-Earth:
Sun stared from the south on the stones of their hall,
From the ground there sprouted green leeks.

Sun turned from the south, Sister of Moon,
Her right arm rested on the rim of Heaven;
She had no inkling where her hall was,
Nor Moon a notion of what might he had,
The planets knew not where their places were.

The High Gods gathered in council
In their Hall of Judgement, all the rulers:
To Night and to Nightfall their names gave,
The Morning they named and the Mid-Day,
Mid-Winter, Mid-Summer, for the assigning of years.

At Ithervale the Aesir met:
Temple and altar they timbered and raised,
Set up a forge to smithy treasures,
Tongs they fashioned and tools wrought;

Played chess in the court and cheerful were;
Gold they lacked not, the gleaming metal.
Then came Three, the Thurse Maidens,
Rejoicing in their strength, from Gianthome.

The High Gods gathered in council
In their Hall of Judgement: Who of the Dwarves
Should mould man by mastercraft
From Brimir's blood and Blain's limbs?

Motsognir was their mighty ruler,
Greatest of the Dwarves, and Durin after him:
The Dwarves did as Durin directed,
Many man-forms made from the earth. . . .

—From *Völuspà* (trans. P. B. Taylor and W. H. A.)

World, End of the

The Fifteen Days of Judgement

"Then there shall be signs in Heaven."—
Thus much in the text is given,
Worthy of the sinner's heeding:
But the other signs preceding
Earth's Last Judgement and destruction,
And its fiery reconstruction,
May be drawn from other channels;
For we read in Hebrew annals
That there shall be altogether
Fifteen Judgement days, but whether
Following or interpolated,
Jerome saith, is nowhere stated.

Day I

On the first day, loud upcrashing,
Shall the shoreless ocean, gnashing
With a dismal anaclysmal
Outrush from its deeps abysmal,
Lifted high by dread supernal
Storm the mountain heights eternal!
Forty cubits of sheer edges,

Wall-like o'er the summit-ridges
Stretching upright forth—a mirror
For the unutterable terror
Of the huddled howling nations,
Smit with sudden desolations,
Rushing hither, thither, drunken,
Half their pleasant realms sea-sunken.

Day II

On the second day, down-pouring,
Shall the watery walls drop roaring
From the ruinous precipices
To the nethermost abysses,
With a horrible waterquaking
In the world-wide cataracts, shaking
Earth's foundations as they thunder.—
Surf-plumed steeds of God Almighty,
Rock and pyramid, forest, city,
Through the flood-rent valleys scourging,
Wide in headlong ebb down-surging,
Down till eye of man scarce reaches
Where, within its sunken beaches,
Hidden from a world's amazement,
Cowers the Deep in self-abasement.

Day III

On the third day, o'er the seething
Of the leprous ocean writhing,
Whale and dragon, orc and kraken,
And leviathan, forsaken
His unfathomable eyrie,
To and fro shall plunge—the dreary
Dumb death-sickness of creation
Startling with their ululation.
Men shall hear the monsters bellow
Forth their burden as they wallow;
But its drift?—Let none demand it!
God alone shall understand it!

Day IV

On the fourth day, blazing redly,
With a reek pitch-black and deadly,
A consuming fire shall quiver
From all seas and every river!

Every brook and beck and torrent
Leaping in fiery current;
All the moats and meres and fountains
Lit, like beacons on the mountains;
Furnace-roar of smolten surges
Scarring earth's extremest verges!

Day V

On the fifth day, Judgement-stricken,
Every green herb, from the lichen
To the cedar of the forest,
Shall sweat blood in anguish sorest!
On the same, all fowls of heaven
Into one wide field, fear-driven,
Shall assemble, cowed and shrinking;
Neither eating aught, nor drinking;
Kind with kind, all ranked by feather,
Doves with doves aghast together,
Swan with swan in downfall regal,
Wren and wren, with eagle, eagle!
Ah! when fowl feel such foreboding,
What shall be the Sinner's goading?

Day VI

On the sixth day, through all nations
Shall be quaking of foundations,
With a horrible hollow rumbling—
All that all men builded crumbling
As the heel of Judgement tramples
Cot and palace, castles, temples,
Hall and minster, thorpe and city;—
All men too aghast for pity
In the crashing and the crushing
Of that stony stream's downrushing!—
And a flame of fiery warning
Forth from sundown until morning
With a lurid coruscation
Shall reveal night's desolation!

Day VII

On the seventh day, self-shattered,
Rifting fourfold, scarred and scattered,
Pounded in the Judgement's mortars,
Every stone shall split in quarters!

Pebble, whinstone, granite sparry,
Rock and boulder—stones of quarry,
Shaped or shapeless, all asunder
Shivering, split athwart and under;
And the splinters, each on other
Shall make war against his brother,
Each one grinding each to powder,
Grinding, gnashing, loud and louder,
Grinding, gnashing on till even,
With a dolorous plea to Heaven.
What the drift?—Let none demand it!
God alone shall understand it!

Day VIII

On the eighth, in dire commotion,
Shall the dry land heave like Ocean,
Puffed in hills and sucked in hollows,
Yawning into steep-down swallows—
Swelling, mountainously lifted
Skyward from the plains uprifted—
With a universal clamour
Rattling, roaring through the tremor;
While, flung headlong, all men living
Grovel in a wild misgiving!
What, O Sinner, shall avail your
Might in solid Earth's own failure?

Day IX

On the ninth day all the mountains
Shall drop bodily, like spent fountains,
All the cloud-capped pride of pristine
Peak and pinnacle amethystine
Toppling, drifting to the level,
Flooding all the dales with gravel;
One consummate moment blasting
All that seems so everlasting—
All men to the caves for shelter
Scurrying through the world-wide welter!

Day X

On the tenth day, hither, thither,
Herding from their holes together,
With a glaring of white faces,
Through the desolate wildernesses

Men shall o'er that mountain ruin
Run as from a Death's pursuing,—
Each one with suspicious scowling,
Shrinking from his fellow's howling—
For all human speech confounded
Shall not sound as once it sounded.
None shall understand his brother—
Mother, child, nor child his mother!

Day XI

On the eleventh day, at dawning,
Every sepulchre wide yawning
At the approach of Earth's Assessor,
Shall upyield its white possessor;—
All the skeletons, close-serried,
O'er the graves where each lay buried,
Mute upstanding, white and bony,
With a dreadful ceremony
Staring from the morn till gloaming
Eastward for the Judge's coming;
Staring on, with sockets eyeless,
Each one motionless and cryless,
Save the dry, dead-leaf-like chattering,
Through that white-branched forest pattering.
What its drift?—Let none demand it!
God alone shall understand it!

Day XII

On the twelfth, the Planets seven
And all stars shall drop from Heaven!
On the same day, scared and trembling,
All four-footed things assembling,
Each after his kind in order—
All the lions in one border,
Sheep with sheep—not needing shepherd—
Stag with stag—with leopard, leopard—
Shall be herded cowed and shrinking,
Neither eating aught nor drinking,
But to Godward bellowing, shrieking,
Howling, barking, roaring, squeaking;—
What the drift? Let none demand it!
God alone shall understand it.

Day XIII

On the thirteenth awful morning
Shall go forth the latest warning,
With a close to all things mortal,
For the Judge is at the portal!
In an agony superhuman,
Every living man and woman,
Child and dotard—every breather—
Shall lie down and die together,
That all flesh in death's subjection
Shall abide the Resurrection!

Day XIV

On the fourteenth, morn to even,
Fire shall feed on Earth and Heaven,
Through the skies and all they cover,
Under earth, and on, and over;
All things ghostly, human, bestial,
In the crucible celestial
Tested by the dread purgation
On that final conflagration;
Till the intolerable whiteness
Dawn, of God's exceeding brightness
Through the furnace-flames erasure
Of yon mortal veil of azure!

Day XV

Last, the fifteenth day shall render
Earth a more than earthly splendor,
Once again shall word be given:
"Let there be new Earth, new Heaven!"
And this fleeting world—this charnel,
Purified, shall wax eternal!—
Then all souls shall Michael gather
At the footstool of the Father,
Summoning from Earth's four corners,
All erst human saints and scorners,
And without revenge or pity
Weigh them in the scales almighty!—
Sinner! Dost thou dread that trial?
Mark yon shadow on the dial!

Ast illi semper modo "cras, cras," umbra docebit.

—Sebastian Evans

Loud howls Garm before Gnipahellir,
Bursting his fetters, Fenris runs:
Further in the future, afar I behold
The Twilight of the Gods who gave victory.

Brother shall strike brother and both fall,
Sisters' sons slay each other,
Evil be on earth, an Age of Whoredom,
Of sharp sword-play and shields' clashing,
A Wind-Age, a Wolf-Age, till the world ruins:
No man to another shall mercy show.

The waters are troubled, the waves surge up:
Announcing now the knell of Fate,
Heimdal winds his horn aloft,
On Hel's Road all men tremble.

Yggdrasil trembles, the towering Ash,
Groans in woe: the Wolf is loose:
Odin speaks with the Head of Mimir
Before he is swallowed by Surt's kin.

From the east drives Hrym, lifts up his shield,
The squamous serpent squirms with rage,
The Great Worm with the waves contending,
The pale-beaked eagle pecks at the dead,
Shouting for joy: the ship Naglfar

Sails out from the east, at its helm Loki,
With the children of darkness, the doom-bringers,
Offspring of monsters, allies of the Wolf,
All who Byleist's Brother follow.

What of the Gods? What of the Elves?
Gianthome groans, the Gods are in council,
The Dwarves grieve before their door of stone,
Masters of walls. *Well, would you know more?*

Surt with the bane of branches comes
From the south, on his sword the sun of Valgods,
Crags topple, the crone falls headlong,
Men tread Hel's Road, the Heavens split open.

A further woe falls upon Hlin
As Odin comes forth to fight the Wolf;
The killer of Beli battles with Surt:
Now shall fall Frigg's beloved.

Now valiant comes Valfather's Son,
Vidar, to vie with Valdyr in battle,
Plunges his sword into the Son of Hvedrung,
Avenging his father with a fell thrust.

Now the Son of Hlodyn and Odin comes
To fight with Fenris; fiercest of warriors,
He mauls in his rage all Middle-Earth;
Men in fear all flee their homesteads;
Nine paces back steps Bur's Son,
Retreats from the Worm, of taunts unafraid.

Now death is the portion of doomed men,
Red with blood the buildings of Gods,
The Sun turns black in the summer after,
Winds whine. *Well, would you know more?*

Earth sinks into the sea, the Sun turns black,
Cast down from Heaven are the hot stars,
Fumes reek, into flames burst,
The sky itself is scorched with fire.

I see Earth rising a second time
Out of the foam, fair and green;
Down from the fells, fish to capture,
Wings the eagle; waters flow.

At Ithervale the Aesir meet:
They remember the Worm of Middle-Earth,
Ponder again the Great Twilight
And the ancient runes of the High God.

Boards shall be found of a beauty to wonder at,
Boards of gold in the grass long after,
The chess-boards they owned in the olden days.

Unsown acres shall harvests bear,
Evil be abolished, Baldur return
And Hropt's Hall with Hoddur rebuild,
Wise Gods. *Well, would you know more?*

Haenir shall wield the wand of prophecy,
The sons of two brothers set up their dwelling
In wide Windhome. *Well, would you know more?*

Fairer than sunlight, I see a hall,
A hall thatched with gold in Gimle:
Kind lords shall live there in delight for ever.

Now rides the Strong One to Rainbow Door,
Powerful from heaven, the All-Ruler:
From the depths below a drake comes flying,
The Dark Dragon from Darkfell,
Bears on his pinions the bodies of men,
Soars overhead. I sink now.

—From *Völuspà* (trans. P. B. Taylor and W. H. A.)

WRITING

Literature is the effort of man to indemnify himself for the wrongs of his condition.

—Emerson

The only end of writing is to enable readers better to enjoy life or better to endure it.

—Dr Johnson

When I stop drinking tea and eating bread and butter I say, "I've had enough." But when I stop reading poems or novels I say, "No more of that, no more of that."

—A. Chekhov

There are two kinds of writers, those who are and those who aren't. With the first, content and form belong together like soul and body; with the second, they match each other like body and clothes.

—Karl Kraus

It costs the writer no more effort to write *fortissimo* than *piano*, or *universe* than *garden*.

Cynicism in literary works usually signifies a certain element of disappointed ambition. When one no longer knows what to do in order to astonish and survive, one offers one's *pudenda* to the public gaze. Everyone knows perfectly well what he will see; but it is sufficient to make the gesture.

—Paul Valéry

Poetry avoids the last illusion of prose, which so gently sometimes and at others so passionately pretends that things are thus and thus. In poetry they are also thus and thus, but because the arrangement of the lines, the pattern within the whole, will have it so. Exquisitely leaning toward an implied untruth, prose persuades us that we can trust our natures to know things as they are; ostentatiously faithful to its own nature, poetry assures us that we cannot—we know only as we can.

—Charles Williams

A man is a poet if the difficulties inherent in his art provide him with ideas; he is not a poet if they deprive him of ideas.

To write regular verses destroys an infinite number of fine possibilities, but at the same time it suggests a multitude of distant and totally unexpected thoughts.

Skilled verse is the art of a profound sceptic.

In poetry everything which *must* be said is almost impossible to say well.

—Paul Valéry

[A poem] begins in delight, it inclines to the impulse, it assumes direction with the first line laid down, it runs a course of lucky events, and ends in a clarification of life—not necessarily a great clarification, such as sects and cults are founded on, but in a momentary stay against confusion.

—Robert Frost

I had towards the poetic art a quite peculiar relation which was only practical after I had cherished in my mind for a long time a subject which possessed me, a model which inspired me, a predecessor who attracted me, until at length, after I had moulded it in silence for years, something resulted which might be regarded as a creation of my own.

—Goethe

Darius

Fernazes the poet on the serious part
Of his epic poem is now at work.
How that the kingdom of the Persians
Was taken over by Darius son of Hystaspes. (From him
Is descended our own glorious monarch
Mithridates, called Dionysos and Eupator.) At this point
Philosophy is called for; he must analyse
The feelings which Darius must have had;
Arrogance perhaps and intoxication? No—rather
A sort of understanding of the vanity of greatness.
Upon this point the poet deeply meditates.

But his servant interrupts him who comes
Running in, and announces the momentous news.
The war with the Romans has begun.
The greater part of our army has crossed the frontiers.

The poet is dumbfounded. What a disaster!
How ever could our glorious monarch now,

Could Mithridates, Dionysos and Eupator,
Give any of his attention to Greek poems?—
To Greek poems, just fancy, in the midst of war!

Fernazes is worried. How unfortunate!
Just as he had it in his grasp with his "Dareios"
Positively to distinguish himself, and his critics,
His envious critics, once and for all to shut them up!
What a putting-off, what a putting-off of all his plans!

And if it were only a hold-up, well and good.
But let us see if we are even safe
Here in Amisos. It isn't a particularly strong town,
The Romans are most frightful enemies.

Can we ever bring it off with them,
We Cappadocians? Can it ever come to pass?
Can we be now a match for the legions?
Great gods, defenders of Asia, help us now.—

None the less in all his trouble and commotion,
Insistently still the poetic notion comes and goes—
Most likely of course arrogance and intoxication;
Arrogance and intoxication must have filled Darius.

—C. Cavafy (trans. J. Mavrogordato)

Start and Finish

Thursday, September 30, 1926

. . . it is not oneself but something in the universe that one's left with. It is this that is frightening and exciting in the midst of my profound gloom, depression, boredom, whatever it is. One sees a fin passing far out. What image can I reach to convey what I mean? Really there's none, I think. The interesting thing is that in all my feeling and thinking I have never come up against this before. Life is, soberly and accurately, the oddest affair; has in it the essence of reality. I used to feel this as a child—couldn't step across a puddle once, I remember, for thinking how strange—what am I? etc. But by writing I don't reach anything. All I mean to make is a note of a curious state of mind. I hazard the guess that it may be the impulse behind another book.

Saturday, February 7, 1931

Here in the few minutes that remain, I must record, heaven be praised, the end of *The Waves*. I wrote the words O Death fifteen minutes ago, having reeled across the last ten pages with some moments of such intensity and intoxication that I seemed only to stumble after my own voice, or almost, after some sort of speaker (as when I was mad). I was almost afraid, remembering the voices that used to fly ahead. Anyhow, it is done; and I have been sitting these 15 minutes in a state of glory, and calm, and some tears, thinking of Thoby and if I could write Julian Thoby Stephen 1881–1906 on the first page. I suppose not. How physical the sense of triumph and relief is! Whether good or bad, it's done; and, as I certainly felt at the end, not merely finished, but rounded off, completed, the thing stated—how hastily, how fragmentarily I know; but I mean that I have netted that fin in the waste of water which appeared to me over the marshes out of my window at Rodmell when I was coming to an end of *To the Lighthouse.*

Tuesday, July 14, 1931

. . . my *Waves* account runs, I think, as follows:—

I began it, seriously, about September 10th 1929.

I finished the first version on April 10th 1930.

I began the second version on May 1st 1930.

I finished the second version on February 7th 1931.

I began to correct the second version on May 1st 1931, finished 22nd June 1931.

I began to correct the typescript on 25th June 1931.

Shall finish (I hope) 18th July 1931.

Then remain only the proofs.

—Virginia Woolf

In general, I do not draw well with literary men: not that I dislike them, but I never know what to say to them after I have praised their last publication. There are several exceptions, to be sure: but then they have either been men of the world, such as Scott, and Moore, etc., or visionaries out of it, such as Shelley, etc.

—Lord Byron

The business man and the artist are like matter and mind. We can never get either pure and without some alloy of the other.

—Samuel Butler II

A poem is never finished, only abandoned.

—Paul Valéry

The artistic temperament is a disease which afflicts amateurs.

—G. K. Chesterton

The manuscript in the drawer either rots or ripens.

—Maria von Ebner-Eschenbach

On a Day's Stint

And long ere dinner-time I have
Full eight close pages wrote.
What, Duty, hast thou now to crave?
Well done, Sir Walter Scott!

—Walter Scott

Most of what I know about the writing of poetry, or, at least, the kind I am interested in writing, I discovered long before I took an interest in poetry itself.

Between the ages of six and twelve I spent a great many of my waking hours in the fabrication of a private secondary sacred world, the basic elements of which were (a) a limestone landscape mainly derived from the Pennine Moors in the North of England, and (b) an industry—lead mining.

It is no doubt psychologically significant that my sacred world was autistic, that is to say, I had no wish to share it with others nor could I have done so. However, though constructed for and inhabited by myself alone, I needed the help of others, my parents in particular, in collecting its materials; others had to procure for me the necessary textbooks on geology and machinery, maps, catalogues, guidebooks, and photographs, and, when occasion offered, to take me down real mines, tasks which they performed with unfailing patience and generosity.

From this activity, I learned certain principles which I was later to find applied to all artistic fabrication. Firstly, whatever other elements it may include, the initial impulse to create a secondary world is a feeling of awe aroused by encounters, in the primary world, with sacred beings or events. Though every work of art is a secondary world, such a world cannot be constructed *ex nihilo,* but is a selection and recombination of the contents of the primary world. Even the purest poem, in the French sense, is made of words, which are not the poet's private property but the communal creation of the linguistic group to which he belongs, so that their meaning can be looked up in a dictionary.

Secondly, in constructing my private world, I discovered that, though this was a game, that is to say, something I was free to do or not as I chose, not a necessity like eating or sleeping, no game can be played without rules. A secondary world must be as much a world of law as the primary. One may be free to decide what these laws shall be, but laws there must be.

As regards my particular lead-mining world, I decided, or rather, without conscious decision, I instinctively felt that I must impose two restrictions upon my freedom of fantasy. In choosing what objects were to be included, I was free to select this and reject that, on condition that both were real objects in the primary world, to choose, for example, between two kinds of water turbine, which could be found in a textbook on mining machinery or a manufacturer's catalogue; I was not allowed to invent one. In deciding how my world was to function, I could choose between two practical possibilities—a mine can be drained either by an adit or a pump—but physical impossibilities and magic means were forbidden. When I say forbidden, I mean that I felt, in some obscure way, that they were morally forbidden. Then there came a day when the moral issue became quite conscious. As I was planning my Platonic Idea of a concentrating mill, I ran into difficulties. I had to choose between two types of a certain machine for separating the slimes, called a buddle. One type I found more sacred or "beautiful," but the other type was, as I knew from my reading, the more efficient. At this point I realized that it was my moral duty to sacrifice my aesthetic preference to reality or truth.

When, later, I began to write poetry, I found that, for me at least, the same obligation was binding. That is to say, I cannot accept the doctrine that in poetry there is a "suspension of belief." A poet must never make a statement simply because it sounds poetically exciting; he must also believe it to be true. This does not mean, of course, that one can only appreciate a poet whose beliefs happen to coincide with one's own. It does mean, however, that one must be convinced that the poet really believes what he says, however odd the belief may seem to oneself.

What the poet has to convey is not "self-expression," but a view of a reality common to all, seen from a unique perspective, which it is his duty as well as his pleasure to share with others. To small truths as well as great, St Augustine's words apply.

"The truth is neither mine nor his nor another's; but belongs to us all whom Thou callest to partake of it, warning us terribly, not to account it private to ourselves, lest we be deprived of it."

ACKNOWLEDGMENTS

Acknowledgment is made to the following publishers and authors or their representatives for their permission to use copyright material. Every reasonable effort has been made to clear the use of the material in this volume with the copyright owners. If notified of any omissions the editor and publisher will gladly make the proper corrections in future editions.

George Allen & Unwin Ltd: "Zero" from *Number: The Language of Science* by Tobias Dantzig. From "Fellowship of the Ring" from *Lord of the Rings* by J. R. R. Tolkien.

Arion: From the *Annales* and *Tragoediae* by Ennius, translated by Janet Lembke. *Arion* (6.3) 1967.

John Baker Publishers Ltd: From *Roman Roads in Britain* by Ivan Margary.

Basic Books, Inc.: From *The Ambidextrous Universe* by Martin Gardner. Copyright © 1964 by Martin Gardner.

Basil Blackwell: From *The Discovery of Mind* translated by Bruno Snell. From *The Klephtic Ballads* translated by John Baggally.

Cambridge University Press, New York: From *Non-Dramatic Literature of the 16th Century* and *The Discarded Image* by C. S. Lewis. From *Góngora* translated by Edward Wilson.

Cambridge University Press, London: From the works of A. N. Whitehead.

Chappell & Co. Ltd: "Take Him." Words by Lorenz Hart. Copyright © 1952 Chappell & Co, Inc. Reproduced by permission of Chappell & Co. Ltd, London.

The Clarendon Press, Oxford: From *Taliessin through Logres* by Charles Williams, 1938. From *The Heroic Recitations of the Bahima of Ankole* by H. F. Morris, 1964. From *Somali Poetry: An Introduction* by B. W. Andrzejewski and I. M. Lewis, 1964. From *A History of Technology* edited by Charles Singer et al., Vol. 1, 1954 (author, E. R. Reach).

Miss D. E. Collins, representing the author's estate, and A. P. Watt & Son: For extracts from the works of G. K. Chesterton.

Constable & Co. Ltd: From "The Concept of Cure" by Anthony Storr, from *Psychoanalysis Observed* edited by Charles Rycroft. From *The Desert Fathers* translated by Helen Waddell.

Curtis Brown Ltd, New York: From *Elective Affinities* by Goethe, translated by Elizabeth Mayer and Louise Bogan. Copyright © 1963 by Henry Regnery Company. Reprinted by permission of Curtis Brown Ltd.

The John Day Company: "Journey to the North" and "Chariots Go Forth to War" from *The White Pony* by Tu Fu, translated by Pu Hsiang-hsing, edited by Robert Payne. Copyright 1947 by The John Day Co. Reprinted by permission of the editor.

J. M. Dent & Sons Ltd: "Samson Agonistes" from *Family Reunion* by Ogden Nash.

Gerald Duckworth & Co. Ltd: From *The Flower Beneath the Foot* and *Concerning the Eccentricities of Cardinal Pirelli* by Ronald Firbank.

Encounter: From *On Science and Culture* by J. Robert Oppenheimer, which appeared in the October 1962 issue.

Evans Brothers Ltd: From *My Memories of Six Reigns* by Princess Marie Louise.

Faber and Faber Ltd: From Chapter VIII, "Experiments", from *History in English Words* by Owen Barfield. "Buildings as Drawn by Girls and by Boys" from *Identity: Youth and Crisis* by Erik H. Erikson. From *Markings* by Dag Hammarskjöld, translated by

W. J. Sjöberg and W. H. Auden. "In the Beginning" from *The Anathemata* by David Jones. "Solvitur Acris Hiems" by Horace, translated by Louis MacNeice, from *The Collected Poems of Louis MacNeice.* "The Gate" from *Collected Poems* by Edwin Muir. "Peter" and an extract from "The Pangolin" from *Complete Poems of Marianne Moore.*

Victor Gollancz Ltd: From *Crowds and Power* by Elias Cannetti.

Granada Publishing Ltd: From "Asphodel, That Greeny Flower" from *Pictures from Brueghel* by William Carlos Williams.

Robert Graves and A. P. Watt & Son: "The Climate of Thought" and "Rhea" from *Collected Poems* by Robert Graves.

John Howard Griffin: From *Black Like Me* by John Howard Griffin.

Grune & Stratton, Inc.: From *Strategies of Family Therapy.* Reprinted by permission of Grune & Stratton, Inc. and Jay Haley.

Michael Hamburger: For the translation of "When from the Heavens . . ." and "Tears" by Friedrich Hölderlin.

Hamish Hamilton Ltd: From *Conversations with Max.* Copyright © 1960 by S. N. Behrman.

Harper & Row, Publishers: From *Through the Valley of the Kwai* by Ernest Gordon. Copyright © 1962 by Ernest Gordon. By permission of Harper & Row, Publishers.

Rupert Hart-Davis: "Park Concert" by James Michie and "The Mole" by Andrew Young.

A.M. Heath & Co. Ltd: From *August for the People* by Nigel Dennis. By permission of Nigel Dennis.

David Higham Associates Ltd: From *Odes of Horace* by James Michie, published by The Bodley Head. From *The Descent of the Dove* by Charles Williams, published by Faber and Faber Ltd. From *The Pendulum* by Anthony Rossiter, published by Victor Gollancz Ltd.

Hodder and Stoughton Ltd: From *The Making of the English Landscape* by W. G. Hoskins.

The Hogarth Press Ltd, Quentin Bell and Angelica Garnett: From *A Writer's Diary* by Virginia Woolf.

The Hogarth Press Ltd and the Literary Estate of the translator: "Darius" from *Poems* by C. P. Cavafy, translated by J. Mavrogodato.

The Hogarth Press Ltd and Alan Hodge: "A Modern Nightmare" from *Collected Poems* by Norman Cameron.

The Hutchinson Publishing Group Ltd: From *Poems* by Ivor Gurney.

John Johnson: "The Thunderstorm" from *Limestone and Other Stories* by Adalbert Stifter, translated by David Luke.

McIntosh and Otis Inc.: From *My Life with the Eskimo* by Vilhjalmur Stefansson.

Macmillan & Co. Ltd, London: "The Last Signal", "She Revisits Alone the Church of her Marriage", "During Wind and Rain" from the *Collected Poems of Thomas Hardy;* "Walcheren Island: Dumb Show" from *The Dynasts* by Thomas Hardy. By permission of the Trustees of the Hardy Estate and Macmillan & Co. Ltd.

The Macmillan Company, New York: From *The Empty Fortress* by Bruno Bettelheim.

Methuen & Co. Ltd: From *King Solomon's Ring* by Konrad Lorenz.

John Murray: From *In the Antarctic* by Frank Debenham. From *Earth's Company* by Leslie Reid.

John Murray and The Houghton Mifflin Co.: "False Security" and "I. M. Walter Ramsden" by John Betjeman.

New Directions Publishing Corporation: From *Rhymes and More Rhymes of a Pfc* by Lincoln Kirstein. Copyright © 1964, 1966 by Lincoln Kirstein.

The New York Review of Books: Passage on James D. Watson by P. B. Medawar. Copyright © 1968 The New York Review. Reprinted with permission from *The New York Review of Books.*

James Nisbet & Co. Ltd: From *The Names of the Stars* by E. J. Webb, and from *The Changing Face of England* by Anthony Collett.

The Observer: "Dreams" by John Davy. Reprinted from *The Observer* of August 13, 1967.

Oxford University Press, New York: From *Christianity and Classical Culture* by C. N. Cochrane.

Oxford University Press, London: "Hunting a Hare" from *Anti-worlds and the Fifth Ace* by Andrei Voznesensky, translated by W. H. Auden.

Penguin Books Ltd: "Deor" and "Wulf and Edwacer" from *The Earliest English Poems* translated by M. Alexander. "Chamber Music" from *Twentieth-Century German Verse* translated by Joseph Weinheber, and passage and poem by Rimbaud, translated by Oliver Bernard. "The Lettuce" and "Cygnet" from *The Penguin Book of Latin Verse* translated by Frederick Brittain.

A. D. Peters & Co.: *Imaginary Book Reviews* by J. B. Norton. Originally printed in the *Daily Express.* Reprinted by permission of A. D. Peters & Company. "Trench Nomenclature" from *Undertones of War* by Edmund Blunden, published by William Collins Sons & Co. Ltd Reprinted by permission of A. D. Peters & Company.

Laurence Pollinger Ltd and the Estate of the late Mrs Frieda Lawrence: "Bibbles", excerpt from "She Goat" and "Tortoise Family Connections" from *The Complete Poems of D. H. Lawrence,* published by William Heinemann Ltd.

Laurence Pollinger Ltd and Holt, Rinehart & Winston, Inc.: "The Middleness of the Road" and "Were I in Trouble" from *The Complete Poems of Robert Frost,* published by Jonathan Cape Ltd.

Princeton University Press: From *Mimesis: The Representation of Reality in Western Literature* by Erich Auerbach, translated by W. R. Trask (Princeton University Press, 1953; Princeton Paperback, 1968). Reprinted by permission of Princeton University Press.

G. P. Putnam's Sons: From *Across the Arctic America* by Knud Rasmussen. Copyright 1927 by G. P. Putnam's Sons.

The Ronald Press Company: From *Learning Theory and Personality Dynamics* by O. Hobart Mowrer. Copyright 1950 The Ronald Press Company, New York.

Routledge & Kegan Paul Ltd: From *Gravity and Grace* and *The Notebooks of Simone Weil* by Simone Weil. "Winter Gold" and "Islands of the Earthly Paradise" from *A Celtic Miscellany* by K. H. Jackson.

Russell & Volkening, Inc.: From *An Alphabet for Gourmets* by M. F. K. Fisher, published by Viking Press Inc. Copyright © 1948, 1949 by M. F. K. Fisher.

Schocken Books, Inc.: From *Franz Rosenzweig: His Life and Thought* by Nahum N. Glatzer. Copyright © 1953, 1961 by Schocken Books, Inc. Reprinted by permission of Schocken Books, Inc.

Scientific American, Inc. and W. H. Freeman and Company: From "Leaf Shape" by Eric Ashby. Copyright © 1949 by Scientific American, Inc. All rights reserved.

Scott Meredith Literary Agency, Inc.: From *The Big Love* by Florence Aadland. Copyright © 1961 by Lancer Books, Inc. Reprinted by permission of the author and her agents, Scott Meredith Literary Agency, Inc., 580 Fifth Avenue, New York, N.Y. 10036.

Martin Seeker & Warburg Ltd: From *My Dog Tulip* by J. R. Ackerley. "The Long Cat" from *Creatures Great and Small* by Colette.

Simon & Schuster, Inc.: From *Dictionary of Cuisine* by Dumas, translated by Louis Colman. Reprinted by permission of the translator.

The Society of Authors: "De Profundis" and an extract from "Time's Wingèd Chariot" by Walter de la Mare. Reprinted by permission of the Literary Trustees of Walter de la Mare and The Society of Authors as their representative. "When the bells justle in the tower" by A. E. Housman. Reprinted by permission of The Society of Authors as the literary representative of the Estate of A. E. Housman, and Jonathan Cape Ltd, publishers of A. E. Housman's *Collected Poems.*

The Souvenir Press Ltd: "The Summit" from *The Mountain of My Fear* by David Roberts.

Sunday Telegraph: "Intercom in Nasakom" by Towyn Mason. Reprinted by permission of the *Sunday Telegraph* and Towyn Mason.

Thames and Hudson Ltd: From *The Informed Heart* by Bruno Bettelheim.

Myfanwy Thomas: "Home", "Roads" and "Rain" by Edward Thomas.

Helen Thurber: From "Soapland" in *My World—and Welcome to It,* published by Harcourt, Brace & World, New York. Originally printed in *The New Yorker.*

A. P. Watt & Son: From *Lucia's Progress* by E. F. Benson. By permission of The Executors of the late E. F. Benson and William Heinemann Ltd.

Weidenfeld (Publishers) Ltd: "A Commandant Reminisces" from *Commandant of Auschwitz* by Rudolf Hoess. From *The Intellectual History of Europe* by Friedrich Heer. "Naming Animals" from *The Savage Mind* by Claude Lévi-Strauss.

The World Publishing Company, New York: From *The Face of Violence* by J. Bronowski. Copyright © 1967 by J. Bronowski.

Yale University Press: "Little City" from *A Beginning* by Robert Horan. Copyright © 1948 by Yale University Press. Reprinted by permission of Yale University Press.

Basile Yanovsky: For passage on "Anesthesia". Copyright © 1970 by Basile Yanovsky.

Professor G. E. M. Anscombe: From *Philosophical Investigations* by Ludwig Wittgenstein. Published by Basil Blackwell.

The Clarendon Press, Oxford: "Poor Poll" from *The Poetical Works of Robert Bridges,* 1936.

INDEX OF AUTHORS, TRANSLATORS, AND OTHER SOURCES

ESSAYS AND REVIEWS

1969–1973

Foreword to the American Edition of *The Pendulum*, by Anthony Rossiter

Nearly all human beings, I should guess, whatever their occupation in life, will recognise from their own experience what Mr Rossiter means by the "Pendulum". Even if we only define them in terms of "high" spirits and "low", we have all had "good" days and "bad" days for which we could see no obvious cause outside ourselves. If we are persons whose vocation in life depends upon using our brains, if, for example, we are scientists or philosophers or artists of some kind, a good day is also one in which our minds function quickly and easily, a bad day one in which our minds function sluggishly and with difficulty. In the case of writers or painters whose concern is with the created world and their reactions to it, they have all experienced moments when "things" around them, whether natural objects like mountains and trees, or human artefacts like chairs and boots, seemed more intensely "there" than usual and endowed with a mysterious "numinous" significance.

One does not have to be a diagnosed manic-depressive to understand what Mr Rossiter is talking about when he says:

> A discarded shirt linked me to the previous evening. Warmth filled my heart as I noticed the worn patch in the carpet. My hair-brushes neatly paired together gave smug approval from the dressing-table. A clean bath towel welcomed me in a rough and friendly manner.

or

> The gate was strong and wise . . . there was no conceit in its stance.

Most of us, too, know that an event as well as an object can have a numinous significance. Reading the following description, one may say "this is rather way out", but one has had similar, if less intense, experiences.

> A nurse was having difficulty in measuring two quantities against each other on a scales. The left dish insisted upon outweighing the other, and I saw in it the bully in life, the one with "the whip hand"; the right dish uncomfortably aloft, seemed to stand small chance, as does "the little man" in life, of exerting its influence. Then, quite suddenly, a small miracle occurred. The nurse equated the scales more nearly to a perfect balance, there was a tremor of delight as the two opposing dishes made a final frictional effort to disagree, and then there was perfection as the dual forces married in harmony. Even in my drowsy state, my heart stirred with joy at this revelation and perfection.

Our experiences when the pendulum swings the other way are no less numinous, but the emotions aroused in us by the object or event change from joy and confidence to panic and dread. There is a vivid description of this in Gerard Manley Hopkins' *Journals.*

> We hurried too fast and it knocked me up. We went to the College, the seminary being wanted for the secular priests' retreat: almost no gas, the retorts are being mended; therefore candles in bottles, things not ready, darkness and despair. In fact, being unwell, I was quite downcast: nature in all her parcels and faculties gaped and fell apart, *fatiscebat,* like a clod cleaving and holding only by strings of root.

One might expect that, when the "good" or "bad" moment is past, when the pendulum is in a median position, that the so-called "sane" would say to themselves, as we say when we wake from a dream, "What I saw and felt was a delusion: now I see things as they really are". But it is not so. Between the swings, the sanest of us have a feeling that a curtain has fallen between reality and ourselves. We say: "For a moment I was granted a vision of a reality behind phenomena which is now withdrawn."

What, then, are the crucial differences between the "sane" and those who have, like Mr Rossiter, at times to be hospitalised? One of them, according to Mr Rossiter's own testimony, is that the insane person identifies a symbolic object with the spiritual truth it symbolises. He tells us that, the first time he went off his head, he had been looking at his dressing-gown.

> My dressing-gown hung from the door. A grey flannel one made from an army blanket. It had red facings. Now it was transformed into an agonised Cruxifixion, its arms, caught on other hooks, outstretched.

In this experience, as such, there was nothing abnormal. But, in his reaction to it, there was, for he knelt down and began to pray to his dressing-gown.

This is one symptom of what he calls the "egocentricity" of the mad. Anybody who has manic-depressive friends will know what he means by this term. The unmistakable sign that someone has crossed either the "manic" or the "depressive" frontier is that a dialogue becomes impossible. In depression he may refuse to speak at all, in mania he may talk for hours without stopping, but his words are not addressed to any listener and, if the latter interposes a remark, this has no influence on his conversation. What is most disturbing about an insane person is that it is impossible to feel compassion for him, in the sense of imaginatively sharing in his suffering, as we can with the merely physically ill. The temptation to treat mental patients sadistically is very strong because, since they cannot see those about them as the persons they actually are but only as symbolic objects, it is difficult not to treat them as "recalcitrant" objects in return.

We are all egocentric, that is to say, each of us thinks: "I am the most important person walking the earth". But so long as we are sane, we add: "important to me. To most other human beings I am of no importance whatsoever, and to God I am neither more nor less important than every other human being". There are, undoubtedly, as Mr Rossiter says, affinities between "the sensations during the high flight" and the experiences of the mystics.

> The deep feeling of the unity of things, universal bliss, a sharing of everything, material and otherwise.

I believe, too, as he does, that both kinds of experience have a common origin,

> An intense spiritual quest after "oneness" and the beatification of mankind.

The difference between them, I would guess, is that the manic-depressive forgets that, for there to be one, there must first be two, so that, either as in the manic phase he "absorbs" the universe, or, as in the depressed phase, the universe absorbs him. In theological terms, one might say that he is without faith in the doctrine of the Holy Trinity, of which George MacDonald wrote:

> It is not the fact that God is all in all that unites the universe: it is the love of the Son to the Father. For of no onehood comes unity; there can be no oneness where there is only one. For the very beginnings of unity there must be two. Without Christ therefore there could be no universe.

In speaking of the insane as "egocentric", we must be careful to distinguish this from egoism or selfishness. The former is not willed by the patient: it now seems quite possible that it is connected with some bio-chemical malfunction, like the accumulation in the brain of an excess of salt. The truly egotistic man knows very well how to handle his neighbours so that he gets his own way at whatever cost to them: the "egocentric" patient puts himself at the mercy of others.

Mr Rossiter has had a particularly tough time, for, in addition to his mental troubles, he has suffered from thrombosis in his legs which required a succession of surgical operations. Never once, though, in his story, does he show the faintest trace of self-pity. The most amusing and at the same time saddest passage in this book is a description of a self-pitier, a certain Captain Ernest Butler. I will not spoil the reader's fun by giving it in full, but I cannot resist one revealing quotation.

> "Mind you, they can't do this op. on everyone, it just doesn't work. . . . But I was lucky; it was a risk, mind you, but I took it."

In helping him to endure unpleasant days, he has had the comforts of being able both to paint—an art of which I am not a competent judge—and to write—here I can say, without any hesitation, write very well—a happy marriage, and a Papa who must be a dear, judging by the following anecdote.

> My father was out shooting. He had just delighted himself by getting a "left and right". "Good shot, Rossiter!" said a voice near by, "you're in fine form to-day". There was a pause and my father's neighbour on the shoot added, "Quite a coincidence, a taxi starting up in the district run by a Rossiter. It's an unusual name". My father fired again, hit another pheasant, winged a second, and did a "double take". "My God—my son must be out of hospital!"

The Pendulum will, no doubt, be of great interest to psychologists as a detailed and accurate description from the inside of a clinical condition. At the same time, anyone who has an interest in human nature, and appreciates the virtues of courage and humor, will, I am sure, read it with fascination and delight.

The Pendulum: A Round Trip to Revelation,
by Anthony Rossiter (1969)

Foreword to *Persons from Porlock and Other Plays for Radio,* by Louis MacNeice

Louis MacNeice wrote a considerable number of radio plays on a wide variety of subjects, and it is quite impossible in one volume to give an adequate representation of the whole range of his work.

As a preliminary to making this selection, I asked myself: "Out of the various themes he treated, which were so well suited to radio that I cannot imagine them being as successful in any other medium?"

I began, therefore, by excluding his dramatisations of already existing prose works, of the *Njal Saga,* for example, and the scene of *Trimalchio's Feast* from the *Satyricon.* These seem to me extremely well done, but this selection is a book to be read, and since good translations, both of the *Saga* and of Petronius, exist, I think the interested reader will prefer to go to the originals.

The most striking difference between radio drama and the ordinary stage play is that in the former everything the characters say is heard primarily as a soliloquy. In a stage play the audience "overhear", so to speak, the remarks which the actors they see address to each other; in a radio play each remark is heard as addressed directly to the listener, and its effect upon the invisible characters in the play is secondary.

Then, unlike the stage play, the radio play, like the movie, permits of almost instantaneous changes in place and time—the Aristotelian Unities are irrelevant to the medium—and a large cast is economically possible. The Elizabethan stage without scenery or proscenium permitted the Elizabethan dramatist, if he so wished, to write, as a modern dramatist cannot, short scenes, but only fairly short, since it takes time for the actors to make their entrances and exits: in a radio play a scene can be only a few seconds long.

This means, I think, that radio drama is an excellent, perhaps the ideal, medium for "psychological" drama, that is to say the portrayal of the inner life, what human beings privately feel and think before and after they perform a public act. For its principal characters, therefore, it demands men and women who are by nature self-conscious and articulate: Hamlet is more suited to radio than Fortinbras.

MacNeice's last play, *Persons from Porlock*, seems to me a magnificent example of such a psychological drama. It covers more than twenty years of the life of Hank, a would-be painter. From the outside, these years are mostly a record of frustration and worldly failure. He starts out with the hope of becoming a "pure" painter. He fails. He becomes a commercial artist but preserves too much artistic conscience to succeed as one. He takes to the bottle, and his girl friend leaves him. He starts painting again and is reduced to beggary. (There is a suggestion that these paintings of his last phase procured him posthumous fame.) In addition, however, to his interest in painting and women, and his alcoholism, he is enchanted by the idea of exploring caves: underground, and only underground, he feels happy and himself. And it is in a cave that he meets his death. I shan't spoil the reader's pleasure by further description. I would only point out that Hank's death is a good illustration of a scene that would only be possible in a radio play. As he is dying, various characters who have played a part in his life appear to him and speak, helping him to arrive at a deeper self-knowledge. If one tries to imagine this scene in a stage play, one realises that it would not work. Firstly, while in the radio play one knows that the other characters are thoughts inside his head, if brought on to the stage they would be visibly external, so that the audience would be puzzled to know—a fatal dramatic flaw—whether they were "real" or tiresomely "symbolic". Secondly, a dying man cannot "do" anything: he can only lie there motionless, and on stage a motionless figure is an undramatic bore.

Several of MacNeice's best radio plays—I wish I had room to include more of them—were dramatised fairy-tales, some, like *The Heartless Giant*, traditional, others, like his best-known play, *The Dark Tower*, and *Queen of Air and Darkness*, his original creation.

Again, the medium of radio seems peculiarly suited to the fairy-tale. To begin with, since the world of fairy-tales is a Secondary World where the laws, inhabitants, events are utterly different from those of the Primary World of our public experience, every fairy-tale is, in a sense, a "psychological" drama, for it deals with our imagined experiences, not our actual ones. Secondly, the fairy-tale world is full of supernatural characters, embodied natural forces, talking animals, and magical transformations. On a visible stage these are very difficult, if not impossible, to make convincing. In the case of a talking animal, for example, the audience is always conscious that it is a human being dressed up as an animal, and it is not possible before the eyes of an audience for a beast to change into a man or vice versa. The disembodied voices of radio, on the other hand, can present such things convincingly, for the imagination of the listener is not spoiled by any collision with visual reality.

In two of the plays I have selected, *Enter Caesar* and *They Met on Good Friday*, MacNeice deals with historical subjects, in the first with Julius Caesar's rise to power, in the second with the complicated and ambiguous relations between the Viking and the native inhabitants in Ireland during the tenth and eleventh centuries.

In considering with what elements in political history radio drama is best capable of dealing, it may be helpful to think first about the medium which is its antithesis, the old silent movie. In the purely visual world of the latter, the audience can tell from the physical appearance of the characters, and what they are wearing, who is physically strong or weak, beautiful or ugly, rich or poor, who gives orders and who obeys them. But if the director wishes to indicate that this character is morally good and that one morally bad, he has to resort to type-casting, which everyone knows is a fake; in real life, villains can look like saints and vice versa. The camera can convey the emotions felt by the characters to the degree that these are visibly manifest in facial expressions or gestures, scowls, grins, laughter, tears, etc., which in practice means their emotions in critical situations. When their faces are still, their feelings remain unknown. If it is essential for the audience to know what somebody says, the director has to resort to the caption which is necessarily very brief and elementary: nobody can make a speech or conduct an argument. As for the thoughts of a character, the camera can tell us nothing whatsoever. On the other hand, the camera is superbly equipped to show the simultaneous actions of a large number of people, as on a battlefield or at a State triumph or funeral. In short, a silent movie on an historical subject can show us very vividly what actually happened, but it can tell us scarcely anything about why it happened.

With the medium of radio drama, it is just the other way round. All physical action and all mass behaviour has to take place, so to speak, "off-stage" as conventional noises, clashing of weapons, cheers, boos, etc. But, because it makes us hear what characters say, even in a dialogue with each other, as a soliloquy, it can express better than any other medium the reasons people give themselves for taking this or that action.

In *Enter Caesar*, its hero never speaks a word. What we hear are a series of political discussions by others, both professional politicians and men-in-the-street about him. Is he a danger to them personally or to the State, or is he a saviour? Would it be good policy to support him or oppose him? In either case, what steps should be taken? The result, to my mind, is most interesting, dramatic, and, in the best sense of the word, educational. It gives those of us who are not, like MacNeice, classical scholars who have read all the historical documents, a clear understanding of the political and social conditions in the Roman Republic after Sulla's death which enabled Caesar to come to power.

It is melancholy to reflect, firstly, that Louis MacNeice is dead and can give us no more poetry, secondly, that, since the advent of television, radio drama is probably a dying art. A dramatic medium in which almost all the effect depends upon the spoken word offers unique opportunities to poets, and it will be a matter for regret if they are going to be deprived of it.

Persons from Porlock and Other Plays for Radio,
by Louis MacNeice (1969)

A Civilized Voice

Alexander Pope: The Education of Genius 1688-1728.
By Peter Quennell. Stein & Day. $7.95.

It is not often that knowledge of an artist's life sheds any significant light upon his work, but in the case of Pope I think it does. Most of his best poems are "occasional"—that is to say, they are concerned not with imaginary persons or events but with the historical and contemporary, with Pope's political and literary friends and enemies, so that without some knowledge about them we cannot properly understand what he wrote and why. (Such knowledge, needless to say, does not explain why he wrote so well.) For example, in the concluding lines of a poem probably written before 1715, Pope (or so I used to think) describes Addison as

Statesman, yet friend to Truth! of soul sincere,
In action faithful and in honour clear;
Who broke no promise, served no private end.
Who gain'd no title, and who lost no friend;
Ennobl'd by himself, by all approv'd,
And prais'd, unenvied, by the Muse he lov'd.

I was, of course, in error. These lines of the "Epistle to Addison" were addressed to James Craggs, his successor as Secretary of State. However, the whole tone of the poem is friendly.

Then, sometime between that date and 1735, Pope changed his opinion and described Addison thus:

> Shou'd such a man, too fond to rule alone,
> Bear, like the Turk, no brother near the throne,
> View him with scornful, yet with jealous eyes,
> And hate for Arts that caus'd himself to rise,
> Damn with faint praise, assent with civil leer,
> And without sneering, teach the rest to sneer.

In understanding this change, we must be informed about Addison's somewhat devious behavior at the time of the almost simultaneous publication of Pope's translation of the *Iliad* and Tickell's.

More mysterious and much sadder is the history of the relationship between Pope and Lady Mary Wortley. She was the one great, passionate love of his life, and though she could not reciprocate, she was obviously very fond of him, at least in the beginning. What caused their estrangement is not clear. Current gossip had various explanations—that Lady Mary had borrowed a pair of sheets from Pope's mother and thoughtlessly sent them back unwashed, or that at an ill-chosen moment he had made fervent advances and she had burst into laughter—but these were almost certainly false. Mr Peter Quennell's explanation, in his *Alexander Pope: The Education of Genius 1688–1728,* is probably as close to the truth as we can get:

> Their quarrel, if a definite quarrel took place, probably originated not in any single episode, but in the very nature, the secret stresses and strains, of their curiously unequal friendship. For Lady Mary, it had been an amusing literary diversion: for Pope, an all-absorbing passion. Pope had the pride that goes with genius; Lady Mary possessed a considerable share of talent, and, to the self-esteem that usually accompanies talent, she added the strain of levity and light-hearted cruelty that she derived from her education as a woman of the world.

Their estrangement seems to have begun in 1722, and the suffering it caused Pope may be guessed from a poem he wrote to Gay:

> Ah friend, 'tis true—this truth you lovers know—
> In vain my structures rise, my gardens grow,
> In vain fair Thames reflects the double scenes
> Of hanging mountains, and of sloping greens:
> Joy lives not here; to happier seats it flies,
> And only dwells where WORTLEY casts her eyes. . . .
>
> What are the gay parterre, the chequer'd shade,
> The morning bower, the ev'ning colonade,
> But soft recesses of uneasy minds,

To sigh unheard in, to the passing winds?
So the struck deer in some sequester'd part
Lies down to die, the arrow at his heart.

Such grief may not excuse the ferocity with which, years later, he was to attack her, but it makes it comprehensible.

Then, we cannot fully understand Pope and any other writers of his period without knowing something about the general climate of thought and opinion by which they were surrounded. It was one of the few historical periods in which one could with accuracy speak of an educated élite who, whether as writers or as readers, shared the same artistic tastes and general ideas about Nature, Man, and Society—a period, therefore, when "originality" and "alienation" were not regarded as the hallmarks of genius. Take the question of religious belief. The uneducated multitude was fanatically anti-Papist. Defoe said that there were a hundred thousand fellows in his time ready to fight to the death against popery without knowing whether popery was a man or a horse. Though not physically persecuted, Roman Catholics were penalized: they could not live within ten miles of London, or attend a university, or serve in public office. But the educated laity, whether Protestant or Catholic, saw no reason that their theological differences should impair their social relations. Pope was born and remained a Roman Catholic, but throughout his life most of his closest friends were Protestant, and had any of them been asked to define precisely the difference between their faiths they would have found it difficult to give an answer.

Pope's statement of faith and his opinion of medieval Catholicism would scarcely have been approved of in Rome:

> Nothing has been so much a scarecrow to them [the Protestants] as the too peremptory and seemingly uncharitable assertion of an utter impossibility of salvation to all but ourselves. . . . Besides the small number of the truly faithful in our Church, we must again subdivide, and the Jansenist is damned by the Jesuit, the Jesuit by the Jansenist, the strict Scotist by the Thomist, &c. There may be errors, I grant, but I can't think 'em of such consequence as to destroy utterly the charity of mankind, the very greatest bond in which we are engaged by God to one another. . . .
>
> I am not a Papist, for I renounce the temporal invasions of the Papal power. . . .
>
> With *Tyranny*, then *Superstition* join'd,
> As that the *Body*, this enslav'd the *Mind*;
> Much was *Believ'd*, but little *understood*,
> And to be *dull* was constru'd to be *good*;
> A *second* Deluge Learning thus o'er-run,

And the *Monks* finish'd what the *Goths* begun.
At length, *Erasmus,* that *great, injur'd* name,
(The *Glory* of the Priesthood, and the *Shame!*)
Stemm'd the *wild Torrent* of a *barb'rous Age,*
And drove those *Holy Vandals* off the Stage.

The truth is, I think, that the religion of all educated persons at the time, whether they knew it or not, was not Christian but Deist. Their political passions ran stronger, but even in politics their love of order was greater than their ideological commitments. Pope and most of his friends were Tories who detested the Whig plutocracy that had come to power with William III. Pope himself may even have had secret Jacobite sympathies, but one cannot believe that the failure of the Jacobites in 1715 and 1745 caused him sleepless nights. What he wanted, he said, was a king who would be "not a King of Whigs or a King of Tories, but a King of England," which "God of his mercy grant his present Majesty may be."

Mr Quennell's book is equally excellent as a biography of a poet whom he admires and as a history of a period he loves and understands. It is beautifully written, scholarly but readable. He has, I am thankful to say, no ugly little secrets to tell us. Though Pope was often devious and unscrupulous in his dealings, his life was surprisingly free from scandal. In his youth, he may sometimes have visited brothels—given his physical disadvantages, what more romantic sexual adventures could he have hoped to have?—but in fact he was much less of a rake than he liked to make others believe. Nor was his life full of exciting incidents. He had three narrow escapes from death:

> First, he had been saved from the horns of a maddened cow at Binfield; secondly when he was a very young man, an imprudent coachman, negotiating a dangerous ford, had almost driven him and his party into a deep hole in the riverbed; last of all, he had nearly been plunged to destruction in Lord Bolingbroke's hurtling coach-and-six.

And Mr Quennell has one or two amusing anecdotes to tell, such as of the time when Pope read parts of his translation of the *Iliad* in the presence of Lord Halifax. On four or five occasions, the noble Lord interrupted:

> "I beg your pardon, Mr Pope," he would say, "but there is something in that passage that does not quite please me. Be so good as to mark the place . . . I'm sure you can give it a better turn." Pope was both puzzled and mortified; and on the journey home in Dr Garth's chariot, he complained that, having thought over the passages criticised, he could not understand the Minister's objections. Garth, however, laughed heartily. . . . "All you need do," says he, "is to leave them just as they are; call on Lord Halifax two or three months hence, thank him for his kind

> observations on those passages, and then read them to him as altered." Pope obeyed the Doctor's instructions and "his lordship was extremely pleased" to observe that his criticisms had proved so effective, exclaiming that the passages he had singled out were now everything they should be.

Then, there was Pope's socially unfortunate meeting with Voltaire:

> As the day drew on and the hour of farewells approached, Pope suggested that he should remain for dinner; and at the dinner table he met Mrs Pope, a plain, modest, round-faced old lady, now over eighty-four years old, who, in her motherly way (writes Owen Ruffhead) noticing that their foreign guest "appeared to be entirely emaciated" and seemed to have a weak stomach, "expressed her concern for his want of appetite"; at which Voltaire gave her "so indelicate and brutal an account of the occasion of his disorder contracted in Italy that the poor lady was obliged immediately to rise from the table."

But Pope's life has little gossip-column interest; most of his days were spent, quietly and industriously, writing, translating, landscape gardening, painting, playing with his dogs and entertaining his friends. (I am curious to know how many of his paintings and drawings have survived. I have myself seen a self-portrait in oils which is first-rate.)

While we are on the subject of the private life of an artist, I must take the opportunity to say how wholeheartedly I approve of Pope's attempt—alas, a vain one—to revise his private letters before letting the public read them, for he pruned them, sometimes changed the name of his correspondent, and pieced together separate items to form a single, more impressive text:

> Like Byron, Pope believed that his letters were bound to interest posterity; and, even in his least studied messages, he clearly had a double purpose: besides communicating with the friends he loved, he was establishing a link between himself and unborn readers. But he had none of Byron's reckless indiscretion; and, as soon as he took up his pen, he assumed the vigilant attitude of the true creative artist. His sense of style, which was immediately brought into play, affected both his use of language and his general handling of his theme. Wherever he felt that the record needed improvement, he hastened to apply the proper touches.

If private letters are to be made public—in my will I have requested my friends to burn mine—it is no more dishonest to revise a letter than a poem.

Then, what a pleasant surprise it is in these days to read of a writer who was an affectionate and dutiful son to both his parents. Mr Pope Senior seems to have been the ideal father for a poet. He encouraged his son but insisted on a high standard of performance. "These are not good rhymes," he would often remark, severely, and send the boy away to turn them better. "Pope was never beaten for interrupting his father's and mother's evening conferences, or thoughtlessly and selfishly tumbling downstairs. . . . In other respects he allowed him to go his way, conduct his education as he pleased, and read the books that most amused him." I do not believe that the average child can educate himself without the imposition of some external discipline, but Pope was not an average child, and in his case such permissiveness succeeded admirably. He taught himself to read by copying printed books. A priest named Banister taught him the rudiments of Latin and Greek and, as his pupil was to say later:

> If it had not been for that I should never have got any language: for I never learned anything at the little schools I was at afterwards.

Thereafter he studied these languages in his own way:

> I did not follow the grammar; but rather hunted in the authors for a syntax of my own: and then began translating any parts that pleased me particularly, in the best Greek and Latin poets: and by that means formed my taste; which, I think, verily, about sixteen, was very near as good as it is now.

Dates are always interesting and can sometimes be startling. One thinks so automatically of Pope as *the* poet of the eighteenth century that one is surprised at being reminded that he died before the century was half over. One is also apt to forget not only how precocious he was but how soon his talents were recognized. That Wycherley, aged sixty-four, should have asked Pope, aged eighteen, to correct and improve his verses is astounding. If not quite as precocious as Rimbaud, Pope was only twenty-one when he composed an important long poem, the *Essay on Criticism*, and twenty-six when he published the second version of *The Rape of the Lock*, an undoubted masterpiece. (Unlike some prodigies, however, he did not peter out early. The *Epistles* and *Imitations of Horace*, written toward the end of his life, are among his best works.) Only someone who was certain not only of his genius but of his contemporary fame could have started collecting his letters at the age of twenty-four and at twenty-five been confident that he could get sufficient subscribers to make it financially possible for him to devote six years to translating the *Iliad*.

To counterbalance the blessings of genius and a happy home, there was, of course, the curse of ill health. At the age of twelve, infected by milk from a tubercular cow, he developed Pott's disease—a tuberculosis of the spine, which turned the originally good-looking boy into an invalid, "the little Pope the ladies laugh at." When one tries to imagine the atrocious suffering and humiliation this must have caused him, one marvels not that he should have sometimes been irrationally suspicious and excessively malevolent but that he should have so often been kind and generous and shown such a gift for friendship. Very few people in his condition would have been brave enough to write an essay on "The Club of Little Men":

> A set of us have formed a society, who are sworn to *Dare to be Short*, and boldly beat out the dignity of littleness under the noses of those enormous engrossers of manhood, those hyperbolical monsters of the species, the tall fellows that overlook us. . . . If any member shall take advantage from the fulness or length of his wig . . . or the immoderate extent of his hat . . . to seem larger and higher than he is, it is ordered, he shall wear red heels to his shoes and a red feather in his hat, which may apparently mark and set bounds to the extremities of his small dimensions.

But what is really important is his poetry, and perhaps the best approach to that is through his views on landscape gardening. During the early part of the eighteenth century in England, the relation between Man and Nature seems to have been happier than ever before or since. Wild Nature had been tamed, but machines had not yet debased and enslaved her. Earlier generations had thought of Nature as a dangerous realm against which men must erect defenses; later generations were to think of Nature as a realm of freedom into which the individual could escape from the constraints of human society. The older view is exemplified by the Baroque gardens of Europe, with their geometrical patterns and topiary work designed to make them look as unlike the Nature outside as possible. But in England landscape gardeners like William Kent held the view that their proper function was "to brush Nature's robe," to confine themselves to adding the final, decisive touches, planting a term here, a sphinx or an obelisk there, or "improving" a corner of the landscape to recall a picture by Lorrain or Poussin. Pope was Kent's enthusiastic disciple. A man who could write "A tree is a nobler object than a prince in his coronation robes" was certainly not afraid of Nature, and he poured ridicule on the old Baroque formalities:

> His Gardens next your admiration call.
> On ev'ry side you look, behold the Wall!
> No pleasing Intricacies intervene,
> No artful wildness to perplex the scene;
> Grove nods at grove, each Alley has a brother,
> And half the platform just reflects the other.
> The suff'ring eye inverted Nature sees.
> Trees cut to Statues, Statues thick as trees;

But he also believed that Nature needed Man's help to realize her beauties to the full:

> Consult the Genius of the Place in all,
> That tells the Waters or to rise, or fall,
> Or helps th'ambitious Hill the heav'n to scale,
> Or scoops in circling theatres the Vale,
> Calls in the Country, catches op'ning glades.
> Joins willing woods, and varies shades from shades,
> Now breaks, or now directs, th'intending Lines,
> Paints as you plant, and, as you work, designs.
> Still follow Sense, of ev'ry Art the Soul,
> Parts answ'ring parts shall slide into a whole,
> Spontaneous beauties all around advance,
> Start ev'n from difficulty, strike from chance.

An equally apt description, surely, of what Pope was after in his poetry and, at his best, succeeded in realizing. Comparing Dryden and Pope, Mr Quennell says:

> Whereas our first reading of a passage by Dryden is usually sufficient to display his genius, Pope, whenever we reread him. is apt to reveal some unexpected subtlety. Dryden's virtues lie on the surface; in Pope's verse, several layers of significance are compressed into a single image; and his imagery has a protean charm that constantly changes and grows beneath the reader's eye.

In his first published poems, the *Pastorals*, Nature is, to be sure, too subordinate to artifice, precision to euphony; the epithets are as abstract and conventional as the Romantics imagined was typical of all Augustan verse:

> Soon as the flocks shook off the nightly dews,
> Two Swains, whom Love kept wakeful, and the Muse,
> Poured o'er the whitening vale their fleecy care,
> Fresh as the morn, and as the season fair.

But already he is capable of writing a memorable couplet which is vivid as well as melodious:

> The moving Mountains hear the pow'rful Call,
> And headlong Streams hang list'ning in their Fall!

And from the *Essay on Criticism* to the last poems, Pope's lapses into conventional diction become very rare; his epithets are almost always both exact and original. The only technical defect I can find in his mature work comes from his ingrained habit of thinking in couplets which are self-contained units. As a result, he sometimes fails to notice that the rhymes of two successive couplets are too similar:

> With arms expanded Bernard rows his *state,*
> And left-legged Jacob seems to emu*late.*
> Full in the middle way there stood a *lake,*
> Which Curll's Corinna chanced that morn to *make.*

It was, naturally, necessary for the poets at the end of the century to get away from the heroic couplet, which by then had become a dead end, and to discover new forms for both long poems and lyrics, but if Wordsworth had Pope in mind as the enemy when he advised poets to write "in the language really used by men" he was singularly in error. Should one compare Pope at his best with any of the Romantics, including Wordsworth, at their best, it is Pope who writes as men normally speak to each other and the latter who go in for "poetic" language. When Wordsworth tries to write according to his theories, the result is nearly always flat; to write well, he has to forget them. In Pope, theory and practice are one. Compare

> Shut, shut the door, good *John!* fatigu'd I said.
> Tye up the knocker! say I'm sick, I'm dead.
>
> (Pope)

> She went from Op'ra, Park, Assembly, Play,
> To morning walks, and pray'rs three hours a day;
> To part her time 'twixt reading and Bohea,
> To muse, and spill her solitary tea,
> Or o'er cold coffee trifle with the spoon,
> Count the slow clock, and dine exact at noon.
>
> (Pope)

> To me the meanest flower that blows can give
> Thoughts that do often lie too deep for tears.
>
> (Wordsworth)

> A voice so thrilling ne'er was heard
> In springtime from the Cuckoo-bird,
> Breaking the silence of the seas
> Among the farthest Hebrides.
>
> (Wordsworth)

To find "natural speech" in the verse of the early nineteenth century, one must go to the least "romantic" and most Popean in spirit of the poets—to the Byron of *Don Juan* and the Tom Moore of *The Fudge Family in Paris.*

The only major poem of Pope's which seems to me a failure is *An Essay on Man.* Occasional lines of great beauty like

> Die of a rose in aromatic pain

do not compensate for the unconvincing and boring Deist theology.

About his translation of the *Iliad,* there will always be two opinions. Those who dislike it say, quite truly, that Pope sees Homer through Vergilian spectacles (his warriors have much more Roman *gravitas* than their Bronze Age originals), that what in Homer is tragic in Pope too often becomes merely grandiose, and that the movement and structure of the English heroic couplet are far removed from those of the Greek hexameter. But when these critics have done their worst, it still cannot be denied that Pope's "translation" is a magnificent English poem, and that no subsequent translator, despite all advances in philological and archeological scholarship, has produced one as readable. To the problem of the metre, there cannot, I believe, be a completely satisfactory solution. Some twentieth-century translators have claimed that the best equivalent is a free six-beat line, but I agreed with Mr Carne-Ross when he wrote recently in *Delos*:

> The claims . . . have, I think, been granted a great deal too readily. It is about the same length, but its lumbering gait is at the furthest possible remove from the supply articulated line of Homer. Most of the time it is verse only by typographical courtesy and its movement is so ill-defined that it falls a ready prey to any other metre whose path it chances to cross.

Today I feel a little less enthusiastic about *The Dunciad* than I felt when I last wrote about it, eighteen years ago. The Second Book in particular I find repellent, as grubby as anything produced by our contemporary "underground." The best things in the first three books are nearly always addenda to the *Essay on Criticism,* passages in which Pope forgets about personalities and writes beautifully about bad writing:

> She sees a Mob of Metaphors advance,
> Pleas'd with the Madness of the mazy dance . . .
> How Time himself stands still at her command,
> Realms shift their place, and Ocean turns to land.
> Here gay Description Ægypt glads with showers;
> Or gives to Zembla fruits, to Barca flowers . . .
> On cold December fragrant chaplets blow,
> And heavy harvests nod beneath the snow.

The Fourth Book, however, is superb throughout, and prophetic of much that we must endure today. Pope had never seen a "behaviorist" or a "social scientist," but he guessed exactly what such creatures would be like:

"Be that my task (replies a gloomy Clerk,
Sworn foe to Myst'ry, yet divinely dark;
Whose pious hope aspires to see the day
When Moral Evidence shall quite decay,
And damns implicit faith, and holy lies,
Prompt to impose, and fond to dogmatize):
Let others creep by timid steps, and slow,
On plain Experience lay foundations low.
By common sense to common knowledge bred,
And last, to Nature's Cause thro' Nature led.
All-seeing in thy mists, we want no guide,
Mother of Arrogance, and Source of Pride!
We nobly take the high Priori Road,
And reason downward, till we doubt of God:
Make Nature still incroach upon his plan:
And shove him off as far as e'er we can:
Thrust some Mechanic Cause into his place;
Or bind in Matter, or diffuse in Space.
Or, at one bound, o'er-leaping all his laws,
Make God Man's Image, Man the final Cause,
Find Virtue local, all Relation scorn,
See all in *Self*, and but for self be born:
Of nought so certain as our Reason still,
Of nought so doubtful as of *Soul* and *Will*."

If only one of Pope's poems could be preserved, my choice would be *The Rape of the Lock*, and Mr Quennell's account of how it came to be written will fascinate anyone who is interested in the factors which enter into poetic composition. The first factor was a historical incident—a feud between two old Catholic families, the Fermors and the Petres, which had broken out because the seventh Lord Petre had stolen a lock of hair from the head of Arabella Fermor. Lord Petre was the ward of Pope's friend John Caryl, who suggested to the poet that he might write a comic poem about the incident which would reconcile the parties by making them both laugh. The second factor was a literary genre, the mock epic—works like *The War of the Frogs and the Mice* (at one time attributed to Homer), Tassoni's *Secchia Rapita*, published in 1622, and Boileau's *Le Lutrin*, finished in 1683, all of which Pope had almost certainly read. To call this a second factor is not to say that it came second in time. Given Pope's literary tastes and talents, it is much more probable that the idea of writing a mock-heroic epic was already in his mind, awaiting a suitable subject. The third factor was a contemporary social fashion. One of the most brilliant passages in the poem, the account of the card game between the Baron and Belinda, might not have been written had not ombre, the particular game Pope describes, introduced into England from Spain in the previous century, recently become all the rage. Lastly, there was an odd book, *Le Comte de Gabalis*, by L'Abbé de Montfaucon de Villars, which Pope happened to read, either in the original or in an English translation, and from which he took his Sylphs and other "lower militia of the sky." Since these did not appear in the first version, I would guess that he had not yet read the book when he began the poem. In any case, he had an extraordinary stroke of good luck, for the Sylphs, etc., were exactly what he needed to play the role in a mock epic played by the Gods in a serious epic. Moreover, as tiny creatures, they were ideally suited to Pope's imagination, fascinated as he always was by littleness.

Aside from its many beauties, *The Rape of the Lock* demonstrates that Pope's imagination was much odder than it is generally supposed to be. I have said that his poetry was like his landscape gardening. The general layout of his Twickenham garden conformed to the general good taste of his time, but it contained one very peculiar feature—the grotto of which Dr Johnson said, rather severely, "Where necessity enforced a passage, vanity supplied a grotto."

> [Pope] encrusted the passage with a rough mosaic of luminous mineral bodies—Cornish diamonds, knobs of metallic ore, lumps of amethyst, spiky branches of coral, coloured Brazilian pebbles, crystals and quartzes, slabs of burnished flint, and rare and interesting "fossile" specimens, amid a rich embroidery of rustic shell-work and scraps of looking-glass cut into angular designs. On the roof shone a looking-glass star; and, dependent from the star, a single lamp—"of an orbicular figure of thin alabaster"—cast around it "a thousand pointed rays." Every surface sparkled or shimmered or gleamed with a smooth sub-aqueous lustre; and, while these corruscating details enchanted the eye, a delicate water-music had been arranged to please the car; the "little dripping murmur" of an underground spring—discovered by the workmen during their excavations—echoed through the cavern day and night.

So, in his poems, Pope will suddenly indulge in a certain "zaniness" which reminds me of Lewis Carroll.

> Here living Teapots stand, one Arm held out,
> One bent; the Handle this, and that the Spout:
> A Pipkin there like Homer's Tripod walks:
> Here sighs a Jar, and there a Goose-pye talks.
> Men prove with Child, as pow'rful Fancy works.
> And Maids turn'd Bottles, call aloud for Corks. . . .
>
> More she had spoke, but yawn'd—All Nature nods:
> What Mortal can resist the Yawn of Gods?
> Churches and Chapels instantly it reach'd;
> (St James's first, for leaden Gilbert preach'd)

Then catch'd the Schools; the Hall scarce kept awake:
The Convocation gap'd, but could not speak. . . .
The Vapour mild o'er each Committee crept;
Unfinish'd Treaties in each Office slept;
And Chiefless Armies doz'd out the Campaign;
And Navies yawn'd for Orders on the Main.

Since Mr Quennell's book is primarily a biography, not a work of literary criticism, it is fitting that in conclusion I return to Pope as a human being. In a period when many writers were hired agents of the government, he showed an admirable integrity. Though not as poor as most of Grub Street, Pope, at least until after the publication of his *Iliad*, was by no means rich, and tempting offers, it seems, were made. In 1717, according to his own account, which there is no reason to doubt, James Craggs, then Secretary at War, offered him

> both a pension of three hundred pounds and complete freedom from all official ties, since he was ready to pay the pension from secret-service funds at his disposal, "without anyone's knowing that I had it." This offer he repeated several times, "and always used to insist on the convenience that a coach would be of to me."

How admirable, too, that, while wholly dedicated to the vocation of the poet, he never became an aesthete—never, that is, regarded his vocation as superior to all others. On the contrary, he wrote:

> To write well, lastingly well, immortally well, must not one leave Father and Mother and cleave unto the Muse? . . . 'Tis such a task as scarce leaves a man time to be a good neighbour, an useful friend, nay to plant a tree, much less to save his soul.

Poetry does not allow us to escape from life, but it does grant us a brief respite from our immediate problems, refreshment for tired spirits and relaxation for tense nerves. As I get older and the times get gloomier and more difficult, it is to poets like Horace and Pope that I find myself more and more turning for the kind of refreshment I require.

The New Yorker, 22 February 1969

To Stephen Spender on his Sixtieth Birthday: Greetings from Auden

Dear Stephen:

How nice to know that we are both "Fish": *Pisces* is a good sign, I think. As you now follow me into our sixties, I hope you feel as content as I do, and as happy to recall that we have known each other for forty-two years. As a school friend of your brother Michael, I had, of course, already heard of you. I remember, for example, hearing your father (what a rum one *he* was!) say in 1924: "My son Stephen is too sensitive for a boarding-school." And, when I first met you, sensitive you seemed to be: it was only gradually that I discovered you were, underneath, as tough as an old boot. One reason for this, of course, has been the extraordinary good health you have always enjoyed. I can't complain about my own, but it makes me jealous to think that you have never had to worry about your waistline.

A birthday is much too personal an occasion for literary criticism and, besides, I would rather read your writings than talk about them. I may, however, speak of your conversation: nobody else I know can, when you are in the mood, be so funny and malicious. I may speak, too, of your work as an editor, since *Encounter* was so important an outlet for me. Alas, all was not what it seemed, but no one who knows you will believe for one second that you were privy to any shenanigans. You are not the stuff of which agents are made.

Among the many things for which I admire you (and Natasha), not the least has been your talent as a parent. To have raised two children who exhibit both common sense and good manners is, in these difficult times, no mean accomplishment.

One last point. From one day to the next, almost, you changed from looking like a Shelley to looking like an Elder Statesman: however did you manage it?

So, a very happy birthday and many even happier returns.

Love,
WYSTAN AUDEN

The Guardian, 28 February 1969
(two-star London edition only)

Papa Was a Wise Old Sly-Boots

My Father and Myself. By J. R. Ackerley. Coward-McCann. $5.00.

My first reason for wishing to review this book is that it gives me an opportunity to make public acknowledgment of a debt which not only I but many writers of my generation owe to Mr Ackerley. He informs us that he became Literary Editor of *The Listener* in 1935, but of his work there he says not a word. Those of us, however, who were starting our literary careers at the time have very good cause to remember how much he did for us: *The Listener* was one of our main outlets. More surprisingly, he says nothing about his intimate friends in the literary world, of whom there were many, including E. M. Forster. He says that he went to work for the BBC because he felt he had failed in his ambition to become a writer himself. On first reading this statement seems absurd: though he published only four books in his lifetime, all were enthusiastically received by the reviewers, and are just as good reading today as when they first appeared. I think, though, I understand what he means, namely, that he discovered that he could not create imaginary characters and situations: all his books were based on journals, whether written down or kept in his head.

In *My Father and Myself*, Mr Ackerley strictly limits himself to two areas of his life, his relations with his family and his sex-life. His account of the latter, except for its happy ending, is very sad reading indeed. Few, if any, homosexuals can honestly boast that their sex-life has been happy, but Mr Ackerley seems to have been exceptionally unfortunate. All sexual desire presupposes that the loved one is in some way "other" than the lover: the eternal and, probably, insoluble problem for the homosexual is finding a substitute for the natural differences, anatomical and psychic, between a man and a woman. The luckiest, perhaps, are those who, dissatisfied with their own bodies, look for someone with an Ideal physique; the ectomorph, for example, who goes for mesomorphs. Such a difference is a real physical fact and, at least until middle age, permanent: those for whom it is enough are less likely to make emotional demands which their partner cannot meet. Then, so long as they don't get into trouble with the police, those who like "chicken" have relatively few problems: among thirteen- and fourteen-year-old boys there are a great many more Lolitas than the public suspects. It is when the desired difference is psychological or cultural that the real trouble begins.

Mr Ackerley, like many other homosexuals, wanted his partner to be "normal." That in itself is no problem, for very few males are so "normal" that they cannot achieve orgasm with another male. But this is exactly what a homosexual with such tastes is unwilling to admit. His daydream is that a special exception has been made in his case out of love; his partner would never dream of going to bed with any other man. His daydream may go even further; he may secretly hope that his friend will love him so much as to be willing to renounce his normal tastes and have no girl friend. Lastly, a homosexual who is, like Mr Ackerley, an intellectual and reasonably well-off is very apt to become romantically enchanted by the working class, whose lives, experiences, and interests are so different from his own, and to whom, because they are poorer, the money and comforts he is able to provide can be a cause for affectionate gratitude. Again, there is nothing wrong with this in itself. A great deal of nonsense has been spoken and written about the sinfulness of giving or receiving money for sexual favors. If I may be forgiven for quoting myself:

> Money cannot buy
> the fuel of Love,
> but is excellent kindling.

No, the real difficulty for two persons who come from different classes is that of establishing a sustained relationship, for, while a sexual relationship as such demands "otherness," any permanent relationship demands interests in common. However their tastes and temperaments may initially differ, a husband and wife acquire a common concern as parents. This experience is denied homosexuals. Consequently, it is very rare for a homosexual to remain faithful to one person for long and, rather curiously, the intellectual older one is more likely to be promiscuous than his working-class friend. The brutal truth, though he often refuses to admit it, is that he gets bored more quickly.

For many years, Mr Ackerley was a compulsive cruiser:

> In spite of such adventures, if anyone had asked me what I was doing, I doubt if I should have replied that I was diverting myself. I think I should have said that I was looking for the Ideal Friend. Though two or three hundred young men were to pass through my hands in the course of years, I did not consider myself promiscuous. It was all a run of bad luck . . . What I meant by the Ideal Friend I doubt if I ever formulated, but now, looking back, I think I can put him together in a negative way by listing some of his disqualifications. He should not be effeminate, indeed preferably normal: I did not exclude education, but did not want it, I could supply all that myself and in the loved one it always seemed to get in the way; he should admit me but no one else; he should be physically attractive to me and younger than myself—the younger the better, as closer to innocence; finally he should be on the small side, lusty, circumcised, physically healthy and clean: no phimosis, halitosis, bromidrosis. . . . The Ideal Friend was always somewhere else and might have been found if only I had turned a different way. The buses that passed my own bus seemed always to contain those charming boys who were absent from mine; the ascending escalators in the tubes fiendishly carried them past me as I sank helplessly into hell. . . . In the "thirties" I found myself concentrating my attention more and more upon a particular society of young men in the metropolis which I had tapped before and which, it seemed to me, might yield, without further loss of time, what I required. His Majesty's Brigade of Guards had a long history in homosexual prostitution. Perpetually short of cash, beer, and leisure occupations, they were easily to

> be found of an evening in their red tunics standing about in the various pubs they frequented, over the only half-pint they could afford or some "quids-in" mate had stood them. Though generally larger than I liked, they were young, they were normal, they were working-class, they were drilled to obedience; though not innocent for long, the new recruit might be found before someone else got at him; if grubby they could be bathed, and if civility and consideration, with which they did not always meet in their liaisons, were extended to them, one might gain their affection.

Frank as he is, Mr Ackerley is never quite explicit about what he *really* preferred to do in bed. The omission is important because all "abnormal" sex-acts are rites of symbolic magic, and one can only properly understand the actual personal relation if one knows the symbolic role each expects the other to play. Mr Ackerley tells us that, over the years, he learned to overcome certain repugnances and do anything to oblige but, trying to read between the lines, I conclude that he did not belong to either of the two commonest classes of homosexuals, neither to the "orals" who play Son-and/or-Mother, nor to the "anals" who play Wife-and/or-Husband. My guess is that at the back of his mind, lay a daydream of an innocent Eden where children play "Doctor," so that the acts he really preferred were the most "brotherly," Plain-Sewing and Princeton-First-Year. In his appendix, he does tell us, however, that he suffered, and increasingly so as he got older, from an embarrassing physical disability—premature ejaculation with the novel and impotence with the familiar. O dear, o dear, o dear.

But then, when he was nearly fifty, a miracle occurred. He acquired an Alsatian bitch named Tulip. (Had Fate sent him an *Aureus* dog instead of a *Lupus*, there would have been no miracle.)

> She offered me what I had never found in my sexual life, constant, single-hearted, incorruptible, uncritical devotion. She placed herself entirely under my control. From the moment she established herself in my heart and my home, my obsession with sex fell wholly away from me. The pubs I had spent so much of my time in were never revisited, my single desire was to get back to her, to her waiting love and unstaling welcome. I sang with joy at the thought of seeing her. I never prowled the London streets again, nor had the slightest inclination to do so. On the contrary, whenever I thought of it, I was positively thankful to be rid of it all, the anxieties, the frustrations, the wastage of time and spirit. The fifteen years she lived with me were the happiest of my life.

Very fittingly, *My Father and Myself* is dedicated to her.

In considering the story of his relationship to his father, let me begin by making two chronological lists.

Roger Ackerley			Joe Ackerley		
Date	*Event*	*Age*	*Date*	*Event*	*Age*
1863	Born in Liverpool.		1896	Born.	
			c. 1906	At school at Rossal.	10
1875	Father financially ruined.	12			
1876	Leaves school and goes to work as a clerk.	13			
1879	Runs away to London and enlists in the Royal House-Guards. Makes friends with Fitzroy Paley Adams (aged 33) who starts to educate him.	16			
			1914	World War One, Enlists.	18
1882	Service in Egypt where he may have contracted syphilis. Discharged.	19			
1883	Adams dies, leaving him a legacy of £500. Re-enlists in the Life Guards. Makes friends with Comte James Francis de Gallatin (aged 30).	20	1916	Wounded.	20
1884	Discharged. Goes to work for a wine-merchant in Liverpool. Lends his legacy to de Gallatin at 20 percent interest.	21			
1885	Father dies. Makes friends with Arthur Stockley (aged 20).	22	1918	Again wounded and a P.O.W. Soon after interned in Switzerland. (Copy for *Prisoners of War.*)	22

Roger Ackerley			Joe Ackerley		
Date	*Event*	*Age*	*Date*	*Event*	*Age*
				Peter Ackerley killed in action.	
1886	de Gallatin engages him to run a pony farm. They travel together in Italy.	23	1919–21	Cambridge.	23–25
1888	At de Gallatin's house, meets Louise Burkhardt, a visitor from Switzerland. They become engaged. Quarrel with de Gallatin, ending in a law-suit.	25	1921–25	Lives at home on an allowance of £350 a year.	25–29
			1923–24	Visits India (Copy for *Hindu Holiday*).	27
1889	Marries L.B.	26			
1892	His wife dies. Receives an allowance from her parents of £2000 a year. Meets the future mother of Joe (a legitimate actress, aged 28) on a Channel boat. Goes into a fruit business, started by Arthur Stockley.	29	1925	Leases flat in Hammersmith from Arthur Needham, an old acquaintance of de Gallatin.	29
1895	Peter "Ackerley" born.	32	1928	Joins Talks Department of B.B.C.	32
1896	Joe born.	33	1929	Father dies.	33
1898	A daughter by Joe's mother.	35			
			1934	Takes Flat in Maida Vale.	38
			1935	Becomes Literary Editor of *The Listener.*	39
1910	Twin daughters by another woman, Muriel.	47			

Roger Ackerley			Joe Ackerley		
Date	*Event*	*Age*	*Date*	*Event*	*Age*
1912	A third daughter by Muriel.	49			
			1945 or 1946	Acquires Tulip. (Copy for *My Dog Tulip* and *We Think the World of You.*)	50
1919	Marries Joe's mother.	56			
			1959	Retires from B.B.C.	63
1929	Dies from the effects of tertiary syphilis.	66	c. 1960	Tulip dies.	64
			1967	Dies in his sleep of a coronary.	71

Needless to say, it was only by degrees that the son discovered some of the more startling facts about the father's life. He tells us that he learned of his illegitimacy (curiously enough, his maternal grandmother was also illegitimate) from his sister, who had heard it from his mother, but he does not say if this discovery was made before or after the marriage. There was, on the face of it, no reason to suspect such a thing. The children were given the name Ackerley and even Roger's business partner, Stockley, believed there had been a registry-office marriage. Though for the first few years, he seems to have been "a week-end father," who only paid them occasional visits, he set up house with them in 1903 and was as attentive and generous to both the children and their mother as they could possibly have wished.

Of his father's second family, Mr Ackerley only learned from a letter he left to be opened after his death, requesting his son to make certain financial provisions for them. For Muriel's children he had shown less paternal concern.

> The birth of the twins was registered by him under an assumed name, he borrowed the name of his mistress; the youngest girl was never registered at all. They were all stowed away in a house near Barnes Common in care of a Miss Coutts. Through dietary ignorance or a desire to save his pocket, she fed them so frugally and injudiciously that they all developed rickets. They had no parental care, no family life, no friends. Their mother whom they did not love or even like, for she had less feeling for them than for her career and reputation, seldom appeared; the youngest girl does not remember to have seen her at all until she was some ten years old. But three or four times a year a relative of theirs, whom they knew as Uncle Bodger and who jokingly called himself Wil-

> liam Whitely, the Universal Provider, would arrive laden with presents. This gentleman, almost their only visitor, they adored. He would come in a taxi with his load of gifts (sometimes with a dog named Ginger, who had perhaps provided him with a pretext for the visit: "I'm taking the dog for a walk," and who, since he was *our* dog, was also therefore another conspirator in my father's affairs, had he but known it.

Then, even after learning from his landlord, Arthur Needham, that the Comte de Gallatin was not only queer but a bold cruiser of Guardsmen, it was only after his father's death that he began to wonder about this friendship and its break-up. It must have been odd to realize that, had some Time Machine monkeyed with their time-spans, it might well have been a thirty-year-old Joe who picked up a twenty-year-old Roger in a bar, and for a short while believed he had found the Ideal Friend.

The Fruit Business did extremely well, so that the household enjoyed every comfort. There was a butler, a gardener, and, evidently, a very good table. Ackerley Senior had an Edwardian appetite in food and drink with all the risks to health which that implies. Like King Tum-Tum, he had to take the waters every year, in his case at Bad Gastein.

As a father, aside from a distressing habit of telling dirty stories, for which he must be excused because it was the convention among his business colleagues, he seems to have been all that a son could reasonably hope for. To begin with, he was good-tempered.

> Even in family quarrels, he seldom intervened, he did not take sides and put people in their places. Whatever he thought, and it was easily guessed, for the faults were easily seen, he kept to himself until, later, he might give it private expression to me in some rueful comment.

Unintellectual businessmen who find they have begotten a son who wants to become a writer are apt to be bewildered and resentful, but he gave his own a liberal allowance and never attempted to make him go into the family business or even take some regular job.

Then he was unshockable. In 1912 he told his two sons that

> in the matter of sex there was nothing he had not done, no experience he had not tasted, no scrape he had not got into and out of.

At the same time, and this seems to me to have been his greatest virtue, he was never nosy. It is quite obvious, for example, that he knew perfectly well what his son's sexual tastes were. In view of some of the characters the latter brought to the house, he could hardly have helped knowing.

> There was a young actor who rendered my father momentarily speechless at dinner one evening by asking him, "Which do you think is my best profile, Mr Ackerley"—turning his head from side to side—"this,

> or this?"; there was an Irishman with a thin, careful curled cyclindrical fringe of a moustache and black paint around the lower lids of his eyes, who arrived in a leather jacket with a leopard-skin collar and pointed purple suede shoes; and an intellectual policeman. "Interesting chap," said my father afterwards, adding, "It's the first time I've ever entertained a policeman at my table."

I don't think Mr Ackerley ever fully appreciated this aspect of his father's character. Speaking for myself, I would say that between parents and their grown-up children, the happiest relation is one of mutual affection and trust on the one hand, and of mutual reticence on the other; no indiscreet confidences on either side. In the following dialogue, it is the father, surely, who shows the greater wisdom and common sense.

> "I've got something to tell you, Dad. I lied to you about Weybridge. I didn't go there at all."
>
> "I know, old boy. I knew you were lying directly I asked you about the floods."
>
> "I went to Turin."
>
> "Turin, eh? That's rather farther. I'm very sorry to have mucked up your plans."
>
> "I'm very sorry to have lied to you. I wouldn't have done so if you hadn't once said something about me and my waiter friends. But I don't mind telling you. I went to meet a sailor friend."
>
> "It's all right, old boy. I prefer not to know. So long as you enjoyed yourself, that's the main thing."

Like all of us, Mr Ackerley had his cross to bear, but I simply do not believe he was as unhappy as his habit of glooming led him to imagine. How many people have had so understanding a father? How many have found their Tulip? How many have written four (now five) good books? How many have been in the position to earn the affectionate gratitude of a younger literary generation? No, he was a lucky man.

The New York Review of Books, 27 March 1969

A Piece of Pure Fiction in the Firbank Mode

A Nest of Ninnies. By John Ashbery and James Schuyler.
E. P. Dutton. $4.95.

My! what a pleasant surprise in these days to read a novel in which there is not a single bedroom scene. Indeed, though as is proper in a comedy, three marriages have been celebrated before it is over and two more are imminent, there are no love scenes. There are, to be sure, some scenes of violence, but the violence is meteorological: the characters can hardly go anywhere without encountering torrential rains. More extraordinary still, though many of them live in suburbia, they all seem, believe it or not, to be happy and, though sometimes bitchy, actually to like each other.

The direct ancestor of the authors is, I should guess, Ronald Firbank. For example:

> "I'm certainly glad I never took up the violin," Alice said. [She plays the cello.] "It's so confusing not to have something to lean on."

> "Would you like to go to some nightclubs? I could take you to one in Montmartre that is frequented by gangsters."
>
> "Anything," Fabia said, "so long as we don't wind up at another Akim Tamiroff festival. However, I'm determined to visit the site of Les Funambules."
>
> "I'm not sure I know where that is," Paul said.
>
> "Frankly, I'd settle for a hot bath and the English weeklies," Alice said as the boat crunched to a stop next to a dock. "But—*vive l'aventure!*"

> The engine gave a brief summary of Elektra's dance of triumph and, like Elektra, died.

The interest all the characters take in the pleasures of the table—the dust jacket informs us that they sit down to eat twenty-one times and drink on twenty-three different occasions—reminds me of the *Lucia* novels of E. F. Benson, but I understand that the authors have not read them. Anyway, it is great fun to read about their gastronomic experiences: hunger is, after all, a more basic passion than sex. In Childs, they are content with cheese fondue on toast tips; at home, they are a bit more fancy:

> The guests took their places at the table. The dinner menu was as follows: salted nuts in small dishes; a relish of olives and celery stuffed with Roquefort cheese spread, consommé madrilène, broiled lamb chops, green peas and new potatoes, tomato aspic salad, baked Alaska. Rolls and demitasse. The demitasse was served in the living room.

Though all the characters (even Nadia, whose father makes all the lead paint for the battleships of France) work for their living—in a Manhattan office, practicing medicine, giving music lessons, dealing in antiques, running a restaurant, etc.—their work never seems to interfere with their play. If one of them goes to Florida or Paris or Rome, all the others are mysteriously able to come too.

Aside from eating and talking, their main preoccupations seem to be music, opera in particular, and French and Italian literature. I think I am right in saying that no reference is made to any American author, though one character does your reviewer the honor of misquoting him. In both fields their tastes are catholic and their knowledge sometimes esoteric.

Not every reader will have heard compositions by Max Reger or be familiar with the works of Sannazaro or Matilde Serao. The youngest of them, Abel, even seems to be a budding composer of the modern school. ("Slightly above their heads, Abel and his cello were accompanying some household tympani in a piece which sounded as though a sofa were being lifted and gently dropped.")

Like many folk tales, the idylls of Theocritus, the *Alice* books, *The Importance of Being Earnest,* the novels of Firbank and P. G. Wodehouse, *A Nest of Ninnies* is a pastoral: the world it depicts is an imaginary Garden of Eden, a place of innocence from which all serious needs and desires have been excluded.

It is possible, I think, that in our time pastoral is the genre best suited to pure fiction. I observe that those contemporary writers who wish to deal with the problems, sufferings and evil of the real world in which we all live seem to be finding fiction in the traditional sense inadequate to their needs, and are turning more and more to some kind of reportage, whether in the first or third person.

A young novelist who is attracted by pastoral should be warned, however, that it is extremely difficult to do well. I am not surprised to learn that, though *A Nest of Ninnies* is only 191 pages long, it took Messrs Ashbery and Schuyler several years to write. Their patience and artistry have been well rewarded. I am convinced that their book is destined to become a minor classic.

The New York Times Book Review, 4 May 1969

Freedom and Necessity in Poetry

What I have to say is really only a gloss on two lines by Goethe:

In der Beschränkung zeigt sich erst der Meister
Und Das Gesetz nur kann uns Freiheit geben.

Most of what I know about the nature of poetry or, at least, about the kind of poetry I am interested in writing or reading, I learned long before the notion of writing poems ever occurred to me. Between the ages of six and twelve I spent a great many of my waking hours constructing a private sacred world, the principal elements of which were two: a limestone landscape based on the Pennine Moors in the North of England, and an industry, lead-mining. It was, unlike a poem, a pure private world of which I was the only human inhabitant: I had no wish to share it with others, nor could I have done so. However I needed the help of others in procuring me the raw materials for its construction. Others, principally my parents, had to provide me with maps, guide-books, text-books on geology and mining machinery, and when occasion offered, take me down real mines. Since it was a purely private world, theoretically, I suppose, I should have been free to imagine anything I liked, but in practice, I found it was not so. I felt instinctively, without knowing why, that I was bound to obey certain rules. I could choose, for example, between two kinds of winding-engines, but they had to be real ones I could find in my books; I was not free to invent one. I could choose whether a mine should be drained by a pump or an adit, but magical means were forbidden.

Then, one day, there came a crisis, I was planning my Platonic Idea of the Perfect Concentrating Mill, and I had to choose between two types of a machine for separating the slimes, called a buddle. One type I felt to be the more "beautiful" or "sacred", but the other one was, I knew from my reading, the more efficient. I suddenly and clearly felt that I was faced with what I can only call a moral choice: I knew it was my duty to resist my aesthetic preference and choose the more efficient.

What, then, did I learn from this somewhat odd activity? Firstly, that the construction of any secondary world is gratuitous, not a utile, act, something one does, not because one must, but because it is fun. One is free to write a poem or to refuse to write one. However, any secondary world we may imaginatively construct necessarily draws its raw materials from the Primary World in which we all live. One cannot, like God, create *ex nihilo.* How much and how many facts one takes can vary very greatly. There are some poems, the songs of Campion, for example, which take almost nothing but the English language, so that, if one tries to translate them into another language, nothing is left of value. There are others, poems, *The Divine Comedy*, for instance, which include a very great deal from the Primary World, its history, its landscape, its theology, its astronomy etc.

Any individual poet, however, is not completely free to choose what raw materials he will use, he can only use those which stir his imagination, those which he finds enchanting or numinous, and this is a matter outside his will to choose or change. A psychologist might, no doubt, be able to explain why, in my childhood, limestone and lead-mining so enchanted me; I only know that, in fact, they did.

Lastly, any secondary world is, like the Primary World, a world governed by laws. These may be very different from the laws of the Primary World, and may vary from one secondary world to another, but for each there are laws. Though a poet has a very wide range of choice in deciding what these laws shall be, his freedom is not unbounded, but must be suited to the contents, just as, while there are many kinds of rules for various card-games, all of them have to fit the fact of a pack of four suits of thirteen cards each ranging from the King to the Ace.

To return to my buddle problem. Though, at the time, I knew I must, against my inclinations, choose the more efficient, it was only later that I came to understand clearly why. Even in an imaginary world a machine cannot escape the law of machinery, namely, that efficiency of function takes precedence over beauty of appearance.

So, in the case of poetry, all poems must submit to the laws of the language in which they are written, which is not the poet's private property. A poet cannot invent his own words or attribute his private meaning to them; he has to use words, however rare, the meaning of which can be found in some lexicon or other. Again, though he may sometimes depart from normal syntax, he can only do this with great care, or what he writes will become unintelligible.

If I try to define in one sentence what a poet does when he writes a poem, I would say this: he attempts to transform a crowd of recollected occasions of experience into a community by incorporating it in a verbal society. I must, therefore, define what I mean by the terms crowd, society and community. A crowd is composed of $N>1$ members whose only relation is arithmetical: they can only be counted. A crowd loves neither itself nor anything other than itself; it exists neither by choice or necessity but by chance. Of a crowd it may be said, either that it is not real but only apparent, or that it should not be. A physicist, for example, assumes that disorderly occurrences in Nature are apparent, not real, and seeks to discover the laws behind the appearance. A poet, on the other hand, knows that he starts from a real crowd of experiences, which it is his duty to transform.

A society is comprised of a definite or an optimum number of members, united in a specific manner into a whole with a characteristic mode of behaviour which is different from the modes of behaviour of its component members in isolation. A society cannot come into being until its component members are present and properly related: add or subtract a member, change their relations, and the society either ceases to exist or is transformed into another society. A society is a system which loves itself, and to this self-love, the self-love of its members is totally subordinate. Of a society it may be said that it is more or less successful in maintaining its existence.

A community is composed of N members united, to use a definition of St Augustine's, by a common love of something other than themselves, God, music, stamp collecting, or what-have-you. Like a crowd and unlike a society, its character is not changed by the addition or subtraction of a member. In a community all members are free and equal. If, out of a group of ten persons, eight prefer beef to mutton and two prefer mutton to beef, there is not a single community with two dissident members, but two communities, a large one and a small one. To achieve actual existence, a community has to embody itself in a society or societies which can express the love which is its raison d'être. A community of music-lovers, for example, cannot just sit around loving music like anything, but must form itself into societies like choirs, orchestras, string quartets, etc. and make music. Of a community it may be said that its love is more or less good. In inorganic nature, communities do not exist, only societies which are submembers of the total system of nature, enjoying their self-occurrence. They can exist among men, and, I think, among some animals, but they do not necessarily exist there.

Poems are verbal societies, but it is important to remember that we use words for two quite different purposes, as a communication code between individuals to request and supply information necessary to our functioning and existence, and as Personal Speech. Many animals have communication codes, and in a social animal, like the bee, this code may be extremely complex, but so far as we know, no animal is capable of Speech proper. Our use of language as a communication code is best illustrated by those phrase-books for tourists visiting foreign countries. Such a phrase as: "Can you tell me the way to the railroad station?" When I address this question to a stranger in the street, I do so because it is information I must have if I am to catch my train. I have no personal interest in the one I ask, nor he, when he answers, any personal interest in me. We might as well be other people.

But we are also capable of Speech. In speech, one unique person addresses one or more other unique persons voluntarily: he could remain silent if he chose. We speak as persons because we desire to disclose ourselves to each other and to share our experiences, not because we need to share them, but because we enjoy sharing them. To understand the nature of speech, we must begin, not with statements in the third person, like *the cat is on the mat,* but with Proper Names, the first and second personal pronouns, words of summons and command, response and obedience. Poetry is personal speech in its purest form. The subject matter of poetry is, as I said earlier, a crowd of recollected occasions of personal feelings and ideas. The nature of the final order of a poem is the outcome of a dialectical struggle between these occasions and the particular verbal society or system into which the poet is attempting to embody them. As a society, the verbal system is actively coercive upon the occasions it is attempting to embody; what it cannot embody truthfully it excludes. As a potential community the occasions are passively resistant to all claims of the system to embody them which they do not recognize as just; they decline all unjust persuasions. A successful poem is, as the psalmist says: "A city that is at unity with itself". In my own case, and I suspect that this is the case with most poets, at any given time, I have two concerns on my mind. On the one hand, certain experiences which seem to me of value; on the other certain problems of language and reflection, style, diction, metre, etc. which interest me. Consequently, I am engaged on a double search: the experiences are looking for their needed form, and the form is looking for the suitable experiences. It is only when these find each other, that I am able to begin writing a poem. The form cannot be selected arbitrarily nor can one say that any given form is absolutely necessary. The nature of any given language limits choice. For instance, in Greek, hexameters and pentameters are a "normal" metre; in English, though they can be written, they sound eccentric. Similarly, though alexandrines and decasyllabics can be written both in French and English, it is not a pure matter of chance, that alexandrines are the staple metre of French verse, and decasyllabics of English.

Poetry is concerned with human beings as unique persons. What men do from necessity or by second nature cannot be the subject of poetry, for poetry is gratuitous utterance. As Paul Valéry said: "In poetry everything that must be said cannot be said well." It is essentially a spoken, not a written word. One can never grasp a poem one is reading unless one hears the actual sound of the words. In so far as one can speak of poetry as conveying knowledge, it is the kind of knowledge implied by the Biblical phrase: "Then Adam knew Eve his wife"; knowing is inseparable from being known. To say that poetry is ultimately concerned with only human persons does not, of course, mean that it is always overtly about them. We are always intimately related to non-human natures and, unless we try to understand and relate to what we are not, we shall never understand what we are. As Emerson wrote:

> Man is an analogist and studies relations in all objects. He is placed in the centre of beings and a ray of relation passes from every being to him. And neither can man be understood without these objects, nor these objects without man. . . . Because of this radical correspondence between visible things and human thoughts, in poetry all spiritual facts are represented by natural symbols.

Again, to say that a poem is a personal utterance does not mean that it is an act of self-expression. The experiences a poet endeavours to embody in a poem are experiences of a reality common to all men: they are only his in that this reality is perceived from a perspective which nobody but he can occupy. What by providence he has been the first to perceive, it is his duty to share with others.

The job of poetry, of all the arts, then, is to manifest the personal and the chosen: the manifestation of the impersonal and the necessity is the job of the sciences. Even there, the word necessity is ambiguous: it might be better to say the unchanging or unhistorical which changes according to unchanging laws. Physics, for example, has discovered the velocity of light, but no physicist can say that the velocity of light must be what in fact it is, that it could not have been different. Like art, pure science is a gratuitous and personal activity, and I am convinced that the stimulus to scientific enquiry is the same as that of artistic fabrication, namely a sense of wonder. As Nietzsche said:

> Art says: "Life is worth living": Science says: "Life is worth knowing".

Scientific knowledge, however, is not reciprocal like artistic knowledge: what the scientist knows cannot know him. Hence the language of science and the language of poetry are at opposite poles. As Wittgenstein has said:

> "It" is not the name of a person, nor "here" of a place, and "this" is not a name. But they are connected with names. Names are explained by means of them. It is characteristic of physics not to use these words.

In fact the natural sciences could not realize their true nature until an impersonal universal language had been invented, from which every vestige of poetry has been eliminated, namely Algebra, of which Whitehead wrote:

> Algebra reverses the relative importance of the factors in ordinary language. It is essentially a written language, and it endeavours to exemplify in its written structure the patterns which it is its purpose to convey. The pattern of the marks on paper is a particular instance of the pattern to be conveyed to thought. The algebraic method is the best approach to the expression of necessity by reason of its reduction of accident to the ghost-like character of the real variable.

One rather curious link between the Arts and the Sciences is the fact that political theories, based like Plato's on analogies to artistic fabrication, or based like those of Leontiev, the Marxist, on analogies to science, both inevitably produce in practice political tyranny.

A poem, or any work of art, is but one secondary world out of an infinite number of possible secondary worlds. Therefore, the poet is free to choose whatever thoughts and words suit this particular poem, and to treat all that don't suit it as if they did not exist. Secondly he aims at producing a verbal object which is complete in itself and will endure without change.

A political state that was really like a good poem would be a nightmare of horror. The population would be fixed by law at a figure: any superfluous or recalcitrant persons would have to be exterminated, and those permitted to exist would be forbidden ever to change their job.

Political analogies from science overlook the fact that science is based on experiment. The scientist forms a hypothesis and then tests it by an experiment, the objects of which are assumed to have no will of their own, or, at least to be incapable of changing their minds. If the experiment falls to confirm his hypothesis, then he must abandon it.

I think Rosenstock-Huessy is substantially right when he says:

> The scientific method cannot lead mankind because it is based on experiment, and every experiment postpones the present moment until one knows the result. We always come to each other and even to ourselves too late so soon as we wish to know in advance what to do.

Needless to say, I do not believe that the Arts can lead mankind, either.

But politics has to do with history-conscious persons who have wills of their own and opinions which they can change. Suppose that as a politician I make the hypothesis that a rational or "scientific" agriculture would be a collectivised agriculture. I collectivise it: the peasants are rebellious and food production drops. Does this disprove my hypothesis? Not necessarily. I can always argue that the apparent failure of my experiment is due to the malice or stupidity of the peasants, and that, if I continue with it long enough, they will change their minds and come to realize that I am right. This means tyranny because in politics there is always a distinction, unknown to science, between truth and justice.

The existence of human beings is dual: as biological organisms made of matter, we are subject to the laws of physics and biology: as conscious persons who create our own history, we are free to decide what that history shall be. A true notion of what is just can only be arrived at by a collaboration between science and art. Without science, we could have no notion of equality: without art no notion of liberty. Justice means recognizing that two apparently contradictory statements are both true, namely, *Hard Cases make bad Law*, and *One law for the ox and the ass is oppression.*

Let me conclude these remarks with a poem which is concerned with both Art and Science, an *Ode to Terminus*, the Roman God of boundaries.

ODE TO TERMINUS

The High Priests of telescopes and cyclotrons
keep making pronouncements about happenings
  on scales too gigantic or dwarfish
  to be noted by our native senses,

discoveries which, couched in the elegant
euphemisms of algebra, look innocent,
  harmless enough but, when translated
  into the vulgar anthropomorphic

tongue, will give no cause for hilarity
to gardeners or house-wives: if galaxies
  bolt like panicking mobs, if mesons
  riot like fish in a feeding-frenzy,

it sounds too like Political History
to boost civil morale, too symbolic of
the crimes and strikes and demonstrations
we are supposed to gloat on at breakfast.

How trite, though, our fears beside the miracle
that we're here to shiver, that a Thingummy
so addicted to lethal violence
should have somehow secreted a placid

tump with exactly the right ingredients
to start and to cocker Life, that heavenly
freak for whose manage we shall have to
give account at the Judgement, our Middle-

Earth, where Sun-Father to all appearances
moves by day from orient to occident,
and his light is felt as a friendly
presence, not a photonic bombardment,

where all visibles do have a definite
outline they stick to, and are undoubtedly
at rest or in motion, where lovers
recognize each other by their surface,

where to all species except the talkative
have been allotted the niche and diet that
become them. This, whatever micro-
biology may think, is the world we

really live in and that saves our sanity,
who know all too well how the most erudite
mind behaves in the dark without a
surround it is called on to interpret,

how, discarding rhythm, punctuation, metaphor,
it sinks into a drivelling monologue,
too literal to see joke or
distinguish a penis from a pencil.

Venus and Mars are powers too natural
to temper our outlandish extravagance:
You alone, Terminus, the Mentor,
can teach us how to alter our gestures.

God of walls, doors and reticence, nemesis
overtakes the sacrilegious technocrat,

but blessed is the City that thanks you
for giving us games and grammar and metres.

By whose grace, also, every gathering
of two or three in confident amity
repeats the pentecostal marvel,
as each in each finds his right translator.

In this world our colossal immodesty
has plundered and poisoned, it is possible
You still might save us, who by now have
learned this: that scientists, to be truthful,

must remind us to take all they say as a
tall story, that abhorred in the Heav'ns are all
self-proclaimed poets who, to wow an
audience, utter some resonant lie.

The Place of Value in a World of Facts: Proceedings of the Fourteenth Nobel Symposium, Stockholm, September 15–20, 1969, edited by Arne Tiselius and Sam Nilsson (1970)

In Defense of the Tall Story

The Artist as Critic: Critical Writings of Oscar Wilde. Edited by Richard Ellmann. Random House. $10.

To my pleasant surprise, *The Artist as Critic,* a collection of Wilde's critical writings selected and introduced by Richard Ellmann, is very much better reading than I had expected. I had never read any of them before, and preconceptions and hearsay can be most misleading. (Two trivial queries: Why include three articles about America which have nothing to do with the arts? And, for Wilde's sake, why open with "The Tomb of Keats," a piece which says nothing new and ends with a poem, an art form for which Wilde, poor man, had no talent whatever?)

"The Portrait of Mr W. H.," for example, turns out to be a very different piece from what I had imagined. No reader of Shakespeare's sonnets can help wondering as to the identity of the young man and the dark lady, but every sane reader realizes that the few certain facts we know provide no answer. Those, some of them great scholars, who claim to have solved the mystery have only exposed their own biases, social and sexual. "The Portrait of Mr W. H.," which is fictional in form, does, to be sure, record a theory—namely, that the young man was a boy actor in Shakespeare's troupe named

Willie Hughes—but this theory is put forward not by the narrator (Wilde?) but by a young queen, Cyril Graham. The narrator would like to believe it, but he sees at once that if the theory is true, then the opening series of sonnets, in which Shakespeare apparently urges his friend to marry, cannot mean what they seem to mean. He examines them in minute detail, and argues with great ingenuity that "marriage" means marriage to Shakespeare's Muse. Needless to say, the argument is unconvincing, and is, I am sure, intended to be so. What Wilde has done is to give us an amusing parody of the way in which such theorists think, and of the extremes to which they are prepared to go to prove their point. Cyril Graham forges a portrait; another character, Erskine, writes the narrator a letter in which he says that for the sake of the theory he is going to commit suicide when, in fact, he is dying of consumption. The narrator himself concludes:

> I have been dreaming, and all my life for these two months has been unreal. There was no such person as Willie Hughes.

The longest essay in this collection, "Intentions," is not, strictly speaking, literary criticism but a highly polemical theory of aesthetics. Every polemical writer has an audience problem. Those whose position he is attacking and wishes to correct seldom read him; those who do are apt to misunderstand him because they take his arguments, his terminology, too literally and fail to realize that the former are deliberately exaggerated and the latter given a special, provocative meaning. The first dialogue in "Intentions," for instance, is entitled "The Decay of Lying," but this is really a polemical way of saying "The Decay of the Tall Story." A lie can be told only in the primary world, where we all live. It is told deliberately, with the intention of deceiving, because the liar hopes to gain some personal advantage by deceiving his listeners. He, on the other hand, who tells a Tall Story has no intention of deceiving—he assumes that his audience will recognize it as a story about an imaginary world—and his motive in telling it is to give pleasure to others. No reader of a folk tale in which animals speak has ever believed that this was a naturalist's description of actual animal behavior, and the whole fun would be lost if he did. What Wilde is attacking is the "naturalistic" theory of art—novelists like Zola and Royal Academy painters who identify "truth" in art with a photographic record of the primary world. The error of naturalism lies in thinking that there is such a creature as a "natural" man. What it calls "human nature" is our "second nature," a highly artificial product of education and environment. Necessity is interesting, so the behavior of animals and plants is interesting as a manifestation of biological laws. Freedom is interesting, so the chosen deeds of human beings when they act as unique persons are interesting. But men's habits, their conditioned social behavior, are the least interesting things about them because they are accidental, and the accidental is never interesting. Only bores study sociology.

I am sure that Wilde would agree with me that there are occasions on which one can say that a work of art is "false." A writer may, out of ignorance, make a statement about the primary world which is false, as when Tennyson, in "Locksley Hall," seems to assert that railroad trains run in grooves. In another way, Yeats' line "I have been changed to a hound with one red ear" seems to me artistically false, not because I know he never dreamed such a thing but because as a Tall Story it is pointless.

Then, when Wilde says that all art is immoral he certainly does not mean that no moral judgments can or should be passed on the characters in a play or a novel. He is asserting, firstly, that the aesthetic interest of a character and his morals are not the same thing. Iago is aesthetically interesting, but no playgoer will think that in consequence he is a good man. In *King Lear*, Edmund is a much more interesting character than Cordelia, but every one knows it is better to be good like her than evil like him. Secondly, Wilde is attacking the kind of reader who thinks a work is immoral if it allows a bad character any success in this world: in order to be moral, it must show that goodness pays and badness does not pay. The good must be rewarded for their efforts by riches and a happy marriage, the bad by prison, infamy, penury, death. Literary works do exist—those of de Sade and Genet and several of D. H. Lawrence's novels, for instance—which I would call immoral. Such works are always perverse sermons: they try to persuade the reader that certain characters and modes of conduct are moral and to be imitated when common sense knows that they are neither. Preaching, however, is a tricky business, and the "heroes" of such authors are always aesthetically boring.

Again, when Wilde urges the importance of doing nothing, this, if taken literally, could only mean that it is better to be dead than alive, for living is action. A man contemplating is doing something, a man talking at considerable length about the importance of doing nothing is doing something. Wilde's opponent is, of course, the Philistine to whom only necessary or useful actions have any value and who dismisses all gratuitous actions, like working at pure mathematics or making works of art, as a waste of time.

Lastly, when Wilde distinguishes between the critic and the creator and stresses the importance of the former, he does not foresee the day when criticism will become a heavy industry, or the appearance of the kind of critic who imagines that works of literature are full of cryptic symbols and meanings which the ordinary reader will never "get" unless he, the critic, deciphers them for him. From his own critical practice, it is clear that Wilde would have disapproved. He is, however, perfectly right when he says that without the critical spirit there can be no art:

> Every century that produces poetry is, so far, an artificial century, and the work that seems to us to be the most natural and simple product of its time is always the result of the most self-conscious effort.

When he says

> So far from its being true that the artist is the best judge of art, a really great artist can never judge of other people's work at all, and can hardly, in fact, judge of his own. That very concentration of vision that makes a man an artist, limits by its sheer intensity his faculty of fine appreciation. . . . A truly great artist cannot conceive of life being shown, or beauty fashioned, under any conditions other than those that he has selected. Creation employs all its critical faculty within its own sphere. It may not use it in the sphere that belongs to others. It is exactly because a man cannot do a thing that he is the proper judge of it

he is exaggerating, probably consciously, but there is a truth in what he says. Many poets and painters have said important and interesting things about their predecessors; very few are to be trusted in their judgments about their contemporaries, and if they are wise they will keep their mouths shut.

I am surprised that our radical student left has not discovered "The Soul of Man Under Socialism." Why wrestle with Marcuse's impenetrable prose when they could find much the same thing said lucidly and elegantly by Wilde?

> If the Socialism is Authoritarian; if there are Governments armed with economic power as they are now with political power: if, in a word, we are to have Industrial Tyrannies, then the last state of man will be worse than the first.

> Disobedience, in the eyes of anyone who has read history, is man's original virtue. It is through disobedience that progress has been made, through disobedience and through rebellion.

> It is only in voluntary associations that man is fine.

Wilde's own literary criticism was limited to short reviews, many of them unsigned. Like anyone else who has had a classical education (one should never forget that Wilde got a First in Mods and a First in Greats), as a critic he is primarily concerned with artistic form and mastery of language. His prose may sometimes be too lush—"Let me play you some mad scarlet thing by Dvořák"—and he sometimes makes statements which are meant to be provocative epigrams but, in fact, are sheer nonsense—"Nothing that actually occurs is of the smallest importance"—but his language is never ungrammatical nor his use of words sloppy. He knew Latin and Greek and French very well. When, as a reviewer, he is savage, which is not often, it is always over some misuse of words or some mistranslation. Though he never claimed to be a scholar, he was remarkably well-read. It is obvious from his review of two books on Sir Philip Sidney—one by J. A. Symonds, the other by Edmund Gosse—that he knew more about the literature of the period than either of them. To come to his reviews after reading "Intentions" is to be in for a surprise. Thus the defender of lying and artificiality writes:

> The arts are made for life, and not life for the arts.

Of Balzac, whom he admires enormously, he says:

> Observation gave him the facts of life, but his genius converted facts into truths, and truths into truth.

And of Morris's translation of *The Odyssey*:

> One merit at any rate Mr Morris's version entirely and absolutely possesses. It is, in no sense of the word, literary; it seems to deal immediately with life itself, and to take from the reality of things its own form and colour.

Then there is an amazing review of Browning, which, with a few alterations in vocabulary, might come out of *Pravda.* Who would ever guess that the following passage was written by the author of *The Importance of Being Earnest*:

> Let any sensible man outside the Browning Society dip into the mysterious volume of literary hocus-pocus that has recently been so solemnly reviewed, and see whether he can find a single passage likely to stir the pulses of any man or woman, create a desire to lead a higher, a holier, and a more useful life in the breast of the indifferent average citizen. . . . Is it possible that Mr Browning can see nothing in the world around him to induce him to make an earnest endeavour to help the people out of their difficulties and to make their duty plain? . . . The people are suffering, and are likely to suffer more; where is the poet who is the one man needful to rouse the nation to a sense of duty and inspire the people with hope?

Poets like Henley and Whitman, who wrote free verse, are obviously not his cup of tea, but he always looks for and acknowledges their virtues. One would have expected him to overvalue small, intricate verse forms; in fact, he is extremely sensible about them:

> I cannot imagine any one with the smallest pretensions to culture preferring a dextrously turned triolet to a fine imaginative ballad. . . . The triolets, and the rondels, and the careful study of metrical subtleties, these things are merely the signs of a desire for perfection in small things, and the recognition of poetry as an art. They have had certainly one good result—they have made our minor poets readable, and have not left us entirely at the mercy of geniuses.

In short book reviews, probably written in a hurry, one does not look for great depth of critical insight, but Wilde's verdict on Ben Jonson seems to me penetrating:

> Pelion more than Parnassus was Jonson's home. His art has too much effort about it, too much definite intention. His style lacks the charm of chance. . . . Literature was as living a thing to him as life itself. He used his classical lore not merely to give form to his verse but to give flesh and blood to the persons of his plays. He could build up a breathing creature out of quotations.

Then, in his review of Swinburne's latest volume, especially when one remembers that at the time Swinburne was the God of the young, it is impressive to find that what Eliot was to say years later in *The Sacred Wood* had already been anticipated by Wilde:

> His song is nearly always too loud for his subject. . . . It has been said of him, and with truth, that he is a master of language, but with still greater truth it may be said that Language is his master. Words seem to dominate him. Alliteration tyrannizes over him. Mere sound becomes his lord. He is so eloquent that whatever he touches becomes unreal.

It is also delightful though—given Wilde's talents—not surprising to come across passages which make one roar with laughter:

> The last President [of the Royal Society of British Artists] never said much that was true, but the present President never says anything that is new, and if art be a fairy-haunted wood or an enchanted island, we must say that we prefer the old Puck to the fresh Prospero. Water is an admirable thing—at least, the Greeks said it was—and Mr Ruskin is an admirable writer; but a combination of both is a little depressing.
>
> Still, it is only right to add that Mr Wyke Bayliss, at his best, writes very good English. Mr Whistler, for some reason or other, always adopted the phraseology of the minor prophets. Possibly it was in order to emphasize his well-known claims to verbal inspiration, or perhaps he thought with Voltaire that "*Habakkuk est capable de tout,*" and wished to shelter himself under the shield of a definitely irresponsible writer none of whose prophecies, according to the French philosopher, have ever been fulfilled.

The Artist as Critic is a volume it is very nice to possess.

The New Yorker, 29 November 1969

Foreword to *G. K. Chesterton: A Selection from His Non-Fictional Prose*

I have always enjoyed Chesterton's poetry and fiction, but I must admit that, until I started work on this selection, it was many years since I had read any of his non-fictional prose.

The reasons for my neglect were, I think, two. Firstly, his reputation as an anti-Semite. Though he denied the charge and did, certainly, denounce Hitler's persecution, he cannot, I fear, be completely exonerated.

> I said that a particular kind of Jew tended to be a tyrant and another particular kind of Jew tended to be a traitor. I say it again. Patent facts of this kind are permitted in the criticism of any other nation on the planet: it is not counted illiberal to say that a certain kind of Frenchman tends to be sensual. . . . I cannot see why the tyrants should not be called tyrants and the traitors traitors merely because they happen to be members of a race persecuted for other reasons and on other occasions.

The disingenuousness of this argument is revealed by the quiet shift from the term *nation* to the term *race*. It is always permissible to criticize a nation (including Israel), a religion (including Orthodox Judaism), or a culture, because these are the creations of human thought and will: a nation, a religion, a culture can always reform themselves, if they so choose. A man's ethnic heritage, on the other hand, is not in his power to alter. If it were true, and there is no evidence whatsoever to suppose that it is, that certain moral defects or virtues are racially inherited, they could not become the subject for moral judgment by others. That Chesterton should have spoken of the Jews as a race is particularly odd, since few writers of his generation denounced with greater contempt racial theories about Nordics, Anglo-Saxons, Celts, etc. I myself am inclined to put most of the blame on the influence of his brother and of Hilaire Belloc, and on the pernicious influence, both upon their generation and upon the succeeding generation of Eliot and Pound, exerted by the *Action Française* Movement. Be that as it may, it remains a regrettable blemish upon the writings of a man who was, according to the universal testimony of all who met him, an extraordinarily "decent" human being, astonishingly generous of mind and warm of heart.

My second reason for neglecting Chesterton was that I imagined him to be what he himself claimed, just a "Jolly Journalist", a writer of weekly essays on "amusing" themes, such as *What I found in my Pockets, On Lying in Bed, The Advantage of having one Leg, A Piece of Chalk, The Glory of Grey, Cheese* and so forth.

In his generation, the Essay as a form of *belles-lettres* was still popular: in addition to Chesterton himself, there were a number of writers, Max Beerbohm, E. V. Lucas, Robert Lynd, for example, whose literary reputations rested largely upon their achievements in this genre. Today tastes have changed. We can appreciate a review or a critical essay devoted to a particular book or author, we can enjoy a discussion of a specific philosophical problem or political event, but we can no longer derive any pleasure from the kind of essay which is a fantasia upon whatever chance thoughts may come into the essayist's head.

My objection to the prose fantasia is the same as my objection to "free" verse (to which Chesterton also objected), namely, that, while excellent examples of both exist, they are the exception not the rule. All too often the result of the absence of any rules and restrictions, of a metre to which the poet must conform, of a definite subject to which the essayist must stick, is a repetitious and self-indulgent "show-off" of the writer's personality and stylistic mannerisms.

Chesterton's insistence upon the treadmill of weekly journalism after it ceased to be financially necessary seems to have puzzled his friends as much as it puzzles me. Thus E. C. Bentley writes:

> To live in this way was his deliberate choice. There can be no doubt of that, for it was a hard life, and a much easier one lay nearby to his hand. As a writer of books, as a poet, he had an assured position, and an inexhaustible fund of ideas: the friends who desired him to make the most of his position were many. But G. K. Chesterton preferred the existence of a regular contributor to the Press, bound by iron rules as to space and time. Getting his copy to the office before it was too late was often a struggle. Having to think of a dead-line at all was always an inconvenience.

Whatever Chesterton's reasons and motives for his choice, I am quite certain it was a mistake. "A journalist", said Karl Kraus, "is stimulated by a dead-line: he writes worse if he has time." If this is correct, then Chesterton was not, by nature, a journalist. His best thinking and best writing are to be found, not in his short weekly essays, but in his full-length books where he could take as much time and space as he pleased. (In fact, in this selection, I have taken very little from his volumes of collected essays.) Oddly enough, since he so detested them, Chesterton inherited from the aesthetes of the eighties and nineties the conviction that a writer should be continuously "bright" and epigrammatic. When he is really enthralled by a subject he is brilliant, without any doubt one of the finest aphorists in English literature, but, when his imagination is not fully held he can write an exasperating parody of himself, and this is most likely to happen when he has a dead-line to meet.

It is always difficult for a man as he grows older to "keep up" with the times, to understand what the younger generation is thinking and writing well enough to criticize it intelligently; for an over-worked journalist like

Chesterton it is quite impossible, since he simply does not have the time to read any new book carefully enough.

He was, for example, certainly intelligent enough and, judging by his criticisms of contemporary anthropology, equipped enough, to have written a serious critical study of Freud, had he taken the time and trouble to read him properly: his few flip remarks about dreams and psycho-analysis are proof that he did not.

Chesterton's non-fictional prose has three concerns, literature, politics and religion.

Our day has seen the emergence of two kinds of literary critic, the documentor and the cryptologist. The former with meticulous accuracy collects and publishes every unearthable fact about an author's life, from his love-letters to his dinner invitations and laundry bills, on the assumption that any fact, however trivial, about the man may throw light upon his writings. The latter approaches his work as if it were an anonymous and immensely difficult text, written in a private language which the ordinary reader cannot hope to understand until it is deciphered for him by experts. Both such critics will no doubt dismiss Chesterton's literary criticism as out-of-date, inaccurate and superficial, but if one were to ask any living novelist or poet which kind of critic he would personally prefer to write about his work, I have no doubt as to the answer. Every writer knows that certain events in his life, most of them in childhood, have been of decisive importance in forming his personal imaginative world, the kinds of things he likes to think about, the qualities in human beings he particularly admires or detests. He also knows that many things which are of great importance to him as a man, are irrelevant to his imagination. In the case of a love-poem, for example, no light is thrown upon either its content or its style by discovering the identity of the poet's beloved.

This Chesterton understands. He thought, for example, that certain aspects of Dickens's novels are better understood if we remember that, as a child, Dickens was expected to put on public performances to amuse his father, so he informs us of this fact. On the other hand, he thought that we shall not understand the novels any better if we learn all the details about the failure of Dickens's marriage, so he omits them. In both cases, surely, he is right.

Again, while some writers are more "difficult" than others and cannot therefore hope to reach a very wide audience, no writer thinks he needs decoding in order to be understood. On the other hand, nearly every writer who has achieved some reputation complains of being misunderstood both by the critics and the public, because they come to his work with preconceived notions of what they are going to find in it. His admirers praise him and his detractors blame him for what, to him, seem imaginary reasons. The kind of critic an author hopes for is someone who will dispel these preconceived notions so that his readers may come to his writings with fresh eyes.

At this task of clearing the air, Chesterton was unusually efficient. It is popularly believed that a man who is in earnest about something speaks earnestly and that a man who keeps making jokes is not in earnest. The belief is not ill-founded since, more often than not, this is true. But there are exceptions and, as Chesterton pointed out, Bernard Shaw was one. The public misunderstood Shaw and thought him just a clown when, in fact, he was above all things a deadly serious preacher. In the case of Browning, Chesterton shows that many of his admirers had misunderstood him by reading into his obscurer passages intellectual profundities when in fact the poet was simply indulging his love of the grotesque. Again, he shows us that Stevenson's defect as a narrator was not, as it had become conventional to say, an over-ornate style but an over-ascetic one, a refusal to tell the reader anything about a character that was not absolutely essential. As a rule, it is journalism and literary gossip that is responsible for such misunderstandings; occasionally, though, it can be the author himself. Kipling would certainly have described himself as a patriotic Englishman who admired above all else the military virtues. In an extremely funny essay, Chesterton convincingly demonstrates that Kipling was really a cosmopolitan with no local roots, and he quotes in proof Kipling's own words.

> If England were what England seems,
> How soon we'd chuck her, but She ain't.

A patriot loves a country because, for better or worse, it is his. Kipling is only prepared to love England so long as England is a Great Power. As for Kipling's militarism, Chesterton says:

> Kipling's subject is not that valour which properly belongs to war, but that interdependence and efficiency which belongs quite as much to engineers, or sailors, or mules, or railway engines. . . . The real poetry, the "true romance" which Mr Kipling has taught is the romance of the division of labour and the discipline of all the trades. He sings the arts of peace much more accurately than the arts of war.

Chesterton's literary criticism abounds in such observations which, once they have been made, seem so obviously true that one cannot understand why one had not seen them for oneself. It now seems obvious to us all that Shaw, the socialist, was in no sense a democrat but was a great republican; that there are two kinds of democrat, the man who, like Scott, sees the dignity of all men, and the man who, like Dickens, sees that all men are equally interesting and varied; that Milton was really an aesthete whose greatness "does not depend upon moral earnestness or upon anything connected with morality, but upon style alone, a style rather unusually separated from its substance"; that the Elizabethan Age, however brilliant, was not "spacious", but in literature an age of conceits, in politics an age of conspiracies. But Chesterton was the first critic to see these things. As a literary critic, therefore, I rank him very high.

For various reasons I have selected very little from his writings on historical and political subjects. Chesterton was not himself an historian, but he had both the gift and the position to make known to the general public the views of historians, like Belloc, who were challenging the Whig version of English History and the humanists' version of cultural history. It must be difficult for anyone under forty to realize how taken for granted both of these were, even when I was a boy. Our school textbooks taught us that, once the papist-inclined and would-be tyrants, the Stuarts, had been got rid of, and the Protestant Succession assured, the road to Freedom, Democracy and Progress lay wide open; they also taught us that the civilization which had ended with the fall of the Roman Empire was re-born in the sixteenth century, between which dates lay twelve centuries of barbarism, superstition and fanaticism. If today every informed person knows both accounts to be untrue, that the political result of the Glorious Revolution of 1688 was to hand over the government of the country to a small group of plutocrats, a state of affairs which certainly persisted until 1914, perhaps even until 1939, and that, whatever the Renaissance and the Reformation might signify, it was not a revolt of reason against fanaticism—on the contrary, it might be more fairly described as a revolt against the over-cultivation of logic by the late Middle Ages—Chesterton is not the least among those persons who are responsible for this change of view. The literary problem about any controversial writing is that, once it has won its battle, its interest to the average reader is apt to decline. Controversy always involves polemical exaggeration and it is this of which, once we have forgotten the exaggerations of the other side, we shall be most aware and critical. Thus, Chesterton's insistence, necessary at the time, upon all that was good in the twelfth century, his glossing over of all that was bad, seems today a romantic day-dream. Similarly, one is unconvinced by Belloc's thesis in *The Servile State,* that if, when the monasteries were dissolved, the Crown had taken their revenues instead of allowing them to fall into the hands of a few of its subjects, the Crown would have used its power, not only to keep these few in order, but also for the benefit of the common people. The history of countries like France where the Crown remained stronger than the nobility gives no warrant for such optimism. Absolute monarchs who are anxious to win glory are much more likely to waste the substance of their country in wars of conquest than plutocrats who are only interested in making money.

Chesterton's negative criticisms of modern society, his distrust of bigness, big business, big shops, his alarm at the consequences of undirected and uncontrolled technological development, are even more valid today than in his own. His positive political beliefs, that a good society would be a society of small property-owners, most of them living on the land, attractive as they sound, seem to me open to the same objection that he brings against the political ideas of the Americans and the French in the eighteenth century: "Theirs was a great ideal; but no modern state is small enough to achieve anything so great." In the twentieth century, the England he wanted would pre-suppose the strictest control of the birth-rate, a policy which both his temperament and his religion forbade him to recommend.

On the subject of international politics, Chesterton was, to put it mildly, unreliable. He seems to have believed that, in political life, there is a direct relation between Faith and Morals: a Catholic State, holding the true faith, will behave better politically than a Protestant State. France, Austria, Poland were to be trusted: Prussia was not. It so happened that, in his early manhood, the greatest threat to world peace lay, as he believed, in Prussian militarism. After its defeat in 1918, he continued to cling to his old belief so that, when Hitler came to power in 1933, he misread this as a Prussian phenomenon. In fact, aside from the economic conditions which enabled it to succeed, the National Socialist Movement was essentially the revenge of Catholic Bavaria and Austria for their previous subordination to Protestant Bismarckian Prussia. It was not an accident that Hitler was a lapsed Catholic. The nationalism of the German-speaking minority in the Hapsburg Empire had always been racist, and the hot-bed of anti-Semitism was Vienna not Berlin. Hitler himself hated the Prussian Junkers and was planning, if he won the war, to liquidate them all.

Chesterton was brought up a Unitarian, became an Anglican and finally, in 1922, was converted to Roman Catholicism. Today, reading such a book as *Heretics*, published in 1905, one is surprised that he was not converted earlier.

If his criticisms of Protestantism are not very interesting, this is not his fault. It was a period when Protestant theology (and, perhaps, Catholic too) was at a low ebb, Kierkegaard had not been re-discovered and Karl Barth had not yet been translated. Small fry like Dean Inge and the ineffable Bishop Barnes were too easy game for a mind of his calibre. Where he is at his best is in exposing the hidden dogmas of anthropologists, psychologists and their ilk who claim to be purely objective and "scientific". Nobody has written more intelligently and sympathetically about mythology or polytheism.

Critical Judgment and Personal Taste are different kinds of evaluation which always overlap but seldom coincide exactly. On the whole and in the long run, Critical Judgment is a public matter; we agree as to what we consider artistic virtues and artistic defects. Our personal tastes, however, differ. For each of us, there are writers whom we enjoy reading, despite their defects, and others who, for all their virtues, give us little pleasure. In order for us to find a writer "sympathetic", there must be some kinship between his imaginative preferences and our own. As Chesterton wrote:

> There is at the back of every artist's mind something like a pattern or a type of architecture. The original quality in any man of imagination is imagery. It is a thing like the landscape of his dreams; the sort of world he would wish to make or in which he would wish to wander; the strange flora and fauna of his own secret planet; the sort of thing he likes to think about.

This is equally true of every reader's mind. Our personal patterns, too, unlike our scale of critical values, which we need much time and experience to arrive at, are formed quite early in life, probably before the age of ten. In "The Ethics of Elfland" Chesterton tells us how his own pattern was derived from fairy-stories. If I can always enjoy reading him, even at his silliest, I am sure the reason is that many elements in my own pattern are derived from the same source. (There is one gulf between us: Chesterton had no feeling for or understanding of music.) There are, I know, because I have met them, persons to whom Grimm and Andersen mean little or nothing: Chesterton will not be for them.

G. K. Chesterton: A Selection from His Non-Fictional Prose,
selected by W. H. Auden (1970); *Prose,* [Autumn 1970]

Translation

> To translate means to serve two masters—something nobody can do. Hence, as is true of all things that in theory no one can do—it becomes in practice everybody's job. Everyone must translate and everyone does translate.—Franz Rosenzweig

> I remember saying to Anatole France that translation was an impossible thing. He replied: "Precisely, my friend; the recognition of that truth is a necessary preliminary to success in the art."—J. Lewis May

Communication Codes and Personal Speech

Each of us is at one and the same time both an individual, a member of the human race and of a certain society, and also a unique person. The term individual is both a biological description—*a* man, *a* woman, *a* child—and a social-cultural one—*an* American, *an* Englishman, *a* lawyer, *a* doctor. As individuals we are the result of natural selection, sexual reproduction and social conditioning. The society or societies to which we belong, however, must be called corporate persons. On the other hand no two individuals are identical. Each of us is also a unique person who can say "I," choose to do this rather than that, and accept the responsibility for the consequences, whatever they may turn out to be. As persons we are called into being, not by any biological process, but by other persons—our parents, our siblings, our friends, our enemies.

Human beings, therefore, use words for two purposes which, though they often overlap, are quite different. As individuals we use words to request and supply information which it is essential for us to know if we are to survive and function properly. Many, perhaps most, animals have such a code—auditory or visual or olfactory signals by which they communicate vital information about food, sex, territory, the presence of enemies. Our use of words as a code is best illustrated by phrase books for tourists abroad, giving the equivalents in other languages for such remarks as:

Where is the railroad station?
What time is it?
I want a double-room with bath.
How much is that?

Provided that the way of living and the social needs of two linguistic groups are more or less the same, exact translation from one language into another is possible. Provided a culture is technologically advanced enough to have a railroad, it will have a word meaning *station*; provided it has a money economy, it will be possible to translate the value of one currency into the other.

But, as we have seen, every society is a corporate person; that is to say every society holds certain general ideas about the nature of man, the world, good and evil, which its individual members take for granted, but which may and, to some degree, always do differ from those of other societies. Here problems of translation begin to arise.

During World War II Roosevelt and Churchill announced as their peace aims the Four Freedoms—Freedom of Speech, Freedom from Fear, etc.—but in scarcely any other language except English can the concept of freedom *from* be exactly translated. Then, anyone whose mother tongue is English and who starts to learn another language very soon discovers words for which we have no exact equivalent so that, when we attempt to translate them, we must either use different English words according to the context, or, in despair, use the foreign word. How, for example, is one to translate the Greek word *polis* or the French word *esprit* or the German word *Schadenfreude*?

As persons we are capable, as the other animals are not, of personal speech. In speech one unique person addresses another unique person by choice—he could have remained silent. We speak as persons because we desire to disclose ourselves to each other and to share our experiences, not because we must, but because we enjoy sharing them. When we genuinely speak, we do not have the words ready to do our bidding; we have to find them, we do not know exactly what we are going to say until we have said it, and we say something new that has never been said in exactly the same way before.

This means that, even if speaker and listener use the same language, they both have to translate, for no two persons speak their mother-tongue in exactly the same way. Suppose, for example, a friend tells me that he has fallen in love. In order to understand him, I have to ask myself two questions. Firstly: "Have I had an experience similar to the one he is describing?" Secondly: "If so, is it the experience I myself would describe as falling in love?" Furthermore, if I am fully to understand either his experience or my own, I must know something about the history of the concept of "falling in love" as it has developed in Western culture, and try to imagine what sense of our experiences people would make who belong to cultures where the concept is unknown.

Language and Time

The author of a literary work writes, consciously at any rate, for an audience who not only speak the same tongue but are also his contemporaries. His translator does the same, only now both the tongue and the times are different. How is the translator to find words in his own language which will convey to his contemporaries the same meaning and emotional overtones which the original had for the author's? Any answer will be guesswork.

Take, for example, the two biblical words *ecclesia* and *presbuteros*, usually translated as *church* and *priest*. In Tyndale's translation of the Bible they become *congregation* and *elder*. Tyndale felt that, in the sixteenth century, the conventional terms would be taken to mean what they meant to Roman Catholics. As a Protestant, he was convinced that the Roman Church had perverted the true Christian faith, that the Apostles and the Early Christians would have been horrified by what the Roman Church and its hierarchy had become. Others, not all of them Catholics, preferred the old terms. Who can say for certain which was right?

Again, take this phrase from Vergil: "Rosea cervice refulsit." Dryden translates it as:

> She turned and made appear
> Her neck refulgent.

Here I think one may say with certainty that Dryden has made a mistake. To be sure, the English word *refulgent* is etymologically derived from the Latin, but it has a neoclassical tone which *refulsit* cannot have had for Vergil's contemporaries. To them, I believe, the effect must have been much nearer that conveyed by Gavin Douglas' translation:

Her nek schane like unto the rois in May

even though no month is mentioned in the original.

One translator of Homer, in an attempt to enable the monolingual reader "to smack the sound, if not the full sense of the Greek," even went so far as to write *hydropot* for "water-drinker."

The Goal of the Translator

A translation in the proper sense is not a "trot." A trot is like a pair of spectacles for the weak-sighted; a translation is like a book in Braille for the blind. The translator, that is to say, has to assume that his readers cannot and probably never will be able to read the original.

As a general rule, I believe that translation should be a work of collaboration. The person responsible for the final version into English, let us say, must not only possess English as his mother-tongue; he must also be a master of it, alive to its subtlest nuances. But very few writers who are masters of their own tongue have equal mastery over another. As his collaborator, therefore, he needs a person who knows some English but whose mother-tongue is the original, or, in the case of dead languages like Greek and Latin, a first-rate philological scholar.

Once, either by himself, or with the help of a collaborator, the translator has learned exactly *what* his author says, his real task begins, the task of capturing in his own tongue the author's tone of voice. Let us say he is translating Goethe. The question he must ask and try as far as possible to answer is: "What, without ceasing to be himself, would Goethe have written, had he thought and written in English?"

In poetry form and content, sound and sense are as inseparable a unity as body and soul, so that any verse translation is to some degree an "imitation" rather than a translation. A poet's imagery can usually be accurately translated because it is derived from sensory perceptions common to all men, whatever language they speak. But effects which depend upon language, like rhymes and puns, are not reproducible. For instance, in no other tongue but English can one make this joke of Hilaire Belloc's:

When I am dead, I hope it may be said:
His sins were scarlet, but his books were read.

Then there are the problems of prosody and meter. Even when two languages possess the same metrical form—sonnets have been written in nearly all European languages—exact copying is very difficult. German and Italian, for example, are polysyllabic and highly inflected; English contains many more monosyllabic words and has very few inflections. In the case of languages like Greek and Latin, whose prosodies are based, not as ours upon stressed and unstressed syllables, but upon long and short syllables, the wise translator will forget all about the original meter.

However closely the verse translator may strive to reproduce what the original says, his first obligation is to produce a good English poem. In trying to do so, he cannot escape from the aesthetic presuppositions of his age as to what is truly "poetic" in form and diction. Thus Dryden translated Vergil and Pope translated Homer into heroic couplets, and it would never have occurred to them to do anything else since, in their time, the heroic couplet was considered the only possible medium for a long serious poem. Again, until this century the only kind of unrhymed verse which was considered to be poetry was the five-foot iambic line of blank verse. It is only since poets have started to write English poems of their own in looser unrhymed forms, that, as translators, they have been able to make similar experiments.

It follows from all this that there cannot be a definitive translation of any important poem which will do for all time. Every generation has to make its own version.

The concluding stanza of Horace's Ode 7, Book IV, runs thus:

Infernis neque enim tenebris Diana pudicum
liberat Hippolytum,
nec Letheae valet Theseus abrumpere caro
vincula Piritheo.

The meter here consists of a dactylic hexameter followed by the second half-line of a pentameter. For it, the Loeb "trot" runs:

For Diana releases not the chaste Hippolytus from the nether darkness, nor has Theseus power to break the Lethean chains of his dear Pirithous.

Here are three versions, one from the eighteenth century, one from the late nineteenth, and the third from the last decade.

Hippolytus, unjustly slain,
Diana calls to life in vain;
Nor can the might of Theseus rend
The chains of hell that hold his friend.

—Samuel Johnson

Night holds Hippolytus the pure of stain,
Diana steads him nothing, he must stay;
And Theseus leaves Pirithous in the chain
The love of comrades cannot take away.

—A. E. Housman

Great is the power of Diana and chaste was Hippolytus, yet still
  Prisoned in darkness he lies.
Passionate Theseus was, yet could not shatter the chains
  Forged for his Pirithous.

—James Michie

None of these versions is without merit. It may be noted that the contemporary acceptance of free verse has allowed Mr Michie to approximate to the original meter. It is rather curious, too, that the version which departs most widely from the Latin is Housman's, who was the greatest Latin scholar of his day. This is not necessarily a criticism. Some English poems which have most successfully captured the spirit of poets like Horace and Juvenal have been imitations after Horace or Juvenal which made no attempt to reproduce the original exactly. Not only can there be no definitive verse translation, but also each translator has to follow his own taste in poetry. As Arthur Waley has written: "The translator must use the tools he knows best how to handle. What matters is that a translator should have been excited by the work he translates, should be haunted day and night by the feeling that he must put it into his own language."

Man in Literature: Comparative World Studies in Translation,
edited by James E. Miller, Jr., Robert O'Neal,
and Helen M. McDonnell (1970)

Foreword to *I Am an Impure Thinker*, by Eugen Rosenstock-Huessy

"A good wine needs no bush," and the same ought to be true for a good book. A foreword should be unnecessary. My reason for writing this one is that when *The Viking Book of Aphorisms* was published, in which Mr Kronenberger and I had included a number of quotations from Rosenstock-Huessy, a reviewer complained that he had never heard of him.

I first heard of him in, I should guess, 1940, when a friend gave me a copy of *Out of Revolution*, of which two chapters are included in this selection. (The whole, I am happy to say, has been re-issued as a paperback by Argo Books.) Ever since I have read everything by him that I could lay my hands on.

I should warn anyone reading him for the first time that, to begin with, he may find as I did, certain aspects of Rosenstock-Huessy's writings a bit hard to take. At times he seems to claim to be the *only* man who has ever seen the light about History and Language. But let the reader persevere, and he will find, as I did, that he is richly rewarded. He will be forced to admit that, very often, the author's claim is just: he *has* uncovered many truths hidden from his predecessors.

I was born and raised in England and always thought that I knew the history of my country between the accession of Henry VIII in 1509 and the accession of William III in 1688 fairly well, but it took a German to show me, what no English historian had done, the connection between the execution of Sir Thomas More in 1535 and the execution of Charles I in 1649, to explain the real meaning of the terms *Restoration* and *Glorious Revolution*, and why the revolutionary and permanent changes made by Cromwell had to be concealed and denied by calling the years from 1640 to 1660 *The Great Rebellion*.

Again, I am a poet by vocation and, therefore, do not expect to learn much about Language from a writer of Prose. Yet, half of what I now know about the difference between Personal Speech, based upon Proper Names, and Second and First Personal Pronouns, words of command and obedience, summons and response, and the impersonal "objective" use of words as a communication code between individuals, I owe to Rosenstock-Huessy. He has also clarified for me many problems of translation, for instance, the historical reasons why one cannot translate *Common Sense* literally into French or *Geist* into English.

Whatever he may have to say about God, Man, the World, Time, etc., Rosenstock-Huessy always starts out from his own experience as a human being, who must pass through successive stages between birth and death, learning something essential from each of them. For this reason I would recommend a reader of this selection to start with the two autobiographical pieces at the end. He will understand better, I believe, when he reads the others, exactly what the author means by his motto *Respondeo etsi mutabor* (I answer even though I have to be changed), and why he attaches so much importance to it.

Speaking for myself, I can only say that, by listening to Rosenstock-Huessy, *I* have been changed.

I Am an Impure Thinker, by Eugen Rosenstock-Huessy (1970)

[A Tribute to Igor Stravinsky]

When the possibility first arose of writing a libretto for Igor Stravinsky, both Chester Kallman and I were scared stiff. In the first place, we felt the awe that younger and less well-known persons very properly feel for the older and famous: in the second, Rumor had it that Stravinsky was a difficult person to work with. Rumor had lied. What we feared to find was a Prima Donna: what in fact we found was a professional artist, concerned not for his personal glory but solely for the Thing-to-be-made. Of Stravinsky the man, I can only repeat what I have said elsewhere about somebody else, namely, that he embodies the truth of Logan Pearsall-Smith's aphorism: "Hearts that are gentle and kind, and tongues that are neither—these make the finest company in the world."

Too often in my life, I have met persons whom I revered but found myself unable to love: less often, I have met persons whom I loved but found myself unable to revere. I have met Igor Stravinsky and find myself able to do both: what a joy that is!

Booklet accompanying a set of recordings, *Igor Stravinsky: Nine Masterpieces Conducted by the Composer* (1970)

Concerning the Unpredictable

The Unexpected Universe. By Loren Eiseley.
Harcourt, Brace & World. $5.75.

> In creation there is not only a Yes but also a No; not only a height but also an abyss; not only clarity but also obscurity; not only progress and continuation but also impediment and limitation . . . not only value but also worthlessness. . . . It is true that individual creatures and men experience these things in most unequal measure, their lots being assigned by a justice which is curious or very much concealed. Yet it is irrefutable that creation and creature are good even in the fact that all that is exists in this contrast and antithesis.—Karl Barth in *Church Dogmatics*

Rather oddly, I first heard of Dr Loren Eiseley not in this country but in Oxford, where a student gave me a copy of *The Immense Journey*, since which time I have eagerly read anything of his I could lay my hands on. His obvious ancestors, as both writers and thinkers, are Thoreau and Emerson, but he often reminds me of Ruskin, Richard Jefferies, W. H. Hudson, whom, I feel sure, he must have read, and of two writers, Novalis (a German) and Adalbert Stifter (an Austrian), whom perhaps he hasn't. But I wouldn't be sure. Some of the quotations in his latest book surprised me. I would not have expected someone who is an American and a scientist to have read such little-known literary works as the "Völuspá," James Thomson's *The City of Dreadful Night*, and Charles Williams' play *Cranmer*.

I have one slight criticism of his literary style, which I will get over with at once. Like Ruskin, he can at times write sentences which I would call "woozy"; that is to say, too dependent upon some private symbolism of his own to be altogether comprehensible to others. For example:

> We refuse to consider that in the old eye of the hurricane we may be, and doubtless are, in aggregate, a slightly more diffuse and dangerous dragon of the primal morning that still enfolds us.

To this objection he has, I know, a crushing reply:

> One of Thoreau's wisest remarks is upon the demand scientific intellectuals sometimes make, that one must speak so as to be always understood. "Neither men," he says, "nor toadstools grow so."

Dr Eiseley happens to be an archeologist, an anthropologist, and a naturalist, but, if I have understood him rightly, the first point he wishes to make is that in order to be a scientist, an artist, a doctor, a lawyer, or what-have-you, one has first to be a human being. No member of any other species can have a special "field." One question his book raises is: "What differences have recent scientific discoveries, in physics, astronomy, biology, etc., made to man's conception, individually or collectively, of himself?" The answer is, I believe, very little.

We did not have to wait for Darwin to tell us that, as physical creatures, we are akin to other animals. Like them, we breathe, eat, digest, excrete, copulate, are viviparously born, and, whatever views we may have about an "afterlife," must certainly suffer physical death in this. Indeed, one result of urbanization has been that, despite what we now know about our ancestry, we feel far less akin and grateful to the animal kingdom than did primitive tribes, with their totem systems and animal folktales.

Speaking of the recognition of Odysseus by his dog Argos, Dr Eiseley says:

> The magic that gleams an instant between Argos and Odysseus is both the recognition of diversity and the need for affection across the illusions of form. It is nature's cry to homeless, far-wandering, insatiable man: "Do not forget your brethren, nor the green wood from which you sprang. To do so is to invite disaster. . . . One does not meet oneself until one catches the reflection from an eye other than human."

Before Descartes, such a warning would have been unnecessary. On the other hand, nothing Darwin and the geneticists have to tell us can alter the fact that, as self-conscious beings who speak (that is to say, give Proper Names to other beings), who laugh, who pray, and who, as creators of history and culture, continue to change after our biological evolution is complete, we are unique among all the creatures we know of. All attempts to account for our behavior on the basis of our pre-human ancestors are myths, and usually invented to justify base behavior. As Karl Kraus wrote:

> When a man is treated like a beast, he says, "After all, I'm human." When he behaves like a beast, he says, "After all, I'm only human."

No; as Dr Eiseley says, "There is no definition or description of man possible by reducing him to ape or tree-shrew. Once, it is true, the shrew contained him, but he is gone." Or, as G. K. Chesterton said, "If it is not true that a divine being fell, then one can only say that one of the animals went completely off its head."

What modern science has profoundly changed is our way of thinking about the non-human universe. We have always been aware that human beings are characters in a story in which we can know more or less what has happened but can never predict what is going to happen; what we never realized until recently is that the same is true of the universe. But, of course, its story is even more mysterious to us than our own. When we act, we do know something about our motives for action, but it is rarely possible for us to say why any thing novel happens in the universe. All the same, I do not personally believe there is such a thing as a "random" event. "Unpredictable" is a factual description; "random" contains, without having the honesty to admit it, a philosophical bias typical of persons who have forgotten how to pray. Though he does use the term once, I don't think Dr Eiseley believes in it, either:

> The earth's atmosphere of oxygen appears to be the product of a biological invention, photosynthesis, another random event that took place in Archeozoic times. That single "invention," for such it was, determined the entire nature of life on this planet, and there is no possibility at present of calling it preordained. Similarly, the stepped-up manipulation of chance, in the shape of both mutation and recombination of genetic factors, which is one result of the sexual mechanism, would have been unprophesiable.

I must now openly state my own bias and say that I do not believe in Chance; I believe in Providence and Miracles. If photosynthesis was invented by chance, then I can only say it was a damned lucky chance for us. If, biologically speaking, it is a "statistical impossibility" that I should be walking the earth instead of a million other possible people, I can only think of it as a miracle which I must do my best to deserve. Natural Selection as a negative force is comprehensible. It is obvious that a drastic change in the environment, like an Ice Age, will destroy a large number of species adapted to a warm climate. What I cannot swallow is the assertion that "chance" mutations can explain the fact that whenever an ecological niche is free, some species evolves to fit it, especially when one thinks how peculiar some such niches—the one occupied by the liver fluke, for example—can be. Dr Eiseley quotes George Gaylord Simpson as saying:

> The association of unusual physical conditions with a crisis in evolution is not likely to be pure coincidence. Life and its environment are interdependent and evolve together.

Dr Eiseley has excellent things to say about the myth of the Survival of the Fittest:

> A major portion of the world's story appears to be that of fumbling little creatures of seemingly no great potential, falling, like the helpless little girl Alice, down a rabbit hole or an unexpected crevice into some new and topsy-turvy realm. . . . The first land-walking fish was, by modern standards, an ungainly and inefficient vertebrate. Figuratively, he was a water failure who had managed to climb ashore on a continent where no vertebrates existed. In a time of crisis he had escaped his enemies. . . . The wet fish gasping in the harsh air on the shore, the warm-blooded mammal roving unchecked through the torpor of the reptilian night, the lizard-bird launching into a moment of ill-aimed flight, shatter all purely competitive assumptions. These singular events reveal escapes through the living screen, penetrated, one would have to say in retrospect, by the "overspecialized" and the seemingly "inefficient," the creatures driven to the wall.

The main theme of *The Unexpected Universe* is Man as the Quest Hero, the wanderer, the voyager, the seeker after adventure, knowledge, power, meaning, and righteousness. The Quest is dangerous (he may suffer shipwreck or ambush) and unpredictable (he never knows what will happen to him next). The Quest is not of his own choosing—often, in weariness, he wishes he had never set out on it—but is enjoined upon him by his nature as a human being:

> No longer, as with the animal, can the world be accepted as given. It has to be perceived and consciously thought about, abstracted, and considered. The moment one does so, one is outside of the natural; objects are each one surrounded with an aura radiating meaning to man alone.

> Mostly the animals understand their roles, but man, by comparison, seems troubled by a message that, it is often said, he cannot quite remember or has gotten wrong. . . . Bereft of instinct, he must search continually for meanings. . . . Man was a reader before he became a writer, a reader of what Coleridge once called the mighty alphabet of the universe.

For illustrations of his thesis, Dr Eiseley begins with an imaginary voyage—Homer's epic the *Odyssey*—and goes on to two famous historical voyages, that of Captain Cook in the *Resolution*, during which he discovered not the Terra Incognita he was sent to find—a rich and habitable continent South and westward of South America—but what he described as "an inexpressibly horrid Antarctica," and Darwin's voyage in the Beagle, during which he found the data which led him to doubt the Fixity of Species. Lastly, Dr Eiseley tells us many anecdotes from his own life voyage, and these are to me the most fascinating passages in the book. Of the *Odyssey* he says:

> Odysseus' passage through the haunted waters of the eastern Mediterranean symbolizes, at the start of the Western intellectual tradition, the sufferings that the universe and his own nature impose upon homeward-yearning man. In the restless atmosphere of today all the psychological elements of the Odyssey are present to excess: the driving will toward achievement, the technological cleverness crudely manifest in the blinding of Cyclops, the fierce rejection of the sleepy Lotus Isles, the violence between man and man. Yet, significantly, the ancient hero cries out in desperation, "There is nothing worse for men than wandering."

Dr Eiseley's autobiographical passages are, most of them, descriptions of numinous encounters—some joyful, some terrifying. After reading them, I get the impression of a wanderer who is often in danger of being shipwrecked on the shores of Dejection—it can hardly be an accident that three of his encounters take place in cemeteries—and a solitary who feels more easily at home with animals than with his fellow human beings. Aside from figures in his childhood, the human beings who have "messages" for him are all total strangers—someone tending a rubbish dump, a mysterious figure throwing stranded starfish back into the sea, a vagrant scientist with a horrid parasitic worm in a bottle, a girl in the Wild West with Neanderthal features. As a rule, though, his numinous encounters are with non-human objects—a spider, the eye of a dead octopus, his own shepherd dog, a starving jackrabbit, a young fox. It is also clear that he is a deeply compassionate man who, in his own words, "loves the lost ones, the failures of the world." It is typical of him that, on recovering consciousness after a bad fall, to find himself bleeding profusely, he should, quite unself-consciously, apologize to his now doomed blood cells—phagocytes and platelets—"Oh, don't go. I'm sorry, I've done for you." More importantly, he reveals himself as a man unusually well trained in the habit of prayer, by which I mean the habit of listening. The petitionary aspect of prayer is its most trivial because it is involuntary. We cannot help asking that our wishes may be granted, though all too many of them are like wishing that two and two may make five, and cannot and should not be granted. But the serious part of prayer begins when we have got our begging over with and listen for the Voice of what I would call the Holy Spirit, though if others prefer to say the Voice of Oz or the Dreamer or Conscience, I shan't quarrel, so long as they don't call it the Voice of the Super-Ego, for that "entity" can only tell us what we know already, whereas the Voice I am talking about always says something new and unpredictable—an unexpected demand, obedience to which involves a change of self, however painful.

At this point, a digression. Last September, I attended a symposium in Stockholm on "The Place of Value in a World of Fact." Most of those present were scientists, some of them very distinguished indeed. To my shock and amazement, they kept saying that what we need today is a set of *Ethical Axioms* (italics mine). I can only say that to me the phrase is gibberish. An axiom is stated in the indicative and addressed to the intellect. From one set of axioms one kind of mathematics will follow, from another set another, but it would be nonsense to call one of them "better" than the other. All ethical statements are addressed to the will, usually a reluctant will, and must therefore appear in the imperative. "Thou shalt love thy neighbor as thyself" and "A straight line is the shortest distance between two points" belong to two totally different realms of discourse.

But to return to Dr Eiseley. As a rule, the Voice speaks to him not directly but through messengers who are unaware of the message they bear. In the following dream, however, he is spoken to without intermediaries:

> The dream was of a great blurred bear-like shape emerging from the snow against the window. It pounded on the glass and beckoned importunately toward the forest. I caught the urgency of a message as uncouth and indecipherable as the shape of its huge bearer in the snow. In the immense terror of my dream I struggled against the import of that message as I struggled also to resist the impatient pounding of the frost-enveloped beast at the window.
>
> Suddenly I lifted the telephone beside my bed, and through the receiver came a message as cryptic as the message from the snow, but far more miraculous in origin. For I knew intuitively, in the still snowfall of my dream, that the voice I heard, a long way off, was my own voice in childhood. Pure and sweet, incredibly refined and beautiful beyond the things of earth, yet somehow inexorable and not to be stayed, the voice was already terminating its message. "I am sorry to have troubled you," the clear faint syllables of the child persisted. They seemed to come across a thinning wire that lengthened far away into the years of my past. "I am sorry. I am sorry to have troubled you at all." The voice faded before I could speak. I was awake now, trembling in the cold.

I have said that I suspect Dr Eiseley of being a melancholic. He recognizes that man is the only creature who speaks personally, works, and prays, but nowhere does he overtly say that man is the only creature who laughs. True laughter is not to be confused with the superior titter of the intellect, though we are capable, alas, of that, too: when we truly laugh, we laugh simultaneously *with* and *at.* True laughter (belly laughter) I would define as the spirit of Carnival.

Again a digression, on the meaning of Carnival as it was known in the Middle Ages and persisted in a few places, like Rome, where Goethe witnessed and described it in February of 1788. Carnival celebrates the unity of our human race as mortal creatures, who come into this world and depart from it without our consent, who must eat, drink, defecate, belch, and break wind in order to live, and procreate if our species is to survive. Our feelings about this are ambiguous. To us as individuals, it is a cause for rejoicing to know that we are not alone, that all of us, irrespective of age or sex or rank or talent, are in the same boat. As unique persons, on the other hand, all of us are resentful that an exception cannot be made in our own case. We oscillate between wishing we were unreflective animals and wishing we were disembodied spirits, for in either case we should not be problematic to ourselves. The Carnival solution of this ambiguity is to laugh, for laughter is simultaneously a protest and an acceptance. During Carnival, all social distinctions are suspended, even that of sex. Young men dress up as girls, young girls as boys. The escape from social personality is symbolized by the wearing of masks. The oddity of the human animal expresses itself through the grotesque—false noses, huge bellies and buttocks, farcical imitations of childbirth and copulation. The protest element in laughter takes the form of mock aggression: people pelt each other with small, harmless objects, draw cardboard daggers, and abuse each other verbally, like the small boy Goethe heard screaming at his father, "*Sia ammazzato il Signore Padre!*" Traditionally, Carnival, the days of feasting and fun, immediately precedes Lent, the days of fasting and prayer. In medieval carnivals, parodies of the rituals of the Church were common, but what Lewis Carroll said of literary parody—"One can only parody a poem one admires"—is true of all parody. One can only blaspheme if one believes. The world of Laughter is much more closely related to the world of Worship and Prayer than either is to the everyday, secular world of Work, for both are worlds in which we are all equal, in the first as individual members of our species, in the latter as unique persons. In the world of Work, on the other hand, we are not and cannot be equal, only diverse and interdependent: each of us, whether as scientist, artist, cook, cabdriver, or whatever, has to do "our thing." So long as we thought of Nature in polytheistic terms as the abode of gods, our efficiency and success as workers were hampered by a false humility which tried to make Nature responsible for us. But, according to Genesis, God made Adam responsible for looking after the Garden of Eden on His behalf, and it now seems as if He expects us to be responsible for the whole natural universe, which means that, as workers, we have to regard the universe *etsi deus non daretur*: God must be a hidden deity, veiled by His creation.

A satisfactory human life, individually or collectively, is possible only if proper respect is paid to all three worlds. Without Prayer and Work, the Carnival laughter turns ugly, the comic obscenities grubby and pornographic, the mock aggression into real hatred and cruelty. (The hippies, it appears to me, are trying to recover the sense of Carnival which is so conspicuously absent in this age, but so long as they reject Work they are unlikely to succeed.) Without Laughter and Work, Prayer turns Gnostic, cranky, Pharisaic, while those who try to live by Work alone, without Laughter or Prayer, turn into insane lovers of power, tyrants who would enslave Nature to their immediate desires—an attempt which can only end in utter catastrophe, shipwreck on the Isle of the Sirens.

Carnival in its traditional forms is not, I think, for Dr Eiseley any more than it is for me. Neither of us can enjoy crowds and loud noises. But even introverted intellectuals can share the Carnival experience if they are prepared to forget their dignity, as Dr Eiseley did when he unexpectedly encountered a fox cub:

> The creature was very young. He was alone in a dread universe. I crept on my knees around the prow and crouched beside him. It was a small fox pup from a den under the timbers who looked up at me. God knows what had become of his brothers and sisters. His parent must not have been home from hunting.
>
> He innocently selected what I think was a chicken bone from an untidy pile of splintered rubbish and shook it at me invitingly. There was a vast and playful humor in his face. . . . Here was the thing in the midst of the bones, the wide-eyed, innocent fox inviting me to play, with the innate courtesy of its two forepaws placed appealingly together, along with a mock shake of the head. The universe was swinging in some fantastic fashion around to present its face, and the face was so small that the universe itself was laughing.
>
> It was not a time for human dignity. It was a time only for the careful observance of amenities written behind the stars. Gravely I arranged my forepaws while the puppy whimpered with ill-concealed excitement. I drew the breath of a fox's den into my nostrils. On impulse, I picked up clumsily a whiter bone and shook it in teeth that had not entirely forgotten their original purpose. Round and round we tumbled for one ecstatic moment. . . . For just a moment I had held the universe at bay by the simple expedient of sitting on my haunches before a fox den and tumbling about with a chicken bone. It is the gravest, most meaningful act I shall ever accomplish, but, as Thoreau once remarked of some peculiar errand of his own, there is no use reporting it to the Royal Society.

Thank God, though, Dr Eiseley has reported it to me. *Bravo!* say I.

The New Yorker, 21 February 1970

Translator's Note [to the Icelandic "Song of Rig"]

Spelt *Audun,* my family name appears quite frequently in the Sagas, so perhaps it is not surprising that my father was fascinated by Iceland, and that I inherited his interest. As a boy, I grew up on English translations of the most important Sagas. As an undergraduate at Oxford I grew to love Anglo-Saxon poetry which, of course, made me curious to learn about the Elder Edda.

Since in Poetry Form and Content, Sound and Sense are as inseparable as Soul and Body, any translation of verse is to some degree an "Imitation" rather than an exact translation. What the chief difficulties are depends upon the idiosyncrasies of the two languages involved and the traditions of their respective literatures. In translating into English from Greek or Latin, for example, the greatest problem is that of metre. Firstly, English prosody is based on stress, Greek and Latin upon vowel quantity. Secondly, in English, even a stressed hexameter sounds eccentric, and unsuited to an "epic" style. In this respect, Old Norse is easier because of its stressed alliterative lines. On the other hand, the kennings, so common in Old Norse poetry, which, like the Homeric epithets, are metrical formulae, often have to be glossed. *Diomedes of the loud war-cry* is self-explanatory. But how is the reader to know that *Grani's Road* means the river Rhine unless he knows that Grani was the name of Sigurd's horse and that Sigurd journeyed down the Rhine?

A poet writes consciously at any rate for an audience who speak the same mother-tongue as he does, and are also his contemporaries. His translator does the same, only now both the tongue and the times have changed. In translating poems like the Elder Edda, which were composed many centuries back, the translators' first question is: "What words can I use which will have the same meaning and emotional overtones for my readers that the original words had for the original audience?" That is to say: "How am I to avoid being falsely archaic on the one hand, and falsely modern on the other?" No answer can be more than guess-work.

Atlantica & Iceland Review, [Spring] 1970

A Russian Aesthete

Against the Current: Selections from the Novels, Essays, Notes, And Letters of Konstantin Leontiev. Edited, with an introduction and notes, by George Ivask. Weybright & Talley. $7.50.

Since I know no Russian, all I can say about Mr George Reavey's translation of *Against the Current,* a selection from the writings of Konstantin Leontiev, is that it reads easily and well. In making his selection, Mr George Ivask has clearly tried, in the limited space at his disposal (two hundred and seventy-three pages), to do justice to all of Leontiev's concerns—as a writer of memoirs and fictionalized autobiography, as an observer of life in the Middle East, as a political theorist, and as a literary critic. Nearly all the extracts are interesting, but, speaking for myself, I wish he had devoted more pages to the literary critic, even if this meant a sacrifice of range. Leontiev's views on most topics were, to put it mildly, extravagant, but in literary criticism he was completely sane and one of the best critics I have read. *Essays in Russian Literature: The Conservative View,* edited and translated by Spencer E. Roberts (Ohio University Press, 1968), prints the whole of his hundred-and-twenty-five-page essay on Tolstoy's novels, which I would recommend to readers who are beguiled by the twenty-four pages of it in this new selection.

Leontiev was born in 1831, the child of minor gentry. He studied medicine at Moscow University, served as a surgeon in the Crimean War and then as a household physician on a country estate. After his marriage, he gave up medicine, entered the Russian Consular Service, and spent ten years in the Middle East, during which time, after being "miraculously" cured of dysentery or cholera while praying to the Virgin, he became devoutly Orthodox. In 1874, he returned to Russia, and from 1880 to 1887 he served on the Censorship Committee. Then he entered the Optina Monastery and, just before his death, in 1891, was consecrated as a monk. In 1851, he met Turgenev, who was impressed by his talent, but they quarrelled later over politics. Leontiev's books, it seems, received little attention, but in the last year of his life he found an admirer in the writer Vasily Rozanov, twenty-five years his junior.

For some mysterious reason, Leontiev's mother, instead of marrying the man she loved, married his brother, whom she did not, and her son evidently shared her distaste:

> My father was one of those frivolous and easily distracted Russians (and gentry, especially) who reject nothing and uphold nothing rigorously. In general, it may be said that my father was neither very clever nor very serious.

His mother, on the other hand, he adored and admired. The reasons he gives for this are revealing:

> She was incomparably more elegant than my father, and because of an inborn instinct, that was very important to me.

From her, he said he learned

> the lessons of patriotism and feeling for monarchy, the examples of a strict order, constant work, and refined taste in everyday life.

Leontiev, that is, was both by nature and by choice an aesthete and a narcissist. Aesthetes and narcissists can be found in every country, but Leontiev was also a Russian, and to me, at least, who was born and bred a British Pharisee, Russians are not quite like other folk. If their respective literatures in the nineteenth century are a guide, no two sensibilities could be more poles apart than the Russian and the British. (The American sensibility seems closer to the Russian. I can imagine a Russian equivalent of *Moby Dick* but not of *Sense and Sensibility*.) Time and time again, when reading even the greatest Russian writers, like Tolstoy and Dostoevski, I find myself exclaiming, "My God, this man is bonkers!" In his introduction, Mr Ivask quotes a remark by Alexander Blok: "It is worth living if only to make absolute demands on life." What a contrast to the advice given by the Red Queen to Alice—"Speak in French when you can't think of the English for a thing, turn out your toes as you walk, and remember who you are"—or this definition by an Anglican bishop: "Orthodoxy is reticence." In British English, even today, the word *enthusiastic* is a pejorative. For this reason, the Russian writers we feel most at home with are Turgenev and Chekhov, though I suspect that if there were any decent translations we should find Pushkin even more to our taste.

Leontiev may extol the virtues of order and constant work, but he does not seem to have practiced them:

> The conflict of ideas in my mind was so violent in 1862 that I lost weight and not infrequently spent whole winter nights in Petersburg without any sleep, with my head and arms resting on a table in a state of exhaustion as a consequence of my martyrlike reflections.

No Englishman could possibly do such a thing. Reading accounts of Russian life, whether in the past or in the present, one gets the impression that the Protestant ethic of self-discipline, prudence, and regular hours has had no influence. Is this the cause or the effect of the despotism under which Russians have always lived? In Russia, says Leontiev,

> only that becomes established which, I repeat, is created somewhat arbitrarily and artificially by the government.

This seems as true of the New Russia of Lenin and Stalin as of the Old Russia of Peter and Catherine.

Western aesthetes have as a rule subscribed to the doctrine of Art for Art's Sake and deliberately averted their eyes from the realms of the political and social. This, to his credit, a Russian aesthete like Leontiev would never do. "The devil," he says, "take art without life!" The socially concerned aesthete, however, who judges society by the standards which apply to works of art, though his negative criticisms may be cogent, is, when it comes to making positive suggestions as to how to correct its defects, almost certain to talk nonsense, often pernicious nonsense. The aesthetic imagination is excited by the extraordinary person, deed, or event; the ethical question "Are these good or evil, just or unjust?" is not its concern. I myself do not believe an artist can entirely ignore the claims of the ethical, but in a work of art goodness and truth are subordinate to beauty. In the political and social realms it is just the other way round; a government, a society that ignores the aesthetic does so at its peril, but the ethical demand for justice must take precedence. Good looks and bearing are always to be admired. Says Leontiev:

> Dzheffer Dem was still young and extremely handsome. His face was pleasantly round, very swarthy and fresh-complexioned. About his whole person, in his huge black eyes, in his small black mustache that was twirled up, in his graceful carriage, in his smooth unhurried gait, in his white hands peacefully held behind his back, there was so much that was inexplicable, of good breeding, calm pride, secret self-assurance, that I cannot put it all into words!

But when, as in this case, their owner is a ruthless killer, one must admit that even the drabbest conformist bank clerk in a frock coat is preferable as a citizen. Or, again:

> "Would you like to have a world in which all people everywhere live in identical small, clean, and comfortable little houses—the way people of middle income live in our Novorossiisky towns?"
>
> "Of course. What could be better than that?" Piotrovsky replied.
>
> "Well, then I am no longer your man," I retorted. "If democratic movements must lead to such terrible prose, I shall lose the last vestige of my feeling for democracy. Henceforth I shall be its enemy!"

Piotrovsky was, of course, wrong in thinking of Suburbia as a Utopia, but he was right in thinking that Suburbia was preferable to slums, however picturesque. Leontiev, incidentally, had to live in neither.

In judging social and political life, what the aesthete overlooks is the fact that while every human being is a unique person, a member of a class of one, very few human beings are extraordinary, whether in looks or talents or character; for the average man to seek to become extraordinary and therefore aesthetically interesting would be unauthentic, and as a rule he knows this. A playwright is free to select his heroes and heroines and ignore the mass of mankind; the politician can ignore no one, and, since they comprise the majority, ordinary men and women are his primary concern, for in politics to ignore usually means to oppress or to kill.

Leontiev's recommendations—at least for Russia, though I do not think he had any hope they would be listened to—were as follows:

> The State should be diversified, complex, strong, class-structured, and cautiously mobile. In general, strict, sometimes to the point of ferocity.

> The Church should be more independent than the present one. . . . The Church should have a mitigating influence on the State, and not vice versa. . . .
>
> The laws and principles of authority should be stricter; people should try to be personally kinder; the one will balance the other.

In coming to such conclusions he did not, as one might have expected, draw analogies from the process of artistic fabrication; he drew them from biology. Unfortunately, biological analogies are equally misleading. An organism lives under the necessity of being itself—an oak tree cannot turn into a butterfly—but it is false to call this necessity "despotism," since it is unconscious, whereas political despotism is consciously imposed. It would seem that all specific social structures are, like individual organisms, mortal, so one can speak of the rise, flowering, and decay of a particular society like the Roman Empire, but only with great caution. Like every species, the human race is potentially immortal, but, unlike all the others, man is a history-making creature whose "nature" is not identical with his social habits. A social animal like the bee could not change its hive-ways without ceasing to be a bee; man can and does continually change his ways. When a particular society disappears, human beings do not disappear but, by choice or necessity, become members of some new kind of society. One may prefer *this* society to *that*, but both are equally *human*.

Living, as we do, in an age when *liberal* has become a dirty word, it may be easier for us than for Leontiev's contemporaries to listen to his objections to the liberal philosophy. Everyone today will agree that the world we have fabricated during the last two hundred years is hideous compared with any fabricated in earlier times. And no one, I think, believes anymore in the liberal dogma of Progress; namely, that all change must be for the better. On the contrary, most of us, both old and young, are terrified of what the future may bring. The nineteenth-century "reactionaries" like Kierkegaard, Nietzsche, and Leontiev prophesied that liberalism, if successful, would produce a drably uniform society, Ortega y Gasset's mass man, and, as we all know, their prophecies have come true, but this, surely, was not what the original liberals intended. On the contrary, they must have hoped that political liberty would encourage diversity, that, granted equality before the law, equality of opportunity, and greater affluence, each individual, freed from the despotism of birth and poverty, would be able to develop into the kind of person he wished. That their hopes were disappointed may, I think, be mainly attributed to two factors, neither of them political in the strict sense. Firstly, to the development of technology. Starting with Locke, the creators of philosophical liberalism were eighteenth-century figures who lived before the Industrial Revolution, so they thought in terms of a society composed mostly of farmers and craftsmen. Machines have no political opinions, but they have profound political effects. They demand a strict regimentation of time, and, by abolishing the need for manual skill, have transformed the majority of the population from workers into laborers. There are, that is to say, fewer and fewer jobs which a man can find a pride and satisfaction in doing well, more and more which have no interest in themselves and can be valued only for the money they provide. Leontiev, like Herzen, was shocked by the materialism and philistine ambitions of the European working class, but what can men who have never known what it is to take pleasure in one's work hope for except more money and more consumer goods? Secondly, the liberals underestimated the desire of most human beings for conformity —their fear of being unlike their neighbors and of standing alone in their opinions and tastes. It is true, as the critics of liberalism said, that the class-stratified societies of earlier times present a picture of much greater variety and aesthetic interest than the egalitarian society we know, but this was only because the class structure compelled the classes to live, dress, and think differently; within each class, whether that of the aristocrats or the peasants, the urge for conformity was probably no less strong than it is today, when, as we know, tight pants and long hair are just as de rigueur for a rebel hippie as a Brooks Brothers suit and a crew cut are for a junior executive.

Before considering Leontiev as a literary critic, I suppose I must say a word about his attitude toward the Christian faith and the Church, though I am loath to do so because I find it repellent. He seems to have been one of those persons who alternate between leading a dissolute life and weeping over their sins, not out of genuine repentance but out of fear of going to Hell. Faugh!

By vocation, Leontiev was a writer, not a political theorist, and when he discusses literature he speaks not as an amateur but with professional authority. Because he believed that Life was more important than Art, his literary preference was for "realism"—novels and poems, that is to say, which try to depict as truthfully as possible the Primary World in which we all live. Thus, comparing *War and Peace* with *Anna Karenina*, he says:

> Is the general trend of *War and Peace* as true in spirit and style to the life of the year 1812 as the trend of *Anna Karenina* is faithful to the spirit and style of our time? It seems to me not so true.

To explain what he means, he tries to imagine what *War and Peace* would be like if Pushkin had written it. He admits at once that it would not be anywhere near as great a novel, but he thinks it would have been more "realistic":

> Pushkin would not have (probably) even called the French marshals and generals, who were running away from themselves in carriages and fur coats, "wicked and insignificant men who have done a great deal of evil," just as the Russian heroes, who were chasing them from Moscow,

probably did not call them that in their soul in the year 1812, but chided them in passion rather than according to the precepts of a tediously moral philosophy.

What Leontiev hated—and I heartily agree with him—was "naturalism" which identifies the "real" with the ignoble and the ugly. As with Karl Kraus, his criticism is never generalized but always specific and concrete: he picks out phrases, verbal habits, even single words which seem to him symptomatic of a literary disease:

> When Tolstoy's Ivan Ilyich uses the "bed-pan," that is all right. Ivan Ilyich is a sick, dying man. I like it here. But when Gogol's Tentetnikov, awakening in the morning, still lies in bed and "rubs his eyes," and his eyes are "small," this is very nasty and unnecessary. . . .
>
> When, at the end of *War and Peace*, the already married Natasha brings out the childbed linen to show it in the drawing room, the green stain on the linen has turned yellow; although this is unattractive and crude, yet it is appropriate here; it has great significance. . . . But when Pierre "dandles" ("dandles," indeed! why not simply "nurses"?) on the palm of his large hand (those hands) that same infant and the infant suddenly soils his hands, this is completely unnecessary and proves nothing. . . . It is ugliness for the sake of ugliness. . . .
>
> These constant repetitions—"hurriedly," "involuntarily," "involuntary," "alien," "alien," "nervously," "pudgy," "pudgy," and so on; "juicy mouth," "toothless mouth"—these frequent psychological scrutinies and unnecessary corporeal observations when we read aloud not only Tolstoy but the majority of our best authors—Turgenev, Pisemsky, Dostoevsky—are sometimes simply intolerable!

Leontiev, with what justice I do not know, thought that Russian writers and readers were more addicted to this vice of "nose-picking" than those of other countries:

> Suppose, for example, it is necessary to say that one of the male characters was frightened. An Englishman would more than likely say, without exaggerating one way or the other, either positively or negatively: "Intensely frightened, James stood motionless, etc." A Frenchman: "Alfred began to tremble. A deathly pallor covered his handsome face. He withdrew, but with dignity." The Russian writer would prefer to express himself thus: "My hero, like a blackguard, got cold feet and trudged off home." Perhaps even better: "dashed off home."

A first-rate critic, as distinct from a run-of-the-mill one, always shows respect for the author he is considering, even in attack. When his author does something he disapproves of, he tries to put himself in the author's place and asks, "What were his reasons for doing this?" So, after objecting to Tolstoy's tendency to "nose-pick," Leontiev is willing to concede that, much as he dislikes it, Tolstoy, given the nature of his readers, was probably justified:

> The Russian reader of our time (especially the reader who occupies a middle position in society) . . . [has been] educated . . . in such a way that a wart will make him believe more strongly in nobility, a snort will make him feel love more intensely, and so on; and if someone "with a nervous gesture pours out a glass of vodka" and then, instead of smiling, "smirks," his confidence will be complete! . . .
>
> Tolstoy . . . has rendered his readers a patriotic service by all this slight, external humiliation of life.

I hope very much that someone will soon publish an English translation of Leontiev's collected critical essays.

The New Yorker, 4 April 1970

Foreword to *The Sorrows of Young Werther* [and] *Novella*, by Johann Wolfgang von Goethe

So far as I know, Goethe was the first writer or artist to become a Public Celebrity. There had always been poets, painters and composers who were known to and revered by their fellow artists, but the general public, however much it may have admired their works, would not have dreamed of wishing to make their personal acquaintance. But, during the last twenty years or so of Goethe's life, a visit to Weimar and an audience with the Great Man was an essential item in the itinerary of any cultivated young man making his Grand Tour of Europe. His visitors in his old age were innumerable, but most of them had actually read only one book of his, written when he was twenty-four. What Goethe felt about this may be guessed from his first version of the Second Roman Elegy.

> Ask whom you will, I am safe from you now, you fair ladies and fine society gentlemen! "But did Werther really live? Did it all really happen like that? Which town has the right to boast of the lovely Lotte as its citizen?" Oh, how often I have cursed those foolish pages of mine which made my youthful sufferings public property! If Werther had been my brother and I had killed him, I could scarcely have been so persecuted by his avenging sorrowful ghost.

The biographers tell us that *Werther* was the product of Goethe's unhappy love for Charlotte Buff, but this is certainly an oversimplification. When writing a novel, an author naturally often makes use of his personal experiences, but a novel is not an autobiography. Goethe, for instance, did not, like his hero, commit suicide. Again, Goethe makes Werther an idle dilettante, who sketches a bit, reads a bit, but is incapable of seriously concentrating on anything. There is an element of self-portraiture in this: all his life, partly out of a temperamental impatience and partly because he was interested in so many things, he found it difficult to finish a work, but idleness was never one of his vices. When he wrote *Werther* he was probably in a disturbed state, for, a year after its publication, he wrote: "I am falling from one confusion into another." The novel seems to me to be one of those works of art in which the conscious and unconscious motives of the creator are at odds. Consciously, that is, Goethe approved of his hero, but his unconscious motive was therapeutic: by cultivating to the extreme, but only in words, the indulgence in subjective emotions typical of the *Sturm und Drang* movement, to get it out of his system and find his true poetic self, just as Byron, after *Childe Harold*, was able to put humorless gloom behind him and realize his true talent as a comic poet. Certainly, the admirers of *Werther* would have been bewildered by these lines written in Goethe's middle-age.

Vergebens werden ungebundne Geister
Nach der Vollendung reiner Höhe streben.
Wer Grosses will, muss sich zusarnmenraffen;
In der Beschränkung zeigt sich erst der Meister,
Und das Gesetz nur kann uns Freiheit geben.

(Unfettered spirits will aspire in vain to the pure heights of perfection. He who wills great things must gird up his loins; only in limitation is mastery revealed, and law alone can give us freedom.)

Living in the twentieth century, not the eighteenth, and knowing, as most of his contemporaries did not, Goethe's later work, *Werther* can still fascinate us, but in a very different way. To us it reads not as a tragic love story, but as a masterly and devastating portrait of a complete egoist, a spoiled brat, incapable of love because he cares for nobody and nothing but himself and having his way at whatever cost to others. The theme of the egoist who imagines himself to be a passionate lover evidently fascinated Goethe, for, thirty years later, he depicted a similar character in Edouard, the husband in *Elective Affinities.*

Had Goethe, from the bottom of his heart, really wanted his readers to admire Werther, why did he introduce the story of the servant who is in love with his widowed mistress? After nursing his love in secret for some time, he finally makes a pass at her, is surprised in the act by her brother and, of course, fired. Shortly afterwards, he shoots the servant who had taken his place, though he has no grounds whatsoever for supposing that the latter had succeeded where he had failed. Goethe not only introduces this character but also makes *Werther*, the future suicide, identify the murderer's situation with his own, thereby making it impossible for the reader to think of suicide as "noble. "Again, if Goethe really wished us to be Werther's partisan in the erotic triangular situation Werther-Lotte-Albert, one would have expected him to make Albert a coarse philistine to whom Lotte is unhappily married, but he does not. Albert is, to be sure, a "square" who does not appreciate Klopstock or Ossian, but he is presented as a good man, affectionate, hard-working, a good provider, and Lotte as a contented wife. Never once does she show any signs of wishing she had married Werther instead. She is very fond of him, but evidently thinks of him as a "brother" with whom she can have interesting conversations. Her weakness, which is in part responsible for the final catastrophe, is a dislike of admitting disagreeable facts: she keeps on hoping that Werther will get over his passion and become just a good friend, when she should have realized that this would never happen, and that the only sensible thing for her to do was to show him the door.

To escape from his own emotional confusion, Goethe became a civil servant at the court of Weimar, where he soon had important responsibilities. Similarly, in a moment of lucidity, aided by the good advice of his friend Wilhelm, Werther realizes that the only sensible thing for him to do is to give Lotte up, go away, and take a job, also, apparently, as some sort of civil servant. The society he now finds himself in is stuffy, snobbish, and conventional, but the Count, his boss, takes a great liking to him, and he seems all set for a successful career. Then a disagreeable but trivial incident occurs.

> [Count C.] had invited me for dinner at his house yesterday, on the very day when the whole aristocratic set, ladies and gentlemen, are accustomed to meet there late in the evening. I had completely forgotten this fact; and it also did not occur to me that subordinate officials like myself are not welcome on such occasions.

The "set" arrive and he senses that the atmosphere is chilly, but, instead of leaving, defiantly remains, is openly snubbed, and finally has to be asked by the Count to leave.

About this several things may be said. In the first place it is the professional duty of anyone in diplomacy or civil service not to forget the habits of the society in which he is living. Secondly, Werther is already well aware that the aristocratic set consider themselves superior to everyone else and, therefore, to himself, for he is not of aristocratic but bourgeois origins. Lastly, if a man thinks the social conventions of his time and place to be silly or wrong, there are two courses of behavior which will earn him an outsider's respect. Either he may keep his opinions to himself and observe the conventions with detached amusement, or he may deliberately break them for the pleasure of the shock he causes. He makes a scandal, but he enjoys it. Werther, by staying on when it is clear that his presence is unwelcome, defies the company, but his precious ego is hurt by their reactions, and he resigns from his post, returns to Lotte and disaster for all, destroying himself and ruining the lives of Lotte and Albert. What a horrid little monster!

Novella, published in 1828, four years before Goethe's death, is an excellent example of a literary genre, the idyll, at which German writers, more than those of any other language group, have always excelled. (I cannot think of a single English work which could be accurately classified as one.) It may be read as a postscript to one of his greatest masterpieces, the epic poem *Hermann und Dorothea*, published in 1798. Like the pastoral, the presupposition of the idyll is a harmonious relation between man and nature, desire and reason, but its descriptions of man and nature are much more realistic, less idealized, than those of the pastoral. An idyll, like a comedy, must end happily, but, unlike a comedy, it is always sober and serious.

In *Novella*, there are two significant locations, the town market and the old castle, and two types of human character, the huntsman and the trainer of wild animals. The market is an image for a good human society, peaceful, industrious, co-operative, prosperous.

> The Princc's father had lived long enough to see, and to put to good use, the day when it became clear that all the members of a state should spend their lives in the same industrious way; that everyone should work and produce according to his faculties, should first earn and then enjoy his living.

> There were mountain people, having come down from their quiet homes among rocks, firs and pines, and mixing with the plains people, who lived among hills, field and meadows; also tradespeople from small towns, and others who had assembled here. After having quietly surveyed the crowd, the Princess remarked to her companion how all these people, wherever they came from, used for their clothing more material than was necessary, more cloth and linen, more ribbon for trimming. "It seems to me that the women cannot pad themselves enough, nor the men puff themselves out enough to their satisfaction."
>
> "And we won't begrudge them that pleasure," said the old gentleman. "People are happy, happiest indeed, when they can spend their surplus money on dressing themselves up and decking themselves out."

The old castle, long a ruin and overwhelmed by the forest, is now being repaired, not, it seems, to make it rehabitable, but as a tourist sight. If I understand Goethe rightly, he is telling a parable about the relation between wild, that is to say untamed, nature and human craft, or *techne.* Man must respect Nature and not try to enslave her: on the other hand, Nature needs Man's help if she is to realize her full potentialities. The daemonic, destructive aspect of Nature is represented in the story by the fire which, for the second time, has broken out in the market and threatens to destroy it. It is to be noticed, however, that a fire in such a place is probably caused by human carelessness: it is not an "Act of God." Man can and should tame Fire, just as, if he will have the sensitivity and the patience, he can tame the lion and the tiger. All too often, however, he regards wild creatures as things to be killed and exploited for his own pleasure. Significantly, in describing the Prince's hunting expedition, Goethe uses a military metaphor.

> . . . the plan was to penetrate far into the mountains in order to harass the peaceful inhabitants of those forests by an unexpected invasion.

It is natural enough that the Princess should be scared when she sees the escaped tiger approaching and that Honorio should shoot it, though, as they are soon to learn, it would have done them no harm unless frightened. Honorio's second thoughts about his deed are more dubious.

> "Give it the finishing stroke!" cried the Princess. "I'm afraid the beast may still hurt you with its claws."
>
> "Excuse me, but it is already dead," the young man answered, "and I do not want to spoil its pelt which shall adorn your sledge next winter."

The same attitude is displayed by the castellan, who is annoyed that he cannot shoot the lion.

> "Why did I take my gun to town yesterday to have it cleaned! If I had had it handy, the lion would not have stood up again; the skin would be mine, and I would have bragged about it all my life, and justly so!"

The Prince, the Princess, Honorio are good people but they are in need of further education, of the lesson in reverence for Life which is given them by the humble family, man, wife and boy, to whom the tiger and the lion belonged. Because they are good people, they are willing to learn even from their social inferiors. It was a fine artistic stroke on Goethe's part to make the chief instructor the child, and let him deliver his message in song, not in prose.

The Sorrows of Young Werther [and] *Novella,* by Johann Wolfgang von Goethe, translated from the German by Elizabeth Mayer and Louise Bogan (1971)

Foreword to *Selected Poems,* by Joseph Brodsky

One demands two things of a poem. Firstly, it must be a well-made verbal object that does honor to the language in which it is written. Secondly, it must say something significant about a reality common to us all, but perceived from a unique perspective. What the poet says has never been said before, but, once he has said it, his readers recognize its validity for themselves.

A really accurate judgement upon a poem as a verbal object can, of course, only be made by persons who are masters of the same mother-tongue as its maker. Knowing no Russian and therefore forced to base my judgement on English translations, I can do little more than guess. My chief reason for believing that Professor Kline's translations do justice to their originals is that they convince me that Joseph Brodsky is an excellent craftsman. For example, in his long poem *Elegy for John Donne* the word *sleep* occurs, if I have counted rightly, fifty-two times. Such repetition might very easily have become irritating and affected: in fact, it is handled with consummate art.

Again, it is clear from these translations that Mr Brodsky commands many tones of voice, from the lyric (*A Christmas Ballad*) to the elegiac (*Verses on the Death of T. S. Eliot*) to the comic-grotesque (*Two Hours in an Empty Tank*), and can handle with equal ease a wide variety of rhythms and meters, short lines, long lines, iambics, anapaestics, masculine rhymes and feminine, as in *Adieu, Mademoiselle Véronique*:

> If I end my days in the shelter of dove-wings,
> which well may be, since war's meat-grinder
> is now the prerogative of small nations,
> since, after manifold combinations,
> Mars has moved closer to palms and cacti,
> and I myself wouldn't hurt a housefly . . .

About the uniqueness and, at the same time, universal relevance of a poet's vision, it is easier for a foreigner to judge, since this does not primarily depend upon the language in which it is written.

Mr Brodsky is not an easy poet, but even a cursory reading will reveal that, like Van Gogh and Virginia Woolf, he has an extraordinary capacity to envision material objects as sacramental signs, messengers from the unseen. Here are a few examples.

> But this house cannot stand its emptiness.
> The lock alone—it seems somehow ungallant—
> is slow to recognize the tenant's touch
> and offers brief resistance in the darkness.
>
> ("The tenant . . .")

The fire, as you can hear, is dying down.
The shadows in the corners have been shifting.
It's now too late to shake a fist at them
or yell at them to stop what they are doing.
("The fire . . .")

A hand that holds a pillow fast
is creeping down a polished bedpost,
making its way to a cloud breast
by this inept and tongue-tied gesture.
A sock, torn on a jagged rock,
twists in the dark; its curve is swan-like.
Its funnel mouth is all agog;
it stares up like a blackened fishnet.
("Enigma for an Angel")

Close your umbrella, as a rook would close
its wings. Its handle-tail reveals the capon.
("Einem alten Architekten in Rom")

It's not quite spring, but something like it.
The world is scattered now, and crooked.
The ragged villages are limping.
There's straightness only in bored glances.
("Spring Season of Muddy Roads")

Unlike the work of some of his contemporaries, Mr Brodsky's seems to stand outside what might be called the Mayakovsky tradition of "public" poetry. It never uses a fortissimo. Indeed, original as he is, I would be inclined to classify Mr Brodsky as a traditionalist. To begin with, he shows a deep respect and love for the past of his native land.

The dogs, moved by old memory, still lift
their hindlegs at a once familiar spot.
The church's walls have long since been torn down,
but these dogs see the church walls in their dreams . . .

For them the church still stands; they see it plain.
And what to people is a patent fact
leaves them entirely cold. This quality
is sometimes called "a dog's fidelity".
And, if I were to speak in earnest of
the "relay race of human history",
I'd swear by nothing but this relay race—
this race of all the generations who
have sniffed, and who will sniff, the ancient smells.
("A Halt in the Desert")

He is also a traditionalist in the sense that he is interested in what most lyric poets in all ages have been interested in, that is, in personal encounters with nature, human artifacts, persons loved or revered, and in reflections upon the human condition, death, and the meaning of existence.

His poems are a-political, perhaps defiantly so, which may explain why he has, so far, failed to win official approval, for I can find nothing in them which the sternest censor could call "subversive" or "immoral". The only lines which could conceivably be called "political" are these:

> Adieu to the prophet who said, "Forsooth,
> you've nothing to lose but your chains." In truth
> there's conscience as well—if it comes to that.
>
> ("A Letter in a Bottle")

a sentiment with which, surely, any good Marxist would agree. As for his artistic credo, no poet would quarrel with

> It seems that what art strives for is to be
> precise and not to tell us lies, because
> its fundamental law undoubtedly
> asserts the independence of details.
>
> ("The Candlestick")

After reading Professor Kline's translations, I have no hesitation in declaring that, in Russian, Joseph Brodsky must be a poet of the first order, a man of whom his country should be proud. I am most grateful to them both.

The New York Review of Books, 5 April 1973; Joseph Brodsky, *Selected Poems*, translated and introduced by George L. Kline (1973); written 1970

Lame Shadows

Tonio Kröger and Other Stories. By Thomas Mann, translated by David Luke. Bantam. $1.25.

Anyone who offers a fresh translation of a prose work—poetry is another matter—is in duty bound to justify his undertaking by explaining why he thinks that earlier versions are unsatisfactory, a task which can only be congenial to the malicious. Dr Luke has felt, quite rightly, obliged to cite some of the errors made by Mrs Lowe-Porter, and anybody who knows German will agree with him that many of these are serious. But he does so with obvious reluctance and concludes by paying her a just tribute.

> Her task, as the exclusive translator of [Mann's] entire work, was, of course, Herculean, and her mistakes were probably as much due to

> understandable haste as to an inadequate knowledge of German. Her achievement deserves credit for its sheer volume, and it would be churlish to deny that her renderings are often by no means infelicitous. My own method in retranslating these six stories was to avoid consulting the existing versions of them until I had at least decided on my first draft for a given sentence or paragraph. The corresponding passage in Mrs Lowe-Porter would then occasionally suggest second thoughts.

Dr Luke had already demonstrated his extraordinary gifts as a translator in his versions of three *Novellen* by Adalbert Stifter, an author who is probably more difficult to "english" than Thomas Mann. Of his latest offering, I can only say that I cannot imagine anybody thinking the job must be done a third time. His brilliant Introduction, too, puts a reviewer in an awkward spot: what on earth is he to say about these six stories which Dr Luke has not already said better?

Five of them are variations on the same theme, the incompatibility of "Life," that is to say, unreflective vitality, innocence, happiness, a "normal" existence, with alienating self-consciousness. The sixth, "*Gladius Dei*," deals with the difference between healthy and decadent art.

In all of them, the chief character feels himself, with a mixture of pride and shame, to be an Outsider. In "The Joker" and "Tristan," he is a contemptible dilettante who imagines that a refined sensibility gives him the right to think of himself as "artistic," though he never gets down to fabricating a satisfactory art object. Before "Tonio Kröger" ends, however, its hero has justified his claim by producing good work. In the farcical and cruel "The Road to the Churchyard," he is simply a drunken failure, in "Little Herr Friedemann," the first written of the stories, a cripple.

This story does not, in my opinion, quite come off. Mann seems to be using the feeling of isolation felt by a cripple as a symbol for that felt by an artist. But cripples and artists both exist in the world and their reasons for feeling isolated are quite different. The cripple's physical deformity is a visible fact, patent to all. He knows this, and is therefore absolutely certain that he can never hope to win the love of a young, beautiful, and "normal" girl. At the age of sixteen, Herr Friedemann, after watching a flirtation between two of his contemporaries, realizes this:

> "Very well," he said to himself, "that is over. I will never again concern myself with such things. To the others they mean joy and happiness, but to me they can only bring grief and suffering. I am done with it all. It is finished for me. Never again."

That he should fail to keep his resolution and fall madly in love with Frau von Rinnlingen is not surprising, but I find it incredible that he should have openly declared his passion. What could he possibly have expected to happen except what did happen—to be rejected with scorn and laughter? An artist's problems, on the other hand, are private to himself unless he chooses to disclose them. He may be, for example, by temperament incapable of falling in love or of fidelity, but if he does fall in love and is reasonably personable to look at, he stands a perfectly good chance of marrying the girl he loves: and a number have.

If I call these stories "dated," I do not mean that they are out-of-date, only that, like most works of art, they could only have been produced at a particular period in social and cultural history. The notion of the alienated artist is a phenomenon of the second half of the nineteenth century. In earlier times we do not find it and, in our own, alienation has become almost a universal problem. The causes for it were, I think, three. Firstly, after the disappearance of patronage, artists ceased to have a professional social status. Individual artists might become famous public figures but, collectively, they ceased to have status in the way that doctors, lawyers, businessmen, farmers, etc., have, whether famous or obscure, successful or unsuccessful.

Secondly, European society in the nineteenth century and, indeed, until the First World War, was still a class-stratified society, in which almost everybody was born into an identifiable "station" and would spend his life in it. (It is to be noticed what a pride Mann's heroes take in their upper bourgeois background, and their feelings of guilt at having chosen "art" instead of going into Father's business.) The artist, that is to say, was a special case. Earlier, this had not been so. In an oral culture, a poet has a social importance irrespective of the aesthetic merit of his work, as the man who makes immortal the great deeds of the past: in a polytheistic culture, as the recounter of its myths, he is a theologian as well as an artist. Then, in any society where the rich and powerful, whether out of genuine love of the arts or because they think it enhances their prestige, include artists in their retinue, the latter have the status of an Upper Servant. Haydn wore the Esterhazy livery.

Lastly, until the Industrial Revolution, writers, composers, and painters were not the only kinds of artists. Cobblers, blacksmiths, carpenters, etc., were equally craftsmen, concerned in giving the objects they made a gratuitous aesthetic value as well as a necessary utility value. In such a society, therefore, it was taken for granted, even by those who never read a book or looked at a picture or listened to music, that beauty was as valuable as utility. But, by the end of the nineteenth century, machine production had reduced most worker-craftsmen to the status of laborers, whose only interest in their labor was as a means of earning their livelihood, and beauty came more and more to be regarded as a social luxury, making both the creators of beautiful things and their specialized public objects of social suspicion.

When a man finds himself a social oddity, he is very apt to alternate between feelings of guilt—there must be something wrong with me—and megalomania—the fact that I am an oddity proves that I am superior to the average mass. Polar opposites as in appearance they look, the two literary doctrines of Naturalism and Art-for-Art's-Sake, as propounded by Zola and Mallarmé, are really both expressions of the same megalomania. The aesthete is, at least, frank about this. He says: "Art is the only true religion. Life has no value except as material for a beautiful artistic structure. The artist is the only authentic human being: all the rest, rich and poor alike, are *canaille*."

The naturalist is more disingenuous. Officially, he says: "Down with all art that prettifies life. Let us describe human life and nature as they really are." But his picture of life "as it really is" is a picture of human beings as animals, enslaved to necessity, who can only manifest behavior and are incapable of personal choice or deeds. But if human beings are really as the naturalist describes them, then they cannot be loved or admired. Who can be? Only the naturalist himself for his accurate clinical observations. Like all kinds of behaviorists, he does not apply his dogmas to himself. He does not say: "My books are examples of behavior, conditioned by blind reflexes." The hidden link between the naturalist and the aesthete is revealed by the total absence in both of any sense of humor.

Aestheticism, as Mann saw very clearly, has an even more pernicious effect upon art lovers than upon the artists themselves. The latter must, at least, work hard in order to win their own self-respect, but their public is passive and does nothing, yet feels itself superior to the Philistines. The nineteenth-century respectable bourgeoisie imagined that a "moral" novel meant one in which the good were rewarded for their virtues by coming into money and a happy marriage, while the bad were punished for their vices by ending in penury and disgrace. This was silly of them, but they were nearer the truth than the aesthetes who, in reaction, denied any relation between art and morality. In "*Gladius Dei*," Mann describes a decadent picture:

> It was a Madonna, painted in a wholly modern and entirely unconventional manner. The sacred figure was ravishingly feminine, naked and beautiful. Her great sultry eyes were rimmed with shadow, and her lips were half-parted in a strange and delicate smile. Her slender fingers were grouped rather nervously and convulsively round the waist of the Child, a nude boy of aristocratic, almost archaic slimness, who was playing with her breasts and simultaneously casting a knowing sidelong glance at the spectator.

Now it is possible to argue that pornography has a legitimate social function, but only on condition that it claims to do nothing except act as a sexual stimulus. If, as in this case, it claims to be not only a work of art but also a religious work of art, then Hieronymus is right: it should be burnt.

In his treatment of the self-conscious sensitive artist vis-à-vis "the bright children of life, the happy, the charming and the ordinary," Mann's irony and humor reveal that, however much he may have been influenced by

Nietzsche, he took him with a grain of salt. As an analyst of Pride, the primal sin of self-consciousness, Nietzsche is the greatest of all psychologists, but he should have accepted it as an unchangeable factor in the human condition. His Super-Man, who combines the self-consciousness of a man with the self-assurance of an animal, is a chimera.

In these stories Mann describes very convincingly the nostalgia felt by his "sensitive" characters for the "normal," but he makes it clear that their conception of the "normal" is subjective and not objective. In clarifying this, he amusingly makes use of an autobiographical fact: he was born with dark hair in Northern Germany where blond hair is the norm. So Tonio (and, incidentally, Spinell in "Tristan") is dark-haired and dark-complexioned. Now, it is natural enough for a person to be attracted by his physically opposite type, as Tonio is by Hans, but if he identifies physical appearance with character traits, he is clearly indulging in a private fantasy. Nobody, for instance, could possibly contend that only fair-haired people are athletes, only dark-haired ones writers. Mann never lets us know what Hans or Ingeborg think of themselves, only what Tonio thinks about them.

Toward the end of the story the following sentence is italicized: *Hans Hansen and Ingeborg Holm walked through the dining-room.* By this device, Mann informs the reader that the sentence is, in fact, untrue: they are not Hans and Ingeborg, but another couple belonging to the same type. It was as types not as persons that Tonio had admired them. To make sure that the reader gets the point, Mann gives us Tonio's verdict on Italy. It is well-known that artists and intellectuals from Northern Europe have often fallen in love with Mediterranean countries, finding them, in contrast to their own, the home of unreflecting happiness and vitality. Not so Tonio:

> All that *bellezza* gets on my nerves. And I can't stand all that dreadful southern vitality, all those people with their black animal eyes. They've no conscience in their eyes, these Latin races.

Though Tonio Kröger is the only representative of the aesthetic in these stories whom one can respect, he is not the most interesting to read about: he talks far too much. Of them all, the one I like best is "Tristan." The title is clearly ironic. Anybody who is familiar with Wagner's opera will recognize at once that Spinell is not Tristan but Melot, the malevolent troublemaker, in disguise. He will also relish the contrast between the aged, melancholic, probably impotent figure of King Mark, and the exuberant, gourmandising Philistine to whom Frau Klöterjahn is married.

My, how times have changed since these stories were written! Less than seventy years ago, it was still possible to raise the question: Is a love for race-horses more "normal," more *echt* than a love for poetry? Today the question would be: Are these different loves the truthful manifestation of personal taste and choice, or have they been assumed in order to be popular in the social circle in which the individual happens to move? (Personal choice and taste do not, of course, exclude learning from other persons: they do exclude group influence.) In all technologically "advanced" countries, fashion has replaced tradition, so that involuntary membership in a society can no longer provide a feeling of community. (The family, perhaps, can still provide it, but families are temporary societies which dissolve when the children grow up.)

In consequence, the word "normal" has ceased to have any meaning. Community still means what it always has, a group of persons united by a love of something other than themselves, be it racehorses or poetry, but today such a love has to be discovered by each person for himself; it cannot be acquired socially. Society can only teach conformity to the momentary fashion, either of the majority or of its mirror-image, the rebellious minority. To belong to either is to be a member, not of a community, but of a "public" in the Kierkegaardian sense. Today, all visible and therefore social signs of agreement are suspect. What a pleasant surprise it would be to meet a crew-cut hippie or a company director with hair down to his shoulders.

The New York Review of Books, 3 September 1970

Robert to the Rescue

The Letters of Robert Browning and Elizabeth Barrett Barrett, 1845–1846. Edited by Elvan Kintner. Belknap Press of Harvard University Press. $30.

Beginning on Friday, January 10, 1845, and ending on Friday, September 18, 1846, R. B. and E. B. B. between them wrote five hundred and seventy-three letters, which in the two-volume edition of *The Letters of Robert Browning and Elizabeth Barrett Barrett, 1845–1846* take up a thousand and eighty-seven pages. I can think of no more striking example, firstly, of the extraordinary energy of the Victorians, and, secondly, of their sense of having plenty of time for everything. In this century, it is impossible to imagine two lovers in the same circumstances writing a third as much. It was the duty of Mr Elvan Kintner, as their editor, to read every single word, and it must be said at once that he has done a magnificent job, which could not be improved on. The annotation is particularly admirable. This, says Mr Kintner,

> undertakes not only to identify people, places, and literary allusions, but to furnish bits of biography, quotations from newspapers and periodicals, cross-references between letters, and even exegesis at a point or two where Browning's prose gets confusing.

As for the text of the letters themselves, he has attempted something more than exactness:

> The holograph letters are full of variant readings, alterations, and cancellations, some of them dramatically decisive, others still legible. Some of these are directly alluded to in the text itself; others provide a reading in depth that clarifies the meaning or the tone or both of a sentence or a letter.

Lastly, his introduction is pleasantly modest in length but gives all the relevant historical facts. I have only one question. Mr Kintner says that at the time "the line between upper middle class and gentry was blurring," which seems to suggest that he thinks that Browning was born into the upper-middle class. Had he not been a poet—the social status of a writer or artist is always something special—I would have said that by birth he belonged to the middle-middle or even lower-middle class. In England, when I was a boy, neither a businessman (someone "in trade," as we said) nor a dissenter was considered *quite* respectable.

Well, for our profit, Mr Kintner has read every word of these letters, but I cannot see any other human being doing the same. The vocabulary of love and endearment, like that of sex, is very limited. To the lovers themselves, there is no such thing as repetition; pledges of undying affection, benedictions, and so on cannot be renewed too often. For the detached outsider, it is otherwise. Luckily for the detached outsider, however, the actual story of Browning's courtship of E. B. B. and their elopement is so extraordinary, so dramatic, even melodramatic, that their correspondence remains the most interesting collection of love letters ever published. Furthermore, their mutual affection aside, both parties are intelligent, well read, highly articulate persons with whom one is glad to become acquainted. Readers of Browning's poetry know how fascinated he was by the grotesque in Nature. Take these lines from "The Englishman in Italy":

> . . . our fisher arrive,
> And pitch down his basket before us,
> All trembling alive
> With pink and grey jellies, your sea-fruit;
> You touch the strange lumps,
> And mouths gape there, eyes open, all manner
> Of horns and of humps,
> Which only the fisher looks grave at,
> While round him like imps
> Cling screaming the children as naked
> And brown as his shrimps.

Every now and again in the prose of his letters one encounters the same kind of vision. For instance:

> What a fine fellow our English water-eft is: "Triton paludis Linnaei"—*e come guizza* (*that* you can't say in another language; cannot preserve the little in-and-out motion along with the straightforwardness!)—I always loved all those creatures God "*sets up for themselves*" so independently of us, so successfully, with their strange happy minute inch of a candle, as it were, to light them; while we run about and against each other with our great cressets and fire-pots.

As for her letters, it is a pleasant surprise to discover what one would never have guessed from her poems: that she possessed a sense of humor. Here is her description of the young men who courted her sister Henrietta:

> Two years ago, three men were loving her, as they called it. After a few months, & the proper quantity of interpretations, one of them consoled himself by giving nic-names to his rivals. Perseverance & Despair he called them . . . & so, went up into the boxes to see out the rest of the play. Despair ran to a crisis, was rejected in so many words, but appealed against the judgement & had his claim admitted—it was all silence & mildness on each side . . a tacit gaining of ground,—Despair "was at least a gentleman," said my brothers. On which Perseverance came on with violent reiterations . . insisted that she loved him without knowing it, or *should* . . elbowed poor Despair into the open streets . . who being a gentleman wouldn't elbow again—swore that "if she married another he would wait till she become a widow, trusting to Providence". . did wait every morning till the head of the house was out, & sate day by day, in spite of the disinclination of my sisters & the rudeness of all my brothers, four hours in the drawing-room . . let himself be refused once a week and sate all the longer . . allowed everybody in the house (& a few visitors) to see & hear him in fits of hysterical sobbing, & sate on unabashed, the end being that he sits now sole regnant, my poor sister saying softly, with a few tears of remorse for her own instability, that she is "taken by storm & cannot help it."

There are other surprises, at least for me. Though I had heard that Elizabeth took some drug, I did not know that this was a mixture of morphine and ether, and the chief item in her household expenses. The later portraits and caricatures of Browning make him look like a man who had never known a day's illness in his life. It turns out that as a young man he was a martyr to nervous morning headaches, and E. B.'s letters to him are almost as full of anxious inquiries and suggested remedies—he should drink wine and put his feet in hot water at night—as his to her. More extraordinary still, after they have decided to get married, Browning writes that he will have to have a separate room because "I could never brush my hair and wash my face, I do think, before my own father: I could not, I am sure, take off my coat before you *now*—why should I ever?"

Since the final outcome of the drama was so completely dependent upon either their discretion or their ignorance, the characters of the supporting cast are perhaps more interesting than those of the protagonists. Firstly, of course, Papa. "Assuredly, Mr Barrett was no monster," says Mr Kintner, and one should never forget that, though a slave owner, he petitioned for Emancipation. (What a curious coincidence it was that both the Brownings and the Barretts should have come from slave-owning families.) At the same time, however, his behavior to his children can only be described as monstrous. Elizabeth was, it seems, his favorite child, and she probably understood his character better than his other children. In her opinion, his basic mistake was one of the intellect rather than the heart—a total misconception, due to a misreading of the Scriptures, as to the rights and duties of a parent. Whatever the cause, the effect on his relations with his children was disastrous, both for them and for him:

> After using one's children as one's chattels for a time, the children drop lower & lower toward the level of chattels, & the duties of human sympathy to them become difficult in proportion. And (it seems strange to say it, yet it is true) *love*, he does not conceive of at all. He has feeling . . he can be moved deeply . . he is capable of affection in a peculiar way—but *that*, he does not understand, any more than he understands Chaldee, respecting it less of course.

In consequence, his family refused him their confidence, would tell him nothing of what they were doing, feeling, and thinking:

> He isolates himself—& now and again he feels it—the cold dead silence all round, which is the effect of an incredible system. If he were not stronger than most men, he could not bear it as he does.

It has always seemed to me most extraordinary that, given both his revulsion at the idea of his children's marrying and his knowledge that Browning was a frequent visitor, he should never have suspected that the relation between him and his daughter was anything more than a literary friendship. The reason, presumably, was that which she gave—his inability to conceive of sexual love. And, of course, if he had no suspicions, nobody else was going to arouse them:

> Let there be ever so many suspectors, there will be no informers . . I suspect the suspectors, but the informers are out of the world, I am very sure:—and then, the one person, by a curious anomaly, *never* draws an

> inference of this order, until the bare blade of it is thrust palpably into his hand, point outwards.

Yet, as Elizabeth realized, had he been a kinder, more demonstrative father, she might never have got married:

> For me, he might have been king & father over me *to* the end if he had thought it worth while to love me openly enough—yet, even so, he would not have let you come too near. And you could not have come too near—for he would have had my confidence from the beginning, & no opportunity would have been permitted to you of proving your affection for me, and I should have thought always what I thought at first.

Then there is the enigmatic figure of Mr Kenyon. To what extent was he conscious of playing the role of Cupid? It was he, a close friend and admirer of both Robert and Elizabeth, who suggested to the former that he enter into a correspondence. Also, as a frequent visitor at Wimpole Street, he was in a position to observe any changes in Elizabeth's manner when Robert's name came up. She records how he sometimes scared her by looking at her through his big spectacles and making such remarks as "But I don't see why I should ask you, when I ought to know him better than you can" and "Now that his book is done, I suppose Mr Browning will come without excuses." It seems probable that he guessed what was happening but preferred not to know for certain. Robert wanted to tell him outright, but Elizabeth advised against it—rightly, I think:

> I know perfectly that either he would be unhappy himself, or he would make us so. He never could bear the sense of responsibility. Then, as he told me today, and as long ago I knew . . he's "irresolute," timid in deciding. Then he shrinks before the daemon of the World—and "What may be said" is louder to him than thunder.

Knowing, too, that, when they did get married, anyone who seemed to have had foreknowledge would be cast by her father into outer darkness, she was anxious to keep the number as small as possible. Her sisters had to know, but neither her brothers nor Robert's parents. She did confide in Mr Gould, her former Greek teacher, who had long been blind. An old servant of her grandparents, Trippy, a real Creole mammy, who disapproved of Emancipation and dined at Wimpole Street every Sunday, had guessed, and so, of course, had her personal maid, Elizabeth Wilson. Trippy was too old and too privileged to suffer, but Wilson would certainly be put into the street without a character, so Elizabeth was determined to take her with them to Italy.

Then, of course, there was Flush, her spaniel and the subject of one of her best poems. As she once wrote to Robert, "I am your Flush and he is mine." Flush obeyed her every wish and nobody else's:

> You would laugh to see me at my dinner . . Flush & me—Flush placing in me such an heroic confidence, that . . after he has cast one discriminating glance on the plate, &, in the case of "chicken," wagged his tail with an emphasis . . he goes off to the sofa, shuts his eyes & allows a full quarter of an hour to pass before he returns to take his share. Did you ever hear of a dog before who did not persecute one with beseeching eyes at mealtimes? And remember, this is not the effect of *discipline.* Also if another than myself happens to take coffee or break bread in the room here, he teazes straightway with eyes & paws . . teazes like a common dog & is put out of the door before he can be quieted by scolding.

Flush, it would seem, was jealous of any rival for her affections, for on July 8, 1846, he bit Robert. According to Elizabeth, Flush repented and forgave, since, when, a little while later, she asked, as she had often done before, "Do you love him?," he wagged his tail for the first time.

Though endearments in themselves are not very interesting, in a correspondence such as this the way in which the writers sign their letters is a revealing indication of the stage of intimacy and trust at which they have arrived. Thus, on January 11, 1845, when answering Robert's first letter, Elizabeth signs herself "Your obliged and faithful Elizabeth B. Barrett." By May 17th, this has become "Ever yours, E. B. B." On May 20th, Robert paid his first visit, and immediately wrote a letter proposing marriage, which she answered:

> You have said some intemperate things . . . fancies, which you will not say over again, nor unsay, but *forget at once, & for ever, having said at all*—& which will die out between *you & me alone,* like a misprint between you and the printer. . . . Your friend in grateful regard.

Only ten days later, this has become "Ever yours, my dear friend"; by July 21st, "May God bless you my dear friend, my ever dear friend!" Her letter of September 16th is simply signed "E. B. B.," possibly because she did not want Robert to overoptimistically misconstrue what she says in it:

> . . . if I were different in some respects and free in others by the providence of God, I would accept . . . the great trust of your happiness . . . & give away my own life and soul to that end. I *would* do it . . *not, I do* . . observe!

By September 26th, she has almost capitulated:

> If He [God] should free me within a moderate time from the trailing chain of my weakness, I will then be to you whatever at that hour you shall choose—whether friend or more than friend

and she finishes with "May God bless you on this [day] & on those that come after, my dearest friend." In her own family, she was known by the nickname Ba, and on December 24th she so signs herself for the first time. Rather oddly, it was not until July 2, 1846, that she first dared to address him as Robert.

Exactly how serious Robert's intentions were when he made his first proposal we shall never know. Elizabeth, certainly and very naturally, thought they were not. For some years, she had been an invalid who had to be carried up and down stairs, there was no objective reason to suppose that her health would improve, and unless it did a marriage would have been out of the question. Miraculously, though, she slowly got better. On January 18, 1846, she was able to write:

> Now, shall I tell you what I did yesterday. It was so warm, so warm the thermometer at 68 in this room, that I took it into my head to call it April instead of January, & put on a cloak & walked down stairs into the drawing room—walked, mind! . . . It was a feat worthy of the day—& I surprised them all as much as if I had walked out of the window instead.

On May 11th, while driving in Regent's Park:

> I wished so much to walk through a half-open gate along a shaded path, that we stopped the carriage & got out & walked, & I put both my feet on the grass . . which was the strangest feeling! . . & gathered this laburnum for you. It hung quite high up on the tree, the little blossom did, and Arabel said that certainly I could not reach it—but you see!

On May 28th, she went out and mailed a letter for the first time, and on June 7th wrote her first letter downstairs in the drawing room. From then on, her excursions and visits become frequent. Mr Kenyon takes her to see the new Great Western locomotive, which terrifies her. With Mrs Jameson, she visits Samuel Rogers' house and is overwhelmed by her first sight of the great Italian painters. Then, on September 5th, she does something which, even for a Victorian spinster in perfect health, would have been considered very daring. On September 1st, Flush had been stolen by a gang of dog thieves, who were holding him to ransom. She now actually goes herself to find the leader of the gang:

> I went . . . with Wilson in the cab. We got into obscure streets,—& our cabman stopped at a public house to ask his way. Out came two or three men . . "Oh, you want to find Mr Taylor, I dare say"! (mark that no name had been mentioned!) & instantly an unsolicited philanthropist ran before us to the house, & out again to tell me that the great man "wasn't at home!—but wouldn't I get out?" Wilson, in an aside of terror, entreated me not to think of such a thing—she believed devoutly in the robbing

> & murdering, & was not reassured by the gang of benevolent men & boys who "lived but to oblige us" all round the cab—"Then wouldn't I see Mrs Taylor," suggested the philanthropist:—and, notwithstanding my negatives, he had run back again and brought an immense feminine bandit . . . fat enough to have had an easy conscience all her life . . who informed me that "her husband might be in in a few minutes, or in so many hours—wouldn't I like to get out & wait" (Wilson pulling at my gown) (the philanthropist echoing the invitation of the feminine Taylor.)—"No, I thanked them all—it was not necessary that I should get out, but it was, that Mr Taylor should keep his promise about the restoration of a dog he had agreed to restore."

The letters written during the last two and a half months of their engagement are exciting reading. In 1845, Elizabeth had nearly gone to Italy herself, but the plan fell through at the last minute. Next year, there was talk in the family of her making the trip, and a close friend, Mrs Jameson, had offered to take her. What *could* she say? She knew Mrs Jameson was to be trusted, but she did not want to burden her with the truth:

> "But *you*! Have you given up going to Italy—?" I said "no, & that I had not certainly"—I said "I felt deeply how her great kindness demanded every sort of frankness & openness from me towards her,—and yet, that at the moment I could not be frank—there were reasons which prevented it . . Would she promise not to renew the subject to Mr Kenyon? not to repeat to him what I said?—& to wait until the whole should be explained to herself?"

On June 28th, Elizabeth copied out passages from travel books about Italy, and she and Robert started discussing where they should settle. Their first idea was La Cava, a town between Naples and Salerno, described as "enchantingly beautiful, very good air & no English." Other possibles were Vietri and Amalfi. Then she learned from an acquaintance that "La Cava is impossible for the winter owing to the damp and cold. At no season should any person remain out at the hour of sunset. . . . Salerno has bad air too near it, to be safe as a residence. Besides, it is totally without the resources of books, good food, or medical advice." Robert thought that the "bad air" was probably an Italian superstition but that it would be better to take no risks. Finally, they decided on Pisa, though somewhat worried about newspaper reports of earthquakes. It is interesting to note that Florence, where they were in the end to make their home, was at this time firmly rejected:

> As for the travelling English, they are horrible, and at Florence, unbearable . . their voices in your ear at every turn . . and such voices!—I got to very nearly hate the Tribune for their sakes.

In addition to where to go, there was the question of how to travel. Would it be less of a strain on her if they went all the way by sea, or crossed over to France and made their way overland? They finally decided on the second alternative. Then there was the embarrassing question, at least for Robert, of Elizabeth's private income of some four hundred pounds a year. Robert had not yet reached the point of earning his living through his writings, and had hitherto depended on an allowance from his father. (On the marriage certificate he describes himself not as Poet or Author but as Gentleman.) Elizabeth drew up the following provisional will:

> In compliance with the request of Robert Browning, who may possibly become my husband, that I would express in writing my wishes respecting the ultimate disposal of whatever property I possess at this time, whether in the funds or elsewhere . . . I here declare my wishes to be . . that he, Robert Browning . . . having, of course, as it is his right to do, first held & used the property in question for the term of his natural life . . . should bequeath the same, by an equal division, to my two sisters, or, in the case of the previous death of either or both of them, to such of my surviving brothers as most shall need it by the judgement of my eldest surviving brother.

At the last minute, two crises occurred. On September 1st, Flush was kidnapped; on September 9th, a Wednesday, Papa announced that the family would be moving to the country, possibly on the next Monday, to stay while the town house was repainted. If this happened, they would have to wait a year, since it would be too dangerous for Elizabeth to travel during the winter. On the Friday, therefore, Robert paid his last visit; on the Saturday, they were married in St Marylebone Church, the two witnesses being a cousin of Robert's, James Silverthorne, and Elizabeth's maid, Wilson. After the ceremony, Elizabeth sent Wilson home and went herself to the house of Mr Boyd, where

> I was made to talk & take Cyprus wine,—& my sisters delaying to come, I had some bread and butter for dinner, to keep me from looking too pale in their eyes—At last they came, & with such grave faces! Missing me & Wilson, they had taken fright,—& Arabel had forgotten at first what I told her last night about the fly. I kept saying, "What nonsense . . . what fancies you do have to be sure" . . trembling in my heart with every look they cast at me. And so, to complete the bravery, I went on with them in the carriage to Hampstead . . as far as the heath,—& talked & looked.

Actually, matters were not quite as urgent as they had feared; they did not leave for a week, and had time to discuss how their calling card was to read. Robert thought:

"Mr & Mrs R. B." on *one* card—with the usual "at home" in a corner. How shall we manage *that* by the way? Could we put "In Italy for a year"?

Elizabeth disagreed:

You must not think of putting any "At *home*" anywhere, or any other thing in the place of it. . . . Put simply the names, as you say, on one card, only without abbreviation or initial, & no intimation of address, which is not necessary, & would be under our circumstances quite wrong.

In the postscript to her last letter, she pays tribute to her maid and, indirectly, to herself:

The boxes are *safely sent*. Wilson has been perfect to me—and *I*. . calling her "timid," & afraid of her timidity!—I begin to think that none are so bold as the timid, when they are fairly roused.

They did not actually get to Pisa until October 15th. In the following April, they moved to Florence, and lived happily for an "ever after" that was to last fifteen years.

To read about these two as human beings is as exciting as it ever was, but our judgment of them as poets has changed. When they met, Elizabeth was a well-known and much admired poet—Poe dedicated *The Raven and Other Poems* to her—while Robert's work was known only to a few. Today, one hundred and twenty-five years later, Browning is rightly ranked with Tennyson as one of the two great Victorian poets, while she is read only by literary historians. I am afraid that George Saintsbury's verdict is just. "Her ear for rhyme," he says, "was probably the worst on record in the case of a person having any poetic power whatever," and cites in evidence

From my brain the soul-wings budded, waved a flame about my body,
  Whence conventions coiled to ashes. I felt self-drawn out, as man,
From amalgamate false natures, and I saw the skies go ruddy
  With the deepening feet of angels, and I knew what spirits can.

On which he comments:

Now only conceive anyone who had just used "budded" suggesting the pronunciation "buddy" for "body" at a few words' distance! These things are horrible and heartrending. They make the process of reading Mrs Browning something like that of eating with a raging tooth—a process of alternate expectation and agony. Nor is the diction much better than the rhyme. This, in some ways, certainly, elect lady appears to have been congenitally destitute of all power of mental association; and you turn not many pages from the "ruddy buddy budding with soul-wings" before you come to a "*confluent* kiss"!

True, I say. But what proportion of her total output have I read? A third? Now that I have read these letters, the first thing I shall do is tackle *Aurora Leigh*.

The New Yorker, 12 September 1970

Portrait with a Wart or Two

Belloc: A Biographical Anthology. Edited by Herbert van Thal. Knopf. $8.95.

If one is interested in an author, one cannot help asking oneself: "Suppose I had to make an anthology from his works, what would I select?" This means, of course, that one will be unfairly prejudiced against any selection which differs from one's own. In the case of a poet, though different readers may have different preferences, their principle of selection will, I think, be the same: they will try to select what, in their opinion, are his best poems, those, that is, which seem most likely to survive the test of time. Thus, I cannot imagine anyone, when making a selection from Wordsworth, including the sonnet "Spade with which Wilkinson has tilled his lands," on the grounds that, bad though it is, only Wordsworth could have written it.

But in the case of a man like Belloc, who wrote not only "pure" literature but was also a prolific journalist, a highly polemical writer about history, politics, public affairs, the problem of selection is much more difficult, because one cannot separate the artistic fabricator from the propagandist, the literary man-of-action. In the case of the former, his personality, his foibles, are, or should be, of no concern to the public; in the case of the latter, they are important and significant.

About Belloc the artist, all readers, whatever their religious and political convictions, will agree on two points. Firstly, he is, like Swift, one of the great masters of straightforward English prose. Even when I find *what* he is saying wrongheaded or absurd, I have to admire *how* he says it, his clarity, vigor, and elegance; and whenever his subject is one to which dogmas are irrelevant, as when he is describing his experiences as a French conscript, or his adventures among savage mountains and on stormy seas, or his visits to little known cities, I am completely enchanted. Secondly, as a writer of Light Verse, he has few equals and no superiors. (His "serious" poems, like the Sonnets, seem to me *bien fait*, but without original vision, an imitation of poetry-in-general.)

Since I, personally, am interested in Belloc the literary artist, not in Belloc the polemicist, my own anthology would consist almost entirely of passages from *Hills and the Sea, The Path to Rome, The Cruise of the Nona, Many Cities,*

Cautionary Tales, *Peers*, and *More Peers*. I would also certainly include, and here I am most grateful to Mr van Thal for reprinting it, since I had never read it before, his magnificent Taylorian lecture, *On Translation*, from which I cannot resist quoting a brief sample.

> If you come across the French word "*constater*," which in point of fact you do in nearly all official documents with which you may have to deal, you must always replace it by a full English sentence, even so ample as, "We note without further comment," or "We note for purposes of future reference," or in another connection, "We desire to put on record." In the same way there are whole French phrases which should justly be put into a shorter form in English. Take such a sentence as this, "*Il y avait dans cet homme je ne sais quoi de suffisance.*" The right translation of this would not be: "There is in this man I know not what of self-sufficiency"; the right translation is rather, more briefly, "There was a touch of self-complacency about him."

I realize, however, that my selection would not realize Mr van Thal's objective of giving "representation to the differing facets of the man and his genius." I can see that, given his aim, it was just and necessary to include an excerpt from Belloc's book on the Jews, because that race was an important concern in his life. Distasteful as I find it, Belloc was right on one point. The refusal of the educated classes in England to admit publicly that anti-Semitism existed, the wish to sweep the problem under the rug, was not going to make matters any better. Actually, since the readmittance of the Jews under Cromwell, I do not think that anti-Semitism has ever been a serious menace in England. It has always flourished more strongly in Roman Catholic and Greek Orthodox countries than in Protestant ones, partly, perhaps, because Protestants have always been devoted, some might say addicted, to the Old Testament. Hitler, it should be remembered, was an Austrian, not a Prussian.

At times, however, I feel that, in his wish to be fully representative, Mr van Thal goes a bit too far. Was it really kind to Belloc's memory to reprint such pieces as "Advice to the Rich," which reads like a malicious parody, or *A Chinese Litany of Numbers*, a series of lists which are neither witty nor profound and could have been assembled by a computer, or the brief note to Compton Mackenzie, which only reveals that, like his friend Chesterton, Belloc knew nothing whatsoever about music? (No one who did could have spoken of "the love-song in Don Juan.")

But in general Mr van Thal has done what must have been an extremely difficult task very well. For example, in representing Belloc the historian, he has wisely concentrated upon his pen-portraits of historical characters, because it is almost impossible to make excerpts from historical narrative without falsifying it. Besides, Belloc was very good at pen-portraits, and they are usually free from bias in the way that his narratives are not. Moreover, he sometimes sees things about his characters which previous historians had missed. I am sure, for example, he is right when he says that Robespierre was not, as popular legend believed him to be, the real power in the Committee of Public Safety, that the real power was Carnot.

Though I am quite certain he was wrong in believing that, but for Henry VIII's marriage to Anne Boleyn, England would have remained Catholic—I am sure she would have become Protestant within a generation—his portrait of Anne herself is very fair. Even more remarkably, so is his portrait of Cromwell.

(Incidentally, it has always struck me as extremely odd and significant that the lands which became Protestant at the Reformation were precisely those which had been least influenced by the culture of *pagan* Rome. England, it is true, lay inside the *limes*, but the Roman influence there seems to have been superficial. It is also true that Ireland lay outside them, but there, because of political circumstances, Catholicism was the chief, perhaps the only, means of maintaining a sense of national identity.)

Again, Mr van Thal has evidently sensed that, if one wants to understand a man's ideas about history and politics, particularly if they are controversial, one has to view them in the context of his time and society. By what other thinkers was he influenced? Whom did he consider the Enemy and what, precisely, did the Enemy think? To understand Belloc, for example, one must know something about the Whig version of English history which had dominated the nineteenth century. But this, by its nature, an anthology devoted to a single author cannot do.

All in all, then, despite some reservations, I think *Belloc* a fascinating compilation. One last picayune complaint. The first two lines of "Lord Finchley" are printed wrong.

> Lord Finchley tried to mend the Electric Light Himself.
> It struck him dead: and serve him right.

should run:

> Lord Finchley tried to mend the Electric Light
> Himself. It struck him dead: and serve him right!

The New York Review of Books, 5 November 1970

Well Done, Sir Walter Scott!

Sir Walter Scott: The Great Unknown. By Edgar Johnson.
Two volumes. Macmillan. $25.

Aside from those giving or taking a course in the History of the English Novel, how many people today, I wonder, read Scott on their own? If I am at all typical, not many, I fear. I have read and reread all of Jane Austen, all of Dickens, all of George Eliot, and most of Trollope, but I have read only about half of Scott's novels, and it is a long time since I opened one. (A few years ago, while working on an anthology, I read all of his poems, but of that more anon.) I knew, though I have never read it, that he wrote an extensive biography of Napoleon, but I never knew till now that he wrote a life of Swift and edited the works of John Dryden so well that when George Saintsbury made a reëdition he left Scott's elaborate apparatus of historical notes alone because they were "thoroughly trustworthy." About Scott the man, I knew that he suffered from a lame right leg, that in 1825 he was trapped in a financial disaster, and that Abbotsford was among the first private houses—perhaps *the* first—to be lit by gas, but that was absolutely all I knew. Professor Edgar Johnson's magnificent and (I am willing to bet) definitive biography—the two-volume *Sir Walter Scott: The Great Unknown,* published by Macmillan—has made me resolve to read Scott's novels again, or for the first time, as soon as I can find the leisure, and I hope other readers will feel the same.

Not the least of Professor Johnson's many merits is that he is not, unlike all too many biographers of artists, under the illusion that knowledge of the life sheds any significant light upon the work; accordingly, he keeps his chapters of historical narrative and his chapters of critical assessment separate. Few writers have led lives interesting enough to deserve a biography, but Scott is one of the exceptions, and readers who have no interest in his writings will still find the story of his life fascinating and inspiring. In it, thank God, there are no ugly secrets. When he was twenty-one, he had the not uncommon experience of falling in love with a girl (in this instance, Williamina Belsches) who married another. Of this he wrote later:

> Broken-hearted for two years—my heart handsomely pieced—but the crack will remain to my dying day.

Yet, two years afterward, he married Charlotte Charpentier, and the marriage, which lasted for twenty-nine years, was obviously a very happy one. Moreover, however painful the earlier experience may have been, he had the sense to realize that it was probably all for the best, since some years later he wrote to a friend in a similar situation:

> . . . assure yourself that scarce one person out of twenty marries his first love, and scarce one out of twenty of the remainder has cause to rejoice

having done so. What we love in these early days is generally rather a fanciful creation of our own than a reality. We build statues of snow and weep when they melt.

In all of Scott's multifarious dealings with others, Professor Johnson has only one incident to describe in which he behaved with anything but scrupulous honesty, and even then the fault was mostly that of his publisher, William Miller. Learning that a Reverend Mr Edward Forster was contemplating an edition of Dryden, Scott suggested that they collaborate. But Miller insisted that only Scott's name appear on the title page, and in the end Forster was squeezed out. Professor Johnson says:

> Though he was not obliged to forego a design he had formed before he and Forster were acquainted, it would at least have been more fastidious to find another publisher than the one who had behaved so shabbily to his associate. Scott had not himself cuckooed Forster out of the nest, but he had allowed Miller to do so. That such sharp practice was not unusual among booksellers does not leave Scott absolutely blameless.

Professor Johnson tells us that he has adhered strictly to the recorded evidence and allowed himself no fictional embellishments, not even of the weather, yet his Life reads like a novel. At every moment the reader feels he is seeing and hearing exactly what went on. That this should be possible is an indication of how vast the collection of available documents must be, and of Professor Johnson's herculean labors in mastering them. He tells us that a Scott bibliography published in 1943 contains almost three thousand items, taking up four hundred pages. There are twelve volumes of Scott's published letters, and enough unpublished to make six more. The Walpole collection of letters written to Scott contains six thousand written by more than sixteen hundred correspondents, etc., etc.

The story of Walter Scott really begins when, at the age of eighteen months, it was found that his right leg was paralyzed. Such a physical handicap, as we know, either destroys a child or inspires him with the determination to transcend it. In Scott's case, it made him a person of heroic courage. Later in life, he was to be faced with perhaps worse sufferings, but he surmounted them all and refused to despair:

> From childhood's earliest hour, I have rebelled against external circumstances.

For the sake of his health, he was sent to his grandmother's sheep farm, at Sandyknowe, near Kelso, with his mother's maid to look after him. This almost ended in disaster. Forced to leave her lover behind in Edinburgh, she conceived a hatred for her charge and was haunted by a desire to cut his throat with a pair of scissors and bury him in a bog. Fortunately, she confessed this to the housekeeper and was sent away in time. At Sandyknowe, he was the only child, and all the household vied with one another to please him and amuse him with stories. The effect of this was a precocious development of his imagination:

> I was wayward, bold, and wild,
> A self-willed imp, a granddame's child,
> But half a plague and half a jest,
> Was still endured, beloved, caressed.

He learned to read very early, and by the time he was six he was evidently a child prodigy, who enjoyed Milton. A distant relative of his mother said that he was

> the most extraordinary genius of a boy I ever saw. He was reading a poem to his mother when I went in. . . . It was the description of a shipwreck. His passion rose with the storm. He lifted his eyes and hands. "There's the mast gone," says he; "crash it goes!—they will all perish!" After his agitation he turns to me "This is too melancholy," says he; "I had better read you something more amusing."

This talent for performance never deserted him, and everybody who met him testified to his extraordinary powers as a mimic and raconteur. John Wilson Croker, the Secretary to the Admiralty, meeting him in 1815, said:

> The Prince [Regent] and Scott were the two most brilliant story-tellers . . . I have ever happened to meet.

Besides telling a story well, he could make very witty remarks, as when he described the Duke of Wellington's style of debate as "slicing the argument into two or three parts, and helping himself to the best."

One might have expected his early experiences as an indulged "only" child, coupled with his lameness—though his leg improved, he was never to be able to walk without a stick—to make him ill at ease with "healthy" boys of his own age, but it didn't. Soon after his return to Edinburgh, he learned to get on with his siblings and become popular among his schoolmates. Most people, I think, tend to be either introverts who are happiest alone and prefer the company of a few close friends to large gatherings, or extroverts who hate to be alone and enjoy life in society. Scott was one of those rare exceptions who took an equal pleasure in solitude and company. As poet and novelist, he could always entertain himself, and he loved solitary walks and rides; at the same time, he was very gregarious. Abbotsford was always crowded with guests, and when he visited London or Paris he was a lion of the drawing rooms and country houses:

> Yesterday I forgot where I was to dine. . . . Fortunately an accident reminded me that my Amphitrion for the day was Lord Castlereagh. Were I to tell this in a stage coach or in company what a conceited puppy I

> would seem, yet the thing is literally true, as well as my receiving three blue ribbands and a marchioness in my hotel in the same day.

Scott was also an exception in that he combined in equal measure a love of imaginative fantasy and a passion for historical fact. It was with good reason that his friends in college nicknamed him Duns Scotus, and his library at Abbotsford contained twenty thousand volumes, including a rare collection of books on the supernatural. Of all English imaginative writers, he must have been the greatest scholar.

Idiosyncrasies are always endearing, and Scott was not without them. He was musically tone-deaf, and, according to his son-in-law, neither his palate nor his sense of smell was refined. He could not distinguish corked wine from sound or tell Madeira from sherry. Uniforms and military gear in general seem to have fascinated him. During the invasion scare of 1796, when he joined the Edinburgh Light Dragoons, he was almost crazily happy:

> At parade no one was prouder in full-dress uniform obtained from a regimental tailor at a cost of £22 and of more than peacock splendor—scarlet coat with blue collar and cuffs and silver epaulettes trimmed with silver lace, white leather breeches, black boots fiercely spurred, and a helmet crested with leopard skin and a red and white hackle.

Indeed, one of his friends was rather shocked:

> Scott is become the merest trooper that ever was begotten by a drunken dragoon on his trull in a hay-loft. Not an idea crosses his mind, or a word his lips, that has not an allusion to some damned instrument or evolution of the Cavalry: "Draw your swords—by single files to the right of front—to the left wheel—charge!"

The working habits of a writer are always interesting, at least to other writers. Like most serious and prolific writers—Balzac and Proust are exceptions—Scott worked by day, not by night. By 1804, he had established his schedule:

> Formerly, when business or enjoyment had taken up the middle of the day, after he was supposed to have gone to bed he had devoted several hours to writing and study. But his doctor told him this course was likely to aggravate the nervous headaches that were the only illnesses he now knew. Consequently he began rising at five in the morning. He lighted his own fire if it was cold; he shaved and arrayed himself carefully in a shooting jacket or whatever garment he meant to wear till dinner time. . . . Before settling down to work he paid a quick visit to the stables to feed his favorite horse. . . . Six o'clock saw Scott at his desk, papers and reference books neatly arranged about him, Camp lying faithfully at his feet, and the two greyhounds Douglas and Percy, as fancy moved them,

> leaping in and out of a window always left open for them . . . When the rest of the household assembled for breakfast around nine, he had already, as he put it, done enough "to break the back of the day's work." . . . After breakfast Scott labored for another couple of hours. . . . By noon, saying, "Out, damned spot," he could close his writing box and be "his own man" for the rest of the day. In bad weather he worked in the afternoon as well, but otherwise he was out and riding by one o'clock.

Ideas evidently came to him quickly and easily. He wrote in his journal:

> And long ere dinner-time I have
> Full eight close pages wrote.
> What, Duty, hast thou now to crave?
> Well done, Sir Walter Scott!

Eight of his manuscript pages, Professor Johnson informs us, were the equivalent of twenty-four pages of print.

Robert Hogg, his secretary in later life, recorded:

> It soon became apparent to me . . . that he was carrying on two distinct trains of thought, one of which was already arranged, and in the act of being spoken, while at the same time he was in advance considering what was afterwards to be said. This I discovered by his sometimes introducing a word which was wholly out of place . . . but which I presently found to belong to the next sentence, perhaps four or five lines further on, which he had been preparing at the very moment that he gave me the words of the one that preceded it.

Such disciplined habits were to stand him in good stead when troubles came upon him. For three years of his middle forties, he suffered from agonizing stomach cramps, caused by gallstones—a condition then inoperable. The pain was so severe that he could not stop himself screaming, and it could be alleviated only by heavy doses of laudanum, which sent him into an acute depression the next day. He worked on. Then, of course, came his financial troubles. Professor Johnson goes into them in the minutest detail, but I think it would take the mind of a chartered accountant to make head or tail of them. All that is clear to me is that though he may have been careless he was not culpable. The easiest course for him to take would have been to declare himself a bankrupt, but his sense of honor forbade it. He worked on. His leg grew worse. He worked on. In 1830, he suffered his first stroke. He worked on. His friends implored him to take things easy. He refused:

> Dr Abercrombie knows better than most people that a man can no more say to his mind "don't think" than Mollie can say to her Kettle "don't boil" when she finds it on a brisk fire.

In 1831, his mind began to fail. When Wordsworth and his daughter, Dora, visited him in September, she asked him to write some verses for her album:

> Wordsworth read them with sad pity in his heart. They revealed how much the noble mind was impaired, "not by the strain of thought, but by the execution, some of the lines being imperfect, and one stanza wanting corresponding rhymes: one letter, the initial S, had been omitted in the spelling of his own name."

In the following year, he died, at the relatively early age of sixty-one, officially from a stroke but in fact from a lifetime of overwork.

His political views I find fascinating and sympathetic. Though he called himself a Tory and strongly disliked the Whigs, he was a Tory of a most peculiar kind. By nature, he was, as Chesterton pointed out, a democrat; that is to say, a man who believed in the equal dignity of all men, whether gentlefolk or peasantry. For this reason, he was disgusted by the meddlesome sort of charity:

> . . . all your domiciliary, kind, impertinent visits—they are all pretty much felt like insults, and do no manner of good: let people go on in their own way, in God's name. How would you like to have a nobleman coming to teach you how to dish up your beefsteak into a French kickshaw? . . . Let the poor alone in their domestic habits, I pray you; protect them and treat them kindly, of course, and trust them; but let them enjoy in quiet their dish of porridge and their potatoes and herrings, or whatever it may be—but for any sake don't torment them with your fashionable soups.

He disapproved of the Game Laws and supported Catholic Emancipation. He did, it is true, oppose Parliamentary Reform. In this he may have been mistaken, but he was quite right in thinking that the immediate effect would be to put power into the hands of the industrialists and the middle class, who were certainly not interested in the sufferings of the poor. His own "Tory" suggestion was the reimposition of income tax, a measure which would hardly have been popular with either the mine-owners and mill-owners or the landed gentry of his time, and it was not until 1842 that the measure was adopted.

Has any serious writer, before or since, and anywhere in the world, had the fantastic success in his own lifetime that Scott enjoyed? In his old age, Goethe became an international celebrity, but very few of his visitors had read anything of his except *Werther*, written when he was twenty-four. But almost everything Scott wrote, whether in verse or prose, was a best-seller from the day of publication. One example, *Marmion* (published in February of 1808), will suffice:

> Even at the staggering price of one and a half guineas [worth today about thirty dollars] the entire first edition of two thousand copies was

> sold out in less than two months. A second of three thousand was hurried through the press and melted away so rapidly that before the end of May a third was thundering out, making a total of eight thousand published in little over three months. Before the end of the year, these were almost exhausted; two editions of three thousand each followed in 1809; two more amounting to five thousand in 1810. In 1811, the poem's fourth year, nine thousand were issued.

When one remembers that the population of England and Scotland at the time was fewer than twelve million, at least half of whom were illiterate, such figures are indeed astonishing.

Nor was his social success any less than his literary. One cannot imagine another writer, even Dickens, being elected president of a scientific body, as Scott was elected president of the Royal Society of Edinburgh (at his first meeting, he startled his audience by reciting to them the ballad of the Laidly Worm), or being put in charge of the social arrangements for a Royal Visit. Scotland has reason to be grateful to Scott for undertaking the task. At his request, George IV restored the Scottish peerages forfeited in 1715 and 1745 and had the famous cannon Mons Meg, which had been carried off to London in 1754, returned to Edinburgh. About the Royal Visit, Professor Johnson has an amusing anecdote to relate:

> The King laughed, called for a bottle of Highland whiskey, drank Scott's health, and desired another glass to be filled for him. When Scott had drained his own glass, he begged the one just touched by royal lips as a keepsake and carefully tucked it away in the skirt pocket of his overcoat. After presenting the St Andrew's Cross he hurried home in excitement to tell all about it, rushed into the drawing room, still in his wet coat, and forgetting about the glass threw himself into a chair—then leaped up with a yell, clapping a hand to his backside. Lady Scott thought he had sat on a pair of scissors. His scar was slight, but the historic glass was smashed to splinters.

Today, Scott's name is still respected, but how much is he read? So far as I know, no critic has attacked his work, and that is always a bad sign. I said at the beginning of this article that I recently read all of his poetry. I am sorry to have to report that in my opinion the long narrative poems fail to hold the attention. I don't know why it should be so, but it seems to me that very few long narratives about historical actions do, once the age of the heroic epic is over. *The Canterbury Tales* are tall stories, in which incident serves only to reveal character; *Orlando Furioso* takes place in a fantastic world, *The Fairie Queen* in a dream landscape. And, after 1770, which are the long poems we most enjoy? *Don Juan*, which, though officially a narrative, is a platform from which Byron can air his views about society; *The Prelude*; *In Memoriam*, which is really a collection of lyrics; "The Ancient Mariner" and *The City of Dreadful Night*, both set in a dream world, not the real one. In the case of Scott, his choice of metre—rhymed octosyllabic or four-stress couplet—was, I think, a mistake. The rhymes come so quickly that they sound forced or pat. Opening *Marmion* at random, I find:

> The tide did now its flood-mark gain,
> And girdled in the Saint's domain:
> For, with the flow and ebb, its style
> Varies from continent to isle;
> Dry-shod, o'er sands, twice every day,
> The pilgrims to the shrine find way;
> Twice every day, the waves efface
> Of staves and sandall'd feet the trace
>
> (Canto II, 9)

Narrative, it seems to me, is better served by unrhymed verse, like the blank verse of *The Idylls of the King*, or by long lines, like the six-beat couplets of Morris's *Sigurd the Volsung*:

> So up and down they journeyed and ever as they went
> About the cold-slaked forges, o'er many a cloud-swept bent,
> Betwixt the walls of blackness, by shores of the fishless meres,
> And the fathomless desert waters, did Regin cast his fears.

What do remain unforgettable are the lyrics which Scott interposes—songs like "Where shall the lover rest," "The toils are pitched and the stakes are set," "Pibroch of Donald Dhu," to cite only three. These are indeed beautiful, original, and nearly always of great rhythmical interest. Scott's most original poetry, however, is to be found in the chapter headings to his novels. For instance:

> Indifferent, but indifferent—pshaw, he doth it not
> Like one who is his craft's master—ne'er the less
> I have seen a clown confer a bloody coxcomb
> On one who was a master of defence.
>
> (*The Monastery*, Chapter 21)

> "Speak not of niceness when there's chance of wreck,"
> The captain said, as ladies writhed their neck
> To see the dying dolphin flap the deck:
> "If we go down, on us these gentry sup;
> We dine upon them, if we haul them up.
> Wise men applaud us when we eat the eaters,
> As the devil laughs when the keen folks cheat the cheaters."
>
> (*Peveril of the Peak*, Chapter 38)

Minor poetry, if you like, but effective, and nobody but Scott could have written it.

Professor Johnson's defense of the novels is able and most convincing. He thinks that many of Scott's admirers, both in his own day and later, misunderstood what he was up to:

> Readers of his own time confused his interest in the past with the fantastic pseudo-medievalism of Walpole's *Castle of Otranto* and the romantic supernaturalism of Coleridge's "Christabel" and "Rime of the Ancient Mariner." Countless later readers have repeated their error. For them the Waverley novels have been costume drama, whose fascination lay in powdered wigs, silk stockings and knee breeches, farthingales, ruffs, hauberks and chain armor, in battlements, dungeons, and flying buttresses, in deeds of derring-do, bloodshed and crashing castle walls.

But in fact, he argues, Scott, far from being a romantic, was essentially an eighteenth-century rationalist. He had little use for either the Wordsworthian cult of Wild Nature or the Byronic cult of the Ego. As for the cult of the Man of Feeling, he wrote, "Of all sorts of parade, I think the parade of feeling and sentiment the most disgusting."

> If his teacher Dugald Stewart had convinced him that there is a core of human nature which for all its variety of forms is fundamentally unchanged, his wide reading from youth upward had been seminal in assembling a host of powerful examples of the richness and variety of human behavior. Another of his teachers, the elder Adam Ferguson, had stressed "the multiplicity of forms" of different societies, and Alexander Fraser Tytler had made him skeptical of the tendency to reduce everything to general principles, the excessive systemization of an insufficient foundation of fact. And, above all, the writings of Edmund Burke had made him aware of the power of custom, of tradition, of deep social, cultural, even ancestral forces, in molding men's minds and hearts. . . . Steering a course between the extremes of innate and external determinism, and between fate and free will, he showed his characters in a thousand ways the result of their heredity, their surroundings, their occupations, and at the same time portrayed the ineradicable essences, even the personal idiosyncrasies, irresistibly asserting themselves through all the impersonal forces.

It is significant, surely, that the critic Georg Lukács, who, as a Marxist, is committed to the cause of "social realism," should so greatly admire Scott. He was, Lukács has written, the "great poet of history, because he has a deeper, and more genuine and differentiated sense of historical necessity than any writer before him."

The New Yorker, 20 February 1971

[A Review of *Hogarth on the High Life*, by Georg Christoph Lichtenberg]

Hogarth on High Life: The "Marriage à la Mode" Series,
from Georg Christoph Lichtenberg's commentaries.
Translated and edited by Arthur S. Wensinger, with W. B. Coley.
Wesleyan University Press. $35.

It is a crying scandal that the writings of G. C. Lichtenberg (1742–99), professor of physics at the University of Göttingen from 1769 until his death, should be almost unknown in the English-speaking world. To begin with, he was an ardent Anglophile who spent some time in England, and in his *Letters from England* (1776–78) described his fascination with the London scene. He himself used to say that he learned how to write good German from learning English. Be that as it may, he is, as Nietzsche and others have recognized, one of the supreme masters of the German language. He is also, which should appeal to the Anglo-Saxon sensibility, extremely funny—a magnificent aphorist. Let one example suffice, his definition of the donkey: "A horse translated into Dutch." This volume, excellently translated by Professor Wensinger and sumptuously produced by the Wesleyan University Press, contains Lichtenberg's commentaries, published in the last years of his life, upon Hogarth's famous engravings, published in 1745. Alas, it is impossible to review, for in order to appreciate the subtlety of Lichtenberg's iconographic and physiognomic insights it is necessary to have both the whole plates and the reproduction of details before one's eyes as one reads; the words of a reviewer are impotent. All he can do is urge anybody who is interested either in the visual arts or in literature to buy this book immediately. He is in for a treat.

Unsigned. *The New Yorker*, 12 December 1970.

Foreword to *Plastic Sense*, by Malcolm de Chazal

M. Malcolm de Chazal is a poet, though he writes in prose (not, thank God, in free verse). His chosen literary form is the aphorism. This is an aristocratic genre. The aphorist does not argue or explain: he asserts. At the same time, however, he addresses his reader as an equal, not as a pupil in need of instruction. It is for the reader to decide, on the basis of his own experience, whether an aphorism be true or false. For example, when Valéry says, "Consciousness reigns but does not govern," I do not feel I have been told a fact hitherto unknown to me, but rather, that I have been made conscious of a fact which, unconsciously, I have always known. On the other hand, reading through *Plastic Sense*, I came upon one statement, only one, "the insect can fathom the lowing of the cow," which seems to me false, that is to say, my reaction is, "What scientific reason is there to suppose that the insect can? Such observations of insects as I have made incline me to think it cannot."

French literature is famous for its aphorists, but, both in style and content, Chazal's are a quite new phenomenon. The language used by most aphorists is abstract and deliberately avoids metaphor and visual imagery: Chazal's is always metaphorical and charged with images. For example, two of the commonest topics for aphorists have been self-love and the difference between the two sexes. Typical "traditional" statements on these topics are:

> We would rather run ourselves down than not speak of ourselves at all.
> (La Rochefoucauld)

> A man keeps another's secret better than he does his own.
> A woman, on the other hand, keeps her own better than another's.
> (La Bruyère)

How different is Chazal's treatment of the same matters:

> The egotist's feelings walk in Indian file.

> Women eat when they talk, men talk when they eat. At table men talk longer between mouthfuls, women while eating. Women preside at breakfast when the courses are negligible and hurried. Men's voices dominate at suppers and banquets when there are long waits between courses.

Even more striking is the difference between the dominant concerns of the French aphoristic tradition and his. Most of them have occupied themselves either with the behavior of Court or High Society, like La Rochefoucauld, La Bruyère, Chamfort, Vauvenargues, or with political life, like de Tocqueville, or with the life of the mind, like Pascal and Valéry. Of French literature in general I do not think it unfair to say that while there have, of course, been distinguished French professional naturalists, French poets and novelists, with the notable exception of Colette, have shown relatively little interest in what in English is meant by "Nature," namely, first, our human experience of all beings, mineral, vegetable, or animal, which we recognize as being "other" than ourselves, and, secondly, those aspects of our own nature which, as sentient creatures, made of matter, who are born, eat proteins, defecate, reproduce sexually, and die, we share with the rest of created beings.

In this sense Chazal is a "nature" poet. He has, like all writers, his forebears, but in his case most of them belonged to other literary cultures than his own, and it does not follow that he must necessarily have read them. For example, here are some observations which one might easily have found in

Plastic Sense, but happen to have been written by others, the first two by Novalis, then three by Thoreau, and the last by Ruskin:

> Are not plants, perhaps, the product of a feminine nature and a masculine spirit, animals the product of a masculine nature and a feminine spirit? Are not plants, as it were, the girls, animals the boys, of nature?
>
> As we manure the flowerbeds for the plants, so they manure the airbeds for us.
>
> The song-sparrow is heard in fields and pastures, setting the midsummer to music—as if it were the music of a mossy rail or fencepost.
>
> A turtle walking is as if a man were to try to walk by sticking his legs and arms merely out of the windows.
>
> The heavens and the earth are one flower. The earth is the calyx, the heavens the corolla.
>
> The Swallow: it is an owl that has been trained by the Graces, it is a bat that loves the morning light, it is the aerial reflection of a dolphin, it is the tender domestication of a trout.

Chazal is a practicing painter as well as writer. (I was, incidentally, first introduced to his writings in the early Fifties by another painter, the late Pavlec Tchelitchev.) Every painter is a lover of "nature" in the sense in which I have used the word, since his primary concern is with the visual appearance of things, including human beings. If what distinguishes us from all other beings is a consciousness of having a Self, this property is not visually manifest. All that can be "seen" are our expressions and our gestures, which all things, animate and inanimate, exhibit likewise.

Anybody, however, who, like a painter, is preoccupied with sensory experience of the world knows that this is rarely, if ever, the experience of one sense only. Rarely, if ever, do we see without at the same time hearing, smelling, tasting, and touching. To testify to this, we have to have recourse to speech: the painter can only record the seen, the musician only the heard, but the writer, thanks to the metaphorical and analogical resources of language, can at least indirectly record our synaesthetic experience of the outer world. As a painter turned writer, Chazal is, as one might expect, a marvelous physiognomist.

> The leaf is all profile; the flower can never be anything but full face, no matter what angle you view it from. If both were profiles, the flower would seem to be riding the leaf like a horseman; and if both were full face, the whole plant would flatten out into a kind of tapestry. So long as the leaf's flatness is wedded to the flower's fullness, we tend to see flowers superimposed on leaves even when the foliage is in the foreground. Because of this, a plant's leaves never "drown out" its flowers.

> The full face always seems nearer than the profile even at the same distance away.
>
> Roses on the bush are sisters on the plant and first cousins in the vase. As one might expect, something of their common character has passed into the vase, thinning out their kinship.
>
> The gestures of the feet are perhaps the most "artificial" part of our step. Our feet have no "natural" gestures except in water. The watery element is the greatest of all simplifiers of gesture. All the gestures of the fish are infantile.
>
> A man uses his fingers more than a child, who depends on his palm. These are, respectively, the carpentry and masonry of gesture.

But he is at his most impressive in his descriptions of experiences which involve more than one sense.

> A voracious sense of smell leans forward on its nostrils like a glutton eating with his elbows on the table.
>
> Fog severs all spatial connections of resemblance or sympathy in nature. Trees wander like lost sheep until the air currents that nip at their heels herd them together. Fog sends each plant off to search its own soul alone in the infinite corners of the schoolroom of space, and puts a dunce's cap on light itself. Fog is the water's "detention room."
>
> Wind is vocalic, water consonantal. A blast of humid air is the essence of all diphthongs. Squalls stutter while hurricanes swallow their words. . . . The noise of water is sound riding horse on sound. The noise of wind is an infantry march of sound. So: a cavalcade of water and the hurricane shifting its feet.

Any collection of aphorisms, especially one as extensive as *Plastic Sense,* cannot and should not be read as one reads a novel or even a volume of poems. There is no need to read the pages in their printed order, and one should not read for too long at a time: fifteen minutes is, perhaps, the maximum. On the other hand, if the author is talented enough, there is no literary genre to which one can return more often and be sure of finding something exciting and thought-provoking which one had missed on earlier readings.

Sens-Plastique has now been a companion of mine for nearly twenty years, and so far as I am concerned, Malcolm de Chazal is much the most original and interesting French writer to emerge since the war.

Plastic Sense, by Malcolm de Chazal,
edited and translated by Irving Weiss (1971);
The New York Review of Books, 6 May 1971

Foreword to *Austria: People and Landscape*, by Stella Musulin

As Baroness Musulin says, with documentary proof, the average Englishman's knowledge of Austrian geography is very vague, and his knowledge of her history almost nil. Even those who have been there are apt to imagine that Salzburg is a city in the Tyrol. When, in 1925, I left England for the first time to attend the Salzburg Festival and then on to Kitzbühel—both sadly changed since then—I don't *think* I made this mistake, but I can't be sure.

As for those who have not, when, a few years ago, President Jonas paid a state visit to England, the Lord Mayor of London kept referring to Australia. It must be admitted, however, that President Jonas's knowledge of England was not very extensive either, for, in the course of a speech, he said: "There has been a historic friendship between Austria and England ever since the time of Richard I." (Austria, perhaps, had reason to be grateful, for the ransom paid to get him back enabled Vienna to build a new city wall.)

That the average man should have a vaguer notion of Austria than of most foreign countries may be partly due to the fact that, when one considers her geography, it seems a miracle that she should exist at all.

> Austria possesses mountain ranges and deep rivers. But it is a curious fact that these natural barriers have not, on the whole, been accepted as political frontiers. The all-important Danube certainly marked the "limes", the northern frontier of the Roman Empire, but it was never an Austrian frontier—today it is not even a provincial boundary. Geologically speaking, the highland plateau north of the Danube forms the southern tip of the great Bohemian massif; climate and vegetation of the Hungarian "puszta" begin in the Vienna basin. The highest alpine range in Austria has never been a state frontier. And it was not until 1918, when mountains already possessed very little strategical significance and would never again have any at all, that it had ever occurred to anyone to declare the Brenner to be a natural and therefore desirable national frontier.

> If we suppose for a moment that England, Scotland and Wales were not an island but were surrounded by land inhabited by related peoples, we might well be surprised that those three countries had ever become one nation.

> If ever a political event took place in defiance of all realistic probability it was the liberation of the eastern provinces of Austria, and part of the capital, from Soviet Russian occupation. Into the almost straight line

> down from the North Sea which divides Europe into two halves, Austria presses forward like a battering ram.

To this day, despite the automobile and mass communications, the inhabitants of the various provinces differ greatly from each other in temperament, dialect, dress, domestic architecture, etc. When, a few years ago, the Austrian Army was on manoeuvres and entered the Tyrol, the peasants rushed out to repel an invasion.

If they have recently developed, as I think they have, a stronger sense of all being Austrians, this is probably due, as Baroness Musulin suggests, to their common experiences, firstly under Hitler and then under the Allied Occupation.

> The case of the amateur historian is this: civilisation means, in part, self-awareness throughout all the stages of cause and effect, and to understand the thought and behavior of people to-day one must know their heritage. To know anything about the psychology of the South Tyrolese, for example, of the Serbs and Croats, of the Czechs and Slovaks, it is essential to dig down a long way. The same is true of the Slovene Carinthians whom we shall happen on later.

This is the task which Baroness Musulin has attempted and, in my opinion as an amateur reader of history, with triumphant success.

She begins with the Vorarlberg, then moves eastward through the Tyrol and the Salzkammergut, then southward to Carinthia and Styria, then northward to Upper and to Lower Austria (where we both happen to live within half an hour's drive of each other), then eastward again to Burgenland, then back to end in Vienna. To each of these areas she devotes a chapter which is more or less complete in itself. This has the advantage for a reader that he can take the chapters in any order he chooses, according to his personal interests or the place he is planning to visit next. To every kind of curiosity, to the lover of scenery, of history, of architecture, of eccentric characters and touching romances, she has something to offer. Anybody, for example, in search of perfect material for a movie, could hardly do better than to consult her accounts of the adventures of Maria Clementine Sobieski, the future bride of the Old Pretender, or of Eva Kraus, *die Hundsgräfin*, with whom Napoleon fell in love when she was a housemaid in Schönbrunn, or of Anna Plochl, the daughter of a Styrian postmaster, with whom the Archduke Johann fell in love when she was twelve and he was thirty-four and finally married after patiently waiting for thirteen years. More suitable material, perhaps, for an historical novelist than a film-director is the life-story of Anna Neumann.

> Anna married six times. This comparatively rapid turnover gave rise to ugly rumour and suspicion among her numerous tenantry, though

> never among her peers, of poisoning or witchcraft. Her biographers consider that she was an extremely able administrator of her husbands' estates which had snowballed into her hands, and that she drove herself to work as a distraction from her grief over the death of her first four husbands whom, uncommon though this may have been, she had married (as she was beautiful as well as rich the choice was ample) for love. Having lost her only daughter, Anna found herself at the age of 76 a fourfold widow with great possessions and no heir other than a step-nephew who had married a nonentity; he was not, Anna thought, a promising founder of a dynasty. Her decision was soon made, and she now married a thirty-year-old man, Ferdinand von Salamanca, Count Ortenburg. . . . Anna's whole intention, it must be realised, was to find a worthy heir, on the assumption that, after her death, the young widower would at once marry a girl who could put the old lady's ambitions into effect. Simply to have given away her estates to any local nobleman was not the answer. To her horror, the plan misfired because Ferdinand was tubercular and within five or six years he was dead. Anna, living at Murau Castle in Styria, was now 82, and failing. There was little time to lose. An old friend, a statesman from the Imperial court, called on her and made a suggestion. How about the twenty-eight-year-old Count Georg Ludwig von Schwarzenberg, whose only barrier to a brilliant career in diplomacy was a lack of private means? Georg Schwarzenberg called at Murau, and she evidently liked what she saw. The odd pair were married.

Baroness Musulin has had both the curiosity and the opportunity to explore all the Austrian provinces in detail, so that she probably knows the country a good deal better than most people who were born there. Very few Austrians, for example, have visited the Mühlviertel, near the Czech border in Upper Austria, which was Adalbert Stifter's country: she has. The same is true of her historical reading. Not many Austrians, in my experience, realize that, for most of the sixteenth century, "practically the entire nobility of Austria, most of the townsfolk, the mining and industrial workers and a section of the peasantry" became Lutherans, so that when, in the seventeenth century under pressure from the Jesuits, the Habsburgs put the screws on, many of the most intelligent and skilful persons in the country were obliged to emigrate, a fact which, in part, explains the character of the Viennese.

The relation between Art and Society is so obscure that only a fool will claim that he understands it. How, as Baroness Musulin asks in her concluding chapter on Vienna, is one to explain the extraordinary eruption of genius in that city which began during the last decades of the nineteenth century and lasted until the late 1920s, manifesting itself in every field, literature, music, painting, philosophy, medicine? When it began the empire was already dying on its feet, and it continued after its total collapse. Why? Even more extraordinary in my opinion were the artistic achievements of men like Nestroy and Adalbert Stifter living in Metternich's police state. More than that, I cannot help wondering if they could have written what they did under a more liberal regime. Talking of Stifter, Baroness Musulin says that he, like the composer Bruckner, "has not travelled well". Of Bruckner this may be true, but of Stifter I would say that he has not travelled, period: until a few years ago nobody had attempted to translate him.

But I must stop and leave the reader to enjoy Austria by himself. I know of few books of this kind that are at one and the same time so instructive and such fun to peruse.

Austria: People and Landscape, by Stella Musulin (1971)

Foreword to *Selected Poems,* by Gunnar Ekelöf

Gunnar Ekelöf was born in 1907 in Stockholm. His father was a wealthy stockbroker who caught syphilis, became insane and died while Ekelöf was still a child; his mother was a member of the petty nobility and does not seem to have shown him much affection. Consequently, he had to find such happiness as he could in a private dream world of his own. Of this early time he wrote:

> My own childhood environment was well-to-do but so far beyond the normal and so unrealistic that there was good room for peculiar kinds of want. . . . I had books, music, beautiful furniture around me, but they forced me to go long roundabout ways before I could feel I had a legitimate right to them.

As Ekelöf grew up, he became engrossed in Oriental mysticism:

> I learned to hate Europe and Christianity and during the morning prayer at school I began to mumble *Om mani padme hum* as a form of protest . . .

In the Royal Library he discovered *Tarjúmán el-Ashwáq* by Ibn el-Arabi which for a long time was his favourite book and from which, he tells us, he first learned what is meant by Symbolism and Surrealism. With the idea of emigrating to India, he went to London to study at the School of Oriental Languages, but abandoned this scheme and returned to Sweden to study Persian at the University of Uppsala. However, a long illness prevented him from completing his studies. It was at this time that he wrote his first poem:

> One night I had an experience that I would have to characterize as a form of ecstasy. It came over me as a shower of shooting stars, and I

> remember staggering a bit on my way home. As often on such occasions, I had had the usual orchestra playing somewhere behind me, and I myself joined in with one instrument after the other. Then it became a poem, my first fairly original one.

Ekelöf's second great and lasting passion was music and, in the 1920s, he went to Paris to study it, but soon became absorbed by the problems of poetic language:

> I placed one word beside another and finally with a great deal of effort managed to construct a whole sentence—naturally not one that "meant something" but one that was composed of word-nuances. It was the hidden meaning that I was seeking—a kind of *Alchemie du verbe.* One word has its meaning and another word has its own, but when they are brought together something strange happens to them: they have an in-between connotation at the same time as they retain their original individual meanings . . . poetry is this very tension-filled relationship between the words, between the lines, between the meanings.

It was in Paris, it would seem, that he wrote many of the poems which appeared in his first book, *Sent på jorden* (*Late on the Earth*), which was published in 1932. This he later described as a "suicidal book":

> I literally used to walk around with a revolver in my pocket. Illegally, for that matter. In my general despair I did everything possible to remain in my dream-world or to be quickly removed from it. I began to gamble and I lost my money, which made my temporary return to Sweden quite definite.

Late on the Earth attracted little critical attention, but by the time of the publication of *Färjesång* (*Ferry Song*) in 1941, he had become recognized as one of Sweden's leading poets.

The translations in this Penguin volume are of two late works, *Dīwān över Fursten av Emgión* (*Dīwān over the Prince of Emgión*), 1965, and *Sagan om Fatumeh* (*The Tale of Fatumeh*), 1966. His last volume, *Vägvisare till underjorden* (*Guide to the Underworld*) was published in 1967. In 1968 he died of cancer of the throat.

The Prince of Emgión had appeared in two earlier poems. Ekelöf relates that, during a spiritualist seance in Stockholm during the thirties, he had asked where his spiritual "I" was to be found. The oracle, a drinking-glass placed upside down, replied: "In Persia and his name is the Prince of Emgión." Later, Ekelöf came to believe that this Prince was of Armenian-Kurdish stock, half a Christian and half a Gnostic.

Dīwān was begun in Constantinople in 1965, and most or all of the poems were written within a period of four weeks. "*Dīwān,*" Ekelöf wrote to a friend, "is my greatest poem of love and passion. I cannot touch it nor see it because I grow ill when I see this blind and tortured man. . . . As far as I can understand, someone has written the poems with me as a medium. . . . Really, I have never had such an experience, or not one as complete."

The character he here refers to is not the Prince, but Digenís Acrítas, the hero of an eleventh-century Byzantine epic romance. Digenís was the son of an Arab father and a Byzantine mother. Captured in battle, he was incarcerated in the prison of Vlacheme, where he was tortured and blinded. In his suffering his principal consolation is the Virgin, to whom he addresses passionate hymns. Though there are references to what are obviously Christian icons, this figure is not the Christian Madonna, but rather the Earth Mother, the Goddess known to us through St Paul as the "Diana of the Ephesians". In *Dīwān* another female figure appears who is human, not divine, perhaps a wife, perhaps a sister or daughter.

The Tale of Fatumeh is an equally sad story. It tells of a generous, loving girl who becomes first a courtesan and then the beloved of a prince, whose child she bears; she is apparently deserted by him and brought to the Harem at Erechtheion, but she is eventually thrown out of the Harem and spends a miserable old age, selling herself to keep alive. Like Digenís, Fatumeh is sustained by her visions. Whatever has happened and may happen, no disaster shall degrade her soul.

Like the Greek poet Constantine Cavafy, Ekelöf sets these poems in a bygone age. Different in sensibility as they are—Cavafy is ironic and detached, Ekelöf passionate and involved—neither chooses the past as an escape: for both it is a means for illuminating and criticizing the present. Although Ekelöf was fascinated by Byzantium, he never idealized it. "Why," he wrote in a letter, "have I become interested in the Byzantine, the Greek life? Because Byzantine life, traditionally and according to deep-rooted custom, is like the political life in *our* cities and states. I am intensely interested in it because I hate it. I hate what is Greek. I hate what is Byzantine. . . . *Dīwān* is a symbol of the political decadence we see around us. *Fatumeh* is a symbol of the degradation, the coldness between persons, which is equally obvious."

Ekelöf had a special numerological theory and considered life an odd number and death an even number. His numerological preoccupation is expressed in his division of *The Tale of Fatumeh* into a *naẓm*, a string of beads, and a *tesbiḥ*, a rosary, each consisting of twenty-nine numbered poems. This plan regrettably had to be abandoned for this version. Some textual emendations have also been made whenever Ekelöf's manuscripts have warranted such action.

W. H. AUDEN
LEIF SJÖBERG

Selected Poems, by Gunnar Ekelöf,
translated by W. H. Auden and Leif Sjöberg (1971)

The Artist's Private Face

The Letters of Thomas Mann,
Volume I: 1889–1942 and Volume II: 1943–1955.
Selected and translated by Richard & Clara Winston. Introduction by Richard Winston. Secker & Warburg. 12 guineas.

These handsomely produced volumes, excellently edited and translated, contain 540 letters, but a fraction of Mann's total output. The German edition contains 1,331, and his daughter Erika estimated that, in his lifetime, he must have written twenty thousand in longhand, quite apart from thousands dictated to a secretary. When Mann was forced to leave Germany in a hurry, much of his earlier correspondence was lost. Consequently, the letters here printed, written between the ages of sixteen and fifty-seven, when Hitler came to power, take up only 191 pages, whereas there are 410 from the last twenty-two years of his life.

Had I been personally responsible for the selection, I would have omitted the extracts from the letters to his future wife Katia, which he wrote in 1904 while courting her, as being too private and personal, but the editors have only printed brief extracts, and none of them are shy-making.

Thomas Mann was not, in my opinion, a "born" letter-writer, as Horace Walpole or Byron or Keats were, not, that is to say, a man to whom writing letters was as much a means of artistic expression as writing poems or novels. He wrote his letters because an occasion called for one. Now and again, but not very often, he says something funny. For example:

> Many happy returns on your birthday, and also forgive us generously for our enormous levity in having brought you into the world. I promise it won't happen again, and, after all, we weren't treated any better.

or (apropos of Huxley's *The Doors of Perception*)

> . . . being rapt over the miracle of a chair and absorbed in all sorts of colour illusions has more to do with idiocy than he thinks.

Then, human nature being what it is, letters written when the writer is very angry are always fun to read. In this collection, there are two real scorchers, one, written in 1936, to the journalist Eduard Korrodi, which led to Mann being deprived of his German citizenship, and one to Prince Hubertus Löwenstein, written in 1940.

Anyone who is interested, not only in Thomas Mann himself, but also in the problems which confront every writer, will hunt through these letters eagerly to learn what he has to say on such matters. Thus, in 1901, as one might expect from the author of *Tonio Kröger,* he writes to his brother Heinrich:

> All literature is death! I shall never understand how anyone can be dominated by it without bitterly hating it.

How different his view forty years later.

> I am an artist. That means a man who wishes to entertain himself—and this isn't a matter to pull a solemn face about. . . . No, in the making of art there can be no question of suffering. Anyone who has chosen so essentially amusing a job has no right to play the martyr in the presence of serious people.

As a specialist, a writer has to be faithful to his artistic conscience. As a citizen, like all men, he has to do his duty by society. Few writers in this difficult century have so clearly recognised as Mann his double responsibility without ever confusing the two. The novels he wrote after Hitler came to power, *Joseph in Egypt, The Beloved Returns, The Transposed Heads* have nothing to do with contemporary events: on the contrary, they are works of "freedom and gaiety." But from the very beginning he knew that it was his duty publicly to denounce the Nazis at whatever cost to himself, and to spend a great deal of his valuable time doing what he could to help their victims. Though luckier than most of the emigré writers in that his books were immediately translated into English and sold very well, his lot was not easy. Every writer thinks of himself as writing for those who share his mother-tongue.

> At bottom I am aware that my books are not written for Prague and New York, but for Germans. The rest of the world has always been an "extra."

For fourteen years he was cut off from his natural audience. Then, like any famous man whose "political" sayings and actions receive wide publicity, he was frequently misunderstood and even maligned. Some of his fellow exiles attacked him because he refused, as a German, to distinguish between "good" and "bad" Germans; during the McCarthy era, he was frequently accused of being pro-Communist; and when, very rightly, he insisted on giving his lecture on Goethe in both West and East Germany, there were many protests. He may have made some political mistakes, like voting for Henry Wallace, but his motives were always honourable.

Every reader of these letters will make his own list of curiosa which particularly catch his attention. I can only give some of mine. I never knew before that the seminal idea for *Death in Venice* was an historical and heterosexual incident, Goethe's infatuation as an old man with the young girl to whom he wrote the "Marienbad Elegy." When Mann received the Nobel Prize in 1930, the most powerful Swedish critic called *The Magic Mountain* an "artistic monstrosity" and said that *Buddenbrooks* was the sole reason for the award.

Mann was very well read in German literature, but he read Adalbert Stifter for the first time when he was forty-two. He does not seem to have read the most famous English novelists: the only two English writers he mentions with unqualified praise are Conrad and, surprisingly, Blake. Was it his friendship with Einstein which enabled him, in February 1944, to prophesy: "Socialism will probably not bring peace; that is more likely to be accomplished by physics through the unleashing of the uranium atom"? Lastly, I was glad to be reminded of an incident which I had forgotten, but which made quite a stir at the time. One of the prosecutors at the Nuremberg Trials quoted some lines which he attributed to Goethe, but which were, in fact, lines which Mann gave Goethe to say in *The Beloved Returns.*

I cannot imagine how any reader under thirty will respond to these letters, but for anyone who, like myself, graduated in 1928, knew Germany well and loved the German language, it is fascinating to compare Mann's reactions and one's own to the same historical events. I find his generally wise, wiser than most of us, and always noble.

The Sunday Times, 3 January 1971

W. H. Auden on George Orwell

The Collected Essays, Journalism and Letters of George Orwell. Edited by Sonia Orwell and Ian Angus. Penguin. Four volumes, 10s each.

Aside from editorial matter, these volumes run to over two thousand pages of small print. Obviously, it is impossible to deal with them adequately in a single review. Few readers, I imagine, are going to read every word, but the editors were right in their decision to let each reader make his own selection, for Orwell was a man of many interests who, for different reasons, can appeal to a wide variety of men. Those, for example, who are primarily interested in Orwell the literary artist will turn first to pieces like "The Spike", "Hop Picking", "Looking Back on the Spanish War", "How The Poor Die", in which he narrates experiences that befell him, and then to the essays on other writers, notably Dickens and Swift, and to his book reviews. Others may prefer his political pamphlets like *The Lion and the Unicorn.* For the historian there are his letters to *Partisan Review,* and for anyone who simply wants a good laugh, there is, of course, "Boys' Weeklies."

On his aims as a writer, he begins by saying:

> My starting point is always a feeling of partisanship, a sense of injustice. When I sit down to write a book, I do not say to myself, "I'm going to produce a work of art." I write it because there is some lie I want to expose, some fact to which I want to draw attention, and my initial concern is to get a hearing.

He realises, however, that this is not the whole truth, for he goes on to say:

> I am not able, and I do not want, completely to abandon the world view that I acquired in childhood. So long as I remain alive and well, I shall continue to feel strongly about prose style, to love the surface of the earth, and to take pleasure in solid objects and scraps of useless information. It is no use trying to suppress that side of myself. The job is to reconcile my ingrained likes and dislikes with the essentially non-individual activities that this age forces on all of us.

Among the writers of this century, he stands out, like Hilaire Belloc, as a master of unadorned English prose. Even when one disagrees with what he is saying, one has to admire the vigour and lucidity with which he says it. Like the Austrian, Karl Kraus, he knew that corruption of the language must corrupt society: hence his admirable essay on "Politics and the English Language". (I wish he had written one on political and military euphemisms.)

As a novelist, he is, I think, most successful when he is least "fictional", that is to say, when he narrates what he himself has personally felt and witnessed. Though I am very glad for his sake that he wrote *Animal Farm* and *1984*, since they freed him from financial anxieties, neither, in my opinion, quite comes off. When one compares his encounters with the poor in the early nineteen-thirties with those of his great predecessor, Henry Mayhew, in the eighteen-fifties, one is struck, and saddened, by the decline in their powers of verbal expression. Compared with the Dickensian exuberance of Mayhew's interviewees, Orwell's seem almost inarticulate. I rather fear the cause may be universal elementary education, which has destroyed their instinctive native speech, but not trained them to do more than read the cheaper newspapers.

About other writers he shows keen insights and astonishing fair-mindedness. Though himself a man of strong political and moral convictions, he is always ready to recognise aesthetic merit in those of whose politics and morals he disapproves: he even manages to say a good word for Dali. Indeed, the only writers whom, it seems to me, he has gotten all wrong are the poets, including myself, who began to publish in the 'thirties, The Movement, as he calls us. We were, he says,

> didactic, political writers, aesthetically conscious, of course, but more interested in subject-matter than technique.

To this, I can only say, that all my life I have been more interested in poetic technique than anything else. What *is* true is that I am technically more conservative, more conscious of my debt to the nineteenth century (Yeats was too, for that matter) than poets like Eliot and Pound. Then, aside from a few plays, very little of the poetry I wrote in that decade was overtly political: basically I have always thought of myself as a comic poet. More seriously, he charges us with refusing to admit that we were bourgeois. The term *bourgeois* like *proletariat*, has no meaning in English-speaking countries, but if he means that I was ashamed to be, like himself, professional upper middle class, I have never thought of myself as anything else. At times, to be sure, I wrote satires about my class, but one can only satirise what one knows at first hand. One final point. I did not have to wait to read *Homage to Catalonia* to know that the Soviet Union was anything but a Utopia, and I was as shocked as he was when the official English left had the nerve to support the Nazi-Soviet pact. The mistake I made was to think: "The Russians are barbarians who have had neither a Renaissance nor a Reformation and have always lived under a tyranny. In an enlightened West, Communism would be different." We have learned better by now, we now know that human nature being what it is, a single party government, whether of the right or the left, cannot be anything but a tyranny.

But, of course, when revolutionary social changes seem necessary, the temptation to adopt a single party government is very great. What Orwell seems to have hoped for was a Socialist (non-Communist) party which would be elected by an overwhelming majority and, like the Swedish Socialist Party, stay in power for decades, so that it would have nothing to fear from rival political parties.

> It will crush any open revolt promptly and cruelly, but it will interfere very little with the spoken and written word. Political parties with different names will still exist, revolutionary sects will still be publishing their newspapers and making as little impression as ever.

He was, I fear, over-optimistic.

As a commentator on the contemporary political and social scene, he reminds me of Cobbett: he exhibits the same independence of party and the same vigour. Both of them, too, were not under the illusion that political action can solve all problems. Thus Orwell:

> There is always a new tyrant waiting to take over from the old—generally not quite so bad, but still a tyrant. Consequently two views are always tenable. The one, how can you improve human nature until you have improved the system? The other, what is the use of changing the system until you have improved human nature?

> In politics one can never do more than decide which of two evils is the lesser.

Today, reading his reactions to events in the war and the immediate years after the war, my first thought is: "O how I wish Orwell were still alive, so that I could read his comments on contemporary events." For example, last year, our mutual friend, Geoffrey Gorer, sent out a questionnaire, asking people to identify their social class—I think he gave them about five options.

Almost all his respondents, he tells me, identified themselves incorrectly. What would he say to that? What would he say about hippie communes, student demonstrations, drugs, trades unions? Would he still be as hopeful about the social benefits of nationalised industries? Would he still call for a higher birth-rate? What he would say, I have no idea: I am only certain that he would be worth listening to.

He did, I think, have one blind spot. His fanatic, essentially religious hatred of Christianity, prevented him from seriously studying the subject. Thus, while I am sure he was well read in Communist literature, I very much doubt if he had read much theology or ecclesiastical history. He seems to have imagined that Christianity, like Manicheism and Buddhism, is an "other-wordly" religion. In fact, from the accession of Constantine to the present day, the charge which all too often can justly be brought against the Churches, both Catholic and Protestant, is that they have been all too "worldly", all too willing to make shady deals with temporal powers that would protect their power and wealth. The English Catholic apologists of this century, Belloc, Chesterton, Beachcomber, etc., all had very definite views about politics, society, history. One may disagree with them—I do myself—but the one thing one cannot accuse them of is a lack of concern for the things of this world. I suspect that the cause of Orwell's obsessive hatred was probably his experiences at his prep-school, St Cyprian's, which seems, when I compare it with the one I attended, to have been exceptionally nasty. I also suspect that his upbringing in early childhood had more effect on his sensibility and character than he realised. If I were asked to name people whom I considered true Christians, the name *George Orwell* is one of the first that would come to my mind. As evidence, I will cite two passages from his writings.

> He was half-dressed and was holding up his trousers with both hands. I refrained from shooting him . . . I had come here to shoot "Fascists", but a man who is holding up his trousers isn't a "Fascist", he is visibly a fellow creature similar to yourself.

> If it were left to me, my verdict on both Hitler and Mussolini, would be: not death, unless it is inflicted in some hurried unspectacular way. If the Germans and Italians feel like giving them a summary court-martial and then a firing squad, let them do it. Or better still, let the pair of them escape with a suitcaseful of bearer securities and settle down as the accredited bores of some Swiss pension. But no martyrising . . . above all, no solemn hypocritical trial of war criminals.

The Spectator, 16 January 1971

The Anomalous Creature

The Fall into Time. By E. M. Cioran, translated from the French by Richard Howard, Introduction by Charles Newman. Quadrangle. $5.95.

The Fall into Time can and, I think, should be read simultaneously in at least two ways, perhaps more. It can be read seriously as a sermon by a latter-day Jeremiah (it is not an accident, surely, that M. Cioran is the son of a Greek Orthodox priest) about The Fall of Man, a passionate denunciation of the mess he has made of his life, a condition which, the preacher says, is better accounted for by theology than by biology.

In listening to such a sermon, one naturally expects some exaggeration; if we are to be roused from our sloth and flattering illusions, the picture must be painted as black as possible. Man, says this preacher, is "an episode, a digression, a heresy, a kill-joy, a wastrel, a miscreant who has complicated everything." Consciousness is an evil, "the quintessence of decrepitude." Knowledge is an evil: "The more we yield to the desire to know, stamped as it is with perversity and corruption, the more incapable we become of remaining *inside* some reality, any reality." Language is an evil: "[Man] will never approach life's inviolate sources if he still has dealings with words."

The preacher, however, is in the anomalous position, of which M. Cioran, I'm sure, is well aware, of being unable to practice what he preaches. To denounce consciousness, he must appeal to the conscious minds of his audience; to denounce knowledge is to claim that he *knows* it is evil; to denounce language he has to use words. Chesterton wrote: "If it is not true that a divine being fell, then one can only say that one of the animals went entirely off its head." To understand Man, that is, individual men must share his madness. So M. Cioran says of one of his forerunners, Nietzsche: "We owe the diagnosis of our disease to a lunatic, more contaminated and scarred than any of us, to an avowed maniac, precursor and model of our own delirium."

M. Cioran, himself, however, is certainly sane by ordinary standards. Only now and again does he say something which, to me, seems crazy. I do not believe that he is a Manichaean, but occasionally he makes remarks which make him sound like one, as when he suggests that God fell when He created the Universe, or when he declares: "No one recovers from the disease of being born, a deadly wound if ever there was one." Then he says that, while everybody's secret wish is to be praised, which is true, we are all ashamed to admit it, which is, surely, false, though, of course, we want to be praised for the right reasons. Then, coming from a writer, I find this observation very odd.

> What writer enjoying a certain fame does not ultimately suffer from it, enduring the discomfort of becoming known and understood, of having a public, however limited it may be? Envious of his friends who loll in the comforts of obscurity, he will do his best to pull them out of it. . . . Write! Publish! he keeps urging furiously.

A writer may suffer from the feeling that he is admired or disparaged for the wrong reasons, but every writer hopes to be read. If M. Cioran really suffered as he says, then, either he would not publish at all, or publish anonymously. Then, judging by myself and the writers I know, our secret and shameful wish is that we could be the only writer alive: the last thing we want to do is encourage competitors.

For the most part, however, M. Cioran carries me along with him. On the mental triad, Faith or Belief, Doubt, and Denial, he has fascinating things to say. Without beliefs of some kind, we cannot really live, far less act.

> Anyone who cherishes the equilibrium of his mind will avoid attacking certain essential superstitions. This is a vital necessity for thinking, despised only by the skeptic who, having nothing to preserve, respects neither the secrets nor the tabus indispensable to the duration of certitudes. . . .
>
> Skepticism has against it our reflexes, our appetites, our instincts. For all its declarations that being is a prejudice, this prejudice, older than ourselves, outdates man and life, resists our attacks, withstands reasoning and proof, since it is also true that whatever exists and manifests itself in duration is based on the undemonstrable and the unverifiable.

The capacity to affirm or believe proceeds, says M. Cioran, from "a depth of barbarism which the majority, which virtually the totality of men have the good fortune to preserve. . . ."

The term "barbarism" obviously has shock value, but I suspect there may be another reason why he uses it. He writes in French, and the French language has no equivalent to the English term "common sense." ("*Bon sens*" is not the same thing.)

M. Cioran distinguishes between two kinds of skeptic, the "pure" skeptic or Negator, and the Doubter. The negator is not really seeking for truth, his goal is endless interrogation and he rarely calls the act of negation in question. The doubter, on the other hand, frequently calls doubt into question.

> The drama of the doubter is greater than that of the negator, because to live without a goal is more difficult than to live for a bad cause.

> Only the "barbarian" in us is capable of creative thought.

> As long as we follow the mind's spontaneous movement, as long as, by reflection, we put ourselves on the level of life itself, we cannot think

> we are thinking: once we do so, our ideas oppose each other, neutralize each other within an empty consciousness. . . . To produce, to "create," is to have the courage or the luck not to perceive the lie of diversity, the deceptive character of the multiple. . . . Illusion alone is fertile, illusion alone originates. . . . All that shimmers on the surface of the world, all that we call interesting, is the fruit of inebriation and ignorance.

I must confess I don't see why diversity should necessarily be a lie, but I think I get the basic idea.

But to regard M. Cioran solemnly as a preacher is not the only way of reading him. He can also be read playfully as a master of language who is having enormous fun handling words. In his most intelligent Introduction, Mr Charles Newman speaks of the temptation to grasp M. Cioran by the aphorism, "to make him into a kind of Gallic Oscar Wilde." Provided one realizes that he is not simply that, I think it is a perfectly legitimate way of reading him.

He has said that all his books are autobiographical, but no writer could be less "confessional." He tells us that a man in good health is always disappointing, but I suspect his own health is good. I hope so, for his sake, since, if it is not, then by his own judgment he is a sadist. He says that, if only there were more boasters and flatterers around, the psychiatrist would be out of a job, but I'm pretty sure he indulges in neither activity. He declares that we should be better off if we were verminous like the animals and smelled of the stable, but I should be surprised to hear that he never takes a bath. He condemns lucidity:

> Consciousness is not lucidity. Lucidity, man's monopoly, represents the severance of consciousness: it is necessarily consciousness of consciousness, and, if we are to distinguish ourselves from the animals, it is lucidity alone which must receive the credit or the blame.

Yet the first thing one notices about these two sentences, or any others by M. Cioran, is how "lucid" they are. Never, in reading him, does one encounter, as one often does when reading Hegel or Heidegger, sentences which make one exclaim: "What the heck does this mean?" For me, the two most interesting authors writing in French who have emerged since the last war are M. Cioran and M. Malcolm de Chazal, both of them aphorists, a literary device which always gives me joy. When, for instance, I read

> He who has never envied the vegetable has missed the human drama

or

> Resign from the race? That would be to forget that one is never so much a man as when one regrets being so

they make me feel anything but gloomy. I say: "Goody! Goody!"

In conclusion, let me say that Mr Richard Howard's translation is magnificent.

The New York Review of Books, 28 January 1971

The Mountain Allowed Them Pride

Deborah: A Wilderness Narrative. By David Roberts. Vanguard. $6.95.

I wonder if the psychologists can explain why it is that mountaineering should so strongly appeal to the intellectual, the book-loving, the introvert, persons for whom conventional athletics, like football or baseball, have no interest. Whatever the reason, one consequence has been that the books written about mountaineering have been of an unusually high literary standard. The first historical account of ascending a mountain for its own sake (no rock-climbing, of course) is by Petrarch, and from the middle of the nineteenth century when serious rock-climbing became popular until the present day, a succession of vivid accounts of expeditions have appeared, starting with Edward Whymper's account of climbing the Matterhorn. David Roberts has already written one excellent book, *The Mountain of My Fear*; *Deborah*, in my opinion, is even finer.

It tells of the attempt by two friends from Harvard—henceforth I shall call them, as they are in the book, Dave and Don—to climb the East Face of Mount Deborah, Alaska, in the summer of 1964. (The Western, and easier, face had been climbed in 1954.) The expedition, that is to say, the time they spent alone together in the wilderness, lasted six weeks.

There are two threads to the narrative. Firstly, it is a detailed factual account of what all mountain climbers have to do and suffer, of carrying heavy loads, being storm-bound for days in a tiny tent, aware all the time of the possibility of being killed by an avalanche or by falling into a crevasse. On the way down, Don twice fell into one with nearly fatal results: the first time it took four hours to get him out, the second time he suffered severe facial injuries. And then of course whoever the climbers are, there is the excitement and worry of wondering: "Shall we succeed?" In this case, they did not. From a high col Dave saw the East Face for the first time at close range.

> The crumbly brown rock towered, flat and crackless, a few degrees less than vertical. A thin splotchy coating of ice overlay most of the rock. Where the rock overhung, great icicles grew. . . . And above, blocking out half the sky, was the terrible black cliff, the six-hundred-foot wall that we had once blithely, back in Cambridge, allowed three days to climb. At its upper rim, nearly a thousand feet above me, hovered monstrous chunks of ice, like aimed cannons at the top of a castle wall. As I

> watched, one broke off, fell most of the six hundred feet without touching anything, then smashed violently on a ledge to my left and bounced out of sight down the precipice.

Curiously, they felt less disappointed than one might have expected.

> Of course we were sad. But as we turned down, we were almost lighthearted, too. The mountain had been fair to us; it had unequivocally said Stop, instead . . . of forcing the decision of failure on us. . . . The mountain had allowed us pride.

During the ascent, both Dave and Don had suffered from anxiety dreams. (As one would expect, neither had sexual dreams.) Thus Dave: "I would be a guest at a buffet dinner where every imaginable delicacy was heaped in inexhaustible piles on a huge table. There would be scores of other guests. . . . But each time I started to eat, someone would interrupt me with a question." After their defeat, the anxiety disappeared, and now he dreamed that "this time I was the host and friend after friend kept showing up and complimenting me on the food."

The second thread of the story is of the greatest psychological interest, a day-by-day account of the personal reactions to each other of two young men united by a love of climbing at which both are equally gifted, but of very different temperaments, living at very close quarters under conditions of great stress.

Of course, we only hear Dave's side of the story, but I don't think Don's would contradict it.

Long before they decided to climb Deborah (it was actually Don who suggested making it a two-man show), Dave had begun to reflect on the differences between them. Dave was quick and impatient, Don slow and methodical. "I loved conversations, but Don preferred to think by himself." Then there was the contrast between their attitudes towards their academic studies. Dave, majoring in mathematics, took exams in his stride; Don, majoring in philosophy, would panic at the prospect almost to the point of a nervous breakdown.

Even their attitudes towards their common love, climbing, were not the same. Dave was approaching their expedition as "an arduous adventure to be got through with, a thing to be conquered, a place to visit for the sake of the wonder and beauty, but from which to return when it began to wear thin." For Don, it was just the opposite, "an adventure to be lived as long as possible, a place to go where he could be at home and relax."

Their first angry argument broke out as they were approaching base camp.

> Don had used the phrase "well-behaved" four or five times to describe the glacier's lack of crevasses . . . we irritably argued the merits of the word "well-behaved." What had really provoked the quarrel, I suppose,

> was the boredom of the hiking. I had started to notice some of Don's mannerisms and, for lack of a better preoccupation, had picked on one of them to vent my frustrations. It was the first time that I recognized a trait of my own. . . . I could not stand for things to go well for too long a stretch; it was as if I needed a regular exercise of hostility.

Since a person's eating habits are always a manifestation of his character, it is not surprising that these were a frequent source of irritation. "I got mad at his deliberate way of spooning his breakfast cereal because it was indicative of his methodicalness, which was indicative of a mental slowness, which was why he disliked and opposed my impatience." For one cause of annoyance, Dave was entirely to blame: he should never have tried to play chess, which he played well, with Don, who did not. No game is any fun unless both sides are equally matched.

To avoid ill-feelings, they found that they had to obey strict rules when it came to dividing things between them, like food and weights.

> The pound was not a fine enough unit; we haggled over ounces. . . . We vacillated between the roles of the accuser ("Come on now, the stove's easily two and a half pounds") and martyr ("It's all right, I'll take it anyway").

Such incidents in isolation can make it sound as if their expedition was a disastrous failure, which it clearly wasn't. As Dave gratefully acknowledges, there were many good moments of warmth, joy and brotherhood. The difficulty for a writer about such moments is that it seems to be a law of language that happiness, like goodness, is almost impossible to describe, while conflict, like evil, is all too easy to depict.

A most fascinating book.

The New York Times Book Review, 7 February 1971

He Descended into Hell in Vain

A Spy for God: The Ordeal of Kurt Gerstein. By Pierre Joffroy. Harcourt Brace Jovanovich. $6.95.

> The man who will not act except in total righteousness achieves nothing. He does not enter the path of progress and he is not true because he is not real. . . . The man who seeks to be true must run the risk of being mistaken, of putting himself in the wrong.—Karl Jaspers

It is very seldom that a book reduces me to tears as this one did. It is the story of a man who, if he had not committed suicide in a French prison in 1945, would almost certainly have been hanged at Nuremberg as a war criminal; yet, on finishing it, I find myself sharing Martin Niemöller's conviction that he was a saint.

> He was tall, with grey-blue eyes, his temples and the back of his neck shaved in the Prussian style. A wide expanse of forehead on a narrow head, big ears that stuck out slightly, a large nose somewhat flattened above a full mouth, of which the firmly modelled upper lip seemed to crush the lower as though by an impulse from within.

Kurt Gerstein was born in 1906, one of seven children. His father was a judge, an upright man according to his standards, which were those of the upper middle class before 1914. Certain things were simply "not done," for example:

> . . . to disobey one's civil and military superiors, to show lack of respect for the Imperial family or for constituted authority, to marry someone of inferior status or to be on too friendly terms with Jews, though these might be quite honorable people.

Even as a child, Kurt Gerstein seems to have been a maverick, estranged both from his parents and his siblings. He never referred to his father as "father" but always simply as *Er*, and the "mother" in his early life was not his own but his Catholic nursemaid Regina, a position later occupied by his Berlin housekeeper, Leokadia Hinz. At school, though he was obviously the brightest in his class, he was often in trouble for not doing his work. After passing his *Arbitur*, he decided to become a mining engineer, a job at which he was very successful. The arts meant nothing to him, but he had a passionate wish to *know*. He displayed many manic traits:

> He drove himself remorselessly. Eating, drinking and sleeping were time-consuming occupations, a waste of substance. . . . He slept less than five hours a night, there was always so much to do.

A devout Christian, in his spare time he ran summer camps for boys, who all seemed to have adored him, though some later felt the need to rebel against his overwhelming personality.

On May 1, 1933, he became a member of the Nazi Party. To those who objected, he said: "You're criticizing it from the outside. No man should pass judgment on matters of which he has not first-hand knowledge. You must go and see for yourself—to Hell if need be."

It was not long before he was in trouble. In 1935, at a performance of a racist play, *Wittekind*, he stood up, wearing his party badge, and shouted "Shame!," for which he was badly beaten up. In September, 1936, he was imprisoned for six weeks for distributing illegal pamphlets of the Confessional Church. As a result he was expelled from the Party, dismissed from the Ministry of Mines, and debarred from public service.

He decided to study medicine, but was presently again in trouble for practicing it before he was fully qualified. In 1937 he married. In July, 1938, he was again arrested on account of his relations, in this case quite innocent, with an opposition group that wanted to restore the Monarchy, and was sent to Welzheim concentration camp near Stuttgart. Fortunately, he had made a good impression on one of his Gestapo interrogators, who managed to get him out after six weeks. His father, who by now had become an ardent Nazi, pulled strings so that, on June 10, 1939, he was readmitted to Party membership.

It was at this time that the Nazi authorities started their euthanasia program for the elimination of the old and incurably sick, and one of their victims in 1941 was Gerstein's sister-in-law, Berta. His reaction to this was to decide to join the Waffen SS which miraculously, in view of his record, he succeeded in doing, and, because of his training as a mining engineer and a doctor, was appointed to their Hygiene Institute in Berlin. This was just at the time when a typhus epidemic had broken out among the German armies in Russia.

> Gerstein, aided by two of his former pupils, Armin Peters and Horst Dickten, proceeded to show what he could do. They devised, first, a delousing apparatus for uniforms, blankets and under-clothes, using high pressure steam, which destroyed not only the lice but also their excrement, and secondly a mobile water-filter unit. Both were approved by the Army and proved highly successful. . . . Later they produced a floating pump for use against mosquitoes, a new type of hospital bed and special delousing vehicles.

As a result, Gerstein soon became a VIP, traveling all over Germany and occupied Europe and with an apparently inexhaustible expense account of which he took full advantage. Everywhere he went, he bought up large stocks of food and rare articles. Interviewed in 1968 by M. Joffroy, Horst Dickten said:

> He had two objects in mind. First, to suborn important people with the princely gifts he made them. It was a triumph every time he got another high-ranking soldier or civil servant in his power—and I may say that there were plenty of them. And this first operation paved the way for the second, which was far more important: helping people in the concentration camps. . . . The goods—mainly food and medical supplies—were either sent in through the aircraft factory at Oranienburg or else smuggled into the camp at night with the help of guards whom we had bribed.

Because of his status as the leading decontamination expert, an invitation to visit Hell was not long in coming. Two doctors came to visit him. "We need two trucks capable of pumping exhaust gas into a closed chamber. Can you suggest a suitable method?" Gerstein roughed out a design on the spot. "You need only fit the trucks with an auxiliary engine." Then, on June 8, 1942, a Major Gunther walked into his office.

> "Lieutenant Gerstein, you are required to procure 260 kilos of prussic acid within the shortest possible time. You will be required to accompany it and to make arrangements for its use in place of the gas at present being used."

The official German euphemism for extermination of human beings was *Entwesung*, in English decontamination, so it was as an expert in exterminating lice that Gerstein came to Belzec and saw with his own eyes exactly what went on. He wrote a report on this in French when a prisoner of war, which M. Joffroy prints in full. Most of the horrors are by now well-known, but on this occasion there was an added touch. After the Jews had been pushed into the chamber and the doors closed, the Diesel pump refused to start, and it took two hours and forty-nine minutes to get it going.

Now that he knew the worst, Gerstein went to everybody he could think of who might be able to get the news to the Allies and the neutral countries, but nobody would believe him. Here are some typical reactions.

> The Papal nuncio: "Go away. Get out!"

> A member of the Dutch Resistance: "I told them [the British]. But they simply refused to believe anything so atrocious."

> An official in the State Department: "It appears to me inadvisable, in view of the incredible nature of these allegations, and our complete inability to give assistance in the event of their being true, to circulate the information in the manner proposed."

> A German Protestant pastor and anti-Nazi: "Your friend is mad."

> The International Red Cross: "We're in a terrible dilemma. A woman member of the Committee is urging us to issue a solemn protest against the persecution of the Jews in Germany. But how can we? If we were to protest, Hitler would denounce the Geneva Convention and we should have to give up all our work in favor of the Allies and on behalf of prisoners of war, the occupied territories, civilian internees and so on."

Gerstein had hoped that the Allied planes would shower leaflets on Germany telling the facts. Whether the Germans would have believed them seems doubtful. It is true that Hitler called off the euthanasia program because the facts had gotten around, and he was afraid of disaffection among Catholic soldiers, but then the facts came from the Germans themselves, not from people with whom they were at war. Anyway the Allies did nothing. He had dirtied his hands in vain. By supplying gas he had made himself an accomplice in crime. He was on occasions able to perform little acts of sabotage, but his only concrete achievement was to modify the gas Zyklon B so that it killed a little less painfully.

Presently he began to arouse suspicions. Some of the doctors in Auschwitz even thought he was planning to blow the camp up. By 1944, the SS had decided he was too slow in delivering and were ordering their gas through another channel. He was acquainted with the generals who were planning to assassinate Hitler, though he believed them mistaken. They simply wanted to get rid of Hitler and then win the war: Gerstein believed that nothing but total defeat could atone for what had been done. How he escaped being arrested and shot remains a mystery. As the Russians advanced, the authorities made plans to eliminate all those who had worked in the camps. Foreigners were to be shot: Germans, like the bestial Captain Wirth, were sent to fight the Yugoslavian Partisans.

When the war ended he surrendered to the French and wrote his report. At first he was allowed a good deal of liberty, but he ended up in the high security prison of Cherche-Midi, charged with "war-crimes, murder and complicity." They seem even to have suspected him of having invented the gas chamber. He might have accepted such a fate for himself, but he was tormented by the knowledge that he had mentioned the names of several people who had tried to do something, with the result that they too, thanks to him, were arrested. On July 26, 1945, he hanged himself in his cell. The body was buried in a communal grave under the name of Gastein, so that "Gerstein" remained on the list of Wanted Persons long after he was dead. At Nuremberg, efforts were made, principally by the Americans, to suppress his report, for what political reasons we shall never know. Finally, on August 27, 1950, a German denazification court sitting on his case ruled that he had been a Nazi and remained one.

M. Joffroy's attention was drawn to the case by a remark of Leon Poliakov in his book *The History of Anti-Semitism*:

> Our personal conviction is absolute. . . . The German Gerstein was a just man among the Gentiles.

At first he was skeptical. He thought his inquiry would only take a few weeks' time and that he would probably find it was simply a case of a man who thought it safer to have a foot in both camps. It took him two years and eight months. His conclusion: "I have not juggled with facts or with texts, and I have accepted as essentially true Gerstein's own account of his situation, having verified most of the details."

Let Karl Barth have the last word:

> Gerstein was a truly remarkable figure such as could only have existed and can only be understood in the context of that time and those terrifying dilemmas.

The New York Review of Books, 11 March 1971

Craftsman, Artist, Genius

I must leave it to others, better professionally qualified than I, to estimate Stravinsky's achievement as a composer. I can, however, I think, speak with some authority about Stravinsky as a paradigm of the creative artist, a model and example from whom younger men, be they composers, painters, or writers, can derive counsel and courage in an age when the threats to their integrity seem to be greater than ever before.

First, let them pay attention to his conception of artistic fabrication. "I am not," he said, "a mirror struck by my mental functions. My interest passes entirely to the object, the thing made." An artist, that is to say, should think of himself primarily as a craftsman, a "maker," not as an "inspired" genius. When we call a work "inspired," all we mean is that it is better, more beautiful, than we could possibly have hoped for. But this is a judgment for the public to make, not the artist himself. True, there have been artists, Hugo Wolf for example, who could create only during periods of intense emotional excitement, but this is a personal accident—most such artists have probably been manic-depressives. It has nothing to do with the value of what they produced in this state. Nearly all persons in a manic phase believe that they are inspired, but very few of them produce anything of artistic value.

Where art is concerned, Valéry was surely right when he said: "Talent without genius isn't much; but genius without talent isn't anything at all." The difference between a pure craft, like carpentry, and art is that when the carpenter starts work he knows exactly what the finished result will be; the artist does not know what he is going to make until he has made it. But, like the carpenter, all he can or should consciously think about is how to make it as well as possible, so that it may become a durable object, permanently "on hand" in the world.

As an illustration of Stravinsky's professional attitude, let me speak from personal experience. When Chester Kallman and I were offered the opportunity to write the libretto of *The Rake's Progress,* we felt, of course, immensely honoured, but at the same time rather alarmed. We had heard that, during the composition of *Perséphone,* there had been great friction between the composer and André Gide over the setting of the French text. Furthermore,

Stravinsky had on more than one occasion expressed the view that, in setting words to music, the words themselves do not matter, only the syllables.

Though, as lovers of music, we both knew that musical and spoken rhythmical values cannot be identical, we were afraid, particularly since Stravinsky had never set English before, that he might distort our words to the point of unintelligibility. But from the moment we started working with him we discovered that our fears were groundless. Going through our text, Stravinsky asked for and marked into his copy the spoken rhythmical value of every word. In one instance, only one, he made a mistake. He thought that, in the word "sedan-chair," the accent in "sedan" fell on the first syllable. When we pointed this out to him, he immediately altered his score. In one number in the opera, the Auctioneer's aria in Act III, scene I, it is dramatically essential that the sung rhythms conform pretty closely to the spoken. They do. In the rest of the work, whatever occasional liberties he took, not one of them struck our English and literary ears as impermissible.

Second, Stravinsky's life as a composer is as good a demonstration as any that I know of the difference between a major and a minor artist. In the case of a minor poet, A. E. Housman, for example, if presented with two of his poems, both of equal artistic merit, one cannot, on the basis of the poems themselves, say which was written first. The minor artist, that is to say, once he has reached maturity and found himself, ceases to have a history. A major artist, on the other hand, is always re-finding himself, so that the history of his works recapitulates or mirrors the history of art. Once he has done something to his satisfaction, he forgets it and attempts to do something new which he has never done before. It is only when he is dead that we are able to see that his various creations, taken together, form one consistent *oeuvre.* Moreover, it is only in the light of his later works that we are able properly to understand his earlier. To illustrate my argument, let me quote two sayings of Stravinsky's.

> I care less about my works than composing.

> The chief problem in being eighty-five . . . is the realisation that one may be powerless to change the quality of one's work. The quantity can be increased, even at eighty-five, but can one change the whole? I, at any rate, am absolutely certain that my *Variations* and *Requiem Canticles* have altered the picture of my whole work. . . .

Last, and most important of all, in his attitude towards the Past and Present, Tradition and Innovation, Stravinsky has set an example which we should all do well to follow. When I contemplate the contemporary artistic scene, I realise how extraordinarily lucky all of those whom we think of as the founders of "modern" art, Stravinsky, Picasso, Eliot, Joyce, etc., were in being born when they were, so that they reached manhood before 1914. Until the

First World War, European society was in all significant respects still what it had been in the nineteenth century. This meant that for these artists the need they all felt to make a radical break with the immediate past was an artistic, not a historical imperative, that is to say, unique for each one of them. None of them would have dreamed of saying: "What kind of music or painting or poetry is 'relevant' to the year 1912?" Nor did they think of themselves collectively as the avant-garde, a term of which Baudelaire, who was certainly himself a great innovator, quite rightly said: "This use of military metaphor reveals minds not militant but formed for discipline, that is for compliance: minds born servile, Belgian minds, which can only think collectively." What each of them felt, I believe, was rather: "It is only by creating something 'new' that I can hope to produce a work which in due time will take its permanent place in the tradition of my art." They were also lucky in their first audiences, who were honest enough to be shocked. Those, for instance, who were scandalised by *Le Sacre du Printemps*, may seem to us now to have been old fogies, but their reaction was genuine. They did not say to themselves: "Times have changed, so we must change in order to be 'with it.'"

In times of rapid social change and political crisis, there is always a danger of confusing the principles governing political action with those that govern artistic fabrication. Thus Plato, dismayed by the political anarchy in the Athens of his time, tried to take artistic fabrication as the model for a good society. Such a theory, if put into practice, must, as we have learned to our cost, result in a totalitarian tyranny, involving, among other things, the most rigid censorship of the arts.

Today in the so-called "free" societies of the West, the most widespread error is the exact opposite of Plato's, namely to take political action as the model for artistic fabrication. To do this is to reduce art to an endless series of momentary and arbitrary "happenings," and to produce in artists and public alike a conformism to the tyranny of the passing moment which is far more enslaving, far more destructive of integrity and originality, than any thoughtless copying of the past.

Once more, Stravinsky:—

> What, may I ask, has become of the idea of universality—of a character of expression not necessarily popular, but compelling to the highest imaginations of a decade or so beyond its time?

This, as we all know, his own compositions have achieved. If any young artist hopes to do the same, let him begin by forgetting all about "historical processes," an awareness of which, as the Master has said, "is probably best left to future and other kinds of wage-earners."

The Observer, 11 April 1971

Louise Bogan 1897–1970

Louise Bogan would certainly, and rightly, have objected to being called a poetess, a term which implies: "For a female, her verse is not bad." She would, however, I think, have gladly and proudly admitted to being a woman poet, for on several occasions she discussed the difference in attitude of the two sexes towards the art of poetry, and the different threats they encounter in trying to write well. Many a man must have had the experience, after telling a woman a funny story, of hearing her ask: "But did it really happen?" The male imagination, it would seem—perhaps because we are biological luxuries—enjoys making things up, creating worlds which have little, if anything to do with the real one. So far as I know, all the writers of nonsense verse have been men. Also, all the poets whom, in a pejorative sense, I would call aesthetes, have been men. Men are tempted, as women, it would seem, are not, to say things and express emotions, not because they believe them to be true or have actually felt them, but because they believe them to be poetically interesting and effective.

For a woman poet, as Louise Bogan said, the danger is different. Her imagination is only stimulated by real events and personal emotional experiences —"crises," as she called them. She is, therefore, not tempted to lie; but she is more tempted than a man to be over-intense in describing them. She finds it harder to attain the objectivity towards and detachment from her experience which all art requires.

Knowing this, Louise Bogan was able to guard against it. Most of her poems are obviously personal, but not one is embarrassing. This poem, for example, is almost certainly, I should say, based on an actual dream, but the significance of the dream has been made valid for everyone.

THE MEETING

For years I thought I knew, at the bottom of the dream,
Who spoke but to say farewell,
Whose smile dissolved, after his first words,
Gentle and plausible.

Each time I found him, it was always the same:
Recognition and surprise,
And then the silence, after the first words,
And the shifting of the eyes.

Then the moment when he had nothing to say
And only smiled again,
But this time towards a place beyond me, where I could not stay—
No world of men.

Now I am not sure. Who are you? Who have you been?
Why do our paths cross?
At the deepest bottom of the dream you are let in,
A symbol of loss.

Eye to eye we look, and we greet each other
Like friends from the same land.
Bitter compliance! Like a faithless brother
You take and drop my hand.

Her standards for judging her own work were extremely severe; in consequence, she was not a prolific poet. The last collection made by herself, *The Blue Estuaries 1923–1968*, contains one hundred and thirty-two poems, which means that her average production of poems she thought worth preserving was less than three per annum.

In judging a poem, one looks for two things: craftsmanship—it should be a well-made verbal object; and uniqueness of perspective—nobody but the author could have written it. Louise Bogan's poems satisfy both criteria. Not one of them is shoddily constructed, and not one reminds one of another poet. Indeed, while in the case of most poets one can detect the influence of other poets, dead or contemporary, a specific influence on her work would be hard to find. One can only say that her work inherits from the general tradition of English poetry, and that, on her personally, modernist experiments and innovations had little or no effect.

One might have expected this to make her as a critic narrow-minded and hostile to experiment, but it did not. On the contrary, she was the kind of reviewer every writer hopes for, someone who judges his work in terms of what he is trying to do, and who takes more pleasure in pointing out virtues than defects. At the same time she was no blurb writer. Take, for example, this admirable passage about surrealism:

> Surrealist poets have gone into the subconscious as one would take a short trip into the country, and have brought back some objects of grisly or erotic-sadistic connotation, or a handful of unrelated images, in order to prove their journey. It has not occurred to them that the journey has been taken many times, that human imagination has, before this, hung a golden bough before the entrance to hell, and has described the profound changes the true journey brings about. It is a journey not to be undertaken lightly, or described without tension of any kind.

Before returning to her poetry, a word should be said about another activity of hers, translation. Goethe's prose is not easy but, in collaboration with Elizabeth Mayer, she produced first-rate English versions of *Werther*, *Novella*, and *Elective Affinities*.

But of course the poems are the main thing. Their range of subject matter may not be very wide, but there is plenty of rhythmical variety, and there are poems which, if unsigned, one would not immediately attribute to her.

For instance, "Animal, Vegetable and Mineral," of which this is one stanza:

Self-fertile flowers are feeble and need priming.
Nature is for this priming, it appears.
Some flowers, like water-clocks, have perfect timing:
Pistil and anthers rise, as though on gears;
One's up and when t'other's down; one falls; one's climbing.

By temperament she was not a euphoric character and in her life she had much to endure. What, aside from their technical excellence, is most impressive about her poems is the unflinching courage with which she faced her problems, her determination never to surrender to self-pity, but to wrest beauty and joy out of dark places.

She clearly had a deep love and understanding of music, and I can think of no other poet in this century and few in others who have written more lyrics which cry out for a composer to set them. To mention only a few, "Roman Fountain," "Song for a Lyre," "To Be Sung on the Water," "Musician," and, finest, perhaps, of all, "Henceforth, from the Mind."

Henceforth, from the mind,
For your whole joy, must spring
Such joy as you may find
In any earthly thing,
And every time and place
Will take your thought for grace.

Henceforth, from the tongue,
From shallow speech alone,
Comes joy you thought, when young,
Would wring you to the bone,
Would pierce you to the heart
And spoil its stop and start.

Henceforward, from the shell,
Wherein you heard, and wondered
At oceans like a bell
So far from ocean sundered—
A smothered sound that sleeps
Long lost within lost deeps,

Will chime you change and hours,
The shadow of increase,
Will sound you flowers

Born under troubled peace—
Henceforth, henceforth
Will echo sea and earth.

It was a privilege to have known her. It will always be a privilege to read her. Our Academy has suffered a grievous loss.

Proceedings of the American Academy of Arts and Letters and the National Institute of Arts and Letters, 1971

The Megrims

Migraine. By Oliver Sacks. University of California Press. $8.50.

There screen'd in shades from day's detested glare,
Spleen sighs for ever on her pensive bed,
Pain at her side, and megrim at her head
—Pope

Dr Sacks's primary purpose in writing this book was, no doubt, to enlighten his fellow practitioners about a complaint of which most of them know all too little. As Dr Gooddy says in his Foreword:

> The common attitude is that migraine is merely a form of mainly non-disabling headache which occupies far more of a busy doctor's time than its importance warrants. . . . Some tablets and the current inelegant cliché of "learning to live with it" are advised by the physician, who hopes he will not be on duty the next time the patient comes for advice. . . . Many doctors are only too pleased when a patient, in desperation, takes himself off to the practitioners of "fringe medicine," almost hoping that the results will be both disastrous and very costly.

I am sure, however, that any layman who is at all interested in the relation between body and mind, even if he does not understand all of it, will find the book as fascinating as I have.

It has been estimated that migraine afflicts at least ten percent of the human race and the true percentage may well be higher, since probably only those who suffer severe attacks consult a doctor. Even if, like myself, one has had the good fortune never to have experienced an attack, we all have known some relative or friend who has had them, so that we can compare their character traits and symptoms with Dr Sacks's detailed descriptions.

Unlike contagious diseases and genetic disabilities such as hemophilia on the one hand, and hysterias on the other, migraine is a classic example of a psychosomatic illness in which physiological and psychological factors play an equal role. As physical organisms we are pretty much the same, that is to say, our bodies have a limited repertoire of symptoms. This makes it possible to diagnose a case of migraine, to distinguish it from, say, epilepsy or asthma. But as conscious persons who can say *I*, each of us is unique. This means that no two cases of migraine are identical; treatment that succeeds with one patient can fail with another.

> A migraine is a physical event which may also be from the start, or later become, an emotional or symbolic event. A migraine expresses both physiological and emotional needs: it is the prototype of a psychophysiological reaction. Thus the convergence of thinking which its understanding demands must be based simultaneously, both on neurology and on psychiatry. . . . Finally, migraine cannot be conceived as an exclusively human reaction, but must be considered as a form of biological reaction specifically tailored to human needs and human nervous systems.

The first part of Dr Sacks's book consists of a series of detailed clinical observations. He distinguishes between three types of migraine, common migraine, popularly called "a sick headache," classical migraine, in which, as in epileptic attacks, there is frequently a distortion of the visual field, and migrainous neuralgia, or "cluster headache," so called because attacks are closely grouped. These descriptions, interesting as I found them, I do not feel qualified to discuss.

I will mention two curious observations Dr Sacks makes. He tells us that the "Nightmare Song" in *Iolanthe* mentions no fewer than twelve migraine symptoms, and that the visions of the medieval nun, Hildegard of Bingen, were clearly visual auras caused by classical migraine.

Part Two is devoted to the questions: "What circumstances trigger off a migraine attack?" and "Is there a migraine personality?" The evidence is bewilderingly diverse. Thus, migraine often runs in families, but Dr Sacks believes this is probably learned from the family environment, not genetically inherited, for many patients have no such family history.

Though classical migraine more commonly attacks young people and males, this is not invariable, and the first attack of common migraine may occur after the age of forty, among women, for example, during their menopause. Classical migraine and cluster headache tend to occur for no discernible reason at regular intervals, varying from two to twelve weeks; common migraine seems more dependent upon external and emotional situations. Some cases resemble allergies: an attack can be caused by bright lights, loud noises, bad smells, inclement weather, alcohol, amphetamines. Others suggest a hormonal origin: migraine is not uncommon among women during their menstrual periods, but very rare during pregnancy.

Such a diversity naturally produces an equal diversity of theories as to the basic cause of migraine. The somatically orientated physician looks for a chemical or neurological solution, the psychiatrist for an exclusively psychological answer. Dr Sacks thinks that both are only half-right. Of the psychological theories the two most accepted are those of Wolff (1963) and Fromm-Reichmann (1937).

> Migraineurs are portrayed by Wolff as ambitious, successful, perfectionistic, rigid, orderly, cautious, and emotionally constipated, driven therefore, from time to time, to outbursts and breakdowns which must assume an indirect somatic form. Fromm-Reichmann is also able to arrive at a clear-cut conclusion: migraine, she states, is a physical expression of unconscious hostility against consciously beloved persons.

Dr Sacks's experiences with his patients have led him to conclude that while many are, as Wolff says, hyperactive and obsessional, there are others who are lethargic and sloppy, and that while, as Fromm-Reichmann says, most migraine attacks are a somatic expression of violent emotions, usually rage, this may be a reaction to an intolerable life situation of which the patient is quite aware, and may also be self-punitive.

> We find, in practice, that sudden *rage* is the commonest precipitant, although *fright* (panic) may be equally potent in younger patients. Sudden *elation* (as at a moment of triumph or unexpected good fortune) may have the same effect. . . . Nor should one claim that all patients with habitual migraine are "neurotic" (except in so far as neurosis is the universal human condition), for in many cases the migraines may replace a neurotic structure, constituting an alternative to neurotic desperation and assuagement.

In Part Three, Dr Sacks discusses the physiological, biological, and psychological factors in migraine. His theories about its biological basis I found particularly interesting and suggestive. Among all animals are to be found two possible reactions to a situation of threat or danger, fight-or-flight and immobilization. He quotes Darwin's description of the second:

> The picture of passive fear, as Darwin portrays it, is one of passivity and prostration, allied with splachnic and glandular activity (". . . a strong tendency to yawn . . . death-like pallor . . . beads of sweat stand out on the skin. All the muscles of the body are relaxed. The intestines are affected. The sphincter muscles cease to act, and no longer retain the contents of the body. . . ."). The general attitude is one of cringing, cowering, and sinking. If the passive reaction is more acute, there may be abrupt loss of postural tone or of consciousness.

He believes that, despite the association between migraine and rage, it is from this passive reaction, tailored to human nature, that migraine is biologically derived. This seems to me very plausible. Before he invented weapons, primitive man must have been one of the most defenseless of all the creatures, being devoid of fangs or claws or tusks or hooves or venom, and a relatively slow mover. It seems unlikely, therefore, that aggression or rage can have been a basic biological instinct in man as it is in the predator carnivores. Human aggression must be a secondary modification of what was originally a feeling of terror and helplessness. As Coleridge said: "In all perplexity there is a portion of fear, which disposes the mind to anger."

Dr Sacks concludes his chapter on psychological approaches to migraine by saying that three kinds of psychosomatic linkage may occur.

> . . . first, an inherent physiological connection between certain symptoms and effects; second, a fixed symbolic equivalence between certain physical symptoms and states of mind, analogous to the use of facial expressions; third, an arbitrary, idiosyncratic symbolism uniting physical symptoms and phantasies, analogous to the construction of hysterical symptoms.

The last part is devoted to the problems of therapy. As in all cases of functional disorders, the personal relation between doctor and patient is of prime importance. "Every sickness is a musical problem," said Novalis, "and every cure a musical solution." This means, as Dr Sacks says, that, whatever method of treatment a physician may choose or be forced to choose, there is only one cardinal rule:

> . . . one must always *listen* to the patient. For if migraine patients have a common and legitimate complaint besides their migraines, it is that they have not been listened to by physicians. Looked at, investigated, drugged, charged: but not listened to.

Dr Sacks recognizes that there are drugs, notably Ergotomine Tartrate and Methysergide, which can relieve the pain of an acute attack, and which it would be heartless to refuse a patient, unless he has other physiological conditions which counterindicate their use, but he regards them as somewhat dangerous palliatives which cannot effect a permanent cure.

His own bias, he tells us, is toward psychotherapy, but he is modest in his claims. He does not think, for example, that the only solution to migraine is depth analysis, for which few patients have either the money or the time. Further, he admits that some patients find a psychotherapeutic approach unacceptable.

> Severely affected patients should be seen on a regular basis, at intervals —approximately of two to ten weeks. The early interviews must be long and searching, in order to expose for both patient and physician the general situation and specific stresses which are involved, while establishing the foundations of the physician's authority and the patient-physician

> relationship; later consultations may be briefer and more limited in scope, and will chiefly be concerned with the discussion of current problems as these are experienced by the patient and expressed in his migraines. Cursory medical attention is disastrous, and an important cause of allegedly "intractable" migraine.

He also recommends the keeping of two calendars, a migraine calendar and a calendar of daily events, which may reveal unsuspected circumstances as provocative of attacks.

"Cure," in his opinion, means finding for each particular patient the best *modus vivendi* for him. This can mean, in certain cases, allowing the patient to "keep" his headaches.

> The attempt to dislodge severe habitual migraines in a pathologically unconcerned or hysterical personality may force the patient to face intense anxieties and emotional conflicts which are even less tolerable than the migraines. The physical symptoms, paradoxically, may be more merciful than the conflicts they simultaneously conceal and express.

Such patients would agree with Marx: "The only antidote to mental suffering is physical pain."

The New York Review of Books, 3 June 1971

Too Much Mustard

The Complete Immortalia. Edited by Harold H. Hart.
Hart Publishing Company. $10.
The Gambit Book of Popular Verse. Edited by Geoffrey Grigson.
Gambit. $7.95.

I strongly suspect Mr Harold H. Hart of being deeply concerned about the problem of overpopulation, for if anything could be calculated to make a reader swear off sex forever, it is his compilation *The Complete Immortalia.*

So far as I know, the making of bawdy verses is almost exclusively a masculine activity, and in all males there is a strong Manichaean streak which finds most bodily functions ridiculous, if not repulsive. The reason for this is, I believe, that we get erections without our consent, and go to the bathroom not because we choose but because we must, and this offends our *amour-propre.* (Hunger is different for, though a natural necessity, we are free to choose what we shall eat.)

All the common terms relating to copulation or excretion sound ugly and derisive, and practically all bawdy verses make sex seem grubby and treat women with aggressive contempt. Of course, nearly all of us find them fun (nearly all "serious" poets have written some) but only, if we are sane, in small doses.

One synonym for bawdy is spicy. In the kitchen, spices are used sparingly to add flavor to the essential elements in a dish: a meal consisting solely of spices would make us throw up, as this volume has made me want to. But then, as a reviewer, I have had to read it straight through from cover to cover. The only proper way to read it would be at the rate of a page a month. *Caveat emptor.*

About *The Gambit Book of Popular Verse* I have nothing to say except that I recommend every lover of poetry to rush out and buy it immediately. Mr Grigson has done a superb job. Even those who, like myself, have been lifelong devotees of popular anonymous verse will find many pieces which they have not read before and unfamiliar versions of many which they have. No limericks.

The New York Review of Books, 4 November 1971

W. H. Auden on the Young Mr Goethe

The Autobiography of Johann Wolfgang von Goethe.
Translated by John Oxenford.
Introduction by Gregor Sebba. Sidgwick and Jackson. £7.50.

How wise it was of Goethe to wait until he was over sixty before attempting to tell the story of his childhood, adolescence and early manhood. Only age can look at youth with objective detachment, see his early self as if it were someone else. Provided, of course, that age has a good enough memory. Presumably, Goethe had diaries and documents to help him out but, even so, his power of recall, his ability to remember every detail of places, personal encounters, even conversations, are astonishing, at least to me.

How wise of Goethe, too, to stop when, at the age of twenty-six, he leaves for Weimar. Before a writer has found his own voice, his immediate experiences, the things he likes to think about, the books he reads, the people he meets who influence him and thereby help him to find his own voice, are more important and interesting than his juvenile writings. But, once he has found his own voice, it is his productions, not his personal life, that are, or should be, of concern to the public.

Goethe does not, thank goodness, like too many autobiographers, ever take his clothes off. "One should never speak," he writes, "publicly at least, of his own faults, or those of others, unless he hopes to attain some useful end thereby," and this maxim he applies to others no less than to himself. Even when he describes persons, like his father, with whom he found relations difficult, or who, like Herder, often criticised him severely, the portrait is always basically sympathetic.

I have only one criticism: whenever he talks about his sentimental attachments to young ladies, to Gretchen, Annette, Frederica, Lili, he becomes a bore. But then, I have yet to read an autobiographer who was not a bore on this subject. One always feels one knows it all already, either from one's own experience, or the experiences of one's friends. In Goethe's case, moreover, his own behaviour in such affairs makes a rather disagreeable impression. The girls he falls for are always girls with whom a permanent relation would be impossible: for a while he makes a great fuss, but presently he bolts. I am inclined to attribute this to his unusually close relationship with his sister which, though it would be silly to call it incestuous, made a mature sexual life difficult for them both. Her marriage was unhappy, and he continued throughout his life to have difficulties. Indeed, so far as his sex-life was concerned, his oniy sensible act was to take Christiane Vulpius as his mistress and later marry her. Some poets with similar problems have been able to transmute them into lyric poetry of a high order. Goethe, in my opinion, could not. He can be marvellous on carefree sensuality, as in the *Roman Elegies*, but, with the exception of the "Marienbad Elegy," which anyway is more about growing old than about love, his romantic lyrics are seldom satisfactory. After reading a number of them, I found myself composing a squib.

How wonderfully your songs begin
With praise of Nature and her beauty,
But then, as if it were a duty,
You drag some god-damned sweetheart in.
Did you imagine she'd be flattered?
They never sound as if they mattered.

But, the girls aside, his autobiography is endlessly fascinating as a picture both of himself, his family, his friends, and of the times in which he grew up. When he was seven, the Seven Years War broke out, and three years later the French occupied Frankfurt and an officer, luckily a nice one, was billeted in his father's house. (I was surprised to learn that both his father and he were passionately pro-Frederick II.) Linguistically, it was a period of exciting change, for, unlike England and France, Germany had not yet developed a standard educated *Hochsprache.*

> The German, having run wild for nearly two hundred years in an unhappy tumultuous state, went to school with the French to learn manners, and with the Romans in order to express his thoughts with propriety. But this was to be done in the mother-tongue, when the literal application of these idioms, and their half-Germanisation, made both the social and business style ridiculous. Besides this, they adopted without moderation the similes of the southern languages, and employed them most extravagantly.

In consequence, the poets had to turn to foreign poets for their models, Klopstock to the Classics, others, like Goethe, first to Racine and then to Shakespeare. Goethe learned to speak and read French fluently, but I doubt if his command of English was as good. Apropos of translations of Shakespeare, he makes a very wise comment.

> I value both rhythm and rhyme, whereby poetry first becomes poetry; but that which is really, deeply, and fundamentally effective, that which is really permanent and furthering, is that which remains of the poet when he is translated into prose. Then remains the pure, perfect substance, of which, when absent, a dazzling exterior often contrives to make a false show, and which, when present, such an exterior contrives to conceal. I therefore consider prose translations more advantageous than poetical, for the beginning of youthful culture; for it may be remarked, that boys, to whom everything must serve as a jest, delight themselves with the sound of words and the fall of syllables, and, by a sort of parodistical wantonness, destroy the deep contents of the noblest work.

In contrast to the formidable reserved *Geheimrat* of later years, the young Goethe seems to have been very outgoing, a charmer and born raconteur, whose conversation entranced older people as much as his contemporaries, and addicted to dressing up in disguise and to practical jokes. For instance, he was once on a drive with Basedow, who was a heavy smoker, a habit Goethe disliked, and a passionate opponent of the doctrine of the Trinity.

> The weather was warm, and the tobacco-smoke had perhaps contributed to the dryness of Basedow's palate; he was dying for a glass of beer; and, seeing a tavern at a distance on the road, he eagerly ordered the coachman to stop there. But, just as he was driving up to the door, I called out to him loudly and imperiously "Go on!" Basedow, taken by surprise, could hardly get the contrary command out of his husky voice. I urged the coachman more vehemently, and he obeyed me. Basedow cursed me, and was ready to fall upon me with his fists; but I repied to him with the greatest composure, "Father, be quiet. You ought to thank me. Luckily, you didn't see the beer sign! It was two triangles put together across each other. Now, you commonly get mad about one triangle; and, if you had set eyes on two, we should have to get you a strait-jacket."

But however much Goethe may have changed during his lifetime, one trait was there from the beginning, an extraordinary wide range of interests, a passionate concern, not only for literature, but also for all natural phenomena. Even to the boy Science was as important as Art. By the time the autobiography ends, he has already become famous as the author of *Werther*. Today, it is difficult to understand how the young men of his generation, on reading such a devastating portrait of a revolting untalented little egoist who didn't care what harm he did to others provided he could get his own way, could have thought of him as a hero to be admired and imitated. It seems clear that, for Goethe, writing the book was a therapeutic act, a way of getting the *Sturm-und-Drang* nonsense out of his system, and he seems to have realised this himself.

> *Werther* produced its great effect precisely because it struck a chord everywhere, and openly and intelligently exhibited the internal nature of a morbid youthful delusion. . . . By this composition, more than any other, I had freed myself from that stormy element, upon which, through my own fault and that of others, through a mode of life both accidental and chosen, through design and thoughtless precipitation, through obstinacy and pliability, I had been driven about in the most violent manner. I felt, as if after a general confession, once more happy and free, and justified in beginning a new life.

Happy? I'm not so sure. Once, quite late in life, Goethe said that he had only been really happy for a few months in his life: this, no doubt, was an exaggeration, but the remark should not be ignored. Goethe's later Olympian Apollonian manner was, I felt sure, a defence mechanism by which he fought off emotional chaos and melancholia. It is significant, I think, that the motive the young student gave for studying anatomy and medicine, was to overcome his natural repugnance to sickness and sick people. All his life, I believe, Goethe found it dangerous to let his thoughts dwell on the unpleasant.

The Spectator, 11 December 1971

Foreword to *Sense & Inconsequence*, by Angus Stewart

In calling his nonsense verses "satirical", Mr Stewart is in error. Satire is angry and optimistic; it believes that, once people's attention is drawn to some evil, they will mend their ways. Nonsense verse is good-humoured and pessimistic: Life with all its difficulties and absurdities has to be accepted—with a laugh. As William Hazlitt wrote: "Man is the only animal that laughs and weeps; for he is the only animal that is struck by the difference between what things are and what they might have been."

The essential difference between Nonsense poetry and all other kinds is that, in the case of the latter an event or an emotion seems to have looked for and, if successful, found adequate linguistic expression, but in Nonsense verse, the relation between subject and language is reversed: the language seems to have created the event. The two principal devices of Nonsense verse are unexpected rhymes and unexpected metrical shifts. For example:

> There was an Old Man of Thermopylae,
> Who never did anything properly
>
> (Lear)

His conduct is dictated, not by his character but by the name of the place he comes from.

Again, in this poem by Mr Stewart, a Proper Name dictates.

> Alas, eternal Brighton Rock!
> Aunt has sent another stock!
> You can go on biting
> But can't eat the writing;
> As far as you bite on
> It still says, Brighton.

Mr Stewart writes in the tradition of Lear, Carroll, Clerihew Bentley and Ogden Nash. The things he makes fun of are absurd but not painful or unpleasant. There is another kind of Nonsense verse, typified by Harry Graham, the Sick Joke.

> In the drinking well
> Which the plumber built her,
> Aunt Maria fell:
> We must buy a filter.

When I was a child, this was the kind of poetry I most enjoyed, and I hope Mr Stewart will try his hand at it some time. In any case, the test of success or failure in Nonsense verse is very simple. Does it make one laugh? Mr Stewart's verses have made me laugh and will, I am sure, make many readers laugh with me.

Sense & Inconsequence: Satirical Verses, by Angus Stewart (1972)

Chester Kallman: A Voice of Importance

The Sense of Occasion. By Chester Kallman.
Braziller. Cloth, $5.95; paper, $2.95.

I can see no reason why the fact that Mr Kallman and I have been close friends for over thirty years should debar me from reviewing him. In my experience, one's feelings about a writer as a person and one's aesthetic judgment of his work affect each other very little, if at all. I have met three poets whose poems I admire enormously whom I thought poor human beings: vice versa, I can think of a number whom I like personally, but whose verses I cannot, alas, appreciate.

Mr Kallman has previously published two volumes of poetry. *Storm at Castelfranco* (1956) and *Absent and Present* (1963). These, most unjustly, received almost no attention, and this neglect I should like to rectify.

The Sense of Occasion is divided into three sections. The first, "Winter's Journey," consists of nine poems about, if not an unhappy, at least a very difficult, love affair. Such a theme is very treacherous: all too easily it tempts the writer into indulging in egocentric self-pity, whining, and fuss.

Mr Kallman has managed to resist these temptations, firstly, thanks to his sense of humor that never deserts him, even in the most tense moments, and, secondly, thanks to his command of linguistic technique, both metrical and rhetorical. He is a difficult poet to quote from because his poems are so tightly knit that any passage depends for its full effect upon its place in the whole. Here, however, is an example:

ANOTHER

One in the morning. Good God. Only One.
My change-point. At the bare
Thought of you, thought of you, just nightmare,
Ends ends ends ends
For the mere worse, and all comparison:
There are no likes of you and none
Whose love makes more demands.
Forgive me your injuries to me. Care.
God help us both if we are in his hands.

The second section, "Theaters," is a miscellany of poems, long and short, on various topics. One of the long ones, "Delphi," seems to be about some mystical vision the author had on that historic spot; I cannot, I must confess, make head or tail of it, but I am sure that the difficulty is not due to the author's incompetence. But no reader, I'm sure, will have any trouble with the charming "The Body's Complaint to the Soul," based, obviously, on Marvell's poem, but in no way an imitation.

Miss Skylark! titivated in
The touchy dungeon of my skin,
Foreseeing, and yet hardly loath,
That morning-after for us both
When I must in the mirror meet
A face unfocused, indiscreet,
And you no longer think you'll fly
To bloodless orders when I die.

For though you wilfully admit—
In order to charge me with it—
Our time for rousing love is past,
You still possess me in one last
Elusive vanity: to prove
A pleasure while intending love.

Nor will he have any problems over "Griselda Sings" with its surprise shock ending.

Even as you swear
You loved and love me:
Would that move me
If anything could
For good now, for ill?
Try if you like,
Act as you will;
I do not know, I know
Only that should
I move I would strike,
Strike to kill.

And this, surely, is a fine example of the "pure" lyric:

SALOME DANCE

There was no theme but this;
There was no other meaning.

There was a dark dream. This.

There was no gleam but this
Sickle sharpened for gleaning.

Heads will fall, it would seem.

The final section, "The African Ambassador," is a very remarkable achievement indeed. To begin with, it is a technical tour de force. All sixteen of the poems are written in lines of six syllables, yet this never becomes monotonous. Most of them use a strict syllabic count, but in a few contiguous vowels are elided. Stanzas vary in length: some have pure rhymes, some half-rhymes, and, by varying their placing, Mr Kallman reproduces, in a six-syllable form, various traditional forms, such as the ballade and terza rima; there is even a triolet:

He knows his place; he knew
No place entirely
A home. Seedy here, nothing new

He knows. His place he knew
Of old with the handsome few;
Now in the majority
He knows his place. He knew
Noplace entirely.

Secondly, Mr Kallman has succeeded in what is one of the most difficult of all tasks, namely, in inventing a myth, or rather, perhaps, a metaphor, that does not remain private to the author but is accessible to all.

As an epigraph to the poem, there is a quotation from Graham Greene:

> . . . to me . . . Africa will always be the Africa of the Victorian atlas, the blank unexplored continent the shape of the human heart.

I can think of two other quotations that are relevant:

The poet has no identity—Keats

. . . though our words be such,
Our lives do differ from our lines by much—Herrick

The Ambassador is both black and Jewish, and so doubly an outsider, and, like all ambassadors, in a sense an exile from his homeland. His job is to represent the interests of the Heart in the country of Consciousness. The "language" of the Heart is nonverbal, but he can only speak to Consciousness in words, and all translation inevitably means transmutation. In every poem, that is, *Wahrheit* is transmuted into *Dichtung*.

Scanning my lines you see
You are what you would be
Were I like you: i.e.
To say a questing bee
Wrings a morning-glory
As a nervous lady
The edge of her hanky
Is to say exactly
Nothing of each. For me
Love appears unlikely.

And this is how he addresses the Patron Goddess of Poetry, the Moon:

I smile, I give no tongue
To my heart-throbs that punctuate
The secrets of a state

They shrink from knowing and you,
Enforcer of the deep,
Serve naught to voice, one night

With asterisks for light
Past appetite and song.

But no quotations can do the poem justice. It must be read in its entirety. I have no hesitation in saying that, in my opinion, "The African Ambassador" is one of the most original and significant poems written in the past twenty years.

Harper's Magazine, March 1972

The Diary of a Diary

Kathleen and Frank. By Christopher Isherwood.
Simon & Schuster. $10.

In reading Mr Isherwood's latest book—since in it he always refers to himself as Christopher, I shall henceforth call him by his first name—it may be helpful to recall the three crises through which, according to Erik Erikson, anybody who merits an autobiography must pass: the crisis of Identity, the crisis of Generativity, and the crisis of Integrity. Roughly speaking, these occur in youth, middle age, and old age respectively, but they usually overlap, and the intensity and duration of each varies from individual to individual.

In the Identity crisis, the young man is trying to find the answer to the question, "Who am I *really*, as distinct from what others believe or desire me to be?" This is a crisis of consciousness. The Generativity crisis is a crisis of conscience. The question now to be answered is: "I have done this and that; my acts have affected others in this way or that. Have I done well or ill? Can I justify the influence that, intentionally or unintentionally, I have had on others?" Both the Identity and the Generativity crises are preoccupied with freedom and choice. The Integrity crisis of old age is concerned with fate and necessity. As Mr Erikson puts it, it demands:

> . . . the acceptance of one's one and only life-cycle as something that had to be and that, by necessity, permitted of no substitutions, the knowledge that an individual life is the accidental coincidence of but one life-cycle with but one segment of history.

As I read it, *Kathleen and Frank* is Christopher's attempt, wholly successful in my opinion, to solve his Integrity crisis. As he himself writes in his Afterword:

> Christopher saw how heredity and kinship create a woven fabric; its patterns vary, but its strands are the same throughout. Impossible to say exactly where Kathleen and Frank and Richard and Christopher begin; they merge into each other. . . . Christopher has found that he is far

> more closely interwoven with Kathleen and Frank than he had supposed, or liked to believe.
>
> And as he went on reading he made another discovery. If these diaries and letters were part of his project, he was part of theirs, for they in themselves were a project too. . . .
>
> By now Christopher's project has become theirs. . . . For once the Anti-Son is in perfect harmony with his Parents, for he can say, "Our will be done!" *Kathleen and Frank* will seem at first to be their story rather than his. . . . Perhaps, on closer examination, this book may prove to be chiefly about Christopher.

Since I am Christopher's junior by only two and a half years, I am bound, of course, to compare his situation with my own. Thus, I cannot imagine myself keeping a personal diary. In mine I enter only social engagements, lately the death of friends, when in the city, household incidents like getting the bathroom wash-basin unclogged, when in the country, natural phenomena like the weather, the first cuckoo, or the first strawberries. But then my professional preoccupation is with verse, not prose. With novelists it is evidently otherwise. It is a well-known fact that Christopher keeps a journal which his friends and admirers all look forward to reading some day. It now appears that he must have inherited this habit from his mother, for the core of his book is a diary which she started as a young girl and continued to keep until, in her seventies, a stroke made writing impossible.

The trouble for the reader of a diary who does not know its author personally is that he can only judge it, firstly, by its entertainment value—it must amuse him—and, secondly, by its historical value, the light it sheds upon the social mores and political events of the time in which it was written. I must frankly confess that, taken by itself, that is to say, without Christopher's comments and explanations, I do not think Kathleen's diary very interesting. For example, one expects from a diarist traveling in foreign countries vivid descriptions of the landscape and acute observations about the inhabitants. These Kathleen cannot provide. The only observation of hers that amused me was her preference—she was a staunch monarchist—for the royal splendor of Madrid to the "republican dullness" of Paris. When she does comment on public events, which is not very often, her remarks are too typical of her class to be considered her own.

What does, however, remain most impressive after one reads Christopher's description of her parents, Emily and Frederick, is that she grew up to be so "normal," not a wild neurotic, for both of them, it seems, were monsters. Emily, says Christopher, was

> a great psychosomatic virtuoso who could produce high fevers, large swellings and mysterious rashes within the hour, her ailments were roles into which she threw herself with abandon.

One is not surprised to learn that, in later life, Kathleen was so suspicious of "illness" that Christopher had almost to die of blood poisoning before he could convince her that he was not being hysterical.

Frederick was a possessive bully with a deplorable passion for photography. (Since I consider the two most evil technical inventions so far to have been the internal combustion engine and the camera, I must also deplore Christopher's interest in the movies.)

In adolescence Christopher rebelled, very naturally, against Kathleen's cult of the past, but I'm not sure that he realizes even now that this was no personal idiosyncrasy, that, had he been in her situation, he would probably have felt the same nostalgia. If she looked back on the early years of her marriage in Wyberslegh Hall as the happiest days of her life, what could be more natural? It was clearly a very cozy home, much nicer than Marple, and later, owing to Frank's military duties, they had often to find temporary homes. Then, in 1915, she became a widow, and what widow can find much cause for rejoicing in either the present or the future?

Kathleen and Frank first met in 1893, their engagement was officially announced in 1902, they were married on March 12, 1903, and Christopher was born on August 26, 1904. Kathleen, it seems, had previously been in love with a young man, generally referred to as "The Child," who jilted her, and neither she nor her friends expected her to get married. Their courtship was prolonged and not without its sticky moments. In the first place. Frank had very little money. Then the very fact that they shared many interests, e.g. literary, made it difficult for them both to decide whether it would not be better if their relationship remained one of brother and sister rather than husband and wife. Fortunately, they finally opted for the second, and it is clear that their married life was exceptionally happy.

Of the two, Frank was the odd character. Though by profession a soldier, Frank had a passion for music—he played the piano very well—play-acting, including playing female roles, and knitting socks, even when on duty. I would have expected his letters to be more "amusing" performances than they are, but it seems that only when telling stories or writing letters to Christopher could he really let himself go. Though he sometimes doubted if soldiering was his real vocation—shortly before World War I he seriously thought of resigning from his regiment—one's final impression is that he was not a misfit in the army. There is, for example, no evidence that his personal tastes ever caused him social embarrassment in an officer's mess. And in one letter, after complaining about his situation, he has to add:

> However there are moments when one feels quite military. Did I tell you about the little man who rushed up to me the other day and told me that he had made enquiries of the sergeants in the Volunteers and he heard I was likely to be most popular—that what the men liked was

a real officer who, when they came in from drill, said something which made their bosoms swell. I can't imagine myself doing this at all!

Then, whatever motives he may have had for sometimes wishing he were a civilian, one of them was certainly not the fear of getting killed. The young Christopher wove a myth about his dead father as the Anti-Hero, but it is obvious that he must have been a very brave man. He first saw battle in the Boer War, when he might very easily have got killed, in which case neither Christopher nor this book would exist. Luckily, he only caught typhoid fever and was invalided home. Then came World War I and in 1915 he was killed.

It seems clear that it was mainly from Frank that Christopher inherited his imaginative gifts. I'm sorry that he did not also inherit his love of music—Kathleen doesn't seem to have been very musical. I am also sorry, as a good little Episcopalian like Kathleen, that he did inherit Papa's addiction to esoteric religions. Frank took up theosophy and Christopher Vedanta. In the matter of religion, I think I was luckier in my youth than he was. I should guess that the church Kathleen attended twice on Sundays was Broad if not Low. My parents, fortunately, were High, so that my first experiences of divine worship were of exciting, dramatic rituals. I was even a boat-boy.

For selfish reasons, I wish Christopher had said a little more about his experiences at St Edmund's School, Hindhead, where we first met in 1915. He was known to us then as "Beesh," a contraction of Bradshaw-Isherwood, and I can personally vouch for his linguistic and imaginative precocity, for it was from his lips that I heard the first witty remark in my life. We were out together on a Sunday walk in the Surrey landscape. "God," he said, "must have been tired when He made this country." About our headmaster "Ciddy" he is not quite fair. It is true that, since they were cousins, their relationship was bound to be difficult. It is also true that Ciddy's temperament was not of the kind that inspires affection in the young. I must say, however, that he was a brilliant teacher to whom I owe a great deal. Incidentally, last October I attended a luncheon in London at which the guests of honor were Miss Mona and Miss Rosa, both, I am happy to say, in fine fettle.

I myself never saw either Wyberslegh or Marple, and the only member of Christopher's family I ever met, outside of Kathleen and his younger brother Richard, was his Uncle Henry, about whom I once wrote a slightly improper poem.

His descriptions of the family and their life in Cheshire are, however, fascinating both personally and historically. Marple Hall was said to be haunted, and both Christopher and Richard had experiences there that were clearly paranormal, i.e. no rational explanation for them is convincing. About one point I am curious. Kathleen seems never to have accepted her father- and mother-in-law as friends: she always referred to them by their surnames. I cannot help wondering if the cause for this was not class consciousness. Her father, Frederick, was, or had been, in the wine business, that is to say, "in trade." In England at that time both the landed gentry and the professional middle class looked down on those "in trade," those in business or in industry, as being not quite gentlemen, however rich they might be.

I have two little bones to pick, one with the author, the other with his publisher. The narrative would be easier to follow if the former had provided genealogical tables and the latter had printed at the top of each page the year with which it is concerned.

A fine book though. I cannot imagine any reader, whatever his social background and interests, not being enthralled by it.

The New York Review of Books, 27 January 1972

A Worcestershire Lad

The Letters of A. E. Housman. Edited by Henry Maas.
Harvard University Press. $11.50.

Mr Henry Maas informs us that Arthur Platt's widow destroyed all Housman's "Rabelaisian" letters to him. I am delighted to hear it. His letters to Moses Jackson have also not yet been made available. I hope they never will be. If the reader of *The Letters of A. E. Housman*, edited by Mr Maas and published by the Harvard University Press, occasionally finds himself yawning or skipping, at least he never feels like a Peeping Tom, and if he hopes to find something titillating he will be disappointed. All he will learn is that Housman took an interest in "naughty" books like *The Whippingham Papers*, *My Life and Loves*, and Corvo's letters, and that he published in a scholarly journal, under the title "Praefanda," an article on obscene phrases in the Latin poets. This is, surely, as Housman himself would have wished. Apropos of somebody who wished to interview him, he wrote:

> Tell him that the wish to include a glimpse of my personality in a literary article is low, unworthy, and American. Tell him that some men are more interesting than their books but my book is more interesting than its man. Tell him that Frank Harris found me rude and Wilfrid Blunt found me dull. Tell him anything else that you think will put him off.

To the letters on everyday and literary topics Mr. Maas has added a forty-two-page supplement of letters on technical classical matters. These will be fully intelligible only to classical scholars, but I think he was quite right to include them. To Housman himself, his scholarship came first, his poetry second: he believed he had been put on earth not to write *A Shropshire Lad* (I never knew before that this title was proposed by A. W. Pollard; Housman's own title had been "Poems by Terence Hearsay") but to produce a definitive edition of Manilius. His choice of this particular Latin poet may have been influenced by his own interest in astronomy, which is Manilius's subject, but the decisive factor was probably that the text presented an exceptional challenge to an editor. He was certainly under no illusions as to Manilius's literary merits. Thus he says, in a letter to Robert Bridges:

> I adjure you not to waste your time on Manilius, He writes on astronomy and astrology without knowing either. My interest in him is purely technical.

Most of the letters in the supplement are concerned with textual minutiae. The only general statement I have found is a judgment on Virgil:

> Virgil's besetting sin is the use of words too forcible for his thoughts.

However, speaking for myself, though I cannot understand much of them, I am fascinated by the glimpses one gets of how the mind of a textual scholar works:

> With *optandum* you require something like *quicquam*, which Estaço obtained by writing *dicere quid*. With *optandum* of course you can supply *uitam* from *uita*; but yet the MS reading is *optandus*. Because Catullus once elides *que* at the end of a verse it cannot safely be inferred that he would elide anything else. I have seen nothing better than Munro's *magis aeuom optandum hac uita*, though it is not all the heart could desire.

Incidentally, I had occasion not so long ago to compare three translations of the last stanza of the Horace Ode, Book IV, 7—one by Dr Johnson, one by James Michie, and one by Housman. To my surprise, the one which departed most widely from the Latin was Housman's. Indeed, had I not known the source, I would have thought that it was a verse from a Housman poem.

About his emotional life little needs to be said. It is now no secret that at Oxford he fell deeply in love with a fellow-undergraduate, Moses Jackson, an experience which, on his own testimony, he was never to repeat. Since Jackson was perfectly "straight," there could be no question of reciprocation. About this, Mr Maas writes:

> Too clear-headed and honest to deceive himself about the nature of this absorption, he was also too well trained in conventional morality to accept it with resignation. The evidence of his poetry suggests that he was overwhelmed with shame.

If by "conventional morality" Mr. Maas means Housman's Christian upbringing, I think he is mistaken. If Housman did feel shame and guilt, this was caused not by the Bible but by classical literature. I am pretty sure that in his sexual tastes he was an anal passive. Ancient Greece and Rome were both pederastic cultures in which the adult passive homosexual was regarded as comic and contemptible.

As to his attitude to life in general, though often labelled a Stoic, he denied this:

> In philosophy I am a Cyrenaic or egoistic hedonist, and regard the pleasure of the moment as the only possible motive of action. As for pessimism, I think it almost as silly, though not as wicked, as optimism. George Eliot said she was a meliorist: I am a pejorist [i.e. someone who believes the world is steadily getting worse].

In his relation to others, he remained all his life a shy and essentially solitary man. His generation was more formal than mine, but even in those days it must have been unusual for a sixteen-year-old boy to sign a letter to his stepmother "A. E. Housman," and it was only in writing to members of his family that he ever used Christian names. Even such intimate friends as A. S. F. Gow and his publisher, Grant Richards, continued to the end to be "Dear Gow," "Dear Richards."

This reserve and distance from others was probably due, I think, to his experiences in early childhood. His mother, after suffering for years from cancer, died when he was twelve, while his father took to the bottle. It is significant, surely, that out of a family of seven—five boys and two girls—only one son and one daughter married and only the latter had children.

"Vanity, not avarice," Housman once wrote, "is my ruling passion," but I don't think he ever realized just how vain he was. A man who refuses honors like honorary degrees from universities or the O.M. from the State declines them not because he feels unworthy but because he feels that no honor can possibly do justice to his merits, and a poet who refuses to be included in anthologies of contemporary verse reveals that he considers himself superior to all of his colleagues. But vanity did not distort Housman's judgment. He was always aware of what he could and could not do:

> I do regard myself as a connoisseur; I think I can tell good from bad in literature. But literary criticism, referring opinions to principles and setting them forth so as to command assent, is a high and rare accomplishment and quite beyond me.

He was also a good judge of his own work. Most of the posthumously published poems are inferior. Of "Hell Gate," which happens to be my favorite poem of his, he says, acutely:

> . . . the whole thing is on the edge of the absurd: if it does not topple over, that is well so far.

As a letter writer, he could when he tried—which, it must be admitted, was not very often—be most entertaining, both vivid and witty:

> This afternoon Ruskin gave us a great outburst against modern times. He had got a picture of Turner's, framed and glassed, representing Leicester and the Abbey in the distance at sunset, over a river. . . . Then he said, "You, if you like, may go to Leicester to see what it is like now. I never shall. But I can make a pretty good guess." Then he caught up a paintbrush. "These stepping-stones of course have been done away with, and are replaced by a be-au-ti-ful iron bridge." Then he dashed in the iron bridge on the glass of the picture. "The colour of the stream is supplied on one side by the indigo factory." Forthwith one side of the stream became indigo. "On the other side by the soap factory." Soap dashed in. "They mix in the middle—like curds," he said, working them together with a sort of malicious deliberation. "This field, over which you see the sun setting behind the Abbey, is now occupied in a *proper* manner." Then there went a flame of scarlet across the picture, which developed itself into windows and roofs and red brick, and rushed up into a chimney. "The atmosphere is supplied—thus!" A puff and cloud of smoke all over Turner's sky: and then the brush thrown down, and Ruskin confronting modern civilisation amidst a tempest of applause.

Housman was one of the very first civilians to travel by air, and the jumbo-jet tourist of the seventies will be interested to learn what it was like to fly in the early twenties:

> It was rather windy, and the machine sometimes imitated a ship at sea . . . but not in a very lifelike manner. . . . The noise is great, and I alighted rather deaf, not having stuffed my ears with the cotton-wool provided. Nor did I put on the life-belt which they oblige one to take. . . . On the return journey we were two hours late in starting because the machine required repairs, having been damaged on the previous day by a passenger who butted his head through the window to be sick.

I knew he had written parodies and comic verse, but I had never seen any. From the few examples quoted in this book, I should like to see more. His parody of Frances Cornford's "Why do you walk through the fields in gloves," though not quite as good as Chesterton's, is amusing enough, and, for a sixteen-year-old, this pastiche of Milton is a remarkable feat:

> Or where, high rising over all,
> Stands the Cathedral of St Paul
> And in its shadow you may scan
> Our late lamented ruler, Anne,
> Or where the clouds of legend lower

Around the mediaeval Tower,
And ghosts of every shape and size
With throttled throats and staring eyes
Come walking from their earthy beds
With pillow cases on their heads
And various ornaments beside
Denoting why or how they died.

In these letters he mentions surprisingly few English authors. Among the poets he approved of were Coventry Patmore, Robert Bridges for his early poems (not the later), Masefield, Blunden, and Edna St Vincent Millay. Among prose writers he admired Wilkie Collins (his only two letters to T. S. Eliot are about him), Arthur Machen, and Aldous Huxley. One suspects that he found the work of most of his contemporaries and juniors antipathetic.

What has fascinated me most is the descriptions these letters contain of the minor headaches which plague an author's life. Anyone who publishes a book these days must expect it to contain misprints and errors in punctuation. (One British reviewer has listed a series of those that occur in this volume.) I had thought that careless printing and proofreading was a recent phenomenon. Apparently it is not so:

> When the next edition of the Shropshire Lad is being prepared, it would save trouble to the compositor as well as to me if he were told that the third edition is almost exactly correct, and that he had better not put in commas and notes of exclamation for me to strike out of the proof, as was the case last time.

> On former occasions the proofs have come to me full of the usual blunders,—numerals wrong, letters upside-down, stops missing, and so on. I have then, at the cost of much labour, removed all these errors. Then, when the last proof has left my hands, the corrector for the press has been turned on to it, and has found nothing to correct; whereupon, for fear his employers should think he is not earning his pay, he has set to work meddling with what I have written.

And every poet will sympathize with Housman over the following:

> I have marked for correction, if possible, certain ugly over-running of words from one line to another. Since these over-runnings existed in neither the 1896 nor the 1900 edition, it seems absurd that they should be necessary in this, which has smaller print than the former and a larger page than the latter.

Then, if, like Housman, an author achieves popular success, there are other nuisances: Requests for autographs from total strangers who hardly ever enclose postage stamps. Requests for a handwritten copy of a poem. Visits by professed admirers who then betray their ignorance of his work:

> I had a visit not long ago from Clarence Darrow, the great American barrister for defending murderers. He had only a few days in England, but he could not return home without seeing me, because he had so often used my poems to rescue his clients from the electric chair. Loeb and Leopold owe their life sentence partly to me; and he gave me a copy of his speech, in which, sure enough, two of my pieces are misquoted.

As regards Mr Maas's editing of these letters, his footnoting seems for the most part excellent. I have only two complaints. I think I know Housman's poems pretty well, but when a poem is identified only as "A Shropshire Lad LXIII," I am flummoxed. Why not quote the first line? Then, in one letter, Housman writes:

> My feelings are much the same as [Aldous] Huxley's; but in my case school is not the cause, for I was quite uninfluenced by my school, which was a small one. I think the cause is in the home.

Surely we ought to be informed as to what Huxley had said.

Naturally, one cannot read Housman's letters without thinking again about his status and achievement as a poet. A minor poet, certainly, which, of course, does not mean that his poems are inferior in artistic merit to those of a major poet, only that the range of theme and emotion is narrow, and that the poems show no development over the years. On the evidence of the text alone, it would be very difficult to say whether a poem appeared in *A Shropshire Lad*, published when he was thirty-seven, or in *Last Poems*, published when he was sixty-three. I don't know how it is with the young today, but to my generation no other English poet seemed so perfectly to express the sensibility of a male adolescent. If I do not now turn to him very often, I am eternally grateful to him for the joy he gave me in my youth.

The New Yorker, 19 February 1972

Down with the "Melting Pot"

To me, Europe, at least its heartland, means the area dominated by the ideals of French culture. Historically, it is of fairly recent date, being the joint creation of the French Revolution and the Congress of Vienna, at which it was settled that Europe was not to be dominated by French bayonets.

In this heartland most of the inhabitants are either Catholics, anti-clericals (sometimes both) or atheists. Anti-semitism, alas, can exist, but there are no ghettos. There is a class of peasant proprietors which is politically potent. There are few hedges to be seen. The standard alcoholic beverage is wine, the standard non-alcoholic drink is coffee. Bathroom fixtures include a bidet, but only luxury hotels supply soap. On checking in at an hotel one has to show one's passport or other means of identification. Opera houses are numerous. In contrast to the United States there is still an excellent railway system: and in contrast to England there are no licensing hours.

It follows from this that officially Protestant countries like Prussia and Scandinavia, or Greece with its Orthodox Church, are, at most, European outlands. With the exception of intellectuals who read European literature either in translation or the original, and have some knowledge of one or two European languages, and perhaps a few members of the aristocracy who have married into European families, the English have never thought of themselves as Europeans. If they visit Canada or Australia they "go overseas"; if they cross the Channel they "go abroad".

Whatever reasons the British man in the street may give for objecting to Britain joining the Common Market they are, I am inclined to suspect, rationalizations of a deplorable prejudice: he thinks that Europeans are not quite "white folks". When this prejudice was born I don't know—it cannot have existed in medieval Christendom—but it was certainly already rampant by the eighteenth century. As one of the characters in Smollett's *Count Fathom* says:

> When an Englishman happens to quarrel with a stranger, the first term of reproach he uses is the name of his antagonist's country, characterized by some opprobrious epithet, such as a chattering Frenchman, an Italian ape, a German hog, and a beastly Dutchman.

I know nothing about economics, so have no idea what the financial effect on Britain will be if she joins the Common Market. I am, however, passionately in favour of her doing so because I think that the British working class will never get over their insularity until they begin going to Europe as workers. It is impossible to work in a foreign country without acquiring at least a smattering of its language and becoming personally acquainted with some of the local inhabitants. They may even have something valuable of their own to contribute. I myself have reason to be grateful to the recent influx into Austria of Yugoslav and Turkish workers. The Austrians do not eat lamb, which is my favourite meat. When I first went there it was very difficult to obtain; now it is much easier.

Tourism, on the other hand, however valuable as a source of revenue to the favoured country, does nothing to improve mutual understanding and good will. Even the educated tourist is all too often only interested in the sights, natural or artistic, and shows little or no interest in the inhabitants of the country he is visiting, or their history. As for the mass tourist, he is interested in nothing, not even in the food. His only reasons for going, let us say to Spain, seem to be, so far as I can see, to sunbathe, a habit of which I disapprove, and to be able to tell his neighbours that he has been there.

When one speculates about the future, whether of Europe or anywhere else, one's fears are stronger than one's hopes. As a poet I am professionally a lover of diversity. In poetry, thank God, there cannot be, as in architecture, such a thing as an international style. How jolly it is, for instance, that a German poet can secure effects which I, writing in English, cannot secure, and that, vice versa, there are things I can say which he cannot.

The worst thing, from my point of view, that could happen to Europe would be if it became a melting-pot in which cultural differences were erased. One cannot, alas, say that this is an impossibility. In my opinion the two most evil technological inventions so far have been the internal combustion engine and the camera, and of the two the latter is the greater menace.

I can envisage a time when people will find traffic congestion so intolerable that they will demand that the petrol-driven automobile be replaced by an electric brougham which creates no fumes and travels at the rate of twenty miles an hour. (Faster speeds damage the human ego by inflating it.) I cannot, however, foresee an end to photographic advertisements or to TV which are already beginning to create a worldwide mass culture.

Politically, the future does not look too bright either, though a change of political regime does not, I think, alter the character of a people so much as the totalitarians would like to believe. I am sure that anything is better than a one-party system whether of right or left. (The only country where it is tolerable is Yugoslavia, but there, though there is officially only one party, in fact there are four, the Slovenes, the Croatians, the Serbs and the Macedonians.)

One has, however, to admit that political life in the non-communist countries is not in a very healthy state either. When I was young I would never have dreamed that I would live to see the day when the greatest threat to the economy would come from the trade unions, which have become power structures indifferent to the common welfare. I am terrified lest, in despair at the inability of democratic governments to deal with industrial disputes or solve such problems as pollution, the electorate should opt for some kind of dictatorship.

My private political solution, which, of course, I know, stands no chance of being adopted is this. Politicians should be elected, like jurors, by lot. This would destroy the party machines. Because there would be no possibility of their being reelected, the elected could vote according to their own conscience. And the computers could work out the proper representation of minority groups.

Still, despite all changes, the Europe I knew as a young man, and grew to love, is still recognizable. Long may she continue to be.

"Europe in 1975," a special section of *The Times*, 23 February 1972

A Genius and a Gentleman

Letters of Giuseppe Verdi. Selected, translated, and edited by Charles Osborne. Holt, Rinehart & Winston. $7.95.

A few years before his death Verdi wrote: "Never, never shall I write my memoirs! It's good enough that the musical world has put up with my notes for so long a time. I shall never condemn it to read my prose." I don't think, however, that he would have any objection to our reading this selection of his letters, admirably translated and edited by Charles Osborne. It contains no embarrassing "human" documents, no love letters, for instance. Whether this is because Verdi never wrote any or because Mr Osborne has had the good taste to omit them, I don't know. Anyway, I am very glad. There is only one letter that could possibly be called "private and confidential," Verdi's reply to his old benefactor, Antonio Barezzi, who had taken him to task for not regularizing his relationship with Giuseppina Strepponi by marrying her.

> I have nothing to hide. In my house there lives a lady, free and independent, who, like myself, prefers a solitary life, and who has a fortune capable of satisfying all her needs. Neither I nor she is obliged to account to anyone for our actions. But who knows what our relations are? What affairs? What ties? What rights I have over her or she over me? . . . I will say this to you. however: in my house she is entitled to as much respect as myself, more even.

As we know, they did finally get married in 1859. All that is puzzling, in view of how obviously well suited to each other they were, is why they did not do so earlier. My guess would be that it was she rather than Verdi who kept putting it off. There is one other piece of information in the letters that leaves me curious. In 1844–45 Verdi came near to a nervous breakdown, suffering severely from psychosomatic headaches and stomach cramps. What can the psychological trouble have been?

As we all recognize, the nineteenth century was the Golden Age of Opera, but I doubt if any of us, whether composers or opera-goers, would have liked to live in it. So far as composers were concerned, they were terribly overworked. It was a common clause in a contract that the finished score of a full-length opera was to be delivered within four months after the composer received the libretto. (Of all the great opera composers of the age, the only one who was not prolific was Bellini, and I have always wondered how this was financially possible for him.)

Then there were problems of copyright. In 1855 the House of Lords decreed that no foreign opera in England would have copyright unless the composer conducted the first performance himself. Then there was censorship. The setting of *Ballo in Maschera* had to be transferred from Sweden to Boston, and changes had to be made in the text of *Rigoletto.* Prima donnas were even more difficult to handle than they are now. (Today, the real pests are the stage directors.) When Sophie Loewe was to sing in *Ernani,* she objected to the opera ending in a trio. She wanted a brilliant cabaletta for herself alone and made the librettist, Piave, write one for her. Luckily, Verdi was adamant. The singer who was to sing Banquo in *Macbetto* objected to also taking the role of Banquo's ghost.

Opera-goers, too, had much to put up with. There were boxes on the stage so that the curtain could not be brought up to the footlights, and there does not seem to have been an orchestral pit as we know it. (I was interested to learn that Verdi, like Wagner, wanted an invisible orchestra.) Then, as now, standards varied, of course, from opera house to opera house. After the premiere of *Giovanna d'Arco* at La Scala, Milan, Verdi was so disgusted that he refused to let them have another for forty-three years, when he gave them the first performance of *Otello.* The worst of all, he thought, was the Paris Opera.

> Everyone wants to pass judgment according to his own ideas, his own taste, and, which is worst of all, according to a system, without taking into account the character and individuality of the composer. . . . If a composer lives for too long in this atmosphere of doubt, he cannot escape having his convictions shaken a little, and begins to correct and adjust, or, to put it better, to look askance at his own work. Thus, in the end, you will have not a work in one piece, but a mosaic. . . . No one, surely, will deny the genius of Rossini. All right, but, despite all his genius, his *Guillaume Tell* has about it this fatal atmosphere of the Opera; and sometimes, though more rarely than in the work of other composers, you feel there's too much here, not enough there, and that it doesn't move with the honesty and security of *Il barbiere.*

In one respect the musical scene has greatly improved since Verdi's time. There are still many lovers of Wagner but no "Wagnerites." We listen to Wagner one evening and to Verdi the next with equal pleasure and admiration. When one remembers the contempt in which the Wagnerites held Verdi as a composer, one is astounded by Verdi's good temper and common sense. He believed that each country should be loyal to its own musical traditions. Thus, for Germans, whose musical founder was Bach, the Wagnerian development was right, but not for Italians, whose music stemmed from Palestrina. Though Verdi wrote a string quartet, a charming if not very important work, he did not approve of Italian string quartet societies: they were right for the Germans, but the Italians should found vocal quartet societies. The chief danger for contemporary composers, he thought, was a lack of simplicity.

> Art which lacks naturalness is simply not art. Inspiration is necessarily born of simplicity. . . . We create big works rather than great works. And from the big are born the small and the baroque.

By simplicity, though, he did not mean *verismo.*

> To copy truth may be a good thing, but to invent truth is better, much better.

> His ideas about musical education are most interesting.

> Practise the fugue constantly, tenaciously, to satiety, until your hands are strong enough to bend the notes to your will. Thus you will learn to compose with confidence, will dispose the parts well, and will modulate without affectation. Study Palestrina, and a few of his contemporaries. Then skip until you come to Marcello, and direct your attention especially to his recitatives. . . . Don't let yourself be fascinated by beauties of harmony and instrumentation, or the chord of the diminished seventh, that rock and refuge of all of us who don't know how to compose four bars without a half-dozen of these sevenths.

> . . . *No study of the moderns!* That will seem strange to many. But when I hear and see so many works today, constructed the way bad tailors make clothes based on a model, I cannot change my opinion. . . . When a young man has undergone strict training, when he has found his own style and has confidence in his own powers, he can then, if he thinks it useful, study these works somewhat, and there will be no danger of his turning into an imitator.

It is clear from his own productions that he practiced what he preached. As a young man he did study very hard until he could make the notes go where he wanted and felt secure enough to obtain the effects he had in mind. But, on his own admission, he was one of the least *erudite* of musicians. He tells us, for instance, that he could not "get" a piece of music by reading the score, and he complained that many people went into ecstasies over much "classical" music when, if they had been honest, they would have admitted they found it boring. Nor did he ever try to ingratiate himself either with critics or the public. He was willing, he said, to accept their hisses on condition that he didn't have to beg for their applause.

Though, unlike Wagner, he did not write his own librettos, he always knew exactly what he wanted and, if he was dissatisfied, could tell his librettist in detail why. Thus he writes to Piave, who was revising *La Forza del destino*:

> You talk to me about 100 syllables!! And it's obvious that 100 syllables aren't enough when you take 25 to say the sun is setting!!! The line "Duopo e sia L'opra truce compita" is too hard, and even worse is "Un Requiem, un Pater . . . e tutto ha fin". First of all, this "tutto ha fin" rhymes with "Eh via prendila Morolin". It neither sounds well nor makes sense. . . .
>
> Then, the seven-syllabled lines!!! For the love of God, don't end lines with "che", "piu" and "ancor".

And here are his instructions to Ghizlanzoni about the finale of *Aida.*

> Duet
> O life farewell, earthly love
> Farewell, sorrows and joys. . . .
> In infinity already I see the dawn,
> We shall be united for ever in heaven.
>
> (Four beautiful twelve-syllabled lines. But to make them suitable for singing, the accent must be on the fourth and eighth syllables.)

And he was equally clear in his mind about details of stage direction. He gave Morelli, who was to direct *Otello,* a precise description of what he wanted Iago to look like, and when he himself directed *Macbetto,* he had Banquo's ghost emerge from a trap door immediately in front of Macbeth's chair, whereas in most other productions he had merely entered from the wings.

Though there was one great tragedy in Verdi's life when, in his middle twenties, he lost both his children and his first wife, one must say that, on the whole, his life was singularly fortunate. The son of an illiterate innkeeper's family, he would never have gotten anywhere had not Barezzi made it financially possible for him to study in Milan. His life with Giuseppina Strepponi was obviously very happy. By the age of forty he was famous, and he might well have never written two of his most beautiful operas had he not, when old, found in Boito the ideal librettist for what he had in mind. (Incidentally, I am astounded to learn from an editorial note by Mr Osborne that, as late as 1863, Boito, in praising Faccio, a composer of whom I have never heard, likened Verdi's music to a "stained brothel wall.") One feels that both as a composer and as a human being Verdi richly deserved his good fortune. In the case of most great men, I am content to enjoy their works. There are very few who make me also wish that I could have known them personally. Verdi is one of them.

The New York Review of Books, 9 March 1972

Telling It the Way It Was

Historical Memoirs of the Duc De Saint-Simon. Volume III, 1715–1723.
Edited by Lucy Norton. Hamish Hamilton. £6.

The third, and final, volume of Lucy Norton's shortened English version of Saint-Simon's Memoirs covers the years 1715–23. It opens, that is to say, with the death of Louis XIV and ends with the death of the Prince Regent, the Duc d'Orleans, Saint-Simon's lifelong friend. It was in these years that Saint-Simon played a prominent part in French political life: under an absolute monarchy he had been without influence and at the end of this period he retired into private life.

In a book intended for the non-specialist, Miss Norton has been right, I think, to make cuts (the Saint-Simon fan will read the whole thing in French). Thus she omits four hundred pages from the year 1718 because they were not written by Saint-Simon but by Torcy. Though I shall have occasion later to take issue with her about a verbal point, her translation reads easily and well, and her editorial notes are all one could require.

Saint-Simon is, in my opinion, the greatest of all "social realist" writers (a term not to be confused with socialist realism or naturalism). His only rivals, so far as I know, are the anonymous authors of the Icelandic Sagas. The social realist begins by asking: "What do I know for certain about my fellow human beings?", and his answer is: "What they do and say in the presence of others who can bear witness to it." If, like Saint-Simon and unlike the authors of the Sagas, he is a personal participant in the events he is describing, he may make guesses as to their unspoken thoughts and motives, but he must admit that guesses are not evidence. Again, as a participator, he can and should express his moral judgment on the behaviour of others, but he must always remember his human limitations and not play God:—

> . . . Praise and blame flow freely over those who stir my emotions, and are used more temperately concerning those to whom I have been indifferent; yet I have always been a staunch supporter of the virtuous and fiercely against dishonest people. . . . Nevertheless . . . I have been infinitely watchful of my likes and dislikes, more especially of the latter so as to keep the balance when writing of people, not only to avoid exaggeration, but to forget personal prejudice, regarding myself as my own enemy, rendering exact justice, and letting the truth everywhere prevail.

The cliché adjective for Saint-Simon is *malicious*, but I do not find him so. To be sure, he had a keen eye for human vices and weaknesses, but he knew that few human beings are wholly evil (his lifelong enemy Cardinal Dubois really seems to have been) and he is always ready to testify to their good qualities:—

> Hard, brutal, apt to take aversions, she had sudden outbursts that were truly alarming, and no one was safe from them. Although possessed of sufficient intelligence and wit, she had no tact, no charm, no gentleness. As I have already said, she was intensely jealous of her rights, and capable of the meanest actions in protecting them. Her figure resembled that of a Swiss guard, and yet she could be a most loyal and tender friend.

He himself thought he was a poor stylist, too profuse with synonyms, overlong, repetitious. This is not true. What made him think so was, probably, that French literature when he grew up was completely dominated by the rules of the Neo-Classic aesthetic, with its doctrine of the three unities and its rigid segregation of the Low and the High Style, the comic and the tragic. Under such rules, social realism is impossible. Historical life in the primary world is full of loose ends, and the coarse, the comic, the noble are always falling over one another. What makes Saint-Simon superior to all other writers of memoirs is his photographic memory, both visual and auditory. When he describes a scene, the reader sees the room, the furniture, where the people in it are standing, what they are wearing, their every movement and gesture, and, of course, hears exactly every word they utter. If any food is served, we are told what the dishes were. Naturally, such accounts take time: Saint-Simon is often witty, but not epigrammatic.

Although, during the Regency, he was closely involved in affairs of state, and frequently asked his opinion, I doubt if, aside from his period as Ambassador to Spain, where he was a very great success, he had much influence on the course of events. Disliking absolute monarchy and the royal minions, he believed that power would best be vested in the great nobles, who were well enough off to be disinterested, and, though himself devout, he disliked all religious persecution. As a politician he was too outspoken, too little of an intriguer. We know what Saint-Simon thought about the Duc d'Orléans, but it is not quite so clear what the latter thought of Saint-Simon, though he was always friendly. Time and time again, the Regent would ask his advice and then do something else. The Regent was famous for his debaucheries, while Saint-Simon, who was unusually happily married, lived decently and soberly, and to many at Court he must have seemed a fuss-pot and goody-goody. One day the Regent delighted him by saying that he was going to turn over a new leaf:—

> The very next day, I learned from persons whom the roués had told, that no sooner was M. le Duc d'Orléans seated with them at supper, than he burst into a loud peal of laughter, saying that he had just pitched me a tale and that I had fallen for it completely. He then recounted all our conversation to everyone's huge amusement, his own included.

The best analysis of Saint-Simon, the writer, that I know of is by Erich Auerbach in *Mimesis*, and it is now that I have a little bone to pick with Miss Norton. There is a famous scene in which Saint-Simon visits the Duc d'Orléans one morning and realises that the end is not far off. Miss Norton's translation runs thus:—

> His appearance terrified me. His head was hanging; his face purple-red: he was so dazed that he did not even see me enter.

In the original the second sentence begins *Je vis un homme.* Surely it is important to translate this literally, for, as Auerbach says, "'I saw a man' (not 'I saw the

Duke') expresses two things: that in the first moment he does not recognise, or refuses to believe, who the man before him is; secondly, that the unfortunate creature is hardly Monsieur le duc d'Orléans any longer but 'only' a man."

Though I happen to detest the medium, these memoirs would surely be ideal material for a TV serial, as would also (let me seize this opportunity to make a plug) E. F. Benson's *Lucia* novels.

The Observer, 12 March 1972

I'll Be Seeing You Again, I Hope

Though I've lived more than half my life in the States, am an American citizen (which I expect to remain), have acquired a short *a* and that wonderful verb *gotten* and have learned to say *aside from* instead of *apart from*, I cannot, of course, call myself an American. I do, however, think of myself as a New Yorker and believe that I shall continue to think so, even in Oxford.

At Oxford I shall be living in a college community which, at my age, I believe is better for me than living in a metropolis. If I had to choose between New York and London, I should probably choose New York with all its perils.

People ask me if I shall miss the "cultural life" here. My answer: I have never taken part in it. Since I like to go to bed very early, I seldom go to the theater or movies or concerts. My cultural life is confined to reading, listening to records of classical music, and solving crossword puzzles, activities I can indulge in anywhere. At this point I must say that the crossword in *The New York Times* frequently drives me up the wall with rage because of the lack of precision in its clues. Time and again, one sees from the letters one has what the word must be, but the clue is inaccurate. The clues in British crosswords may be more complicated, but they are always fair. E.g. *Song goes dry for a ruined Dean.* Answer: *Serenade.*

The sole advantage of a metropolis, admittedly a great one, is that, there, one's friends are easily accessible. No change in one's life can be unaccompanied by sorrow, and my mind is preoccupied at the moment by the thought of the many dear friends I have, both in the city and outside it, and how much I am going to miss them.

New York, however, is not simply a metropolis: It is also a city of neighborhoods, and I consider myself extremely fortunate in the one where I have lived for the past twenty years. (To me, it will always be *The Lower East Side*, never *The East Village*.)

Whoever invented the myth that America is a melting pot? It is nothing of the kind and, as a lover of diversity, I say thank God. The Poles, the Ukrainians, the Italians, the Jews, the Puerto Ricans, who are my neighbors, may not be the same as they would be in another country, but they keep their own characteristics. It is a neighborhood of small shops where they know one personally, and how nice they have all been to this Wasp! Let me take this opportunity to thank in particular Abe and his coworkers in the liquor store; Abe the tobacconist; On Lok, my laundryman; Joseph, Bernard and Maurice in the grocery store at Ninth and Second Avenue; Harold the druggist; John, my mailman; Francy from whom I buy my newspaper, and Charles from whom I buy seeds for my Austrian garden. God bless you all! And now I must begin to think about the problems of packing. The heart sinks.

The New York Times, 18 March 1972

A Poet of the Actual

Anthony Trollope. By James Pope Hennessy. Little, Brown. $10.

Every reviewer, I'm sure, must be conscious of having to read more quickly than one should. If the book is bad, little harm is done, but if, as in this case—*Anthony Trollope,* by James Pope Hennessy—it is both good and long, he knows that he cannot do proper justice to it. If Trollope's biography was to be written at all, Mr Pope Hennessy, who has already displayed his remarkable gift for the genre in his Life of Queen Mary, was the obvious man, for his grandfather was almost certainly the model for Phineas Finn. As a rule, I am opposed to biographies of writers, but in Trollope's case, for a number of reasons, I approve. To begin with, Trollope wrote an autobiography, published posthumously, which, though probably accurate so far as it goes, leaves out a great deal. What puzzles me is why he wrote one at all, for he himself asserted that no man has ever written a truthful record of his inner life:

> Who could endure to own to a mean thing? Who is there that has done none?

Then, he was not simply a novelist. As an employee of the Post Office, he was also a man of action, and a most successful one. Then, he was an addicted traveller, forever "banging about" the world. More important, he happened to be what one would never suspect from his writings—a very eccentric character who might well, though he would have hated to admit it, have come straight out of a novel by Dickens. James Russell Lowell thus describes their meeting:

> Dined the other day with Anthony Trollope; a big, red-faced, rather underbred Englishman of the bald-with-spectacles type. A good roaring

positive fellow who deafened me (sitting on his right) till I thought of Dante's Cerberus. . . . He and Dr Holmes were very entertaining. The Autocrat started one or two hobbies, and charged, paradox in rest—but it was pelting a rhinoceros with seed-pearl—

Dr. You don't know what Madeira is in England?

T. I'm not so sure it's worth knowing.

Dr. Connoisseurship with us is a fine art. There are men who will tell a dozen kinds, as Dr Waagen would know a Carlo Dolci from a Guido.

T. They might be better employed!

Dr. Whatever is worth doing is worth doing well.

T. Ay, but that's begging the whole question. I don't admit it's worse doing at all. If they earn their bread by it, it may be worse doing (roaring).

Dr. But you may be assured—

T. No, but I mayn't be asshorred. I don't intend to be asshorred (roaring louder).

As he grew older, he got even louder. A friend described him as "crusty, quarrelsome, wrong-headed, prejudiced, obstinate, kind-hearted and thoroughly honest old Tony Trollope."

In view of which it seems only fitting that his fatal stroke should have been brought on, as it appears, firstly by a fit of rage at a noisy German band and then by a fit of laughter as one of the assembled company read aloud from Anstey's *Vice Versa.*

Trollope has told us himself about his exceptionally wretched childhood and early manhood. His father was clearly a little crazy. Suffering acutely from migraines, he became a calomel addict who ruined his law practice by an ungovernable temper. Anthony's elder brother, Tom, said of him:

> I do not think it would be an exaggeration to say that for many years no person came into my father's presence who did not forthwith desire to escape from it. . . . Happiness, mirth, contentment, pleasant conversation seemed to fly before him as if a malevolent spirit emanated from him.

Their mother, the famous authoress, seems to have had great charm, but Tom was so obviously her favorite child that Anthony felt neglected.

To any observer who met him during the first twenty-six years of his life, his future must have looked grim, for, as a schoolboy and as a clerk in the Post Office, he was unsociable, dirty, slovenly, and lazy both in his person and in his work. The transformation effected by his move to Ireland, where, within two or three years, he became a compulsive writer, an efficient civil servant, a passionate fox hunter, and a happily married man, would be incredible in a novel. Yet it happened. Why? My own guess is that for the first time in his life he found himself a member of the ruling class; there were, Mr Pope Hennessy tells us, more British soldiers in Ireland at that time than there were in the whole of India, and he was in a position to give orders and see that they were obeyed. From then on, his life pattern was fixed, and in due course it led to fame and wealth.

Mr Pope Hennessy is probably the only person now living who has read all of Trollope's sixty-five books, the majority of which are in two or three volumes, and he devotes a good many pages to describing and assessing the little-known ones. For this I am most grateful to him. Like everybody who reads Trollope at all, I have read the Barchester novels and several others, but I had never even heard of *He Knew He Was Right*, which Mr Pope Hennessy thinks one of the best, and what he says about it makes me eager to read it at the first opportunity.

At this point, a personal digression. I was born a member of the upper professional middle class—clergymen, lawyers, doctors, etc.—and the world I knew as a child was still in most respects the world of Barchester. There were rich and poor clerical livings, often in the gift of laymen, and there were endless squabbles between High, Broad, and Low churchmen. The Married Women's Property Acts had made things more difficult for fortune-hunting young males, but the snobberies were still the same. Persons in business or industry, however rich, were "in trade"—i.e. not quite gentlemen—and Dissenters came in through the back door, not the front.

I find Trollope's insistence that writing novels is a craft like making shoes, and his pride in the money he got by writing them, sympathetic. He was aware, of course, that craft and art are not the same: a craftsman knows in advance what the finished result will be, while the artist knows only what it will be when he has finished it. But it is unbecoming in an artist to talk about inspiration; that is the reader's business. Again, Trollope would never have denied that his primary reason for writing was that he loved the activity. He once said that as soon as he could no longer write books he would wish to die. He believed that he wrote best when he wrote fastest, and in his case this may well have been true: a good idea for a novel stimulated his pen. Though large sales are not necessarily a proof of aesthetic value, they are evidence that a book has given pleasure to many readers, and every author, however difficult, would like to give pleasure.

To preach, as Trollope did, the Protestant work ethic is fine, provided one is aware, as he was not, of the difference between a worker—i.e. someone who is paid to do what he enjoys doing—and a laborer whose job has no interest in itself: he does it only because he must, in order to feed himself and his family. Trollope's failure to make this distinction is responsible for his unfeeling, even cruel attitude toward the Irish peasants, the West Indian slaves, and the Australian aborigines.

Of Trollope's virtues as a novelist, Henry James said, very rightly:

> His first, his inestimable merit was a complete appreciation of the usual. . . . Trollope will remain one of the most trustworthy, though not one of the most eloquent, of the writers who have helped the heart of man to know itself.

For "usual" one might substitute "actual," and the most actual of actualities in the modern world is surely money. Important as they are to us, our emotions are less actual, for we are frequently deceived about what we feel, whereas we always know exactly how much money we have. Money is a medium of exchange which affects all our relations with others. As Walter Sickert said, "Nothing knits man to man like the frequent passage from hand to hand of cash." Money is the necessity that frees us from necessity. Of all novelists in any country, Trollope best understands the role of money. Compared with him, even Balzac is too romantic. It is odd that Dickens, who, like Trollope, had known poverty in early life, should have shown so little insight into the problem. Mr Pope Hennessy says:

> In *David Copperfield* and in *Oliver Twist* the little heroes' penury is turned off like a tap at the appearance on the scene of a fairy godmother and a fairy godfather. These transformation scenes are pantomimic, delightful, and illogical, but they have little or nothing to do with reality. . . . Trollope's attitude to money was neither romantic nor . . . cynical. . . . In Trollope's very earliest novels—the Irish ones—money is already a predominant theme, money in the ugly shape of unpaid land rents, of contested wills or of the unhappiness of Trollope's first heiress-orphan, Miss Fanny Wyndham. When he turned to England for the source-material for his novels, his increasing pessimism about the British upper and middle class began to show itself. . . . In Trollope's accounts of all this there is no cynicism, but only humor and sadness. . . . His simmering distaste for what he saw is reflected in successive novels until, in the year 1873, it boiled over and goaded him into writing that bitter satire on London society *The Way We Live Now.*

About the relation between money and love, Trollope knew that (if I may be excused for quoting myself)

> Money cannot buy
> the fuel of Love,
> but is excellent kindling.

To Trollope himself, making money was a proof of his manhood, of doing better than Papa. In this he was more American than European, for in Europe, till recently, most wealth had been inherited.

Trollope believed that

> the object of a novel should be to instruct in morals while it amuses. . . . The novelist creeps in closer than the schoolmaster, closer than the father, closer almost than the mother. He is the chosen guide, the tutor whom the young pupil chooses for herself.

I wish more modern novelists shared his belief, though today one would probably speak of "values" rather than "morals." If the Victorians were sometimes a little too reticent about sex, at least they knew that sex is a private, not a public, activity. If I have to choose, I prefer veils to nudity. (Actually, when they are read carefully, Trollope's novels turn out to be much less prudish than one thought at first.) The task of teaching morality is not easy; the Victorians and, indeed, most novelists have tried to solve it by making their bad characters come to a bad and unhappy end, their good characters to a good and happy one. Of course, both they and their readers knew perfectly well that in real life the righteous often have to beg their bread while the ungodly flourish like a green bay tree. But they were in a real dilemma. It seems to be a law of the imagination that bad characters are more fun to write and read about than good ones. As Simone Weil wrote:

> Imaginary evil is romantic and varied; real evil is gloomy, monotonous, barren, boring. Imaginary good is boring, real good is always new, marvellous, intoxicating. "Imaginative literature," therefore, is either boring or immoral or a mixture of both.

The New Yorker, 1 April 1972

Doing Oneself In

The Savage God: A Study of Suicide. By A. Alvarez.
Random House. $7.95.

Though I have been fascinated by this book, I am not sure that I am the proper person to review it. As a Christian, I am required to believe that suicide, except when it is an act of insanity, is a mortal sin, but who am I to judge, since at no time in my life have I felt the slightest temptation to commit it, any more than I can imagine myself going off my head or indulging in sadistic or masochistic acts? Of course, like everybody else, I have my "good" and "bad" days, but I have always felt that to be walking this earth is a miracle I must do my best to deserve. It would be most ungracious of me if I did not, seeing what an extraordinarily lucky life I have had. I was the favorite child of my parents; I have enjoyed excellent health; I am a worker not a laborer, i.e.

I have been paid by society to do what I enjoy doing; I have been reasonably successful; and I have a number of wonderful friends whom I love dearly. This does not mean that I want to live forever: at present I feel that I would like *le bon Dieu* to take me at the canonical age of seventy, though I fear He will not.

I can imagine two situations in which suicide would be a rational act. If someone contracts a painful and incurable disease and knows, moreover, that the cost of medical treatment is going seriously to deplenish the estate he has to leave his heir, to put an end to his life would certainly be rational: whether it would also be moral, I can't decide. Then I think of the case of a French Resistance fighter who is arrested by the Gestapo and is afraid that, under torture, he may give away the names of his colleagues: in this case suicide would be not only rational but his moral duty.

Mr Alvarez's opening and closing chapters describe personal experiences, one the death of his friend, the poet Sylvia Plath, the other his own, fortunately unsuccessful, attempt at suicide. I will discuss these later. The rest of his book is concerned with the history of attitudes toward suicide and the theories put forward to account for it.

In associating with the suicide the epic hero and the martyr, Mr Alvarez seems to me to be stretching his net too wide. Though it is usually the fate of the epic hero to fall in battle, that is not his goal: his goal is to slay the enemies of his people, and by his valiant deeds to win immortal glory on earth. The martyr does not sacrifice his life for the sake of any particular social group, but for all mankind. He does not, incidentally, die by his own hand, but by the hands of others. In the special case of Christ, the God-Man, he dies to redeem sinful mankind: the ordinary martyr dies to bear witness to what he believes (it can be Christian or Marxist) to be saving truth, to be shared with all men, not reserved as an esoteric secret for a few.

The Church from the beginning had always condemned the Stoic attitude toward suicide, but, during the persecutions, she discovered that there was an ethical-psychological problem which no one had foreseen, namely, that a man might insist upon getting himself martyred, not in order to bear witness to the truth on earth, but in order to win for himself immortal glory in Heaven. In other words, his real motive could be the pride of the epic hero. The Church found herself having to preach caution and discourage her converts from insisting upon martyrdom when it could possibly be avoided. Only when the choice lay between martyrdom and apostasy was martyrdom to be chosen. The paradigm was the story of the Passion. Far from rushing joyfully upon death, Christ, in the Garden of Gethsemane, prays in agony that the cup shall pass from Him.

The suicide proper dies by his own hand. This may be, as was the case with most of the famous Roman suicides, because he knows that if he does not kill himself he will be killed, and self-killing seems less degrading. But I would define a suicide in society as we know it as someone who for one reason or another finds his life subjectively intolerable. I stress the word subjectively because in circumstances that would seem to an outsider objectively intolerable, as in concentration camps or for sufferers from gross physical deformities, suicide appears to be rare. Mr Alvarez quotes a very moving passage by the wife of Osip Mandelstam.

> Whenever I talked of suicide, M used to say: "Why hurry? The end is the same everywhere, and here they may even hasten it for you." . . . In war, in the camps and during periods of terror, people think much less about death (let alone suicide) than when they are living normal lives. Whenever at some point on earth mortal terror and the pressure of utterly insoluble problems are present in a particularly intense form, general questions about the nature of being recede into the background. . . . Who knows what happiness is? Perhaps it is better to talk in more concrete terms of the fullness or intensity of existence, and in this sense there may have been something more deeply satisfying in our desperate clinging to life than in what people generally strive for.

Money is an objective fact and when they lose it, some people, as during the Wall Street crash, kill themselves, but in such cases I suspect that money has become a private symbol for their personal worth. To those, like Chatterton, who have always been poor, this cannot happen. I think Mr Alvarez is wrong when he says: "Suicide was a solution to a practical problem."

What we all ask from others is mutual understanding. In the case of physical pain, this presents no difficulty: we can all sympathize, that is, feel with someone else's toothache. We can also all share in another's happiness, for we are all happy in the same way. It is otherwise when we are mentally unhappy, for each of us is unhappy in his own unique way, so that we can never imagine exactly what another is suffering. Even two persons, both with suicidal feelings, cannot, I think, completely understand each other. Mr Alvarez's definition of suicide as *The Closed World* applies to all mental unhappiness.

In consequence, no theory, sociological or psychological, of why people commit suicide is satisfactory. For instance, in the case histories of many suicides it is found that they lost a loved one in childhood, but so have many people who do not kill themselves. Again, if, as Freud believed, there is a death instinct, which I rather doubt, it must be active in all men, yet the majority do not cut short their lives. Climate has been invoked as a factor, but though their climate is the same, the suicide rate is high in Sweden but low in Norway. Protestantism, it has been alleged, is more conducive to suicide than Catholicism, but Austria, a Catholic country, has the third highest suicide rate in the world. A pessimistic philosophy of life certainly has no influence. Schopenhauer and Thomas Hardy lived to a ripe old age.

If suicide has become commoner in this century than in previous ones, I do not think this can be attributed to our particular social and political problems, for social-political life has been very grim throughout history. What does seem to play a role in suicide as in art is fashion. (Think of the effect on the young at the time of *Werther.*) The late Middle Ages were grim enough, no anesthetics or plumbing, lepers, the Inquisition, plundering mercenaries, yet the poetry of the period, the writings of Chaucer, Langland, Douglas, Dunbar are happy. Today happy art is regarded by many as rather vulgar.

Mr Alvarez's first chapter is an account of the last few years in the life of his friend, the poet Sylvia Plath. I understand that her husband, Ted Hughes, thinks it inaccurate, and I am in no position to judge. It does seem clear from the facts that she intended her successful attempt to fail, as her two previous attempts had. Mr Alvarez says, and I agree with him:

> . . . for the artist himself art is not necessarily therapeutic: he is not automatically relieved of his fantasies by expressing them. Instead, by some perverse logic of creation, the act of formal expression may simply make the dredged-up material more readily available to him. The result of handling it in his work may well be that he finds himself living it out . . . when an artist holds up a mirror to nature he finds out who and what he is: but the knowledge may change him irredeemably so that he becomes that image.

The moral, surely, is that one should be very cautious in what one chooses to write about.

In our aesthetic judgments I think Mr Alvarez and I would usually agree—one would not call good poetry what the other would call bad. But in our personal tastes, i.e. the writers we really take to our hearts, it is clear that we differ.

Reading those he calls the Extremist Poets, Plath, Hughes, Berryman, I greatly admire their craftsmanship, but I cannot sympathize fully with what they are doing. The poetry which is really my cup of tea, that, for example, to name two modern Americans, of Frost and Marianne Moore, whether tragic, comic, or satiric, is always firmly rooted in staid common sense. Mr Alvarez's taste, whether in modern poetry or in the poetry of the past, seems to be for the extreme. For example, he obviously loves John Donne whom, great as he is, I find an insufferable prima donna; give me George Herbert every time.

Mr Alvarez's concluding chapter is devoted to his own unsuccessful attempt at suicide. It is most moving to read but rather puzzling. For instance, he tells us that, as a child, he kept repeating endlessly to himself *Iwishiweredead*, but he cannot tell us just why this was so. The statistics, he tells us, show that:

> The incidence of successful suicide rises with age and reaches its peak between the ages of fifty-five and sixty-five. In comparison, the young are great attempters: their peak is between twenty-five and forty-four.

Mr Alvarez was thirty-one and already established in the literary world before he swallowed forty-four sleeping pills, but at home, so that he was found by his wife just in time to save him. To the outsider an attempted suicide has about it the aura of a sick joke. (Cowper's account, quoted in this book, of his desperate and always thwarted efforts to kill himself is pure black farce.) Mr Alvarez's reactions to his failure are fascinating and cheer my heart.

> The truth is, in some way I had died. The overintensity, the tiresome excess of sensitivity and self-consciousness, of arrogance and idealism, which came in adolescence and stayed on beyond their due time, like some visiting bore, had not survived the coma . . . I was disappointed. Somehow, I felt, death had let me down; I had expected more of it. I had looked for something overwhelming, an experience which would clarify all my confusions. But it turned out to be simply a denial of experience. . . . Months later I began to understand that I had had my answer after all. . . . Once I had accepted that there weren't ever going to be any answers, even in death, I found to my surprise that I didn't much care whether I was happy or unhappy; "problems" and "the problem of problems" no longer existed. And that in itself is already the beginning of happiness.

I congratulate him. That is what I mean by common sense.

The New York Review of Books, 20 April 1972

Wilson's Sabine Farm

Upstate. By Edmund Wilson. Macmillan. £4.50.

I believe I have gotten more sheer pleasure out of *Upstate* than from any other books by Edmund Wilson that I have read. I feel in duty bound, however, to warn younger readers that they may not feel the same. One's preoccupations, intellectual and emotional, when one is twenty are very different from what they are when one is fifty and over.

The main theme of *Upstate* is the relation between the author and an old house in Upper New York State, Talcottville, which he inherited from his mother in 1951. Very few young people own the house they live in, so that the joys and headaches of being a householder can mean nothing to them. Talcottville had belonged to his family for generations, so that, on inheriting it, one of Mr Wilson's first psychological tasks was to understand and become reconciled to his family ghosts. The young man whose first task is to discover who he is, as distinct from what others believe or expect him to become, has, naturally, to forget, if not rebel against, his family. Mr Wilson himself tells us that he was entranced by Talcottville as a child—it was there that he discovered that his future vocation was to become a man-of-letters—but by the time he was an undergraduate at Princeton, visits there bored him. Again, unless they happen to be naturalists, most young people are more interested in human beings than in Nature. In *Upstate* Mr Wilson displays, what I don't recall finding in his earlier books, both a passionate interest in Nature and a remarkable gift for describing Her vividly. For instance:

> You pass an abandoned quarry and pick your way through a queer broken-up terrain: great square blocks of stone, like the bed of Dry Sugar River, with deep straight-fissured crevices between them, but here disguised by having been grown over so that the crevices have grassy lips and from a distance look like a field. This formation continues through more woodland, in the open places sprigged with everlasting—after which you come to a clearing partly framed by big maples, but lined on one side by a row of cottonwoods diffusing a pleasant fragrance. Now appears a great pit, from which rises a kind of rock pyramid, made of more or less square-cut blocks. One cannot tell whether this object is natural or erected by human hands, somehow in connection with the quarry. Traversing this field to the left, you soon hear the roar of a river. You find yourself at the top of the glen, at the bottom of which the stream gushes out in what is at first a small torrent.

> My Showy Ladyslippers, brought me and expertly planted by the Weilers, are almost all blooming now, and I am extremely proud of them. Five are in flower or bud—though the one that has flowered is as yet rather measly. It is as if the plants themselves had contrived with much taste the combination of deep-pink pouches and white ribbon-like streamers, of smooth surfaces and speckled interiors, with the piquancy of the single dots of yellow and red. I feel that they are exquisite independent beings who are, nevertheless, willing to live here.

Lastly, the young like to be regaled with accounts of dramatic events and romantic encounters. In the years covered by this book there was, to be sure, one dramatic event in Mr Wilson's life, his trouble with the Income Tax Authorities but, since he has devoted a book to it, he mentions it here only in passing. As for Romance, the only encounter that remotely resembles one is a Father-Daughter relationship that developed between the author and a young Polish girl, Mary Pcolar, who gave him lessons in Hungarian while he tried to teach her some political history. His wife complained that he seemed to get on better with her than with his own children to which he replied that, when there is an age difference, he could only feel close to someone to whom he felt he had something to teach. This I can understand. It is at least certain that, once they have reached adolescence, the last thing children want from Papa is a tutor.

In 1915, when Mr Wilson was twenty, I was eight years old: that is to say, we inhabited different universes. Today I feel that, in all essential respects, we are contemporaries so that I can directly compare his experiences and reactions to them with my own, noting where they agree and where they differ. Some of the differences are, of course, temperamental, but those which fascinate me most are due to the fact that Mr Wilson was born and brought up in the States, while I was born and brought up in England. The older I get, the more I realise that, while class snobbery is a contemptible vice, class consciousness, knowing what class one belongs to—it doesn't matter which—is vital to any psychological security. (A man should, I think, be a gentleman, not a cad, but gentlemen and cads are to be found in all classes.) Mr Wilson and I belong to the same class, called in England Upper Middle Class Professional. One of his grandfathers was a Presbyterian Minister: both of mine were Anglican Clergymen. His other grandfather was a physician as was my father. His own father was a lawyer like one of my uncles. Both of us received what was then an élite education: Mr Wilson went to a boys' boarding school and Princeton, I to a boarding school and Oxford.

The experiences and attitudes of the Professional Class in England and in America are not, however, quite the same. In England, there was always a distinction between the Gentry, who owned land, and the Professional Class which rarely did. This, so far as I can make out, was not so in America. Then American Professionals have never looked down on, as we did, persons in business or industry, however rich they might be, as socially inferior, "in trade" as we used to say. (The only respectable "trades" were Banking and Book Publishing.) But the most striking social difference between the United States and, not only England but any European country, lies in matters of religion. In all European countries, even where there is separation of Church and State, it is always the case that one denomination is normal and respectable, all the others eccentric. In New England at first, I suppose the Presbyterians and, later, the Unitarians occupied this position, but by the nineteenth-century, instead of anything remotely resembling a State Church, there remained only what Henry James called "The multiplied signs of theological enterprise". In England, when I was young, Dissenters, Baptists, Methodists and the like, came in through the back door, not the front. In many American communities, they are the leading citizens. On the other hand, because of the old Roman Catholic families like the Norfolks, Roman Catholics could not be regarded as necessarily socially inferior, as was the case for some time in the States when most Roman Catholics were foreign immigrants.

One of the most fascinating chapters in this book is the one Mr Wilson devotes to the various freak sects which, until quite recently, flourished in Upper New York State. Of these, the most extraordinary of all was the Oneida Community, founded by John Humphrey Noyes (b. 1811).

> There were forty families involved, selected by Noyes from the best New England stock, and their mating was subjected to a rigid discipline. The women—fifty-nine of them—were obliged to sign the following pledge:
>
> (1) That we do not belong to ourselves in any respect, but that we belong first to God, and second to Mr Noyes as God's true representative.
>
> (2) That we shall have no rights or personal feeling in regard to child-bearing which shall in the least degree oppose or embarrass him in his choice of scientific combinations. . . .
>
> The men had to subscribe to equivalent submissions, and each, if he wanted to mate, had to apply to a Central Committee in order to impregnate a given woman . . . The proposal of the applicant, if granted, had always to be conveyed through a third person. If the Central Committee should calculate that the union of two persons, on account of their qualities, was likely to be specially desirable, they could be ordered to breed together. What was called "Special Love"—that is, what we call falling in love—was dreaded and always discouraged: the lovers would be separated and sometimes punished.

Today, in Mr Wilson's part of the world, religion, both sane and freakish, is on the wane. (The Jesus Freaks do not seem to have got there yet.) In his own town, Boonville, there is only one church left—of what denomination he does not say—served by a visiting minister.

Since the decay of the railroads, it is almost impossible to live in the American countryside without a car, but Mr Wilson is one of those rare Americans who have never learned to drive. From this deficiency he seems to have profited. He tells us that he can only really talk to his children when they are driving him around, and some of his chauffeurs have become good friends, among them a certain Albert Grubel, whose ruling passion seems to have been *Schadenfreude.*

> . . . the day before Memorial Day [he] said that the papers predicted about two hundred and sixty car accidents for the holiday. The next day he asked me whether I knew how many there had been—from the paper he gathered that they had been runnin' double. Then he told me that in April two women had gone out in a car and disappeared, and then they found them at the bottom of a lake under two feet of water.

In addition to Talcottville, where he likes to spend his summers, Mr Wilson also has a house in Wellfleet on Cape Cod, where he spends the winter. This would seem an ideal arrangement. Unfortunately, his wife Elena, does not like the climate of Upper New York State and is scared by the landscape, so that she only comes for short visits and much of the time he is alone.

Though he seems to have been very lucky in finding people to look after him, he is sometimes reduced to a depressing bachelor's diet.

> Glyn's wife is a delightful cook and has produced a welcome relief from the chipped beef, canned hash and canned baked beans which, when Elena is not here with me, are usually all I can think of.

Having, like Elena, grown up in Europe, I can understand what she feels about the landscape. I have never lived in the American countryside, but I know that, within an hour's drive of Manhattan, where Nature, aside from the weather, has been obliterated, the road may pass through untamed forests with not a human habitation in sight. In Europe, since at least the sixteenth century, there has been no untamed Nature. The relationship between Man and Nature is conceived of as a happy and fruitful marriage between equals. They may sometimes have rows, but essentially both trust and love each other. To Americans, on the other hand, unless they happen to be professional lovers of the wilderness, Nature, even today, is thought of as a formidable antagonist to be conquered and made to submit.

I have noticed that, when an American talks about "Conservation" he usually means preserving a wilderness in its primitive state. In Europe, as the woods behind my Austrian house testify, it means looking after Nature, seeing that she is well-kempt and well-mannered. My sentiments, like Elena's are wholly European.

Mr Wilson and I were both, thank God, brought up on the Protestant Work Ethic but, though I generally think of myself as fairly industrious, he makes me feel a lazybones. I know I haven't the energy nor, I suspect, the talent, to become proficient, as he has, in difficult foreign languages like Russian, Hungarian and Hebrew. Of his own working habits he says that what he likes is, first, the dedicated toil and then the orgy, by which term I think he means good food and drink at a large party. He confesses that, at his age, he finds it difficult to talk to strangers, but he seems happy to have a lot of friends around him at the same time, whereas I like to see them one, or at most two, at a time. One statement of his astounds me. He says that he cannot write without having first washed his hands: mine don't get washed until I take my evening bath.

In our literary tastes we seldom disagree. He thinks more highly of Genet than I do and does not care for Trollope whom I adore, but then my childhood was spent in Barchester. I wish he would write a piece about E. F. Benson's *Lucia* books, now fortunately available in paper-back. I rank them among the finest English comic novels written in this century.

Like most places in the States, Boonville is not what it was. Juvenile hoodlums and snowmobiles have already arrived, and there is a prospect of a four-lane highway which will run in front of Mr Wilson's door. But he has reached an age when it is honest to say:

> That the old life is passing away, that all around me are anarchy and what seems to me stupidity, does not move me much any more. I have learned to read the papers calmly and not to hate the fools I read about. As long as my health holds out, I shall have to go on living, and I am glad to have had some share in some of the better aspects of the life of this planet and of northern New York.

Nobody can accuse him of being an "escapist" for much of his writing has been *engagé* and not in his youth only: *Apologies to the Iroquois* is a late work.

The proper social function of the old is, in my opinion, to become, in their own persons and here and now, an example of what is meant by the civilised life. *Upstate* is testimony that this is precisely what Mr Wilson has done.

Books & Bookmen, June 1972

To an Old Friend [Cecil Day-Lewis]

In the nineteen-thirties, according to the critics, there existed a strange Chimera named *Daylewisaudenmacneicespender*. It is true that all four of us were undergraduates at Oxford who got to know and like each other personally. (William Empson had the good luck to go to Cambridge, so was treated as an individual.) It is also, of course, true, that intellectuals of the same generation, confronted by the same political and social events, are likely to show certain characteristics in common, though these are more likely to be in the realm of ideas than in the realm of literary style.

But what poets of the same generation have in common is the least interesting thing about them. What really matters is the way in which they differ, for every genuine poet, major or minor, is unique, a member of a class of one. Here are two stanzas, one written early, one late.

> What life may now decide
> Is past the clutch of caution, the range of pride.
> Speaking from the snow
> The crocus lets me know
> That there is life to come, and go.

> But when we cease to play explorers
> And become settlers, clear before us
> Lies the next need—to redefine
> The boundary between yours and mine;
> Else, one stays prisoner, one goes free.
> Each to his own identity
> Grown back, shall prove our love's expression

Purer for this limitation.
Love's essence, like a poem's shall spring
From the not saying everything.

No reader, acquainted with our works, could think for five seconds that these could have been written by MacNeice, Spender or myself. If it was one of our lot, it could only have been Day-Lewis.

A label like "Poets of the Thirties" is particularly aggravating because it seems to suggest that they conveniently stop writing when the decade is over. None of us, I am thankful to say, did, and I don't think any of us ever want to hear about that tiresome decade again.

There are some poets, A. E. Housman, for example, who show no poetical development, that is to say, if confronted with two poems of his, both of equal merit, it would be very difficult, on the evidence of the text alone, to say which was written first. Day-Lewis was not one. As he wrote in his excellent introduction to the Penguin *Selected Poems*:

> My later work, as far as I may judge, presents a good deal more variety both in subject matter and in verse forms, a more sensuous appeal, and a greater flexibility of line, than my earlier . . . What happens, as far as I can make out, is that I have some deep violent experience which, like an earthquake, throws up layers of my past that were inaccessible to me poetically till then. During the last war, for instance, I found myself able to use in verse for the first time images out of my own childhood. The new material thrown up, the new contours which life presents as a result of the seismic experience, may demand a new kind of poem. It is here that change of technique appears.

I gather from this that he must have sometimes had the same experience as myself. An idea for a poem suggests itself which one has to turn down for one of two reasons: *no longer* or *not yet.*

Had he been asked to define his profession, I think he would have said, as I do, A Man of Letters, a term which, today, is most unfashionable. In addition to the poems, there were the translations, the fiction, the lectures, the work as a publisher, the public recitals of verse and music in collaboration with Jill Balcon, and then at the end, of course the Laureateship. If his official occasional poems as Poet Laureate are not, it must be confessed, very interesting, how many of such written by his predecessors have been? Very few. Rudyard Kipling, who, of all poets in our history was, by temperament and talent, ideally suited to the post, never held it. I like to think of the poems he might be writing today about such matters as Student Demonstrations, Porn, Trade Unions, Women's Lib. They would make a lot of people very cross, but they would be fun to read.

But this is not the occasion for a literary essay and, from now on, I shall drop the surname.

I don't remember exactly how I first met Cecil, but it was certainly very soon after I came up to Oxford in 1925. At that time he was sharing digs with Rex Warner, whom, incidentally, I have never quite forgiven for losing his excellent translations of Maximian's Elegies. Cecil introduced me to the later Yeats, and I introduced him to Hardy, Frost and Edward Thomas. I can't recall who first discovered Emily Dickinson or Gerard Manley Hopkins. Much as we admired him as a man, an editor, a critic and a poet, neither of us was poetically influenced by Eliot, but, then, who has been? I am always surprised when students in the States want courses in Contemporary Literature. That we regarded as our business and would never have dreamed of asking our tutors to tell us about it.

Another interest we had in common was music. Cecil possessed a good tenor voice and I used to accompany him in Elizabethan songs. In company, then and later, he could be most amusing and witty but, so far as I know, he never wrote a comic poem. Humour, including black humour, he reserved for his fiction.

When I went down in 1928, I went to Berlin and, during the next twelve years, travelled extensively. Cecil was much more insular and did not cross the Channel, I believe, until after the war. Neither of us had private means and could not yet hope to earn our living by our pens, so we both became schoolmasters. That I did so was largely his doing. Cecil had been teaching at a prep school in Scotland, but in 1930 moved to a school in Cheltenham. Thanks to his recommendation, I succeeded him. When, twenty-six years later, I succeeded him as Professor of Poetry, I'm sure he had a hand in it.

I happen to be both a lover of poetry and a Whodunit addict, but it must have been a source of enormous satisfaction to Cecil to know that, as Nicholas Blake, he could give pleasure to thousands who would never dream of reading Day-Lewis. In his early days, his detective Nigel Strangeways exhibited certain traits of behaviour which, I am proud to believe, were taken from me.

In later days we did not see as much of each other as I should have liked. The Atlantic is a wide ocean. It was sheer bad luck that, the only time when Cecil was in the States, to deliver the Charles Eliot Norton Lectures, should have been the one winter when I was not in New York but in Berlin. When we did meet, however, it was just as if we had seen each other yesterday.

Thank you, Cecil. It was a great privilege to have been permitted to know you.

The Sunday Times, 4 June 1972

Introduction to *The Spirit of Man: An Anthology*, compiled by Robert Bridges

An adolescent, who knows the names of very few writers and has read very little of their work, treats any anthology as a literary guide-book. He wants to be introduced to authors who, from the selections given, strike him as being his cup-of-tea, whom he would like to read more of. My own generation, for example, is eternally grateful to *The Spirit of Man* because it printed for the first time poems by Gerard Manley Hopkins. We were enormously impressed and when, a few years later, Bridges published a selection from his work, we rushed out to buy it. I, personally, am also grateful because it introduced me to Canon Dixon who, though already published, was almost unknown, and I have been a great admirer of his poetry ever since. (I wish I could say the same about D. M. Dolben.)

Now, reading the book again after many years, I see that I never realised what an extremely idiosyncratic compilation it is. The conventional anthology attempts to give an equitable representation of the authors in the period which it covers. That is to say, unless it is specifically devoted to minor authors, it will give more space to major ones and, except for epics and dramas, it will usually give a poem in its entirety. Furthermore, the anthologist will not be governed by his personal taste alone: if his aesthetic judgement tells him that a poem is historically important, he will include it, even though he doesn't care much for it. Lastly, it is rare for an anthologist to include both verse and prose selections in the same volume.

Of his own intentions, Bridges writes:

> Whatever merit or attractive quality it may have, will lie in its being the work of one mind at one time; and its being such implies the presence of the peculiarities and blemishes that mark any personality and any time: these he has not sought to avoid.

Let us consider the time first. *The Spirit of Man* was published in January 1916, that is to say, in the middle of World War I. I should guess that Bridges thought of his prospective readers as being mostly civilians with sons and loved ones at the Front. For such, the time was one of fear, often grief, and anxiety as to the final outcome. His primary purpose in compiling it, therefore, was not so much literary, to give aesthetic pleasure, as ethical, to offer consolation to hearts in suffering and distress and to strengthen the wills of the dejected. For this reason, the prose selections are as important as the poetic, and, in both cases, they tend to be short. Again, since the main impact on the reader is intended to be *what* is said rather than *how* it is said, the names of the authors are not, as in most anthologies, included in the text, but assigned to an appendix.

Aside from Classical authors, the Bible, a few philosophers like Spinoza, mystics like Kabir, and one or two quotes from Tolstoi and Dostoievski, the only non-English-speaking authors represented are French—France was our ally at the time—and their contributions are printed in their own tongue. There are no selections from German authors, like Goethe or Nietzsche, though the latter certainly had some savage things to say about his fellow-countrymen. It would seem obvious to conclude that this omission was due to the fact that we were at war with Germany, but I am not quite sure. It is possible that Bridges did not know German literature very well. I entertain this possibility, because there are no selections from Italian authors, like Dante or Petrarch, either. Though, so far as I recall, Italy had not yet become our ally when the anthology was compiled, Bridges could easily have included them in a later edition.

As for Bridges' personal tastes, I find them rather strange, though it must be remembered that he was not compiling a conventional anthology. In the index, there are more entries under *Shelley*, a poet whom I cannot myself read with pleasure, than under either *Shakespeare* or *Milton*. After these three, his favourite English poets seem to be Keats, Blake, Dixon, Coleridge and Wordsworth. There are only two selections from Tennyson, and none from Dryden, Pope or Browning. His favourite French prose-writer seems to be Amiel, his favourite French poet Rimbaud, a judgement with which I heartily concur, but it seems a bit odd to find no Racine, Victor Hugo, Baudelaire or Verlaine. Of his contemporaries, the only poets he quotes are Yeats, Masefield and Lascelles Abercrombie. There is no Hardy or Housman, though the latter was a personal friend. I suspect that he omitted them because he felt that, in war-time, their poems would be too depressing.

His own contributions, all but one of them, are translations, and all but one are imitations of classical metres, Hexameters, Elegiacs, Alcaics, Scazons, which are scanned, not, as is usual in English verse, by stress but, as in Greek and Latin, by vowel quantity. He was obviously proud of them and, as a great admirer of prosodic virtuosity, I think he had every right to be.

Now that we know more about the series of appalling diplomatic blunders on all sides which led to the outbreak of the First World War, one may take issue with Bridges for, in his Preface, laying the whole blame upon Prussia, but one must remember that, at the time, every Englishman thought the same. What remains wholly laudable is the complete absence from *The Spirit of Man* of any patriotic flag-wagging. There is no Kipling, for example.

There remains the question: what, fifty-six years after its first publication, will a modern reader make of the book? Has it still a valuable spiritual function? I would say, emphatically, yes. The world has greatly changed, but one cannot say that the future looks any brighter than it looked in 1916: indeed, it may well look worse. Bridges' words ring as true to-day as they did then.

> Our habits and thoughts are searched by the glare of the conviction that man's life is not the ease that a peace-loving generation has found it or thought to make it, but the awful conflict with evil which philosophers and saints have depicted; and it is in their abundant testimony to the good and beautiful that we find support for our faith, and distraction from a grief that is intolerable to face, nay impossible to face without that trust in God which makes all things possible.

The Spirit of Man: An Anthology,
compiled by Robert Bridges (1972)

The Poet of No More

Tennyson. By Christopher Ricks. Macmillan £3.95.

I must begin by apologising to Professor Ricks. What follows is less a review of his excellent book, the best study of Tennyson I have read, than a series of personal reflections on the poet suggested to me by reading it.

When I was a small child, the only poetry I liked was comic, like Belloc's *Cautionary Tales*, or sick jokes like Graham's *Ruthless Rhymes for Heartless Homes.* The first "serious" poetry I remember enjoying was *In Memoriam*, which my father used to read aloud to me. When I started to write poetry myself, it might have been expected that I would have written imitations of Tennyson, but I didn't. I must have instinctively guessed what I only consciously realised years later: that Tennyson, like Eliot, was an extremely idiosyncratic poet by whom it is impossible to be influenced, since one will only produce the palest of imitations. Eliot has told us who his early models were—dramatists like Webster and Tourneur and French Symbolists like Laforgue—and I think a reader would guess this, even if he hadn't been told. But, reading Tennyson's early verse, I find myself unable to spot a model. We know that when he was fourteen he was deeply upset by Byron's death: but Byron certainly had no influence. It has been said that he was influenced by Keats and Coleridge, but I can't see it. I think that Milton may have had an effect, particularly through poems like "Lycidas", but I am not sure. How early the Tennysonian style was formed may be seen from the fact that he could take lines he had written years before and incorporate them in a new poem. Thus, the famous lines in "Ulysses"—

> To follow knowledge like a sinking star,
> Beyond the utmost bound of human thought

—are to be found in one of his Trinity College notebooks.

I knew that his childhood had been unhappy, but, until I read Professor Ricks, I didn't realise just how awful it was. To have had a grandfather who disinherited his father and didn't like his grandchildren either, a father who, though an Anglican priest, was a drunkard and at times a dangerous paranoiac, and a Calvinist aunt who assured him as a child that he was damned, must have been terrifying experiences. What astounds me is that they didn't turn the mature Tennyson into a militant atheist. Nor had I realised before that the nervous breakdown he suffered in the early 1840s was as severe as in fact it was: so severe that his friends were seriously afraid that he might go mad or commit suicide.

Most readers will agree, I think, that, in depicting states of melancholia, loneliness or desertion, Tennyson is the greatest poet who ever lived. But not all of them, perhaps, realise how difficult it is to deal with such subjects without indulging in self-pity. To me, his most amazing achievement is that, even in his bleakest poems, there is no trace of self-pity. It is, perhaps, a sense of this danger that has turned so many melancholics—Sydney Smith and Edward Lear, for example—into wits and comic writers. As Nietzsche said, "every joke is an epitaph on an emotion." A striking example of this is Byron. So long as he indulges his melancholia, in works like *Childe Harold*, he is a bore: he only became great when he took to writing comic poetry. So far as I know, Tennyson never wrote any comic verses, except unintentionally. (Presumably neither his wife nor anyone else dared tell the old boy that the lines

"The curse is come upon me," cried
The Lady of Shalott

were funny.) He could, however, be amusing in conversation. It is told that he once dined at Balliol, when Jowett was Master. In Senior Common Room afterwards he recited a new poem. Jowett said: "I shouldn't publish that poem if I were you, Tennyson." After a few seconds of speechless rage, Tennyson replied: "Well, if it comes to that, Master, the sherry you served us before dinner was filthy."

If he did not write comic verse, his occasional poems to his friends are enchanting. Professor Ricks says: "If one may distinguish the favourite from the best, I should say that 'To E. FitzGerald' is my favourite among Tennyson's poems." I myself would find it hard to choose between that poem and "To E. L., on His Travels in Greece", "To the Rev. F. D. Maurice" and "The Daisy". Rather oddly, it is in these poems that his poetic model is obvious—namely, Horace.

Tennyson was not a narrator and not a dramatist, but he might have made a superb librettist. If only he had found an English Berlioz to work with (a Verdi would have been too sane), what remarkable works they might have turned out. *Maud* has always struck me as a libretto *manqué*. Even the bellicose ending, which is painful to read, might have been most effective if set to martial music.

From childhood on Tennyson was fascinated by the sound of words: "When I was eight, I remember making a line I thought grander than Campbell, or Byron, or Scott. I rolled it out, it was this: 'With slaughterous sons of thunder rolled the flood.'" But he never became, as Swinburne often did, the slave of sound, for his visual imagination was as keen as his auditory sensibility. It doesn't matter where you open his poems, the imagery is as vivid as the pattern of vowels and consonants is delectable.

I saw
The smallest grain that dappled the dark Earth,
The indistinctest atom in deep air,
The Moon's white cities, and the opal width
Of her small glowing lakes, her silver heights
Unvisited with dew of vagrant cloud.

("Timbuctoo")

He spoke; and, high above, I heard them blast
The steep slate-quarry, and the great echo flap
And buffet round the hills, from bluff to bluff.

("The Golden Year")

The hedgehog underneath the plantain bores,
The rabbit fondles his own harmless face.

("Aylmer's Field")

Reading Professor Ricks's comments and observations convinces me that he is exactly the kind of critic every poet dreams of finding. No poet wants either uncritical admirers or decoders who discover in his poems secret symbols and meanings which never entered his mind. But every poet thinks of himself as a craftsman, a maker of verbal objects: what he hopes for is that critics will notice the technical means by which he secures his effects. Alas, so few critics do. Professor Ricks is a happy exception. I had known the following stanza by heart for years:

And bless thee, for thy lips are bland,
  And bright the friendship of thine eye;
  And in my thoughts with scarce a sigh
I take the pressure of thine hand.

But, until Professor Ricks pointed it out to me, I had never noticed that the internal rhymes in the last two lines re-enact the abba stanza form:

  And in my thoughts with scarce a *sigh*
I take the pressure of thine *hand.*

How delighted Tennyson would be to know that someone at last has spotted this.

The Listener, 10 August 1972

A Saint-Simon of Our Time

In the Twenties: The Diaries of Harry Kessler. Translated by Charles Kessler, with an Introduction by Otto Friedrich.
Holt, Rinehart & Winston. $10.

Count Kessler's diaries begin when he was fifty, three days before the Armistice, and end in 1937, a year after the outbreak of the Spanish Civil War, when he was an exile living in Paris. Mysteriously, there are no entries between New Year's Eve, 1933, and May 25, 1935.

Like Saint-Simon, though deeply involved in politics he does not seem to have exerted a decisive influence on events. Before the war, apparently, he had collaborated with Bernard Shaw in an effort to improve Anglo-German relations. Later he went on several diplomatic visits, to Warsaw, to London, to Genoa. His most ambitious plan was to reorganize the League of Nations. Perceiving, quite rightly, that a league based on national sovereignty would be impotent to deal with any serious crisis, he proposed a league made up of international collectivities—labor unions, churches, professional groups, etc.—but nothing came of it.

Unlike Saint-Simon, who was only concerned with France, Kessler was one of the most cosmopolitan men who ever lived. Partly educated in France and England, he was completely at home in both. There is hardly anyone in political or artistic circles in either country whom he does not seem to have met. The only notable exceptions, so far as I can make out, were Winston Churchill and T. S. Eliot.

At this point I should like to take a slight exception to the description on the dust-jacket of the 1920s as an "era of cultural renaissance." There were, to be sure, important figures like Brecht, Weill, and the Bauhaus Group who were creations of that decade, but most of the greatest writers, musicians, and painters had started their careers before 1914. What had changed were their audiences, who were now ready to appreciate them. Furthermore, I am unwilling to apply the term "renaissance" to a period which saw the rise of such asinine movements as Dada and Surrealism.

Count Kessler was known as the "Red Count," but he was never a communist. He was a pacifist and a liberal. For Germany he thought the only viable form of government would be a Socialist Republic, but I doubt if he would have made this a must for all countries. It was rather that he hated the Hohenzollerns and the German military cast. Of the Kaiser, he writes:

> He was both shy and intemperate, screaming his head off to hide his embarrassment. His brutality and his cheap posturing were means of self-protection and self-deception, a purely personal matter for which all of us are now paying the price by way of political destruction and economic ruin. This rabbit roaring like a lion would be history's most ridiculous monster if his performance had not resulted in such suffering and rivers of blood. The mendacity of his behavior undermined policy and the state, substituted sham and show for sound Prussian tradition, and distorted the perspective of almost the entire nation.

Not that he imagined that, with the abdication, the Golden Age had arrived. Of nearly all the political figures, whether right or left, he took a dim view. Even Rathenau, whose life he was later to write, struck him at first as "an adept at striking false attitudes and displaying himself in a freakish posture." About most of the others he was scathing.

> Here the regal proletarian Scheidemann, inflated like a peacock in his brief glory, wandered round arm in arm with Preuss and Erzberger, deliberating affairs of state. As they passed up and down, the Gothic trappings quivered slightly in the breeze. I joined them. Erzberger, with his baggy cheeks and sly, sensual lips, received me smilingly. He always looks like someone who has fed well and is in the process of giving a tip. What with Scheidemann being pompous in his concertina trousers and Preuss a sheer monstrosity, the three of them constituted the quintessence of German humdrumness.

> [Noske] has indeed something of a bear with a nose-ring about him. Though "unemployed," he looks prosperous enough, travels first class, wears brand new yellow boots, and consumed during the journey large quantities of ham rolls and beer. Were there not so much innocent blood on his hands, he would be a slightly comic, almost likeable figure. Where, in that immense frame of his, he keeps his social conscience and his Social Democratic red heart is another matter and his own secret.

Nor do foreign politicians fare much better at his hands.

> . . . Radek made a mischievous speech, assuming the mask of youthful ardour. From behind it, and his flashing spectacles, there suddenly crept into his face an expression somewhere half-way between that of Facta and a wolf and at the same time having something of the look of a street urchin after a particularly successful prank.

> In addition to that indefinably youthful appearance which characterizes an English boy past school-leaving age, he [Chamberlain] has a

> clean-shaven sharply contoured, lean face. It carries little trace of intellect, but resembles that of a boiling chicken or a bad reproduction of features on a fine old medal executed in relief.
>
> His delivery was abominable. He stuttered, continually corrected himself, from time to time got stuck, and was evidently undecided as to how much he should or should not say. . . . Never in my life have I experienced so lamentable a performance on the part of a Foreign Minister in a Parliament. . . . How such a helpless, awkward, indecisive, vague man is expected to discuss the world's most serious problems with some degree of good sense is incomprehensible. I would not let him act for me even in eviction proceedings.

Though he disapproved of the methods of fascism and the intellectual stagnation which resulted, he was inclined, in 1927, to believe that Mussolini might be a genuine statesman. At the same time, however, he pointed out that the popular notion of Mussolini as the man who made the trains run on time and made the postal system efficient was a myth. Italian trains had been as punctual and Italian post as unreliable before his coming to power as after.

On the subject of communism he quotes an interesting though, I think, erroneous view of Rathenau's.

> The current Russian version is like a magnificent play performed as melodrama by third-rate actors. Germany, if Communism should come in, will give just as appallingly crude a performance. We lack the men to handle such an extremely complicated system. It requires more delicate and sophisticated talent than we possess. We have nobody of the requisite stature, though the British and Americans may. German organizational capacity is confined to parade-ground style; Bolshevism demands the staff college touch.

I am a little surprised that so acute a political observer as Kessler should never have remarked on the basic weakness of the Weimar Republic, namely its multiplicity of parties and factions. A one-party system, whether right or left, must become a tyranny, but a parliament consisting of more than two or, at most, three parties must be unstable and impotent to put through urgent reforms.

Hitler? Let us leave him till later.

For someone of my generation in England, who was too young for the First World War to be real, reading these diaries has been a curious experience. They forcibly remind me, firstly, of how unpolitical we were and, secondly, of how safe we felt. Having known neither civil violence, political executions and assassinations, nor inflation, we all thought the world was still as it had been before 1914. As an undergraduate, I had a few friends, like Hugh

Gaitskell and Richard Crossman, who were interested in politics, but they were intending to make politics their profession. The rest of us couldn't have cared less what was happening politically either in England or elsewhere. My own interests were in literature and music. I read the *Times Literary Supplement*, but I would never have dreamed of opening a daily newspaper.

As for myself, though I think Isherwood and Spender would agree with me, my really significant experiences when I went to Berlin in 1928 were not cultural, exciting though the cultural life of the city was at the time. They were two. For the first time I realized that the world was no longer a safe place, that the foundations were shaking. And then, as a foreigner, stammering in ungrammatical German, I had no class status, and so could make friends with members of the working class in a way I could never have done at home. Both parties would have been too conscious of their accents.

In his account of his experiences in the world of arts and letters Kessler has certain things to say which I, at least, never knew before. I never knew that he had collaborated with Hofmannsthal in planning the scenario for *Der Rosenkavalier.* I had never heard of a translation by Edward and Victoria Sackville-West of Rilke's *Duino Elegies,* which they made for his Cranach Press. And I was surprised to learn that Einstein could not understand why the public should be so interested in his theories.

> When Copernicus dethroned the earth from its position as the focal point of creation, the excitement was understandable because a revolution in all men's ideas really did occur. But what change does his own theory produce in humanity's view of things? It is a theory which harmonizes with every reasonable outlook or philosophy and does not interfere with anybody being an idealist or materialist, pragmatist or whatever else he likes.

Well, then, Hitler. It is easy to understand, given the political circumstances, why Napoleon, Mussolini, Lenin, and Stalin came to power. From books like these diaries and Otto Friedrich's *Before the Deluge,* we know of the various political maneuvers that went on in Germany, but to this day it remains a complete mystery how such an unprepossessing-looking and illiterate creature as Hitler could have become dictator. Even as a demagogic orator he was greatly inferior to Goebbels. Much as I dislike the invention, I think McLuhan is right in thinking that, had television then existed, Hitler would never have made it. One notices, too, that he never made a fireside chat on the radio: there was always a background of a cheering crowd.

Had England and France acted when he reoccupied the Rhineland, he might well have been overthrown by an army *Putsch.* We did not act because, by then, public opinion in both countries felt the Allied occupation had been unjust. Once that point was passed, he was firmly in the saddle and, but for his insanity in insisting upon a war, he would have remained where he was until he died a natural death. To lay the blame upon the character of the German people is too easy a way out. Kessler says, I think rightly:

> I have through the years come to recognize two characteristics as being absolutely and inalterably basic to all Germans, but especially the younger generation, whether they belong to the left or right, the Communists, the Nazis, the Social Democrats or the middle class: escape into metaphysics, into some sort of "faith," and the desire for discipline, for standing to attention and receiving orders or issuing them. The German, because of some feeling or other of insecurity, is through and through a militarist and through and through an escapist into some kind of beyond or Utopia, and the awful part is that he mixes them together!

Or, as one of Kessler's cultural heroes, Nietzsche, said: "Definition of Germanics—obedience and long legs."

But why just *this* kind of faith? Aside from party functionaries, the SS and the Gestapo, to whom Nazism was their profession, it is impossible to estimate how many Germans between 1934 and 1939 were convinced Nazis. Heroes like Niemöller and Bonhoeffer are rare: the average man in all countries thinks about his job and his family and does as he is told if the consequence of disobedience will bring disaster to both.

One thing that surprises me very much is that Kessler never once refers to *Mein Kampf*. Can it be that he never read it? After reading it, I and my friends were convinced that a Second World War was only a matter of time. In Hitler's determination to be the master of Europe and Russia there was something profoundly self-destructive. As Count Keyserling observed:

> According to his handwriting and his physiognomy, Hitler . . . clearly falls into the potential suicide category, a man looking for death. He embodies a fundamental trait of the German nation, which has always been in love with death and to whom the tribulation of the Nibelungs is a constantly recurrent basic experience.

There was a story in England current when the defeat of Germany was certain that, at the end of the war, Hitler would come out of his Berchtesgarten house, remove his moustache, and say: "I am British Agent Number 567. Germany is destroyed." But no reading of *Mein Kampf* or any other Nazi literature could have prepared one for Belsen and Auschwitz, and one is not surprised to learn that when Kurt Gerstein informed the British and Americans of what was happening, they refused to believe him. All one can say is that, in history, nothing is so silly or so horrid that it cannot happen.

Mr Kessler's translation reads very well and the editorial notes are all one could wish for. I have only two complaints. For my taste there are too many cartoons by George Grosz. When one has seen one of them, one has seen them all. Then, once, or twice—I don't see why since he generally doesn't—he anglicizes the titles of operas and plays. It took me some time to realize that the Hofmannsthal play he calls *A Hard Case* was *Der Schwierige*.

The New York Review of Books, 31 August 1972

Other People's Babies

The Rise and Fall of the British Nanny. By Jonathan Gathorne-Hardy. Hodder and Stoughton. £3.95.

"The Nanny Block," writes Mr Gathorne-Hardy in his marvellously researched and beautifully written (if, at times, a bit repetitious) study, "should be viewed as a mountain of ice which grew during the 1830s, '40s and '50s, reached its height between 1890 and 1914, and then slowly melted and crumbled, but was still very sizeable in 1939, still recognisably the same shape, and which after the Second World War finally and swiftly disappeared."

From my own experience I would have said that there was a serious decline after the first World War. My parents were not wealthy, but, until 1914, they employed a cook, a parlour-maid and a nanny. My mother helped with the cooking and I and my brothers with the washing-up. Had we been younger, I very much doubt if they could have afforded a nanny. Of the prep-school boys I taught in the '30s, very few, I think, had had a nanny, while in my generation they all would have had.

If, comparing my own childhood experiences with those described in this book, I find Mr Gathorne-Hardy's portrait of the nanny overdramatic. I realise that this was inevitable. Only those whose emotional relationship, for good or evil, to their nanny was exceptionally important are likely to have much to say about her. Sometimes, like Churchill's Nanny Everest, she was exceptionally loving: sometimes, like Curzon's Miss Paraman, she was exceptionally cruel. Then there are those to whom, for one reason or another, nanny took the place of mother, so that, when she left, they suffered a traumatic experience. Lastly, in a few cases, like Byron's, a nanny sexually "interfered" with her charge.

But I cannot believe that such nannies were typical of their kind. Mr Gathorne-Hardy himself says his mother was the most important figure in his childhood and that he can only dimly recall his nanny. In my own case I cannot remember her at all. A psychologist might argue, of course, that this is a proof of repressed emotions, but I don't believe it. Naturally, I cannot remember being toilet-trained. I suspect this was done early, but it must have been done sensibly because I have suffered no ill effects in later life, What I do remember very vividly from the nursery is being taught table-manners. If one rejected a dish, one was told to remember "the starving Armenians," if one gobbled, to leave something for "Mister Manners." One was not allowed to refuse a dish but, if one disliked it, one was given only a small helping, And I recognise every word of an imaginary mealtime conversation by M. A. Gibbs which Mr Gathorne-Hardy quotes:

> "May I get down, Nanny?"
>
> "Not until you have finished your bread and butter, dear."
>
> "But Nanny—"
>
> "Eat up your bread and butter dear. Not too fast, dear, and don't cram your mouth like that. It is bad manners" . . .
>
> "It's all gone now, so may I get down, Nanny?"
>
> "If you say please, dear."
>
> "Please, Nanny."
>
> "Wait till I take your bib off and then say grace."
>
> "For what wehavereceivedmaythelordmakeustrulythankfulamen. May I get down now, Nanny? Please."
>
> "Yes, dear, you may."

As one of his correspondents writes, the ideal situation is one in which both parents love their children and can afford a really nice nanny, so that the child is wrapped in treble security. Such a situation, thank God, was mine. A fairly strict discipline, if not irrational or brutally imposed, is surely a good thing, both in the nursery and the school. Polite behaviour is always an asset, and to acquire a timetable of when to eat, excrete, work and sleep, is very useful in adult life.

Some of Mr Gathorne-Hardy's most fascinating chapters are concerned with the social status of the nanny. All seem to have been of working-class origin. What made them choose to become nannies? In many cases, of course, it was a genuine love of children which made it seem a vocation but, even then, there is something mysterious about preferring to look after other people's children rather than one's own, for nannies rarely married. Sometimes the motive may have been social snobbery, a desire to play a part in the lives of the rich and powerful. But often, I suspect, the motive was a simple desire for security. A nanny was provided with food, clothing and accommodation. One question which the book does not discuss and which I would like to know more about is the question of accent. It seems that they must somehow have acquired an upper-class accent because, if they hadn't, their charges would have acquired a lower-class one. How did they manage this?

In Victorian and Edwardian times there was a popular masculine myth which declared that sexual intercourse was enjoyed only by women of the Lower Orders; a lady would, like Lady Hillingham, close her eyes, open her legs and think of England. Mr Gathorne-Hardy advances the theory that this was because, for upper-class males, their first intimate physical contacts, being pot-trained, washed, cuddled and spanked, were with their nannies. This is ingenious but not, to me, convincing. I think it more likely that it was a rationalising excuse for consorting with prostitutes, of which there were enormous numbers. A girl does not become a prostitute because she is lustful but because she is poor. However, if she is to succeed in her profession, she must at least pretend to enjoy it.

I wish I had the space to discuss the early chapters of this book, describing the upbringing of children in the pre-nanny ages, but I must confine myself to the last one, in which Mr Gathorne-Hardy gives two examples of what can happen to children who have been deprived both of parents and of nannies. The first of these was a group of six German-Jewish children whose parents had been gassed, had lived for three years in a concentration camp and were then brought to a country house in Sussex—

> The children's positive feelings were centred exclusively on their own group. It was evident they cared greatly for each other and not at all for anybody or anything else. They had no wish other than to be together and became upset when they were separated from each other, even for short moments. . . . On walks they were concerned for each other's safety in traffic, looked after children who lagged behind, helped each other over ditches, and carried each other's coats. In the nursery they picked up each other's toys.

The second, in this case the result of a deliberate educational policy, tells us what happens to children brought up under the kibbutz system:—

> . . . because they have never learned to do so, they cannot form deep attachments to individuals. There is a flatness of emotion between single people, a physical and psychical distance. . . . Intimacy, comradely friendship, is praised in theory and dreaded in practice. . . . Not that the kibbutzniks don't feel strong emotions. Their group-centred feelings are very strong indeed and rewarding.

I suppose it may be a satisfactory way of life. All I can say is, and I suspect that Mr Gathorne-Hardy would second me, thank God I had both a mummy and a nanny.

The Observer, 3 September 1972

An Odd Couple

Munby, Man of Two Worlds: The Life and Diaries of Arthur J. Munby 1828–1910. By Derek Hudson. Gambit. $12.50.

To his friends and acquaintances, who included such people as Rossetti, Ruskin, Swinburne, Thackeray, and Browning, Munby was a member of the professional upper middle class, a tall, handsome bachelor, a barrister (though he hated Law) who loved parties, the theater, the opera, was a member of the Athenaeum Club and the Society of Antiquities, and a gifted minor poet. From the examples of his work which Mr Hudson gives us, I would say that he was at his best when his model was Clough and least successful when his model was Tennyson, a poet whom it is impossible to be influenced by: the result is always Tennyson and water.

His friends also knew that he had a strong social conscience, acquired at Cambridge under the influence of F. D. Maurice's Christian Socialist Movement, that he was an unpaid teacher of Latin, first at the Working Men's College and later at the Working Women's College, and that he served on the Ecclesiastical Commission. Whether they knew that he was a skilled draftsman and an avid collector of photographs, though he did not take them himself, we don't know. Given the subjects of his sketches and photographs, I should guess that they didn't.

But of his taste in women they certainly hadn't the remotest inkling. This seems to have been acquired in childhood.

> This evening at nine we had prayers in the library as usual: my father sitting at the centre table & reading for the twentieth time one of those good sincere old sermons, full of the simple Calvinistic Protestantism of thirty years ago. I am on the sofa by my mother: at the far end of the room the servants sit in a row against the wall: last and lowest in rank, and next the door, sits Maggie the kitchenmaid. She is directly opposite me: let us observe what effect the good old sermon has on her. At first she sits bolt upright: her white cap is relieved against the paper on the wall; her smooth black hair is neatly combed behind her large red ears; her rosy wholesome face is bright & clean; she wears a brown plain "frock" and black apron; her ruddy hands lie folded in her lap. Her big round eyes are wide open, staring at nothing, or glancing sometimes with vague interest up at the busts on the top of the bookcases.
>
> . . . Oh kitchen-Maggie! The long grave periods . . . of that excellent sermon, how little they are valued by your rustic mind! And so, perhaps, it is more or less with all of us. Yet do we think the reading of these sermons useless? Certainly not. The formal good they do may be small. Their value comes from the scenes they create and the associations they leave behind.

Had his friends heard rumors of his obsessive interest in colliery women, fisher-girls, milkwomen, female acrobats, they would probably have given it a cynical explanation. Prostitution in Victorian London was a major industry, which may be partly explained, perhaps, by the life-situation of the Victorian "lady." Whereas the "gentlemen" had their work, either in the professions or, in the case of the gentry, in looking after their estates, their wives had nothing whatever to do except bear children. All the household work was done by servants and even their children were looked after by nannies and governesses. Their lives, however physically easy, must often have been psychologically difficult, for idleness seldom makes people either more intelligent or nicer. In Munby's case, however, I am convinced that his interest was aesthetic rather than sexual. He would have agreed with Van Gogh, who wrote:

> As far as I know there isn't a single academy where one learns to draw a digger, a sower, a woman putting the kettle over the fire or a seamstress. . . . I think that, however correctly academic a figure may be, it will be superfluous, though it were by Ingres himself, when it lacks the essential modern note, the intimate character, the real action. . . . I ask you, do you know a single digger, a single sower, in the Old Dutch school? Did they ever try to paint "a laborer"? Did Velasquez try it in his water-carrier or types from the people? No. The figures in the pictures of the old master do not work.

And, on his side, Van Gogh would certainly have appreciated Munby's drawings and photographs of brawny and sooty-faced working women.

In order that we should understand Munby's character, Mr Hudson was right, I'm sure, to print his many descriptions of chance and fleeting encounters with working-class girls both before and after his crucial encounter with Hannah Cullwick, but they are, to me at least, rather boring. What did interest me was the reaction of the women colliery workers in Lancashire to Lord Shaftesbury's Act of 1842, forbidding the employment of women underground. Though in the long run this was, no doubt, a good thing, twelve years later it was still resented, not only by management but also by the women themselves. In the first place, in mining areas there were often no other jobs available, so that they were thrown out of work. In the second, they seem to have enjoyed working underground.

> One told him she "liked it reet well—would like well to work below again—used to draw with belt and chain—liked it better than working up here." Another agreed she had been "like a horse or a dog," but said that surface work was harder "and we were warm in't pit. I only wish I was at it again," she added.

The crucial encounter in both their lives occurred on May 27, 1854 when Munby was twenty-five and Hannah had just turned twenty-one. She was born in Shifnal, Shropshire, the daughter of a saddler and a housemaid, and went to work at the age of eight. When they met she was the scullery maid to Lady Louisa Cotes, who was in London for the season. She had had a curious premonition:

> . . . at tea one day i saw a man's face clearly as could be in the fire . . . it was such a nice manly face with a moustache—i little thought i shd see

> such a face, but in 54 i *did* see it. . . . My brother had been to see me & i walked with him part of his way home—i'd my lilac frock—a blue spotted shawl & my black bonnet on, & an apron. When i had kiss'd Dick & turn'd again & was crossing for the back street on the way to Grosvenor St a gentleman spoke to me, & i answer'd him—that was Massa's face that i'd seen in the fire. . . .

Munby's account of their meeting runs as follows:

> . . . she was brought to me, a surprise of all surprises, by Him who brought Eve to Adam. . . . A tall erect creature, with light firm step and noble bearing: her face had the features and expression of a high born lady, though the complexion was rosy & rustic, & the blue eyes innocent and childlike: her bare arms and hands were large and strong, and ruddy from the shoulder to the finger tips; but they were beautifully formed . . .
>
> A robust hardworking peasant lass, with the marks of labour and servitude upon her everywhere: yet endowed with a grace and beauty, an obvious intelligence, that would have become a lady of the highest.
>
> Such a combination I had dreamt of and sought for; but I have never seen it, save in her.

His photographs of her confirm this description. Unlike the colliery girls, she was slender, but her biceps measured thirteen and a half inches in circumference.

At first neither of them seems to have thought of marriage. As Hannah was to write after they did get married:

> . . . i made my mind up that it was best & safest to be a slave to a *gentleman*, nor wife & equal to any vulgar man—still with the wish & determination to be independent by working in service and without the slightest hope o' been rais'd in rank either in place or by being married.

At first one is tempted to classify her simply as a masochist, but the more one reads both her diaries and Munby's, the more superficial and inadequate such a classification becomes. Hannah was evidently a person who took a craftsman's pride in performing her lowly tasks as efficiently as possible.

> How shamed ladies'd be to have hands & arms like mine, & how weak they'd be to do my work, & how shock'd to touch the dirty things even, what i black my whole hands with every day—yet such things must be done, & the lady's'd be the first to cry out if they was nobody to do for 'em—so the lowest work i think is honourable in itself and the poor drudge is honourable too providing her mind isn't as coarse & low as her work is, & yet loving her dirty work too.

Such an attitude may have been commoner among Victorian servants than we are apt, today, to imagine. Their pay was meager, their work arduous and often dirty, but they knew that they were performing duties which were essential to the functioning of the society in which they lived, and to know that one is needed is always a source of psychological satisfaction. They must also have observed that many of their mistresses, for all their wealth and leisure, were bored and unhappy.

While they were "walking out," a situation which lasted for nearly nineteen years, Munby and Hannah had to be very careful not to be seen together by anyone who might recognize them and would have immediately assumed that they were having an affair, which was not the case. Once, indeed, she was dismissed from a job because other servants had seen them together and reported the fact to her employer. And after their marriage, which had to be kept a secret from all except her relatives, when she came to live with Munby at Fig Tree Court, she had to play the role of a servant in front of guests and other occupants, one of whom was Asquith, and could only be a wife when she and Munby were alone. But she seems to have enjoyed this, not as a masochistic humiliation but as a game which it was fun to play as well as possible.

> "When do you have your dinner?" I thought it best to say, as she retired. "About one o'clock, Sir," my wife answered. "Then perhaps you had better do the bedroom." "Very well, Sir," said she, quite gravely: and soon she reappeared with all her housemaid's gear, and slid as quiet as a mouse behind our backs into the bedroom, and drew the curtain behind her but did not shut the door: for I knew that she was secretly enjoying the conversation, though I could hear her vigorously emptying slops and lustily making the bed. Peacock, however, took no more notice of her presence there than if she had been a dog: he continued talking, in his clever rambling way; pouring out miscellaneous learning antiquarian and philosophical, talking Spinoza and Berkeley, reading Kingsley's poems aloud, reciting ballads of his own.

When he had gotten rid of Peacock, and they were alone together, Hannah said:

> "But as for him, he'll go mad, with his talk about not trusting our senses, and the things we see not being real! How do I know it's you that kiss me, or you I've loved these twenty years? Why, God gave us our senses, & if we can't trust them, what *can* we trust?

They were married in 1873 when Munby was forty-four and Hannah was thirty-nine. Only her relatives were allowed to know. At first all went well, but in 1878 their relationship began to be difficult. For this I think Munby was largely to blame. The double life in Fig Tree Court no longer amused him. He had taken a cottage, Wheeler's Farm in Pyrford, which was associated with another girl, Sarah Carter, with whom he had had a flirtation, which cannot have been pleasant for Hannah. He also seems to have wished he were again a bachelor: on one occasion he writes of the joys of being alone. Sex, it is clear, was never very important to him. He may well have been sexually impotent, for there were no children by the marriage.

Even had he wanted Hannah to live with him in Pyrford, it would have been impossible because in a small country community this would have meant social calls on the vicar and others, which would have been embarrassing. Though, as the photographs show, Hannah could look like a lady, she could not act like one or, probably, speak like one. She was highly intelligent, Munby had taught her French and to read aloud to him from the best literature, but it seems unlikely that he could have cured her Shropshire accent. At the same time Munby was unwilling to give up his social life. Hannah evidently felt both lonely and embittered. Munby's diary for 1880 and 1881 contains no mention of her, and, though they probably corresponded, he kept none of her letters. In 1882, thank goodness, their relations improved, and in 1888 he rented her a cottage in Hadley, Shropshire, where he paid her frequent visits. In 1903, Hannah left Hadley and went to live in Shifnal where she had been born. In his diary for 1906, Munby describes the following scene.

> "I say, Massa," she exclaimed, "*what* a good job, as I arena a lady! One thing, I should hate to be stuck up, an' dress fine, an' keep that nesh an' prim, an' talk affected. . . . But now, I can sweep an' scour, an' clean your boots, an' clean grates, an' get coals in, an' all the jobs as I've always bin used to in service, an' I can talk my own plain talk, an' I can do everything for you—aye, an' I can read out to you as well as any lady could!" And she threw her arms around him & kissed him.

Hannah died in 1909 and Munby in 1910.

If he were alive today, where could he look for emotional satisfaction? In his day, domestic servants were the largest employed class in London. Now only the very rich can afford any. Moreover, the replacement of coal stoves by gas and electric, the disappearance of the chamber pot, inventions like vacuum cleaners, washing-up machines, etc., have abolished all "dirty" work. I think Mr Hudson is right when he says that the country today where Munby would feel most at home is Soviet Russia.

This book is the most fascinating private document of Victoriana to be published since Kilvert's diaries. Mr Hudson has done us a great service.

The New York Review of Books, 19 October 1972

A Kind of Poetic Justice

The New Oxford Book of English Verse 1250–1950. Chosen and edited by Helen Gardner. Oxford £3.25.

As a fellow anthologist, I cannot, of course, read this book without wondering what I should have done had I been in Dame Helen Gardner's shoes. At least I know the difficulties. The Oxford Books of Verse are intended to be official and standard works. This means that the anthologist must subordinate his, or her, personal literary taste to his duties as a literary historian.

For example, in his *Oxford Book of Modern Verse* Yeats was far too self-indulgent. He happened to dislike the poetry of Wilfred Owen, but he should not, on that account, have left him out. This error Dame Helen never makes. I suspect, though I cannot, of course, be certain, that she takes as little pleasure in Shelley's poetry as I do, but he is adequately represented. The only change in her selection that I would have made would be to substitute for "To Maria Gisbourne in England, from Italy" an extract from *The Triumph of Life*, which seems to me his best poem. Sometimes one has the good luck to find one's personal taste and one's sense of a poet's historical importance in agreement. Dame Helen, for example, obviously loves Yeats and Eliot, and her selections from them could not be bettered.

Secondly, an anthologist has to be constantly on his guard against being a slave to the taste of his age. This Sir Arthur Quiller-Couch failed to do. In 1900, the Metaphysical poets had been forgotten and most critics still agreed with Matthew Arnold's description of Dryden and Pope as "Classics of our Prose." Dame Helen has corrected that. In 1900, too, the most popular modern poet was Swinburne. Today, I suspect, hardly anyone reads him, but Dame Helen has not omitted him on that account: indeed, she prints one more poem than Quiller-Couch did. Again, also, I believe, under the influence of Matthew Arnold, comic or nonsense verse was considered unworthy company for "serious" poetry. Miss Gardner knows better and has included excellent selections from Lear and Lewis Carroll. I am surprised, therefore, by her selection from Thomas Hood. Hood's "serious" poems, which is all she prints, seem to me Keats and water, but his comic verse entitles him to the rank of a major poet.

Then every anthologist knows that, due to the exigencies of space, an anthology is weighted in favour of the writer of short lyrics and against those whose major achievements are in long poems, dramatic or narrative. It is possible, for instance, to do justice to Clare, but not to the Elizabethan dramatists or Milton or Wordsworth or Byron. Quiller-Couch included no extracts from long poems; Dame Helen has, though she does not, and I think wisely, print passages from plays.

Of her 945 pages, she devotes only twenty-four to the age between Langland and Skelton. Langland only gets eight lines, and the only Scotch poet of the period represented is Dunbar: there is nothing from Henryson, Gavin Douglas or King James I. Aside from the problem of space, I imagine she felt, probably rightly, that the average reader would not understand Middle Scots and that it is impossible to modernise the original text.

Like every lover of poetry, I have my special private pets, and I looked eagerly to see what she had done with Campion, George Herbert and William Barnes. Her Campion and Herbert selections seem to me admirable, though, in the case of the latter, I was sorry that she did not have the space to include his longest poem, "The Sacrifice," which also seems to me his greatest: in the case of Barnes, however, I feel I could have done better, but, then, one is always jealous about one's pets.

For obvious space reasons, Dame Helen has limited her list of poets writing in English to those who were or are British citizens. However, she makes an exception in the case of Ezra Pound. It is true, of course, as we all know, that he did enormous services to British poets, but so have some other Americans. I know, for instance, how much I owe to Robert Frost and Marianne Moore. T. S. Eliot is a problem. Though for many years a British citizen, was his poetic sensibility really British? I should be inclined to say no. The opening words of *The Waste Land*, "April is the cruellest month," could not possibly have been written by someone who grew up in this country.

Every poet, I suspect, resents being anthologised. In his introduction Quiller-Couch wrote:—

> Having set my heart on choosing the best, I resolved not to be dissuaded by common objections against anthologies—that they repeat one another . . . or perturbed if my judgment should so often agree with that of good critics. The best is the best, though a hundred judges have declared it so.

The kind of anthologist a poet hopes for is someone who, faced with two poems of equal merit, will print the less well-known. Alas, this rarely happens. Of the four pieces of mine which Dame Helen prints, three are old warhorses which have constantly been anthologised. For all I know or care, they may be quite good, but I never want to hear about them again. I must not forget, however, that, like all poets, I am vain.

But of all modern poets, the one who has been most shabbily treated by anthologists is Walter de la Mare, and I am sorry to see that Dame Helen has followed her predecessors in only printing some of his earlier poems. Surely, she should have included extracts from "Time's Wingèd Chariot," in my opinion his greatest poem. This would not have been difficult since, though long, it is, like *In Memoriam*, a sequence of lyrics. Still, Dame Helen has undoubtedly done an excellent job.

The Observer, 29 October 1972

Evangelist of the Life Force

Bernard Shaw: Collected Letters 1898–1910. Edited by Dan H. Laurence. Dodd, Mead. $25.

Surely, George Bernard Shaw possessed more energy, physical and mental, than any other man who ever lived. I am not surprised to learn that he suffered from migraine: How else could Nature persuade him to take a rest? *Bernard Shaw: Collected Letters 1898–1910*, superbly edited and indexed by Professor Dan H. Laurence, covers a period of twelve years. Professor Laurence says that he has cut passages which seemed to him repetitious or trivial. (He has also corrected the spellings, for Shaw, it seems, like his fellow-Irishman Yeats, was a poor speller.) Even so, they run to nearly a thousand pages. When one remembers all the other things he was doing—writing and often directing his plays, sitting on committees, writing tracts, making public speeches, and indulging in hobbies like photography and playing the pianola—it hardly seems credible.

The volume opens shortly before Shaw's marriage to Charlotte Payne-Townshend and his decision to give up being a dramatic critic. Though already well known as a critic of both music and drama, and as a stump orator, he was virtually unknown as a playwright. By the time it ends, his plays are being performed frequently in many countries, and he is sometimes referred to as "the Millionaire Socialist." Though the letters, quite rightly, are printed in chronological order, I would advise the reader to start by reading some of the extended correspondence with certain individuals rather than to try reading the volume straight through; he will find it less exhausting. I would particularly recommend the letters to Archibald Henderson, his future American biographer, to Siegfried Trebitsch, his German translator, and to William Archer, the translator of Ibsen.

In the correspondence with Archer, I was startled to discover, they both indulged in what in the Middle Ages was called "flyting"; that is to say, they showered each other with insults out of sheer high spirits.

Here is Archer on Shaw:

> . . . you have done nothing really big, nothing original, solid, first-rate, enduring. If you were to die tomorrow, what would happen? In the his-

> tory of literature, you would find a three-line mention,—like that we now give to Peacock or Beddoes—as an eccentric writer, hard to classify, whose writings a few people still remember with pleasure. . . . I don't mean to say that I despair of you as a dramatist; but I am bound to confess that *Man & Superman* rather dashes my hopes. I think, with all your extraordinary talents, you want a measure of mental discipline before you can produce a real work of art, which it is rather late to think of your attaining. I don't despair but I am not sanguine.

And here is Shaw on Archer:

> You really are a very curious character. You admit the superiority of my talent and wit. You are quite wrong. Incredible as it sometimes seems, you have just as much talent and wit as I have. You have all the tools of the trade; but you have no conscience. . . . There is an absolute gratuitousness about your perversity that is inexplicable unless one sees you as a sort of child in fairyland who has never learnt to live in the world and who resents the intrusion of moral problems as angrily as it joyfully welcomes the advent of the poetic glamor.

On the evidence of the text alone, who would imagine that they were friends?

Though they will always be important to historians, the average reader, particularly if he is under sixty, will find the letters in which Shaw expresses his political and social views the least interesting. Our world is so utterly different. I myself was interested by his views on the Boer War. Most of the Liberal Left were pro-Boer. He thought that both sides were in the wrong. Though he did not foresee Apartheid, he forecast that if the Boers won the war, which in the long run they did, it would be good for England but bad for South Africa. He tells us that in his youth he was unpolitical but was converted to Socialism by Henry George, though without ever swallowing his single-tax theory. From then on, he was, as Chesterton said, a great Republican; that is, a man who cared passionately about the Public Thing but not, like Scott and Dickens in their different ways, a Democrat:

> The Social-Democratic federation and the Socialist League aimed at being big working-class organisations. I wanted something in which I could work with a few educated & clever men of Webb's type.

Like all the Fabians, Shaw thought that the average worker was too ignorant and too lazy to know where his true political interests lay. Shaw was also a Puritan, and the Puritans are always a minority group. He was a vegetarian, I believe also a teetotaller who even disapproved of tea, and he seems to have thought the sexual act repulsive. He objected to marriage as a social institution on the ground that it gave official license to unbridled sensuality, and his own marriage was, by mutual consent, never consummated.

His quarrel with the censorship in his day was that it licensed plays like *The Notorious Mrs Ebbsmith*, which he thought immoral, but refused to license a moral tract like *Mrs Warren's Profession*. He would, I am certain, be deeply shocked by the modern toleration of Porn. But then, nearly everyone—I know that I do—believes in censorship on condition that he or she can be the censor. Some would be permissive about sex but severe about political opinions they disapproved of, and vice versa. It is in keeping with his puritanical nature that he thought certain people, like the murderer Rayner, should be exterminated—as painlessly as possible, of course, but still put to death.

His own description of his style of public speaking reveals him as an elitist:

> As I have always had to try to make my audience think new things, I have never had the successes of the orator who is the mouthpiece of his audience. But I have once or twice been the most unpopular man in a meeting and yet carried a resolution against the most popular orator there by driving in its necessity. . . . I never practised speaking as an art or an accomplishment. . . . I needed it as a weapon, as an instrument, as a means to the end of making people listen to what I had to say.

Though unorthodox, Shaw was a profoundly religious man. In his youth, he tells us:

> I simply bolted Darwin without chewing him because I was so very anxious to get rid of "the argument from design," Paley & the watch, &c&c. I did not notice that, as Butler used to say, Darwin banished mind from the universe. It was not until "neo-Darwinism" began to apply the doctrine practically—politically in dynamite, and socially in vivisection—that I began to see that to the ordinary man Darwinism meant simply the application of a pigeon fancier's ideals to all the social problems. Secularism is not a philosophy of life: it is only an attempt to leave life out of the question because no rationalistic, materialistic explanation of it has been found.

His doctrine of the life force, which owes something to Schopenhauer and Nietzsche but more, I think, to Samuel Butler, he defines as follows:

> My doctrine is that God proceeds by the method of "trial and error," just like a workman perfecting an aeroplane. He has to make hands for himself & brains for himself in order that his will may be done. He has tried lots of machines—the diphtheria bacillus, the tiger, the cockroach; and he cannot extirpate them except by making something that can shoot them or walk on them, or, cleverer still, devise vaccines & anti-toxins to prey on them. To me the sole hope of human salvation lies in teaching Man to regard himself as an experiment in the realization of God, to regard his hands as God's hand, his brain as God's brain, his purpose

> as God's purpose. He must regard God as a helpless Longing, which longed him into existence by its desperate need for an executive organ.

How far he was from being an atheist or even a freethinker may be seen from his views about the education of children:

> I am not a believer in the possibility of what is called Secular Education. You must either give children religious reasons for behaving themselves or else use the brute force of the cane. I object to the cane. And as to modern science and ethics, I know too much about them to imagine that they are any less superstitious than the creeds of the sects.

How one would like to read a tract by Shaw about behaviorism!

On one occasion, while bathing, he nearly got drowned, and in a letter to H. G. Wells he gives a fascinating description of his reactions to the prospect of immediate death:

> My reflections were of the most prosaic kind: I utterly failed to rise to the occasion dramatically. Chiefly I damned my folly for having postponed altering my now obsolete will, which I had brought down to Llanbedr for the purpose. My affairs were not in order: Charlotte would be a widow and would never make out about my translators, whose contracts are all higgledy pigg. . . . Conclusions. Whenever you get a serious call at the apparent approach of death, you may depend on it that your imagination is only at play, and that your organism hasn't the slightest intention of dying. . . . If anybody had suggested a discussion on religion or immortality or the ethical aspect of my past to me, I should have given him my last kick for obtruding such heartlessly unreal and irrelevant stuff on me under such circumstances. Nothing of the kind occurred to me for a moment. The business inconvenience of my death preoccupied me completely.

I think that most of us in such a situation would feel the same. What Shaw, however, does not seem to have realized is that the situation of a man who knows he is dying of some disease is very different. He has the time to set his affairs in order, and he may very well be grateful for spiritual advice if it is given in the right way.

The general impression Shaw's letters give is of a man who was not only very intelligent but also good and generous. There was only one trait in his character which I, at least, find unsympathetic; namely, his behavior toward women other than his wife. He seems to have fitted his own definition of a philanderer:

> A philanderer is a man who is strongly attracted by women. He flirts with them, falls half in love with them, makes them fall in love with him, but will not commit himself to any permanent relation with them, and

often retreats at the last moment if his suit is successful—loves them but loves himself more—is too cautious, too fastidious, ever to give himself away.

His letters to Erica Cotterill make painful reading. This talented but mentally unbalanced young lady fell madly in love with him and bombarded him with pash notes. He should have soon realized that for both their sakes he should avoid all communication. Instead, he sent her theatre tickets, invited her to his house, where she behaved hysterically, and wrote her long letters full of fatherly advice. The advice was sound enough, but in her condition she could only interpret it as meaning that she might make him. It was not until five years later that he did what he should have done long before: dictate a letter to be signed by his wife, forbidding her the house.

To most people, Shaw means Shaw the dramatist, so they will turn most eagerly to the letters in which he talks about the drama, acting, stage directing, and his opinions of other dramatists. He is curiously unfair to Shakespeare, whom he accuses of taking his morality ready-made. But who knows what Shakespeare's personal views on any subject were? Whereas Shaw had to invent his characters, all of whom, including the women, were variants of himself, most of the raw material for Shakespeare's plays came from others. The opinions uttered by his characters are appropriate to their characters and situation. "As flies to wanton boys are we to the gods: they kill us for their sport" is, as Shaw says, a frightful blasphemy, but in the context it is dramatically right, and who on earth ever imagined that Shakespeare is speaking personally?

Shaw was evidently a superb stage director. Professor Laurence describes his methods thus:

> His system was based largely on musical principles. . . . Invariably Shaw would begin by reading the play in its entirety to the assembled cast, thus indicating his basic intent as to rhythms, pacing, intonation, and accent. He would annotate the actors' scripts musically: Robert Loraine's *Don Juan in Hell* script, his widow recalled, "twinkled with crotchets, crescendoes, and minims; with G clefs, F clefs, and pianissimos." Actors embarking on long speeches were given a specific pitch on which to begin, and were instructed at specific points to modulate to another pitch. As Shaw told a performer on a later occasion, "Begin at a low pitch and drag the time a little; then take the whole speech as a crescendo—p to ff.". . .
>
> He violated most of the directorial rules, "feeding" readings of lines to performers, or handing them series of final instructions on changes in blocking and interpretation just hours or minutes before an opening performance. Yet his actors loved him, for he was patient, considerate, tactful, open to suggestion, respectful of disagreement, and tolerant of innovation.

Shaw was often accused of having no interest in passion, of being interested only in logic. This is a half-truth. We have all observed that when a man is acting logically it never occurs to him to justify his actions, either to himself or to others. When, however, in the grip of some passion or other, a man is behaving irrationally, he has to invent "reasons" to persuade himself and others that his behavior is really rational. It was such rationalizations rather than the passions themselves which fascinated Shaw's imagination.

The impression we get today from Shaw's plays cannot be the same as that of his first audiences. The trouble about a theatre of ideas as a theory is that ideas lose their dramatic impact as soon as they cease to be novel. His plays continue to live not because of his ideas but because of his fascinating characters and the wonderful eloquence of their speech. Only two of his characters, I think, must be judged as failures: Marchbanks and Dubedat. It is impossible to portray a poet or a painter on the stage, because the dramatist cannot produce the poems and the paintings which would convince the audience that they are what they claim to be. All we get is the artistic temperament, and that, as Chesterton said, is a disease which afflicts amateurs, and was certainly not a complaint from which Shaw himself ever suffered. I can only repeat something I wrote fifteen years ago. Now that we have got used to them, what impresses us most about Shaw's plays is their musical quality. He has told us himself that it was from *Don Giovanni* that he learned how to write seriously without being dull. For all his claims to be just a propagandist, his writing has an effect nearer to music than the work of most of those who have claimed to be writing "dramas of feeling." His plays are a joy to watch, not because they purport to deal with social and political problems but because they are such wonderful examples of conspicuous waste; the conversational energy displayed by his characters is so far in excess of what their situation requires that, if it were to be devoted to practical action, it would wreck the world in five minutes. The Mozart of English Letters he is not, for the music of the Marble Statue is beyond him; the Rossini, yes. He has all the brio, humor, cruel clarity, and virtuosity of that master of *opera buffa*.

The New Yorker, 25 November 1972

Happy Birthday, Dorothy Day

A Harsh and Dreadful Love: Dorothy Day and the Catholic Worker Movement.
By William D. Miller. Liveright. $8.95.

I assume that all readers of *The New York Review of Books* know something about the activities of the Catholic Worker movement, even if they have never read its newspaper or visited one of its hostels or communal farms. So, since the philosophical outlook that inspired it was Peter Maurin's Christian "Personalism," most of what I have to say will be "personal" in a lay sense. Let me begin by saying that I am eternally grateful to Dorothy Day for conveying to me the nicest poetical compliment I have ever received. She had been in jail in the old Women's Prison at Eighth Street and Sixth Avenue for protesting against air-raid warnings. There the prisoners got a shower once a week. It so happened that a poem of mine had recently appeared in *The New Yorker*, of which the last line ran: "Thousands have lived without love, not one without water." One of Dorothy Day's co-inmates was a whore who went off to her weekly shower quoting it. "My God," I thought, "I haven't written in vain."

Those who joined the movement deliberately chose, like St Francis and his followers, a life of poverty. The problem about such a choice is that, while it is possible to choose poverty rather than riches, to live on nothing at all is, in any modern society, impossible. A communal farm—the Catholic Workers had several—may become self-supporting, but the land has first of all to be bought. As for their hostels, which looked after the poor, deserving and undeserving, these, obviously, could only be run at a financial loss. This meant, especially since it refused to accept ads for its paper, that the Catholic Worker movement was dependent for its survival upon the voluntary donations of others, most of whom were probably better off.

Somehow or other these contributions always managed to arrive, often, it must have seemed, miraculously, in time to stave off catastrophe. I once made a contribution myself. My conscious motive in doing so was my admiration for what the movement was doing to help the down-and-out, but unconsciously, I fear, I was trying to allay my conscience for not doing likewise. I don't think God has ever called me to a life of voluntary poverty, but if He did, I know I should resist violently. I am far too worldly, far too fond of my creature comforts. Moreover, I cherish my privacy. Hard as I should find the monastic life, I should find it a great deal easier than working in a Catholic Worker's hostel where, it seems, one is never alone for a second.

Dorothy Day and her colleagues were often accused of being "soft" on communism, even of being communist agents, and she certainly had no hesitation in working with communists if she felt they had a just cause. She recognized clearly enough the difference between the communist sense of community and her own:

> Communism has said, with the evidence of history to back it, that historical Christianity has been only a pawn in centuries of international rivalry and warfare. It, to the contrary, offers men the idea of the universal state and universal peace. But from the Worker's Christian point of view, this universality is an illusion, since it can never be anything more than a point running in the track of time. Communism's promised com-

> munity represents a deification of historical time, an attitude against which the Christian must rebel, since real love has no fulfillment except in the completion of time.

But she did not realize, I feel, the profound difference between Marxism as a *Weltanschauung*, and as a form of state government. She thought the former, and I agree, with its passion for social justice and its utopian daydream of the state withering away, closer to the Christian view of the world than capitalism with its greeds and ruthless competitiveness. (It is a long time, incidentally, since capitalism had any coherent philosophy of its own.) But capitalism with all its defects is in practice preferable to a one-party system, whether of right or left, which must inevitably become a tyranny. The Catholic Worker movement would never have been tolerated in Russia.

On political issues Dorothy Day has always shown enormous courage and, usually, common sense. At the time of the Spanish Civil War, when the Catholic press was almost unanimous in support of Franco as the leader of a holy crusade against atheistic communism, *The Catholic Worker* was the only paper to support the Loyalists. Though it probably foresaw that, if the latter won, the Church would be persecuted, it thought that a Christian must always choose to be persecuted rather than to persecute. During the Thirties, *The Catholic Worker* took an equally firm stand against racism and the anti-Semitism of Father Coughlin and the Brooklyn *Tablet*; and, after the war, against the anticommunist hysteria of the McCarthy era and, later, against the American involvement in Vietnam.

There is only one point on which I take issue with Dorothy Day—some of her colleagues, it seems, felt the same—namely, her assertion that all sides were equally to blame for the outbreak of World War II. She wrote:

> We believe that Hitler is no more personally responsible than is Chamberlain or Daladier or any other leader. The blame rests upon the peoples of the entire world, for their materialism, their greed, their idolatrous nationalism, for their refusal to believe in a just peace, for their ruthless subjection of a noble country. Capitalism's betrayal came more quickly in Germany because of the Versailles Treaty, and Nazism flowered as a logical result.
>
> . . . Hitler is incidental; the war must have come sooner or later under the circumstances.

This, I'm sorry to say, I think nonsense. To begin with, it seems to imply that history is wholly determined by blind anonymous forces and that individuals play no part. Those of us who knew Germany well and followed the events there closely felt certain that, from the moment Hitler came to power, which he might very easily not have done, a second world war was only a matter of time. Ironically enough, if England and France had reacted when he reoccupied the Rhineland, Hitler would almost certainly have been ousted by a military *Putsch.* They did not react because, by that time, public opinion in both countries felt that the Allied occupation had been unjust.

We all know that war is a horrible thing and that, whoever is to blame for starting it, atrocities will be committed on both sides; but the blame for World War II, surely, lies with Germany and Japan (Russia, because of the Nazi-Soviet Pact, cannot be altogether exonerated), not with England, France, or America.

Dorothy Day's pacifism, as distinct from her historical analysis, is another matter. It is always legitimate for a person to say: "My conscience forbids me to kill another human being under any circumstances." I should have thought it possible for such a person to enlist in the army, provided he could be in a medical corps, devoted to saving lives not taking them, but, perhaps, he could not feel certain that such a job would be assigned to him. In that case, he must declare himself a conscientious objector whatever the consequences. Fortunately, both in England and America, COs were assigned to jobs in work camps; in Germany or Russia, if there were any, they were liquidated.

In the case of Vietnam, I find my personal conscience and my impersonal historical analysis in complete agreement. Luckily for me, I am too old to have to make a decision, but I wholeheartedly sympathize with those draftees who, instead of registering as COs, publicly burn their draft cards or abscond to Canada.

Rather oddly, and to the dismay of some of her coworkers, when Castro seized power in Cuba, Dorothy Day abandoned her hitherto uncompromising pacifist postion. She did not deny that Castro had made much use of firing squads, but she excused him on the grounds that his revolution had been for the poor, and if one had to choose between the violence done the poor by the acquisitive bourgeois spirit of many Americans and the violence of Castro, which was aimed at helping the poor, then she would take the latter.

> We do believe that it is better to revolt, to fight, as Castro did with his handful of men . . . than do nothing.

What I had not realized until I read Mr Miller's book was how rapidly success came to the movement. First published in 1933, by 1935 *The Catholic Worker* reached a circulation of 65,000 copies, and very soon Worker hostels were started in many American cities besides New York.

As the Franciscans had discovered in the Middle Ages, any "leftish" Christian way of life attracts not only potential saints but also cranks of all kinds, and Mr Miller gives some amusing accounts of the sort of thing the movement had to put up with.

> It was an unusual group at the farm that summer—a circumstance that for the Catholic Worker was completely usual. There was a man just out of Sing Sing who planted flowers, a seminarian who brought six pigs . . . and an ex-circus performer who would do cartwheels down the hill in back of the house when the moon was full.

At another farm:

> A cabal developed against Dorothy Day, the leader of which was the head of one family that lived on the upper farm. . . . Emphasizing "the priesthood of the laity," he gathered about him a group of which his family was the center. This man designated one of the group its "spiritual adviser," and then proceeded to bedeck his person with symbols of authority, insisting on the performance of solemn obeisances from the others—bowing, kneeling, and the like—and when they ran afoul of his edicts, penances were imposed. . . . The women were forbidden to speak unless spoken to, and were compelled to knock on the doors of even their own kitchens if men were present.

Then, in the Sixties, came the middle-class hippies with their promiscuity and drugs. They were too much even for Dorothy Day's tolerance, and she turned them out, observing that their behavior was

> . . . a complete rebellion against authority, natural and supernatural, even against the body and its needs, its natural functions of child bearing. It can only be a hatred of sex that leads them to talk as they do and be so explicit about the sex functions and the sex organs, as instruments of pleasure. . . . This is not reverence for life, this certainly is not natural love for family, for husband and wife, for child. It is a great denial, and is more resembling Nihilism than the revolution which they think they are furthering.

In diagnosing, correctly in my opinion, their attitude to life as a form of Manichaeism, she reminds us that, today as in the Middle Ages, all groups that try to live a Christian life without compromise attract heretics, persons, that is to say, who, disgusted by the worldliness of the Church Visible, attribute this to Her theology, and the kind of theology they adopt in its stead is nearly always Manichaean.

To this temptation Dorothy Day never succumbed. She was always aware that, because we live in time, the existence of the Church as a temporal and social organization is essential; that, without Her, she would never have heard of the Gospels, in the light of which she could criticize Her failings.

> Where else shall we go, except to the Bride of Christ, one flesh with Christ? Though she is a harlot at times, she is our Mother. . . . Love is

indeed a harsh and dreadful thing to ask of us, of each one of us, but it is the only answer.

This year the Catholic Worker movement will be sixty-nine years old and Dorothy Day herself has just turned seventy-five. I need not wish her a happy birthday because I am certain it will be.

The New York Review of Books, 14 December 1972

Marianne Moore 1887–1972

With the death of Miss Marianne Moore we have lost both a major poet and a great lady—I speak in terms of character, not class. In the case of most writers, I am content to enjoy their works. It is not often that I find myself also wishing I could have known them personally. Among them are George Herbert and William Barnes, whom, of course I could not meet, but I count it among one of the greatest privileges in my life that I can say I was personally acquainted with Miss Moore.

Next to her unique tone of voice, utterly unlike any one else's, what immediately strikes me both about the poet and the person is her perfect manners, never too loud or fussy or off-key. Like most people she was repelled by the cobra, but she knew that this was not the cobra's fault.

Distaste which takes no credit to itself is best. Like all well-mannered people she loved order and precision.

> . . . . And as
> Meridian-7 one-two
> one-two gives, each fifteenth second
> in the same voice, the new
> data—"The time will be" so and so—
> you realize that "when you
> hear the signal," you'll be
>
> hearing Jupiter or jour pater, the day god—
> the salvaged son of Father Time—
> telling the cannibal Chronos
> (eater of his proxime
> newborn progeny) that punctuality
> is not a crime.*

Different as they are in every other respect, her poems have one characteristic in common with Dryden's: both are always firmly rooted in staid

*From "Four Quartz Crystal Clocks," *Collected Poems*, The Macmillan Co., New York, 1951.

common sense. Here are a few statements by Miss Moore herself which all poets would do well to ponder.

> Humility, indeed, is armor, for it realizes that it is impossible to be original, in the sense of doing something that has never been thought of before. Originality is in any case a by-product of sincerity; that is to say, of feeling that is honest and accordingly rejects anything that might cloud the impression, such as unnecessary commas, modifying clauses, or delayed predicates.
>
> One writes because one has a burning desire to objectify what it is indispensable to one's happiness to express.
>
> Do the poet and scientist not work analogously? Both are willing to waste effort. To be hard on oneself is one of the main strengths of each. Each is attentive to clues, each must narrow the choice, must strive for precision.
>
> Must a man be good to write good poems? The villains are not illiterate, are they? But rectitude has a ring that is implicative, I would say. And with no integrity, a man is not likely to write the kind of book I read.*

I could wish that this occasion could have been devoted to a reading of her poems instead of a prose piece by someone else, but, as she would be the first to agree, conventions must be obeyed. Just how she developed her extraordinary syllabic stanzas—when, in 1935, I first read them, I couldn't hear them—must, of course, remain a mystery. In an interview with Mr Donald Hall, she said that prose writers, like Dr Johnson, Burke and Sir Thomas Browne, had had more influence on her style than other poets. In the same interview, when asked "How does a poem start for you?", she replied:

> A felicitous phrase springs to mind—a word or two, say—simultaneously usually with some thought or object of equal attraction: "Its leaps would be set to the flageolet"; "Katydid-wing subdivided by sun, till the nettings are legion." I like light rhymes, inconspicuous and un-pompous conspicuous rhymes . . . I have a passion for rhythm and accent, so blundered into versifying. Considering the stanza the unit, I came to hazard hyphens at the end of the line, but found that readers are distracted from the content by hyphens, so I try not to use them.†

As all readers of her poems know, many of them are about animals, usually exotic ones. Her approach is that of a naturalist, but really their theme is almost always the Good Life. Sometimes, as in the bestiaries, she sees an animal as an emblem—the devil-fish, so frightening to look at because of

* *Predilections*, Viking Press, New York, 1955.
† *A Marianne Moore Reader*, Viking Press, New York, 1961.

the care she takes of her eggs, becomes an emblem of charity, the camel-sparrow an emblem of justice, the jerboa-rat an emblem of true freedom as contrasted with the false freedom of the conqueror—and sometimes, as in the beast fable, the behavior of animals is presented as a moral paradigm. Occasionally, as in *Elephants*, the moral is direct, but, as a rule, the reader has to perceive it for himself.

Here is Miss Moore on that animal Man.

. . . Among animals, *one* has a sense of humor.
  Humor saves a few steps, it saves years. Unignorant,
    modest and unemotional, and all emotion,
  he has everlasting vigor,
    power to grow,
      though there are few creatures who can make one
      breathe faster and make one erecter.

Not afraid of anything is he,
    and then goes cowering forth, tread paced to meet an obstacle
at every step. Consistent with the
  formula—warm blood, no gills, two pairs of hands and a few hairs—that
  is a mammal; there he sits in his own habitat,
        serge-clad, strong-shod. The prey of heat, he, always
          curtailed, extinguished, thwarted by the dusk, work partly done,
        says to the alternating blaze:
          "Again the sun!
            anew each day; and new and new and new,
            that comes into and steadies my soul"*

As a final thank-you to Miss Marianne Moore for all she has given us, I can only quote the last stanza of a poem I wrote for her eightieth birthday.

For poems, dolphin-graceful as carts from Sweden,
our thank-you should be a right
good salvo of barks: it's much too muffled to say,
"how well and with what unfreckled integrity
it has all been done."

Proceedings of the American Academy of Arts and Letters and the National Institute of Arts and Letters, 1973

* *Collected Poems*, The Macmillan Co., New York, 1951.

Preface to *Selected Songs of Thomas Campion*

Thomas Campion is the only man in English cultural history who was both a poet and a composer. (Rather oddly, there seems to be no record of where or how he received a professional musical education.) Tom Moore was also a musician, but he wrote his songs for traditional Irish tunes, even if he may sometimes have modified them. Campion's songs can, of course, be enjoyed as spoken verse without their music, but they would not be what they are or sound as they do if he had not, when he wrote them, been thinking in musical terms. Again, if one forgets that he was a composer, one is tempted to write off his *Observations in the Art of English Poesie* as just one more wrong-headed attempt of a humanist to "classicize" English poetry. It is true that, in theory, he condemns rhyme as barbarous, but, in practice, aside from the examples he gives in the book—which are, by the way, much better than earlier generations thought them—he wrote only one unrhymed poem, the Sapphics of *A Book of Ayres, XXI.* Even in so classical an experiment as *Canto Secundo,* the asclepiadians are rhymed. Again in his *Masques,* one would have expected the speeches to be in blank verse, the one unrhymed form which has always been found acceptable in English poetry—but in fact, he always rhymed them. If he took more pride in his Latin poems than his English, which he called "superfluous blossoms of my deeper studies," nobody who knows anything about poets will take this too seriously. All he probably meant was, firstly, that he found writing Latin verses more difficult and, secondly, that he knew very few of his contemporary poets who could write them at all.

The real significance of Campion's *Observations* is that a poet writing in English need not think about vowel length,only about stress. A composer, no matter what language he is setting, must think about both.

Though we have no proof, I feel reasonably certain that the prosodic principles of Greek and Latin poetry, in which one long syllable is regarded as equivalent to two short syllables, and a syllable, short in itself, becomes long when followed by more than one consonant, were derived from music. When I was a boy and, in Campion's time, too, I imagine, the rhythms of Latin verse were not understood by the English, for we simply stressed the long syllables which, in fact, meant treating all syllables as of equal length. For example, we recited the first half line of the *Aeneid* thus:

Árma virúmque canó

Musically, this is in waltz time, and the first two feet are not, quantitatively, dactyls as they should be, but tribrachs.

The quantitatively correct musical setting is in march time.

Because of the secondary beat in a musical bar, this means that quantitative dactyls, if scanned by stress, become bacchics. In fact, the musical rhythms of an accentual prosody are the reverse of a quantitative one. In English, as Campion realized, it is iambic or trochaic verse that is in march time. Then, though he does not, I believe, discuss it, he must have known, as a composer, that when sung at slow tempi, words can change their metrical value. Thus, when spoken, the line

O sacred head sore wounded

is iambic or trochaic: but, when sung to Bach's chorale, it becomes spondaic.

In my opinion, Campion is the greatest master in English poetry of what the French symbolists called *la poésie pure.* If I have to admit that he is, nevertheless, a minor poet, this is because I believe that "major" poetry is, necessarily, "impure." What he has to offer us is a succession of verbal paradises in which almost the only element taken from the world of everyday reality is the English language. Since words, unlike musical notes, are denotative, his songs have to be "about" some topic like love or religion, but the topic is not itself important. As C. S. Lewis has written:

> His poetry is as nearly passionless as great poetry can be. There are passions somewhere in the background, but a passion, like a metre, is to Campion only a starting point: not for moral or intellectual activity but for the creation of a new experience which could occur only in poetry. By the time he has finished, the original, the merely actual, passion hardly survives as such: it has all been used. This happens as much in his religious as in his erotic pieces.

For this reason, I cannot imagine a translation of his poems into another tongue which would have any value or meaning whatsoever. Change the sound of a syllable or the rhythm of a line, and all is lost. To explain what I mean, let me try to analyze four stanzas.

1. In Myr/tle Ar/bours on / the downes	(8)	a
The Fai/rie Queen / Proser/pina,	(8)	x
This night / by moone/-shine lead/ing merr/ie rounds	(10)	a
Holds a watch / with sweet love,	(6)	b
Down the dale, /up the hill;	(6)	c
No plaints / or groans / may move	(6)	b
Their holy / vigill.	(5)	c

Lines 1, 2, 3, and 6 are straightforward iambics, but variety is provided by the varying number of feet, 4, 4, 5 and 3, and the much lighter final stress of *Proserpina* compared with *dowries, rounds,* and *move.* Also, this line is a refrain which occurs in every stanza and does not rhyme. Lines 4 and 5 are linked by metre—each consists of two cretics—but not by rhyme. Though, in isolation from the other stanzas, one would be inclined to scan line 7 as

Their ho/ly vig/ill

after looking at the other stanzas, I think Campion means us to read it as an adonic.

2. Fountain / of health, / my soules / deepe wounds / recure (10) a
Sweet showres / of pit/ty raine, / wash my / unclean/nesse pure (12) a
One drop / of thy desir/ed grace (8) b
The faint / and fad/ing heart / can raise, / and in / ioyes
be / some place (14) b
Sinne and Death, / Hell and temp/ting Fiends / may rage; (10) c
But God / his own / will guard / and their / sharp paines /
and griefe / in time / asswage (16) c

Lines 4 and 6 are in regular iambics but of different lengths. In line 1, Campion inverts the first foot, and in line 2 the fourth. Line 3 *can* be read as four iambs but, since in the first stanza the corresponding line runs

Lord light me to thy blessed way

I think that Campion probably means us to scan it as a spondee, a choriamb and an iamb. In line 5 something occurs which is very rare in spoken verse, but not infrequent in musical setting: the first two feet are molossoi:

3. All my desire, / all my delight / should be,
Her to enioy, / her to unite / to mee:
Envy should cease, / her would I love / alone:
Who loves / by lookes, / is sel/dome true / to one.

Heroic couplets are one of the commonest verse forms in English, but Campion gives them a completely new movement in the first three lines by inverting the first and the third foot, so that they scan as two choriambs followed by an iamb.

4. The lov/ers teares/ are sweet, / their mov/er makes / them so; (12)
Proud of / a wound / the blee/ding Sould/iers grew (10)

Poore I / alone, / dreaming, / endure (8)
Griefe that / knowes nor / cause, nor / cure. (7)

Here Campion inverts the first foot in line 2. In line 3, he makes the first foot a spondee and inverts the third. In line 4, by lopping off a syllable, he shifts the rhythm from iambic to trochaic. To appreciate his virtuosity, one has only to rewrite the stanza in regular iambics.

The lovers teares are sweet, their mover makes them so,
And proud of wounds the bleeding Souldiers grew.
But I, alone, in dreams endure
A Griefe, that knowes nor cause, nor cure.

If asked to name one's favorite poets, it would be meaningless to answer Dante or Shakespeare or Goethe, about whose greatness we are all agreed. One can only name one or two minor poets for whom one feels a particular personal affection, so that, while every competent critic would agree that they are good, one probably rereads them more often and with more delight than most people do. In my own case, the two names I would cite are William Barnes and Thomas Campion.

Selected Songs of Thomas Campion, selected and prefaced by W. H. Auden, introduction by John Hollander (1973)

Introduction to *George Herbert: Selected by W. H. Auden*

Reading a poet whose work I admire, it is only very seldom that I find myself wishing: "Oh, how I would like to have been an intimate friend of his!" There are some, like Byron, whom I would like to have met once, but most, I feel, would either, like Dante and Goethe, have been too intimidating, or, like Wordsworth, too disagreeable. The two English poets, neither of them, perhaps, major poets, whom I would most like to have known well are William Barnes and George Herbert.

Even if Isaak Walton had never written his life, I think that any reader of his poetry will conclude that George Herbert must have been an exceptionally good man, and exceptionally nice as well.

He was born in Montgomery Castle on 3 April 1593, the fifth son of Sir Richard Herbert and Lady Magdalen Herbert, to whom Donne dedicated his elegy "Autumnal Beauty", and his uncle was Lord Herbert of Cherbury. By birth, that is to say, he enjoyed a secure social position. In addition Nature had endowed him with the gifts of intelligence and personal charm.

Educated at Westminster School and Trinity College, Cambridge, he became a Fellow of the latter in 1616, and was appointed Public Orator to the University in 1620. He was not only an excellent Greek and Latin scholar, but also fluent in Italian, Spanish and French, and an accomplished amateur musician who played the lute and composed songs.

For a young man of his breeding and talents one would have prophesied a great future in the world. He soon attracted the attention of two powerful and influential figures, the Duke of Richmond and the Marquess of Hamilton and, when they met, King James I took great fancy to him.

His own ambition was as great as his opportunities. He seems to have dreamed of one day becoming a Secretary of State and this led him somewhat to neglect his duties as Public Orator in order to attend the Court. The Academic Life, evidently, was not altogether to his taste. Walton tells us:

> . . . he had often designed to leave the university, and decline all study, which he thought did impair his health; for he had a body apt to a consumption, and to fevers, and other infirmities, which he judged were increased by his studies. . . . But his mother would by no means allow him to leave the university or to travel; and though he inclined very much to both, yet he would by no means satisfy his own desires at so dear a rate as to prove an undutiful son to so affectionate a mother.

This is confirmed in the poem "Affliction".

> Whereas my birth and spirit rather took
> The way that takes the town;
> Thou didst betray me to a lingring book,
> And wrap me in a gown.
> I was entangled in the world of strife,
> Before I had the power to change my life.
>
> Yet, for I threatned oft the siege to raise,
> Not simpring all mine age,
> Thou often didst with Academick praise
> Melt and dissolve my rage.
> I took thy sweetned pill, till I came where
> I could not go away, nor persevere.

Though he writes in another poem, "The Pearl":

> I know the wayes of Pleasure, the sweet strains,
> The hillings and the relishes of it;
> The propositions of hot bloud and brains;

one does not get the impression from his work that the temptations of the flesh were a serious spiritual menace to him, as they were to Donne. Nor did he suffer from religious doubts: in the seventeenth century very few people did. His struggle was with worldliness, the desire to move in high circles, to enjoy fame and power, and to such temptations he might very well have succumbed, had not his two aristocratic patrons and then, in 1625, King James, all died, thus dashing his hopes of immediate preferment.

For the first time he began to consider seriously the possibility of taking Holy Orders, a course which his mother had always prayed for. Most of his friends disagreed, thinking the priesthood too mean an employment, too much below his birth and natural abilities. To one such counsellor, he replied:

> It hath been formerly adjudged that the domestic servants of the King of heaven should be of the noblest families on earth; and though the iniquity of the late times have made clergymen meanly valued, and the sacred name of priest contemptible, yet I will labour to make it honorable by consecrating all my learning, and all my poor abilities, to advance the glory of that God that gave them.

These words show that Herbert was under no illusion as to the sacrifice he would have to make, and to come to a definite decision was clearly a struggle, for he was not ordained a priest until 1630 when he was made Rector of Bemerton, a tiny rural parish on Salisbury Plain. In the previous year he had married Jane Danvers after a courtship of only three days, and the marriage turned out to be a very happy one. In 1633 he died of consumption at the age of only forty.

Since none of his poems were published during his lifetime, we cannot say for certain when any of them were written, but one suspects that it was from the two and a half years of indecision that many of them, particularly those which deal with temptations and feelings of rebellion, must date.

Since all of Herbert's poems are concerned with the religious life, they cannot be judged by aesthetic standards alone. His poetry is the counterpart of Jeremy Taylor's prose: together they are the finest expressions we have of Anglican piety at its best. Donne, though an Anglican, is, both in his poems and his sermons, much too much of a *prima donna* to be typical.

Comparing the Anglican Church with the Roman Catholic Church on the one hand and the Calvinist on the other, Herbert writes:

A fine aspect in fit aray,
Neither too mean, nor yet too gay,
    Shows who is best.
Outlandish looks may not compare:
For all they either painted are,
    Or else undrest.

She on the hills, which wantonly
Allureth all in hope to be

By her preferr'd,
Hath kiss'd so long her painted shrines,
That ev'n her face by kissing shines,
For her reward.

She in the valley is so shie
Of dressing, that her hair doth lie
About her eares:
While she avoids her neighbours pride,
She wholly goes on th' other side,
And nothing wears.

Herbert, it will be noticed, says nothing about differences in theological dogma. The Anglican Church has always avoided strict dogmatic definitions. The Thirty-Nine Articles, for example, can be interpreted either in a Calvinist or a non-Calvinist sense, and her Office of Holy Communion can be accepted both by Zwinglians who regard it as a service of Commemoration only, and by those who believe in the Real Presence. Herbert is concerned with liturgical manners and styles of piety. In his day, Catholic piety was typically baroque, both in architecture and in poets like Crashaw. This was too unrestrained for his taste. On the other hand, he found the style of worship practised by the Reformed Churches too severe, too "inward". He would have agreed with Launcelot Andrewes who said: "If we worship God with our hearts only and not also with our hats, something is lacking." The Reformers, for instance, disapproved of all religious images, but Herbert thought that, on occasions, a stained-glass window could be of more spiritual help than a sermon.

Doctrine and life, colours and light, in one
When they combine and mingle, bring
A strong regard and aw; but speech alone
Doth vanish like a flaring thing,
And in the eare, not conscience ring.

Walton tells us that he took enormous pains to explain to his parishioners, most of whom were probably illiterate, the significance of every ritual act in the liturgy, and to instruct them in the meaning of the Church Calendar. He was not a mystic like Vaughan: few Anglicans have been. One might almost say that Anglican piety at its best, as represented by Herbert, is the piety of a gentleman, which means, of course, that at its second best it becomes merely genteel.

As a Christian, he realized that his own style of poetry had its spiritual dangers:

. . . Is there in truth no beautie?
Is all good structure in a winding stair?

But as a poet he knew that he must be true to his sensibility, that all he could do was to wash his sweet phrases and lovely metaphors with his tears and bring them

to church well drest and clad:
My God must have my best, even all I had.

He is capable of writing lines of a Dante-esque directness. For example:

Man stole the fruit, but I must climb the tree,
The Tree of Life to all but only Me.

But as a rule he is more ingenious, though never, I think, obscure.

Each thing is fully of dutie:
Waters united are our navigation;
Distinguished, our habitation;
Below, our drink; above, our meat;
Both are our cleanlinesse. Hath one such beautie?
Then how are all things neat?

He is capable of clever antitheses which remind one of Pope, as when, speaking of a woman's love of pearls for which some diver has risked his life, he says:

Who with excessive pride
Her own destruction and his danger wears.

And in a most remarkable sonnet, "Prayer", he seems to foreshadow Mallarmé.

Church-bels beyond the starres heard, the souls bloud,
The land of spices; something understood.

Wit he had in abundance. Take, for example, "The Church-Porch". Its subject matter is a series of moral maxims about social behaviour. One expects to be utterly bored but, thanks to Herbert's wit, one is entertained. Thus, he takes the commonplace maxim, "Don't monopolize the conversation", and turns it into:

If thou be Master-gunner, spend not all
That thou canst speak, at once; but husband it,
And give men turns of speech: do not forestall
By lavishnesse thine own, and others wit,
As if thou mad'st thy will. A civil guest
Will no more talk all, then eat all the feast.

A good example of his technical skill is the poem "Denial". He was, as we know, a skilled musician, and I am sure he got the idea for the structure of this poem from his musical experience of discords and resolving them. The first five stanzas consist of a quatrain, rhymed *abab*, followed by a line which comes as a shock because it does not rhyme:

O that thou shouldst give dust a tongue
To crie to thee,
And then not heare it crying! all day long
My heart was in my knee,
But no hearing.

But in the final stanza the discord is resolved with a rhyme.

O cheer and tune my heartlesse breast,
Deferre no time;
That so thy favours granting my request,
They and my minde may chime,
And mend my ryme.

This poem and many others also show Herbert's gift for securing musical effects by varying the length of the lines in a stanza. Of all the so-called "metaphysical" poets he has the subtlest ear. As George Macdonald said of him:

> The music of a poem is its meaning in sound as distinguished from word . . . The sound of a verse is the harbinger of the truth contained in it . . . Herein Herbert excels. It will be found impossible to separate the music of his words from the music of the thought which takes shape in their sound.

And this was Coleridge's estimate:

> George Herbert is a true poet, but a poet *sui generis*, the merits of whose poems will never be felt without a sympathy with the mind and character of the man.

My own sympathy is unbounded.

George Herbert: Selected by W. H. Auden (1973)

Introduction to *A Choice of Dryden's Verse*

In a volume of this size it is clearly impossible to give an adequate representation of the whole range of Dryden's literary activities. I began, therefore, by deciding to ignore his plays. In my opinion, despite some fine rhetorical speeches, they are rather boring. The conventions and style of French Classical Tragedy on which they are modelled do not, I believe, suit either the

English language or the English sensibility. What translations of Racine or Corneille have really been successful? The Restoration dramas which have survived are comedies in prose like those of Congreve and Wycherley. Then, for all the time he spent writing plays, I do not think Dryden was by nature a playwright, because he cannot create imaginary characters in whom one can believe. His imagination was only genuinely aroused by historical reality, friends and enemies whom he knew personally, events of which he had first-hand knowledge. Then I have excluded his "translations" in the strict sense. As for his translation of the *Aeneid,* I agree with C. S. Lewis that it is too "classical", that Gavin Douglas' translation is nearer to what Virgil must have sounded like to his contemporaries. Pope's *Iliad* is also too "classical" to be homeric, but it is a much finer English poem. The *Fables* are another matter, for in them Dryden makes no claim to be translating Chaucer or Ovid or Boccaccio. He writes his own poem as an "imitation after the manner of". Lastly, with the greatest regret, I felt that there was no room to include any of his prose criticism, though this is of the highest historical and aesthetic importance.

Dryden's lifetime (1631–1700) coincided with the most violent and revolutionary changes in political, religious and social life which England has so far experienced. When he was born, Charles I claimed to rule by Divine Right: then came the Civil War, Charles' execution, the Protectorate, The Restoration and, finally, the "Glorious Revolution" of 1688. In such a period it must always be a temptation for the average citizen, and particularly for one of Dryden's temperament, to support whichever side seems to be winning and to desert it when it seems to be a lost cause, and, in his youth, Dryden does seem to have been a bit of a time-server. His readiness to write a panegyric on Cromwell and two years later a panegyric on Charles II is a little disturbing. I am quite convinced, however, that his conversion to Roman Catholicism was not, as Macaulay believed, a worldly act, but perfectly genuine. He must have known that, even if James II succeeded in abolishing the political and educational disabilities imposed on Roman Catholics, there was not the remotest chance of the Anglican Church, still less of the Dissenters, rejoining the Catholic Fold.

Any persecution of Protestants, as under Queen Mary, was out of the question. From a worldly point of view, he would have had nothing to fear either from the State or from his public, had he remained an Anglican. In fact, as we know, James was overthrown and Dryden lost his Poet Laureateship.

In discussing Dryden as a poet, I am painfully aware that anything I say can only be a feeble echo of Professor Mark Van Doren's magnificent study. When I was an undergraduate, most of my elders, I think, still agreed with Matthew Arnold's dictum: "Dryden and Pope are classics of our Prose." Such a view is, I hope, outmoded, but, in approaching the work of any poet, it is essential that a reader should not expect from him a kind of poetry which he cannot write and, usually, does not want to. Dryden, for example, has no imaginative insight into violent personal emotions, such as sexual love. Though he takes an interest in cosmological theories like that of Lucretius, he shows no concern for non-human nature in the Wordsworthian sense. Nor can one imagine him having any kind of mystical experience like Traherne or Blake. His attempts at what the Metaphysical poets called Wit are seldom successful, as is evidenced by many stanzas in *Annus Mirabilis,* e.g.:

> On high-rais'd decks the haughty Belgians ride,
> Beneath whose shade our humble frigates go:
> Such port the elephant bears, and so defied
> By the rhinoceros, her unequal foe.

The Stuffed Owl printed Stanza V of *Threnodia Augustalis* as an example of bad, because unintentionally comic, verse.

> . . . Like helpless friends who view from shore
> The labouring ship, and hear the tempest roar;
> So stood they with their arms across
> Not to assist, but to deplore
> Th' inevitable loss.

Here I disagree: I think Dryden meant to be funny. Lastly, he lacks what I would call Fantasy. He could not, for example, have written these lines by Pope:

> Here living Teapots stand, one arm held out,
> One bent; the Handle this, and that the Spout:
> A Pipkin there like *Homer's Tripod* walks;
> Here sighs a Jar and there a Goose-pye talks.
> Men prove with Child, as powr'ful Fancy works,
> And Maids turn'd Bottles, call aloud for Corks.

On the other hand Dryden is pre-eminent in English Literature as the poet of Common Sense. His lines have no undertones, as Pope's often have: they mean exactly what, on first reading, they seem to say. He is the ideal poet to read when one is weary, as I often am, of Poetry with a capital P, the mannerisms and obscurities of the symbolists, the surrealists and their ilk.

His literary Godfather was, of course, Ben Jonson, but his real ancestor, in my opinion, is Dunbar. Both of them thought of themselves as professional "makars" of verbal objects, whose imagination was excited by actual occasions, almost any occasion and Dryden is, without any doubt, the greatest Occasional Poet in English.

He does not "rise" to the occasion: he elevates it. Whether he is eulogising or satirising, events and persons that in real life may have been unimportant are transfigured by his verse into events and persons that really matter to the reader. Dryden is also the master of argument in verse. The extracts in this volume from *Religio Laici* and *The Hind and the Panther* will, I hope, give some idea of his powers of ratiocination, but they are inadequate: both poems should be read *in toto.* When one compares them with Pope's exercise in argument, *The Essay on Man,* Dryden's superiority is immediately apparent. One reason for this is that his subject matter is more interesting than Pope's but the main reason is, I believe, that, while both employ the end-stopped couplet, Pope tends to think in terms of single couplets, while Dryden thinks in terms of paragraphs.

In Dryden's day there was competition between two kinds of rhymed decasyllabics, the end-stopped couplet developed by Waller and Cowley, and the enjambed couplet, an extreme example of which are the Satires of Donne.

> Graius stays still at home here, and because
> Some preachers, vile ambitious bawds and laws,
> Still new, like fashions, bid him think that she
> Which dwells with us, is only perfect, he
> Embraceth her, whom his godfathers will
> Tender to him, being tender; as wards will
> Take such wives as their guardians will offer, or
> Pay values. Careless Phrygius doth abhor
> All, because all cannot be good: as one,
> Knowing some women whores, dares marry none.

Though Dryden sometimes uses enjambement, he does so very sparingly, and the example he set made the end-stopped couplet the standard verse medium for non-lyrical poems of any length for over a century. When one compares his couplet with Pope's, one notices that he is much freer in his distribution of accents. Pope believed that a pause should always be made after either the fourth or the fifth or the sixth syllable, so that his lines almost always break into two halves, complementary or antithetical. Dryden, influenced perhaps by blank verse, knows no such limitations. His pauses may come anywhere and often they do not come at all. E.g.:

> Drawn to the dregs of a democracy

> Of the true old enthusiastic breed.

> To the next headlong steep of anarchy

> But baffled by an arbitrary crowd

Like all poets, both of them make use of alliteration for reasons of sound and sense, but Dryden's use of it is much more conspicuous than Pope's.

> In friendship false, implacable in hate,
> Resolved to ruin or to rule the state;

> And pricks up his predestinating ears

> This general worship is to praise and pray,
> One part to borrow blessings, one to pay;

Pope disapproved of using an alexandrine to make a triplet. Dryden employs it, but with discretion and always to good effect.

> Firm *Dorique* Pillars found your solid Base:
> The Fair *Corinthian* Crowns the higher Space;
> Thus all below is Strength, and all above is Grace.

> What Help from Arts Endeavours can we have!
> *Guibbons* but guesses, nor is sure to save:
> But *Maurus* sweeps whole Parishes, and Peoples ev'ry Grave.

If Dryden's songs are not as prosodically interesting or as varied in theme as those of the Elizabethans, like Campion and the anonymous madrigal poets, this is not altogether his fault. What composers, except Purcell, were there in his time to write for? Aside from the Odes for music, most of his songs are Light Verse, but all of them are settable, sometimes perhaps, too easily so.

Had I been compiling this selection simply for my own amusement, I might well have printed all his Prologues and Epilogues and nothing else. In them, as in few poems, one hears the speaking voice, neither too soft nor too loud, of a civilised man, defending the cause of civilisation both in social manners and in the Arts. I suspect that those who deny that Dryden is a poet believe that all poems should "sing". I don't agree.

Let George Saintsbury have the last word.

> One feels, however much one may worship the earlier Caroline fancy and the later Romantic imagination—however conscious one may be that Dryden is not Blake or Coleridge, Shelley or Keats, Tennyson or even Browning—a sort of indignation at having to apologise in any way for him. We may with him, prosodically as well as poetically, as a whole be on Earth and not in Heaven. But (as Browning has been mentioned) his Earth is so good that it seems a little impertinent, and more than a little ungracious, to inquire, while we are on it, whether Heaven is not best.

A Choice of Dryden's Verse, selected with an introduction by W. H. Auden (1973)

Foreword to *Goldsworthy Lowes Dickinson*, by E. M. Forster

I first read this book when it came out in 1934. Rereading it now, it seems to me even better than I remembered. I have only one criticism. If I had been Forster, I would not have quoted so extensively from Goldie's verses. In my opinion, poetry was an art for which he had little talent. This may, I realize, be a matter of personal taste rather than critical judgement. Goldie was devoted to the poetry of Shelley, which I have always found unreadable. On the other hand, he shared my admiration for Goethe, though, according to Forster, "he was soon confronted with the immense boringness of Goethe, and few Englishmen have faced it so frankly, and so successfully outstared it". I myself only find Goethe boring when, as in *Dichtung und Wahrheit*, he talks about his romantic attachments to a series of young ladies; on any other topic I find him endlessly fascinating.

That this biography should be the great book it is, seems to me a miracle. To begin with, it is not easy to write justly and objectively about a personal friend, a situation which, Goldie wrote, when asked to review a book by Forster, "leads us Cambridge people to under-estimate virtues and gifts for fear of being too partial". Then nothing is more difficult than writing an interesting book about a really nice person. The biographer of a monster, like Wagner, has a far easier task. Bad behaviour always has a dramatic appeal. Forster imagines Mephistopheles asking him why a memoir of Goldsworthy Lowes Dickinson needs to be written, and when he answers, "My friend was beloved, affectionate, unselfish, intelligent, witty, charming, inspiring," the devil says, "Yes, but that is neither here nor there, or rather it was there but it is no longer here." Forster can only reply:

> These qualities in Goldie were fused into such an unusual creature that no one whom one has met with in the flesh or in history the least resembles it, and no words exist in which to define it. He was an indescribably rare being, he was rare without being enigmatic, he was rare in the only direction which seems to be infinite: the direction of the Chorus Mysticus. He did not merely increase our experience: he left us more alert for what has not yet been experienced and more hopeful about other men because he had lived. And a biography of him, if it succeeded, would resemble him; it would achieve the unattainable, express the inexpressible, turn the passing into the everlasting. Have I done that? *Das Unbeschreibliche hier ist's getan*? No. And perhaps it only could be done through music. But that is what has lured me on.

There were other difficulties too. Though Goldie travelled to America, India, China, a civilization with which he fell in love, he had no dramatic adventures there.

> It is difficult to think of a life where so little happened outwardly. He was never shipwrecked or in peril, he was seldom in great bodily pain, never starved or penniless, he never confronted an angry mob nor went to prison for his opinions, nor sat on the bench as a magistrate, nor held any important administrative post, he was never married, never faced with the problems of parenthood, had no trouble with housekeeping or servants.

Normally, the chief source of material for a biographer is his subject's letters. Forster quotes from a number of Goldie's, and I find them most interesting, but he warns us that they are of small value compared with his conversation.

> When he spoke to his friends or spoke of them . . . he vibrated to wave after wave, and as he turned his head from guest to guest at one of his lunch parties one felt that a new universe was seated on every chair. That was his strength, that was his glory, and if that could be communicated in a biography he would appear for what he was: one of the rarest creatures of our generation. His letters are a misleading substitute; they tend to exhibit him as merely sympathetic and kind.

In 1905, Forster tells us, Goldie's literary reputation was so high that it was believed that he "would easily beat Pater and Gobineau, and even creep up towards Voltaire and Mr Bernard Shaw". If he is little read today, this is not due simply to changes in fashion. He never claimed to be writing for posterity: nearly all of his books are concerned with the immediate issues of his time, political, religious, educational or what-have-you. Then his style when lecturing or talking to small groups seems to have been superior to his written prose. One of his younger friends wrote:

> You know I always find a "but" about Goldie's writing. He would be so inclined to clarity in conversation (with me anyway) but so beautifully unclear with his pen. I get mesmerized when I read anything he writes (except *John Chinaman*) and then have to read it all over again.

On which Forster comments:

> There frequently is this hypnotic effect, although the argument is taut and the language apposite. Something is wrong—or perhaps too right—with the style.

It is only when he is describing Goldie's eccentricities that one feels Forster has an easy job.

> He was not practical, and I can still hear him damning his sleeve-links in the morning because they wouldn't go in, or his hot-water bottle at night because it puffed in his face when he filled it. He swore constantly, and no wonder. For he was unhandy with "so called inanimate objects". They were always splashing or scalding him, or beating a merry retreat at the moment he needed them most, "Here you are, yes of course," he would say, lifting a sheet of paper, and there beneath it, after the locksmith had been sent for, would be the bunch of keys. . . .
>
> He is said to be the only man who could make a Corona type upside down. He struck the keys rapidly and violently, thinking of what he thought and not of what he did, with the result that he doubled

> lines, halved them, threw capitals in the air, buried numerals in the earth, broke out into orgies of ?????? or %%%%%%, and hammered his ribbon to shreds. George becomes "Geroge", Gerald "Gerlad", perhaps "perhpas", and there are even happier transformations such as husband into "humsband", and soul into "soup". A semicolon in the middle of a word means "l".

Forster first met Goldie at a lunch in 1898. Lunch was not a success, and Forster left it "unprepossessing and unprepossessed". A few weeks later, however, on Forster's returning a play he had borrowed and confessing that he hadn't liked it, the smile on Goldie's face came as a revelation of what charm could mean.

> Charm, in most men and nearly all women, is a decoration. It genuinely belongs to them, as a good complexion may, but it lies on the surface and can vanish. Charm in Dickinson was structural. It penetrated and upheld everything he did.

He seems, also, to have had the even rarer gift of creating charm in others. In a letter he wrote "Lennie —— (?) gets nicer and nicer", and Forster comments:

> Lennie's surname is indecipherable, but that he got nicer and nicer there is little doubt: most of the people who constantly saw Goldie did that, though he did not realize why.

And I have never heard of a finer tribute to anyone than Forster's reaction when he learned of Goldie's death:

> He never staged himself as an invalid. He was chiefly occupied in saving us trouble and in sparing our feelings. Oddly enough he succeeded. A character of his strength manages to sustain those who cling to it, and I have "minded" more the deaths of people I have loved much less.

It must always be harder to draw a convincing portrait of a real person than of a fictional character, since, in the first case, the author is free to make the facts and situations what he pleases. I can only say that I find Forster's Goldie as living and convincing as any of the characters in his novels. Then, of course, one is frequently delighted by passages the authorship of which one would immediately guess, if one didn't know it already. For example, this passage about Goldie's unhappiness at his preparatory school:

> But these amenities lay at the edge of his life. Its centre was covered with rubbish and worry. And at its opposite edge lay an imbecile boy whom he sometimes kicked in order to ingratiate himself with his schoolfellows. He made no special confession to his parents about this; it was not a crime like the potatoes, nevertheless it haunted him.

One matter puzzles me a little. In view of Goldie's passionate interest in the League of Nations, I should have expected to find references to Count Kessler, the German who proposed that the League be made up, not of representatives of sovereign states, but of various interest groups, the professions, the churches, the trades unions, etc., on the ground that the League as constituted would be powerless to act in any case of serious conflict between the major powers. This idea, I should have thought, would have appealed to Goldie, but there is no mention of Kessler in Forster's book, nor of Goldie in Kessler's diaries, and it seems to be the case that they never met.

Goldworthy Lowes Dickenson and Related Writings,
by E. M. Forster (1973)

How Can I Tell What I Think Till I See What I Say?

There is only one trait that is common to all poets without exception, a passionate love for their native tongue. This means that the phrase *Poets are born, not made* must be false, for babies are born speechless. What psychological conditions encourage such a love is anybody's guess. Perhaps, such phrases as "my mother tongue" and "the milk of the word" are significant.

★ ★ ★

I may be generalising too much from my own experience, but I suspect that, for children who may later decide to become poets, the kind of verse that will appeal to them most will be comic or nonsense verse, not "serious" poetry. In my own case, my early favourites were Hoffman's *Shock-Headed Peter,* Belloc's *Cautionary Tales,* Harry Graham's *Ruthless Rhymes for Heartless Homes* and, of course, Edward Lear and Lewis Carroll.

In comic verse the role of language is so much more obvious. It seems as if it is the language, its rhymes and metrics which has the power to create the event, not, as in serious poetry, the event in the poet's mind which looks for its fit linguistic expression. For example:

In the drinking well
Which the plumber built her,
Aunt Maria fell:
We must buy a filter.

★ ★ ★

When he first begins to write verses, the surest sign that poet-to-be has real talent is that he is more interested in playing with words than in saying anything original. Originality, if he ever achieves it, will come later.

★ ★ ★

There have been times and places, in the Wales of the Middle Ages, for example, when would-be poets received a professional education like lawyers and doctors. Today they have to educate themselves, and the results are not always satisfactory. If I had to take a class in "writing poetry", I would entirely ignore all questions of critical judgement and taste, and devote the time to questions of fact, that is, to prosodic analysis, rhetoric and philology, the history of the language. Every poet (and every critic of poetry, too) should know the difference between a bacchic and a choriamb, and be able instantaneously to spot the use of epanorthosis or chiasmus. Alas, all too few of them do or can.

★ ★ ★

Whatever else it may be, the making of a work of art is a form of play, that is to say, not something which the maker must do, like eating or sleeping, but something which he finds it fun to make. That is why formal poetry is the norm. Everyone knows that one cannot play a game without rules. One can make the rules what one likes, but one's whole fun and freedom comes from obeying them. There have been poets, Whitman and D. H. Lawrence, for example, who convince one that they had to write in free verse, but they are the exceptions. To succeed in writing free verse, a poet must have an infallible sense for line endings. All too often one feels that the line endings are purely arbitrary and that the whole thing should have been written out as a prose poem.

★ ★ ★

In most cases though not, perhaps, in all, the initial impulse to write a serious poem comes, I believe, from the sense of awe and wonder aroused in the poet's imagination by beings or events that he finds sacred or numinous. This response is involuntary: it cannot be willed. Some of these beings have seemed sacred to all imaginations at all times, for example the Moon, the four elements, and those beings which can only be defined in terms of non-being, darkness, silence, nothing, death. Others, like kings, are only felt to be numinous in certain cultures.

It is rare for a poem, even a love poem, to be based on a single such encounter. In the poet's memory there are usually a number of such experiences, apparently unrelated to each other, that is to say, a crowd. This crowd the poet attempts to transform into a community by embodying it in a verbal society where, if he is successful, the feelings all become members of the same community, loving each other and it. A poem may fail in two ways. It may exclude too much and so be banal, or it may attempt to embody more than one community at the same time, and so be chaotic.

★ ★ ★

Speaking for myself, at any given time my mind is preoccupied with two interests, one thematic, the other formal or linguistic, matters of metre, diction, etc. The theme searches for the form which can most adequately embody it; the formal concern looks for those aspects of a theme with which it can deal most adequately. When the two finally come to an agreement, I am able to write a poem.

★ ★ ★

Not only in youth but at all stages in their writing careers, most poets are conscious of a model, some predecessor who can help them to find their own true path. In finding such models other people can seldom help. Occasionally, an older person, because he has read more, may be able to make a fruitful suggestion to a young poet, but only on condition that he knows the latter, his sensibility and interests, very well.

★ ★ ★

In choosing one's models, it is possible to make mistakes. My first models, Thomas Hardy, Edward Thomas and Robert Frost, were, I think, wholly beneficial, but I have come to the conclusion that Yeats and Rilke, both, of course, great poets, were, for me, bad influences, the former by tempting me into an over-inflated rhetoric, the latter by making some of my poems too *schöngeistig*, too much Poetry with a capital P. Needless to say, the fault was entirely mine, not theirs.

★ ★ ★

In writing poetry, men and women, it seems to me, have quite different problems. A woman finds it hard to detach herself sufficiently from her experience, to make her poems conform to Wordsworth's definition "emotion recollected in tranquility". A man, on the other hand, can all too easily become an aesthete, that is to say, make statements, not because he believes them to be true, but because he thinks they sound poetically effective.

★ ★ ★

The difference between a major and a minor poet is not one of poetic quality. Indeed, a major poet is likely, in the course of his career, to write more bad poems than a minor one. The difference between them is this. In the case of a minor poet, if one takes two poems of his, both equally good but written at different times, it is impossible, on the evidence of the text alone, to say which was written first. In the case of a major poet, on the other hand, one can always trace his development in time; he writes differently in youth, in middle age and when old.

★ ★ ★

Poets themselves have little interest in why or how they started to write poetry. Their primary concern is with what they should write next. In an age, like ours, of rapid social and technological change, this has its dangers. To ask "What sort of poetry should I write at the age of sixty-five" is a sensible question, but to ask "What should I write in the year 1972?" is sheer folly. It can only result in a submission to the fashion of the moment, a desperate attempt to be "with it". Plato tried to model political life on artistic fabrication: this, as we know, can only lead to political tyranny. The error made by all too many artists today is the exact opposite: they try to model artistic fabrication on political action so that, instead of trying to make an artistic object of permanent value, they surrender to the tyranny of the immediate moment and produce meaningless "happenings". Political and artistic history are quite different. The only alternative to a political act is another one. In the case of a work of art there are two alternatives, another work of art or no work of art.

★ ★ ★

Achilles could only kill Hector once, and in Troy, but the Iliad can always be re-read and translated into other tongues.

★ ★ ★

Again, while the history of science exhibits progress, the history of art does not. No work of art can supersede another. In time every successful new work of art takes its permanent place in the tradition.

★ ★ ★

Poems are primarily personal utterances, addressed to other persons. What a poem means is the outcome of a dialogue between the words on the page and the person who happens to be reading it, that is to say, its meaning varies from person to person. Personal utterance, however, is not to be confused with self-expression. The experience a poet attempts to embody in a poem is that of a reality common to us all. It is only his in that it is perceived from a perspective which nobody but himself can occupy. From the poet's point of view, the ideal reaction of a reader to something he has written is: "My God, I really knew that all the time, but I never realised it before."

★ ★ ★

Whatever useful functions it may perform, nothing could be less like a work of art than a dream.

★ ★ ★

Since he is a human being, every poet is, of course, an individual as well as a person. He is born into a particular society at a particular moment in historical time, and, however unique the perspective from which he views it, the world he sees and most of the ideas by which he interprets it are necessarily those of his society and his age. Here again he must practise critical detachment lest he allow conventional responses to falsify his vision. But he must accept his society and his age as facts with which he has to deal. This does not mean that he must swim with contemporary fashion: he can and should reject much that others accept. But he must know clearly what he is rejecting and why. If he tries to think of himself as a disembodied angel, free from all limitations, all relations to his contemporary neighbours, what he makes will be false.

★ ★ ★

Because its maker is an individual, every genuine work of art exhibits the quality of *nowness*, which enables an art historian to give an approximate date and place for its making. Because he is a person, it also exhibits the quality of *permanence*: it continues to be relevant long after its maker and society of which he was a member have passed away.

★ ★ ★

The arts cannot change the course of history. The political and social history of Europe would have been what it has been if Dante, Shakespeare, Goethe, Titian, Michelangelo, Mozart, Beethoven, etc., had never existed.

★ ★ ★

"The sole aim of writing", said Dr Johnson, "is to enable readers a little better to enjoy life or a little better to endure it." To this I would only add that works of art are our chief means of breaking bread with the dead, and without communication with the dead a fully human life, I believe, is not possible.

★ ★ ★

Let me finish, as I began, with language. Whatever his duties as a citizen, a poet, *qua* poet, has only one political duty. Everything he writes must be a model example of the correct and subtle use of his mother tongue, which is always in danger of being corrupted by journalism and the mass media. I call this political because, when words lose their meaning, physical force takes over.

New Movements in the Study and Teaching of English,
edited by Nicholas Bagnall (1973)

The Gift of Wonder

All lovers of poetry, I imagine, would rather quote from poems they admire than talk about them. Once read or listened to, their merits should be immediately apparent. One feels this all the more strongly in the case of a poet whom, like Chesterton, one suspects to be out of fashion and little read. Aside from a few stock anthology pieces, like "The Donkey" and "Lepanto", how many of his poems are known to the contemporary reading public?

Not very many, I fear. Editorial footnoting, as distinct from aesthetic judgment can, however, sometimes be essential. *The Divine Comedy*, for example, is full of references to the names of persons and places with which the contemporary reader, even if he is Italian, is unacquainted, and he needs to be informed of the facts. When Chesterton is obscure, this is usually because the stimulus to his poem came from some public event with which he assumed his readers were familiar, but which has now been forgotten. "A Song of Swords" is prefaced by a newspaper cutting: "A drove of cattle came into a village called Swords, and was stopped by the rioters." But, since I know nothing about this incident in Irish history, I cannot make head or tail of the poem. With the help of a footnote, perhaps I could. I know a little more about the history of World War One, but the meaning of "The Battle of the Stories" (1915) eludes me and I would welcome editorial assistance. In only one of his poems, "The Lamp Post", do I feel that my lack of comprehension is Chesterton's fault. It seems to be based upon some private mythology of his own, which neither I nor any other reader can be expected to decipher.

Consciously or unconsciously, every poet takes one or more of his predecessors as models. Usually, his instinct leads him to make the right choice among these, but not always. In Chesterton's case, for example, I think that Swinburne was a disastrous influence. That he should ever have allowed himself to be influenced by Swinburne seems to me very odd, when one thinks how utterly different their respective views about Life, Religion and Art were, but he was and always to his harm. It is due to Swinburne that, all too often in his verses, alliteration becomes an obsessive tic. In Anglo-Saxon and Icelandic poetry where the metrical structure is based upon alliteration, its essential function is obvious. In modern verse, based upon regular feet and rhyme, alliteration can be used for onomatopoeic effects, but only sparingly: in excess it becomes maddeningly irritating. The other vice Chesterton acquired from Swinburne was prolixity. Too often one feels that a poem would have been better if it had been half the length. "Lepanto", it seems to me, exhibits both faults.

He sees as in a mirror on the monstrous twilight sea
The crescent of his cruel ships whose name is mystery;
They fling great shadows foe-wards, making Cross and Castle dark,
They veil the plumèd lions on the galleys of St Mark;
And above the ships are palaces of brown, black-bearded chiefs,
And below the ships are prisons, where with multitudinous griefs,
Christian captives, sick and sunless, all a labouring race repines
Like a race in sunken cities, like a nation in the mines.
They are lost like slaves that swat, and in the skies of morning hung
The stairways of the tallest gods when tyranny was young.
They are countless, voiceless, hopeless as those fallen or fleeing on
Before the high Kings' horses in the granite of Babylon.

In the case of his longest and, perhaps, greatest "serious" poem, *The Ballad of the White Horse*, I do not, however, I am happy to say, find the length excessive. When, for example, Elf the Minstrel, Earl Ogier and Guthrum express in turns their conceptions of the Human Condition, what they sing could not be further condensed without loss. Here Guthrum.

"It is good to sit where the good tales go,
    To sit as our fathers sat;
But the hour shall come after his youth,
When a man shall know not tales but truth,
    And his heart shall fail thereat.

"When he shall read what is written
    So plain in clouds and clods,
When he shall hunger without hope
    Even for evil gods.

"For this is a heavy matter,
    And the truth is cold to tell;
Do we not know, have we not heard,
The soul is like a lost bird,
    The body a broken shell.

"And a man hopes, being ignorant,
    Till in white woods apart
He finds at last the lost bird dead;
And a man may still lift up his head
    But never more his heart.

"There comes no noise but weeping
    Out of the ancient sky,
And a tear is in the tiniest flower
    Because the gods must die.

"The little brooks are very sweet,
    Like a girl's ribbons curled,
But the great sea is bitter
    That washes all the world.

"Strong are the Roman roses,
    Or the free flowers of the heath,
But every flower, like a flower of the sea,
    Smelleth with the salt of death.

"And the heart of the locked battle
    Is the happiest place for men;
When shrieking souls as shafts go by

And many have died and all may die;
Though this word be a mystery,
  Death is most distant then.

"Death blazes bright above the cup,
  And clear above the crown;
But in that dream of battle
  We seem to tread it down.

"Wherefore I am a great king,
  And waste the world in vain,
Because man hath not other power,
Save that in dealing death for dower,
He may forget it for an hour
  To remember it again."

Guthrum's pessimistic conclusions about the nature of the internal and invisible life are based, it should be noticed, upon his observations of objects in the external and visible world, clouds and clods, flowers, a dead bird, etc. Chesterton, however different his conclusions, does the same. Both in his prose and in his verse, he sees, as few writers have, the world about him as full of sacramental signs or symbols.

Wherein God's ponderous mercy hangs
On all my sins and me,
Because He does not take away
The terror from the tree
And stones still shine along the road
That are and cannot be.

Men grow too old for love, my love,
Men grow too old for wine,
But I shall not grow too old to see
Unearthly daylight shine,
Changing my chamber's dust to snow,
Till I doubt if it be mine.

I would not call him a mystic like Blake, who could say: "Some see the sun as a golden disk the size of a guinea, but I see a heavenly host singing Holy, Holy, Holy." Chesterton never disregards the actual visible appearance of things. Then, unlike Wordsworth, his imagination is stirred to wonder, not only by natural objects, but by human artifacts as well.

Men grow too old to woo, my love,
Men grow too old to wed:
But I shall not grow too old to see
Hung crazily overhead

Incredible rafters when I wake
And find I am not dead.

Probably most young children possess this imaginative gift, but most of us lose it when we grow up as a consequence, Chesterton would say, of the Fall:

They haven't got no noses,
The fallen sons of Eve;
Even the smell of roses
Is not what they supposes;
But more than mind discloses
And more than men believe . . .

The brilliant smell of water,
The brave smell of a stone,
The smell of dew and thunder,
The old bones buried under,
Are things in which they blunder
And err, if left alone . . .

And Quoodle here discloses
All things that Quoodle can,
They haven't got no noses,
They haven't got no noses,
And goodness only knowses
The Noselessness of Man.

In verses such as these, there is little, if any, trace of Swinburnian influence. Behind them one detects the whole tradition of English Comic Verse, of Samuel Butler, Prior, Praed, Edward Lear, Lewis Carroll and, above all, W. S. Gilbert.

It was from such writers, I believe, that Chesterton, both in his verse and his prose, learned the art of making terse aphoristic statements which, once read or heard, remain unforgettably in one's mind. For example:

Bad men who had no right to their right reason,
Good men who had good reason to be wrong . . .

God is more good to the gods that mocked Him
Than men are good to the gods they made . . .

And that is the Blue Devil that once was the Blue Bird;
For the Devil is a gentleman, and doesn't keep his word.

But Higgins is a Heathen,
  And to lecture rooms is forced,
Where his aunts, who are not married,
  Demand to be divorced . . .

For mother is dancing up forty-eight floors,
For love of the Leeds International Stores,
And the flame of that faith might perhaps have grown cold,
With the care of a baby of seven weeks old.

I cannot think of a single comic poem by Chesterton that is not a triumphant success. It is tempting to quote several, but I must restrain myself. Instead, I recommend any reader unacquainted with them to open *The Collected Poems* (Methuen) and sample "The Shakespeare Memorial" (p. 156), "Ballade d'une Grande Dame" (p. 190) and "A Ballade of Suicide" (p. 193). His parodies of other poets are equally good, especially those of Browning and Kipling.

I shall, however, now quote from a volume called *Greybeards at Play* originally published in 1900, reprinted in 1930, not included in the *Collected Poems* and now, I believe, out of print. Until it was sent me by John Sullivan, Chesterton's bibliographer, I had never heard of its existence. I have no hesitation in saying that it contains some of the best pure nonsense verse in English, and the author's illustrations are equally good.

The million forests of the Earth
Come trooping in to tea.
The great Niagara waterfall
Is never shy with me . . .

Into my ear the blushing
Whale Stammers his love. I know
Why the Rhinoceros is sad,
—Ah, child! 'twas long ago . . .

Come fog! Exultant mystery—
Where, in strange darkness rolled,
The end of my own nose becomes
A lovely legend old.

Come snow, and hail, and thunderbolts
Sleet, fire, and general fuss;
Come to my arms, come all at once—
Oh photograph me thus! . . .

The Shopmen, when their souls were still,
Declined to open shops—
And Cooks recorded frames of mind
In sad and subtle chops . . .

The stars were weary of routine:
The trees in the plantation
Were growing every fruit at once,
In search of a sensation.

The moon went for a moonlight stroll,
And tried to be a bard,
And gazed enraptured at itself;
I left it trying hard.

Surely, it is high time such enchanting pieces should be made readily available.

By natural gift, Chesterton was, I think, essentially a comic poet. Very few of his "serious" poems are as good as these. (His one translation from Du Bellay makes one wish he had done many more.) But here is a poem of his which any poet would be proud to have written.

THE SWORD OF SURPRISE

Sunder me from my bones, O sword of God,
Till they stand stark and strange as do the trees;
That I whose heart goes up with the soaring woods
May marvel as much at these.

Sunder me from my blood that in the dark
I hear that red ancestral river run,
Like branching buried floods that find the sea
But never see the sun.

Give me miraculous eyes to see my eyes,
Those rolling mirrors made alive in me,
Terrible crystal more incredible
Than all the things they see.

Sunder me from my soul, that I may see
The sins like streaming wounds, the life's brave beat:
Till I shall save myself as I would save
A stranger in the street.

G. K. Chesterton: A Centenary Appraisal,
edited by John Sullivan (1974)

Renderings

English Biblical Translation. By A. C. Partridge Deutsch. £3.75.

Professor Partridge is that happy exception, a scholar who does not write for his fellow-scholars only but for the general public, yet at the same time without the least hint of condescension.

Very few readers of the Bible today know any Hebrew or Aramaic or Latin or Greek so that, if they are to judge an English translation, they must be informed by those who do of the linguistic problems involved. This is precisely what Professor Partridge supplies. To take a minor and in itself not directly biblical example, how many people know that the traditional identification of the fruit of the Tree of the Knowledge of Good and Evil with the apple is due to the fact that the Latin word for apple *malum* has a homonym which means evil?

Any translation of the Bible involves peculiar problems of its own. We can and should read the Bible, as we read Homer or Shakespeare, for its aesthetic beauty and historical information, but this, at least in the case of Jews and Christians, is not our primary concern. To us, the Bible is Holy Writ, the Word of God, from which we derive our dogmas or absolute metaphysical presuppositions, our social and religious imperatives, our concepts of the purpose of the Cosmos and the meaning of human existence.

The first task of a translator of classical literature is to find English words which are equivalent in tone and impact to those which the original words must have had on the author's contemporaries. For example, I think C. S. Lewis is right when he criticises Dryden in his translation of the *Aeneid*, when he is describing Dido's neck, for translating *refulgens* as *refulgent*. This, he complains, is far too "classical", and Gavin Douglas's version "as fresh as is the rose in May" is nearer to what the word would have conveyed to Virgil's hearers, though the phrase is not literal.

But a translator of the Bible cannot assume that he is introducing readers to a text of which they hitherto knew nothing. He has to reckon with Tradition, with centuries of interpretation, expounded from pulpits to the learned and unlearned alike. He may, on certain points, take issue with Tradition, but he has to reckon with it. As C. S. Lewis, discussing Tyndale's substitution of *congregation* for the traditional translation of *ecclesia* as *church*, wrote:

> The business of a translator is to write down what he thinks the original meant. And Tyndale sincerely believed that the mighty theocracy with its cardinals, abbeys, pardons, inquisition, and treasury of grace which the word *Church* would undoubtedly have suggested to his readers, was in its very essence not only distinct from, but antagonistic to, the thing St Paul had in mind whenever he used the word "ecclesia" . . . Thomas More, on the other hand, believed with equal sincerity that, the "Church" of his own day was in essence the very same mystical body which St Paul addressed; from his premise it followed of course that *Church* was the only correct translation. Both renderings are equally tendentious in the sense that each presupposes a belief. In that sense all translations of scripture are tendentious.

Professor Partridge's book, however, is primarily concerned with language, not doctrine. He investigates the various English versions from Wycliffe down to the Jerusalem Bible and the New English Bible, and gives copious illustrations of the linguistic and syntactical differences between them. Though he is scrupulously fair, I get the impression that he feels as I do, namely that, useful as later versions can be in clarifying obscurities, the King James Bible still remains the most satisfactory version. To begin with, its translators still possessed a feeling for ritual and ceremonious language which today has been almost entirely lost. In the second place, the English language had become in all essential respects what it is today so that the Authorised Version is no more difficult to follow than Shakespeare. Needless to say in both cases archaic usages occur, but any good etymological dictionary, like Chambers, will explain them. Take for example, the translation of *agape* as *charity* in

> Though I speak with the tongues of men and of angels, and have not charity, I am become as sounding brass or a tinkling cymbal.

No modern reader will imagine for five seconds that St Paul is using the word in its contemporary sense. To substitute for it, as most modern versions do, the word *love* seems to me mistaken for two reasons. Firstly, the word fails to make the important distinction between *agape* and *eros*: secondly, if *charity* has lost its original force, at least it has not become, as in recent times the word *love* has, utterly debased. And again, why, in addressing God, substitute *You* for *Thou*? Except among Quakers, we no longer employ the second person singular in addressing intimates: this means that we can use *Thou* as a mark of particular respect. It also prevents that yodelling noise, common in modern liturgies, *You who.*

Finally, I would say that, quite aside from its superior literary qualities, the very archaisms of the King James Bible are a religious asset. The first Christians had no linguistic problems because they expected the Parousia to occur in their lifetime: with us it is different. We are conscious of nearly two thousand years of Christian tradition behind us which it is our duty to transmit to future generations. Though only 350 years old, at least the King James Bible reminds us that Christianity did not begin with us, that tradition is, as Chesterton said,

> the democracy of the dead. Tradition refuses to surrender to the small arrogant oligarchy of those who merely happen to be walking around.

I have come to the conclusion that the ritual parts of the Book of Common Prayer should be conducted, not in English but in Latin. The rite, as distinct from the Ministry of the Word, that is to say, Lessons, Gospels, Epistles, Sermons, is the link between the dead and the unborn. As such, it requires a timeless language which, in practice, means a dead language—something which the Greek and Russian Orthodox Church, orthodox Judaism and until recently, the Roman Catholics have always realised.

This is not to deny, of course, that advances in Biblical scholarship are immensely valuable. I know how much I owe personally to the scholarly introductions to the books in the, as yet incomplete, Anchor Bible. Thanks to them, I can return with increased understanding to the version of the Scriptures I was brought up on.

New Statesman, 2 February 1973

An Odd Ball

Peter Yakovlevich Chaadayev. *Philosophical Letters and Apology of a Madman*. Translated and edited by Mary-Barbara Zeldin. University of Tennessee Press. $7.50.

I first heard of Chaadayev last summer from the Russian poet, Josif Brodsky. On consulting other experts in Russian literature, I found that they all agreed with him that Chaadayev was an important figure in Russian Cultural history. I tried in England to procure an English translation, but in vain. Then, thanks to one of Brodsky's translators, Professor George Kline, I learnt of this one. Though it has been out for four years, I imagine that, like myself, few readers have ever heard of the author.

In her admirable introduction, Professor Zeldin tells us that many facts about Chaadayev's life are obscure. Of Lithuanian descent, he was born, perhaps in 1792, perhaps in 1796, and died in 1856. He studied at Moscow University, then joined the Semenovsky Guards, with whom he fought at Borodino and was later a member of Alexander I's honor guard when he entered Paris in 1814. On returning to Russia, he soon became a close friend of Pushkin's, who in one poem addresses him. thus:

Come, to our country let us tend
The noble promptings of the spirit.
Comrade, believe: joy's star will leap
Upon our sight, a radiant token;
Russia will rouse from her long sleep;
And where autocracy lies, broken,
Our names shall yet lie graven deep.
(trans. Babette Deutsch)

In 1821, for reasons which remain obscure, he resigned his commission, and in 1823 he left Russia for Western Europe, where he spent the next three years and got to know Schelling and Herzen. On his return, he found his situation, both politically and financially difficult. The eight *Philosophical Letters*, originally written in French and addressed to a lady whose name is not given, were completed by 1831. Circulated in manuscript, they had aroused interest and approval among many, but, when part of the first letter was published in Russian in *The Telescope*, there was a scandal. For this Professor Zeldin suggests two reasons.

> In manuscript the Letter was considered private and the reader could exclude himself from the target of its devastating criticism; moreover, agreement with the unprinted Letter's opinions constituted no danger, whereas to express "public" approval of such views or merely to defend the right to state them would, under the police state of Nicholas I, be tantamount to courting disaster.

Abroad he had some champions. Herzen, for instance:

> It was a shot that rang out into the dark night. Whether it was something foundering that proclaimed its own destruction, whether it was a signal, a cry for help, tidings of dawn or of the fact that there would be no dawn, in any event, it forced all to awake.

The result of the publication for Chaadayev personally was that he was kept under house arrest and daily medical supervision—it is curious to learn that "medical" treatment of dissenters is not a recent Russian invention—his papers were confiscated, and he was forbidden to publish anything again. A few months later, he began composing *Apology of a Madman* in which he retracted, or at least modified, some of his earlier views, but neither this nor the other Letters were published in his lifetime.

His writings seem to me to be a little repetitious, but perhaps this is a good thing, for his arguments are complex and not always easy to follow.

His most radical criticisms of Russia are to be found in the first two Letters. His first complaint is that, unlike the nations of the West, Russia was a country without historical traditions.

> We belong to none of the great families of mankind; we are neither of the West nor of the East, and we possess the traditions of neither. Somehow divorced from time, we have not been touched by the universal education of mankind. That wonderful interconnection of human ideas in the succession of the centuries, that history of the human mind which brought man to the state in which he is today in the rest of the world, has had no influence upon us.
>
> Cast a look upon the many centuries in our past, upon the expanse of the soil we inhabit, and you will find no endearing reminiscence, no venerable memorial, to speak to you powerfully of the past, and to reproduce it for you in a vivid and colorful manner. We live only in the narrowest of presents . . .

For this he seems to hold the schism between the Byzantine and Catholic Church largely to blame.

> While the Christian world marched on majestically along the road marked out for it by its divine Creator, carrying along generations, we, though called Christians, stuck to our place. The entire world was being rebuilt, while we built nothing. . . . We were Christians, but the fruits of Christianity were not ripening in us.

Though, in the *Apology*, he was to admit that he had exaggerated

> in not giving its due to that church, so humble, at times so heroic, which alone attenuates the emptiness of our chronicles, on which devolves the honor of our ancestors' every act of courage, every great sacrifice.

I don't think he ever realised that the schism was chiefly the fault of the West. With a little give and take, the theological implications of the *Filioque* Clause could have been settled to the satisfaction of both sides, but the West, under Frankish influence, tried to high-pressure it through, and then, after the sack of Constantinople in the Fourth Crusade, reconciliation was clearly impossible.

He was, however, of course, right in thinking it a disgrace that Russia should have adopted serfdom in the sixteenth century, long after it had been abolished in the West. One should add, though, that, as under feudalism, the Russian nobility was not free either: in order to keep their estates, they had to serve in the armed forces or the Diplomatic Service.

The later and, to me, more interesting Letters are primarily concerned with theological problems. His main thesis seems to be this. If God created us, then the laws of our spiritual and moral nature cannot be, like criminal laws, laws *for*, but must be, like the laws of our physical nature, laws *of*, laws, that is to say, which we can defy but cannot break, any more than I can defy the Law of Gravity by jumping out of the window or the Laws of Biochemistry by getting drunk, and the consequences of defiance must be as inevitable as a broken leg or a hangover.

There is, however, a profound difference between the laws of the physical cosmos and the laws of our inner life, as creatures created in the image of God. The laws of the cosmos, which, incidentally, God did not reveal to us but left it to us to discover, are laws of necessity: no atom can be disobedient. As conscious beings, we possess what we call Free Will. Before Man fell, the laws of his moral nature must, presumably, have seemed as obvious and impossible to dispute as physical laws. That is no longer the case. We are often very uncertain of just what we *ought* to do. But there is no such activity as being free to will anything we choose.

> All our activity is but the effect of a force which drives us to place ourselves in the general order of things, in the order of dependence. Whether we consent to this force or whether we resist it is immaterial; we are always under its sway . . . This is how I conceive the principle of

> the mental world and in this way, as you see, it corresponds perfectly to the principle of the physical world. But one of these principles appears to us as an irresistible force to which everything inevitably submits, whereas the other seems to us to be no more than power which is combined with our own power and is, to some extent capable of being modified by our own power. . . . This in no way prevents us, when we accept freedom as a given fact, from recognizing that passivity is the reality of the moral order, just as it is of the physical order. All powers of the mind, all its means of cognition come to the mind only from its docility. The mind is powerful only because it is submissive. All human reason needs to know is to what it must submit.

The search for such knowledge, Chaadayev says, involves all mankind and the whole of human history. He quotes Pascal:

> The whole succession of men is one man who exists always.

and he would certainly have agreed with Goethe:

> Only all men taken together make up mankind, only all forces in their co-operation the world. If one person promotes only what is beautiful, another only what is useful, only the two of them jointly constitute a human being.

Hence the all-important role played by tradition, for an idea must go through a certain number of generations to become the patrimony of mankind.

> This is the *milieu* in which all the marvels of the intellect occur. Doubtless this hidden experience of the ages does not come as a whole to every fraction of mankind, but it forms the mental substance of the universe. It runs in the blood of all human races, it mingles with their fibre; finally, it carries on those other traditions, yet more mysterious, which have no source on earth, which were the starting point for all societies. It is a fact that in the tribe most remote from the great movement of the world one always finds a certain number of ideas, more or less clear, of the Supreme Being, of good and evil, of justice and injustice. . . . Whence come these ideas? No one knows: traditions, that's all. There is no way to reach their source; children have learned them from their fathers and mothers, that is their whole genealogy.

This is not, of course, to deny the crucial role played, both for good and evil, by "great" individuals whose names we know.

As a Christian, Chaadayev naturally believed that the two most important persons in history have been Moses and Christ, but he did not think that the Old and New Testaments had made the significance of either monotheism or the Incarnation clear and self-evident once and for all. Christian tradition, continuously developing through time, is as important as the Scriptures. For instance, only modern science could have finally buried that god in whom many people who thought themselves to be Christians had undoubtedly believed, namely, a Zeus without Zeus' vices. It is only recently that we have learned that we cannot speak of famines, plagues, lightning as "Acts of God".

As for Christ:

> When the Son of God said that He would send the Spirit to men and that He himself would be in their midst eternally, do you suppose that he had in mind that book that was composed after His death, where his words and deeds are more-or-less well told and where some of the writings of His disciples have been collected? Do you suppose he believed that this was the book which would perpetuate His teaching on earth? Surely this was not His thought. He meant that after Him would come men who would so well lose themselves in contemplation of Him and in the study of His perfection, who would so fill themselves with His teaching or the lesson of his life, that they would morally be at one with him; that these men following upon one another across all future ages, would hand down to one another His whole thought, His whole Being; this is what He meant and what is not understood.

Other historical figures of whom he thought highly were Mohammed and, rather oddly, Epicurus, whom he considered less impractical than the Stoics and less vague and weak than the Platonists. As one might expect, he disapproved of Socrates and Marcus Aurelius, but Homer heads his list of baddies.

> In our view the baleful heroism of passions, the turbid idea of beauty, the unbridled love of earth: all these come from him . . . It is only the Greeks who decided to idealize and deify vice and crime. The poetry of evil is thus found only among them and the nations who inherited their civilisation.

This, to me at least, seems nonsense. I cannot think of any work which more pitilessly exposes the error of polytheism than the *Iliad.* The Olympians, as there depicted, are a sorry lot indeed, whom nobody in their senses could possibly admire. The human beings in the poem, Hector, Achilles, Priam, whatever their faults, are morally infinitely superior.

Unlike most of the Russian Westernisers of his time, Chaadayev was not a political revolutionary. Like the Slavophiles, he sought spiritual and religious solutions to social problems, but unlike them, he believed these could only be sought in the West, not in the East.

> We are simply a nation of the North, and in our ideas as well as in our climate far removed from the scented Vale of Kashmir and the holy

> shores of the Ganges. A few of our provinces neighbor the empires of the East, granted, but our centers are not there, our life is not there, and they will never be there unless the earth's axis shifts or a new cataclysm once again hurls the nature of the South into the glaciers of the polar regions.

Given his admiration for the united Christendom of the Middle Ages and his dislike of schism, one would have expected him to become a Roman Catholic but, apparently, he never did. He was, however, a firm believer in submission to authority, to superior individuals, and had no faith in the common sense of the Common Man. When he came to write *Apology of a Madman,* he had studied Karamzin's *History of the Russian State,* from which he acquired an enormous, perhaps exaggerated, admiration for Peter the Great, with whom, in his opinion, a genuine Russian history began. There are passages in the book which, to-day, are a little disquieting. He seems to have thought that, precisely because Russia was the last great country to become civilised, she might be destined to be the future hope of mankind, but that her mission could only be fulfilled under some kind of autocracy.

> Our might terrifies the world, our empire stretches over one-fifth of the globe; but all that, we must confess, we owe only to the authoritative will of our princes and the assistance of the physical conditions of the country we inhabit.
>
> Fashioned, moulded, created by our rulers and our climate, we have become a great nation only by dint of submission. Scan our chronicles from beginning to end: on each page you will find the profound effect of authority, the ceaseless action of the soil, and hardly ever that of the public will. However, it is also true that, in abdicating its power in favor of its masters, in yielding to its native physical climate, the Russian nation gave evidence of profound wisdom.

Whether her present-day rulers still believe, as, officially, they must, in Russia's messianic mission is not quite certain, but there is no doubt whatsoever that they believe in submission to their will. In saying such things, it is possible that Chaadayev was exaggerating in order to ingratiate himself with the Tsar: it is also possible that he was more of a Slavophile than he himself realised.

Written for, but not published in, *The New Yorker,* February 1973

Veni, Vici, VD

The Dark Fields of Venus: From a Doctor's Logbook. By Basile Yanovsky, M.D. Harcourt Brace Jovanovich. $7.95.

In general, I disapprove of modern permissiveness in writing about sexual matters, but I realize that, even twenty years ago, this book could probably not have been published. Nobody could call it pleasant reading but, in my opinion, it should be required reading, especially for young people. A wall slogan in one clinic announces: "VD strikes one person every two minutes." It is the duty of everyone to be as well informed about venereal disease as possible. At present, ignorance and misconceptions are all too common.

The book consists of 327 vignettes of daily life in a VD clinic. Dr Yanovsky, in addition to being a medical man, is a distinguished novelist and a member of the Russian Orthodox Church. In consequence he is interested in his patients as human beings. In many cases, he found that personal questions were resented, but he discovered how to get round that.

> . . . if I hold a pen in my hand and look at the chart, I can ask the most impertinent questions and always get a reply. That is considered objective, scientific, and of possible use in the treatment.

But before considering the patients, let us listen to what he tells us about the clinics themselves—staff, organization, shortcomings, etc. As one might expect, though there is plenty of money for medicines, there is very little for anything else. The toilets are usually filthy, the water fountains don't work, the elevators are often out of order, and there is not enough space for the doctors to park their cars. But the most exasperating feature is the organizational setup.

> The best pages of Kafka, Beckett, and Ionesco hardly equal the absurdity of NYC arrangements. . . . Out of the twelve or thirteen steps through which the poor VD customer is forced to move, one half of the total . . . require him to go back to the waiting-room, sit down, and wait again. . . . This *danse macabre* adds at least one hour to the patient's waiting time, besides being absurd and humiliating. . . .
>
> If, furthermore, one keeps in mind that our clerks take about fifteen to twenty minutes to admit a patient, and that when they have finally written out his papers, they do not rush to bring them to the doctor but accumulate three or four charts at a time, since, as they put it, "they are not messengers," then the absurdity of the patient-flow arrangement becomes obvious. Sometimes there are several doctors standing around, waiting for a chart to be filled out in order to do some work. The shortage is less of doctors than of intelligent, literate clerks.

Then there is one group of workers at the clinics about whom Dr Yanovsky has serious misgivings, namely the VD "detectives," of whom there are more than a hundred in New York City. Their job is to detect and follow up all syphilitics and their contacts and, lately, gonorrhea contacts as well. This means that now

> . . . all the sexual contacts of a man during the last two weeks before his visit—and with our customers that usually means several women or men—all those named and identified by the unfortunate lover, must be reached by the investigators. The women are called up at their homes or jobs, visited or written to, and finally (through motivation or fright) brought into the clinic. Here, regardless of the result of the medical examination, they are classified G 90 and given 4,800,000 units of penicillin—unless they claim to be allergic to it. One can imagine what family conflicts and even tragedies are created by this interference in the private lives and the bedrooms of people. Notice that those who can afford to consult a private physician escape all the official reports and investigations and are never asked for their contacts.
>
> Thus, unexpectedly, a most progressive, liberal-minded institution, the Health Department, works at transforming our society into a police state. Personally, if I had to choose between freedom, privacy, and gonorrhea on one side and no freedom, no privacy, and no gonorrhea on the other, I would opt for the first alternative.

It is obvious, from reading this book, that there is another matter of organization which could be improved. There are certain noninfectious complaints, urethritis in men and trichomoniasis in women, the symptoms of which resemble VD. Naturally, sufferers come to the VD clinic, only to be told that they cannot be dealt with there and must go to a hospital. Surely, it would save time and trouble for everyone if there could be a department for them in the same building.

One of the great problems in diagnosing VD for certain is that extraneous factors, such as antibiotics, malaria, vaccination injections, heroin, etc., can give a positive reaction when the patient is tested. I have had personal experience of this. One year I had just returned from Austria and went for a general medical checkup. The Wassermann test gave a doubtful positive! Luckily my physician was a personal friend so that, when I told him it was impossible, he believed me. "There is," he said, "a more reliable test." (I think it must be what Dr Yanovsky calls the FTA test.) "It will cost you twenty-five dollars, but we'll send a blood sample to Albany." Sure enough, I was OK. I then asked myself if anything unusual had happened lately. Yes, just as I was leaving the house in Austria, I was stung by a bee. I asked my friend if he thought that bee venom could have possibly affected the Wassermann. He thought it might have. I don't suppose any test is one hundred percent foolproof but, when one thinks of the emotional complications that might arise from even a suspicion of infection, surely the authorities should use only the most foolproof test they know of.

The subjects of Dr Yanovsky's vignettes cover almost every kind of human beings except the chaste and the self-disciplined—married and single heterosexuals, whores, homosexuals, transvestites, lesbians, businessmen who go on Saturday night "sprees," those who go steady, and those who are promiscuous and indulge in group sex. Patients over sixty are rare and there tend to be more females than males, for many men, it seems, go to a private doctor but send their girl friends to the clinic. A great many have little or no English, which makes communication difficult. When asked, for example, if they are allergic to penicillin, they sometimes think the term means "liking to take." Then about one fifth of the patients are junkies, so that finding a vein into which to inject penicillin can be a problem, but at least junkies are not afraid, as so many patients are, of a needle.

The most tiresome are the hypochondriacs who, though they have no symptoms, insist on frequent checkups ("Isn't that what you're paid for?") and complain to the Central Office if the overworked doctor becomes impatient. But it is rare, it seems, for any patient to write to the Central Office to thank the Health Department for the courtesy, kindness, and efficiency of the doctors: they only write when they think they have something to complain about.

Some of the information Dr Yanovsky conveys has surprised me. Many young males like their girls to bite and scratch them, and come to the clinic with scars and scabs which they fear may be infected. Menstruation no longer seems a protection to a woman.

> Lately, a lot of rectal gonorrhea has been showing up in our literature. That's why the Central Office issued a recommendation to take routinely rectal smears of every woman patient. But we don't follow these instructions. We simply have too much to do.

Then, though I knew of course that a person under treatment must abstain from sex, liquor, spices, I never knew before that he should also abstain from riding a motor bicycle. Nor had I realized, though I should have guessed, that one consequence of mass tourism in Europe has been a sharp rise in the number of patients after the summer vacation.

As Dr Yanovsky says, most people know more about their cars than about their bodies, and this ignorance has probably increased, thanks to recent medical research. The public as a whole now believes that science has all the answers, so that it need not worry. If anything goes wrong, wonder drugs can quickly put it right. About possible side effects from penicillin, for example, the average person knows nothing, and, if they occur, he is apt to hold the doctor personally responsible.

Today very few people are "afraid" of VD, though they may fear the pain of a needle. Some men, it seems, can be frightened by being told that VD may render them incapable of begetting children, not because they want to become fathers, but because the thought offends their male egos. Moreover, very few VD patients show any shame or guilt or remorse, or even a sense of personal responsibility for the acts which brought them to the clinic. Many of the young, it seems, regard catching syphilis or gonorrhea as inevitable, like coming down with the flu. Some blame it on alcohol, as if drinking was not an act of human will. Others just say with a grin, "You know how it is." The true meaning of this expression has been admirably defined by Karl Kraus.

> When a man is treated like a beast, he says: after all I'm human. When he behaves like a beast, he says: after all I'm only human.

Some argue that promiscuity provides "multiple experience," others that "it solves a lot of problems."

What is to be done? In the atmosphere of VD clinics as they now are, places where medicine is separated from the rest of life, very little.

> You can't moralize with our young patients. You can't talk to them about Western civilization, the church, or education, for all these are parts of the establishment and responsible for the mess we are in. But they are not down on all religion. They like to hear about Hindu practices, Far Eastern rites, Yoga technique. These have nothing to do with our police or politics. . . .
>
> It is pathetic how these young people, ready to blow up the entire establishment, revere science, which is so important a part of it. Herein lies their greatest contradiction: "Culture, *no!* Penicillin, *sí!*"

About possible improvements, Dr Yanovsky has some suggestions to make, though he is under no illusion that they could be adopted overnight.

> Why not have music, poetry, discussions on the meaning of life, love, and art while they are waiting for their smears and blood tests? Perhaps even free coffee? Sort of an agape.
>
> To separate medicine from ethics, philosophy, religion, and art is absurd. We must allow a new form of clinic to come into being, like the new theater, school, or church. But it must come spontaneously. It can't be planned by the Commissioner and his deputies in the Central Office. There must be an openness, a readiness to let it develop, to nurture it wherever it shows itself in the bud.

I have deliberately refrained from quoting dialogues between Dr Yanovsky and his many patients because I think readers would prefer to read them for themselves. When they have, I am certain that they will come to the same conclusion as his.

They are after something else, and sex is only a substitute, which, apparently, does not satisfy them. It is the job of a teacher, philosopher, or physician to make this clear to every pupil, neighbor, or patient that comes his way.

Every time I stick in my needle I feel: penicillin is not enough!

The New York Review of Books, 22 February 1973

Larkin's Choice

The Oxford Book of Twentieth Century English Verse.
Edited by Philip Larkin. Clarendon Press. £3.

My first reaction, after reading this anthology was: "My God! what a hard-working and conscientious reader Mr Larkin must be." Though he is a little younger than myself, I'm sure he has reached an age when one tends to reread poems that one already knows and likes and to neglect poems by younger writers, unless personally recommended by someone whose critical judgment one trusts. This natural tendency Mr Larkin has overcome. Beginning with Wilfred Scawen Blunt (1840–1922) and ending with Brian Patten (born 1946), he prints selections from no less than 207 poets.

There are many poems which I had never read before, including a most entertaining one by G. D. H. Cole, but not one seems to me unworthy of inclusion. As for omissions, I have only detected two. There is nothing by Gordon Bottomley, a Georgian poet who wrote at least one very fine poem, and nothing by W. J. Turner. Yeats, to be sure, overly represented the latter, but I think it is unjust to exclude him altogether.

About his principles of selection Mr Larkin writes:

> In the end I found that my material fell into three groups: poems representing aspects of the talents of poets judged either by the age or by myself to be worthy of inclusion, poems judged by me to be worthy of inclusion without reference to their authors, and poems judged by me to carry with them something of the century in which they were written. Needless to say, the three groups are not equal in size, nor are they mutually exclusive.

Because of their official aura, I sometimes wonder if it would not be better if the various Oxford Books of Verse were compiled by an Editorial Board rather than by a single editor. It would, at least, prevent reviewers, especially if, like myself, they happen to have compiled anthologies of their own, from complaining that the single editor's choices are not those which they would have made, had they been doing the job.

All of us have our favourite poets and our favourite poems, so that no two anthologists would produce the same anthology. Had I, for example, been editing this anthology instead of Mr Larkin, my selection from Housman would have included "Hell Gate," my selection from Walter de la Mare extracts from "Time's Wingèd Chariot," but how unimportant such cavillings are.

Basically, I am happy to see Mr Larkin's taste in poetry and my own are in agreement. Both of us like poems to be well made and show decorum. Neither of us likes poems which are shoddily made or lacking in Common Sense. The only difference which I think I can detect is that I believe I enjoy comic verse more than he does. He has, to be sure, an extensive selection from John Betjeman, a comic or, at least, a "serio-comic" poet, but ignores such delights as E. C. Bentley's Clerihews, or the nonsense verses in Chesterton's *Greybeards at Play*.

But this is as it should be. No two persons' tastes, thank God, are identical.

I don't suppose there could be a volume comparable to this one, entitled *The Oxford Book of Twentieth Century American Verse*, because no American university press enjoys the peculiar status of the Clarendon Press, but I find myself speculating upon what the differences between them would be, if there were. I'm sure, for example, that one would immediately detect a difference between poems written about Nature by English poets and by American. Thus the opening words of *The Waste Land*, "April is the cruellest month," could not possibly have been written by anyone brought up in England. The American climate, outside California, is violent, the English is mild.

Then, for centuries, no European has had any firsthand experience of an untamed wilderness. Nature, to us, is a friendly Mother Earth, whom we can trust. To Americans, on the other hand. Nature has been virgin and hostile, a *Dura Virum Nutrix* to be subdued by force. I have noticed that when an Englishman and an American talk about Conservation they mean different things. Both, of course, are against the ruthless exploitation of Nature, but, to an Englishman conservation means preserving a "cultured" landscape; to an American preserving the wilderness in its virginal state.

Then, I think that their conception of their vocation is not the same in English and American poets. An English poet, I believe, still thinks of himself as a "clerk," a member of a professional brotherhood, with a certain social status irrespective of the number of his readers, and as taking his place in an unbroken historical succession. Every American poet, on the other hand, to some degree feels that the whole responsibility for contemporary poetry has fallen upon his shoulders, that he is a literary aristocracy of one. There are dangers, of course, in both attitudes. An English poet has to be constantly on his guard against becoming too "cosy" and conformist, an American against crankiness and self-parody.

Mr Larkin must forgive me this, perhaps irrelevant, digression. I congratulate him most warmly upon his achievement.

The Guardian, 29 March 1973

Rhyme and Reason

The Oxford Book of Children's Verse. Edited by Iona and Peter Opie. Oxford £2.25.

I can imagine an anthology with the same title in which the choice of selections was based on the question: "What kind of poetry does a twentieth-century child enjoy?" This, very wisely in my opinion, the Opies have not attempted. Beginning with Chaucer and ending with Ogden Nash, they have confined themselves to verses composed by adults specifically for children. As they point out, very few nursery rhymes and no ballads were "originally compositions for the young." At first I was surprised to find no verses, like counting-out rhymes, associated with children's games, especially since the Opies are the world experts on the subject. On reflection, I think I see why. In their opinion, such verses were composed *by* children not *for* them.

Until the close of the eighteenth century children were regarded, not as persons with a mentality peculiar to their age, but as potential adults, differing from the latter only in that they had not yet acquired the knowledge and codes of behaviour which a decent adult must have. Accordingly, most poems for children written before Wordsworth are didactic. Either, like those of Isaac Watts, they give moral instruction—the titles of the selections from him here printed are "Against Quarrelling and Fighting," "Against Idleness and Mischief," "For the Lord's Day Evening," "Our Saviour's Golden Rule," "The Sluggard," "Cradle Hymn"—or they are mnemonics for remembering such things as the number of days in the months. (I wish the editors could have found room for some of the mnemonic rhymes in Kennedy's *Shorter Latin Primer*, e.g.:—

> Nouns denoting males in ă
> Are by meaning mascula,
> And masculine is found to be
> Hadria, the Adriatic Sea

Or the extraordinary mnemonic I had to learn in an Algebra Class:—

> Minus times Minus equals Plus:
> The reason for this we need not discuss.

In this period, there are some poems, like Prior's "To a Child of Quality, Five Years Old" which, though ostensibly addressed to a child, were really written to flatter its parents, not for the child to read. These, quite rightly, they have omitted.

One happy result of the editors' principle of selection, combined with their scrupulous dating, is that their anthology will delight not only lovers of poetry but also students of cultural history. I knew, for example, that "There was a sick man of Tobago" was the Limerick which prompted Lear to write his, but I never knew before that this was the third of "Anecdotes of Four Gentlemen," published in 1821, and probably written by Richard Scrafton Sharpe.

Knowing that poets who write for children, unlike those who write for adults, may begin early but sometimes only begin when they become grandparents, the editors have, in the interest of history, wisely listed their authors, not by the date of their birth, but by the date of their first known publication.

Before the nineteenth century it is generally easy to detect which poems were written for children only and which for adults only. After that, owing to the change in the conception of the child's nature, it is not. While there are good poems which children cannot appreciate because they deal with experiences which they are too young to have known, there are no good poems that children appreciate which lose their appeal when they grow up. All poets know this. Some, like Lear and Carroll, may have originally written with a children's audience in mind, but they certainly hoped that adults would read them too. Others, writing comic verses like the clerihews of Bentley or Chesterton's nonsense quatrains in *Graybeards at Play*, may have written them to amuse adults, but I'm sure they hoped some children would find them funny. And in both cases their hopes have certainly been fulfilled.

This presents an anthologist with a problem. Exactly which poems should he include in a book of children's verse, and which should he omit? One thing is certain: whatever poems the Opies have omitted, this was not due to ignorance. Most anthologists are notoriously lazy but, as their selections, their foreword and their notes demonstrate, they have really done their homework. Verse for children happens to be a hobby of mine, but they have printed a number which I had never come across before. Two of their selections particularly delighted me. They print eight poems by that most unjustly forgotten author, William Brighty Rands. For example:—

> . . . You friendly Earth, how far do you go,
> With the wheatfields that nod and the rivers that flow,
> With cities and gardens, and cliffs, and isles,
> And people upon you for thousands of miles?
>
> Ah, you are so great, and I am so small,
> I tremble to think of you, world, at all;
> And yet, when I said my prayers today,
> A whisper inside me seemed to say
> "You are more than the Earth, though you are such a dot:
> You can love and think, and the Earth cannot."

And, though the originals were written in German, they print three poems from Heinrich Hoffmann's *Struwwelpeter* in the excellent English versions published in 1848. I'm sorry, though, they did not include my favourite, "The Story of Little Suck-a-Thumb."

There is one omission which surprises me. There are no selections from Harry Graham's *Ruthless Rhymes for Heartless Homes.* These were certainly written for children, and I adored them as a child.

One little question. Had I been the editor, I don't think I would have dared print Rose Fyleman's "There are fairies at the bottom of our garden." Because of the contemporary slang meaning of the word *fairy*, it is impossible to read the poem without giggling. One can, I believe, still speak of a fairy tale, but if I had to speak of fairies, I myself would now refer to them as elves.

But this is a trivial matter. *The Oxford Book of Children's Verse* is a volume all parents and all lovers of poetry should possess.

The Observer, 20 May 1973

Between Crossfires

Hammarskjöld. By Brian Urquhart. Knopf. $12.50.

The long and magnificently researched *Hammarskjöld*, by Brian Urquhart, is not a biography in the conventional sense. Though it contains some amusing personal anecdotes, which I will refer to later, it seems to me less the life story of the man than a day-to-day history of the activities of the United Nations Secretariat during the eight years when Hammarskjöld was Secretary-General. He is only the central figure in the way that a commanding general is the center of a history of a campaign. It is the general's responsibility to make the final decisions and issue orders, but unless he is served by loyal and efficient subordinates he is impotent. Save for men like Ralph Bunche, Andrew Cordier, Rajeshwar Dayal, and—though he is too modest to say so—Mr Urquhart himself, Hammarsjköld could have achieved very little.

As someone who was a member of the Secretariat from its inception, Mr Urquhart overestimates, I think, the general knowledge of the average reader. Thus, though he does give a glossary of acronyms, every time he mentions one I found myself having to refer to it again, since I had forgotten what the letters stand for. Then, he will refer to Article 99 of the United Nations Charter as though everybody had read it. I, for one, never have. Fascinating though it is, I think that the reader who is not a professional diplomat will find some of this book hard going.

When, after the First World War, the League of Nations was formed, Count Kessler, who had been the German Minister to Poland, suggested that it might be better if its delegates, instead of being the official representatives of sovereign states, were representatives of various interest groups—the professions, the trades unions, the churches, and so on—because otherwise, he thought, the League would be unable to act in the case of any serious conflict between the major powers. His suggestion was not adopted. Whether it could have been after the Second World War, I don't know, but it wasn't. The United Nations was constituted as its successor. In consequence, Hammarskjöld and his staff could act successfully only when the major powers, whatever their differing interests, felt that a compromise was better than war. If, as in the case of Hungary, their differences were irreconcilable, the Secretariat could do nothing.

Even for so able a man as Hammarskjöld, the position of the Secretary-General is enormously difficult. To begin with, he has no intelligence service of his own and must rely on such information as he can get from governments and public sources. This is often unavailable or unreliable. Thus Hammarsjköld could not know of the private agreement between England and France to land troops at the Suez Canal until they had done so. And the Secretariat is wholly dependent financially upon what the General Assembly cares to vote it, and this is seldom wholly adequate. As Hammarsjköld himself said, the member governments seemed to expect the Secretariat to go on a lion hunt without being willing even to provide it with a bird gun. The salaries the Secretary-General can offer those who work for him cannot compare with what they could earn as state diplomats or in business. Perhaps this is not altogether a bad thing, for the lovers of money, power, and prestige will not apply; only those will be attracted who are willing to work anonymously and impartially for the cause of international justice.

Lastly, there is the problem of the relation between the Secretary-General and the press during delicate negotiations:

> When information is withheld, journalists understandably enough fall back on speculation. Such speculation, although usually inaccurate, is often near enough to the truth to be accepted as such by large sections of public opinion, and even by governments. The Secretary-General in particular must maintain the absolute discretion on which his confidential relationship with governments is based. The parties to a conflict, on the other hand, may sometimes find it advantageous to leak part of the story to the press in order to build up public support for their own position, and on occasion such activities grow into a fully orchestrated press campaign.

When Hammarsjköld was elected, in 1953, morale in the Secretariat was at a low ebb. It was in the McCarthy era, and it was widely alleged that many of the staff were Communists or Communist sympathizers. This Hammarsjköld dealt with rapidly and effectively. He insisted that the right to fire anyone should be vested in himself, and, should it seem necessary for him to fire someone, compensation should be paid. He also insisted that any accusations should be based on provable fact, not rumor. He forbade members of the Secretariat to take part in any outside political activity other than voting in elections, and he demanded that anyone on his staff who had complaints or political objections to make should bring them to him, not speak of them to outsiders. At first, it seems, some of the Secretariat were alarmed by these ideas, but they soon learned to trust him as a scrupulously just man who would defend them against all outside pressures.

In dealing with the press he showed himself a master:

> Over the years, he perfected a technique of escaping into a cloud of metaphor or abstraction, with a style at the same time articulate and obscure, brilliant but hard to grasp, apparently forthright but often uninformative. His performances evoked a grudging admiration among the journalists, who not infrequently found themselves, at the end of a long press conference in which important matters had ostensibly been discussed, with no spot news and little to write about.

One French journalist called him "the most charming oyster in the world."

His public speeches, Mr Urquhart tells us, were more impressive to read than to listen to, for he spoke in a flat, toneless voice. This was evidently deliberate; he wished to avoid cheap, oratorical effects. On one occasion, however, when Khrushchev, at a General Assembly, attacked him savagely and demanded his resignation, he answered in a ringing voice which earned him an ovation.

From the beginning, Hammarsjköld had very clear ideas of the roles that the Secretary-General could and could not play. Like a good judge, he should be passionately interested in the problems set him, but completely disinterested. In the last speech he made in Oxford he said:

> He is not requested to be a neuter in the sense that he has to have no sympathies or antipathies, that there are no interests which are close to him in his personal capacity or that he is to have no ideas or ideals that matter to him. However, he is requested to be fully aware of those human reactions and meticulously to check himself so that they are not permitted to influence his actions. . . . In the last analysis, this is a question of integrity, and if integrity in the sense of respect for law and respect for truth were to drive him into positions of conflict with this or that interest, then that conflict is a sign of his neutrality and not of his failure to observe neutrality.

And, of course, in any violent dispute both parties will interpret such impartiality as a bias in favor of the other side. During the Congo crisis, for example, Hammarsjköld said:

> From both sides the main accusation was a lack of objectivity. The historian will undoubtedly find in this balance of accusations the very evi-

> dence of that objectivity we were accused of lacking, but also of the fact that very many Member Nations have not yet accepted the limits put on their national ambitions by the very existence of the United Nations.

This does not mean that he thought it either possible or desirable for the Secretariat to usurp the functions of national governments:

> The Secretary-General's initiative . . . is, in principle, a supplementary one. When governments reach a deadlock, he may be the person to help them—and help them with their complete acceptance—out of the deadlock. . . . If governments are seized of a matter, if there is no deadlock, if discussions are going on and if contacts have been established . . . the Secretary-General—no matter how concerned he may be—should keep back.

As a mediator, however, the Secretary-General has one great advantage: he has no pressure group behind him. Consequently,

> he can talk with much greater freedom, much greater frankness, and much greater simplicity in approaching governments than any government representative can do.

Not infrequently, the political parties to a dispute are willing to make mutual concessions but, for political reasons, dare not say so in public. In such cases, provided the Secretary-General is a man whose discretion they can trust, they can tell him in private what they are prepared to concede.

Hammarsjköld's great innovation was, of course, to visit foreign capitals in his official capacity to make personal acquaintance with their leaders (Chou En-lai, Ben-Gurion, Nasser, the King of Laos), hear what they had to say, and express his own opinions. He did not, naturally imagine that such visits would solve the political problems of the world for good and all, but he did hope, and, as it turned out, rightly, that he might be able to relieve tensions, at least momentarily. That he was able to do so testifies to his extraordinary integrity and charm. However they might differ politically, almost all the men he met on these journeys liked him and trusted him, and their liking and trust was reciprocated. (Incidentally, I met Chou En-lai in Hankow in 1938, and I am very happy to find that Hammarsjköld's high opinion of him confirms my own impression. The three politicians I have met in my life whom I most admire are Hammarsjköld, Chou En-lai, and Teddy Kollek, the Mayor of Jerusalem.)

Hammarsjköld said:

> Chou En-lai to me appears as the most superior brain I have so far met in the field of foreign politics. . . . As I said to one of the Americans, "Chou is so much more dangerous than you imagine because he is so much better a man than you have ever admitted."

So, too, with Nasser:

> When he encountered unflattering talk about him, Hammarsjköld told Nasser, he invariably gave one reply: "However that may be, he has never gone back on anything he said to me personally."
>
> Nasser answered, "I wish to maintain that record."

And with Ben-Gurion:

> This aristocratic and determined Swede . . . was not, at first sight, the sort of person whom Ben-Gurion would trust or like, but Hammarsjköld and Ben-Gurion quickly perceived each other's exceptional personal qualities and over the years of often violent disagreement they developed a strong friendship and mutual sympathy which was reinforced by a common taste for conversation on broad philosophical subjects.

Hammarsjköld appeared to have an unerring sense of the kind of thing the person he was talking to would be interested in. Thus, the King of Laos was delighted to find that he and Hammarsjköld seemed to share a love for the classical French diplomacy of the eighteenth century, after which "we both happily embarked," Hammarskjöld wrote later, "on an intense discussion of the acute problems of Laos without ever mentioning them by name."

Even Khrushchev, after Hammarskjöld was safely dead, had to admit that he had been a great man.

As the years went by, Hammarsjköld came more and more to feel that one of the principal functions of the U.N. was to look after the "underdeveloped" countries—to provide them with technical and financial aid and defend their political interests. By "underdeveloped" countries he meant, naturally, poor countries. In the old days, no one imagined that if persons or nations were poor it was their own fault, and, if rich, that this was due to their superior moral virtues. But this, it seems, is no longer the case, so shy-making euphemisms have to be used: at first one could speak of "underdeveloped" countries, but no longer. He was thinking chiefly of the newly emergent states in Africa, and he realized clearly what formidable problems they faced. In the nineteenth century, the colonial powers had divided Africa up among themselves without any regard for economic or tribal facts. As Sekou Touré, the President of Guinea, remarked, "You Western democracies already had a nation when you got a national government, but many of us are expected to govern a country without a nation." And it is amusing, though not surprising, to learn that one local administrator in the Congo asked Ralph Bunche, "The U.N.—what tribe is that?"

Though recognizing the difficulties, Hammarskjöld was, perhaps, a little over-optimistic about the ability to solve them:

> There is something very shocking in the idea that new States must take so-called irresponsible stands. I myself do not believe it for a moment.

> . . . It is quite natural that they, like all of us, will have to find their way through a political system and a framework of procedures which so far have been unknown to them.

He was not quite prepared, I think, to find in the Congo an inverted racism —understandable, in view of the colonial past—and some people objected to his recruiting Swedes and Irish for the U.N. force, on the ground that because they were white they were no better than the Belgians. And though he wanted technical assistants and advisers from the "developed" countries to be replaced as soon as possible by locals, he underestimated

> the psychological problems at the receiving end and the possibility that governments and officials in newly independent countries, however great their need for expertise, might not welcome a new visitation of foreign experts, however high-minded and selfless.

Hammarskjöld's other innovation was, in situations of crisis, such as the Suez Canal and the Congo, when war, interstate or civil, seemed imminent, to recruit a U.N. armed force to help keep the peace. Such a force, he thought, should not be permanent, for different circumstances might require different kinds of recruits:

> To have one ready-made suit hanging somewhere in New York or stored I do not know where and to hope that it will fit the situations in various parts of the world is just to dream. We cannot afford, or usefully have, a wardrobe sufficiently rich and varied to be able to pick out just the right suit as the situation arises. It is much better to have the cloth and go into action as a good tailor quickly when the need arises.

He had very definite ideas about what such a force could and could not do. It could not be sent to any country without the consent of the government concerned. If attacked, it could defend itself, but otherwise it must maintain complete neutrality. In the Congo, where—as was not so at Suez—fighting had already broken out, he allowed the Opération des Nations Unies au Congo a little more freedom of action. Under certain circumstances it could close radio stations and airports, especially if it was requested to do so by competent authorities. Even political leaders could be arrested by the U.N. force if it was requested to do so by both the central government and the provincial authorities.

Mr Urquhart's account of what happened in the Congo, detailed and fascinating as it is, is a little hard to follow on a first reading, and I shall look forward to rereading it, slowly, when I get the opportunity.

As we all know, in the beginning the U.N. intervention in the Congo misfired. Hammarsjköld's original representative in the Congo had been his trusted Indian friend Dayal. Unfortunately, Dayal had been accused, quite unjustly, it seems, of being pro-Lumumba and pro-Communist. In consequence, he had become so unpopular with some of the leaders in Katanga that Kasavubu refused to take responsibility for his safety, and with great reluctance Hammarsjköld decided, after he had been recalled to New York for consultation, not to send him back, and so Conor Cruise O'Brien, a member of the Irish Foreign Service, was approached by Cordier. Hammarsjköld and O'Brien met but briefly in New York before O'Brien left for the Congo, and "neither seems to have got any real idea of the other's character or way of thinking."

As I said at the beginning, there are not many revealing touches in this book about Hammarsjköld the man, but the few it does contain are all good. For example, in Beirut he took an afternoon walk:

> The Lebanese security men, used to riding in cars, were soon exhausted, and one of them, puffing painfully, drew abreast of Ranallo to inquire if Hammarsjköld was married. When told that he was not, the security man remarked, "That is the reason he can walk so fast at his age."

His habit of working late into the night was notorious, but I had supposed that as soon as he had finished he would drop off. This, I find, was not the case:

> When in the small hours Hammarsjköld at last adjourned the discussions, he asked Dayal if he had any books, since in the hurry of departure he had neglected to bring enough to read. Dayal produced a work on Hindu mysticism, *A Vision of the Soul*, and when they met at eight o'clock the next morning Hammarsjköld returned it, saying he had found it most refreshing and illuminating.

His dinner in Sochi, on the Black Sea, with Khrushchev and Mikoyan seems to have been hilarious. He had been praising Pasternak. When Mikoyan objected, he replied that

> it was essential to keep aesthetic judgment apart from political considerations. The Secretary-General had no views on literature, but Mr Hammarsjköld as an individual had the right to such views, provided he also accepted the consequences. When Mikoyan asked if Hammarsjköld approved of the antisocial actions of the hero of the book. Hammarsjköld retorted that the general view that *Crime and Punishment* was a very great novel did not mean that he and Mikoyan thought it was a good idea to murder old widows.
>
> In an effort to change the mood of the conversation, Hammarsjköld proposed a toast to "honest sinners now on record." Both Khrushchev and Mikoyan were disconcerted and asked if he meant "repentant sinners," and, when Hammarsjköld replied in the negative, they refused to drink the toast. After a discussion of the relative merits of Soviet authors

and bourgeois émigrés, Hammarsjköld proposed a new toast to "living Soviet art." When Khrushchev asked what he meant by that, Hammarsjköld said each should define it for himself, and Khrushchev and Mikoyan finally joined in the toast.

As we know from his *Markings*, Hammarsjköld the private person was a great lover of poetry, himself a good minor poet, and a religious contemplative. But as a public figure he was aware that the transition from poetry and contemplation to action is not easy. There is a passage in a letter to the Swedish poet Erik Lindegren which might serve as a footnote to this statement in *Markings*—"In our era, the road to holiness necessarily passes through the world of action":

> We all remain free to form our personal life in accordance with standards which otherwise may find their expression in poetry. But obligation to action, especially in the political field, is more of a danger than of a privilege. At the present phase, events on all levels and the basic stone-age psychology of men make it rather difficult to translate contemplation into action and to make action the source material for contemplation.

The New Yorker, 26 May 1973

Indestructible

Conversations with Klemperer. Edited by Peter Heyworth. Gollancz. £3.

Commissioned by the Canadian Broadcasting Corp. and the Westdeutsche Rundfunk, these conversations, some in English, some in German, were taped in the summer and autumn of 1969. Extracts were broadcast in May 1970 on the occasion of the conductor's eighty-fifth birthday. Quite rightly, Peter Heyworth has done some editing. As he says:

> However well prepared, conversation inevitably meanders. Subjects are raised, dropped, returned to and discussed in different contexts, and in the struggle to produce from the English and German texts a reasonably coherent narrative I have unavoidably done violence to both versions. That was not the only cause for editorial intervention. Dr Klemperer's English has a flavour of its own and, where possible, I have tried to preserve this. But it is one thing to *hear* someone use a language in an effective if unorthodox manner, and quite another to *read* it. The number of adjectives Dr Klemperer uses is, for instance, limited. But spoken with the inflection of a voice that contains an altogether exceptional

> range of expression, is at times harsh, mocking or distant and at others caressing, quizzical or plaintive, that shortcoming is not as apparent as it would be in a written text.

Two things about Dr Klemperer have most greatly impressed me. Firstly, his astounding toughness, both physical and mental. I remember hearing him conduct in 1941 at the New School for Social Research in New York: he had recently recovered from a brain-tumour operation and could not wield a baton. "This man is not long for this world," I said to myself. How wrong I was, and how glad I am that I was! He seems to be accident-prone. He had a bad fall in Leipzig in 1930, in Montreal in 1951 he broke a hip, in 1958 he sustained third-degree burns, and he had another bad fall in 1969. Then, psychologically, he tells us, he has often suffered from the manic-depressive pendulum. On top of that, there were the years of exile in the States, where he never felt at home and was often poor and unemployed.

Secondly, I am amazed by his generosity to other conductors, a virtue which is hardly conspicuous in that band of prima donnas. He will, of course, criticise performances by, say, Toscanini or Karajan, but, when he does, he never fails to mention other performances which he thought excellent. He speaks of one young conductor whom he thought terrible, but he does not give his name.

Both Klemperer's parents were musical, and in 1900 it was decided that he should become a professional pianist. Some years later he decided to abandon this career, and for a rather odd reason:

> I was always so nervous that my hands became wet. James Kwast said to me, "You always play much better at lessons than in public. You are not the same in public". And he was right.

Judging by his experiences in a *Realgymnasium*, he cannot have been altogether surprised by Hitler. He was a bright boy, but he could only come out second in the class, no matter how high his marks, because a Jew could not be first.

As is well known, it was Mahler, the conductor whom above all others he admired, who procured him his first regular job in Prague. Hitherto he had only conducted as stand-in. One thing he tells us about Mahler surprised me: Mahler did not like the songs of Hugo Wolf, though, as students, they had shared lodgings. Incidentally, I wish I could appreciate Mahler's music more than I do. *Das Lied von der Erde* and *Kindertotenlieder* I love, but I find his symphonies, like those of his compatriot Bruckner, terribly long-winded. Dr Klemperer, it seems, does not like any of Strauss's operas after *Elektra.* I wonder if he has ever heard *Arabella.* He feels, like most of us, that Strauss should have left Germany when Hitler came to power. Yet, if he had, he might never have written *Metamorphosen.*

Much as he dislikes the term "modern", Dr Klemperer has never closed his ears to contemporary composers. He was one of the first people to recognise the talents of both Stravinsky and Schoenberg. Though the latter could be very "diffy", he took lessons with him and says he was an excellent teacher. Apparently, they never discussed atonal music. He confesses that he cannot "get" Webern but is willing to concede that the fault may be his. It would take too much space to go into his experiences with the many orchestras he conducted or the tiffs that sometimes occurred, amusing reading as they are, but I think it is worth mentioning that he reckons the greatest success he has ever had was conducting *Lohengrin* in Hamburg in 1910. In the last two chapters he discusses the art of conducting and the Conductor as Composer. About the former, he says:

> The art of conducting lies in my opinion in the power of suggestion that the conductor exerts . . . The conductor's hand should give the musicians the opportunity to play as though they were quite free. The players are hindered when the conductor beats too emphatically.

Dr Klemperer has himself been a prolific composer: he has written a number of operas, symphonies, quartets, and a big *Missa Sacra*. His music, he says, is rooted in tonality, and he ends this chapter by observing that

> I don't feel neglected. All right, my music is not often performed. If audiences were to like my music, I should be very happy. I believe that one day, I don't know when, they will say, "Yes". I mean, *I* believe it; that's my own hope.

I'm sure all readers of this fascinating book will wish that his hope comes true.

New Statesman, 1 June 1973

Progress Is the Mother of Problems (G. K. Chesterton)

The Ancient Concept of Progress. By E. R. Dodds.
Oxford University Press. $13.75.

Those, I hope they are many, who have read two of his earlier books, *The Greeks and the Irrational* and *Pagans and Christians in an Age of Anxiety*, will know that Professor Dodds is that rare creature, a very learned scholar who wishes to share his thoughts not with his fellow scholars only but also with intelligent readers who are not specialists in his field, which in this day and age means persons who cannot read Greek. They will also, I think, have received the impression that, as a man, he is a rationalist and a believer in the "liberal values," but at the same time acutely conscious of the difficulties and dangers inherent in both rationalism and liberalism.

The present volume consists of twelve papers, the first written in 1929, the last in 1971, covering a wide range of subjects. This makes the task of a reviewer very difficult, since each chapter deserves a review to itself.

Progress is a term with many different meanings. Before men can conceive of progress or decadence, they must have had personal experience of change. Thus primitive tribes, living by hunting or agriculture, whose way of life has remained the same for generations can have no idea of progress and usually credit such inventions as fire, weapons, agricultural tools either to a god or to a cultural hero.

Objectively speaking, there is only progress if B supersedes A. Thus, in the arts, though there are periods of flowering and sterility, there is no such thing as progress, only change. The plays of Shakespeare do not supersede the plays of Aeschylus, or the music of Mozart the music of Monteverdi. In the sciences, on the other hand, there is progress: the cosmos of Copernicus superseded the cosmos of Ptolemy, as the discoveries of modern astronomy have superseded Copernicus. In the case of the pure sciences, I think one can say that this progress is also an intellectual and moral good. In the case of technology this is not necessarily so. The modern camera and automobile improve upon their predecessors in that they are more efficient at what they set out to do, but one can think, as I do, that both are evil implements which should never have been invented. In recent years we have learned that discoveries in the pure sciences can have disastrous technological applications: we now realize better than our forebears did the truth of Goethe's dictum, "We need a categorical imperative in science as much as we need one in ethics."

It is only in social and political history that progress must mean a moral change for the better, which is why there are few times—the early fifth century in Athens, the eighteenth and nineteenth centuries in England and France—when people have been able to believe in it. It is much easier to believe in a lost paradise, either the golden age of Hesiod or the fall of Adam in Genesis, and in the myth of eternal recurrence for, as Professor Dodds says, these have deep unconscious roots in human experience.

> In the one case, perhaps, the individual experience of early infancy, when life was easy, nature supplied nourishment, and conflict did not exist; in the other, the eternally repeated drama of the recurrent seasons on which all agricultural life depends.

Though his second chapter is entitled "The *Prometheus Vinctus* and the Progress of Scholarship," Professor Dodds obviously does not mean progress as I have defined it. Aside from the discovery of new papyri and new archaeological evidence, scholarship is much more like an art than a science. A good work of scholarship, like a good work of art, exhibits two qualities: nowness—it has not been done before; and permanence—it will not be rendered obsolete by later scholars.

> What the outside critic does not always sufficiently realize is that the questions which are central for the classical scholar today are for the most part materially different, and nearly always differently formulated, from those on which attention was focused a hundred or even fifty years ago. . . . What we find in any document depends on our own interests, which in turn are determined, at least in part, by the intellectual climate of our own age. . . . [There has been] a shift in the focus of attention from textual questions to the study of dramatic technique on the one hand, and on the other to the problem of relating the individual work of art to the social and cultural background out of which it grew.

Before turning to the religious views of the dramatists, the reader might see what Professor Dodds has to say about the religion of the average uneducated man in ancient Greece. The gist of his argument seems to be that the closest we can come to that religion is by studying the religious habits of Greek peasants today, living in the country away from the cities. To be sure, as Christians they have what their ancestors did not, a Bible and an organized church, but to arrive at what they really believe it would be as silly to read theologians like Augustine and Aquinas, as in olden times it would have been to read Aeschylus and Plato. The literate in classical Greece read Homer, but nothing could be less like a sacred book than the *Iliad*. The gods, as Homer depicts them, are a frivolous, sorry lot who must be feared because they can take or save one's life, but whom nobody could possibly admire or regard as a model. His human characters, whatever their faults, are infinitely more admirable.

It seems clear that to the Greek peasant today the most important religious festivals are still concerned, as they always were, with the seasonal activities of sowing, a time of anxiety, and harvest, with luck, a time of relief, and with the crucial stages of life—birth, puberty, marriage, death. The ritual actions they perform are, to them, magical rites, designed to promote fertility and ward off misfortune.

Here are a few examples Professor Dodds gives of continuity despite all historical change. Mountaintops were held to be holy ground in ancient Greece: they still are, though now they are the home of Elijah, not Zeus. Once, to purge evil influences which had accumulated during the winter, the Greek chewed buckthorn: today, on the first of Lent, he chews garlic and onion. Now as then a dish of gruel, called *panspermia*, is offered in churchyards on the day when it is believed the dead revisit their homes.

The name Artemis has disappeared but there is someone called The Great Lady, who is the mistress of wild animals. There is no longer a home altar to the goddess of the hearth, but every Greek cottage contains an icon. Heracles and local heroes are no longer invoked, instead a local saint, one's name saint, or the Blessed Virgin. Once, before fording a river, the Greek washed his hands; today he crosses himself. I suspect that, until very recently, such practices continued in all peasant communities which were not influenced by the Reformation.

Professor Dodds devotes a chapter each to the *Prometheus Vinctus* and the *Oresteia*, both by Aeschylus, to *Oedipus* by Sophocles, and to the plays of Euripides. Some scholars have been worried because *Prometheus Vinctus* is so obviously what Russians would call "an anti-god play." Aeschylus seems to have gone out of his way to make Zeus as unsympathetic as possible. Nine times he is referred to as a "new" ruler, an insult in Greek because it implies that his sovereignty lacks proper sanction. Then the two characters who speak for him, Cratos and Hermes, are both presented as nasty brutes. How is this to be reconciled with the known fact that Aeschylus worshipped Zeus? Some scholars have gone as far as attributing the play to an unknown atheist. Professor Dodds demonstrates convincingly that this is unnecessary. In the play Prometheus predicts:

> Subduing his stubborn temper, Zeus shall come at last to a pact of friendship with me, and the will shall be his and mine.

And we know from the fragments we possess of the *Lyomenos* that such a reconciliation did take place.

What has led scholars astray is that, brought up on Plato, Aristotle, and Christian beliefs, they could not conceive of a god who grows up, learns lessons, and changes for the better, that the rude tyrant of the *Prometheus* would finally become lovable and good. They should have noticed that, in the *Oresteia*, a similar change of heart occurs. The Furies, the spirits of vengeance, by their own choice become the Eumenides, the ministers of blessing.

It is curious to me that, in both cases, it is the immortals who change their characters. In Homer or the tragedians, it seems to me that the mortals never do: they are what they are for better or worse. Hippolytus, for example, could not have sacrificed to Aphrodite without ceasing to be Hippolytus, or Pentheus become reconciled with Dionysus without ceasing to be Pentheus. It seems to me, though of course I may be wrong, that the ancient Greeks lacked the notion of what we mean by temptation, and that the reason for this is that they failed to make a distinction between will and desire. Thus one cannot call a Homeric hero brave, because one cannot imagine him feeling fear. It is not till Plato that the notion of human moral improvement appears, and even in Plato only the exceptional man can do it on his own.

How different is the world of Shakespeare. To the Greeks, suffering and misfortune are signs of the displeasure of the gods. In Shakespeare, both in his tragedies and his comedies, they are to be accepted, not as penalties for the particular sins of the sufferer, but as occasions for grace or as a process of purgation. Those who try to refuse suffering not only fail to avoid it but are plunged deeper into sin and sufferings. In the comedies, suffering leads to self-knowledge, repentance, forgiveness, love: in the tragedies to self-blindness, defiance, hatred. Thus there is no point before he actually murders Desdemona at which it would have been impossible for Othello to control his jealousy, discover the truth, and convert the tragedy into a comedy. Vice versa, there is no point in a comedy like *The Two Gentlemen of Verona* at which a wrong turning could not be taken and the conclusion be tragic.

I try to imagine what Shakespeare would have done had he written a tragedy about Oedipus. I think he would have opened with Oedipus taking two vows, never to strike a man in anger and never to marry. He would then put him in two situations, First, a man does him a great wrong; secondly he meets a woman and they both fall passionately in love. Shakespeare would then have shown us Oedipus arguing that the man could not possibly be his father, or the woman his mother, but in what he says the audience would perceive that he was rationalizing, that, in both cases, it was only too possible.

A Greek tragedy is the story of an exceptional man who falls from glory to ruin. His personal defect which brings this about is *hybris*, his belief that no misfortune can touch him, a defect which can only occur in someone who has hitherto been exceptionally fortunate. Consequently, when I watch or read a Greek tragedy, I identify myself with the chorus, never with the hero. A Shakespeare tragedy, however, is not only a feigned history but also a parable which has a significance for each one of us, irrespective of our station in life, for in Shakespeare the fatal flaw is pride, imagining that one is the only really unique person in the world, something which we all without exception do.

The fifth century BC was at first a period of intense curiosity and reexamination of tradition in civic, political, social, and religious conduct, and of the relation between law and nature. For this Professor Dodds suggests two causes.

> One was the growing complexity of the social and economic structure, which compelled the introduction of a multitude of new laws. These had no sanction of antiquity, and at Athens at least they were continually being changed. . . . The other was the widening of the Greek horizon which made possible the beginnings of comparative anthropology . . . Herodotus declared that we ought not to laugh at any people for thinking their own laws the best—which is a confession of the relativity of Law.

The Sophist Hippias said that law is a tyrant and thought that nationalism, created by custom, should be less binding than the international bond between fellow intellectuals. Antiphon thought that barbarians and Greeks were equally human, with the same natural needs, and that the requirements of the laws are most of them at war with nature. Alcidamas was the first Greek explicitly to condemn slavery.

Such "liberal" views, such faith in applied intelligence were, alas, short lived. Instead of social and political emancipation, there came civil wars, wars between cities, brutality, and dictatorships. Also, education was a costly luxury available only to the rich.

> This had its inevitable reaction on the character of the teaching. The Sophists depended for their livelihood upon their fees. . . . Hence demand exercised a dangerous control over supply. What such men as Protagoras would have liked to teach, if I understand them rightly, was simply the art of citizenship; what the discontented aristocrats of Athens required them to teach was something more specific—the art of acquiring personal power in a democratic society.

To speak of the individual only, ignoring the community, of nature only, ignoring law, can have fatal results.

> Suppose Nature whispers that democratic justice and obedience to the will of the people are also an arbitrary convention, that man was created free to be himself and push the weak to the wall. . . . Nature became the slogan of the robber-individual and robber-society, as "the survival of the fittest" was in the later nineteenth century and as "realism" is today.

History is a grim subject. As Lord Acton said: "Neither paganism nor Christianity ever produced a profound political historian whose mind was not turned to gloom by the contemplation of the affairs of men," for history seems to be largely dominated by the forces of unreason and by chance. In his earlier thinking, when he was concerned with the philosopher and not with the man in the street, Plato seems to have been a rationalist in the strict sense, someone, that is, who believed that all problems could be solved by reason alone, but he changed his mind.

> The less Plato cared for actual humanity, the more nobly he thought of the soul. The tension between the two was resolved for a time in the dream of a new Rule of the Saints, an élite of purified men who should unite the incompatible virtues of the Yogi and the Commissar, and thereby save not only themselves but also society. But when that illusion faded, Plato's underlying despair came more and more to the surface, translating itself into religious terms, until it found its logical expression in his final proposals for a Servile State, to be ruled not by

> the illuminated reason, but (under God) by custom and religious law. The "Yogi," with his faith in the possibility and necessity of intellectual conversion, did not wholly vanish even now, but he certainly retreated before the "Commissar" whose problem is the conditioning of human cattle. On this interpretation the pessimism of the Laws is not a senile aberration: it is the fruit of Plato's personal experience of life.

He even went so far as to speak of the "errant cause," alias "necessity," which shares with mind the responsibility for the constitution of the universe.

I don't quite understand what Professor Dodds means when he calls Euripides an irrationalist, because I don't see how irrationalism can be a conscious doctrine. We are all capable of behaving like madmen, but when we do so we are not conscious of what we are doing. Euripides had a deep respect for what is now called the unconscious and would probably second Blake, who declared:

> Energy is the only life, and is from the Body; and Reason is the bound or outward circumference of Energy.

The man who refuses to come to terms with his unconscious, to marry heaven and hell, who tries to "repress" his unconscious, will sooner or later be overwhelmed by it as Pentheus is destroyed by Dionysus. But Euripides' portrait of Dionysus is not a pretty one, and I cannot see him personally taking part in a Dionysian orgy, any more than I can imagine him, had he lived in Germany during the 1930s, becoming a Nazi.

There are two chapters which I do not find myself competent to discuss properly. The first is on Plotinus, but I have never yet read the *Enneads*, though I certainly shall when I get the chance. I was fascinated to learn that Plotinus was the first man to make a verbal distinction between the ego and the psyche.

The second, the last and longest, is about supernatural phenomena in classical antiquity. In this case, I must confess that psychical research is not my cup of tea. I have no doubt that phenomena like ESP, telepathy, clairvoyance, and precognition occur, but they seldom seem able to do anything really useful like predicting the result of the Derby. In modern times most people, I suppose, who consult mediums wish to communicate with some dead loved one, but if the afterlife is anything like the drivel mediums talk, I don't want to hear about it. Luckily for them, the ancients believed that only the unquiet dead, those who had died untimely or by violence, were earthbound and available, so their company was not desired, except by necromancers who wished to do harm.

The ancients seem to have had no words for telepathy or clairvoyance: what interested them most was precognition, obtained by examining entrails, divining by lots, consulting mediums or oracles, and in dreams or ecstatic states. They did not have a crystal ball, but they did have what Professor Dodds calls "scryers," brightly lit mirrors or water into which oil had been poured, and, in AD 371, there is mention of an instrument very like a ouija board. Both then and today there seem to be cases of mediums who can reveal the whereabouts of lost objects. There appears to be one now living in Holland who is consulted by the police to locate missing corpses.

But enough. This is a fascinating volume.

The New York Review of Books, 28 June 1973

Praiseworthy

The Church Hymnary: Third Edition. Oxford. £1.40.

Though commissioned by the Presbyterian Churches of Scotland, England and Ireland, this hymnbook contains nothing, either doctrinally or liturgically, which even the highest Anglican will find unacceptable. There are, for example, no references to Predestination. If I were a parish priest or a church organist, I would do my utmost to persuade my congregation and choir to accept it. It is infinitely superior to either *Hymns Ancient and Modern* or *The English Hymnal.*

To begin with, it is much better organised. In their Introduction the editors say:

> Since a Church hymnal is essentially a liturgical book, the Committee, in determining the order in which the hymns are arranged, has borne in mind that the Order of Holy Communion is normative for worship in the Reformed Church . . . The central act of Christian worship from the beginning was understood as a unity, the structure of which involved a double action: (a) the "Liturgy of the Word" based on the reading and exposition of the Scriptures; and (b) the "Liturgy of the Faithful", sometimes called "the Liturgy of the Upper Room"—that is, the Holy Communion or Lord's Supper.

Accordingly, they have divided their book into eight sections, entitled "Approach to God", "The Word of God: His Mighty Acts", "Response to the Word of God", "The Sacraments" (i.e. Baptism and Holy Communion), "Other Ordinances" (e.g. Confirmation, Marriage, Funeral Services), "Times and Seasons", "Close of Service" and "Personal Faith and Devotion". In each section, hymns intended for children are printed last. Moreover, they have not confined themselves to hymns in the usual sense: the Sacrament section, for instance, includes the Apostles' Creed, the Nicene Creed, the Sanctus, the Benedictus and the Agnus Dei. (I'm sorry they have not included that excellent poem, the Athanasian Creed.) Though, as I said, I hope many Anglican churches will adopt it, I think we shall need our Psaltery as well. It is the custom in the Presbyterian Church to sing rhymed metrical versions of the Psalms. Consequently, of the seventy-nine Psalms the editors print, only twenty-two are given in the unrhymed Biblical form to which we are accustomed to chant them.

A digression. Since I was brought up on it, I resent any alterations to Coverdale, but then, since I know no Hebrew, I do not notice when he mistranslates. Thus, I understand that the phrase, "because of the noise in the water-pipes" really means the noise, presumably faint, made by underground streams in a limestone country. But when I was young it gave the organist such a wonderful opportunity to make his instrument roar.

In saying that I think we shall need our Psaltery, I do not mean that I do not welcome the Scotch and French-Genevan metrical versions. I was first introduced to them when, as a prep-school master in Scotland, I had to escort the boys to church on Sunday, and I well remember how enormously impressed I was by both the text and the tune of the metrical version of Psalm 124, "Now Israel may say, and that truly".

The editors have only made two "modernisations" to which I strongly object. In one version of the Lord's Prayer, they have "Our Father who art in Heaven". Why? Nobody can ever have thought that the pronoun *which* meant that God is neuter. Then, they open the Nicene Creed (but not the Apostles' Creed) with *We believe* instead of *I believe.* We may be all right for children, but an adult has to accept personal responsibility for his Faith. At least, though, they have not dropped the term *Holy Ghost* as some "with-it" congregations now do, presumably on the theory that a child might imagine the Third Person of the Trinity to be some kind of spook. But could not a child equally well imagine the *Holy Spirit* to be some kind of hard liquor?

There is one problem which confronts anybody in our age who is compiling a hymnbook, namely, the fact that social and historical changes have made certain kinds of imagery, which in earlier times were perfectly acceptable, embarrassing. Thus, in hymns of adoration, it has become impossible to use the court language of an absolute monarch. A phrase like *By prostrate spirits day and night / Incessantly adored* now sounds slightly comic. In our age, the more we love and reverence someone, the less likely we are to give them titles: those we reserve for officials. Modern warfare has become so horrible and ignoble, that military metaphors as in "Onward Christian Soldiers" are now impossible.

The trouble about reviewing a hymnbook is that the music is just as important as the words, but in a literary periodical one cannot give musical quotations. I can only say that those responsible for the music have shown extraordinary scholarship and good taste. There are all kinds of composers, ancient and modern—Gelineau, for instance—of whom I had never heard, but who have written excellent tunes. I was afraid, because contemporary musical taste is apt to look down on them, that "Victorian" composers like John Bacchus Dykes and W. H. Monk might have been omitted, but, thank goodness, they are still there.

For a book of this size, and one which is beautifully printed as well, £1.40 seems in these days extraordinarily cheap. I only hope this means that a great many people will buy it.

New Statesman, 29 June 1973

Responses to the Near East

Flaubert in Egypt: A Sensibility on Tour. A Narrative Drawn from Gustave Flaubert's *Travel Notes and Letters.* Translated from the French and edited by Francis Steegmuller. Little, Brown. $8.50.

There is no doubt whatever that, both as translator and as editor, Mr. Francis Steegmuller has done an excellent job on *Flaubert in Egypt: A Sensibility on Tour*, but I strongly suspect that Flaubert would disapprove of his efforts. The greater part of the book consists of extracts from travel diaries kept by Flaubert and his companion, Maxime du Camp. In the case of the latter, this presents no problem, since he himself published them. But when he suggested to Flaubert that he do likewise, Flaubert did not agree:

> He rejected my advice, saying that travel, like the humanities, should serve only to "enliven one's style," and that incidents gleaned abroad might be used in a novel, but not in a straight account. Travel writings were to him the same as news items, he said, a low form of literature, and he had higher aspirations.

As a rule, I believe, a writer's wishes should be respected. There are exceptions, of course, and perhaps Flaubert's journal is one of them, for it certainly makes interesting reading. But his letters to his friend Louis Bouilhet raise serious problems of taste, and had I been Mr Steegmuller I would have made extensive cuts in them. To me, one of the most distressing symptoms of the contemporary cultural scene is the blurring, almost the obliteration, of the distinction between the private and the public life. In writing a private letter to an intimate friend of the same sex, it is natural if a man tells of his sexual adventures and employs the four-letter words, but I cannot imagine anyone wanting such descriptions to be read by the general public. Certainly not Flaubert. His early readers may have been shocked by the plot and characters of *Madame Bovary*, but not by its language or imagery.

In 1849, at the age of twenty-seven, Flaubert was going through a difficult period. His father, his sister, and a close friend, Alfred Le Poittevin, had all recently died, his first draft of *La Tentation de Saint-Antoine* had turned out a fiasco, and he had no precise ideas as to what he should write next. He did, it seems, think of the name Madame Bovary while in Egypt—a name adapted from that of a hotelkeeper in Cairo—but, as Mr Steegmuller says:

> [She was] not Emma Bovary as we know her, but the heroine of the story imagined in Blois or of, simply, whatever provincial novel he might write.

It was not until after his return to France that Louis Bouilhet suggested that he base his novel on the life story of Delaunay, and Flaubert immediately assented.

It is evident from both his notebooks and his letters that during his travels Flaubert suffered frequently from depressions and doubts about his future as a writer:

> What is it, oh Lord, this permanent lassitude that I drag about with me? . . . Deianira's tunic was no less completely welded to Hercules' back than boredom to my life.

> As for me, I think about what I have always thought about—literature; I try to take hold of everything I see; I'd like to imagine something. But what, I don't know. It seems to me that I have become utterly stupid.

> Am I about to enter a new period? Or is it the beginning of complete decadence? And from the past I go dreaming into the future, where I see nothing, nothing. I have no plans, no idea, no project, and, what is worse, no ambition.

> The thing we all lack is not style, nor the dexterity of finger and bow known as talent. We have a large orchestra, a rich palette, a variety of resources. We know many more tricks and dodges, probably, than were ever known before. No, what we lack is the intrinsic principle, the soul of the thing, the very idea of the subject. We take notes, we make journeys: emptiness! emptiness! We become scholars, archeologists, historians, doctors, cobblers, people of taste. What is the good of all that? Where is the heart, the verve, the sap? Where to start out from? Where to go?

His low spirits may have been partly due, I suspect, to his being separated from his mother. The relation between them seems to have been too close and emotional to be healthy:

> The next day, Thursday—atrocious day, the worst I have ever spent. I was not supposed to leave until the day after the next, but I decided to go at once; it was unbearable. Endless strolls with my mother in the little garden. I set my departure for five; the clock seemed to stand still. I put

> my hat in the living room and sent my trunk on ahead to the station; it would take me only a minute to get there.
>
> Finally I got away. My mother was sitting in an armchair beside the fire, and in the midst of caressing her and talking with her I suddenly kissed her on the forehead, rushed from the room, seized my hat, and ran out of the house. How she screamed when I closed the door of the living room behind me! It reminded me of her scream just after the death of my father, when she took his hand.

He keeps speaking with loving nostalgia of his study in her house, which he had left exactly as though he were going to return the next day, with the book he had been reading open on the table and his dressing gown thrown over a chair, and when, in a letter, she suggests that he might take a job on his return, a main reason for refusing is that they would be separated.

Their relation in part explains Flaubert's fascination with brothels, where sex could be divorced from emotion. Indeed, one would not have been surprised if it had made him a homosexual, though it did not. In a letter to Louis Bouilhet, he tells of going to bed with a *bardash*, or boy prostitute. Sartre, Mr Steegmuller informs us, wrote an article in which he argues that this was impossible, but, from what one knows about Flaubert's character, I would say that he was a man who would try anything once.

On the whole, Flaubert and du Camp got along together very well, though there seem to have been a few difficult moments. Du Camp was a passionate photographer—Flaubert did not share his interest—and a very nervous one, who went into a tizzy if his pictures failed to come out right, which must sometimes have been rather trying for his companion. Vice versa, on one occasion it was du Camp who lost his temper. During a particularly difficult trip in scorching weather, with nothing to drink, Flaubert kept talking about the lemon ice at Tortoni's. Du Camp suggested that they change the subject, but it was no good:

> I knew Gustave. I knew that nothing could stop him when he was in the grip of one of his morbid obsessions, and I made no further reply, hoping that my silence would silence him. But he began again, and seeing that I didn't answer he began to shout, "Lemon ice! Lemon ice!" I was at the end of my tether and had a horrible thought: "I'll kill him!" I said to myself. I drew my dromedary up close beside him and took his arm: "Where do you want to ride? Ahead or behind?" He answered, "I'll go ahead." I reined in my dromedary, and when our little troop was two hundred paces ahead of me I resumed my way.

But such contretemps were rare. Perhaps the very difference in their temperaments helped to make them good travelling companions. Du Camp was physically hyperactive; Flaubert would have liked to travel stretched out on a sofa and not stirring, watching landscapes and cities pass by before his eyes. Both were given commissions by the French government which would recommend them to French officials in Egypt: du Camp was charged by the Institut de France to take photographs and "squeezes," Flaubert by the Ministry of Agriculture and Commerce to collect information that might interest it—a task that he seems to have totally ignored.

They landed in Alexandria and went on to Cairo, from which they visited the Pyramids, then up the Nile to Wadi Haifa via Esna (where Flaubert had an affair with a famous courtesan, Kuchuk Hanem), on to Luxor and Kara, then across the desert to the Red Sea, and finally back to Cairo.

To illustrate their respective styles of description, I must limit myself to three examples, the first two by Flaubert, the last by du Camp:

> Return to Wadi Haifa in the dinghy, with Maxime. Little Mohammed is as he was this morning. We are rocked by the wind and the waves; night falls; the waves slap the bow of our dinghy, and it pitches, the moon rises. In the position in which I was sitting, it was shining on my right leg and the portion of my white sock that was between my trouser and my shoe.

> A caravan passes us coming the other way; the men swathed in *kufiyehs* [head-cloths] (the women are thickly veiled) lean forward on the necks of their dromedaries; they pass very close to us, no one speaks; it is like a meeting of ghosts amid clouds. I feel something like terror and furious admiration creep along my spine; I laugh nervously; I must have been very pale, and my enjoyment of the moment was intense. As the caravan passed, it seemed to me that the camels were not touching the ground, that they were breasting ahead with a shiplike movement, that inside the dust cloud they were raised high above the ground, as though they were wading belly-deep in clouds.

> Every time I visited a monument I had my photographic apparatus carried along and took with me one of my sailors, Hadji Ismael, an extremely handsome Nubian, whom I had climb up onto the ruins which I wanted to photograph. In this way I was always able to include a uniform scale of proportions. The great difficulty was to get Hadji Ismael to stand perfectly motionless while I performed my operations; and I finally succeeded by means of a trick whose success will convey the depth of naïveté of these poor Arabs. I told him that the brass tube of the lens jutting from the camera was a cannon, which would vomit a hail of shot if he had the misfortune to move—a story which immobilized him completely, as can be seen from my plates.

Yet, interesting and articulate as these two companions can be, my depressing conclusion, after reading this book, is that neither of them was a nice character. When I read Mario Praz's *The Romantic Agony*, in which he discusses the influence on many nineteenth-century writers of the Marquis de Sade, I thought his thesis a little far-fetched. Now I think I see what he was driving at. Compared with France, Egypt at the time of their visit was a country of fantastic brutality. There were incessant cudgellings, castrations of slaves for harems, tortures like the bastinado, and nailing dishonest shopkeepers by the ears to their shops, and ceremonies like the *Doseh*, in which, Flaubert writes:

> a man on horseback rides his mount over the backs of a number of other men stretched out on the ground like dogs. This celebration is repeated at certain times of the year, in Cairo only, in memory and as perpetuation of the miracle performed by a certain Moslem saint who rode his horse into Cairo over earthenware jars without breaking them. The *cadi* who reënacts this ceremony cannot hurt the prostrate men, just as the saint didn't break the jars. If the men die, it is due to their sins.

There is no reason whatsoever to suppose that Flaubert and du Camp were either practicing sadists or masochists, like Swinburne. It is natural, too, that, as tourists, they should be interested in such spectacles. But what shocks me is their "objectivity": never do they show the least signs of disapproval or disgust.

Much as I admire Flaubert the Novelist, particularly for his *L'Education Sentimentale* and *Bouvard et Pécuchet* (I was curious to discover that the 1911 edition of the *Encyclopædia Britannica* takes a dim view of the latter), I have reluctantly come to the conclusion that Flaubert the Man is somebody I would have run miles to avoid meeting.

The New Yorker, 2 July 1973

Books Which Mean Much to Me

Though I shall only mention books which mean much to me, a person's reasons for reading can be so various that I cannot confine myself to a single volume.

For example, one can read in order to learn something new. Thus, I do not subscribe to any literary periodical but I do take the *Scientific American*. What one seeks to learn need not necessarily be pleasant. I cannot ima-gine anyone enjoying *Black Like Me* by John Howard Griffin, but I think every white American should read it. There is a substance which, when injected into the skin, darkens the pigmentation so that a white man can pass for a black one: when the injections are discontinued, he regains his normal color. These injections the author took and in his book he describes his experiences in the Deep South as a Pseudo-Negro. It's pretty grim reading.

Then there are reference books which one consults to check up on facts, As a poet writing in English, I could not live without the thirteen-volume *O.E.D.*, and have two copies, one in Oxford, one in Austria. I also find the 1911 edition of the *Encyclopaedia Britannica* extremely useful.

Then there are books to browse in. Because of their great length and the nature of their subject matter, one cannot read them straight through from cover to cover but, opening them at random, one can be sure of finding something interesting. For me the greatest of all "browse" books is Mayhew's *History of the London Poor.* Mayhew was, without any doubt, the finest reporter who ever lived. Reading his interviews with poor persons of both sexes and various occupations, a ten-year-old boy, a man who combed the sewers for coins, the Queen's rat-catcher, a kept woman, a street prostitute, etc., it is difficult to believe that they were not tape-recorded, so exactly does he catch the tone of voice, the vocabulary and speech idiosyncracies of each. My next favorite browse is, I think, Thoreau's *Journals*, which I find endlessly fascinating. A book somewhat similar in subject matter is Gilbert White's *Natural History of Selbourne*, but this is small enough to read straight through, and I do so every year. Another is Anthony Collett's *The Changing Face of England*, but I should hesitate to recommend it to an American reader, since, to appreciate it to the full, one must have, as I do, a great love for the English countryside, so well-cared-for and well-mannered. As a rule I find American "Nature" too raw and untamed for my taste.

Lastly, of course, there are the self-contained worlds of fiction and poetry, which one reads solely for pleasure. Aside from whodunits, I am not an avid reader of fiction, but there are three English novelists whom I can always reread. The first is Anthony Trollope. His charm for me is probably nostalgia for the past, since the world I lived in as a child before 1914 was in all essentials the world of Barchester. The other two are both creators of imaginary and comic Edens where nothing serious can happen, Ronald Firbank and the E. F. Benson of the *Lucia* novels. The latter deal with the social and cultural goings-on of two rival blue-stockings in an English village. There are six of them, all available in Signet Books and, much as I dislike the medium, I think they would make an ideal T.V. serial. I thought at first they might be too "British" for American readers, but so far every single American of either sex whom I have introduced to them has fallen in love with them.

Naturally, I read a lot of poetry, but not much of it is contemporary. To express one's admiration of the great geniuses like Dante and Shakespeare would be superfluous, since one's reasons for admiring them are obvious. I shall, therefore, finish these reflections by naming four poets, none of them, perhaps, major poets, who are personal pets of mine, whose poems I treasure and whom I wish I could have known personally. They are Thomas Campion, George Herbert, William Barnes and Edward Thomas.

Mademoiselle, September 1973

A Russian with Common Sense

The Letters of Anton Chekhov. Selected and edited by Avrahm Yamolinsky. Viking. $15.

No two sensibilities, in both social and artistic matters, could be more foreign to each other than the British and the Russian. (America and Russia are much more akin.) The only British novel I can imagine having been written in Russian is James Hogg's *Confessions of a Justified Sinner*, and the only Russian I can imagine writing in English is the author of what Avrahm Yarmolinsky, as editor and translator, has assembled for the Viking Press in *The Letters of Anton Chekhov.* There is no exact equivalent in any other language, so far as I know, for the term "common sense." Historically a creation of 1688, it implies a distrust of all enthusiasm and excess, of fanaticism, whether religious or political, and of lack of self-control in personal behavior. Tolstoy and Dostoevski are great geniuses, but common sense is not a quality they exhibit. Speaking of *The Kreutzer Sonata*, Chekhov complains of

> the audacity with which Tolstoy discourses on what he knows nothing about and what, out of stubbornness, he does not want to understand. Thus, his judgments on syphilis, on foundling asylums, on women's abhorrence of copulation, etc., not only can be controverted but also are a direct exposure of a man who is ignorant, who throughout the course of his long life had never gone to the trouble of reading two or three books written by specialists.

Or again:

> Shrewdness and justice tell me that there is greater love for man in electricity and steam than in continence and abstention from meat. War is an evil and law is an evil, but it does not follow that I must needs go about in bast sandals and sleep atop the oven with the hired hand and his wife.

Turgenev is much more levelheaded, but his portraits of women are often grotesque:

> All of Turgenev's women and girls are unbearably contrived and, forgive the term, false, except Bazarov's mother, and mothers generally, especially society ladies. . . . Liza, Yelena, are not Russian girls, but some sort of Pythias, vaticinating, abounding in pretensions not befitting their

rank. Irina in *Smoke* and Odintzova in *Fathers and Children*, generally lionesses, volcanic, seductive, insatiable, questing for something, all of them are rubbish.

With Chekhov's description of how cultured people should behave, Jane Austen would have been in complete agreement. (He is writing to a brother who was an alcoholic.) Cultured people, he writes,

> do not raise a rumpus over a hammer or a lost eraser. . . . They respect the property of others and therefore pay their debts. They are candid and dread lying as they dread fire. . . . They do not belittle themselves to arouse compassion in others. . . . They cannot fall asleep in their clothes, see the cracks in the wall full of insects, breathe foul air, walk on a spittle-covered floor, eat off a kerosene stove. They seek as far as possible to tame and ennoble the sexual instinct. . . . They do not swill vodka offhand. . . . They drink only when they are free, on occasion. For they need *mens sana in corpore sano.*

Such a way of life was evidently not his experience in childhood, for in a letter to another brother he says:

> Despotism and lying mangled our childhood to such a degree that one feels queasy and fearful in recalling it. Remember the horror and revulsion we felt when at dinner Father would raise hell over the soup being too salty or curse out Mother as a fool.

His chief criticism of his fellow-countrymen is that they lack good manners and a work ethic:

> We, so the newspapers say, love our great country, but how is that love expressed? Instead of knowledge—inordinate brazenness and conceit; instead of work—laziness and swinishness; there is no justice; the concept of honor does not go beyond "the honor of the uniform." . . . What is needed is work; everything else can go to the devil. The main thing is to be just—the rest will be added unto us.

Then, among Russian writers, Chekhov seems to have been the only one who understood the everyday role of money in social relations. Indeed, his sole rival anywhere is Trollope. Like the latter, Chekhov's father had been a bankrupt, and from quite early on he himself had had to send part of his meagre earnings to help out his family. But he never became either a miser or a spendthrift, and when, in later life, his financial situation became easier, he was most generous in helping those less fortunate than he. When his friend A. S. Suvorin offered him a loan so that he could buy some property, he replied:

> Should the purchase go through, I shall take advantage of your offer and accept fifteen hundred rubles from you, but please only on condition,

> an indispensable one, that you will regard this sum as a usual debt; that is, without regard to kinship or friendship. You will not interfere with my liquidating it, without allowing me any rebates or concessions. Otherwise, this debt of mine will put me in a position such as you can guess. . . . When I was beginning to work for *New Times* . . . I promised myself to write as often as possible in order to get more—and there is nothing bad about this. But when we became better acquainted and when you became an intimate friend, my sensitiveness reared. . . . I began to fear that our relationship might be darkened by someone's thinking that I needed you as a publisher, not as a human being, etc., etc. All this is foolish, offensive, and only proves that I attribute great importance to money, but I cannot help it. . . . I was born, grew up, was schooled, and began writing in an environment in which money played a shockingly large part.

Chekhov would probably never have become so sane a writer if he had not also practiced medicine. For him there was no nonsense about the Two Cultures:

> Anatomy and belles lettres have an equally illustrious origin, the very same goals, the very same enemy—the devil—and they have absolutely nothing to wage war about. . . . If a man knows the theory of the circulation of the blood he is rich; if, over and beyond that, he masters the history of religion and the lyric "A wondrous moment I recall," he becomes not poorer but richer; ergo, what we are dealing with is only pluses.

> I don't doubt that the study of the medical sciences seriously affected my literary work; they significantly enlarged the field of my observations, enriched me with knowledge, the true value of which for me as a writer can be understood only by one who is himself a physician; they also had a directive influence, and, probably because I was close to medicine, I avoided many mistakes. Acquaintance with the natural sciences, with the scientific method, kept me always on my guard, and I tried, wherever possible, to bring my writings into harmony with scientific data, and where this was impossible, I preferred not to write at all.

In his assessment of the political and social problems of his time, Chekhov was neither a reactionary nor a revolutionary: essentially, he was an apolitical who believed in what are now called the Liberal Values. He could not share the Populists' romantic idealization of the village commune, or *obshchina*:

> The *obshchina* lives by agriculture, but when agriculture begins to be affected by technological culture, it falls to pieces, for the *obshchina* and technological culture are incompatible concepts. By the way, the *obshchina* is responsible for our nationwide drinking and profound ignorance.

And he took a dim view of the intelligentsia as a group:

> As long as it is made up of students, young men and women, they are fine, honorable people, our hope, Russia's future; but no sooner do these students strike out on their own, become adults, than our hope and Russia's future go up in smoke, and all that remains in the filter are dacha-owning doctors, greedy officials, and thievish engineers. . . . I do not believe in our intelligentsia, hypocritical, insincere, hysterical, uncultivated, lethargic; I don't believe in them even when they suffer and complain, for their oppressors emerge from their own viscera. I believe in individuals. I see a hope for salvation from distinct personalities scattered here and there throughout Russia—be they intellectuals or peasants, they are a power, though few in number.

He was perhaps overly optimistic about the capacity of the sciences to insure social progress, but nobody in his time could have possibly foreseen some of the consequences of applied science.

Most of the great letter-writers have been persons, like Horace Walpole, for whom writing letters was their natural mode of literary expression. The average novelist or playwright or poet, preoccupied with his particular medium, seldom writes letters except out of necessity. Chekhov is one of the happy exceptions. When one remembers that he was a prolific author, it is astounding that he should have taken the time and trouble to write so many long and entertaining letters as he did.

As I read them, some things have surprised me. Firstly, his extreme diffidence and doubts about the value of his work, not only when he was a young man but throughout his life. He keeps saying that he doesn't think he is really a dramatist and that his stories are boring, despite the fact that he became well known quite early, for when he was only twenty-eight he received half of the Pushkin Prize. As a rule, self-denigration is really a demand for flattery, but I am sure that in his case it was not. Some of his early work may have had only an ephemeral value, yet his major works are so obviously masterpieces that his doubts seem very odd. I knew, of course, that he died of tuberculosis, but I never knew before how much he had suffered all his life from ill health. He had his first serious hemorrhage in 1897, but he had found blood in his sputum as early as 1884. In addition, he kept being plagued by a number of physical, or psychosomatic, ailments—migraines, hemorrhoids, bowel trouble, irregular pulse, and so on.

His most fascinating letters, I feel, and I am sure many readers will agree, are those he wrote in 1890 about his trip through Siberia to visit the penal colony of Sakhalin, on which he wrote a long report. He had already developed a great talent for the description of nature. Here is a passage from a letter written in 1888.

> Imagine yourself perched on a mountain eight thousand feet high. Now please walk, in your mind, to the edge of the abyss and look down, far down. You see a narrow floor, along which a little white ribbon is twisting—the white-haired, grumbling Aragva. Before you see it, little clouds, groves, ravines, rocks, meet your gaze. Now lift your eyes a bit and look ahead of you: mountains, mountains, mountains, and on them insects—cows and human beings. Look up, and there is a terrifyingly deep sky. A fresh mountain breeze blows.

But the landscape and inhabitants of Siberia, so utterly unlike anything he had seen before, made him write even more vividly:

> On entering a Siberian bedroom at night, you are not assailed by the peculiar Russian stench. True, handing me a teaspoon, an old woman wiped it on her behind, but then they will not serve you tea without a tablecloth, people don't belch in your presence, don't search for insects in their hair; when they hand you water or milk, they don't put their fingers in the glass; the plates and dishes are clean, kvas is as transparent as beer.

> The inhabitants don't observe the fasts, and eat meat even during Passion Week; the girls smoke cigarettes and the crones smoke pipes—that's the accepted thing. It's strange, at times, to see peasant women with cigarettes. And what liberalism! Ah, what liberalism!

> The air on board the steamer becomes red-hot from the talk. People aren't afraid to speak out here. There is no one to make arrests and no place to which to transport anyone—play the liberal to your heart's content. . . . There are no secret denunciations. A fugitive political can go freely by steamer all the way to the ocean without any fear of the captain turning him in. This laissez-faire can also be explained in part by the total indifference to everything that is going on in Russia. Everyone says, "What's it to me?"

On Sakhalin itself, he had to work like a dog. He was not allowed to meet any of the political prisoners, but he interviewed some ten thousand convicts. His experiences were grim. He was present at a flogging, which gave him nightmares. But what distressed him most was the condition of the children:

> I saw hungry children, thirteen-year-old girls who were prostitutes, fifteen-year-old pregnant girls. Girls start in as prostitutes at the age of twelve, sometimes before menstruation. Church and school exist only on paper; it is the convict environment, the convict setup that shape the children. . . . I did not find any contagious diseases in Sakhalin; there is

> very little inherited syphilis, but I saw blind children, filthy, covered with sores—all conditions caused by negligence.
>
> Of course, I shall not settle the problem of the children. I do not know what should be done. It seems to me that charity and remnants of sums allotted to prisons and the like will not do. I believe it is wrong to rely on philanthropy, which in Russia is fortuitous, and on remnants which don't materialize. I prefer the State Treasury.

In 1892, cholera broke out in the country district where he lived. With characteristic decency, Chekhov immediately put literature aside and devoted himself to looking after the peasants. This meant considerable financial hardship for him, since he refused to accept any remuneration for his services. He had no assistants and had to act simultaneously as physician and as medical orderly, and spend a great deal of time begging from the rich for funds—an activity at which he seems to have been successful. The area he serviced included twenty-five villages, four factories, and a monastery, so one can imagine how exhausted he must have got.

How typical, too, of the man that he should have been immediately convinced of Dreyfus's innocence—a conviction in which he never wavered, even though it led to an estrangement with his lifelong friend Suvorin. Then, in a very late letter, he writes to Sholom Aleichem:

> As for my published stories, they are wholly at your disposal, and their translation into Yiddish and their publication in a collection for the benefit of the Jews victimized in Kishinev would give me nothing but heartfelt pleasure.

My, what a nice person!

In his introduction, Mr Yarmolinsky tells us that the Soviet authorities have censored surprisingly little, and then more often for reasons of prudery than of ideology. I myself disapprove of the publication of anybody's love letters, but in what I at first assumed to be a complete edition of Chekhov's letters it would, I suppose, be necessary to include all the letters (there are seventy-five in this book) he wrote to his mistress, later his wife—the actress Olga Knipper. These are not in the least shy-making—they are most high-spirited—but to me, at any rate, they are very repetitious. After reading two or three with great enjoyment, I felt that I had read them all. But I find I was wrong in thinking that Mr Yarmolinsky had translated the complete letters, and he did not in fact need to print so many letters to Olga Knipper. Yet this is a very minor matter. His volume makes wonderful reading.

The New Yorker, 3 September 1973

"I have a ferocious bee in my bonnet"

I have a ferocious bee in my bonnet that is enraged by contemporary liturgical reforms and new translations of the Bible. As an Episcopalian, I was brought up on the *King James Bible* and the *Book of Common Prayer* of 1662. Both were composed at exactly the right moment, when the English language had already become more or less what it is today, so that they are no more difficult to follow than Shakespeare, but the ecclesiastics of that time still possessed a feeling for the ritual and ceremonious which today we have almost entirely lost.

No one praying "Our Father which art in heaven" will think that the relative pronoun means that God is neuter. Nor, reading "Though I speak with the tongues of angels and have not charity" will think that Charity means what it means today. If uncertain, he has only to consult a dictionary. To replace the term, as modern versions do, by *Love* not only blurs the distinction between *agape* and *eros* but also uses a word which in our culture has become totally debased. Again, some with-it congregations have now dropped the title "The Holy Ghost," presumably on the theory that some child might imagine the Third Person of the Trinity to be some kind of Spook. But why should a child not imagine that "The Holy Spirit" was some kind of hard liquor?

It is only since this liturgical reform nonsense started that I came to realize why, when Thomas Cranmer introduced the liturgy in the vernacular, there were riots. I have come to the conclusion that we Episcopalians should have done the exact opposite of the Roman Catholics and said: "Henceforth we will recite the *Book of Common Prayer* in Latin." (There happens to be an excellent translation.) The Rite, as distinct from the Ministry of the Word (that is, lessons from the Bible and sermons), is the link between the dead and the unborn. This calls for a timeless language which, in practice, means a dead language. This, until recently, Roman Catholicism, the Orthodox Churches, Orthodox Judaism, and Islam have understood. (For the first Christians, of course, language was no problem, because they expected the Parousia to occur in their lifetime.)

There is another area of church life, however, where I believe reform is urgently needed, and nothing is being done. There is, as Lichtenberg said, a great difference between believing something *still* and believing it *again.* The transition can never have been easy and in our time it is seldom made without a hiatus of disbelief. To confirm children sometime between the ages of eleven and fourteen, as the Roman Catholics and Episcopalians usually do, is absurd, for no child is capable of making a personal commitment. I think that, as in the Orthodox churches, babies should be admitted to Communion after Baptism, but that Confirmation should be postponed until a person is sufficiently sure of his or her identity to say "I believe" with assurance, and today this will seldom occur before the age of twenty or more.

Vogue, October 1973

An Odd Ball in an Odd Country at an Odd Time

St John of the Cross: His Life and Poetry. By Gerald Brenan, with a translation of the poetry by Lynda Nicholson. Cambridge University Press. $11.95.

Nobody has done more to arouse an interest in Spanish literature among English-speaking readers than Mr Brenan. His scholarship is impeccable and his prose style felicitous.

Spain in the fifteenth and sixteenth centuries was a very strange country and I am very glad I didn't have to live in it. First, there was the Jewish Problem. When the rule of Islam was over, a good many Jews, whether out of conviction or for worldly reasons, were baptized and became known as the New Christians. By the middle of the fifteenth century they had become the Spanish middle class.

> They controlled the silk and cloth industry, they collected the royal and ecclesiastical revenues and many of the best offices in the church, notably the canonries, were filled by them. The judges, lawyers, doctors and apothecaries came mostly from their ranks and a contemporary account gives them as numbering one third of the population in the larger cities.

(The only disability they seem to have suffered under was that they were forbidden to bear arms.) Consequently, they were more hated by the masses than those who had kept their Jewish faith.

Recent research has uncovered an interesting story. St Teresa's grandfather, Juan Sánchez de Cepeda, a prosperous merchant, suddenly announced his conversion to Judaism and apostatized along with his wife and children. Soon after, a tribunal of the Inquisition was set up in Toledo. Faced with the alternative of returning to the Church or being burned at the stake, he not unnaturally chose the former. Why did he renounce Christianity in the first place? Mr Brenan suggests that, at the time, it was physically safer to be a Jew than a New Christian. In several cities there had been riots in which the merchant quarter had been sacked, while the Jewish quarter was left untouched. It is also probable, though not proven, that St John of the Cross was partly Jewish. His uncles had been in the silk trade.

Secondly, there were in Spain in the fifteenth and sixteenth centuries the extraordinarily complicated goings-on in the Carmelite order, and it is with these that Mr Brenan's book is mostly concerned. The first positive information about them comes from a Greek monk called Phocas, who visited Mount Carmel in 1185 and found a community of anchorites living there in seclusion and great austerity. In 1258, when the Saracens were closing in, most of them emigrated, a great many to England.

The Carmelites expanded rapidly in Spain, but began to find their rule too austere, and in 1432 Pope Eugenius gave them a milder one which was general until, in 1562, St Teresa founded a reformed branch, emphasizing poverty, fasting, and prayer. The laxer branch became known as Calced Carmelites, St Teresa's as Discalced. The history of the relations between them, the feuds, the intrigues would make a fascinating if very depressing movie. Much depended upon the attitude of the authorities in Italy. The Carmelite General Rubeo, who had first been in favor of the reform, turned against it. The papal nuncio Ormaneto backed it, but then he died and his successor, Sega, was strongly prejudiced against it and gave his support to Rubeo's emissary, Tostado, who placed all Carmelite houses under the direction of the Calced.

In October, 1577, there was a terrible scene.

> Teresa's term as prioress had lapsed, her successor had come and gone and now a third choice had to be made. There were two parties among the nuns—the strict party who wanted Teresa back and the lax party who wanted someone else. Tostado sent down the provincial to superintend the affair with instructions to make sure that the Calced candidate was elected, and he, thinking he could best secure this by frightening the nuns, threatened to excommunicate any of them who should vote for Teresa. But in spite of this, fifty-five of them, encouraged by Fray Juan de la Cruz's exhortations, declared their intention to vote for her, and they formed a majority. . . . The provincial took his stand by the grille, abusing and excommunicating those nuns who voted contrary to his wishes and striking, crumpling and burning their voting papers. But even this did not produce the effect that he wanted. He therefore gave orders that none of the recalcitrant nuns should attend mass or enter the chapel or see either their confessors or their parents until they had voted as he desired. When they once again refused to do this he declared the election null and void, excommunicated them a second time and appointed the nun who had obtained the lesser number of votes as prioress.

Fray Juan de la Cruz's role in this was not forgotten, and in December he was arrested and cast into prison. Before describing his experiences there, I should say something about his early career.

He was born in 1542 and baptized under the name of Juan de Yepes y Alvarez. His father, Gonzalo de Yepes, orphaned at an early age, was brought up by his uncles who were in the silk trade, joined them and seemed all set for a prosperous career, but then he fell in love with a poor silk weaver, Catalina Alvarez, and married her. Outraged, his uncles cut him off. He became a silk weaver himself and died twelve years later, leaving his widow and three sons in great poverty. Juan seems to have inherited from him an indifference to worldly success: what the father was prepared to sacrifice for Eros, the son was prepared to sacrifice for Agape.

His mother could not support him and he was placed in an orphanage, where he was taught to read and write. Attempts were made to train him for some manual job, but he proved totally incompetent. He spent some time working in a hospital for incurable syphilitics—rather an odd occupation, surely, for a boy—but its administrator noticed his love of reading and got him enrolled in a grammar school run by Jesuits. For someone with his tastes and talents, the priesthood seemed the obvious profession, but he was already determined to forsake the world and, at the age of twenty-one, joined the Carmelite order and adopted the name Fray Juan de San Matías. He then went to study in the Carmelite college attached to the University of Salamanca.

The turning point in his career came in 1567 when he met St Teresa. He had become discontented with the relaxed rule of the Calced Carmelites and was thinking of joining the Carthusians. St Teresa persuaded him to remain and assist her in her reforms, and in November, 1568, he changed his name to Fray Juan de la Cruz.

Though he became her confessor and she said she never had a better one, relations between them were not always easy. She immediately recognized his saintliness, but his incapacity in practical affairs may have sometimes irritated her, and he may have sometimes thought her too concerned with the things of this world.

> We hear of him mortifying her by handing her an unusually small host at communion when he knew that she liked large ones, giving his reason for this that she was too fond of *gustos* or spiritual consolations . . . and she once remarked: "If one tries to talk to Padre Fray Juan de la Cruz of God, he falls into a trance and you along with him."

From his student days on, his reproaches of the conduct of others, however just, seem to have caused great offense. "Let us be off—that devil is coming," his fellow students would say. Later in life, there were two men, Diego Evangelista and Fray Francisco Crisóstomo, both of whom he had reproved for leaving their priories too often to preach elsewhere, who became his mortal enemies and, when the opportunity arose, took vengeance.

> In appearance, Juan de la Cruz was a very small man [under five feet] with dark hair and complexion, a face round rather than long and a slightly aquiline nose. His glance, we are told, was gentle. He grew a slight beard and went bald early. . . . Unlike Teresa, he was singularly devoid of all those vivid and arresting features that one calls personality. We see an inward looking, silent man with downcast eyes, hurrying off to hide himself in his cell and so absent-minded that he often did not take in what was said to him.

> But now back to his experiences in prison. Physically this was sheer hell.

> His bed was a board laid on the floor and covered with two old rugs so that, as the temperature of Toledo sinks to below freezing point in winter and a damp chill struck through the stone walls, he suffered greatly from the cold. Later when the summer came round he suffered equally in his stifling closet from the heat. Since he was given no change of clothes during the nine months that he was in prison, he was devoured by lice. His food consisted of scraps of bread and a few sardines—sometimes only half a sardine. These gave him dysentery.

Then he was frequently scourged, the marks of which he bore to the end of his life.

> His tunic, which was clotted with blood from his scourgings, stuck to his back and putrified. Worms bred in it so that his whole body became intolerable to him.

But then something extraordinary happened. After some six months he was given a new jailer who took pity on him and gave him a new tunic. He also gave him a pen and ink so that he could "compose from time to time a few things profitable to devotion." One evening St John heard a young man singing a popular love song in the street outside.

> I am dying of love, dearest. What shall I do? Die.

He fell into an ecstasy and started writing his most famous poem, "The Spiritual Canticle," and composed several others.

In order to allow him some fresh air, his new jailer would leave the door of his cell open while the friars were taking their siesta. This gave him the opportunity to loosen the staples screwed into the door to hold the padlock, and on the fourteenth of August, 1578, he, miraculously, considering his enfeebled state, managed to escape.

His next ten years were peaceable and happy, living in various priories, acting as a confessor and also, no doubt, having mystical visions. Then, in 1588, when Nicolas Doria, a former Genoese banker who had joined the Carmelites, ten years before, was elected vicar-general, he was soon again in trouble.

> Inflexible, calculating, despotic, with great business capacity and drive, he [Doria] had his own ideas on how the Discalced should be governed and wished to be free to carry them out. In doing so he would show no respect for persons.

He set up a consulta, composed of six elected councilors, sitting in perpetual session, which would impose its authority on all priories and convents, irrespective of their special problems. To this St John of the Cross was strongly opposed. He believed that no prior should be re-elected after his two-year term because he was convinced that power always corrupts, and he advocated election by secret ballot. His popularity with the nuns and his reputation for sanctity brought Doria to the conclusion that here was the enemy he must destroy. He sent Fray Diego Evangelista down to Andalusia to collect evidence of Juan's scandalous conduct.

> Diego would question them minutely for hours on end, and, if he could not get what he wanted by threats would misconstrue and falsify what they had said and then, without giving them what he had written to read through, order them to sign.

One nun was made to declare that Fray Juan had kissed her through the grille, but, as St Teresa had previously observed:

> If a friar questioned a not very intelligent nun for several hours on end he could make her say anything he wanted because nuns were easily frightened and accustomed to obeying their superiors.

San Juan refused to defend himself and by the beginning of 1591 was deprived of any office. In September he was taken ill with an inflammation of his right foot and went to the priory of Ubeda. Unfortunately its prior was his other old enemy, Fray Francisco Crisóstomo, who treated the dying man very harshly. On December 14 Juan died. What followed was, by modern standards, ghoulish. The crowd rushed into the priory. One of them bit off his toe, others took snippings from his hair or tore off his nails. His body reached Segovia minus an arm, a foot, and several fingers. Later the remaining limbs were cut off and, except for an arm given to Medina del Campo, and a finger or two bestowed elsewhere, were restored to Ubeda. Segovia kept only the head and trunk.

In 1675 he was beatified and canonized in 1720.

I find the man and his life as fascinating as Mr Brenan does. I wish, though, I could share his enthusiasm for the poems, but I can't. I can sense their musical felicities and appreciate the love of God's creation which they exhibit. (In his prose works he could write: "All the beauty of the creatures, compared to the infinite beauty of God, is the height of deformity," which smacks to me of Gnosticism. But in the poems, if there is any inclination toward heresy, it is toward Pantheism.) But I am forced to confess that the poems bore me. I should, however, very much like to read translations, if there are any, of a poet I had never heard of, Garcilaso, who introduced into Castilian poetry the Italian hendecasyllable and was, so Mr Brenan tells us, the main poetic influence on St John of the Cross, though Garcilaso's subject matter was entirely secular.

I have no objection to "religious" poetry as such. For example, I love George Herbert's poems, but they deal with experiences like guilt, contrition, prayer, Divine Providence, etc., of which I have some first-hand knowledge. But I do not believe it is possible to write a satisfactory poem about the mystical union. I think I understand why, when theologians like Gregorius, St Bernard, and St Peter Damian wanted to describe this experience, granted to very few people, to the average Catholic, they should have resorted to the erotic poetry of the Song of Songs. What they seem to be saying is that there are only two human experiences in which ego-consciousness is completely obliterated, the mystical union and the sexual orgasm. The difficulty about this is that the average reader is apt to take what they intended to be an analogy as an identity and to imagine the mystical union as being itself an erotic experience. Thus, when one looks at Bernini's famous sculpture of St Teresa in ecstasy, what one sees is a woman in orgasm. I'm perfectly certain that the two experiences must be totally different. Agape and Eros are not the same. No, I'm sorry, for me St John of the Cross's poems simply don't work. Give me Góngora every time.

The New York Review of Books, 1 November 1973

Where Are the Arts Going?

It may be possible for the social historian, dealing with human beings en masse and using statistical techniques, to make some credible forecasts, but even he cannot foresee the historical effect of certain, as yet unborn individuals, and certain, as yet unthought of technological inventions. The history of the last two hundred years would be very different if Napoleon, Lenin and Hitler had not been born, nor the internal combustion engine and the camera invented, but no one, writing in 1773, could have foreseen them.

Prophecies about the future of the arts are even more futile, for every work of art is the creation of a unique person. Suppose that, instead of Picasso, Stravinsky, Joyce and Eliot, four other artists had been born, twentieth-century art would be very different from what it is.

A further complication is caused by artistic fashion, which may at the time seem very significant, but may shortly be replaced by another. The Dadaists and Surrealists no doubt believed that their works were the Art, or Anti-Art, of the Future but, though they undoubtedly influenced their successors, they have failed to dominate them. In the last few years we have been plagued by the attempt of would-be artists to model artistic fabrication on political action, so that, instead of attempting to produce works that shall be permanently "on-hand" in the world, they have gone in for "Happenings". This folly, I hope and believe, will be short-lived.

In my opinion, the last thing an artist should think about is the future of his art in general. I don't mean, of course, that a poet, for example, should not read the poems of his juniors and judge what he likes or dislikes. What he must never do, however, is ask "Am I With-It?" For him, the only cogent question is "What should I do next?"

I myself—I cannot speak for others—have always felt it enormously important to be one's age, that is to say, the moment I believe I have learnt to write a certain kind of poetry satisfactorily, I feel I must drop it and attempt something else. Of course, I may fail, but it is my artistic duty to try. I have often had the experience of a poem suggesting itself to me which I have had to reject for one of two reasons, either "no longer" or "not yet".

This also means that at different periods in one's life one needs different poetic models. A helpful model is an older poet whose sensibility is sufficiently near to one's own to be suggestive, but not so close as to make one write inferior imitations. When I started writing poems, my models were Thomas Hardy, Edward Thomas and Robert Frost. At the present time, they seem to be Horace and Goethe in his "classical" period. I have always loved Horace but, when I was younger, I knew I could not get anything from him: today, I believe I can.

Observer Magazine, 4 November 1973

Death at Random

Twentieth Century Book of the Dead. By Gil Elliot. Scribner's. $7.95. Ballantine Books. $1.65 (paper).

I must begin by saying that I found this book maddeningly repetitious, and its style far too fancy for my liking. Nevertheless, I think it a book everybody should read. It does not tell us anything new, but it rubs our noses in facts which we would prefer to forget.

Mr Elliot's general thesis may be summed up thus. Until quite recently, the majority of human deaths were caused by what he calls the "micro-violence" of nature, famines, floods, diseases, etc. This is no longer the case. Modern medicine has greatly increased the average natural life expectancy. (It has been reckoned that in the Bronze Age this was only seventeen years.) But in this century, thanks to the development of war machinery, far more deaths have been caused by the "macro-violence" of man.

Mr Elliot devotes separate chapters to violence in Russia, China, the other countries involved in World War I and World War II. In passing, he refers to other conflicts, such as the Mexican Civil War and the Armenian massacres. Not being a professional statistician, I am in no position to check his figures, but they seem to me credible. His conclusion:

> Of the 110 million man-made deaths in this century, sixty-two million died in conditions of privation, forty-six million from guns and bombs, or *hardware,* and two million from *chemicals.*

Under deaths from privation, Mr Elliot included deaths in labor and concentration camps, even if their inmates were shoved into gas chambers.

The First World War caused a profound change in the conventional attitude toward warfare. Hitherto, the ruling classes in all countries had subscribed to a warrior ethos, derived from Homer and the Knights of the Round Table. However at variance with the actual facts this may have been, they sincerely thought of those they were fighting as persons, like Achilles and Hector, whom they could name and respect, so that the military professions were considered noble. When I was a small boy, when we had cherry or plum pie, we used to count the stones in order to predict our future careers. Our list ran as follows: *Army, Navy, Law, Church.*

Before 1914, the politicians in all states would have agreed with Kant:

> No state at war with another state should engage in hostilities of such a kind as to render mutual confidence impossible when peace will have been made.

The replacement of the horse by mechanical means of transport, and the invention of heavy artillery and bombs, destroyed this ethos. Hitherto, at the end of a war, monuments had been erected to the memory of famous generals and admirals. In 1918, in all countries, monuments were raised to the Unknown Soldier, about whom nothing is known except that he lost his life. For all anybody knows, he may, personally, have been a coward. Honor, that is to say, is paid to the warrior not as a hero but as a martyr.

One would have thought that the obvious conclusion to draw would have been to say: "Henceforth, war is no longer a permissible form of political activity." Alas, as we know, it was not. Technological warfare has alienated soldiers not only from the enemy but also from what they themselves do, but this alienation is not without its attraction, because it removes any sense of personal responsibility. A sniper who shoots an enemy soldier, even though he does not know his name, knows just what he has done. He can say: "*I* have shot this man." But for someone who lets off a big gun or drops a bomb, there can be no relation between his personal act of pressing a lever and its results. He will never know whom he has killed. So why should he care?

This raises the problem of aggression. Aggression in human beings cannot be an inborn instinct as it is in the predator carnivores. Before he had learned to fashion weapons, man must have been one of the most helpless of the mammals, having neither fangs nor talons nor hoofs nor venom, and unable to move fast. His instinct, in the presence of danger, must have been to flee or to hide. Human aggression, that is to say, is a secondary modification of fear. Man is the only animal who lets the sun go down, not upon his wrath, but upon his funk. When he did manage to invent weapons, this created a special problem for, as Konrad Lorenz says:

> There is only one being in possession of weapons which do not grow on his body and of whose working plan, therefore, the instincts of his species know nothing and in the usage of which he has no corresponding inhibitions.

Aggressive feelings which are derived from fear are very difficult to deal with. A carnivore, if conscious, could give a rational answer to justify his actions: "I must kill in order to live." But when human beings fear each other, this is a subjective feeling which it is often impossible objectively to disprove. Furthermore, in any "advanced" society, most of its citizens feel they are impotent to affect the decisions of their rulers, and are afraid of the consequences should they refuse to obey their orders. As Mr Elliot says:

> . . . it is just as likely, if we are being causal, that the large wars of the century were "because of" passivity, not aggression in individual human beings.

It is, unfortunately, also true that it is, scientifically, easier and quicker to devise means of producing death than of saving life. An antibiotic, for example, has to be tested over time, for germs may develop strains that resist it. But with bacteria, nerve gases, etc., intended to kill, it is immediately clear if one has succeeded.

> If you can deaden the nerves to lessen surgical pain, you can also paralyze the nerves for hostile purposes . . . the attempt to connect the subtle detail and variety of human behavior with physiological processes is delicate—difficult—hypothetical—frustrating—open-ended. But if you approach it from the angle of the death-application, you can most certainly by drugs and surgery ensure the deadening of great areas of human behavior, and thus become a magician freed from irritating difficulties.

Today, since the invention of nuclear weapons, we have to live with the possibility of "total death." This makes war an absurdity for, as Eugen Rosenstock-Huessy has written:

> The warrior provides for his grandfather and his grandson at the cost, if necessary, of his life. But his sacrifice only makes sense within a time span of at least three generations. There can be no genuine soldier or army unless there is a past to hand on to the future after the war is over.

What, then, are we to do? The only logical conclusion would be disarmament, but this, of course, would have to be total. In the "developed" countries we may well need more police than we have, but there is no logical reason why any state should maintain an army; yet so long as governments, for ideological or economic or racial reasons, are afraid of each other, they will continue to arm. Mr Elliot tells us that, today, there are more persons bearing arms in the world than ever before.

I myself have two proposals to make, though I know perfectly well they will not be adopted. I should like to see the members of all governments elected, like jurors, by lot. This would destroy the party machines, those elected could vote according to their consciences, since there would be no question of re-election, and the computers could work out the proper representation of minority groups. Then, in all countries, I would like to see all matters of foreign policy taken out of the hands of men altogether and entrusted to women, preferably wives and mothers. Furthermore, while men would still be permitted to make machines, it should be for women to decide what machines should be made. There is in all males, I believe, a strong Manichaean streak, an unacknowledged secret contempt for matter, both animate and inanimate. Whitehead wrote:

> Scientific reasoning is completely dominated by the pre-supposition that mental functionings are not properly part of nature.

This may not hold for all scientists, but it certainly holds for the majority, especially for those whose researches are involved with technology. The consequence of this Manichaean kind of Cartesianism has been that instead of concluding that since, so far as we know, man is the only rational and self-conscious creature in the universe, he is responsible for helping it to realize what it cannot do without him, just as a gardener is responsible to the plants he grows, scientists have assumed that they have absolute power to do with nature whatever they like without any responsibility.

Mr Elliot writes:

> We seem to be moving towards a condition in which, despite the sentimental writhings about "nature" over the past two hundred years, we shall actually achieve a more intimate relationship with nature than human

> beings have known since pre-historical times. The difference is that this will be an intimacy based on consciousness, not blindness. For the human individual this implies the ultimate recognition of himself as a *conscious being* who is *part of nature.*

I wish I could feel as optimistic as he seems to be. So far the effect of Darwinism on the popular consciousness seems to have been to use our kinship with the higher mammals as an excuse for bad behavior. As Karl Kraus has written:

> When a man is treated like a beast, he says: "After all I'm human."
> When he behaves like a beast, he says: "After all I'm only human."

As Mr Elliot says, we have now to acquire a new consciousness of death. This is very difficult in situations of random or total death because, while those who die in this way were persons with names of their own, who could say *I* and generally wished to live, to the rest of us they are nameless and faceless numbers. We can all mourn the deaths of those whom we have known and loved, but to care in the same way about the dead we did not and could not have known is almost impossible. We can at least, however, bear in mind Goethe's dictum: "Only all men taken together make up mankind, only all forces in their co-operation the world."

Mr Elliot seems to have curious notions about the Christian conception of death. He is, of course, at liberty to say, "I do not believe in the dogma of the resurrection of the body" (the Creed, incidentally, says nothing about the immortality of the soul). But to say, as he does,

> The Christian notion of immortality is a false resolution of life and death, an assertion that they are the same . . .

is simply not true. Christianity has always taken the reality of death extremely seriously. After all, it believes that Christ died to save sinners.

I agree with him fully, however, when he says:

> Fact is not superior to myth. Technology is not more efficient than religion. However much factual and technical knowledge we acquire, we shall always have to live with the unpredictable.

As a footnote to which, let me quote once more from Rosenstock-Huessy.

> The scientific method cannot lead mankind because it is based upon experiment, and every experiment postpones the present moment until one knows the result. We always come to each other and even to ourselves too late as soon as we wish to know in advance what to do.

The New York Review of Books, 12 December 1974

Some Reflections on the Arts

Every genuine work of art exhibits two qualities, Nowness—an art-historian can assign at least an approximate date to its making—and Permanence—it remains on hand in the world long after its maker and his society have ceased to exist.

★ ★ ★

This means that, in the history of Art, unlike the history of Science, though there are periods of flowering and sterility, there is no such thing as Progress, only Change. Shakespeare does not supersede Aeschylus or Mozart Monteverdi, in the way that the Copernican picture of the Cosmos, for example, superseded the Ptolemaic.

★ ★ ★

Consequently, one of the greatest blessings conferred on our lives by the Arts is that they are our chief means of breaking bread with the dead, and I think that, without communication with the dead, a fully human life is not possible.

★ ★ ★

The more we love the Arts, however, the more careful we must be not to overestimate their importance. Dr Johnson said: "The sole aim of writing is to enable readers a little better to enjoy life or a little better to endure it." I myself would modify this slightly and say that every work of art, no matter how sad or even tragic, fills the reader, the listener, the viewer, with joy. Every good work of art is a utopia and, to those who love Art, this brings the danger of aestheticism, of forgetting that, while all is well in the work of art, all is not well in the world, and in consequence neglecting one's duties to society. There have been certain writers like Hobbes, Locke, Voltaire, Rousseau who have affected the course of history, but they were not primarily artists. Though, as individuals, we would have been deprived of much pleasure, I think the social and political history of Europe would have been what it has been if Dante, Shakespeare, Goethe, Titian, Michelangelo, Beethoven, Mozart, etc., had never lived.

★ ★ ★

By all means let a poet, if he wants to, write an "*engagé*" poem, protesting against this or that social evil or injustice, so long as he doesn't imagine that it will alter anything: the person who will most profit from it is himself, for it will enhance his literary reputation among those who feel the same as he does. In trying to improve the world only two things are effective, political action and straight journalistic rapportage of the facts. The poet, qua poet, has only one political duty: by his own example, to try to preserve the purity of language against corruption and misuse, for, when words lose their meaning, then physical force gives the orders.

★ ★ ★

I am thinking of conditions in the West. In Russia it may be different. [There the] writer may have a political effect because he says something the people can learn nowhere else, and the fact that he risks his liberty, perhaps his life, to say it, gives him a moral authority which we in the West can never have.

★ ★ ★

In conclusion, a few words about the writing of poetry, the only art of which I have first-hand experience. On hedonistic grounds I am a fanatical formalist. A Poem is, among other things, a verbal game. Everyone knows that you cannot play a game without rules. You can make these what you like, but your whole fun and freedom lies in obeying them.

★ ★ ★

The subject matter of a poem is composed of a crowd of recollected occasions of feeling, among which the most important are recollections of encounters with "numinous" beings or events. This crowd the poet attempts to transform into a community by embodying it in a verbal society. At any given time I have two things on my mind, a Theme which is preoccupying me, and problems of verbal form, diction, metre, etc. The theme looks for the right form: the form looks for the right theme. When the two come to an agreement, I can write a poem.

★ ★ ★

One is sometimes asked what is meant by a poem. This is a pseudo-question. The meaning of a poem is the outcome of a dialogue between the words on the page and the particular person who happens to be reading it. The interpretation can only be false if the reader does not know the contemporary meaning of the words. Thus, in reading Milton, one must know that, in his day, *inexpressive* meant inexpressible, not, as to-day, lacking in expression. The ideal response I hope for from a reader is that he should say: "My God! I knew that all the time, but never realised it before." Then I would know that I had said something objectively true, not mere self-expression.

Apparently unpublished; written probably 1973

An Odd Fish

Heinrich Heine. *Selected Works.* Translated and edited by Helen M. Mustard. Poetry translated by Max Knight. Random House. $12.50.

Every literate person in America or England has heard of Heine as they have heard of Goethe, but very few, I suspect have read much of his writings. To most, he is the poet who wrote the words to which composers like Schubert,

Schumann and Brahms composed some of their most beautiful *Lieder*. I myself am a little better informed, but only a little. I had, I believe, read all of his poetry, but, until now, I had never read a line of his prose, and I am most grateful to Professor Mustard for making this selection, which I have found fascinating, if frequently infuriating. Heine was a very prolific writer, and it must have been difficult to decide exactly what to select. Aside from four letters to August Lewald, in which Heine displays his utter ignorance of music, Professor Mustard has concentrated on his full length works, two of them, *The Harz Journey* and *Buch Le Grand*, written before he came to settle in Paris, and two, written between 1832 and 1835, *The Romantic School* and *Concerning the History of Religion and Philosophy in Germany*. For obvious personal reasons, I'm sorry she could not find room to include *English Fragments*, because I am curious to know just why he disliked the English so much, especially when, as Professor Mustard says, one would have expected him to approve of the political set-up in England. In one of his poems he writes:

> I might go to England, but
> coal fumes make the air too thick;
> and the English—just their smell
> gives me cramps and makes me sick.

Did the Parisians really smell much nicer?

What often makes Heine difficult to interpret is that he belonged to that comparatively rare human species, the *Romancier*. A liar knows the difference between truth and falsehood. The Romancier cannot distinguish between fact and fiction. To him there is no distinction between what he imagines as having happened and what really happened. To take a very minor example. From 1825 on, the year in which he became a Protestant, he declared that he was born in 1799, when, in fact, he was born in 1797. I'm convinced that he believed what he said, for there can have been no worldly advantage in such a falsification.

This trait makes him a snare for biographers. He is said, upon what factual evidence I do not know, to have fallen in love with his cousin, Amalie, a millionaire's daughter and, after her marriage, with her sister, Therese, but Professor Mustard is, surely, right when she says:

> It is surely wrong, as earlier critics have consistently done, to interpret the many love poems Heine wrote in the '20's to his infatuation with these two girls; in fact, it seems a mistake to interpret them as directly autobiographical. The *Book of Songs* would have been written even if Amalie and Theresa Heine had never existed.

Then, what is one to make of the following "incident" he relates in *The Harz Journey*?

> I suddenly seemed to hear something shuffling and clumping in the corridor outside my room like the uncertain gait of an old man. Finally my door opened, and slowly Doctor Saul Ascher walked in. Cold chills ran through the very marrow of my bones, I shook like aspen leaves, scarcely daring to look at the ghost. . . . Tottering as always, supporting himself on his Spanish cane, he approached me and in his customary drawling dialect he said cordially, "Don't be frightened, and don't think I'm a ghost. What is a ghost? It is a delusion of your imagination if you think you are seeing me as a ghost. What rational connection would such a phenomenon have with reason? Reason, I say, reason—" And now the ghost proceeded to an analysis of reason, cited Kant's *Critique of Pure Reason*, Part 2, Division 1, Book 2, Section 3, the distinction between phenomena and noumena, then constructed the problematic belief in ghosts, piled one syllogism on the other, and concluded with the logical proof that there are absolutely no ghosts. Meantime cold sweat ran down my back, my teeth chattered like castanets, in mortal terror I nodded unconditional agreement at every argument with which the ghostly Doctor proved the absurdity of all fear of ghosts, and he demonstrated so zealously that once he absent-mindedly pulled a handful of worms out of his watch pocket instead of his gold watch and, noticing his error, stuck them back again with nervous haste. "Reason is the highest—" then the clock struck one and the ghost vanished.

An entertaining story, but who could possibly believe it actually happened? This would be perfectly credible as a dream, but Heine says he was wide awake.

Both in his poetry and in his prose, Heine is at his best when he is being comic or satirical. How vivid and original is this description:

> He was a peculiar, thin figure. A small head, sparsely covered with gray hair that extended across his narrow forehead right to his greenish, dragon-fly eyes, his round nose sticking far out, mouth and chin, on the other hand, timidly retreating towards his ears. This miniature face seemed to be made of a soft, yellowish clay such as sculptors mold their first models from; and when his thin lips closed tightly, several thousand fine, semi-circular wrinkles were drawn across his cheeks. The little man said not a word, and only occasionally, when the older lady whispered some friendly remark to him, did he smile like a pug-dog with a cold.

But when he tries to write "beautifully" or "romantically," the results are less satisfactory.

> There is such a wonderful murmuring and rustling, the birds sang fragmentary songs of yearning, the trees whisper as with a thousand girls' tongues, and as if with a thousand girls' eyes the unusual mountain

flowers gaze at us and stretch out to us their strangely broad, curiously notched leaves, the merry sunbeams flash playfully back and forth, the pensive little plants tell each other green fairy tales, everything is as though enchanted, becoming more and more mysterious, an ancient dream comes to life, the beloved appears—alas that she vanishes again so quickly!

Reading such a passage, I understand what Karl Kraus meant when he said, surely the most devastating comment of one writer about another ever made: "Heine was the Moses who struck the rock of the German Language and out gushed—eau-de-Cologne." This is also true of his sentimental lyrics. If one can forget the wonderful music composers set them to, and read them in cold blood, one is not moved.

In both his two long books, *The Romantic School* and *History of Religion and Philosophy*, Heine has a good deal to say about religion, but before reading them, one should first consider Heine's own religion. In 1825 he became a Lutheran. Though he admired Luther greatly, both as a man and the creator of a Standard German—hitherto, there had only been regional dialects—his reason for becoming one was almost certainly a worldly one. It was impossible for an unbaptised Jew to become a lawyer or a university professor. At the time he was writing the books mentioned above, he professed himself a pantheist, a disciple of Spinoza. In 1841, seven years after he set up house with Crescentia Eugénie Mirat, he married her in a Catholic ceremony, and in 1854, he announced that he had returned to a belief in a personal God.

> Yes, I have returned to God like the prodigal son after having watched over the Hegelian sheep for a very long time. Was it misery that drove me back? Perhaps a less miserable reason. Homesickness for Heaven overwhelmed me and drove me on through forests and ravines, over the giddiest mountain paths of dialectics. On my way I found the god of the pantheists but he was no use to me. . . . If you want a God who can help, you also have to accept his being a person. His transcendence, and his holy attributes, his infinite goodness, infinite wisdom, infinite justice, and so on. We then get immortality of the soul thrown in, so to speak, like the nice meat bone that the butcher gives free to the customers he is satisfied with.

In his pantheistic period he was a rabid anti-Catholic. He had good reason to complain of the religious and literary intrigues of the Catholic party, and the vindictiveness of their personal attacks, though it must be remembered that such behaviour was not confined to them, but in his description of the nature of Roman Catholicism, he talks utter rubbish. He declares that the Roman Church had always been Manichean or Gnostic, regarding the world of Matter as the domain of the Devil, and attributing all evil to the flesh. Christianity, whether Catholic or Protestant, is based upon three absolute pre-suppositions: firstly, that God created the material Cosmos, secondly, that, at a certain point in historical time, the Word was made Flesh and dwelt among us, and, thirdly, that the primal sin from which all the others, including the carnal sins of Lust and Gluttony proceed, is Pride. Pride has so little to do with Matter that it cannot be represented pictorially. One can make a picture depicting Vanity; for Pride one can only hang a mirror on the wall. The extreme asceticism, that of the desert eremites, escaping from the profligacy of the big cities, came early and did not last long, and, even then, the Church announced that anyone who abstained from wine on a feast-day was guilty of sin. To be sure, Catholicism believed that some people have a vocation for the contemplative life and should remain celibate, but it has never imagined that the average man or woman was so called. Adultery was a sin, but marriage was a Sacrament. As for the celibacy of the clergy, the most sensible ruling seems to me to be that of the Greek and Russian Orthodox Churches. Monks and those ambitious for High Office, such as a Bishopric, should remain celibate, but the parish priest should be married.

Heine's conviction that nothing good could ever come out of Catholicism led him to make some very odd statements about art in Renaissance Italy, which he admired.

> . . . just as in Wittenberg they protested in Latin prose, so in Rome they protested in stone, in color, and in ottava rima. . . . The painters in Italy perhaps carried on a much more effective polemic against clericalism than the Saxon theologians. The voluptuous flesh in Titian's painting—all of this is Protestantism.

I can understand someone saying, with approval or disapproval, that Titian's paintings are more Pagan than Christian, but to call them Protestant is absurd. In actual fact, the Lutheran Church, by abolishing images, stained-glass windows and highly colored vestments, and centering the rite upon the sermon, offered their congregations far less in the way of sense-pleasure than the Roman Church. The real charge that can be legitimately brought against both is that they have all too often been too this-worldly, all too ready to make shady deals with secular powers which they thought could further their interests.

Politically, Heine thought of himself as a liberal who desired social change, but he was a liberal of a rather peculiar kind. He knew nothing and cared less about the man-in-the-street and the peasant. It would seem that, aside from his mistress and future wife, the only people he met were intellectuals. Speaking of the kind of revolution he desired to see, he says:

> The political revolution that is based on the principles of French materialism will find in the pantheists not opponents, but allies, allies, how-

> ever, who have drawn their convictions from a deeper source, from a religious synthesis. . . . We are fighting not for the human rights of the people, but for the divine rights of mankind. We do not want to be sans-culottes, nor simple citizens, nor venal presidents: we want to found a democracy of gods, equal in majesty, in sanctity, and in bliss. You demand simple dress, austere morals, and unspiced pleasures, but we demand nectar and ambrosia, crimson robes, costly perfumes, luxury and splendor, the dancing of laughing nymphs, music and comedies.

Can he seriously have believed that a world could be built in which such luxuries would be available to the entire population? I, personally, am very shocked to learn that he seems to have admired that evil genius, Napoleon, whom the English should have hanged from the yard-arm and cast the corpse into the sea. It's just possible that he expressed this admiration in order to ingratiate himself with his French friends, but I fear it isn't.

It's a great relief to turn to Heine, the literary critic, where he shows himself to have been very well informed and full of valuable insights. The German Romantic School, as he defines it, in a reaction against the "classical" literature of the Renaissance, turned for inspiration to the literature of the Middle Ages. One gets the impression that he disapproved. For one thing, many of its exponents, like his pet-hate, Schlegel, and Novalis were catholic converts. This does not mean that he desired a return to classicism: for example, he loved the old German folk-songs collected by Brentano and Arnim in *The Boy's Wonderhorn.* His two favorite authors, he tells us, were Lessing and Herder.

His feelings about Goethe were mixed. Like many of his generation he deplored Goethe's apparent indifference to social and political matters. (Actually, though veiled in irony, many of his epigrams and aphorisms are much more critical of the society in which he lived than most readers realise.) But Heine never, as many who felt the same way did, denied his poetic greatness. Of the thousands of visitors Goethe received in later life, very few of them had read anything but *Werther.* Heine had the good intuition to realise that writing *Werther* was, for Goethe, a therapeutic act by which he got the Sturm und Drang follies out of his system. Heine was one of the first critics to point out that the book is a devastating portrait of a horrid little egotist, who should have been drowned at birth. I was delighted to learn that Heine thought very highly of the *West-östlicher Divan,* a work which was so little read that the first edition did not run out until this century. Wieland's poetry was much more widely read at the time than Goethe's. Rather oddly, as a fellow pantheist, Heine thought its doctrine had led Goethe astray into wasting his time on Anatomy, Optics, Botany, etc., instead of with the loftiest concerns of mankind. Aside from the enormous pleasure Goethe got from such studies, without them he could never have written two of his most beautiful and original poems. *Die Metamorphosen der Pflanzen* and *Metamorphosen der Tiere.*

About Goethe's masterpieces, Heine says:

> They adorn our dear fatherland as beautiful statues adorn a garden, but they are, after all, statues. You can fall in love with them, but they are sterile; Goethe's works do not beget deeds as do Schiller's. A deed is the child of the word, and Goethe's beautiful words are childless.

But surely, the same thing could be said about Dante and Shakespeare and all the greatest poets. How many deeds, for that matter, did Heine's words beget?

He was, however, absolutely just when he wrote:

> It was disgusting that Goethe was afraid of any writer with originality and praised and eulogized all the insignificant nobodies. He carried such praise so far that at last it was considered a testimonial of mediocrity to have been praised by Goethe.

He does not mention Hölderlin, which means, presumably, that in 1832 when he wrote *The Romantic School*, Hölderlin's poems had not yet been published.

About Heine's descriptions of and comments upon German philosophers, I do not feel competent to pass judgement since I have read so little of them. I can only repeat his answers to two questions. Why, in the nineteenth century, were all the famous philosophers, Lessing, Kant, Fichte, Marx, not to mention Wittgenstein and Heidegger in this, Germans? Between Descartes and Bergson, how many French philosophers are now remembered? And in England, Jeremy Bentham and J. S. Mill are small beer in comparison.

Heine's view was that German philosophy was a child of Lutheranism. In it there arose a rigid literalism, and the letter of the Bible ruled just as tyrannically as tradition had once ruled. In reaction to this, intellectuals started to ask—"Just what exactly does this word mean?" Then the Lutheran emphasis on Faith rather than Works forced people to ask: "What exactly are the grounds upon which Religious Faith can be justified?"

About German as a language, Heine says:

> German . . . is not merely adequate for metaphysical investigations, but is far more suitable than Latin. The latter, the language for generals' orders, a language for administrators' decrees, a legal language for usurers, a lapidary language for the stone-hard Roman people. It became the appropriate language for materialism. Though Christianity, with truly Christian patience, struggled for more than a thousand years to spiritualize this language, it did not succeed. . . . In no other language than in our beloved German mother tongue could Nature have revealed her most secret workings.

[*Unfinished.*]

Unpublished. Perhaps written for *The New York Review of Books*, September 1973

FOREWORDS AND AFTERWORDS

Forewords and Afterwords

Selected by Edward Mendelson

[*1973*]

FOR

HANNAH ARENDT

The Greeks and Us

[See "Introduction to *The Portable Greek Reader*", *Prose II*, p. 354.]

Augustus to Augustine

[See *Prose II*, p. 226.]

Heresies

[See *Prose V*, p. 202.]

The Protestant Mystics

[See "Introduction to *The Protestant Mystics*", *Prose V*, p. 42.]

Greatness Finding Itself

[See *Prose IV*, p. 283.]

Shakespeare's Sonnets

[See "Introduction to *The Sonnets*, by William Shakespeare", *Prose V*, p. 92.]

[Except for "A Tribute", which Auden newly revised and retyped, the essays in this book were set from marked copies of earlier printings. The textual notes (p. 774) list Auden's minor cuts and revisions in some of the essays.]

A Civilized Voice

[See p. 347.]

Werther and *Novella*

[See "Foreword to *The Sorrows of Young Werther* and *Novella*", p. 412.]

Italian Journey

[See "Introduction to *Italian Journey*", *Prose IV*, p. 324.]

Mr G

[See *Prose V*, p. 356.]

Portrait of a Whig

[See *Prose III*, p. 273.]

Søren Kierkegaard

[See "Introduction to *The Living Thoughts of Kierkegaard*", *Prose III*, p. 285.]

A Knight of Doleful Countenance

(Second Thoughts on Kierkegaard)

[See *Prose V*, p. 361.]

Grimm and Andersen

[See "Introduction to *Tales of Grimm and Andersen*", *Prose II*, p. 390.]

Edgar Allan Poe

[See "Introduction to *Selected Prose and Poetry*, by Edgar Allan Poe", *Prose III*, p. 215.]

Tennyson

[See "Introduction to *A Selection from the Poems of Alfred, Lord Tennyson*", *Prose II*, p. 203.]

A Very Inquisitive Old Party

[See *Prose V*, p. 374.]

The Greatest of the Monsters

[See *Prose V*, p. 389.]

A Genius and a Gentleman

[See p. 503.]

A Poet of the Actual

[See p. 510.]

George Macdonald

[See "Introduction to *Visionary Novels of George Macdonald*", *Prose III*, p. 477.]

A Russian Aesthete

[See p. 405.]

Lewis Carroll

[See "Today's 'Wonder-World' Needs Alice", *Prose IV*, p. 414.]

Calm Even in the Catastrophe

[See *Prose IV*, p. 209.]

An Improbable Life

[See *Prose V*, p. 19.]

A Worcestershire Lad

[See p. 495.]

C. P. Cavafy

[See "Introduction to *The Complete Poems of Cavafy*", *Prose IV*, p. 290.]

A Marriage of True Minds

[See *Prose IV,* p. 348.]

The Poet of the Encirclement

[See *Prose II,* p. 198.]

Un Homme d'Esprit

[See "L'Homme d'Esprit", *Prose III,* p. 590.]

One of the Family

[See *Prose V,* p. 166.]

Walter de la Mare

[See "Introduction to *A Choice of de la Mare's Verse*", *Prose IV,* p. 396.]

G. K. Chesterton's Non-Fictional Prose

[See "Foreword to *G. K. Chesterton: A Selection from his Non-Fictional Prose*", p. 384.]

Lame Shadows

[See p. 419.]

A Consciousness of Reality

[See *Prose III*, p. 419.]

Private Poet

[See *Prose V*, p. 112.]

A Voice of Importance

[See "Chester Kallman: A Voice of Importance", p. 487.]

A Tribute

Though I have always loved his music—when I was sixteen I bought his *Easy Piano Duets*—I must leave it to others, better professionally qualified than I, to estimate Stravinsky's achievement as a composer. I can, however, I think, speak with some authority about Stravinsky as a paradigm of the creative artist, a model and example from whom younger men, be they composers, painters or writers, can derive counsel and courage in an age when the threats to their integrity seem to be greater than ever before.

First, let them pay attention to his conception of artistic fabrication.

> I am not a mirror, struck by my mental functions. My interest passes entirely to the object, the thing made.

An artist, that is to say, should think of himself primarily as a craftsman, a "maker", not as an "inspired" genius. When we call a work "inspired", all we mean is that it is better, more beautiful than we could possibly have hoped for. But this is a judgement for the public to make, not the artist himself. True, there have been artists, Hugo Wolf, for example, who could only create during periods of intense emotional excitement, but this is a personal accident—most such artists have probably been manic-depressives. It has nothing to do with the value of what they produced in this state. Nearly all persons in a manic phase believe that they are inspired, but very few of them produce anything of artistic value.

Valéry, surely, was right when he said: "Talent without genius isn't much, but genius without talent isn't anything at all." The difference between a pure craft, like carpentry, and art is that when the carpenter starts work he knows exactly what the finished product will be, whereas the artist never knows just what he is going to make until he has made it. But, like the carpenter, all he can or should consciously think about is how to make it as well as possible, so that it may become a durable object, permanently "on hand" in the world.

As an illustration of Stravinsky's professional attitude, let me speak from personal experience. When Chester Kallman and I were offered the opportunity to write the libretto of *The Rake's Progress*, we felt, of course, immensely honored, but at the same time rather alarmed. We had heard that, during the composition of *Persephone*, there had been great friction between the composer and André Gide over the setting of the French text. Furthermore, Stravinsky had on more than one occasion expressed the view that, in setting words to music, the words themselves do not matter, only the syllables.

Though, as lovers of opera, we both knew that musical and spoken rhythmical values cannot be identical, we were afraid, particularly since Stravinsky had never set English before, that he might distort our words to the point of unintelligibility. But, from the moment we started working with him, we discovered that our fears were groundless. Going through our text, he asked for and marked into his copy the spoken rhythmical value of every word. In one instance, only one, did he make a mistake. He thought that, in the word *sedan-chair*, the accent in *sedan* fell on the first syllable. When we pointed this out to him, he immediately altered his score. In one number in the opera, the Auctioneer's aria in Act III, scene 1, it is dramatically essential that the sung rhythms conform pretty closely to the spoken. They do. In the rest of the work, whatever occasional liberties he took, not one of them struck our English and literary ears as impermissible.

Second, Stravinsky's career as a composer is as good a demonstration as any that I know of the difference between a major and a minor artist. In the case of a minor artist, A. E. Housman, for example, if presented with two of his poems, both of equal artistic merit, one cannot, on the basis of the poems themselves, say which was written first. The minor artist, that is to say, once he has reached maturity and found himself, ceases to have a history. A major artist, on the other hand, is always re-finding himself, so that the history of his works recapitulates or mirrors the history of art. Once he has done something to his satisfaction, he forgets it and attempts to do something new which he has never attempted before. It is only when he is dead that we are able to see that his various creations, taken together, form one consistent *oeuvre*. Moreover, it is only in the light of his later works that we are able properly to understand his earlier.

> The chief problem in being eighty-five is the realisation that one may be powerless to change the quality of one's work. The quantity can be increased, even at eighty-five, but can one change the whole. I, at any rate, am absolutely certain that my *Variations* and *Requiem Canticles* have altered the picture of my whole work.

Last, and most important of all, Stravinsky, in his attitude towards Past and Present, Tradition and Innovation, has set an example which we should all do well to follow.

When I contemplate the contemporary artistic scene, I realise how extraordinarily lucky those whom we think of as the founders of "modern" art, Stravinsky, Picasso, Eliot, Joyce, etc., all were in being born when they were, so that they reached manhood before 1914. Until the First World War European society was in all significant aspects still what it had been in the nineteenth century. This meant that, for these artists, the need they all felt to make a radical break with the immediate past was an artistic, not a historical, imperative, and therefore unique for each one of them. None of them would have dreamed of asking: "What kind of music or painting or poetry is 'relevant' in the year 1912?" Nor did they think of themselves collectively as the avant-garde, a term of which Baudelaire, who was certainly himself a great innovator, quite rightly said:

> This use of military metaphor reveals minds not militant but formed for discipline: minds born servile, Belgian minds, which can only think collectively.

What each of them felt, I believe, was rather: "It is only by creating something 'new' that I can hope to produce a work which in due time will take its permanent place in the tradition of my art." They were also lucky in their first audiences who were honest enough to be shocked. Those, for instance, who were scandalised by *Le Sacre du Printemps* may seem to us now to have been old fogies, but their reaction was genuine. They did not say to themselves: "Times have changed, so we must change in order to be 'with it.'"

In times of rapid social change and political crisis, there is always a danger of confusing the principles governing political action and those that govern artistic fabrication. Thus Plato, dismayed by the political anarchy in the Athens of his day, tried to take artistic fabrication as the model for a good society. Such a theory, if put into practice, must, as we have learned to our cost, result in a totalitarian tyranny, involving, among other things, the most rigid censorship of the arts.

To-day in the so-called "free" societies of the West, the most widespread error is the exact opposite of Plato's, namely, to take political action as the model for artistic fabrication. To do this is to reduce art to an endless series of momentary and arbitrary "happenings", and to produce in artists and public alike a conformism to the tyranny of the passing moment which is far more enslaving, far more destructive of integrity and originality, than any thoughtless copying of the past.

Once more, Stravinsky:

> What, may I ask, has become of the idea of universality—of a character of expression not necessarily popular but compelling to the highest imaginations of a decade or so beyond its time?

This, as we all know, his own compositions have achieved. If any young artist hopes to do the same, let him begin by forgetting all about "historical processes", an awareness of which, as the Master has said, "is probably best left to future and other kinds of wage-earners."

Markings

[See "Foreword to *Markings*", *Prose V*, p. 81.]

Papa Was a Wise Old Sly-Boots

[See p. 360.]

The Justice of Dame Kind

[See *Prose IV*, p. 412.]

Concerning the Unpredictable

[See p. 397.]

The Megrims

[See p. 478.]

Deborah

[See "The Mountain Allowed Them Pride", p. 465.]

The Kitchen of Life

[See "Introduction to *The Art of Eating*", *Prose V*, p. 37.]

As It Seemed to Us

[See *Prose V*, p. 134.]

ADDENDA TO PREVIOUS VOLUMES

ADDENDA TO PREVIOUS VOLUMES

Some addenda to *Prose II* may be found in *Prose III*, p. 613; they include a previously unpublished note on E. M. Forster written for the book catalogue *We Moderns: Gotham Book Mart 1920–1940* (December 1939), and a few trivial additions to the appendices.

The following items include addenda to *Prose I*, *III*, and *IV*, and a few further addenda to *Prose II*.

A Letter to the Editor of *The Listener*

A review by V. Sackville-West of Edmund Blunden's *Poems*, in the *Listener*, 10 December 1932, included an obvious allusion to reviews of Auden's *Poems* (1930) that had appeared in recent weeks: "He [Blunden] proves, indeed, that a straining after orginality very often defeats its own ends, for by his own calm and traditional methods he manages to be quite as impressive—I put it mildly—as the latest young disciple of Mr Eliot from Oxford or Cambridge." Auden's response appeared two weeks later in the section headed "Points from Letters". Sackville-West's book-length poem *The Land* had been published in 1927.

MODERN POETRY

No review in this lovely age seems to be complete without a sneer. As one of "the latest disciples of Mr Eliot from Oxford or Cambridge" in Miss Sackville-West's review of Mr Blunden's poems (*Listener*, December 10), I protest—to put it mildly—against being taught bad manners by my elders.

Mr Blunden is a fine poet and is very properly recognised as such. But whoever said he wasn't? Not we. Miss Sackville-West's own poem, "The Land", was good (I don't know how it sold but I hope well), yet she talks as if we had collared all the sales. Of course, our work isn't so impressive nor so good: we are ten years younger. We hope to do better next time.

We can't help feeling that Miss Sackville-West knows that the great audience she speaks to wants to be reassured about "modern" poetry. ("Miss West's a clever woman. She's read a great deal. She told me there's nothing in it".)

Helensburgh W. H. Auden

The Listener, 24 December 1930

Also in *Prose I*, a note ought to have mentioned the reference work *Contemporary British Literature: A Critical Survey and 232 Author-Bibliographies*, by Fred B. Millett; third revised and enlarged edition (London: Harrap, 1935), in which the editor thanks Auden among many other authors "for their generosity in sending him notes on their professional and unprofessional interests". The biographical note on Auden is one of the few that says nothing about the writer's interests, but it seems to be based on details (and a misspelling) that Auden supplied: "Born at York, the youngest son of Dr G. A. Auden, F.R.C.P. Educated at St Edmunds [*sic*] School, Gresham's School, and Christ Church, Oxford. Specialized in biology and English literature. Teaches at the Downs School, Colwall, North Malvern."

Also in *Prose I*, a note ought to have mentioned a story told to me by Stephen Spender: At Gresham's School, probably around 1923 or 1924, Auden and Michael Spender, signing themselves "Amici", sent to a London daily paper a letter about public schools, which, when printed, caused a mild sensation at the school.

In *Prose II*, the appendix "Endorsements, Commissioned Texts, and a List" (p. 498) ought to have included Auden's comment on the back flap of the jacket of *About People: A Book of Symbolical Drawings*, by William Steig (New York: Random House, 1939): "This book of drawings is one of the most fascinating I have ever seen. Mr Steig's fantastic comments on human nature are as impressive as the Proverbs of Goya." A few months after writing this comment, Auden reviewed the book in the *Nation* (*Prose II*, p. 49). Steig had written to Random House in an undated letter, perhaps around October 1939: "I think a statement by Auden would be nice and I have a notion he might like the book" (Columbia University Library) It is unclear whether Steig's notion was based on direct or indirect contact with Auden.

Also in *Prose II*, the appendix "Lost and Unwritten Work" (p. 506) ought to have noted that Auden told Alan Ansen on 3 October 1947 that he was preparing a selected edition of Alexander Pope and discussed possible choices; nothing seems to have come of this. Possibly Auden had been commissioned to prepare this selection for the Rinehart Editions series, and later asked to edit instead the volume of Edgar Allan Poe's *Selected Prose and Poetry* (1950). A Rinehart Edition of Pope, edited by W. K. Wimsatt, appeared in 1951.

In *Prose III*, the headnote to the appendix "Auden as Anthologist and Editor" (p. 622) ought to have noted that for the anthology *The World's Best*, edited by Whit Burnett (New York: Dial, 1950), Auden selected "The Massacre of the Innocents" from "For the Time Being" as an example of his work; the editor's headnote about Auden concludes: "In connection with [the excerpt], Mr Auden did not feel that he had anything to say about it. 'You might point out,' he added, 'that it is far harder to pick a representative piece in poetry than it is in prose.'"

Also in *Prose III*, the headnote to the appendix "Public Lectures and Courses" (p. 636) has a brief note on a course that Auden taught at the Poetry Center of the 92nd Street YM-YWHA in New York, starting on 19 October 1955. (Two weeks in December were skipped, and the course ended 25 January 1956.) The title was "Form and Style in Poetry"; it was limited to thirty-five students. The course is described in a typescript note (probably used in preparing a lost descriptive leaflet) in the Center's archives: "A series of twelve lectures and discussion periods in which the text will be The Sonnets of Shakespeare. Sutdents will be expected to learn one sonnet by heart each week and some of them may be asked to write papers requiring the use of a good library." An assignment sheet, also in the Center's archives, is headed "Form and Style in Poetry[.] Auden[.] 11 January 1956":

If three iambs be taken as the norm but inversion of any foot be allowed, then possible variations are as follows:

I. – · / – · / – · a (fem)
· – / – · / · – b (masc)
· – / · – / – · a
– · / · – / · – b

II. · – / – · / – · c (fem)
– · / – · / · – d (masc)
– · / · – / – · c
· – / · – / · – d

Write a song to this pattern with the rhymes as indicated.

In *Prose IV*, the textual note to “Statement by W. H. Auden on Cultural Freedom” (p. 922) ought to have mentioned that Auden’s note was reprinted in a leaflet *A Word about the Congress* (London, 1964).

Also in *Prose IV*, the textual note to “Are the English Europeans?” (p. 935) ought to have mentioned that, as early as 1957, Auden had sketched a similar piece, opening with a list of the characteristics of Europe; he wrote the sketch after receiving an invitation to an unidentified Conférence Européenne de Culture. In 2013 the incomplete manuscript was in the stock of Sevin Seydi Rare Books, London.

Also in *Prose IV*, the textual notes to *The Dyer’s Hand* (p. 945) ought to have pointed out that *Selected Essays*, a paperback edition published by Faber & Faber in 1964, included ten essays chosen by Auden at Faber’s request. These were “Reading”, “Writing”, “The Prince’s Dog”, “Brothers & Others”, “The Joker in the Pack”, “D. H. Lawrence”, “Robert Frost”, “Dingley Dell & The Fleet”, “Genius & Apostle”, and “Postscript: Christianity & Art”. The same textual notes omitted to report that the second clothbound impression (1964) of the 1963 Faber edition of *The Dyer’s Hand* introduced corrections to the text that were made separately from those in the original Random House edition; all the corrections that were made to this second Faber impression were also, as far as I can see, eventually made to the later Random House and Vintage Books editions, as noted in *Prose IV*.

APPENDICES

APPENDIX I

Auden as Anthologist and Editor

Auden's selections of works by single authors are described in the notes to their introductions. These works are: *Persons from Porlock and Other Plays for Radio,* by Louis MacNeice (p. 344); *G. K. Chesterton: A Selection from His Non-Fictional Prose* (p. 384); *Selected Songs of Thomas Campion* (p. 559); *George Herbert* (p. 562); and *A Choice of Dryden's Verse* (p. 567).

In collaboration with Branko Brusar, Auden translated a number of poems by Nikola Šop; one of them, "Cottages in Space", was published in *Encounter,* November 1969, with a note headed "W. H. Auden writes": "Considered by many of his compatriots to be the best living Croatian poet, Nikola Šop was born at Jajce, Bosnia, in 1904. He was crippled for life during Hitler's bombardment of Belgrade in 1941. 'Cottages in Space' is taken from his volume *Space Poems* (1957)."

An Unsigned Introduction to Icelandic Prosody

In 1969 Faber & Faber published a book of translations of Icelandic poetry under the title *The Elder Edda: A Selection,* Translated from the Icelandic by Paul B. Taylor & W. H. Auden, Introduction by Peter H. Salus & Paul B. Taylor, Notes by Peter H. Salus. The poems had been translated into English by Taylor and the translations had been revised and rewritten by Auden. Although the title page attributes the introduction to Salus and Taylor, the second of its six sections, titled "Prosody", was written anonymously by Auden; Taylor wrote to Jason Epstein at Random House on 27 July 1968, "Auden added the section on prosody" (Columbia University Library). The manuscript of the book seems to have been sent to Faber & Faber around August 1968, but was not published until 8 December 1969. An American edition of the book was published by Random House in 1970.

PROSODY

A reader brought up on English poetry since Chaucer—or, for that matter, on Greek and Latin poetry—may at first have some difficulty in "hearing" Icelandic verse, for he will find nothing he can recognize as a metrical foot, that is to say, a syllabic unit containing a fixed number of syllables with a fixed structure of either (as in English) stressed and unstressed syllables or (as in Greek and Latin) long and short syllables.

In English verse, lines are metrically equivalent only if they contain both the same kind of feet, and the same number of syllables. But in Icelandic verse, as in Anglo-Saxon, all lines are metrically equivalent which contain the same number of stressed syllables: the unstressed syllables preceding or succeeding these may vary between none and three (occasionally more).

The principal meters in Icelandic poetry are two: Epic Meter (*fornyrðislag*: "old verse") and Chant Meter (*ljoðaháttr*).

Epic Meter

This is essentially the same as the meter of *Beowulf*. Each line contains four stresses and is divided by a strongly marked caesura into two half-lines with two stresses each. (In printing Icelandic verse, the convention has been to leave a gap between the two half-lines: in our translations we have printed the whole line as it is normally printed in an English poem.)

The two half-lines are linked by alliteration. The first stressed syllable of the second half-line must alliterate with either or both of the stressed syllables in the first: its second stressed syllable must not alliterate.

All vowels are considered to alliterate with each other. In the case of syllables beginning with *s*, *sc* (*sk*) can only alliterate with *sc*, *sh* with *sh*, and *st* with *st*, etc.: similarly, voiced and unvoiced *th* can only alliterate with themselves.

In Icelandic poetry, unlike Anglo-Saxon, the lines are nearly always end-stopped without enjambment, and are grouped into strophes varying in length from two to six or seven lines, the commonest strophe having four.

De*p*árt! You sháll not *p*áss through
My *t*áll gates of *t*ówering stóne:
It befíts a *w*ife to *w*índ yárn,
*N*ót to *k*nów a*n*óther's húsband.

Chant Meter

The unit is a couplet, the first of which is identical with the standard line of Epic Meter: the second contains three stresses instead of four (some hold that it only contains two), two of which must be linked by alliteration.

If you knów a *f*áithful *f*ríend you can trúst,
  Gó *ó*ften to his h*ó*use:
*G*ráss and brámbles *g*rów quíckly
  Upón an un*t*ródden *t*ráck.

Speech Meter and Incantation Meter

Though these are officially classified as separate meters, they are better thought of as variations on Epic Meter and Chant Meter respectively. There is no case of a poem written entirely in either, nor even of a long sustained passage within a poem.

In Speech Meter (*málaháttr*), each half-line contains an extra stress, making six in all.

*L*íttle it *í*s to denÝ, *l*óng it *í*s to trável

In Incantation Meter (*kviðuháttr*), two couplets of Chant Meter are followed by a fifth line of three stresses, which is a verbal variation on the fourth line.

I know a tenth: if troublesome ghosts
  Ride the rafters aloft,
I can work it so they wander astray,
  Unable to find their *forms,*
  Unable to find their *homes.*

Quantity

In Icelandic verse, vowel length plays a role, though by no means as important a one as in Greek and Latin. For example, if a line ends in a single stressed syllable (a masculine ending), this may be either short or long: but if it ends in a disyllable, the first of which is stressed (a feminine ending), the stressed syllable must be short. For example, *Ever* would be permissible: *Evil* would not.

Icelandic, like Greek and Latin, is an inflected language: modern English has lost nearly all its inflections. This means that, in modern English, vowels which are short in themselves are always becoming long by position, since, more often than not, they will be followed by more than one consonant. For example, in the line

Of Man's first disobedience, and the fruit

there is, if it is scanned quantitatively, only one short syllable, *dis.*

Quantitative verse, as Robert Bridges has demonstrated, *can* be written in English, but only as a virtuoso feat. In our translations, therefore, we have ignored quantity. Also now and again, though actually very seldom, we have ignored the strong caesura between the two half-lines, when it seemed more natural to do so.

Auden Selects or Comments on His Own Work

For a few anthologies edited by others Auden made and commented on his choice of his own poems or commented on a selection made by others.

For *This Is My Best: In the Third Quarter of the Century,* edited by Whit Burnett (Garden City: Doubleday, 1970), one of a series of volumes in which writers chose their best work, Auden chose "Thanksgiving for a Habitat", "The Cave of Making", and "The Common Life"; the book reprinted his cover letter, obviously not intended for publication:

Dear Mr Burnett:

Although I have selected three poems for *This Is My Best* I find it very difficult to comment on my own work. It's simply not my business. Will you excuse me?

W. H. Auden

For *Let the Poet Choose,* edited by James Gibson (London: Harrap, 1973), Auden selected two poems, which appeared beneath this headnote:

Every poet, I think, complains about the laziness of anthologists, who simply copy each other. Also no poet wants to hear again about his old war-horses. They may be good poems but he is bored by the thought of them.

As regards my own work, I have some unfavourites but no favourites. Naturally I am more interested in what I have been writing fairly recently than in the distant past. The two I pick are both in *City without Walls.*

The first, "In Due Season", I choose because it is the only English poem since Campion written in accentual asclepiads; the second, "Prologue at Sixty", because I think the alliterative metre is not badly handled.

For *Preferences: 51 American poets choose poems from their own work and from the past,* edited by Richard Howard (New York: Viking, 1974), Auden chose his own "In Due Season" and Thomas Campion's "What faire pompe". Howard's commentary quotes Auden's description of his poem as "an attempt to write an English poem in the First Asclepiadean (spondee, choriamb, choriamb, iamb), the original model is Horace, *Odes,* Book I, no. 1"; Auden's reference to Campion's poem as "the only other example that I know of"; and his further comment: "The difference between Campion and me is that Campion could not decide whether to scan by vowel quantity or by stress: some lines do one, some another. Mine is purely accentual and ignores vowel length altogether."

Editorial and Advisory Boards

Auden served as editor or adviser for a number of magazines and series; see the corresponding appendix in *Prose V* for notes on those that he joined before 1969. He was also listed as a "Patron" of Writers and Scholars International, the publishers of *Index on Censorship*, from the first issue of the magazine, in Spring 1972, through the Autumn 1973 issue; see also pp. 731–32.

APPENDIX II

Lectures and Speeches

This appendix includes texts and reports on Auden's lectures and speeches to public and quasi-public audiences such as the participants in a funeral or the memberships of learned societies and comparable groups.

Auden made a month-long reading tour in the United States and Canada in February-March 1971. He seems to have read and commented on his poems, but gave no lectures as he had done on earlier tours. He also participated in a panel discussion on theatre and the visual arts at the University of Toronto (see p. 726).

Memorial Tribute to David Protetch

David Protetch was Auden's physician in New York and a friend since Auden taught in 1941–42 at the University of Michigan, where Protetch had been a student. Protetch died on 2 May 1969. Auden, then in Austria, seems to have drafted this tribute almost immediately thereafter. The text below is from a typescript (headed "Obituary"), now in the Berg Collection, that Auden sent to Protetch's sister Carole, perhaps in the hope that it could be read at the memorial service on 7 May. A draft is in a notebook in the Berg Collection.

David Protetch was my personal physician as well as my personal friend. As the son of a physician, I was brought up, rightly I think, to be suspicious of the medical profession with its pretensions to omniscience. But in David Protetch I found a member in whom I had absolute trust. He was one of the very few doctors I have met who practiced what Sir William Osler preached when he said: "Care for the individual patient more than for the particular disease from which he is suffering." In consequence, both his diagnosis and his prescribed treatment always turned out accurate and effective. He had, it must be admitted, one defect, also rare among doctors: he habitually undercharged his patients.

A diabetic from early youth, he had always to contend with ill-health, and in the last few years, this became a desperate struggle to keep going at all, but his fortitude under conditions which I should have thought intolerable filled me with admiring amazement.

For him, death was, I should guess, a merciful release, but for his patients it is a catastrophe: "To whom shall we go now?"

The Recent Nobel Foundation Conference in Stockholm on "The Place of Value in a World of Fact"

Auden spoke on this topic at the Columbia University Seminar on the Nature of Man, 15 January 1970, held in the home of Dr Ruth Anshen, who edited various series of books to which Auden had contributed essays. The mimeographed minutes of the meeting, in the Columbia University archives, included a transcript of Auden's talk and the discussion that followed; the text below is reproduced from the transcript, with its original square-bracketed additions and some further light emendation, but with contributions by others omitted or abridged.

Excerpts from this transcript, lightly edited for publication, appeared almost a year later in *Columbia Forum,* Winter 1970, under the title "They Had Forgotten How to Laugh and How to Pray". After the set-off quotation from Goethe near the end of the piece, the text below follows the published text, which has a few sentences absent from the mimeographed transcript, from "On the last evening" through "All distinctions of rank are abolished."; after which the printed text continues, "Goethe describes how he heard a small boy screaming at his father,". All this replaces the following passage in the mimeographed transcript: "Again, the mock abuse from which all distinctions of rank are excluded. There is a small boy screaming at his father,". Possibly the published text at this point was based on a lost recording of Auden's talk; conceivably Auden read proofs of the published text and supplied the additional material. The not-very-good philosopher mentioned in the fourth paragraph was Henry D. Aiken.

Brief excerpts from the *Columbia Forum* text appeared as an op-ed piece in the *New York Times,* 2 February 1971, under the title "Forgotten Laughter, Forgotten Prayer."

I was asked to start off with my impressions about Stockholm. . . . They [the Nobel Foundation] had the idea that they would get thirty-five people together to discuss "The Place of Value in a World of Fact." . . . Now, the first surprising thing was that the students estimated that our average age was sixty-nine . . . which made me actually, being nearly sixty-three, quite a chicken. But anyway, all of us there were aware of the world before World War I, and presumably were brought up before permissiveness came in. I can speak for myself—and I am sure I speak for most of the people there—that in that time one naturally, as in every generation, had to fight for one's independence; [but] I don't think I ever questioned their [my parents'] values. I might think their taste in pictures wasn't very good or something; but, on the whole, when I hear about young people now, questioning their parents' values—it was not a thing which, I think, we did.

And it's curious to think that at that time, when I grew up—of course I grew up in England—somebody could write, without thinking there was anything surprising, "I traveled alone to Bonn with a boring maid."

[Now, to return to the conference,] . . . what was interesting to me were the people who were not there. Most of the people were scientists. Koestler, who organized the thing, though, of course, he has written novels, calls himself an interdisciplinary writer and didn't speak as a novelist. The only representatives of the arts who were there were myself and Gombrich, an art historian. That was all right, because we all know artists can't do very much.

I found it rather odd that we had only one philosopher—and I am sorry to say not a very good one. . . . Though Margaret [Mead] was there, we didn't have any real historian. If one is thinking about the future, what kind of knowledge about the past will you need? That can vary. I think that at this particular point in history, the things we have to study—and here we need the help of historians—are the various European revolutions, starting, let us say, with the papal revolution, then coming on to the Reformation, the English Revolution, the American Revolution, the French Revolution, the Russian Revolution. These things have to be studied; we can learn from them. The rejection of the past, I think, is all nonsense. I must say, I agree very much, about tradition and the past, with a remark by Chesterton, when he says, "Tradition means giving votes to that obscurest of classes, our ancestors. The democracy of the dead refuses to surrender to the arrogant oligarchy of those who merely happen to be walking around," which I think is admirable. Then again, needless to say, there was no theologian. I think an obvious person we should have invited was Austin Farrer.

Now, I think the title, though I know what Koehler meant in his book, *The Place of Value in a World of Fact*, was slightly unfortunate, because basically we were there to discuss how we could make the world better. The word "value" to me has too much economic connotation. If I say a painting by Cézanne is "valuable," I mean in an auction it gets a great deal of money. It's quite different from what I mean if I say it's a great painting. And I also don't think any man who is in love with a girl says to her, "I think you are valuable." I think the word "value" is a very questionable word to use.

Incidentally, I may say, as most people there were scientists, that I know how prima donnaish artists can be; I never realized that scientists are just as bad!

I must tell you about certain things that surprised me. A biologist got up . . . and claimed to be a Cartesian. Now really! I think it might still be possible for somebody who builds bridges or dams to hold the Cartesian position; it's certainly not possible for a biologist, and I don't think it's even possible any more for a physicist. The whole Cartesian thing really is based on a presupposition, which Whitehead once said—which is no longer true, I think—that scientific reasoning is completely dominated by the presupposition that mental functionings are not properly part of nature.

Well, certainly the physicists have changed their mind about that. For example, Heisenberg says, "The scientist no longer confronts nature as an objective observer, but sees himself as an actor in this interplay between man and nature. The scientific method of analyzing, explaining, and classifying is unconscious of its human limitations, which arise out of the fact that by its intervention science alters and refashions the objects of its investigation." In other words, you cannot make the distinction between *res extensa* and *res cogitans* any more.

And then I couldn't believe my ears when I heard people calling for a series of ethical axioms. Now, the idea of an axiom comes from mathematics. You can have a series of axioms for Euclidean geometry; you can have another series of axioms for another kind of geometry. There is no possible question of talking about one being better than another. And to suppose that anything we know about how to behave, or that when we talk about right and wrong, that this is based on logic, seems to me to be an utter misunderstanding of how human beings work at all. The statement, "A straight line is the shortest distance between two points," and the statement, "Thou shalt love thy neighbor as thyself," belong to two completely different worlds of discourse. If we think how in practice we ever learn anything about ethics and behavior, it is in a series of commandments: "You should do this." "You shouldn't do this." It is always stated in the imperative.

With that comes another thing—and this again comes back to the Cartesian thing—that in the sphere of growing up, all of us as children do in fact start with "*credo ut intelligam.*" If I was a baby and I didn't believe, when my parents said to me that there is a word for a thing, I should never learn to speak, obviously. Belief *must* always precede doubt—this seems to me to be quite clear.

Now, about the development from Darwin on in biology: to what extent has it changed our view of human nature? In my view, very little indeed. Human beings have always known that, like other mammals, they were born viviparously, they have to die, they have to reproduce sexually, they have to eat, they have to defecate, and so on. This we have always known. The curious thing actually is that in spite of our scientific knowledge—now this may not have anything to do with the sciences, it may simply have to do with technological society—that, in fact, we probably feel far less contact with the animal world than a hunting tribe did. We are always being told, whether we start from Copernicus or whether you come on to Darwin, that the result of this was to *humble* human beings so that they would realize that they were not as grand as they thought. I see no evidence that this happened at all. We got much more conceited, in my opinion.

On the other hand, I have great suspicion about the motives now of people who use the fact that we are descended from primates, to try to prove that we are just the same; because, I think, what they are really trying to do is to tell us that we don't have to bother about how we behave. Here again, if I may quote Chesterton, who said, "If it is not true that the Divine Being failed, then one can only say that one of the animals went entirely off its head."

We both can behave better and much worse than the animals. Various people have gone into this. For example, Konrad Lorenz points out that the problem of aggression in human beings . . . is so serious, [because,] first of all, our weapons are not part of our bodies, so that there are no built-in physiological and psychological inhibitions to using them. And second, no animal lets the sun go down on his wrath; we, because we have memory, can do this. On the other hand, one must remember that no animal forgives another animal.

Now, though I think, as I say, that the knowledge through Darwin and biology of our direct connection with more primitive creatures has *not* made much difference to our idea of ourselves, the advances in astronomy and physics have complete changed our picture of the physical universe, because previously it was thought of as a static and full thing which did not change. We now know it to be a process, a history. We have always known that our history as a species was part of a story, but we did not know that this was also true of the universe in a much more mysterious way.

This brings me on to something: I heard people talking in Stockholm about random events. Now, it is one thing to say an event is unpredictable. I think the use of the word "random" betrays a metaphysical presupposition that there can be no such thing as teleology. But, if somebody says that one event is random, why shouldn't all thoughts be random events, in which case why should I believe a word anybody says?

I personally do not believe in random events. I believe in miracles and I believe in providence. Take, for example, the question of the "invention" of photosynthesis, which was certainly completely unpredictable, and without it life as we know it could not be. All I can say about it is that this was a very providential event. Again, I know that, knowing what I know about the process of human reproduction and how long we have been here on earth, it is almost a statistical impossibility that I should be walking this earth. How can I take it except as a miracle, which I must do my best to deserve?

Then, if you think for a moment about natural selection, it seems to me that disaster is often predictable. For example, it is quite obvious that if you were to get a sudden violent climatic change, as you did in the ice age, a great many species would be wiped out. But, I don't think that success is predictable. What we observe is that whenever there is an ecological niche vacant, somehow or other some creature fills it. In some cases, the history is extremely complicated—take the case of a parasite like the liver fluke. Now, if you ask me only to believe that this is the result of random mutations—and as you probably know most random mutations that we observe are lethal—put through the sieve of natural selection, I think this is much crazier than believing in fairies.

How could this come about? I will have to say that I think that a lot of people who were present in Stockholm had forgotten two of the three worlds which I think essential for life. I will tell what the three worlds are first of all. They [those at Stockholm] were speaking from the point of view of the *vita activa*, by which I include all purposive action; [but] it does not mean you know your purposes will be realized. It includes politicians, it includes artists, scientists, bus drivers, and so on.

But, I think, they have forgotten two things. If you think about human beings, it seems to me there is one . . . activity which is unique to them—and that comes into the *vita activa*—and that is the activity of personal speech, of which animals are not capable; they are not even capable of calling each other by name. Then, animals are not capable of laughter, and they are not capable of prayer.

What I felt about a number of the people at Stockholm was that they had forgotten how to laugh—and by that I don't mean the Voltairean smile of reason, I mean belly laughter, which I shall talk about in a moment as the spirit of carnival—and how to pray.

If I talk about prayer, I think the petitionary side of it is purely a preliminary, superficial thing, because it is quite involuntary. Naturally, we are always asking: Can I marry the girl I love? Can I sell my house? Or whatever. But prayer really begins at the point at which one listens to a voice. I am not going to argue with people [about this]; I would call it the voice of the Holy Spirit, you could call it the inner light. The only things you cannot call it, you cannot call it reason, and you cannot call it the superego, because the superego could never say anything new.

[In prayer, then,] you listen and you are told, "Now, do this." It is often something you don't want to do. So, the motto over the world of prayer is *Respondeo etsi mutabor*, "I reply even though I am changed." Now, when I saw that these people had forgotten it, I knew that any and all of them had at least prayed once in their lives, when they heard a voice telling them, "You are to serve science." This was addressed to them not as scientists, but as human beings. . . .

On the other side . . . I should say a few words, first of all, about the *vita activa*. This is purposeful action in which we take responsibility for the results of our actions, whatever they may be. Here, of course, there is no question of equality. There is independence, interdependence, but not equality. I can't say a scientist is equal to an artist, or even that a man is equal to a woman; they are different . . .

If you take the world of prayer, here we are all equal in the sense that each of us is a unique person, with a unique perspective on the world, a member of a class of one. The myth of our common descent from a single ancestor, Adam, is a way of saying that as persons we are called into being, not by any biological process, but by our parents, our siblings, our friends, our enemies, and so on. This is where one listens to be told what one is to do next; and there is always something new.

On the other side is what I would call—connected with laughter as I think of it—the spirit of carnival, as exemplified in the Saturnalia, in medieval carnival, and the Roman carnival brilliantly described by Goethe in February of 1776. In the world of the *vita activa* there is no question of equality. There is a special kind of equality in the case of prayer. In the case of carnival, there is complete equality.

Essentially, what is carnival about? Here the great writers about it are Rabelais and Dickens. It is a common celebration of our common fate as members of our species. Here we are, mortal, born into the world, we must die, and this applies to everybody, so that there is a mixture. This is what laughter also implies, because laughter is both an act of protest and an act of acceptance. There is joy in the fact that we are all in the same boat, that there are no exceptions made. On the other hand, we cannot help wishing that we had no problems—let us say, that either we were in a way unthinking like the animals or that we were disembodied angels. [But] this is impossible; so we laugh because we simultaneously protest and accept.

In the world of carnival there is absolute equality. All distinctions of rank and even of sex are abolished. The women dress up as men, the men dress up as women. We discard our selves; we can wear masks. It is also a world of grotesque and parody; we wear grotesque masks, grotesque noses, and things. It is a world of mock obscenity, mock abuse, mock blasphemy.

On the question of blasphemy, I was reading a book by a Russian about Rabelais, who tried to think that the private parodies of religious rites were a protest against religious beliefs. But, of course, this is all nonsense. First of all, if the ecclesiastical authorities had thought so, they would have very soon stopped it. The fact is that blasphemy, of course, always implies belief, just as literary parody does, as Lewis Carroll pointed out: you can't parody an author you don't admire. So that, all blasphemy implies belief, and it is no accident that carnival comes just before Lent, which is a time for fasting and prayer.

This is a time when, naturally, there is mock obscenity, there is mock aggression. I will just give you a passage here from Goethe, describing one scene:

> Here come young fellows dressed up as women, one of whom seems to be far advanced in pregnancy. They are all strolling up and down peacefully, until suddenly the men start to quarrel. The brawl gets more and more violent, until both sides draw huge knives of silver cardboard and attack each other with them. The women cry murder and try to part them, pulling them this way and that. The bystanders intervene just as if they believed that the affair was in earnest. Meanwhile, as if from shock, the pregnant woman is taken ill. A chair is brought, and the others give her aid. She moans like a woman in labor and the next thing you know she has brought forth some monstrous creature into the world to the great amusement of the onlookers. The players and the troupe move on to repeat the performance or some farce like it elsewhere.

On the last evening of carnival, everyone appears in the streets carrying a lighted candle—an obvious symbol of life. Everyone tries to blow out the candles of others, or to relight his from theirs if his is blown out. All cry, "*Sia ammazzato*" ("Drop dead!") All distinctions of rank are abolished. Goethe describes how he heard a small boy screaming at his father, "*Sia ammazzato, il signor padre!*"

Now, all these things seem to me essential. Without the carnival, prayer tends to become Pharisaic or gnostic. Of course, without the *vita activa*, we should all perish in style. Without prayer, carnival turns ugly and dirty and instead of the inner voice, there comes the voice of the demagogue, because people without prayer have forgotten how to address others, and they try to keep it objective—and then there is trouble for that.

It seems to me, for example, that the hippies are trying—and quite rightly because this tends to disappear in a technological civilization—they are trying to revive the spirit of carnival. Unfortunately, it will fail, insofar as they reject the active life of work in between, it seems to me. Now, that is something valuable we can learn from them.

Trying to think about what changes have come about through astronomy and physics in our position in the physical universe, I look at it this way. It is true—and from a Christian point of view this seems to me essential—that it is absolutely right that the physical universe should exist *etsi Deus non daretur*, as if God did not exist. It has to be purged of all kinds of polytheism, which is then expecting, on the earth, God to do for us what we are supposed to do for him.

It seems to me that just as Adam was put in the Garden of Eden to dress it, we are here to look after the universe. By that, I think, in the end, one has to help the universe realize goals which it cannot realize itself. Of course, this is introducing again the idea of teleology, which we know has become a dirty word.

If I want to use an analogy, I say that in regard to the inorganic universe, I see our relation rather like that of a sculptor. No sculptor whom I have ever spoken to thinks of enforcing his forms on nature. He thinks: "I lay bare, I realize in a stone, a form that is latently there."

In regard to living things, I think the analogy, possibly, is that of the good animal trainer. I think a well-trained sheep dog has realized his dogginess, so to speak, more than a wild dog, just as a spoiled lap dog has had his dogginess debased. Therefore, I think we might have a decent world if it were universally recognized that to make a hideous lampshade, for example, is to torture helpless metals. And that every time we make a nuclear weapon, we corrupt the morals of a host of innocent neutrons below the age of consent.

Discussion

In the discussion that followed his prepared remarks, Mr Auden emphasized his point that the hippies were making a mistake in wanting carnival and the dissolution of individuality all of the time. You just can't have a perpetual festival, he said. . . .

. . . Mr Auden noted that the hippies seemed to be trying to get back to tribal life, although the sexual mores of the tribe would not seem to agree with the sexual freedom in hippie life. . . . Mr Auden commented that their fascination with astrology, with its inherent determinism, seemed to oppose their announced love of freedom. . . .

Mr Auden said he was alarmed by two separate aspects of the hippie movement:

> First, one sometimes feels that their lack of interest in the past betrays a lack of belief that they have a future. [Second,] this thing of taking your clothes off on the stage and doing all those things . . . [makes] me wonder if they can have any real friends, because surely there is an essential difference between the public and the private life. You take off your clothes in private; sex is a private matter.

Challenged by Dr Roger Shinn for making such a strong, almost "Cartesian," distinction between "axioms" and "moral commands," Mr Auden supported the distinction by pointing out that it was reflected in the grammar of each kind of statement: "All ethical things are in the imperative; axioms are in the indicative." . . . [Against an argument that mathematics uses imperatives interchangeably with indicatives:] Mr Auden replied: "I am not sure it's really quite true, because you couldn't possibly talk about one form of mathematics being better than another, could you?" Dr Morton Smith: "You could for a purpose." Mr Auden: "Yes, but then you need to bring in a purpose. And I defy you to create a series of axioms which are to everybody ethically compelling."

. . . Mr Auden repeated that he was only maintaining that what we know of our evolution has not really changed our conception of what we are. . . . Mr Auden replied that

> human beings have always known that there was historical change. . . . I don't think it was ever thought that human beings didn't change. People have always known, first of all in their personal lives, that you went through various stages, that you changed. . . .

Mr Auden replied . . . that men have "always known that change occurred. . . . There have been historians for quite a long time; from Herodotus to Thucydides on, we have written records of historians. Maybe a tribe doesn't have a sense of historical change—this may occur—but from the moment there were civilizations, surely people were aware of historical change."

. . . Mr Auden responded:

> There is, of course, a difference between the arts and the sciences in that you cannot, in the arts, talk about progress . . . [while,] in a sense, new scientific discoveries supersede the past. You cannot say that the art of any period supersedes the art of a previous period. There is this profound difference.

> And one other thing—if you ask me what the value of art is on the whole, I will say that it is, generally speaking, the chief medium through which we are able to hold communion with the dead. Homer is dead; his society is gone. But the *Iliad* is still relevant. . . . I personally think that . . . an artist must, essentially, always be a traditionalist in one sense, because, after all, what does one try to do? One tries to make an object which will permanently be on hand in the world. This is what one tries to do. All the odds are against one, but I am not going to attempt anything less.

. . . Mr Auden replied that he agreed that science was much nearer to action than to art. "Art is making. The artist," he said, "is *homo faber.* One makes something, an object." To Dr Anshen's proposal that the artist through art also makes himself, Mr Auden demurred: "No, oneself is completely dispensable."

. . . Mr Auden agreed that the introduction of alien artistic influences "had been going on a long time." He continued:

> In the eighteenth century, for example, Eastern art began to be an influence. Now we live in a world where more or less all things are available. Of course, you adapt them to your own purposes; but, I think, this has probably been always so. To take an obvious example, we can go back to the Romans, when the Roman poets adopted Greek models, which . . . if you think of what people like Horace did, changed the whole prosody of Latin.

After some further discussion, Mr Auden announced that he must depart. "The older I get, the more sleep I want," he said. . . .

Work, Carnival and Prayer

Auden delivered this lecture to various audiences before and during the lecture tour he made in February and March 1971 and, after returning from the tour, sent the typescript to one of his hosts, R. Sherman Beattie, then at Ball State University, Muncie, Indiana. He kept a second, slghtly revised copy, now lost, for later use. After Auden's death Beattie offered his typescript to *The Episcopalian* for unauthorized publication; the magazine divided the text into four parts but printed only the first three (in its issues for March, April, and May 1974) before the magazine changed its format and direction.

Auden read from the lost second typescript when he delivered the first Cheltenham Lecture at the annual Cheltenham Festival of Literature, 13 November 1972. A recording of it was made by Martin Rabius.

The text below is edited from the typescript that Auden gave to Beattie and which is now in the Berg Collection, but I have incorporated the minor revisions heard in the 1972 recording. I have also followed many minor revisions and rearrangements marked in the typescript. After the paragraph that begins "Criminal laws are" (p. 692) Auden scrawled "lucky sick powerful", presumably as a cue to make *ad lib* remarks on the ways in which human beings perceive these conditions as rewards or punishments. After the paragraph that begins "The Incarnation, however" (p. 697) Auden wrote "Friday's Child", a cue to read the poem, as he does in the recording. In the paragraph that begins "Again, one frequently" (p. 698), after "I don't pretend that I can prove them", Auden wrote what seems to be a note to himself: "[two illegible words] in [Rosenstock-]Huessy". After the paragraph that begins "As a Christian, I do not" (p. 699) Auden wrote, then deleted, a mostly illegible sentence: "[illegible] from [?changes] [illegible] no civilization can endure". Most of Auden's quotations are abridged and modified.

To-day, all of us, whatever our religious and political convictions, are conscious of the threat of disaster: we all realise that, if we continue to plunder and poison our earth as we are doing, we shall make it uninhabitable in the not-so-distant future, if we have not already destroyed ourselves with nuclear weapons. The questions: "What is Man's true status in Nature? What are our responsibilities to the Cosmos?" have become more urgent than ever before.

In trying to answer them, those of us who are Christians or Jews may very properly begin by asking: "What are the implications of the story of Creation as given in the first two chapters of Genesis?"

In Chapter One we are told:

> Firstly, that the creation of human beings is only the last in a series of creative acts by God.
>
> Secondly, after each of them, the phrase "And God saw that it was good" is repeated.
>
> Thirdly, in blessing human beings, God uses the same phrase which he uses in blessing the animals: "Be fruitful and multiply."
>
> Lastly, it is to be noticed that, in the phrase "Male and female created He them", the pronoun is in the *Third Person Plural.*

That is to say, though human beings, unlike minerals and plants and the other animals, have been made "in the image of God", a phrase we will consider later, like everything else in the universe, inanimate and animate, we are God's creatures, and, like all living creatures, we are biological organisms who reproduce their kind.

Let us briefly compare this notion of the Divine with two others, the gods of Greek mythology and the God of Greek philosophy.

The gods of mythology are not the creators, either of the material universe or of men. In their natures they are indistinguishable from men: their desires are the same. They only differ from us in that they are immortal and invulnerable, while we are neither. As Pindar wrote:

There is one
race of men, one race of gods, both have breath
from a single mother. But sundered power
holds us divided. So that we are nothing, while
for the other the brazen sky is established
their sure stronghold for ever.

There seems to be no logical reason why the gods should concern themselves with men at all, but the vicissitudes of human existence seem to indicate that they do. They do not love mortals, except sometimes in a sexual sense, and they do not expect mortals to love them. What they demand is the fearful respect which the Lower Orders owe to their betters. If this respect is withheld they become angry and they have the power to reward or punish as they choose. The expression of fearful respect which they seem to prefer is blood sacrifice, either human or animal.

As Lord de Tabley has written:

They cry to the nations
"We strike if you pray not.
We bend down our eyes along
Temple and grove,
Searching the incense curl
And the live smell of blood;
Hating the worshipper,
Craving his prayer."

If men, individually or collectively, are to succeed in any activity, they must find the god concerned with that activity and pay him the reverence he demands. In Homer and, I think, in Euripides, there is no pretense that the gods are "good." Aeschylus and Sophocles do entertain the notion that they may be righteous, but the moral demands they make on men are, like criminal laws, imposed from above on creatures already in existence, and it is left to the gods, when a man breaks one, to decide when and how he shall be punished. In Greek tragedy the tragic flaw of the hero is *hybris.* The hero believes that like the gods, he is invulnerable, until the gods demonstrate that he is not. I will discuss later the difference between *hybris* and the Christian sin of pride: I will merely say now that the temptation to *hybris* can obviously only occur to someone whose life so far has been exceptionally happy and successful. He must be stronger, better looking, richer and happier than most men.

It is clear that the polytheistic pantheon could be reduced to a monotheistic Zeus without changing its character. Such a Zeus would have one, but only one, characteristic in common with the God of the Bible. Both are persons who can speak to men and to Whom men can answer.

This is not the case with the God of Greek philosophy, with the Platonic Ideas or Aristotle's First Cause. Like the polytheistic gods, the *to Theon* of philosophy did not create the material universe—God and the World are co-eternal—but, unlike them and like the Biblical God, He or It is absolutely good and to be loved not feared by men. But the relation is one-sided. We, by virtue of being rational creatures can love God in the sense of trying to imitate Him—even matter can imitate him by adopting regular motions—but God, being impersonal, cannot love us. As Aristotle expressly says: "God has no need of friends, neither, indeed, can he have any." The source of human evil and suffering is not sin, but the misfortune of being souls who are imprisoned in matter, which is by nature inferior and peccable.

Both the gods of polytheism and the god of philosophy are alike in that belief in either is not a matter of faith. Worldly success and failure are self-evident facts: logical reasoning leads to inevitable conclusions. For the Biblical God, however, no proofs of His existence are waterproof. But if, by faith, we believe in Him, and the account of how we were created, certain conclusions follow:

(1) The basic ground for loving God must be gratitude, not fear. Thanks to Him, we exist, and existence is a good. As the Prophets kept reminding Israel: "He delighteth not in the smell of burnt offerings. What is pleasing to Him is a true and contrite heart."

(2) However we are to account for Evil and Sin, we are not to attribute them to the fact that we are not disembodied angels but creatures of flesh and blood, with the desires, like hunger and sex, which go with that condition.

(3) Wittgenstein must be right in saying: "Ethics does not treat of the world. Ethics must be a condition of the world, like logic." That is to say, the laws of man's spiritual nature must, like the laws of his physical nature, be laws-*of*, laws which out of ignorance or choice, he can *defy*, but can no more *break* than he can break the law of Gravity by jumping out of the window or the laws of biochemistry by getting drunk, and the consequences of defying them must be as inevitable and as intrinsically related to our natures as a broken leg or a hangover. As Kin Hubbard wrote: "We are not punished for our sins but by them". In other words, it is not God we should be afraid of, but ourselves, and of the Evil One who is Prince of this world.

All theological language is necessarily analogical, but it was singularly unfortunate that the Church, in speaking of sin and the punishment for sin, should have chosen the analogy of Criminal Law which, as we have seen, is compatible only with a polytheistic cosmology, not with the Biblical conception of God as Creator.

Criminal laws are laws-*for*, imposed upon men who are already in existence, with or without their consent, and, with the possible exception of capital punishment for murder, there is no logical or intelligible relation between the nature of the crime and the penalty inflicted for committing it.

What led the Church into using this disastrous analogy, was, I think, the fact that, both in the Old and the New Testament, ethical laws are stated, as they are in Criminal Law, in the Imperative, not the Indicative—"Thou shalt not commit adultery"—"Thou shalt love thy neighbor as thyself." There are two reasons, I believe, why the Imperative has to be used. Firstly, it is a necessary pedagogical technique, as when a mother says to her small child—"Stay away from the window"—because the child does not yet know what will happen if he falls out of it. In the case of physical laws, we soon learn the consequence of defying them, though even this certain knowledge does not prevent us from destroying ourselves with alcohol or drugs. But in the case of spiritual laws, the consequences are not immediately perceptible to the senses and take effect only gradually. Secondly, because we are all of us in sin, an axiomatic ethical formulation, like saying—"A straight line is the shortest distance between two points"—would be ineffective because we each think of ourselves as the exception to any rule, like a madman who jumps out of the window because he believes he can fly. Furthermore, all sin tends to become addictive: if we persist in it, it is not long before, though we are unhappy, we come to prefer bondage and misery to freedom and joy. As Simone Weil wrote: "Sin is unconscious misery and, for that reason, guilty misery. All sin is an attempt to fill voids." The state of terminal addiction is what we mean by damnation. Since God has given us the freedom either to accept his love and grace and obey the laws of our created nature, or to reject and defy them, He cannot prevent us from going to hell and staying there if that is what we insist upon. In granting us free will, he has, in a sense, chosen to limit His Omnipotence. But, unless, at the same time, He has chosen to limit His Omniscience, the Calvinist doctrine of Predestination is an inevitable conclusion. My own belief is that, just as we have to have faith in God, God has to have faith in us and, considering the history of the human race so far, such "faith" may be even more difficult for Him than it is for us. Though I know it has been labelled a heresy, under the influence, I suspect, of Greek philosophy, I am a convinced Patripassionist.

Let us turn now to the second Chapter of Genesis. Here, in speaking of human beings, the singular has replaced the plural of the First Chapter.

God forms Adam out of the dust, breathes into his nostrils the breath of life and he becomes a living soul whom God addresses as Thou and to whom he answers with I, and the reason given for there being two sexes is not biological but psychological—It is not good that man should be alone. This account helps to clarify what was meant in the first chapter by saying that man is made in the image of God. Every human being, that is to say, is at once, like the other animals, an individual member of a species, Homo Sapiens, and a unique person, a member of a class of one, who can say *I*, an I which is a trinity-in-unity. As St Augustine says: "I am willing and knowing: I know that I am and will: I will to be and to know." The myth of our common descent from a single ancestor, Adam, is a way of stating the fact that, as persons, we are called into being, not by any biological process, but by other persons, God, our parents, our teachers, our siblings, our friends. As individuals, we are countable, comparable, replaceable: as persons we are uncountable, incomparable, irreplaceable. As individuals we exhibit behavior: as Persons we are capable of choosing to act in one way, and refusing to act in another, and of accepting the future consequences of our acts, whatever they may be.

This might be easier for us, if our awareness of ourselves as individuals and as persons could be kept distinct. Unfortunately, they cannot, because man is a history-creating creature who has been able to develop after his biological evolution was complete. Consequently, we can use the indefinite article to mean various things. As a biological description—a man, a woman, a child, a redhead—and to indicate membership in some particular cultural or social group—an Englishman, a doctor, etc. Cultures and professions have been created by persons and so are to be thought of as corporate persons, but those who belong to them are individuals, not persons, to the degree that their modes of thinking and behaving are conditioned by the group to which they belong, and not personally chosen by them.

It is this duality of our nature that tempts us into Pride, the sin which Christian theologians have always regarded as the Primal Sin, from which all the others issue. I want, however, to try and describe Pride with as few theological presuppositions as possible.

My senses tell me that the world is inhabited by a number of human individuals whom I can count and compare with each other, and I do not doubt the evidence of my senses. It requires, however, an act of faith on my part to believe that they enjoy a personal existence as I do, that when I hear them say I, they mean what I mean when I say it, for this my senses cannot tell me. Nor can they tell me that what I see them doing is an act of free choice, for I cannot see them choose, I can only see what in fact they do. Even in the case of my parents, or a lover, where I tell myself that to me they are real persons, it is all too easy for me to endow them with an imaginary I, pleasant or unpleasant, which has nothing to do with their real one.

Vice versa, my own personal existence is to me self-evident. What, where I am concerned, calls for an act of faith, is to believe that I, too, like everyone else, am a human individual brought into the world by an act of sexual intercourse and exhibiting socially conditioned behavior, to believe, that is to say, that the Self of which I am aware and I are an indissoluble unity, for my immediate experience is of a Self, both physical and mental, which I am inhabiting like a house or driving like a motor-car.

The refusal to make these two acts of faith is what constitutes the sin of pride.

And what are the consequences? In relation to others, it ends by my regarding them as objects to be either ignored or exploited for my own advantage. In dealing with them my philosophy is materialist and behaviourist.

In my relation to myself, two consequences are possible. To the degree that I am pleased with the self that has been given me, like the Pharisee in the parable, I take the credit to myself and think that my advantages over others are due to my superior merit. To the degree that I am dissatisfied with myself—and those who are completely satisfied with themselves are very rare—I shall either turn on others and God in a passion of envy and resentment, or refuse to take responsibility for my actions, which is another form of Phariseeism, that is to say, instead of saying simply like the Publican—God be merciful to me a sinner—I shall say—Yes, I know I take bribes and that is a bad thing to do, but I can't help it because Mother didn't love me. In dealing with myself my philosophy is Gnostic and Manicheean.

As an antidote to pride man has been endowed with the capacity for prayer, an activity which is not to be confined to prayer in the narrow religious sense of the word. To pray is to pay attention or, shall we say, to "listen" to someone or something other than oneself.

Whenever a man so concentrates his attention—be it on a landscape, or a poem or a geometrical problem or an idol or the True God—that he completely forgets his own ego and desires in listening to what the other has to say to him, he is praying. Choice of attention—to attend to this and ignore that—is to the inner life what choice of action is to the outer. In both cases a man is responsible for his choice and must accept the consequences. As Ortega y Gasset said: "Tell me to what you pay attention and I will tell you who you are." The primary task of the schoolteacher is to teach children, in a secular context, the technique of prayer.

Petitionary prayer is a special case and, of all kinds of prayer, I believe the least important. Our wishes and desires—to pass an exam, to marry the person we love, to sell our house at a good price—are involuntary and therefore not in themselves prayers, even if it is God whom we ask to attend to them. They only become prayers in so far as we believe that God knows better than we whether we should be granted or denied what we ask. A petition does not become a prayer unless it ends with the words, spoken or unspoken—"Nevertheless, not as I will, but as Thou wilt." Perhaps the main value of petitionary prayer is that, when we consciously phrase our desires, we often discover that they are really wishes that two-and-two should make three or five, as when St Augustine realised that he was praying: "Lord, make me chaste, but not yet."

Be that as it may, the essential aspect of prayer is not what we say, but what we hear. I don't think it matters terribly whether one calls the Voice that speaks to us the Voice of the Holy Spirit, as Christians do, or the Reality Principle, as psychoanalysts do, so long as we do not confuse it with the voice of the Super-Ego, for the Super-Ego, being a social creation, can only tell us something we knew already, whereas the voice that speaks to us in prayer always says something new and unexpected, and very possibly unwelcome. The reason why I do not think the label matters that much is because I know the most convinced atheist scientist has prayed at least once in his life, when he heard a voice saying: "Thou shalt serve Science."

Now, let us return to Genesis. There God entrusts Adam with two tasks which he is to do for himself, not expect God to do for him. Firstly he is to give the animals their Proper Names. To give someone or something a Proper Name is to acknowledge it as having a real and valuable existence, independent of its use to oneself, in other words, to acknowledge it as a neighbor. As Thoreau said: "With knowledge of the name comes a distincter recognition and knowledge of the thing." We cannot, however, treat a neighbor rightly, unless we realise that he, or it, is not a copy of ourselves. Hence one role of science is to rescue us from animism and totemism. As Wittgenstein said: "*I* is not the name of a person, nor *Here* of a place, and *This* is not a name. But they are connected with names. Names are explained by means of them. It is also true that it is characteristic of physics not to use these words."

Secondly, God commanded Adam to till and dress the Garden of Eden, but he did not give him gardening lessons. Adam was to discover for himself what he must do. Man is to use the powers of observation, foresight and intelligence with which he has been endowed to act upon and modify his environment. Man, from the beginning, that is to say, was created a worker—work was not imposed upon him as a result of the Fall.

If it is not good that man should be alone, it is equally not good for him to be idle and do nothing, and the consequence of idleness is boredom and unhappiness. Perhaps that is why it is so hard, according to the Gospels, for a rich man to enter into the Kingdom of Heaven.

Then the model given for all work and, as the Latin word implies, for all culture, is agriculture. This helps to clarify the phrases in the first Chapter—"replenish the earth and subdue it: and have dominion . . . over every living thing that moveth upon the earth." Every good gardener knows that success in his work depends upon a friendly collaboration between himself and Nature. Though it is for him to issue commands and for Nature to obey them, he cannot be a tyrant who commands by whim or enforces obedience by violence. Only those commands can be fruitful which it is in the true interests of Nature as well as his own to obey. The proper relation of a gardener to his flowers and vegetables is that of a father to his children, and a good father is always willing to learn from his children. There are insects that farm, but they can never improve on what instinct wills them to do. Human work always implies both respect for tradition, for past experience and an openness towards the future, a readiness to experiment and innovate.

It has been repeated ad nauseam that the psychological effect of the rise of the natural sciences, the effect of such discoveries as those made by Galileo, Darwin and Freud has been to reduce man's pride and conceit. Nothing could be more untrue. In the medieval cosmology, the earth was only the centre of the Universe in that it was its lowest point, so that all movement towards the earth was downward.

The revolution effected by the sciences has been exactly the opposite. Science has had two effects, one, from a Christian point of view, admirable, the other pernicious.

On the one hand it has liberated man from a misplaced humility before a false god. The god whose death Nietzsche announced was not the true God, though, undoubtedly, he was the god in whom many people who imagined they were Christians believed, namely a Zeus without Zeus's vices, ruler, lawgiver, rewarder, punisher, the god nicely described by William Blake in his translation of Doctor Thornton's Tory translation of the Lord's Prayer:

> Our Father Augustus Caesar, who art in these thy Substantial Astronomic Telescopic Heavens, Holiness to Thy Name or Title, & reverence to Thy Shadow . . . For thine is the Kingship or Allegoric Godship, & the Power, or War, & the Glory, or Law, Ages after Ages in thy descendants, for God is only an Allegory of Kings & nothing else.

Such a god is not a creator of Nature but, like Zeus, a god of Nature, so that it was possible to think of natural catastrophes like Flood, Fire, Famine, Pestilence as "Acts of God", a phrase which is to be found to this day, I believe, in Insurance Policies. If there were such things, then, not only would man be powerless to alter them, but also it would be impious for him to try.

The great achievement of the sciences has been to demythologise the Universe. Precisely because He created it, God cannot be encountered directly in the Universe—a storm, for example, is a natural phenomenon, not as in polytheism the wrath of Zeus—, just as when I read a poem, I do not encounter the author himself, only the words he has written which it is my job to understand. The Universe exists *etsi Deus non daretur.*

Such a discovery was inevitable and, in itself, good. Unfortunately, however, as a whole, Christians failed to realise that it entailed a revision of their idea about their faith. As Charles Williams, discussing the Renaissance, wrote:

> Had chances been different, there might have been a revival of the old wisdom of Christ as *anthropos*; the secrets of Christendom might have enriched with new significance the material world. It was not to be; the

anthropos had been forgotten for the *theos*, and now the other anthropos, the Adam of St Augustine, the *homo sapiens* of science, preoccupied European attention.

Thus, if we ask, as Christians: "Why, since science has made untenable a belief in a God who manifests his existence by direct action in the cosmos, is it possible for us, as Christians, still to believe in God's existence, and not become atheists", our only answer can be: "Because we believe in the Incarnation." Williams speaks of the revival of old Wisdom, for earlier theologians had already sensed this. Thus St Anselm wrote:

> *quod fide tenemus de divina natura et ejus personis* praeter incarnationem, *necessariis rationibus sine scripturae auctoritate probari possit.*

> What we hold by faith about the divine nature and its persons, *except for the incarnation*, can be proved by necessary reason without the authority of the Scriptures.

Commenting on this sentence, Rosenstock-Huessy writes:

> "Except" means that the necessary reasons cannot explain our traditions and memories of the historical life and death of the founder of the Church. Anselm says, in another place, that he could prove negatively that mankind could not have found peace without this historical experience. In other words, theology can go as far as to prove the negative situation of the world and a humanity without the Incarnation. From this assertion, it is clear that the fact that is exempted from reasoning, the Incarnation, is not an annex. It is present *all* the time in the mind of those reasoning. The combination of speculation and tradition, then, is quite subtle: the historical experience forces the speculation onto a level it could not possibly attain otherwise. For instance, a world and a humanity without the incarnation can be proven to be incomplete, to be in the red, to give a sound basis for despair and pessimism and agnosticism. If this is so, the co-habitation of two sequences of facts is the basis of theology in all its mental activity. Christianity is not based on a myth or a legend. It is its honor to be an historical faith, based on events plus reason. (*Speech and Reality*)

The Incarnation, however, remains a matter of faith not reason. The pagan gods often appeared to mortals disguised as human beings, usually for sexual reasons. So long as they were so disguised, no mortal was expected or could recognize their divinity. But at the moment of apotheosis, when they shed their disguise and appeared as they really were, it was impossible to doubt it. Christ, on the other hand, appears on earth as a man, looking like any other man, yet making the assertion: "I am the Way, the Truth, the Life: None cometh unto the Father save through me." And, even after his resurrection, he does not appear to the whole world, only to a few disciples, to whom he entrusts the task of preaching a fact to the world which they cannot prove.

The less happy effect of science, which is not due to the nature of science itself, but to the sinfulness of men, including scientists, has been that, having dethroned an imaginary Zeus, we have set Man in his place as a superhuman ruler who can do anything he likes with impunity, one for whom, as for all tyrants, whatever is possible is necessary.

The effect of Darwin on the public in general was certainly not to make him humbler. Men did not have to wait for Darwin to know that, like all mammals, they are viviparously born, must devour proteins, i.e. other lives, defecate, copulate and die. Indeed in pre-industrial societies, they felt a far closer kinship to the animal kingdom than most of us do. They did however believe that more was expected of men than of the rest of creation, that they could be guilty in the eyes of God of sins, while the rest of creation was morally innocent. To-day, the knowledge that man is a biological species evolved out of less complex creatures, is used only too often as an excuse for bad behavior. As Karl Kraus wrote:

> When a man is treated like a beast, he says: "After all I'm human."
> When he behaves like a beast, he says: "After all, I'm only human."

For example, the phenomenon of aggression in animals has been used to justify human violence as being only "natural". Such justification overlooks two facts. Firstly, no animal can let the sun go down upon its wrath: we, gifted with memory, can and all too often do. Secondly, as Konrad Lorenz has pointed out:

> All living beings have received their weapons through the same process of evolution that moulded their impulses and inhibitions: for the structural plan of the body and the system of behaviour of a species are parts of the same whole. There is only one being in possession of weapons which do not grow on his body and of whose working plans, therefore, the instincts of his species know nothing, and in the usage of which he has no corresponding inhibitions.

Again, one frequently hears scientists speak of "random" events as if this was a demonstrable scientific fact. It is not. To say that an event is "unpredictable", at least in our present state of knowledge, is a factual description. To call an event random conceals, without admitting it, a metaphysical presupposition, which lies outside the realm of science altogether, namely the dogma that there cannot be such a thing as Providence or miracles. As a Christian, I believe in both, by faith: I don't pretend I can prove them. For instance the invention of photosynthesis without which life as we know it would not exist was certainly unpredictable. I can only say, though, that it was a damned lucky event for us. As for miracles, I think the best definition is that of Rosenstock-Huessy: "A miracle is the natural law of a unique event." Biologically speaking, it is almost a statistical absurdity that I should be walking the earth instead of a million other possible people. But how can I regard this fact except as a miracle which I must do my best to deserve. Moreover, I am pretty certain that the most dyed-in-the-wool behaviorist thinks of himself, whatever his conviction, as being "meant" to exist.

To-day the consequences of this are becoming only too obvious. We all realise that Goethe was right when he said: "We need a categorical Imperative in the natural sciences as much as we need one in ethics." We are finding out to our cost that we cannot enslave Nature without enslaving ourselves. If nobody in the universe is responsible for man, then we must conclude that man is responsible, under and to God, for the Universe. This means that it is our task to discover what everything in the universe from electrons upwards could, to its betterment, become, but cannot without our help. This means re-introducing into the sciences a new notion of teleology, long a dirty word. For our proper relation to living creatures the analogy might be that of a good gardener or a good trainer of animals. A well-trained, well-treated sheep-dog is more of a dog than a wild one, just as a stray, terrified by ill-usage, or a spoiled lap-dog, has had its dogginess debased. For our relation to non-living matter, the analogy might be that of a sculptor. Every sculptor thinks of himself, not as someone who imposes forcibly a form on stone, but as someone who reveals a beautiful form already latent in it. The world will be a more pleasant place when it is generally realised that, every time we make an ugly lampshade, we are torturing helpless metal, every time we make a nuclear weapon, we are corrupting the morals of a host of innocent neutrons below the age of consent.

As a Christian, I do not believe we can achieve this, unless we listen to the voice of the Living God who can be personally encountered, not in the natural universe, but only in prayer.

There are two characteristics of man which the Bible does not mention. He is the only creature who can laugh and the only creature who can play-act, that is to say, pretend to be somebody else.

By laughter, I do not mean mocking titters or the superior Voltairian smile, though we are, alas, capable of them both. I mean what we call "belly" laughter.

As Hazlitt said: "Man is the only animal that laughs and weeps; for he is the only animal that is struck by the difference between what things are and what they might have been." Laughter originates in protest but ends in acceptance. A man in a passion of any kind cannot be made to laugh: if he laughs, it is a proof that he has mastered his passion. True laughter is unaggressive:

we cannot wish people or things whom we find amusing to be other than they are. True laughter is, as we say, "disarming".

Our capacity for and love of play-acting is a puzzling trait which has not, in my opinion, received the psychological scrutiny it deserves. Many animals indulge in playful acts—e.g. kittens play at hunting—but they play themselves. Some animals have been genetically conditioned, for protective reasons, to imitate another species—e.g. there are moths that look like hornets—but they do not identify themselves with the species they imitate. The closest human parallel would be the criminal who undergoes facial surgery in order to escape being recognised.

Human beings also play games, like football or bridge, but as games-players we remain ourselves. We may also perform rites in which someone *represents* another being, a god, for instance, but he does not have to *imitate* him, anymore than an ambassador has to imitate the mannerism of the sovereign whom he represents.

But when we play-act we imitate the words, gestures and actions of some person other than ourselves, and at the same time, unlike a madman who thinks he is Napoleon or Jesus Christ, we remain aware that we are not the person whose role we have assumed. Why on earth should we enjoy doing this? My own conclusion is that the impulse behind play-acting is a longing to escape into a world of pre-lapsarian innocence. This is true, also, of our love of games, but between games and play-acting there is one important difference. When we play football or bridge, our game actions are in themselves innocent, i.e. outside the realm of ethical judgement. But when we imitate another human being, we imitate a sinner, and at the same time are not guilty of his sins. If, for example, I play the part of Macbeth, I am not accountable, either to God or the police, for the murders of Duncan and Banquo. If I play Falstaff, I am not responsible for any of his ridiculous behavior. This means, however, that my imitation cannot be complete: all my imitative actions must be mock-actions. If my part calls for me to hate another character and ultimately to stab him, I must not really hate or stab the actor who is playing him: I must only appear to do so. Thus, it is only in play-acting that human beings can approximate to the moral innocence of the animals.

If this is so, it may help to explain the social and religious function of Carnival, a celebration known equally well to Paganism and to medieval Christianity, but now, at least in industrialised and Protestant cultures, largely and, in my opinion, disastrously forgotten.

Here are some extracts from a description of the Roman Carnival as observed by Goethe in February 1788.

> Young men disguised as women of the lower classes are usually the first to appear. They embrace the men, they take intimate liberties with the

women, as being of their own sex, and indulge in any behaviour which their mood, wit or impertinence suggests.

One young man stands out in my memory. He played the part of a passionate quarrelsome woman perfectly. "She" went along the whole length of the Corso, picking quarrels with everyone and insulting them, while her companions pretended to be doing their best to calm her down.

Here a *pulcinella* comes running along with a large horn dangling from colored strings between his thighs. As he talks to women, he manages to imitate with a slight, impudent movement the figure of the God of gardens. . . .

Now an advocate elbows his way quickly through the crowd, declaiming as if he were addressing a court of justice. He shouts up at the windows, buttonholes the passers-by, whether in fancy dress or not, and threatens to prosecute every one of them. To one he reads out a long list of ridiculous crimes he is supposed to have committed, to another an exact tabulation of his debts. He accuses the women of having *cicisbei,* the girls of having lovers. . . .

Now and then a masked fair lady mischievously flings some sugar-coated almonds at her passing friend to attract his attention and naturally enough, he turns round to see who has thrown the missile. But real sugared confetti is expensive, so a cheaper substitute must be provided for this kind of petty warfare, and there are traders who specialise in plaster bonbons, made by means of a funnel, which they carry in large baskets and offer for sale to the crowd. No one is safe from attack, everyone is on the defensive, so now and then, from high spirits or necessity, a duel, a skirmish or a battle ensues. Pedestrians, coachmen, spectators alternately attack others and defend themselves. . . .

Here comes a group of men, wearing short jackets over gold-laced waistcoats, and with their hair gathered up in nets which hang down their backs. With them are other fellows, dressed up as women, one of whom seems to be far advanced in pregnancy. They are all strolling up and down peacefully until, suddenly, the men start to quarrel. A lively altercation ensues, the women get mixed up in it, and the brawl gets more and more violent, until both sides draw huge knives of silver cardboard and attack each other. The women cry murder and try to part them, pulling them this way and that. The bystanders intervened, just as if they believed the affair was in earnest, and try to calm both parties down.

Meanwhile, as if from shock, the pregnant woman is taken ill. A chair is brought, and the other women give her aid. She moans like a woman in labor, and the next thing you know, she has brought some misshapen creature into the world, to the great amusement of the onlookers.

Then on the last day of Carnival everyone comes into the street carrying a lighted candle, an obvious symbol of life. Then, [?says] Goethe:

> "*Sia ammazzato chi non porta maccolo*:" "Death to anyone who is not carrying a candle." This is what you say to others, while at the same time you try to blow out their candles. No matter if it belongs to a friend or a stranger, you try to blow out the nearest candle, or to light your own from it first and then blow it out. . . . This evening the true meaning of *sia ammazzato* is completely forgotten, and it becomes a password, a cry of joy, a refrain added to all jokes and compliments . . . All ages and all classes contend furiously with each other. A boy blows out his father's candle, shouting "*Sia ammazzato il Signore Padre!*" In vain the old man scolds him for this outrageous behavior; the boy claims the freedom of the evening and curses his father all the more vehemently.

To the exhibition of mock sexuality and mock aggression Goethe describes should be added another feature typical of most medieval carnivals, mock religious rites which the Church authorities had the good sense to tolerate. They seemed to have realised that what holds good for literary parody holds good for all parody, namely, that one can only successfully parody something one loves and respects.

The world of Carnival, then, is the antithesis of the everyday world of work and action. Since nothing is organised, it is not a drama but a succession of what to-day are called "happenings" and everybody plays the role of his own choice. During Carnival all human beings, irrespective of sex or age or worldly status, are equal. At this point we should remember two things. Firstly, that Carnival lasts but a brief while, a week at most, and secondly that this week immediately precedes Lent, the season dedicated to fasting, repentance and prayer. In both worlds we are all equal, but for different reasons: during Carnival we are all equal before Nature as members of the same biological species: in prayer, we are all equal in the eyes of God as unique persons. The only occasion upon which both forms of equality are simultaneously asserted is during Mass, at which we both pray and eat. As biological organisms we must all alike assimilate other lives in order to live. As conscious beings, the same holds good on the intellectual level: all learning is assimilation. As children of God, made in His image, we are required in turn voluntarily to surrender ourselves to being assimilated by our neighbors according to their needs. One might define the difference between Hell and Heaven by saying that the slogan of Hell is *Eat or be eaten*, of Heaven *Eat and be eaten.*

In the world of work, on the other hand, whatever the political form of state, there cannot be such a thing as equality. Instead there is, what is lacking in Carnival, interdependence. In the world of work, he who does something for me which I cannot do for myself is my superior. Thus, if I take a taxi, the driver is, for the time being, my superior, and I recognize this fact by paying him money. If I give a course in English poetry, I am superior to my pupils because I know more about the subject than they do: If I don't, then I have no right to be teaching at all. In the world of work, that is to say, we are never equal, but we are always neighbors, members one of another.

I said earlier that I deplore the disappearance in most industrialised societies of a sense of Carnival and what it means, because I do not think that a fully human life is possible without due attention being paid to the three worlds I have outlined. If I understand rightly what it is the hippies are really after, I would say that they are attempting to recover a sense of Carnival, and in so far as they are, they should command our respect and be encouraged. Unfortunately, however, they seem to reject the world of Work, and would like life to be an unending carnival. The consequence of this can only be, firstly, boredom, because one cannot play-act for very long and, secondly, to overcome the boredom, stimulants like drugs and the turning of mock-actions into real ones, i.e. the fun will turn ugly, the mock-obscenity into real grubbiness, the mock aggression into real violence.

But Carnival has its proper and necessary place. Without it, prayer almost inevitably becomes Pharisaic or Gnostic, and when men think only of work and ignore both prayer and carnival, then they lose all humility, all reverence either for God or the natural universe, all sense of their neighbor, and become the tyrannical exploiters of nature and each other, which is the most obvious characteristic of the societies in which we now live.

Prayer, Work, Laughter, we need them all.

Phantasy and Reality in Poetry

Auden delivered this lecture to the Philadelphia Association for Psychoanalysis on 12 March 1971 as its annual Freud Memorial Lecture. The text below is an edited version of the manuscript in the Berg Collection. A diplomatic transcript by Katherine Bucknell, with an extensive introduction and notes, appeared in *"In Solitude, for Company": Auden after 1940* (Auden Studies 3), edited by Katherine Bucknell and Nicholas Jenkins (1995). In the text below I have silently inserted a few words that were obviously intended; doubtful insertions are in square brackets; bracketed insertions that begin with a question mark are my attempts to read illegible words or to make sense of a passage altered by illegible revisions.

A page of the manuscript seems to be missing immediately after Auden's brief list of his nursery library (p. 708); the missing page may perhaps have begun with additional entries in the list. This missing page (numbered 13) seems to have been marked to indicate that the quotation from *Struwwelpeter* (typed on a surviving page numbered "13a") should be inserted in it. I have filled the gap before the quotation with a sentence adapted from a similar passage in *A Certain World* (p. 42), and have filled the gap after the quotation with the two words "It so". It is at least possible that Auden discarded (or misplaced) the entire page and improvised a few words before and after the quotation somewhat in the manner of the patching that I have done here.

In inviting me to deliver the Freud Memorial lecture, you have done me a great honor, but one, also, for which I am only too conscious of my lack of qualifications. As regards Freud himself, there are only two points upon which, as a poet, I have the authority to pass judgements, one positive, and one negative. Firstly, his command of German. Here I would say, without hesitation, that the three great masters of the German language in this century, all of them, curiously enough, from the Hapsburg Empire, have been Freud, Karl Kraus and Kafka. Secondly, as you know, Freud believed that Shakespeare's plays were written by the Earl of Oxford. Here, again, I can say categorically that he was mistaken. I have read many of Freud's [?writings,] as well as other psychoanalytic literature. Some, like *The Interpretation of Dreams* and *On Wit*, have made a lasting impression and I think I understand them. Others, like *Totem and Taboo* and *Moses and Monotheism* I have found impossible to swallow. In the case of most human activities, they cannot be fully understood except from the inside, and this is always presumably the case in psychoanalysis. Anyone like myself who has not had the experience of being analysed, is in no position to assess the truth or falsehood of its findings.

It seems to me therefore I must confine myself in this lecture to the one subject I do know from the inside, namely the Art of Poetry. This also entails that much of what I have to say must be autobiographical, for which I must ask you to excuse me. I should like to believe that my experiences are not peculiar to myself but are fairly typical of all poets, but I cannot be certain.

Freud remarked once that poets had anticipated many of his findings. To what extent is this true? Well, poets, and indeed, all artists, have always known that every human being is an individual member firstly of the biological species, *Homo sapiens*, subject to the drives innate to that species, and a member of various social groups, cultural, and occupational, that have conditioned him to typical social behaviour, but that at the same time every human being is a unique person who can say I and is capable of deeds, that is to say, of choosing to attend to this rather than that, to do this rather than that, and accept personal responsibility for the consequences, whatever they may be, and they are never fully predictable.

If we were not both individuals and persons there could be no art. If we were only individuals, we should all be the same, and art could tell us nothing. If we were only persons, everyone's experience would be unique, and communication would be impossible.

This is also the case, surely, in most medicine and above all in psychotherapy. It is possible, maybe, for a surgeon to assume that all human beings are the same or ought to be, that is to say, when he finds a body that is abnormal, this is his reason for operating. But no physician, still less a psychotherapist can work with such an assumption. If all your patients were the same, the process of analysis, by which the patient discovers things for himself, would be unnecessary. You could tell him at once what was wrong. But if every patient were only unique, you would be helpless, for neither your own experiences as an analyzand, nor anything you have learned from treating another patient, would be of any help to you, in treating this one.

Secondly, poets have always known that the life of the human mind was a historical life which cannot be reduced to or explained in terms of physics or chemistry. That is to say the word *cause* has a different use in history than it has in the physical sciences. In physics, to say *A is the cause of B* is to say *if A then necessarily B.* But in history it means that the occurrence of A provided B with a motive for occurring. That is why history can be understood backwards, but the future is never predictable with any certainty.

Freud was perhaps the first psychologist to realise this. Speaking for myself, what I admire most about Freud the man is that his love of truth was great enough to give him the courage to transcend the materialist, even mechanistic, scientific philosophy which went almost unchallenged when he was growing up. Had one asked a doctor in the 1880s or '90s to forecast the future of psychology, he would almost certainly have replied somewhat as follows.

> It seems probable that we shall soon be able to describe all mental events in terms of physical events in the brain, but even if we cannot, we may safely assume:
>
> (1) The behaviour of the mind can be explained in terms of stimulus and response. Similar stimuli will necessarily produce similar responses.
>
> (2) Mental development is like physical growth, i.e. the mind passes from a younger or earlier phase into an older or later one. The process can be arrested or become morbid, but two phases cannot exist simultaneously any more than an oak can be an acorn at the same time.
>
> (3) The neuroses and psychoses must be typical diagnostic entities, identical in every patient. To discover the cure for one means to discover the procedure which is effective independently of the individual doctor or individual patient.

One has only to read a few lines of Freud to realise that one is moving in a very different world, one in which there are decisive battles, defeats, victories, where things happen that need not have happened and even things which ought not to have happened, a world where novelties coexist with ancient monuments, a world [*illegible words*] that has to be described with analogical metaphors. Given his upbringing, one would have expected Freud to become a behaviourist. But as we know, he did not. About understanding history backwards he wrote:

> So long as we trace the development from its final stage backwards, the connexion appears continuous and we feel we have gained an insight which is completely satisfactory and even exhaustive. But if we proceed in the reverse way, if we start from the premises inferred from the analysis and try to follow these up to the final result, then we no longer get the impression of an inevitable sequence of events which could not be otherwise determined. We notice at once that there might have been another result, and that we might have been just as well able to understand and explain the latter.

For instance when he first heard patients tell him that in early childhood they had been sexually assaulted by their parents, he very naturally assumed that this had been the case. It must have required enormous courage to come to the conclusion that such tales were phantasies, for if an imaginary event can be as effective as a real event, then one is out of the realm of physics and determinism altogether.

To break with the *Weltanschauung* in which one has been raised is never easy, and for Freud it must have been particularly difficult because a psychology without a secure scientific basis can all too easily become woozy like Christian Science or Theosophy. For this reason, he often, I think, uses, what I would call a Descartian vocabulary, which one has to translate in order to understand him. For example, he speaks of a mature sexual relation as "Object love." In my vocabulary, what he really means is Subject love. That is to say, is it not precisely the neurotic who regards other people, both sexually and socially as objects, either to be exploited, or as objects, whom he can endow with any imaginary personality that he prefers. Is it not the mark of maturity to be able to recognize others as persons, as subjects, in their own right?

The second link between poetry and psychoanalysis is that poets have always understood—it is intrinsic to their art—the importance of symbolic and metaphorical language, though, as I hope to explain later, our conception of the symbol and the metaphor differ in some respects from yours.

Well, then, what kind of persons become poets? Freud has a passage on this which, I am sorry to say, I consider if not totally erroneous, at least a grave distortion of the truth. He says:

> An artist is in rudiment an introvert, not far removed from neurosis. He is oppressed by excessively powerful instinctive needs. He desires to win honor, power, wealth, fame and the love of women: but he lacks the means for achieving these satisfactions. Consequently, like any other unsatisfied man, he turns away from reality and transfers all his interest

and his libido too, to the construction of his life of phantasy. In this way he achieves, through his phantasy, what originally he had achieved only in his phantasy.

When I look at my fellow human beings, I see first that they divide into two classes. Firstly those, and they are the lucky minority, who discover, usually in adolescence, what occupation in the world they feel they must devote their lives to. Then there is the majority who, whether for psychological or social reasons have no marked preferences, and accept whatever jobs their education and social circumstances suggest.

Those who do discover a vocation, fall roughly into two classes which one might call extrovert and introvert, though I don't think the terms are accurate. There are those who feel called to a life of action, either among other human beings, like the politician, or into nature like the engineer. There are those whose interest is not in action, but in contemplation and discovery of hitherto unrealised truths. To this group I think, poets and scientists and psychologists belong.

Now it is clear that an adolescent who feels called to be either a man of action or a man of contemplation, whatever he may hope for if he is successful, has not yet obtained his reward. The great difference between the man of action and the man of contemplation, is that the former must receive public recognition in his lifetime, or if he doesn't he is simply a failure. The man of action, therefore, can truthfully be said to desire public power and fame. With the man of contemplation it is otherwise. What matters to him most is that he should perceive some new aspect of truth which he is convinced is of permanent importance. So far as recognition in his lifetime is concerned, of course he hopes for it, but the only judgement that matters is those of his peers. Public fame is of minor importance. In old age Freud did, as a matter of fact, become a world-famous figure, but suppose he had died shortly after the publication of *The Interpretation of Dreams*, which as we all know, at first hardly sold any copies. He would have died in relative obscurity. But any disappointment he may have felt at the time at not being recognised was obviously a very minor matter compared with his conviction—that he had written a book of permanent importance—so it is with artists. Cézanne, for example, was unrecognized in his lifetime, but he knew he was a great painter.

In addition to honour, power, fame, Freud mentions wealth and the love of women. Aside from the obvious fact that for a would-be poet to hope for wealth would be insane, I very much doubt if wealth is a common ambition. Naturally, we all hope to earn enough money to keep ourselves and our families decently housed, clothed and fed, and of course, our standard of what is decent can vary considerably, but how many people really want more than that. As for the love of women, surely most people's idea of a satisfactory sexual life is a happy marriage, however difficult that may be to achieve, rather than to [?pursue] a lot of women in succession.

If you ask me, what distinguishes a poet from other people is not, as Freud seems to think, excessively powerful instinctual needs—but rather an exceptional love of and mastery of language, and language is not his private property, but the [?possession] of the linguistic group into which he is born. Further the poet, [?as opposed to the magician, is one whose imagination is stimulated by arbitrary restrictions.]

And now I must start getting autobiographical. My father was a physician and a classical scholar, and my mother had a university degree at a time when it was very rare for a woman to have one. I was the youngest of three brothers, and I think the favorite child.

My parents, of course, sometimes had their rows, but I would say that their marriage was reasonably happy. What connection, if any, with the Oedipus complex, the following observation has, I don't know, but I have often asked friends the following question. "Suppose you had been an intimate male friend of your father, or an intimate female friend of your mother; your father comes to you and says, 'I am thinking of marrying this girl. What do you think?' And your mother asks, 'I am thinking of marrying this man. What do you think?'" And I find my friends agreeing with me that one would have said, "I don't think she is the right girl or he is the right man for you." This seems to me rather odd because of course, if they had followed one's advice, one would not exist.

Anyway, I was born, thank goodness, and had the luck to grow up in a house full of books, both scientific and literary, so that I always knew that art and science were complementary and equally humane.

I was read to, and taught myself to read when I was four years old. As a reader, one remains in what I would call the nursery stage, so long as the only judgment one passes on a book is: I like this I don't like that, so long, that is to say, as one has not yet come to the point of passing an aesthetic judgment. Here, then are some of the favourite items in my nursery library:

Poetry. H. Belloc, *Cautionary Tales*
Harry Graham, *Ruthless Rhymes for Heartless Homes*
Hoffmann, *Shock-headed Peter*
Prose Fiction. All of Beatrix Potter.
Hans Andersen, *The Snow Queen*
George MacDonald, *The Princess and the Goblin*
Jules Verne, *The Child of the Cavern*, *Journey to the Centre of the Earth*
Rider Haggard, *King Solomon's Mines*

Shock-headed Peter was an English translation of *Struwwelpeter*, and my favorite poem in the book was "The Story of Little Suck-a-Thumb":

One day, Mamma said: "Conrad, dear,
I must go out and leave you here.
But mind now, Conrad, what I say,
Don't suck your thumb while I'm away.
The great tall tailor always comes
To little boys who suck their thumbs;
And ere they dream what he's about,
He takes his great sharp scissors out
And cuts their thumbs clean off—and then,
You know, they never grow again."

Mama had scarcely turn'd her back,
The thumb was in, Alack! Alack!

The door flew open, in he ran,
The great long red-legged scissor man.
Oh! children, see! the tailor's come
And caught our little Suck-a-Thumb.
Snip! Snap! Snip! the scissors go;
And Conrad cries out—Oh! Oh! Oh!
Snip! Snap Snip! They go so fast,
That both his thumbs are off at last.

Mamma comes home; there Conrad stands,
And looks quite sad, and shows his hands;
"Ah!" said Mamma, "I knew he'd come
To naughty little Suck-a-Thumb."

It so happened that I was a compulsive nail-biter—my mother would put bitter-aloe on my fingers, but I simply licked it off and got down to work—but I knew perfectly well that Conrad's fate would not be mine, because the scissor-man was a figure in a poem, not a real person. Very different is the fear aroused in me by spiders, crabs, and octopi which are, I suspect, symbols to me of the castrating *vagina dentata.*

Before discussing the significance of my prose-reading, I should like to mention an incident which happened when I was six. It was Christmas time and my favourite uncle was staying with us. He came down with influenza. I and my next brother were playing rather noisily. My mother came in and said "You must be quiet because Uncle Harry is ill." Whereupon I said "I wish he would die." When I was very properly spanked for this, I remember feeling: "But they don't understand. Of course I don't really wish him dead. I am very fond of him."

Later reflection on this incident has taught me the profound difference between wish and desire. A desire, like hunger or lust, is real, that is to say grounded in the present state of the self, and if I express it, I mean exactly what I say. But all wishes are fantastic, a refusal to accept reality, so that however varied the form of expression the wish takes, all wishes have the same meaning. "I wish that things were other than they are." In saying that I wished my uncle would die, I simply meant, "I wish that circumstances were not as they are, and that I could go on playing." If you ask me why my wish was expressed as a wish for his death, I would answer: because when I was little I loved shocking my elders. I should like to think I have outgrown that, but my friends assure me I haven't.

This leads me to think that a wish expressed in sexual terms does not necessarily mean what it seems to mean.

It is in the light of these remarks that I would have you see how poets regard the symbol. For us, what is important is the manifest object itself, which has completely absorbed its latent meaning if any, and frankly [the latter] does not interest us much. Then I would say that to the degree that, in analysing dreams, you can ignore the manifest content and concentrate upon the latent, you are dealing not with true symbols but with allegorical signs.

For instance, I like tall factory chimneys. If you tell me that they are phallic symbols, you may be right but all I can say is that if such a factory chimney were to turn before my eyes into a phallus, I should not be shocked, but I should be very cross. Which reminds me of a remark Freud once made which has always enchanted me: There are times when a cigar is simply a cigar. Experience convinces me that however the process of symbol formation occurs, the main impetus behind it is not repression: it is something much more like a passion for not minding one's own business. The other animals may find eating and mating sufficient for a lifetime: we do not.

But to return to my books about mining. Most of what I know about the writing of poetry, or at least of the kind I am interested in writing, I discovered long before I thought of becoming a poet. Between the ages of six and thirteen I spent a great many of my waking hours in constructing a private secondary sacred world, the basic elements of which were (*a*) a limestone landscape mainly derived from the Pennine Moors in the North of England, though until I was twelve I only knew these from photographs, and (*b*) an industry—lead-mining. Trying my hand at a little self-analysis, I note, firstly that, even aside from the man-made caverns of mines, a limestone country is full of natural caverns and underground streams. Then, looking at the cross-sectional diagrams of mines in my books, I realize that they are like stylised pictures of the internal anatomy of the human body. As for my passion for lead-mines, I note, firstly, that the word *lead* rhymes with *dead* and that lead is or was used for lining coffins: secondly, that mining is the one human activity that is by nature mortal. Steam-engines may render stage-coaches obsolete, but this cannot be foreseen. But when a mine is opened, everyone knows already, that however rich it may turn out to be, sooner or later it will become exhausted, and be abandoned.

Of this constructed world I was the only human inhabitant. Although I equipped my mines with the most elaborate machinery, I never imagined any miners. Indeed when I visited real mining areas, I preferred abandoned mines to working ones. Yet, whatever the unconscious relation between my sacred world and death may have been, I contemplated it not with fear or grief but with intense joy and reverence.

Though constructed for and inhabited by myself alone, I needed the help of others, my parents in particular, in collecting the raw materials for its construction. Others had to procure for me the necessary textbooks on geography and mining machinery, maps, catalogues, guide books, photographs and, when occasion offered, to take me down real mines, tasks which they performed with unfailing patience and generosity.

From this private activity, I learned various things which I was later to discover also applied to the fabrication of public works of art. Man possesses two quite different kinds of imagination which, following Coleridge, I will call the Primary Imagination and the Secondary Imagination. The concern of the Primary Imagination, its only concern, is with sacred beings. The sacred is that to which it is obliged to respond: the profane is that to which it cannot respond and therefore does not know. A sacred being cannot be anticipated: it must be encountered. All imaginations do not recognize the same sacred beings, but every imagination responds to those it recognizes in the same way. The impression made upon the Primary Imagination by a sacred being is of an overwhelming but undefinable importance—*I am that I am* is what every sacred being seems to say. The response of the Primary Imagination is a passion of awe, which may range in tone from joyous wonder to panic dread. Some sacred beings seem to be sacred to all imaginations at all times. The Moon for example, Fire, Snakes and those four important beings which can only be defined in terms of non-being: Darkness, Silence, Nothing, Death. Some, like Kings, are only sacred to all within a certain culture, some only to members of a social group, like the Latin language among humanists. An imagination can acquire new sacred beings, and it can lose old ones to the profane. Sacred beings can be acquired by social contagion, but not consciously. One cannot be taught to recognize a sacred being: one has to be converted.

To return to my early private world. In constructing it, I learned certain principles which I was later to find applied to all artistic fabrication. Though every work of art is a secondary world, such a world cannot be constructed *ex nihilo*, but is a selection and recombination of elements taken from the primary world we all live in.

Then, in constructing my private world, I discovered that though this was a game, i.e. something I was free to do or not as I chose, no game can be played without rules. A secondary world must be as much a world of law as the primary. One may be free to decide what these laws shall be, but laws there must be.

In my case I decided—or rather, without conscious decision I instinctively felt—that I must impose two restrictions upon my freedom of phantasy. In choosing what objects were to be included, I was free to select this and reject that on condition that both were real objects in the primary world, to choose for example between two kinds of water-turbine, which could be found in a textbook on mining machinery or a manufacturer's catalogue: I was not allowed to invent one. In deciding how my world was to function, I could choose between two practical possibilities—a mine can be drained either by an adit or a pump—but physical impossibilities and magic means were forbidden. When I say forbidden, I mean that I felt, in some obscure way, that they were morally forbidden. Then, there came a day when the moral issue became quite conscious. As I was planning my Platonic Idea of a Concentrating Mill, I ran into difficulties. I had to choose between two types of a certain machine for separating the slimes, called a buddle. One type I found more sacred, but the other type was, I knew from my reading, the more efficient. At this point I realised that it was my moral duty to sacrifice my symbolic preference to reality or truth.

The kind of activity I have been describing is the work of what I call the Secondary Imagination, which is of another character and at another mental level—for it is an activity of the conscious mind. It is active not passive, and its categories are not the sacred and profane but the beautiful and the ugly. Beauty and Ugliness pertain to Form not to Being. The Primary Imagination only recognizes one kind of being, the sacred, but the Secondary Imagination recognizes both beautiful and ugly forms. A beautiful form is as it ought to be, an ugly form as it ought not to be. Observing the beautiful, the Secondary Imagination has the feelings of satisfaction, pleasure, absence of conflict. Observing the ugly, the contrary feelings. It does not desire the beautiful, but an ugly form arouses in it a desire to correct its ugliness and make it beautiful. It does not worship the beautiful; it approves of it and can give reasons for its approval. It approves of regularity, spatial symmetry, temporal repetition, law and order; it disapproves of loose ends, irrelevance, and mess. In addition it has a sense of humor and a love of play.

Lastly, it is social and craves agreement with other minds. If I think a form beautiful and you think it ugly, we cannot help agreeing that one of us must be wrong, whereas if I think something sacred and you think it is profane, neither of us will dream of arguing the matter.

If symbols are the creation of the Primary Imagination, metaphors are the creation of the Secondary. A metaphor is a conscious analogy, and is judged by other conscious minds by its aptness. Since it is a conscious creation, the question of repression cannot arise. We can and often do use sexual language to describe the non-sexual. For instance, one metaphor from agriculture, ploughing the ground and planting seed in Mother-Earth. Even more striking is the extremely daring language used by the mystics like St John of the Cross, who openly use the orgasm, an experience which most people have had, as a metaphor for the union of the soul with God, an experience which very few people have had, because, common to both, is the experience of total self-forgetfulness.

Perhaps nothing is more repugnant to the Secondary Imagination than dreams. Speaking for myself, I find my own dreams, however physiologically and psychologically necessary, seem to me boring in exactly the same way that lunatics are, that is to say, repetitive, devoid of punctuation or any sense of humor, and insanely egocentric. Only once in my life have I had a dream which, on conscious consideration, seemed interesting enough to write down.

Given my passionate interest as a boy in mines, both I and my parents naturally assumed that, when I grew up, I would become either a mining engineer or a geologist. So at Public School I studied science and won a scholarship to Oxford in biology. It was not to be. One Sunday in March 1922, I was walking across a field with a school friend, when he asked me if I ever wrote poetry. "Good God, no," I said. "The idea has never occurred to me." "Why don't you," he replied, and at that moment I discovered my vocation.

When I ask myself why my friend's suggestion met with such an unexpected response, I now realize that, without knowing it, I had been enjoying the poetic use of language for a long time. I had read the technological prose of my books on mining in a peculiar way. A word like *pyrites*, for example, had not, to me, been simply an indicative sign, it was the Proper Name of a Sacred Being so that, when I heard an aunt pronounce it as *pirrits*, I was shocked. Her pronunciation was more than wrong; it was ugly; ignorance was impiety. Proper Names in the strict sense are poetry in the raw. What I think the poet attempts to do is to give experiences their Proper Name. Language is prosaic to the degree that it does not matter what particular word is associated with an idea, provided the association once made is permanent. Language is poetic to the degree that it does matter. In Genesis Adam was told by God to give names to all creatures: Adam the namer was the proto-poet, not the proto-prose-writer.

The immediate consequence of deciding to write poetry was that I had to forget my personal fantasies completely, and concentrate on learning how a poem is written. Before, that is to say, I could woo my own Muse, I had to woo Dame Philology. A beginner's efforts cannot be called bad. They are imaginary, an imitation of poetry in general. The next stage for the young poet is to get a transference upon some particular poet, with whom he feels an affinity—in my case it was Thomas Hardy—whose work he imitates. It is impossible to do a recognizable imitation of a poet without attending to every detail of his diction, rhythms and habits of sensibility. In imitating his Master, the young poet learns that, no matter how he finds it, there is only one word or rhythm or form that is the right one. The right one is still not yet the real one, for the apprentice is ventriloquizing, but he has got away from poetry in general; he is learning how a poem is written. Then if the apprentice is destined to become a poet, sooner or later—in my case when I was twenty—a day arrives when he can truthfully say for the first time: All the words are right and all are genuinely mine.

But it was still to be many years before I could do anything with my lead-mining world of my childhood. My first attempt was in 1940 when I was thirty-three; I tried to describe what I had felt at the age of twelve, when I first saw my sacred landscape with my own eyes. Needless to say, my description of my experiences is, historically, a fiction: what I wrote was an interpretation of them, in the light of, as you will see, later reading in Theology and Psychoanalytic literature. Here it is.

Whenever I begin to think
About the human creature we
Must nurse to sense and decency,
An English area comes to mind,
I see the nature of my kind
As a locality I love,
Those limestone moors that stretch from Brough
To Hexham and the Roman Wall,
There is my symbol of us all.

. . .

Always my boy of wish returns
To those peat-stained deserted burns
That feed the Wear and Tyne and Tees,
And, turning states to strata, sees
How basalt long oppressed broke out
In wild revolt at Cauldron Snout,
And from the relics of old mines
Derives his algebraic signs
For all in man that mourns and seeks,
For all of his renounced techniques,
Their tramways overgrown with grass,
For lost belief, for all Alas,
The derelict lead-smelting mill,
Flued to its chimney up the hill,
That smokes no answer any more
But points, a landmark on Bolt's Law,
The finger of all questions. There

In Rookhope I was first aware
Of Self and Not-Self, Death and Dread:
Adits were entrances which led
Down to the Outlawed, to the Others,
The Terrible, the Merciful, the Mothers;
Alone in the hot day I knelt
Upon the edge of shafts and felt
The deep *Urmutterfurcht* that drives
Us into knowledge all our lives,
The far interior of our fate
To civilise and to create,
Das Weibliche that bids us come
To find what we're escaping from.
There I dropped pebbles, listened, heard
The reservoir of darkness stirred:
"*O deine Mutter kehrt dir nicht*
Wieder. Du selbst bin ich, dein' Pflicht
Und Liebe. Brach sie nun mein Bild."
And I was conscious of my guilt.

Then in 1948, I visited Italy for the first time, and in Florence, wrote a poem, "In Praise of Limestone," which again was related to my childhood phantasies. The lead-mines, of course, could not come in, because there aren't any in Florence, but the limestone landscape was important to me as a connecting link between two utterly different cultures, the northern guilt-culture, I grew up in, and the shame-culture of the Mediterranean countries, to which I was now exposed for the first time. Here is the poem.

["In Praise of Limestone"]

Then in 1965, I tried again to write directly about my original sacred landscape.

["Amor Loci"]

I have however once written a poem which I intend every reader to read as if he or she were dreaming it. The initial idea came, not from a dream, but from a painting I saw of Christ's Agony in the Garden. In the foreground was the kneeling figure of Christ; nearby, on the ground, the disciples asleep. In the background some soldiers were crossing a little bridge. Visually they look quite harmless and there is nothing to show whither they are going. It is only because one has read the Gospel story, that one knows that, in fact, they are coming to arrest Jesus: I thought then that, suppose instead of a static painting, one were to make a film of this event. Then one would see the soldiers getting nearer and nearer until they reached a point where it would be obvious what they were coming to do. Before this, according to the gospel, Jesus had woken his disciples, and then, after his arrest, they all forsook him and fled. It occurred to me then, but not before, that I and, I fancy, nearly everybody, have had a nightmare in which one is pursued by some malignant power, and that since this was a general experience, not private to myself, a poem might be based on it. In my own case, the pursuer used to be a steam-roller. That obviously might not be felt by readers as hostile. I have never dreamed of being pursued by soldiers, and I don't know whether others have, but since soldiers are by profession aggressive, it seemed to me that they could function for all readers as a symbol. For dramatic purposes, I wanted a second person in the poem besides the dreamer, so, for those disciples who ran away, I substituted a single figure, whom the dreamer loves and trusts, i.e. the reader can choose whatever image suits him or her—but who in the end deserts the dreamer leaving him to face the terror alone. Again, I have never personally had this experience in dreams of this kind. Well here is the poem:

["O what is that sound which so thrills the ear . . ."]

If you ask me to describe the process of poetic composition I would say this—The subject matter of a poem is comprised of a crowd of historical occasions of feelings and thought recollected from the past. The poet presupposes that this crowd is real, i.e. a real disorder, but should not be, and attempts to transform it into a community by embodying it in a verbal society. In this he differs from the scientist whose subject matter is a crowd of natural events at all times, but who presupposes that this crowd is not real but only apparent, and seeks to discover the true place of events in the system of nature.

The verbal society of a poem, like any society in nature, has its own laws: the laws of syntax are analogous to the laws of physics: metrical and rhyme schemes are more like the laws of biology.

The nature of the final poetic order is the outcome of a dialectical struggle between the recollected occasions of feeling and thought and the verbal system. As a society the verbal system is actively coercive upon the occasions it is attempting to embody; what it cannot embody truthfully, it excludes. As a potential community, the occasions are passively resistant to all claims of the system to embody them which they do not recognise as just: they decline all unjust persuasion.

In writing a poem, the poet can work in two ways. Starting from an intuitive idea of the kind of community he desires to call into being, he may search for the verbal system which will most justly incarnate that idea, or starting with the idea of a certain kind of verbal system, he may look for the community which it is capable of embodying most truthfully. In practice he nearly always works simultaneously in both directions, modifying his conception of the ultimate nature of the community at the immediate suggestions of the system, and modifying the system in response to his growing intuition of the future needs of the community.

A verbal system cannot be selected completely arbitrarily, nor can one [say] that any given system is absolutely necessary. The poet searches for one which imposes just obligations of feeling and thought. "Ought" always implies can, so that a system whose claims cannot be met must be scrapped. But the poet has to beware of accusing the system of injustice, when what is at fault is the laxness and self-love of the feelings upon which it is making its demands. A poem can fail in two ways: it may exclude too much and so be banal, or it may attempt to embody more than one community at once and so be disorderly.

The two great dangers which a poet has constantly to guard against, are what I would call autoeroticism and narcissism.

A poet must never make a statement simply because he thinks it sounds poetically exciting or effective: he must also believe it to be true. This does not mean of course that one can only appreciate a poet whose beliefs happen to coincide with one's own: It does mean however that one must be convinced that the poet really believes what he says, however odd the belief may seem to oneself.

The second danger lies in the poet's imagination that an experience is of any poetic importance simply because he personally has had it. A valid experience is some perception of a reality common to all men: it is only mine in that it is perceived from a unique perspective which nobody but myself can occupy, so that it's my pleasure and duty to share it with others. From the poet's point of view, the ideal response of a reader to his poem is: "Why, I knew that all the time, but never realised it till now." A good poem, one might say, is like a successfully analysed patient: both have become, what the Psalmist says of Jerusalem, "A city that is at unity in itself." For this very reason I am sceptical as to the value of trying to psychoanalyse a successful work of art as if they were patients. It is only in the case of bad works of art, that I can conceive of analysis throwing light on the reason why it is bad.

As to our purposes in what we do, they are not, I believe, too dissimilar. At least we both can or should be modest about what we can achieve. The sole aim in writing, wrote Dr Johnson, is to enable readers a little better to enjoy life or a little better to endure it. Is that so different from what Freud once said to someone who consulted him upon whether to be analysed or not. "I don't suppose," he said, "we can do much for you, but perhaps we can turn your hysterical misery into ordinary human unhappiness."

An Address at the Event "Lyrik 70"

Auden gave this talk, in a German translation prepared for him by Stella Musulin, at the event "Lyrik 70" at Schloß Neulengbach, Austria, on 20 May 1971. The German text was published in *Podium*, Vienna, April 1971, without the opening sentence and the concluding paragraph. The original English text, in a typescript formerly in the possession of Stella Musulin, was first published as "Neulengbach Speech" in *"In Solitude, for Company": W. H. Auden after 1940,* edited by Katherine Bucknell and Nicholas Jenkins (1995) (Auden Studies, 3). In the paragraph that begins "There are periods", the typescript has "those of [another *mistyped and deleted*] culture than his own"; probably Auden intended either to retype "another" or to insert "other" following "culture" but did neither, so I have used the first of these possible emendations in the text below.

Sehr Verehrter Herr Landeshauptmann, meine Damen und Herren.

I hope you will pardon me if I speak somewhat personally. I do so, not out of vanity, but because I do not wish to give the impression that I am attempting to lay down absolute laws which are valid for all. I give you my experiences as a poet, in the hope that you will be able to compare them with yours, and form your own judgment about them.

Most of what I know about the writing of poetry, or at least about the kind I am interested in writing, I discovered long before I took any interest in poetry itself.

Between the ages of six and twelve, I spent a great many of my waking hours in the fabrication of a private secondary sacred world, the basic elements of which were (a) a limestone landscape mainly derived from the Pennine Moors in the North of England and (b) an industry—lead-mining.

It is no doubt psychologically significant that my sacred world was autistic—that is to say, I had no wish to share it with others nor could I have done so. However, though constructed for and inhabited by myself alone, I needed the help of others, my parents in particular, in collecting its basic materials; others had to procure for me the necessary text-books on geology and machinery, maps, catalogues, guide-books and photographs, and, when occasion offered, take me down real mines, tasks which they performed with unfailing patience and generosity.

From this activity, I learned certain principles which I was later to find applied to all artistic fabrication. First, whatever other elements it may include, the initial impulse to create a secondary world is a feeling of awe aroused by encounters, in the Primary World, with sacred beings or events. This feeling of awe is an imperative, that is to say, one is not free to choose the object or the event that arouses it. Though every work of art is a secondary world, it cannot be constructed *ex nihilo,* but is a selection from and a recombination of the contents of the Primary World. Even the "purest" poem, in the French Symboliste sense, is made of words which are not the poet's private property, but the communal creation of the linguistic group to whom he belongs, so that their meaning can be looked up in a dictionary.

Secondly, in constructing my private world, I discovered that, though this was a game, or rather precisely *because it was a game*—that is to say, not a necessity like eating or sleeping, but something I was free to do or not as I chose—it could not be played without rules. Absolute freedom is meaningless: freedom can only be realised in a choice between alternatives. A secondary world, be it a poem, or a game of football or bridge, must be as much a world of law as the Primary, the only difference being that in the world of games one is free to decide what its laws shall be. But to all games as to real life, Goethe's lines apply.

In der Beschränkung zeigt sich erst der Meister,
Und das Gesatz nur kann uns Freiheit geben.

As regards my particular lead-mining world, I decided, or rather, without conscious decision I instinctively felt, that I must impose two restrictions upon my freedom of fantasy. In choosing what objects were to be included, I was free to select this and reject that, on condition that both were real objects in the Primary World, to choose, for example, between two kinds of water-turbine, which could be found in a text-book on mining machinery or a manufacturer's catalogue: but I was not free to invent one. In deciding how my world was to function, I could choose between two practical possibilities—a mine can be drained either by an adit or a pump—but physical impossibilities and magic means were forbidden. When I say forbidden, I mean that I felt, in some obscure way, that they were morally forbidden. Then there came a day when the moral issue became quite conscious. As I was planning my Platonic Idea of a concentrating-mill, I ran into difficulties. I had to choose between two types of a certain machine for separating the slimes, called a buddle. One type I found more sacred or "beautiful", but the other type was, I knew from my reading, the more efficient. At this point I realised that it was my moral duty to sacrifice my aesthetic preference to reality or truth.

When, later, I began to write poetry, I found that, for me, at least, the same obligation was binding. That is to say, I cannot accept the doctrine that, in poetry, there is a "suspension of belief". A poet must never make a statement simply because it sounds poetically exciting: he must also believe it to be true. This does not mean, of course, that one can only appreciate a poet whose beliefs happen to coincide with one's own. It does mean, however, that one must be convinced that the poet really believes what he says, however odd the belief may seem to oneself.

Between constructing a private fantasy world for oneself alone and writing poetry, there is, of course, a profound difference. A fantasy world exists only in the head of its creator: a poem is a public verbal object intended to be read and enjoyed by others. To become conscious of others is to become conscious of historical time in various ways. The contents of a poem are necessarily past experiences, and the goal of a poem is necessarily in the future, since it cannot be read until it has been written. Again, to write a poem is to engage in an activity which human beings have practiced for centuries. If one asks why human beings make poems or paint pictures or compose music, I can see two possible answers. Firstly all the artistic media are forms of an activity peculiar to human beings, namely, Personal Speech. Many animals have impersonal codes of communications, visual, olfactory, auditory signals, by which they convey to other members of their species vital information about food, territory, sex, the presence of enemies etc., and in social animals like the bee, such a code may be exceedingly complex. We, too, of course, often use words in the same way, as when I ask a stranger the way to the railroad station. But when we truly speak, we do something quite different, we speak as person to person in order to disclose ourselves to others and share our experiences with them, not because we must, but because we enjoy doing so. This activity is sometimes quite erroneously called "self-expression". If I write a poem about experiences I have had, I do so because I think it should be of interest and value to others: the fact that it has till now only been my experience is accidental. What the poet or any artist has to convey is a perception of a reality common to all, but seen from a unique perspective, which it is his duty as well as his pleasure to share with others. To small truths as well as great, St Augustine's words apply.

> The truth is neither mine nor his nor another's; but belongs to us all whom Thou callest to partake of it: warning us terribly, not to account it private to ourselves, lest we be deprived of it.

Then the second impulse to artistic fabrication is the desire to transcend our mortality, by making objects which, unlike ourselves, are not subject to natural death, but can remain permanently "on hand" in the world, long after we and our society have perished.

Every genuine work of art, I believe, exhibits two qualities, Nowness and Permanence. By Nowness I mean the quality which enables an art-historian to date a work, at least, approximately. If, for example, one listens to a composition by Palestrina and one by Mozart, one knows immediately that, quite aside from their artistic merits, Palestrina must have lived earlier than Mozart: he could not possibly have written as he did after Mozart. By Permanence, I mean that the work continues to have relevance and importance long after its creator is dead. In the history of Art, unlike the history of Science, no genuine work of art is made obsolete by a later work. Past science is of interest only to the historian of science, not to what scientists are doing at this moment; past works of art, on the other hand, are of the utmost importance to the contemporary practitioner. Every artist tries to produce something new, but in the hope that, in time, it will take its proper place in the tradition of his art. And he cannot produce anything significantly original unless he knows well what has already been done, that is to say, he cannot "rebel" against the past without having a profound reverence for it.

There are periods in history when the arts develop uninterruptedly, each generation building on the achievements of the previous generation. There are other periods when radical breaks seem to be necessary. However when they are, one will generally find that the "radical" artist does not disown the past, but finds in works of a much earlier period or in those of another culture than his own, the clue as to what he should do now. In my own case, for example, I know how much I owe to Anglo-Saxon and Medieval Poetry.

When I review the contemporary artistic scene, it strikes me how extraordinarily fortunate men like Stravinsky, Picasso, Eliot, etc., that is, those persons we think of as the founders of "modern" art, were in being born when they were, so that they came to manhood before 1914. Until the First World War, western society was still pretty much what it had been in the nineteenth century. This meant that for these artists, the felt need to create something new arose from an artistic imperative, not a historic imperative. No one asked himself: "What is the proper kind of music to compose or picture to paint or poem to write in the year 1912?" Secondly, their contemporary audiences were mostly conservative, but honestly so. Those, for instance, who were scandalised by *Le Sacre du Printemps*, may seem to us now to have been old fogies, but their reaction was genuine. They did not say to themselves: "Times have changed and we must change with them in order not to be left behind."

Here are a few statements by Stravinsky to which the young, whether artists or critics would do well to listen and ponder over.

> In my youth the new music grew out of, and in reaction to, traditions, whereas it appears to be evolving to-day as much from social needs as interior artistic ones. . . . The status of new music as a category is another incomparable. It had none at all in my early years, being in fact categorically opposed, and often with real hostility. But the unsuccess of composers of my generation at least kept them from trading on success, and our unsuccess may have been less insidious than the automatic superlatives which nowadays kill the new by absorbing it to death.
>
> The use of the new hardware naturally appears to the new musician as "historically imperative"; but music is made out of musical imperatives, and the awareness of historical processes is probably best left to future and different kinds of wage-earners.

In times, like our own, of rapid social change and political crisis, there is always a danger of confusing the principles governing political action and those governing artistic fabrication. The most important of such confusions are three.

Firstly, one may come to think of artistic fabrication as a form of political action. Every citizen, poets included, has a duty to be politically "engagé", that is, to play a responsible part in seeing that the society of which he is a member shall function properly and improve. But the poet, qua poet, has only one political function. Since language is his medium, it is his duty, by his own example, to defend his mother-tongue against corruption by demagogues, journalists, the mass-media etc. As Karl Kraus said: *"Die Sprache ist die Mutter, nicht das Magd, das bedankens"*, and when language loses its meaning, its place is taken by violence. Of course, the poet may use poetical and social events as subject-matter for poems—they are as much a part of human experience as love or nature—but he must never imagine that his poems have the power to affect the course of history. The political and social history of Europe would be what it has been if Dante, Shakespeare, Goethe, Michael Angelo, Titian, Mozart, Beethoven, etc., had never existed.

Where political and social evils are concerned, only two things are effective: political action and straightforward, truthful, detailed journalistic rapportage of the facts. The Arts are powerless.

The second confusion, of which Plato is the most famous example, is to take artistic fabrication as the model for a good society. Such a model, if put into practice, is bound to produce a tyranny. The aim of the artist is to produce an object which is complete and will endure without change. In the "city" of a poem, there are always the same inhabitants doing exactly the same jobs for ever. A society which was really like a good poem, embodying the aesthetic virtues of order, economy and subordination of the detail to the whole, would be a nightmare of horror for, given the historical reality of actual men, such a society could only come into being through selective breeding, extermination of the physically and mentally unfit, absolute obedience to its Director, a large slave class kept out of sight in cellars and the strictest censorship of the Arts, forbidding anything to be said which is out of keeping with the official "line."

The third confusion, typical of our western "free" societies at this time, is the opposite of Plato's, namely to take political action as the model for artistic fabrication. Political action is a necessity, that is to say, at every moment something has to be done, and it is momentary—action at this moment is immediately followed by another action at the next. Artistic fabrication, on the other hand, is voluntary—the alternative to one work of art can be no work of art—and the artistic object is permanent, that is to say, immune to historical change. The attempt to model artistic fabrication on political action can therefore, only reduce it to momentary and arbitrary "happenings", a conformism with the tyranny of the Immediate moment which is far more enslaving and destructive of integrity than any conformism with past tradition.

At this point, a little digression on the subject of "free" verse, which seems now to be almost universal among young poets. Though excellent examples, the poems of D. H. Lawrence, for example, exist, they are, in my opinion, the exception, not the rule. The great virtue of formal metrical rules is that they forbid automatic responses and, by forcing the poet to have second thoughts, free him from the fetters of self. All too often, the result of not having a fixed form to be true to, is a self-indulgence which in the detached reader can only cause boredom. Further, in my experience, contrary to what one might expect, the free-verse poets sound much more like each other than those who write in fixed forms. Whatever freedom may do, it does not, it would seem, make for originality.

What then, can the Arts do for us? In my opinion, they can do two things. They can, as Dr Johnson said, "enable us a little better to enjoy life or a little better to endure it." And, because they are objects permanently on hand in the world, they are the chief means by which the living are able to break bread with the dead, and, without a communication with the dead, I do not believe that a fully human civilised life is possible.

Perhaps, too, in our age, the mere making of a work of art is itself a political act. So long as artists exist, making what they please or think they ought to make, even if their works are not terribly good, they remind the Management of something managers need to be reminded of, namely, that the managed are people with faces, not anonymous numbers, that *Homo Laborans* is also *Homo Ludens.*

And now, I hope those of you who know no English will forgive me if I conclude these remarks with a light poem of my own, entitled "Doggerel by a Senior Citizen".

APPENDIX III

Responses to Questionnaires

This appendix includes Auden's responses to questionnaires supplied by newspaper and magazine editors, responses that he understood would be printed under an explanatory headnote.

Around the early 1970s, for *Harper's Dictionary of Contemporary Usage*, edited by William and Mary Morris (Harper & Row, 1975), Auden responded to a series of questionnaires sent out by the editors to 136 members of their "Panel of Consultants on Usage". In the editors' dedication of their book to Auden and H. L. Mencken, Auden is said to have "contributed to this work in its early stages". The questionnaires asked whether, for example, "alright" may be used in place of "all right" or "nauseous" in place of "nauseated", and whether "Rev." may be used as a form of address. The book included a selection of responses from the panel, among them eighteen brief comments by Auden, although, when he wrote them, he seems not to have expected them to be printed. (His answers to the three examples above were: "I might use it—but I don't.", "Never! Never!", and "One says, 'Father.'")

Neglected Books

American Scholar is the quarterly magazine of Phi Beta Kappa. For its Spring 1970 issue, "the Editors asked a number of distinguished men and women to name that book published in the past quarter of a century that they believed to have been the most undeservedly neglected." Auden responded briefly:

Rhymes of a Pfc by Lincoln Kirstein (New Directions, 1964). The best volume of poems directly about World War II.

On Rhythm

Agenda was a little magazine edited by William Cookson mostly devoted to contemporary English poetry and informed by the editor's admiration for Ezra Pound. In its "Special Issue on Rhythm" (Autumn 1972 – Winter 1973) twenty-two poets responded to a questionnaire headed with these two sentences: "The purpose of this questionnaire is to seek practical answers from poets concerning their methods and intentions in the disposition of their poems upon the page. We are not investigating the absolute nature of rhythm so much as the rhythmic intention behind the print." Twenty questions followed, divided under the headings "General Points", "Vers Libre", "Syllabics", and "Metrical Verse". To the extent that Auden answered the questionnaire, he seems to have in mind the following questions. Under the heading "General Points": "How conscious are you of rhythmical considerations?", "Is the disposition of your poems on the page influenced by its visual appearance at all, or purely rhythmical considerations?", and "How do you regard the line-end: (a) as a minute pause inevitably, (b) as a pause only when punctuated, or (c) as a pause, any way, but one lengthened by punctuation?" Under the heading "Syllabics": "How do you define for your own purposes 'a syllable'? What do you do about the slurring of syllables that occurs in speech?"

On hedonistic grounds, I am a fanatical formalist. To me, a poem is, among other things, always a verbal game. Everybody knows that one cannot play a game without rules. One may make the rules what one likes, but one's whole fun and freedom comes from obeying them.

There are a few poets—D. H. Lawrence, for example—whom one feels had to write in free verse, but they are the exceptions, not the rule. Those who do must have an infallible sense for line-endings. So often, when reading "free" verse, I can see no reason why a line ends where it does; why the poet did not write it out as a prose-poem.

At any given time, I have two concerns on my mind, a subject which interests me and formal problems of metre, diction, etc. The Subject looks for the right Form, the Form for the right Subject. When the two finally come together, I can write a poem. For example, a few years ago, I was preoccupied with the, to us, strange and repellant ways of the Insects. At the same time, under the influence of Goethe in his middle "classical" period, I was wondering whether it would be possible to write an English poem in accentual hexameters. The outcome was a poem about Insects in hexameters.

A pause should *always* be made at the end of a line, longer if there is punctuation at its end, shorter if there is enjambment without punctuation.

When writing a poem based on syllable count alone and ignoring stresses, I usually, but not invariably, follow the latin habit of eliding contiguous vowels separated by *h* or *w*. But in reading the poem aloud I pronounce them both. Thus *now imagines* I count metrically as three syllables, but I pronounce them as four.

I have written one or two short poems based, like some of Bridges's, on vowel length not stress. But because of the uninflected nature of English, which is always making vowels long by position, it is impossible to write a poem of any length in this way without resorting to fancy diction.

I don't bother about the visual appearance of a poem on the page, except in one respect. If it is written in long lines, the printer must so set it that there are no run ons.

APPENDIX IV

Auden on the Air

This appendix lists Auden's radio and television talks, readings, and discussions. Other broadcasts almost certainly occurred but have left no trace.

A few of the items listed below include a note indicating that a recording is in the British Library Sound Archive; the Archive seems also to have recordings made from other broadcasts but these are not catalogued clearly enough to be identified with confidence. I have not listed occasional broadcasts by BBC Radio 3 and American radio stations of commercial recordings of Auden's poems.

Auden read three poems in a recording from the "Poetry International 69" festival, London, broadcast in the BBC Third Programme, 21 July 1969. The poems are absent from a transcript at the BBC Written Archives Centre.

Auden read from his recent work in *Release*, BBC-2 television, 25 October 1969.

"W. H. Auden: '. . . poetry may be a very humble occupation'" was the title of an interview with Göran Bengtson, recorded at the Nobel Symposium in Stockholm, and broadcast by Sveriges Television, 7 December 1969. A transcript was at one time in Bengtson's possession.

An interview with Mosheh Dor was broadcast in "Literary Corner", Israel Broadcasting Authority, First Programme, 17 April 1970. The interview was published in *Maariv*, Tel-Aviv, 10 April 1970, and in his *Le-galot le-adam aḥer* (1974), pp. 25–27.

Auden was interviewed by Alexander Walker in the series *Options: A Selective Look at the Arts*, BBC Radio 4, 28 June 1970. A transcript is in the BBC Written Archives Centre.

Auden read a group of poems in a recording from the "Poetry International '70" festival, London, broadcast in the BBC Third Programme, 2 August 1970.

Auden spoke about the job of the librettist in a brief talk in the interval of a performance of *Elegy for Young Lovers* at the Edinburgh International Festival, BBC Radio 3, 29 August 1970.

Auden talked with Pete Morgan and Dennis Brutus "about poetry today" in the programme *Orbit*, BBC Radio 4 Scottish Home Service, 27 September 1970 (recorded 28 June 1970).

Some filmed remarks on George Orwell were broadcast in "The Road to the Left: An Essay on George Orwell", BBC-1 television, 10 January 1971; later rebroadcast in the United States by Public Broadcast Service stations. A newspaper review quoted Auden: "The dilemma, if you are politically *engagé*, the temptation to omit facts which are distasteful to you" (Mary Holland, *Observer*, 17 January 1971).

Auden was interviewed by Bronwyn Drainie for *Weekday*, CBC Television, broadcast around 11 February 1971.

A panel discussion at the University of Toronto on theatre and the visual arts, 10 February 1971, with Auden, Marshall McLuhan, Buckminster Fuller, Jack McGowran, and A. N. Jeffares, was recorded and broadcast on radio, apparently by the CBC, on an unknown date. An edited transcript was published in *Theatre and the Visual Arts*, edited by Robert O'Driscoll and Lorna Reynolds (Irish University Press, 1972).

An interview with R. Sherman Beattie was broadcast by WCSI, Columbus, Indiana, around 25 February 1971. A recording is in a private collection.

Auden was a guest on the interview program *Barry Farber*, WMAL, Washington, 30 March 1971.

Auden read an updated version of "The Unknown Citizen" in *The Great American Dream Machine*, broadcast by National Educational Televison and Public Broadcasting Service stations, 31 March 1971.

"A Little Better to Enjoy Life", a recorded interview with Robert Fulford, was broadcast in *Man Alive*, CBC Television, 24 May 1971.

Auden read some poems in a recording from the "Poetry International" festival, London, broadcast in BBC Radio 3, 18 July 1971.

A recorded interview with Kevin Byrne was broadcast in *Books and Writers*, BBC Radio 3, 10 August 1971, and later in the series *Profile* in the BBC World Service.

"W. H. Auden talks with Hans Keller on Music" was broadcast in BBC Radio 3, 20 November 1971. Some quotations are reported by David Wade, "The Woes of Others", *The Times*, 27 November 1971, and Peter Porter, "I and We", *New Statesman*, 3 December 1971; Keller recalled his conversation with Auden before the broadcast in "The Words and the Music", *Sunday Times*, 1 February 1981. A recording is in the British Library Sound Archive.

An interview with Douglas Cooper, one of a weekly series of interviews, was broadcast by WRTC, Trinity College, Hartford, 2 March 1970, and later distributed (without indication of its origin) as a tape cassette under the title *Distinguished Contemporary: W. H. Auden* (Pelham, N.Y.: Sound Perspectives, 1974).

A brief interview with Leonard Harris about his return to Oxford was included in *The Six O'Clock Report*, WCBS-TV, New York, 16 February 1972.

Auden read and introduced some poems for "Auden at 65", BBC Radio 3, 21 February 1972. A recording is in the British Library Sound Archive.

Auden described his views on poetry in *Comment!*, NBC Television Network, 27 February 1972. A transcript appears below (p. 729).

Auden appeared briefly on the news program *Today*, NBC Television Network, 6 March 1972.

Auden was a guest on *The Dick Cavett Show*, ABC Television Network, 31 March 1972.

"W. H. Auden on the arts and political commitment" was the newspaper listing for a talk in BBC Radio 3, 1 April 1972.

"Arbeit, Karnival, Gebet", a translation by Isabella Levitin of a version of "Work, Carnival and Prayer" (p. 688), was broadcast in *Nachtstudio*, Bayerischer Rundfunk, 24 July 1972. I do not know whether it was read by Auden.

Some of Auden's reading at the 1972 Poetry International was included in "Best of Poetry International", *Aquarius*, ITV, 27 July 1972.

The BBC has a recording of readings titled "Auden in London", apparently broadcast 1 August 1972, perhaps in *The Arts Worldwide*, BBC Radio 3.

Auden was one of a group of poets who read and discussed their favorite poem by Philip Larkin, "Larkin at 50", BBC Radio 3, 9 August 1972. A recording is in the British Library Sound Archive.

Auden's reading of "Loneliness" was included in "Poet's Corner", *Aquarius*, London Weekend Television, 12 August 1972. This program of excerpts from the "Poetry International 72" festival had also been shown at the Young Vic, London, 25 June

1972, and excerpts were included in a film titled *A Plethora of Poets: The Best of Poetry International 1972 and 1973,* distributed in 1975 by the Centre for Internationalising the Study of English, St. Paul, Minnesota.

Further readings by Auden at "Poetry International 72" were broadcast in a programme with that title, BBC Radio 3, 21 August 1972. A recording is at the BBC.

Auden and Sir John Gielgud were interviewed by Michael Parkinson in *Parkinson,* BBC-1 television, 7 October 1972. Excerpts were published as "Art and the Dead", *Listener,* 26 October 1972; other excerpts appeared in Parkinson's *Parkinson: Selected Interviews from the Television Series* (1975), pp. 44–45, and, differently edited, in his *Parky's People* (2010), pp. 324–25.

At a party at Faber & Faber, Auden read "Doggerel by a Senior Citizen"; a recording was broadcast on BBC Radio 3, 9 October 1972.

A recorded interview with Christopher Blount was broadcast in *PM,* BBC Radio 4, 19 October 1972. A recording is in the British Library Sound Archive.

"Poems for the BBC", poems commissioned from and read by seventeen poets, including Auden's "Nocturne", was broadcast in BBC Radio 3, 13 November 1972.

"Why Shun a Nude Tag?" was a broadcast of excerpts from *A Certain World,* including a brief appearance by Auden, *Aquarius,* London Weekend Television, 3 December 1972.

Auden discussed thrillers and crime fiction in *Omnibus File,* BBC-1 TV, 3 December 1972.

"Tennyson, 80 Years On", BBC Radio 3, 8 December 1972, was a discussion among John Betjeman, Robert Lowell, Hallam Tennyson, Auden and others. A transcript, including Auden's one comment (justifying his published comment that Tennyson was "undoubtedly the stupidest" English poet), was published as "A Colloquium on Tennyson", *Listener,* 8 March 1973, pp. 302–5. A recording is in the British Library Sound Archive.

Auden and Mary McCarthy spoke about old age in "Growing Old: Decay or a New Experience?", *Something to Say,* Thames Television, 28 December 1972.

Auden was interviewed by Richard Crossman in *Crosstalk,* BBC-1 TV, 28 January 1973. Excerpts were published as "Remembering and Forgetting: W. H. Auden talks to Richard Crossman about poetry", *Listener,* 22 February 1973. "Londoner's Diary", *Evening Standard,* 29 January 1973, quotes Auden's correction of his statement in the broadcast that he had not altered the text of his poem "Hell is neither here nor there".

Auden's readings at the "Poetry International 72" festival were broadcast as "Auden in London", 10 March 1973

Auden read five of his poems in *Full House,* BBC-2 TV, 7 April 1973.

"Poetry International", BBC Radio 3, 13 July 1973, included some of Auden's readings from the 1973 festival.

"Poets on Poetry: W. H. Auden Talks with Patrick Garland", BBC-1 TV, 5 November 1973, was a posthumously- broadcast interview and readings. A report appeared as "Poets on Poetry—Auden and others", *Listener,* 8 November 1973.

In addition, Auden recorded nine of his poems for the British Council on 14 February 1973 (British Council tape 186), but it is unclear whether these were ever broadcast.

"COMMENT!" WITH EDWIN NEWMAN

Auden appeared on the NBC Sunday morning television program *Comment!* on 27 February 1972. As in other broadcasts of this series, the journalist Edwin Newman introduced four separate guests who had probably been recorded earlier in the week. Before Auden spoke, Newman explained that he had recently announced his return to Britain and that his "subject today is the rules that govern him as a poet." The following transcript appeared in a periodical that published full transcripts of each program, *National Broadcasting Company, Inc. presents Comment! with Edwin Newman,* with the same date as the broadcast.

I think, the best way of explaining my views about the nature of poetry, I can explain by a little piece of autobiography. Between the ages of six and twelve, I spent a great many hours of my waking life constructing a private, sacred world of my own, based on two things: on a certain kind of limestone landscape of the Pennine Moors, and an industry, lead mining.

Now, no doubt it's psychologically significant that this was an autistic world; I couldn't share it with other people, and I didn't want to. Then I discovered that though making this world was a game, something I didn't have to do, like eating and drinking, but which I could do if I wanted to, I found that you cannot play a game without rules. You may make rules for what you like, but a secondary world is just as much a world of law and order as the primary world.

For example, I found out almost instinctively, making this world, that I could choose, shall we say, between two kinds of water turbine. But they had to be real turbines that I could find in catalogues of machinery, I wasn't free to invent one.

Again, I could have a mine drained either by an adit or by a pump. But magic means were forbidden. These were the rules I found myself putting down. I found that this applies in writing poetry, too.

I think there are a few poets—D. H. Lawrence being an obvious example—who you feel have to write in free verse. But they are the exception. And if you do it, you've got to have an infallible sense of line endings, which most people who write in free verse don't.

Then, lastly, I discovered that though, of course, a poem must be beautiful, the poet must not be an aesthete. He must not say things because he thinks they sound poetically effective. He must believe them to be true. And I discovered this in a curious way in making this private world. And I realized it was my moral duty to choose the efficient one, to sacrifice my personal, aesthetic preferences to truth. And I find these things have stood me in good stead.

Then there's one other little thing that, as a writer, has always interested me: that I think it's extremely important to be one's age. There are certain ways you should write when you're thirty, and there are certain things you should write when you're nearly sixty-five, as I am now.

I would say, you can get an idea for a poem and you have to turn it down for one of two reasons: I'm sorry, no longer; or, I'm sorry, not yet. And at different times in one's life one has different models, I think. I know in the book I've just finished that the models have been Horace and the classical Goethe.

Now, I've always loved Horace, but when I was younger, I knew I couldn't use him. Now I think I can. It's important to be one's age. But the fatal mistake that some people make is not to say, "What should I write at sixty-four?" but "What should I write in 1971?" That's absolutely fatal.

APPENDIX V

Endorsements

A publicity flyer with the heading "Gerard Malanga Is Available", offering to book Malanga for poetry readings, printed by Andy Warhol Films, New York, in 1969, included one sentence by Auden: "These are the best poems I have ever read of anyone under 25 writing in America today."

An advertisement for *The Public Life*, a "bi-weekly journal of politics" edited in New York by Walter Karp and H. R. Shapiro, appeared in the *New York Review of Books*, 16 January 1969; it included a comment by Auden: "Hard-hitting and very well-written, *The Public Life* should be read by every citizen who cares for the Public Thing and believes it is too important to be handed over to professional politicians whatever their party." This also appeared in many later advertisements in the *New Republic*, *The Public Life* itself, and other journals, and, around 1973, in advertisements for a successor publishing company, Praxis Publications.

A brief comment on Eugen Rosenstock-Huessy appeared on the front flap of the dust jacket of *Judaism despite Christianity: The Letters on Christianity and Judaism between Eugen Rosenstock-Huessy and Franz Rosenzweig* (University: University of Alabama Press, 1969): "Rosenstock-Huessy . . . continually astonishes one by his dazzling and unique insights." It also appeared in advertisements for the book. Without the ellipsis, it appeared again on the front jacket of Rosenstock-Huessy's *Speech and Reality*, introduction by Clinton C. Gardner (Norwich, Vermont: Argo Books, 1970), and on other books by Rosenstock-Huessy. It may derive from a letter to a publisher.

A comment by Auden appeared on the front cover of the dust jacket of Anthony Rossiter's *The Golden Chain* (London: Hutchinson, 1970): "I am enormously impressed. I don't know anyone, except possibly Virginia Woolf, who has such a sense of the poetry of objects, of the visible as a world of sacramental signs." The same comment, attributed to a letter from Auden to Rossiter, 12 August 1969, was printed in the leaflet announcing an exhibition of recent paintings and drawings by Rossiter at the John Whibley Gallery, 7–25 April 1970. It also appeared in leaflets announcing further exhibits of Rossiter's work and in other publicity material.

Auden's one-word comment, "Enchanting", on Anne Fremantle's memoir *Three-Cornered Heart* (New York: Viking Press, 1970) appeared in a publisher's advertisement in the *New York Times Book Review*, 29 November 1970, but not on the book itself.

A brief comment on V. S. Yanovsky's *Of Light and Sounding Brass* (New York: Vanguard, 1972) appears on the front jacket flap and on various advertisements from the publishers (e.g. *Publishers' Weekly*, 28 August 1972): "A very original and fascinating novel indeed."

Probably around 1972, at Stephen Spender's request, Auden wrote a blurb for the magazine *Index on Censorship*. Auden's typescript, on the same page with a brief note to Spender, is in the magazine's archives, but was perhaps never printed. The following transcript corrects a few typing errors and emends some punctuation:

In my opinion *Index* is a most valuable and important publication. Dealing as it does with Censorship in all states and parts of the world, it cannot be called cheerful reading, but the more widely read it is the better. What particularly impresses me about *Index* is its lack of ideological bias. In principle, no doubt, its editors subscribe to the liberal belief that freedom of speech and freedom of artistic expression are socially and politically desirable, but they would not, I think, say that Censorship should never under any circumstances be applied. They try to ascertain the true facts and let the reader decide for himself.

The back cover of a book of poems by Joseph Francis Murphy, *Black Diamonds* (Old Greenwich: Devin-Adair, 1973), has a sentence from a letter by Auden (27 March 1971) about Murphy's previous book, *Night Visions*: "I found the poems original and moving".

A publisher's advertisement for Janet Flanner's *Paris Was Yesterday* (London: Angus & Robertson, 1973), *TLS*, 22 June 1973, included one sentence by Auden: "I found it fascinating and, since I am a Francophobe, I know it must be."

Auden's comment on Oliver Sacks's *Awakenings* (London: Duckworth, 1973), from a letter to Sacks, appeared in the publisher's advertisements in the *Listener*, 22 November 1973, *New Statesman*, 30 November 1973, and probably elsewhere: "Have read *Awakenings* and think it a masterpiece." The same sentence appeared on the dust jacket or paperback cover of later editions of the book.

A comment on *The Magic of Lewis Carroll*, edited by John Fisher (London: Nelson, 1973), appears on the front flap of the dust jacket "An enchanting book." The same comment appeared in a publisher's advertisement, *TLS*, 31 August 1973. The same book and jacket were published in the United States by Simon & Schuster.

The back cover of a book of poems by N. J. Loftis, *Black Anima* (New York: Liveright, 1973), notes that his poems have "been highly praised by, among others, W. H. Auden".

At some time probably after the early 1970s, publicity for Babette Deutsch's *Poetry Handbook: A Dictionary of Terms* (first published 1957; second edition, 1962; third edition, New York: Funk & Wagnalls, 1969) began to use a quotation from Auden: "Excellent, both in its accuracy and its clarity." Auden may have written this comment after deciding not to write a similar book of his own (see p. 741).

Three years after Auden's death, a book of poems by the popular folksinger Rod McKuen, *The Sea Around Me . . . The Hills Above* (London: Elm Tree Books, 1976), quoted a comment by Auden on its front jacket flap and rear cover: "Rod McKuen's poems are letters to the world and I am happy that some of them have come to me and found me out." When a similar but not identical collection, *The Sea Around Me*, appeared the next year (New York: Cheval Books, 1977), Auden's comment, quoted on the front jacket flap, had been rewritten posthumously: "Rod McKuen's poems are letters to the world and I'm happy that many of them came to me and found me out." Later still, on Rod McKuen's web site (www.mckuen.com), Auden's comment had changed again and now read: "Rod McKuen's poems are love letters to the world and I am happy that many of them came to me and found me out." In one detail, this later version may be more authentic than even the earliest one, as printed in 1976, because Auden may well have written "love letters to the world" and not "letters to the world" as the 1976 version has it.

APPENDIX VI

Letters to the Editor and Other Public Statements

This appendix includes Auden's letters to editors on topical subjects, and briefly lists group letters and statements to which he added his signature. Such group letters became far more common in the 1960s than they had been earlier, and Auden, like many other writers, offered his signature freely for worthy causes.

On 9 May 1972, having asked me a few days earlier to be his literary executor, Auden wrote to me: "on my decease, I want a notice to appear in the American and British Press requesting any friends who have letters from me to burn them when they're done with them, and on no account to show them to anybody else". After his death, I carried out this instruction in letters to the editors printed in the *TLS* and the *New York Times Book Review.*

Policy on Insurance: Cancel

This letter to the editor of the *New York Times* was published on 11 December 1970; a draft is in a notebook in the Berg Collection. A response from the president of the New York Association of Insurance Agents, published on 19 December, confirmed that the policy described by Auden had "reached crisis proportions in this state".

To the Editor:

I have just had an experience, which, on making inquiries, I find is by no means unique, but I have not seen it mentioned in the press. For over ten years I have held a burglary insurance policy. I have always paid the premiums promptly, and have never, I am thankful to say, ever had to make a claim.

A few days ago I received a letter from the insurance company, informing me that my policy will not be renewed owing to "underwriter reasons," a somewhat obscure phrase, which I can only interpret as meaning that they consider me too great a risk. Why?

I live on St Mark's Place which, since it is well lit and always crowded with people, is probably safer than most streets in the city, and my apartment building has a self-locking front door. As we all know, burglaries are on the increase and, had the company written to say that, under these circumstances, they must increase the premium, I should understand their reasoning.

Naturally, I don't expect insurance companies to be in the business for their health, but, surely, it is also their function to provide a public service. Are householders in New York City to be left without any protection whatever against possible losses? The question seems to me to merit public discussion.

W. H. Auden

New York, Dec. 1, 1970

Saying No

Auden's letter to the editor of the *New York Review of Books*, published under the heading above in the issue dated 1 July 1971, responded to W. S. Merwin's letter in the 3 June 1971 issue headed "On Being Awarded the Pulitzer Prize." Merwin wrote that he had been informed that he had won the prize for poetry for 1971 and that he was pleased to know of the judges' regard for his work. "But", he continued, "after years of the news from Southeast Asia, and the commentary from Washington, I am too conscious of being an American to accept public congratulation with good grace, or to welcome it except as an occasion for expressing openly a shame which many Americans feel, day after day, helplessly and in silence." He concluded: "I want the prize money to be equally divided" between a painter who had been blinded by a police weapon while he watched a demonstration from a roof "and the Draft Resistance." Merwin's polite letter of disagreement appeared beneath Auden's letter. ("Hinterholz, Austria" is a misinterpretaton of Auden's street address, Hinterholz 6, Kirchstetten, Austria, which he presumably typed in the local manner, with the town above the street name, leading an American editor to misread "Hinterholz 6" as a town followed by a postcode.)

To the Editors:

As a fellow citizen whose views on American foreign policy are, I should guess, pretty much the same as his, as a fellow poet and, let me add, an admirer, and as a one-time member of the Pulitzer Poetry Prize jury, I feel it is my duty to say that, in my opinion, Mr W. S. Merwin's public refusal to accept the prize money, as reported in your *Review* of June 3, was an ill-judged gesture.

To begin with, it implies that the Pulitzer juries are politically official bodies, which they certainly are not. On the contrary, if there were, as, thank God, there is not, a living American poet of major importance who openly supported our intervention in Vietnam or George Wallace, as Yeats came out in favor of Macduffy's Blueshirts, I think it highly unlikely that he would be awarded the Pulitzer Prize for Poetry.

Secondly, Mr Merwin has no right, if he does not wish to receive the money, to dictate to others how it shall be spent. I should have thought the obvious thing for him to do, feeling as he does, was to accept the money and then privately donate it to the causes he has at heart.

Lastly, the impression made on the reader by his gesture is the exact opposite of what, I am certain, he intended: it sounds like a personal publicity stunt. His position, if carried to its logical conclusion, would require him to abstain from any publication in the United States, for every time a magazine publishes a poem of his, or a member of the public buys one of his volumes, a poet receives "public congratulation."

W. H. Auden
Hinterholz, Austria

Mr Auden and the Laureateship

A story in *The Times*, 24 May 1972 ("W. H. Auden is favourite to become the new Poet Laureate"), reported that Auden's "New York agent" (presumably Perry Knowlton) "was sure he would not mind becoming a British citizen." This prompted an outraged letter from Elizabeth Rex, to which Auden refers in his letter, published 31 May 1972 under the heading above:

Sir, I was amazed and distressed to read in Mrs Elizabeth Rex's letter of May 26 that my New York agent is reputed to have conjectured that I would not mind becoming a British citizen again if, thereby, I could become Poet Laureate.

Even if I coveted the post, which I don't, to do such a thing for such a motive, I should regard as contemptible.

Yours, etc,

W. H. Auden,
3062 Kirchstetten.
Bez. St. Pölten, Hinterholz 6,
N-Ö, Austria.
May 27.

[A Letter about "Prematurity and Uniqueness in Scientific Discovery"]

Auden's letter to the editor of *Scientific American*, March 1973, responds to Gunther S. Stent's "Prematurity and Uniqueness in Scientific Discovery", published in December 1972, which carried the subhead, "A molecular geneticist reflects on two general historical questions: (1) What does it mean to say a discovery is 'ahead of its time'? (2) Are scientific creations any less unique than artistic creations?"

Sirs:

I was delighted by Mr Stent's article in your December issue, which demonstrates so convincingly that scientific research and artistic fabrication have much more in common than most people suppose. There are, however, certain differences between them to which I should like to draw the attention of your readers.

Every good work of art exhibits two qualities, Nowness and Permanence. Thanks to the former, it is possible for an art historian to give at least an approximate date for its making; thanks to the latter, it remains "on hand" in the world long after its maker and his society have disappeared. This means that, in the history of Art, there is Change but no Progress. Mozart does not supersede Monteverdi in the way that I suppose one must say that the Copernican picture of the universe superseded the Ptolemaic. It is only bad art which is superseded—by another kind of bad art. As we all know, much of the poetry, fiction, music, painting, etc., produced in any period is bad, though it may, temporarily, enjoy great popular success. Scientists are in the fortunate position of being judged by their peers, not by the general public. I should be curious to learn if it is possible for a scientist to say: "Much of the research being done at this time is worthless."

As for Prematurity, I can see that it is possible to call Mendel's work premature because, by the time it became known, genetics had already advanced beyond him. One cannot say that Cézanne's paintings were premature because, since they offended contemporary canonical taste, it was some time before their value was appreciated, since, as I said, in art there is no progress, whereas scientific discoveries are of permanent interest only to the historian of Science, not to scientists qua scientists.

W. H. Auden
Christ Church
Oxford

[A Letter about Translations of Cavafy]

The following self-explanatory letter to the editor of the *New York Times Book Review*, 11 March 1973, was evidently written at Rae Dalven's instigation using quotations she supplied.

To the Editor:

Lawrence Durrell, in his review of *C. P. Cavafy: Selected Poems*, translated by Edmund Keeley and Philip Sherrard, in your issue of January 21, states that the arrival of Messrs Keeley and Sherrard on the modern Greek translation scene, "marks quite a definite and definitive stage," in the process of making Cavafy fully available in English. I do not question Mr Durrell's right to his opinion, but his casual references to earlier translations make me wonder if he has read all of them—and this would seem to me the only fair basis for his sweeping judgment.

I wonder for instance if he has read *The Complete Poems of C. P. Cavafy*, translated by Rae Dalven and published in 1961 by Harcourt Brace Jovanovich. I had long been interested in Cavafy and I found Miss Dalven's translations so satisfactory that I wrote an introduction to the volume. The book is still in print in the original edition, and has been in paperback since 1966.

My opinion of the translation was corroborated by a series of eminent and knowledgeable writers. C. M. Bowra reviewed the volume for *The New York Times Book Review* on May 28, 1961. "Miss Dalven's translations," he wrote, "are scholarly, lucid and careful. She aims first and foremost at making the intellectual meaning clear, and with Cavafy this is of first importance. If she avoids any attempt to repeat his rhyme-schemes, she is not to be blamed, and has gained more than she has lost by her decision. Since English words tend to be shorter than Greek, her versions are rather more compressed than the originals, but this too strengthens their substance. Cavafy is a poet for our age, and this volume cannot fail to appeal to many readers who will see in its dramatic contents a sharp analysis of their own troubles."

Moses Hadas, then professor of Greek at Columbia University and an authority on Greek literature, in reviewing the book for *Herald Tribune Books* spoke of Miss Dalven's "carefully wrought volume." Lionel Trilling of Columbia University, in an essay on the book, said that "Miss Dalven's translation gives to the English-speaking world virtually a new poet in the English language."

The volume was also published in England in 1961 by Hogarth Press. It was cited as one of the outstanding books of 1961 by E. M. Forster, who wrote in the London *Observer* of January 14, 1962: "Rae Dalven's translation (the second complete one to appear in this country) should further increase his fame, and she adds a bibliographical note containing facts not widely available." (The other complete translation Mr Forster refers to was that of John Mavrogordato, whose name Mr Durrell also omitted from his review.)

Miss Dalven's translation was favorably reviewed in the *Times Literary Supplement* soon after it was published, and as late as April 2, 1970, it was one of the books which were discussed in a long front page article called "Problems of Poetic Translation in Modern Greek." The author had this to say about Miss Dalven's translations: "Miss Rae Dalven has studied the originals closely and gives an extremely interesting account of Cavafy's prosody and methods of versification, the best so far to appear in English."

Surely a translation of Cavafy which has been praised so highly by so many distinguished scholars and critics deserves to be considered in a review that passed judgment on all previous translations.

W. H. Auden
Oxford, England

Letters and Statements Signed by Auden and Others

In keeping with the times, from the mid-1960s onward, Auden joined many other writers in signing letters of political protest. What follows is a brief listing of these, together with a few other joint letters and communications signed by Auden.

"U.S. Group Appeals to Spain on Basques", *New York Times*, 20 December 1970, reported the text of a telegram urging the Spanish government not to impose the death penalty in a military trial; the newspaper listed fifteen names "among the signers".

"School of Arts", *New York Review of Books*, 7 January 1971, printed the text of a letter to the president of Columbia University, with twenty-eight signatures, protesting cuts in the course offerings at the School of the Arts.

"Freedom Plea for Wife of Soviet Sculptor", *Times*, 21 October 1971, printed the text of a letter delivered to the Soviet ambassador in London, with five signatures (Henry Moore, Arthur Rubenstein, Yehudi Menuhin, Auden, and Stephen Spender), asking the authorities to allow the wife of Alexander Zlotnick to follow him out of the Soviet Union.

"Human Image Debased", *Times,* 12 February 1972, a letter on nudity in public performances, was signed by seven poets, not including Auden. However, "The Times Diary", 10 March 1972, reported that a copy of the letter sent to Auden was returned with his signature some weeks after publication. This copy is now in the Berg Collection.

"Detained in Russia", *Times,* 23 June 1972, printed the text of two letters, the second with twelve signatures including Auden's, calling attention to a hunger strike by the wife of the poet David Markish protesting injustices done to her husband and his mother.

The nomination of Stephen Spender as Professor of Poetry at Oxford was signed by eleven names listed in the *Oxford University Gazette,* 17 May 1973.

"Andrei Amalrik", *Times,* 10 July 1973, with five signatures, protested an imminent new trial for this Russian essayist and historian.

APPENDIX VII

Auden and the Liturgy

Auden was twice involved tangentially with revisions to the liturgy of the Episcopal Church in the United States. This appendix includes events from the periods covered by both *Prose V* and *Prose VI.*

In 1964 the Episcopal Church, prompted by Bishop Daniel Corrigan, director of the Home Commission, commissioned the people and clergy of St Mark's-in-the-Bouwerie, New York, to draft an ecumenical liturgy in contemporary language for use by students. A small group of parishoners worked on the text in 1965. The rector, Michael Allen, wrote that the work

> finally involved W. H. Auden, who is also a member of this parish. I took it over to him and we spent an afternoon on stylistic matters—no fundamental re-write, but the re-working of various phrases. The little phrase "and we are very deaf" is Auden's.

Auden's phrase occurs in "The Preparation", in a prayer by the president and assembly: "Holy Spirit, speak to us. Help us to listen for we are very deaf. Come, fill this moment."

The full text was printed as "The Eucharistic Liturgy, as prepared by the people and clergy of St Mark's-in-the-Bouwerie, New York, for use on special ecumenical occasions", *New Christian* (London), 14 July 1966; an accompanying article, "Local Liturgy", by the Bishop of Woolwich, John A. T. Robinson, included the letter from Michael Allen quoted above. The liturgy and Robinson's essay are reprinted in Robinson's *But That I Can't Believe!* (1967). The liturgy alone was reprinted in various books and collections on the liturgy, e.g. *Word and Action: New Forms of the Liturgy*, with an introduction by John C. Kirby (1969), *The Experimental Liturgy Book*, edited by Robert F. Hoey (1973). Later reprintings tend to omit the source of the text.

For the Protestant Episcopal Church in the United States, Auden served on the Drafting Committee for a revision of the Psalter in the Book of Common Prayer. On 20 December 1967 Auden accepted an invitation to serve on the newly created committee; he "served until his return to England [in 1972] required his resignation" (*The Prayer Book Psalter Revised*, 1973, p. 1). Auden wrote to J. Chester Johnson, later a member of the committee: "my own role is a very minor one, since I know no Hebrew. All I can do is to try and persuade the scholars not to alter Coverdale unless there is a definite mistranslation" (28 January 1971).

Although initially skeptical, Auden became an effective member of the committee and proposed at least three revisions that his colleagues accepted. (These were identified to J. Chester Johnson by the Custodian of the Standard Book of Common Prayer, Canon Charles Mortimer Guilbert.) In Psalm 27:6, he proposed "secrecy" in place of "secret places". In Psalm 42:9, he proposed "cataracts" in place of Coverdale's "water pipes" and the 1928 Prayer Book's "water floods", in "One deep calls to another in the noise of your cataracts". In Psalm 95:5, he proposed "molded" for the earlier "prepared" in "his hands have molded the dry land". These three readings first appeared in 1973 in *The Psalter, Part I: A Selection of the Most Frequently Appointed Psalms* (Prayer Book Studies 23), and were reprinted in later editions of the revised Psalter (*Services for Trial Use: Authorized Alternatives to Prayer Book Services,* 1971, and *The Prayer Book Psalter Revised,* 1973) and eventually in the revised Book of Common Prayer first published in "Proposed" form in 1977 and in final form in 1979.

Johnson also reports that Auden successfully argued for the retention of some earlier readings, among them "Jerusalem is built as a city that is at unity with itself" in Psalm 122.

APPENDIX VIII

Lost and Unwritten Work

Around 1970, the National Council of Churches and the Union Theological Seminary in New York sponsored the creation of the U.S.A. Task Force on the Future of Mankind and the Role of the Christian Churches in a World of Science-Based Technology. Auden seems to have been named as a member of this task force but never attended its meetings. A report was published by the task force in the form of a book: *To Love or to Perish: The Technological Crisis and the Churches,* edited by J. Edward Carothers, Margaret Mead, Daniel D. McCracken and Roger L. Shinn (New York: Friendship Press, 1972). The back cover listed thirty-eight names under the heading "The list of those whose insights have contributed to this volume reads like pages from a Who's Who of Great American Thinkers"; Auden's name was included in this list despite protests from some of the organizers that he had not participated in any way and had written nothing for the report.

In 1970 the *New Yorker* invited Auden to review the first three volumes of a new edition of Samuel Pepys's diaries; he replied by telegram on 9 September "Would like Pepys if he can wait till November"; in the cover letter with which he sent his typescript of "Well Done, Sir Walter Scott!" on 16 November, he wrote: "I don't think I can tackle the Pepys. For one thing, I think that, for the general reader, one should wait till the whole thing is out" (New York Public Library).

In 1971, in discussions with Nikos Stangos, an editor at Penguin Books, Auden agreed to write a book about poetic form. Later that year Random House offered to publish it in the United States. Early in 1972, Auden saw Babette Deutsch's *Poetry Handbook* (1957; second edition, 1962; third edition, 1969). On 29 February 1972 his agent reported to Random House: "he tells me that he's discovered that Babette Deutch has done a book very similar to the one on poetic form that he had in mind and he has decided not to go ahead with the project" (Columbia University Library). See p. 732 for his comment on her book.

Auden was commissioned in 1973 to write a preface to a collection of poems by Ogden Nash but died before writing it.

Around July 1973 Auden agreed to prepare a new edition of his *Oxford Book of Light Verse* (1938) and asked me to collaborate with him, but he died before the project went any further.

Auden agreed to write a foreword to *Forest Poets: An Anthology,* a collection published by the Waltham Forest Arts Council in connection with the 1973 Forest Festival, but died before he could do so. The pamphlet reports: "It is regretted that Mr W. H. Auden who was to have written a foreword to this Anthology died suddenly in Austria on the 29th September."

TEXTUAL NOTES

A Certain World

Auden began collecting quotations for use in his essays and reviews in the early 1940s, perhaps earlier. By the 1960s he had compiled perhaps a few hundred five-by-eight-inch cards, each with a quotation. (The cards are now lost; I saw them in a box on Auden's desk in the late 1960s.) Perhaps around 1966 he began planning what he called a "scrap book" based on these quotations, and in January 1967 signed a contract for it with the American publisher Funk & Wagnalls, apparently at the suggestion of William Cole, who was then working with the firm. Cole later affiliated himself with the Viking Press, and Auden's contract with Funk & Wagnalls was cancelled in November 1967, in favor of a new contract with Viking, who eventually published the book under the imprint, "A William Cole Book".

Auden was actively collecting material by the summer of 1967, when he preserved the excerpt by John Davy (collected under "Dreams") in the *Observer*, 13 August 1967. In mid-October 1968 he wrote to his agent Perry Knowlton: "The Commonplace Book is finished but has to be typed properly when I return [from Austria]. Viking should be warned that it is an *enormous* tome" (reported by Knowlton in a letter to William Cole). The typescript was prepared by a secretary (with at least one page retyped by Auden) and seems to have been submitted in November 1968. Auden's original title was "A Certain World, Compiled by W. H. Auden". Cole noted in an internal memo on 26 February 1969 that Auden did not want it to be called (as Cole wished) "W. H. Auden's Commonplace Book", but "A Certain World": "He says, 'it is surely the only autobiography I'll ever write, and that is my title.'" He agreed, however, to allow it to be identified as part of a series projected by Cole under the name "The Commonplace Book Series" or "The Viking Commonplace Books." On 23 March 1969 another memo from Cole confirmed that Auden did not want "A Commonplace Book" in the title or subtitle. After further wrangling at Viking, and with Auden's assent, the subtitle "A Commonplace Book" was at last added to the book. (It was printed above the title, in smaller type.)

In his memo of 26 February 1969 Cole also wrote that Auden agreed to make a typographical distinction between the quotations and his comments, with his comments printed "in a clear italic, or whatever typeface the designers may decide." This method was not used in the printed book, which instead indented Auden's comments a quarter-inch from the left margin. In the present edition, I have conformed to the practice used throughout these volumes: Auden's comments are printed across the full width of the page, and quotations are indented from both margins.

The index is either Auden's work or the work of a secretary; Cole reported in his 26 February 1969 memo that he had now received it from him.

Elisabeth Sifton, then an editor at Viking, prepared a memo in January 1969 suggesting a few changes in the contents and arrangements. Auden rejected all of these except one: he accepted her suggestion that, in his comment under "Black" (p. 32), "white" should be added after "living" in the description of John Howard Griffin as "the most heroic living American". Although Auden accepted the change for diplomatic reasons, I have restored his original text, because the change obscures his moral point, which is that Griffin, by temporarily darkening his skin, had voluntarily taken upon himself the sufferings that were imposed involuntarily on darker-skinned persons; Auden was pointing to the heroism of Griffin's voluntary suffering, not (as Elisabeth Sifton thought) falsely suggesting that Griffin's temporary suffering was greater than the suffering of those who endured race prejudice all their lives.

During the spring and summer of 1969 Viking checked and corrected many of Auden's quotations, and the book was set in type around the end of the year. Auden wrote to Louis Kronenberger on 15 January 1970: "Am just correcting the galleys of the Scrap Book" (Princeton University Library).

Auden's typescript and the galley proofs included four items that were omitted from the printed text because Viking could not obtain copyright permission: under "Love, Romantic" (p. 173) the book omits Brecht's "The Cranes" (restored here, from Auden and Kallman's translation of *The Rise and Fall of the City of Mahagonny*, written 1960, published 1976); in the same entry, preceding "Take Him" by Lorenz Hart (p. 179), the book omits (and I have not been able to restore) "Adelaide's Lament" ("It says here") by Frank Loesser, from *Guys and Dolls*; and, under "War" (p. 299), the book omits Brecht's "Song of Fraternization" (restored here; translated by Auden as one of the "Eight Songs from *Mother Courage*" in *City without Walls*, 1969).

The fourth omitted item was the entry "Words, Long", which an editor at Viking marked in the final proofs with questions about inconsistencies between the letter counts and the actual words. Instead of checking the originals, Auden marked the whole entry "better delete". I have restored the entry from the typescript, correcting Auden's slight miscopying of the original words.

Auden himself deleted from the typescript a quotation that he had used as the first quotation under "World, Creation of the" (p. 313), the poem by Goethe that begins "When the world, in its uttermost depths", translated by David Luke.

On 20 August 1969 Auden wrote to Michele Medinz at Viking, in reply to a lost letter apparently relaying Michael Hamburger's concerns about the use of his translations from Hölderlin: "I had originally intended, when quoting poems written in foreign languages to print the original text followed by an English prose translation, but this seemed to make the book too long" (Edinburgh University Library).

The Viking Press published the book on 26 June 1970. A few pages of excerpts appeared in *Atlantic*, May 1970, under the title "Auden in the Looking Glass".

Auden prepared a set of "Addenda" for the British edition published by Faber & Faber on 3 May 1971. Although he wanted his additions to be integrated into the main text, Faber was not willing to pay for resetting and reindexing the book, so the additions were segregated in a section at the back headed "Addenda". I have integrated these items into the main text, placing them at the locations indicated by Auden's markings in his copy of the American edition (Harry Ransom Center). The additional items are as follows:

Ants
Death (the quotations from Henley and Dickens)
Fish
Imagination (the quotation from Wittgenstein)
Landscape, Industrial
Marriage (the quotation from Dickens)

Mnemonics (one added item by Spaeth, "On the chord we are starting")
Names, Proper (the quotation from Wittgenstein)
Non-Sequitur, A
Parrot, A
Songs ("The Meeting of the Waters" by Moore)
War ("War Song" by Davidson)
Windmill, A

In setting these additions Faber listed the two quotations for "Death" as if they were separate entries each with the title "Death", listed "The Meeting of the Waters" as a separate item (not, as intended, part of the entry "Songs"), and listed "War Song" as a separate item (not, as intended, part of the entry "War"). Auden's marked copy does not indicate a location for the two-line addition to "Mnemonics", but I have placed it above the existing entries in order to preserve the chronological sequence of composers.

The typescript and galleys lack the foreword, which must have been written at the last minute. A page proof of the foreword shows that in the paragraph fragment after the quotation, an editor inserted "it is" between "when" and good" in the final sentence, probably without Auden's knowledge, so I have restored his reading. In the penultimate paragraph an editor also seems to have changed "share in common" to "have in common", losing the moral force of Auden's verb, which I have restored.

In the typescript the first word of each heading is in uppercase letters and the other words in upper- and lowercase. I have followed the printed book by using upper- and lowercase throughout. I have in some places restored Auden's layout where the publisher's changes obscured the structure of the quotation, and have restored Auden's capitalization where it was, I think, mistakenly reduced by an editor. In the heading "Humanists, the" I have restored the definite article, mistakenly removed by a copy-editor.

Within individual entries, Auden's typescript makes a fairly clear distinction between descriptive subheads supplied by Auden above excerpts from other writers (subheads that are printed here in italics slightly indented from the left) and the original titles of reprinted pieces (printed here in centered italics). The publisher misunderstood this distinction, and gave the same treatment to both kinds of headings. I have restored the distinction made in the typescript. In some instances, the titles are not original to the author but are titles that Auden had devised for earlier books that he had edited, e.g. the title "Enclosure" for the verses by John Clare under the heading "Enclosure".

Where Auden used two or more quotations from the same author in sequence, the typescript gives the name of the author after each quotation; I have followed the book in printing the author's name beneath only the last item in the sequence.

Auden's prose quotations extensively abridge and modify the originals. Where Viking's copyeditor replaced Auden's quotation with the original, I have retained the copyeditor's version, but I have not tried to correct Auden's other wholesale changes in his sources. The copyeditor who checked some of Auden's quotations (for example, from Dryden) used some modern editions where Auden had used early ones, and the copyeditor reduced capitals and italics to match the modern text. In such instances I have restored the formatting of the typescript.

Where the printed text attributes translations to others, "slightly modified by W. H. A." Auden's typescript has only "slightly modified".

Under "Anagrams" a copyeditor added at the end "and one L"; Auden's typist had mistakenly added a second "L" in "O. Cromwel" earlier in the paragraph, leading to this needless correction (which Auden accepted in proof).

Under "Cygnet" I have restored some of the original word order of the quotation in order to undo nonsense but have otherwise left Auden's approximate transcription unchanged.

Under "Friday, Good" in the section that begins "Just as we", Auden wrote, "None of us, I'm certain, will imagine ourselves"; a copyeditor changed "ourselves" to "himself", but Auden's usage may make a theological point, so I have restored it.

Under "Homer and Seeing" I have undone a copyeditor's mistaken repunctuating of the passage that quotes Odysseus; Auden notably abridged and modified this entire excerpt.

Under "Spoonerisms", in the fourth line, "that falls beyond my pane" may have been a typist's mistaken regularization of "that palls beyond my fane"; it is unchanged in the only other published text of the poem, in *Nineteen Poems by Robert Morse* (1981), which is perhaps derived from *A Certain World.*

Under "Translation" I have restored Auden's placement of the titles of the French and English versions of the ode on Namur; in the printed book these appear as headings.

Under "Voyages" Auden or his typist mistakenly omitted three lines from Edward Lear's list of phrases; an editor noticed the omission, but inserted an ellipsis instead of restoring the three lines, which I have restored.

I have silently corrected any German and French misspellings that I noticed and have emended (I hope) the mistyped Greek in "Parrot, A", one of the items that appeared in the addenda to the Faber edition and which Auden may not have proofread. I have corrected the attribution of one quotation: under "Mind, the Human" the quotation that begins "I have drawn from the well" (p. 200) is implicitly attributed in the printed text to Lichtenberg, as it is printed as the first of two quotations from Lichtenberg; Auden similarly attributes it to Lichtenberg in *The Viking Book of Aphorisms* (1962). I have attributed it instead to Karl Kraus. Under "Names, Proper" I have restored the attribution of "Star Names" to E. J. Webb; after Auden read the final proofs, this name was mysteriously replaced in the printed book by the name of the author's better-known brother, C. C. J. Webb. I have removed "von" from Auden's rendering of the name Dietrich Bonhoeffer and corrected Felix Gilber to Felix Gilbert. The entry attributed to "J. P. Richter" should perhaps be given the name under which he published, "Jean Paul". Under "Dogs" the attribution to C. G. W. St John should perhaps read Charles St John. I have made a few silent, trivial corrections to the acknowledgements and index.

Under "Choirboys" the author of the quatrain was Corney Grain.

Under "Hitler" the excerpts quoted by H. Rauschning are now regarded as forgeries by Rauschning.

Under "Mind, the Human" the quotation "When we think a thing" is from *Punch.*

Under "Puns" the "French authoress" was Louise de Vilmorin.

Under "Dons, Humor of", in the poem by A. D. Godley, the final line is pronounced "Save beta minus query."

Under "Nursery Library, My" the book by Thomas Sopwith is *An Account of the Mining District of Alston Moor, Weardale and Teesdale*; the unidentified authors are: *Mines and Miners: or Underground Life*, by Louis Simonon; *Machinery for Metalliferous Mines*, by Edward Henry Davies; *The Edinburgh School of Surgery before Lister*, by Alexander Miles; and *Dangers to Health*, by T. Pridgen Teale. I have restored in Auden's list the English title *Shock-headed Peter*, not the original *Struwwelpeter* (misprinted *Strewel Peter*) by which it was replaced by a copyeditor.

Under "Saints" the two persons of sanctity were Charles Williams and Dorothy Day.

Under "Words, Last" the aristocratic lady was the Marquise de Pompadour.

Viking's copyeditor altered a few attributions, e.g. replacing the pseudonym Beachcomber with J. B. Morton.

For many longer quotations, Auden's typescript listed some specific sources which the publisher omitted for the sake of consistency. Some but not all were listed in the acknowledgements. These were (listed here by entry and author, and slightly regularized):

"Acronyms": Towyn Mason, *The Sunday Telegraph*, 24 December 1967. "Aging": John Gower, *Confessio Amantis*, Book VIII. "Anagrams": D. A. Borgmann, *Language on Vacation*. "Behaviorism": Anthony Storr, "The Concept of Cure", *Psychoanalysis Observed*, ed. Charles Rycroft (Constable, 1966). "Birds": Loren Eiseley, *The Immense Journey* (Gollancz, 1958). "Calvin": C. S. Lewis, *Non-Dramatic Literature of the Sixteenth Century*. "Camps, Concentration": Bruno Bettelheim, *The Informed Heart*. "Cats": Colette, *Creatures Great and Small*, tr. Enid McLeod (Secker & Warburg, 1951). "Chef, Life of a": Alexandre Dumas, *History of Cuisine*. "Childhood": Bruno Bettelheim, *The Empty Fortress*; Erik Erikson, *Identity: Youth and Crisis*. "Children, Autistic": Bruno Bettelheim, *The Empty Fortress*. "Climber, A Professional": David Roberts, *The Mountain of My Fear* (Vanguard Press, 1968). "Cosmos, The Medieval": C. S. Lewis, *The Discarded Image*. "Cuckoo, The": Edward A. Armstrong, *The Folklore of Birds* (Collins, 1958).

"Dark Ages, Thank God for the": Charles Norris Cochrane, *Christianity and Classical Culture*; Erich Auerbach, *Mimesis*. "Day, Times of": Gavin Douglas, Aeneid, Book XII, Prologue. "Dogs": Konrad Lorenz, "The Perennial Retainers" [in *King Solomon's Ring*]; J. R. Ackerley, *My Dog Tulip* (Secker & Warburg, 1956); Frank Debenham, *In the Antarctic* (John Murray, 1952). "Dreams": John Davy, *Observer*, 13 August 1967. "Easter": Francis Kilvert, *Diary*. "Eating": Elias Canetti, *Crowds and Power*; Alexandre Dumas, *Dictionary of Cuisine* (tr. Louis Colman); E. F. Benson, *Lucia's Progress*. "Eclipses": Benjamin John Armstrong, *Armstrong's Norfolk Diary*, ed. H. B. Armstrong (Hodder & Stoughton, 1963); Virginia Woolf, *A Writer's Diary* (Harcourt Brace, 1953). "Enclosure": W. G. Hoskins, *The Making of the English Landscape* (Hodder & Stoughton, 1955). "Eruptions": Goethe, *Italian Journey*. "Eskimos": Vilhjalmur Stefansson, *My Life with the Eskimo* (1913); Knud Rasmussen, *Across Arctic America* (Putnam, 1927).

"Fatigue": John Franklin, *Narrative of a Journey to the Shores of the Polar Sea* (1823). "God": Charles Williams, *The Descent of the Dove*. "Hangman, The": J. Bronowski, *The Face of Violence* (World Publishing Co.). "Hitler": quoted by H. Rauschning, *The Voice of Destruction* (1940; Felix Gilbert, *Hitler Directs His War* (Oxford, 1950). "Honor, Sense of": *The Klephetic Ballads in Relation to Greek History* (Blackwell, 1936). "Horse, Evolution of the": Leslie Reid, *Earth's Company* (John Murray, 1958). "Hospital Talk": Anthony Rossiter, *The Pendulum* (Gollancz, 1966). "Humanists, The": C. S. Lewis,

Non-dramatic Literature of the Sixteenth Century. "Hygiene, Personal": Mrs Florence Aadland, *The Big Love.*

"Imagination": Anthony Rossiter, *The Pendulum*; Goethe, *Italian Journey.* "Jackdaws": Konrad Lorenz, "The Perennial Retainers" [in *King Solomon's Ring*]. "Journalism": Nigel Dennis, *August for the People.* "Landscape: Basalt": Anthony Collett, *The Changing Face of England.* "Landscape: Cultivated": Goethe, *Italian Journey.* "Landscape: Fens": Charles Kingsley, *Prose Idylls: New and Old.* "Landscape: Limestone": Anthony Collett, *The Changing Face of England.* "Love, Romantic": Lorenz Hart, *Pal Joey.* "Machines": Bruno Bettelheim, *The Empty Fortress.* "Madness": J. Ruskin, letter to Carlyle, 23 June 1878; Anthony Rossiter, *The Pendulum*; J. Haley, *Strategies of Psychotherapy* (Grune and Stratton, 1963). "Man": David Jones, *The Anathemata.* "Marriage": Goethe, *Elective Affinities.*

"Names": C. Lévi-Strauss, *The Savage Mind* (1966). E. J. Webb, *The Names of the Stars* (Nisbet & Co., 1952). "Neighbor, Love of One's": Ernest Gordon, *Through the Valley of the Kwai.* "Opera, Soap": James Thurber, *The Beast in Me.* "Owls, Barn": Charles Waterton, *Essays on Natural History.* "Plants": Eric Ashby, "Leaf Shape", from *Plant Life* (Simon & Schuster, 1949). "Puritanism": C. S. Lewis, *Non-dramatic Literature of the Sixteenth Century.* "Reformation, Vocabulary of the": Owen Barfield, *History in English Words.* "Renaissance, The": Charles Williams, *The Descent of the Dove.* "Roads": Ivan D. Margary, *Roman Roads in Britain* (Phoenix House, 1955); Anthony Collett, *The Changing Face of England.* "Royalty": Max Beerbohm, as reported by S. N. Behrman in *Portrait of Max*; Princess Marie Louise, *My Memories of Six Reigns.*

"Science": Robert Oppenheimer, *Encounter* (October 1962); Charles Nicolle, *Biologie de l'Invention.* "Seasons, The Four": Anon. tenth-century, tr. Kenneth Hurlston Jackson, *A Celtic Miscellany* (Harvard, 1951). "Sparrows": John Clare, *Nature Notes.* "Time": E. R. Reach, "Primitive Time Reckoning", *A History of Technology*, vol. 1 (Oxford, 1954). "Translation": C. S. Lewis, *Non-dramatic Literature of the Sixteenth Century.* "Voyages": Goethe, *Italian Journey*; Edward Lear, *Journals of a Landscape Painter in Corsica.* "War": O. H. Mowrer, *Learning Theory and Personality Dynamics* (Ronald Press, 1950); Bruno Bettelheim, *The Empty Fortress* (Free Press, 1957). "Water": Anthony Collett, *The Changing Face of England.*

Essays and Reviews

1969–1973

Foreword to the American Edition of *The Pendulum*

Page 341.

Anthony Rossiter (1926–2000) was a painter, teacher, and writer who was a friend of many poets in Britain and America. He made a series of oil portraits of Auden. Rossiter had been taught in art school by Auden's old friend Robert Medley, who perhaps introduced them.

This book was first published in Britain in 1966; the title of Auden's essay is "Foreword to the American Edition". That edition was published 15 September 1969, although it had originally been announced for publication on 22 April but was delayed after the dust jackets were lost in the publisher's warehouse.

The passage in the book that Auden does not give "in full" appears in *A Certain World*, under "Hospital Talk".

Foreword to *Persons from Porlock and Other Plays for Radio*

Page 344.

The three other plays in the book are *Enter Caesar*, *East of the Sun and West of the Moon*, and *They Met on Good Friday*. A note (conceivably written by Auden) printed below the cast list of *Persons from Porlock* reads: "It was Louis MacNeice's last production. When he went into the studio, after an expedition to the Yorkshire moors to record potholing effects, the illness which was to cause his death was already on him, and he died on 3 September [1967]."

A draft of Auden's foreword is in a notebook in the Berg Collection. Although the essay is headed "Foreword", the title page of the book reads "*Persons from Porlock and other plays for radio* with an introduction by W. H. Auden". The book was published by the British Broadcasting Corporation on 25 September 1969.

A Civilized Voice

Page 347.

No typescript of this review has been found in the *New Yorker* archives. A draft is in a notebook in the Berg Collection.

In the paragraph fragment that begins "If private letters" (p. 351) the request to his friends that Auden reports having written in his will did not in fact appear there, although he stated this preference often in conversation and asked me to publish it after his death.

In the paragraph that begins "About his translation" (p. 356) Mr Carne-Ross is D. S. Carne-Ross with whom Auden was associated through the National Translation Center, publisher of *Delos* (see *Prose V*, p. 487). In the paragraph that begins "Today I feel" (p. 356) Auden had last written about Pope thirty-two years earlier, not eighteen, but his 1936 essay (published in 1937, *Prose I*, p. 141) had been reprinted in *Essays in Criticism* in 1951 and Auden mistook the reprint for the original.

Auden included this essay in *Forewords and Afterwords* (1973) with no significant changes in the text.

To Stephen Spender on His Sixtieth Birthday

Page 359.

Spender learned that Auden had been asked by the *Guardian* to write a birthday greeting for him, and his feelings were hurt when he did not see it in the newspaper delivered to his doorstep on the day. He learned only after Auden's death that Auden had in fact written the birthday message and that the *Guardian* had printed it, but only in the second of the three daily editions of the paper, not the final ("three-star") edition that was distributed in central London. It seems to have been one of two pieces that were replaced in the final edition by a film review. A draft is in a notebook in the Berg Collection.

Papa Was a Wise Old Sly-Boots

Page 360.

As he reports in this review, Auden seems to have met Ackerley through the *Listener*, and remained on friendly terms with him all his life.

In an interview with Jon Bradshaw in 1969 (published in *Esquire*, January 1970 and the *Observer Magazine*, 7 November 1971, and in different form in the British edition of *Harper's Bazaar*, February 1970) Auden said:

> one of my great ambitions is to get into the *O.E.D.* as the first person to have used in print a new word. I have two candidates at the moment, which I used in my review of J. R. Ackeley's autobiography. They are "Plain-Sewing" and "Princeton-First-Year." They refer to two types of homosexual behavior.

Plain-Sewing is mutual masturbation; Princeton-First-Year is frottage. Auden's ambition was fulfilled posthumously when both words were defined in the third volume (1982) of the *Supplement to the Oxford English Dictionary*.

In the chronological lists I have removed the italicization of the name Tulip and have expanded the dates to include the first two digits of each year (18 or 19); in the original text these were dropped wherever it was possible to do so without a loss in clarity.

For the distinction between lupus and aureus dogs, see *A Certain World*, under "Dogs". King Tum-Tum was Edward VII.

Auden included this essay in *Forewords and Afterwords* (1973). He deleted his haiku and the brief sentence that preceded it but made no other changes to the text.

A Piece of Pure Fiction in the Firbank Mode

Page 368.

Auden had known Ashbery and Schuyler since the early 1950s. He had selected Ashbery's *Some Trees* for the Yale Series of Younger Poets and Schuyler had worked for him as a typist in Ischia.

The Childs restaurant chain offered low-priced meals in elegant settings.

Freedom and Necessity in Poetry

Page 370.

This was Auden's contribution to the fourteenth Novel Symposium; other speakers included Jacques Monod, Jerome Bruner, E. H. Gombrich, Gunnar Myrdal, Linus Pauling, Arthur Koestler (who wrote a novel partly about it, *The Call-Girls*, 1972), Konrad Lorenz, and Margaret Mead. The book was published in Stockholm by Almqvist & Wiksell in December 1970 and by John Wiley in the United States and Britain in 1971. The theme of the symposium, "The Place of Value in a World of Facts", was the title of a book by Wolfgang Köhler (1938).

The Swedish compositor seems to have had difficulty interpreting Auden's typescript. I have made some slight emendations to spelling and punctuation, for example, inserting a hyphen in "lead-mining", and correcting "N < I" (where Auden seems to have used the wrong sign and the compositor misread a letter for a numeral) to "*N* > 1". In the second paragraph ("Most of what") I have deleted an extraneous "hours" after "great many". In the one-sentence paragraph that begins "Needless to say" (p. 376) I have emended "that The Arts for the arts, can" to "that the Arts can", although Auden may have intended something different. In the paragraph that follows I have emended "do historiconscious [*sic*] with persons who" to "do with history-conscious persons who".

A mimeographed leaflet, headed "Nobel Symposium 14[:] Abstract | Freedom and Necessity in Poetry | W. H. Auden", seems to have been distributed to participants before the symposium, presumably together with other such abstracts. It differs in many details from Auden's address. A lightly emended text follows; the ellipsis at the end of one section is present in the original.

FREEDOM AND NECESSITY IN POETRY

Man as Individual

Individual is (a) a biological description—a member of the species, Homo Sapiens, a man, a woman, a child, etc. (b) a social-historical description, what we are by "second nature"—a Swede, an Englishman, a taxi-driver etc. As individuals we are the product of sexual reproduction and social conditioning. We are subject to biological and socio-economic necessity. We do not act but exhibit behavior, characteristic of the species and societies of which we are willy-nilly members. As individuals our goal is to stay alive and perpetuate our species. As individuals we are countable, comparable, replaceable.

Man as Person

As persons who can say "I", each of us is unique, with a unique perspective on the world. We are called into personal existence, not by any biological process, but by other persons, our parents, our siblings etc. (The Myth of Adam). As persons we are not subject to necessity, but are free to choose to attend to this rather than that, to do this rather than that, but precisely because we are free, we *must* accept responsibility for the consequences of our attentions and acts whatever they may turn out to be. As persons we are free to form communities, i.e. "groups of rational beings united by a common love of something other than ourselves" (St Augustine)—God, music, stamp-collecting or what have you. As persons our goal is to be happy. As persons we are uncountable, incomparable, irreplaceable.

Happiness

To be happy a man must feel (a) free, not compelled by nature or others to do what he does not like or thinks he ought not to do—(b) important; what he does is needed or admired by others.

Labor, Play and Work

The laborer has no freedom—what he does he must do in order to eat and rear a family—but he has importance. His job exists because society needs what he does.

The player has freedom but no importance. His play is of no concern to others. For play to have any importance, an element of necessity must be introduced, i.e. all games are played according to rules. The players are free to choose what these rules shall be, but, once they have chosen them, they must obey them. These rules introduce an element of importance by making the game difficult to play, i.e. a test of skill.

The worker, lucky man, feels both free and important. What he does is what by taste and talent he enjoys doing (to him, that is, his work is play). At the same time, what he does is needed and rewarded by society (to the latter, his work is labor).

Words and the Individual

Most animals have some kind of code of communication, auditory, visual or olfactory signals, by which individual members of the species convey vital information about food, mates, presence of enemies, etc. As individuals we use words in the same way. If I ask a stranger the way to the railroad station, I do so because I need the information. Neither I nor the stranger have any interest in each other—we might be two other people. Further, when I am using words as a code, the words are not mine—I already know in advance what I am going to say. As may be seen from Phrase-books for tourists in a foreign country, words used as a communication code are more or less exactly translateable into other tongues. . . .

Words and Persons

As persons, we are capable of Speech in the proper sense, i.e. of choosing to disclose ourselves to other persons as a gratuitous act. So far as we know, no other animal can do this. To grasp the nature of Speech, we must begin, not with third-person code statements like *The Cat is on the Mat,* but with Proper Names, The First and Second Personal Pronouns, words of summons and response, command and obedience. Proper Names are untranslateable, and one may say that when we truly speak, the meaning of what we say will be different for every listener. When I truly speak, I do not know what I am going to say until I have said it: I have to "find" the words. Poetry is Speech in its purest form.

The three kinds of Pluralities

Crowds. Societies. Communities.

What the Poet does

The subject matter of a poem is a crowd of recollected occasions of thought-feelings. This crowd the poet attempts to transform into a community by embodying it in a verbal society. He may work in two ways. Starting from an intuition of the kind of community he desires to call into being, he may then search for the kind of society (the poetic form) which will most justly embody it, or starting with a certain form, he may search for the kind of community which it can most truthfully embody. In practice, he generally does both simultaneously, modifying his conception of the community at the suggestions of the form and modifying the form in response to the needs of the community.

Permanence and Nowness

A successful poem exhibits two qualities. (a) Permanence. It continues to be relevant after its maker and the society of which he was a member have disappeared. (b) Nowness. It is possible for a literary historian to date it approximately.

Poems as verbal Utopias and their relation to the actual historical world.

What kind of poems can and/or should be written at the present time?

In Defense of the Tall Story

Page 378.

Auden responded to William Shawn's invitation to review this book on 26 April 1969: "*The Artist as Critic* sounds interesting, but I can't make a definite promise to write about it until I have read it" (New York Public Library). He wrote his review in early May, and asked Shawn on 30 May 1969 whether it had been received: "Some two weeks ago I sent you my piece on the Wilde book." The corrected typescript is in the New York Public Library.

FOREWORD TO *G. K. Chesterton: A Selection from His Non-Fictional Prose*

Page 384.

Auden's editor at Faber & Faber, Charles Monteith, wrote to Auden's British literary agent Graham Watson on 27 July 1967 that Faber had proposed this selection "some time ago" and that Auden wanted to edit it. Auden described his plans to Chesterton's bibliographer John Sullivan on 21 August 1967: "The selection I have in mind will be drawn mostly from his non-fictional prose, though, of course, I shall include some poems" (Berg Collection). No poems appeared in the book he eventually prepared.

Auden seems to have worked on the book during the summer of 1969; he sent "a Contents list of my Chesterton selection" to the poet Michael Ffinch on 24 July [1969] (letter formerly in the stock of the bookseller Michael Silverman). Faber & Faber published the book on 26 January 1970.

Auden seems to have given a copy of the typescript or proofs to the American semi-annual *Prose*, edited by the poet and publisher Coburn Britten from an address a few yards away from Auden's New York flat. The text in *Prose* is titled "G. K. Chesterton's Non-Fictional Prose".

In the book the foreword is preceded by a list headed "Sources" in three columns: the first column lists the publication dates of the fifteen books by Chesterton listed in the second column; the third column lists the essays taken from each book. For a few books, the third column is blank because Auden neglected to spell out the details. A few of the books are mistitled or misdated or both; Chesterton's collection *The Thing* (1929) is dated with a question mark, no one at Faber having taken five minutes to walk from Russell Square to the British Museum Library to find the date in the catalogue.

Most differences between the book and the *Prose* texts were evidently made by the magazine's editor to accommodate separate publication. In the first sentence the magazine has "work on a selection for a publisher". In the paragraph fragment that beings "Whatever Chesterton's reasons" (p. 385) the magazine has "my selection" for "this selection" and "I took" for "I have taken". Similarly, in the paragraph that begins "For various reasons" (p. 388) the magazine has "I selected" for "I have selected"; in the same paragraph, the book version has a comma after "and it is this", which the magazine (followed here) omits. In the paragraph that begins "At this task of clearing" (p. 387) the magazine has "demonstrated" for "demonstrates".

In the paragraph that begins "The disingenuousness" (p. 384) I have followed the magazine in printing "extraordinarily", not "extraordinary". In the paragraph fragment that begins "Chesterton's literary criticism" (p. 387) I have added a comma after "like Dickens", and in the paragraph that begins "On the subject" (p. 389) I have emended "truth faith" to "true faith" (a correction introduced in *Forewords and Afterwords*).

Auden included this essay in *Forewords and Afterwords* (1973); the text and title were taken from the magazine version and had no significant changes.

The "ineffable Bishop Barnes" (p. 389) was Ernest William Barnes, the scientifically minded low-church Bishop of Birmingham who tried to combine relativity and Christianity through a variation on Hegelian dialectic.

Translation

Page 390.

Auden wrote this essay late in 1969 as the introduction to an anthology of translations for use in American high schools and sold only to such schools, not through the book trade. It was published on 27 April 1970, by Scott, Foresman, of Glenville, Illinois, publisher of many similar textbooks. The first word of the book's title, *Man in Literature: Comparative World Studies in Translation*, soon became an embarrassment, and a 1976 reprint changed the title to *Of Time and Place: Comparative World Literature in Translation*; the contents were unchanged.

The title page of the book has "Introduction by W. H. Auden" but the essay itself is titled only "Translation".

Foreword to *I Am an Impure Thinker*

Page 395.

This book was published on 15 November 1970 (the copyright date was 5 October 1970), by Argo Books, Norwich, Vermont, a publisher that exists to publish books by and about Rosenstock-Huessy. The title page calls this piece an "Introduction by W. H. Auden" but the piece itself is headed "Foreword".

[A Tribute to Igor Stravinsky]

Page 396.

This was one of a group of brief tributes printed in the 48-page booklet included in a boxed set of six disks with reissued recordings, published by Columbia Records around August 1970. What Auden "said elsewhere about somebody else" was what he had written (perhaps suppressing his real feelings) about Maurice Bowra in 1967 (*Prose V*, p. 355).

Concerning the Unpredictable

Page 397.

Auden's corrected typescript is in the New York Public Library; an editorial notation has the date 18 December 1969, perhaps the date it was filed at the *New Yorker*. He added the final sentence in ink.

Auden included this review in *Forewords and Afterwords* (1973), omitting only the parenthetical identification of the publisher that in the *New Yorker* text followed the title of the book under review.

Translator's Note

Page 405.

Atlantica & Iceland Review was a glossy quarterly published in Reykjavík to promote Icelandic culture and tourism. "The Song of Rig" was "translated from the Icelandic with notes by Paul B. Taylor, W. H. Auden and Peter H. Salus"; it had not been included in their selection *The Elder Edda.*

A Russian Aesthete

Page 405.

Auden was friendly with George (Yuri) Ivask, the editor of the book, perhaps having met him through his friends V. S. Yanovsky and Isabella Levitin. Auden evidently proposed a review to the *New Yorker*, and he mailed the typescript to William Shawn on 14 April 1969 with a brief cover note: "Herewith my Leontiev piece." His note and his corrected typescript are in the New York Public Library. The text in the magazine rewrites the opening sentence in the typescript: "Since I know no Russian, all I can say about Mr George Reavey's translation of this selection from the writings of Konstantin Leontiev (*Against the Current*, Weybright & Talley) is that it reads easily and well."

Auden included this review in *Forewords and Afterwords* (1973); the text omits only the names of the two publishers that the magazine had printed in the first paragraph.

For a note on the never-identified Anglican bishop who defined othodoxy as reticence, see the notes to the introduction to *The Protestant Mystics* (*Prose V*, p. 524).

Foreword to *The Sorrows of Young Werther* [and] *Novella*

Page 412.

Goethe's novel and novella were translated by Auden's great friend Elizabeth Mayer in collaboration with Louise Bogan. In addition to writing the foreword, Auden translated the song in *Novella.*

Auden had told Jason Epstein that he might be willing to write a foreword, but was surprised when Random House asked him for it in May 1968. He wrote to Bernice Hoffman on 24 May 1968: "I didn't realize that a preface to *Werther* and *Novella* would be needed so soon, and I cannot write one unless I have a copy of the translation very soon" (Columbia University Library). Nothing happened at that time, but Random House asked again about the foreword in January 1970; Auden submitted it on 12 March 1970.

The book was published by Random House on 2 February 1971.

Auden included this foreword in *Forewords and Afterwords* (1973) under the title "*Werther* and *Novella*".

Foreword to *Selected Poems*, by Joseph Brodsky

Page 417.

George L. Kline began work on this volume in the Penguin Modern European Poets series in 1968. Kline was introduced to Auden by Arcadi Nebolsine, a professor of Slavic literature whom Auden met through the New York theological group The Third Hour. Kline asked Auden to write a foreword to the selection, and Auden agreed probably in May 1969. Auden wrote to Kline on 16 December 1969 that he would need to see Kline's introduction before writing his foreword. His pocket diary records that he wrote the foreword on 19 April 1970. A draft is in a notebook in the

Berg Collection, which also has a nonauthorial typescript apparently prepared by Kline.

The book was published by Penguin Books on 29 November 1973. An American edition, with Auden's text unchanged, was published in New York by Harper & Row in 1974.

The text here is that of the book. The text in the *New York Review of Books* (which was followed by Kline's introduction to the book) has some changes required by separate publication: in the second paragraph, at the end of the sentence that begins "Knowing no Russian", the magazine adds "about the poems of Joseph Brodsky." And in the third paragraph the magazine has "the translations" for "these translations." In the same paragraph, the magazine mistakenly has "rhymes and meters" for "rhythms and meters" (probably a compositor's eyeskip; Auden mentions rhymes later in the same sentence).

Lame Shadows

Page 419.

Auden seems to have met David Luke, a German don at Christ Church, during his years as Professor of Poetry at Oxford. Luke led the campaign to invite Auden to return to Christ Church in 1972.

Since the 1930s Auden had used the phrase "lame shadow" to refer to the ideal figure that a wounded ego seeks to find in persons different from himself, as Mann's Aschenbach does in Tadzio. Auden seems to have picked up the phrase from the psychologist John Layard, who may have adapted it from Jung's concept of the shadow. H. T. Lowe-Porter had been Mann's translator during his lifetime.

Auden included this review in *Forewords and Afterwords* (1973), omitting the final sentence.

Robert to the Rescue

Page 424.

The *New Yorker* text conforms to the magazine's house style by inserting after the title of the book "(edited by Elvan Kintner, and published at thirty dollars, by the Belknap Press of Harvard University Press)". Auden's typescript is not in the magazine's archives in the New York Public Library.

Portrait with a Wart or Two

Page 434.

Auden's quotations are, unusually, only slightly approximate.

Well Done, Sir Walter Scott!

Page 437.

Auden sent the corrected typescript of this review to William Shawn on 16 November 1970 with a cover letter: "Herewith a piece on the Scott biography." The title in the typescript lacks the exclamation mark (New York Public Library). The reference to the title and publisher in the first paragraph reads in the typescript, "(*Sir Walter Scott, The Great Unknown. Macmillan. Two volumes. 1279 pp.*)"

[A Review of *Hogarth on the High Life*]

Page 446.

Auden sent this piece to William Shawn on 28 November 1970, reporting in a cover letter: "Herewith all I can manage to do with one of my favorite authors. I've tried to explain why." (New York Public Library) The *New Yorker* printed the review as one of the unsigned items under the heading "Briefly Noted". A manuscript is in a notebook in the Berg Collection.

Foreword to *Plastic Sense*, by Malcolm de Chazal

Page 446.

The book was published in New York by Herder and Herder on 19 April 1971. The *New York Review of Books* text introduces paragraph breaks (followed here) before "In this sense, Chazal is a 'nature' poet" and "Anybody, however", and minor editorial changes (Toqueville for de Tocqueville). The magazine also adds a footnote to the title of the book in the first paragraph: "Originally published in Paris in 1948. A translation by Irving Weiss will be published this spring by Herder and Herder." A corrected typescript of Auden's foreword, almost identical to the printed text, is in the Berg Collection.

The translator was a friend of Auden in Ischia and later in New York.

Foreword to *Austria: People and Landscape*, by Stella Musulin

Page 450.

Stella Musulin was an English journalist of Welsh ancestry who had married an Austrian baron. She and Auden became close friends soon after he settled in Kirchstetten. A draft of Auden's foreword is in a notebook in the Berg Collection.

This book was published by Faber & Faber on 8 November 1971; an American edition, retitled *Austria and the Austrians*, was published in New York by Praeger in 1972.

Foreword to *Selected Poems*, by Gunnar Ekelöf

Page 453.

After completing their translation of Hammarskjöld's *Markings* Auden and Leif Sjöberg collaborated on translations of a number of twentieth-century Swedish poets; their translations of Ekelöf were the only ones collected in book form before Auden's death. This book was published by Penguin Books on 25 November 1971; an American edition was published in New York by Pantheon in 1972.

The Artist's Private Face

Page 456.

John Whitley was literary editor of the *Sunday Times* and presumably commissioned this review.

Thomas Mann was Auden's father-in-law through his marriage to Erika Mann. The point of the reference to Adalbert Stifter was that he was Austrian, not German.

W. H. Auden on George Orwell

Page 458.

Maurice Cowling was literary editor of the *Spectator*. This was Auden's first review for the magazine since 1961.

In the paragraph that begins "Today, reading", in the sentence that, as printed, reads, "Almost all [of the respondents to a questionnaire by Geoffrey Gorer] . . . identified themselves correctly", I have emended "correctly" to "incorrectly". In the book that Gorer based on his questionnaire, *Sex and Marriage in England Today* (1971), the table that lists respondents' self-identification of their social class and the actual status of their professions seems to suggest that perhaps two-thirds of them misidentified their class.

"Beachcomber" was the columnist J. B. Morton, who wrote for the *Daily Express*.

The Anomalous Creature

Page 462.

I have corrected what may have been Auden's typing error, "*Bon sense*".

The Mountain Allowed Them Pride

Page 465.

David Roberts, who was teaching at the time at Hampshire College, was acquainted with Auden. The title of his first book, *The Mountain of My Fear*, was a phrase from Auden's poem "Three Dreams"; Auden quoted from the book in *A Certain World*.

Auden included this essay (without its final one-sentence paragraph) in *Forewords and Afterwords* (1973) under the title "*Deborah*"; the design of the *New York Times Book Review* displayed the title of the book under review as if it were the title of the review, with a descriptive tagline (used in this edition as the title) printed in smaller type above it.

He Descended into Hell in Vain

Page 467.

The printed text has a slightly larger than normal break before the thrid from last paragraph ("M. Joffroy's attention"), which may reflect a break in Auden's typescript. In the first of Auden's three references to the author of the book he writes "M. Joffroy", in the other two "Mr Joffroy"; I have adopted the French form throughout.

Craftsman, Artist, Genius

Page 472.

Stravinsky died on 6 April 1971. This piece seems to have been commissioned by Terence Kilmartin, literary editor of the *Observer*, although no correspondence about it survives in the *Observer* archive. A typescript is in the Berg Collection.

Auden included this piece in *Forewords and Afterwords* (1973); the text was a carbon-copy typescript (mailed to me on 10 May 1972), based on, but substantially revised from, the original printed text, and titled "A Tribute" (p. 662).

Louise Bogan 1897–1970

Page 475.

One of the "Commemorative Tributes of the American Academy of Arts and Letters" printed by the American Academy of Arts and Letters in its *Proceedings* in the year following the death of a Fellow of the Academy.

The Megrims

Page 478.

Auden became friendly with Oliver Sacks in the late 1960s, possibly through their common friend Orlan Fox who had briefly lived in Auden's flat. Auden wrote the review in late March and early April 1971. Shortly after the review appeared he wrote to Sacks:

> In *The New York Review of Books*, dated June 3rd, appears my review of *Migraine.* I hope you will find it alright. The printer, not me, have [*sic*] made a Freudian slip in one quote: *beloved persons* appears as *beloved parents.*

Auden reprinted the review in *Forewords and Afterwords* (1973), with the printer's Freudian slip corrected.

In the second to last paragraph the magazine (followed by *Forewords and Afterwords*), after the italicized "*modus vivendi*", also italicizes "for him". The italicization of the last two words is at least plausible, but is uncharacteristic of Auden's style, and it seems likely that he mistakenly continued to underline the last two words after underlining the first.

The "Dr Gooddy" who wrote the foreword was Dr William Gooddy.

Too Much Mustard

Page 482.

Geoffrey Grigson was an early champion of Auden's work as editor of the magazine *New Verse* in the 1930s.

W. H. Auden on the Young Mr Goethe

Page 483.

Auden printed the poem separately as "To Goethe: A Complaint" in *Epistle to a Godson* (1973)

Foreword to *Sense & Inconsequence*

Page 486.

Angus Stewart, who also wrote novels and stories, was the son of the critic and novelist J. I. M. Stewart ("Michael Innes") who was Auden's contemporary at Christ Church and a don when Auden was Professor of Poetry. The book was published in London by the bookseller Michael deHartington on 10 August 1972.

Chester Kallman: A Voice of Importance

Page 487.

Auden submitted this review to the *New York Times Book Review*; its editor, John Leonard, told me he was embarrassed by it because the newspaper forbade him to assign books to reviewers who were close to the author, but he did not wish to offend Auden, so he passed it on to *Harper's Magazine*, which printed it. Kallman's book was published on 13 December 1972; Auden probably wrote his review around the same time. A first-draft typescript in the Berg Collection is titled "A Voice of Importance", the title he used when he reprinted the essay without change in *Forewords and Afterwords* (1973).

The three poets whom Auden thought poor human beings were probably Yeats, Brecht, and Frost.

The Diary of a Diary

Page 491.

"Ciddy" was Cyril Morgan-Brown, headmaster of St Edmund's; Miss Mona was his sister, Miss Rosa his daughter, who, as Rosamira Bulley, contributed to *W. H. Auden: A Tribute*, edited by Stephen Spender (1975). The "slightly improper poem" was "Uncle Henry", first printed in *Collected Shorter Poems 1927–1957* (1966) but written around 1931.

A Worcestershire Lad

Page 495.

Auden asked on 27 July 1971 to review this book for the *New Yorker*, and when the magazine agreed, asked on 18 August that it be airmailed to him in Austria. He mailed his typescript on 6 September 1971. The typescript title was "A Gloucestershire Lad", presumably corrected to Worcestershire by the magazine's fact checkers (New York Public Library). Some pages of an earlier typescript draft, also titled "A Gloucestershire Lad", are in the Berg Collection, together with a partial carbon copy of the *New Yorker* typescript.

In the paragraph that begins "In these letters" (p. 499) I have moved the parenthesis "(not the later)" after "early poems" instead of after "Bridges"; an editor who corrected Auden's typescript for the *New Yorker*, seeing that this was part of a list of poets, not of poems, had too hastily corrected Auden's typescript text, "the early poems of Robert Bridges (not the later)", to "Robert Bridges (not the later) for his early poems". In making this change, I follow the text collected in *Forewords and Afterwords* (1973).

Auden compared the three versions of Horace in "Translation" (p. 390). The British reviewer who corrected errors was Christopher Ricks, in the *Sunday Times*, 15 August 1971.

Down with the "Melting Pot"

Page 500.

This was Auden's contribution to a supplement published jointly by *The Times*, *Le Monde*, *La Stampa*, and *Die Welt*. In "Auden Europeanised" (*Encounter*, May 1972) Peter Sharratt discusses mistranslations and other variants among the three continental versions, and observes that only the English text, after "the officially Protestant countries like", omits "Prussia and". Probably an editor refused to think of Prussia as a country; I have restored it here.

A Genius and a Gentleman

Page 503.

In the paragraph that begins "It is clear" (p. 505) I do not know why "erudite" is italicized but have let the italicization stand.

Auden included this review in *Forewords and Afterwords* (1973) with no significant changes.

Telling It the Way It Was

Page 506.

Auden wrote to Terence Kilmartin, literary editor of the *Observer*, 19 December 1971 (*Observer* Archives):

> Peter Heyworth tells me that you have been wondering if I would do occasional reviewing for *The Observer*.
>
> I should love to. I have two rules. (1) I won't review contemporary poetry. (2) I won't review a book unless I basically like it.

In the paragraph fragment after the first set-off quotation I have removed the newspaper's italicization of "cliché".

Auden sent me a cutting of this review, asking, in reference to *Forewords and Afterwords*, "Do you think this might go along with the *Pope* piece." Rightly or wrongly, I decided against including it.

I'll Be Seeing You Again, I Hope

Page 509.

Auden's impending return to Oxford was first reported in the *New York Times*, 7 February 1972; the paper seems to have commissioned this piece a short time later. Letters about the crossword clue appeared on 5 and 11 April 1972, one puzzled by it, the other explaining it. (For Auden's explanation, see "President's Address", *Prose V*, p. 132.)

A Poet of the Actual

Page 510.

Auden's corrected typescript was dated by the *New Yorker* 8 March 1972, presumably the date it was received (New York Public Library).

Auden had reviewed Pope-Hennessy's *Queen Mary* in 1960 (*Prose IV*, p. 266). (His surname was hyphenated in that book, though not in his biography of Trollope.) Auden's haiku is quoted from the "Postscript" to "The Cave of Nakedness".

This review appears in *Forewords and Afterwords* (1973) with no significant changes.

Doing Oneself In

Page 514.

Auden's quotations are approximate, for example, neglecting to italicize "had" in the first sentence of the final quotation.

Wilson's Sabine Farm

Page 518.

Auden's only contribution to *Books & Bookmen*, a British monthly for a literate popular audience, edited by Frank Granville Barker. The magazine commissioned reviews from well-known writers; Auden's name was printed in especially large type on the cover.

Some of Auden's punctuation reflects the rhythms of speech, not writing; I have not tried to correct it. However, in the paragraph that begins "In 1915" (p. 520) I have reduced his capitalization of Twenty and Eight and have emended "that is, say," to "that is to say,".

To an Old Friend

Page 523.

Cecil Day-Lewis died on 22 May 1972. The newspaper printed this piece under a relatively small-type heading, "Cecil Day-Lewis's distinguished contemporary W. H. Auden contributes a salute" followed by the larger-type title "To an Old Friend".

Introduction to *The Spirit of Man*

Page 526.

This facsimile edition of Bridges's 1916 anthology was published by Longman on 4 December 1972, although dated 1973 on the copyright page. A corrected carbon-copy typescript of Auden's introduction is in the Berg Collection; the printed text is slightly revised from the typescript. I have made minor adjustments to punctuation.

The Poet of No More

Page 528.

This review was probably commissioned by the editor of the *Listener*, Karl Miller.

A Saint-Simon of Our Time

Page 531.

The break before "For someone" (p. 533) may be Auden's, or it may be one of the many breaks (ignored in this edition) that the *New York Review of Books* introduces in order to break up the visual appearance of a page. In this instance, it seems plausible to retain it. The magazine has a footnote after "Otto Friedrich's *Before the Deluge*": "Harper and Row, 1972."

In the set-off quotation that begins "Radek made" Facta is Luigi Facta, the Italian prime minister.

Other People's Babies

Page 536.

Auden abridges his quotations from the book. "Lady Hillingham" never existed, and the quotation attributed to her by Gathorne-Hardy seems to have existed mostly in oral tradition, perhaps originally as a joke.

An Odd Couple

Page 538.

Auden wrote to William Shawn at the *New Yorker* on 12 May 1972: "A month or two ago a volume of memoirs by a Victorian eccentric called Munby appeared in England which, from the reviews, sounded fascinating. If and when it is published in the U.S., could I have it to review for The New Yorker?" Apparently before he got a reply, he wrote again to Shawn on 8 July 1972: "I find that I seem to have promised to do it for The New York Review of Books, who have sent me a copy, so feel in duty bound to cry off. I'm very sorry." An incomplete carbon-copy typescript is in the Berg Collection; the magazine added the first two paragraph breaks.

A Kind of Poetic Justice

Page 544.

Auden's quotation from Quiller-Couch adds "so" before "often".

Evangelist of the Life Force

Page 546.

The title of Auden's typescript has a hyphen in "Life-Force". The magazine noted the date 12 September 1972, presumably the date it was received. In the typescript, the publishing details are listed beneath Auden's title and the sentence that follows "take a rest?" begins: "These letters, superbly edited". The magazine's text inserts the publication details after the title of the book.

Auden wrote about Shaw "fifteen years ago" in "Crying Spoils the Appearance" (*Prose IV*, p. 95).

Happy Birthday, Dorothy Day

Page 551.

Auden's poem was "First Things First". In 1956 he contributed $250 to the Catholic Worker movement, when its shelter had been fined for violations of the fire code. (The $250 gift was reported in the press; he seems also to have made a larger gift with no publicity.)

Marianne Moore 1887–1972

Page 556.

One of the 1972 "Commemorative Tributes of the American Academy of Arts and Letters", published in its *Proceedings*. Auden seems mistakenly to have expected it to be read aloud for him at the annual ceremonial of the Academy while he was in Europe; thus his reference to "this occasion". His quotations are approximate. Auden's own poem was "A Mosaic for Marianne Moore".

Preface to *Selected Songs of Thomas Campion*

Page 559.

This book was conceived by the publisher David R. Godine, in Boston, who commissioned an introduction from Auden. Godine expected a historical and critical account, not the technical analysis that Auden provided (and which Godine later said he could not understand), so he commissioned John Hollander to provide an additional, separate introduction. A draft (in a notebook) and a photocopy of a non-authorial typescript (with queries from an unknown editor and Auden's handwritten replies) are in the Berg Collection. In the penultimate sentence I have restored the final "do", wrongly omitted by the editor.

After many delays in production, the book was published on 15 September 1973, but with a printed date of 1972.

In the opening paragraph I have removed the italicization of "Sapphics". In the first of the metrical examples ("In Myrtle Arbours") I have emended the printed text by omitting the vergules printed (apparently mistakenly) after the last word in the first, fifth, and sixth lines.

Introduction to *George Herbert*

Page 562.

This was a volume in Penguin's "Poet to Poet" series that also included Crabbe edited by C. Day Lewis, Tennyson edited by Kingsley Amis, and others. Auden seems to have contracted to edit this book around the autumn of 1971. A draft of his introduction is in a notebook in the Berg Collection. Random House wanted to publish the book in the United States, but Penguin had world rights, and published it on 22 February 1973.

Introduction to *A Choice of Dryden's Verse*

Page 567.

This was one of a long series of selections of individual poets published by Faber & Faber; Auden had earlier edited *A Choice of de la Mare's Verse* (*Prose IV*, p. 396). This volume was published on 21 May 1973. A photocopy of a corrected carbon-copy typescript of the introduction is in the Berg Collection; I have followed the typescript in restoring some paragraphing and italicization.

In a list of contents for *Forewords and Afterwords* (1973) that Auden sent to me on 8 April 1973, he listed (after "Shakespeare's Sonnets") "John Dryden (if I get the text from Faber's on time)". The essay did not arrive in time, and was not included in the finished book.

Foreword to *Goldsworthy Lowes Dickinson*, by E. M. Forster

Page 571.

This edition was part of the Abinger Edition of E. M. Forster, edited by Oliver Stallybrass. It was published by Edward Arnold, in London, on 2 August 1973.

Auden reviewed the first edition of this book in 1934 and wrote a retrospective piece about it in 1938 (*Prose I*, pp. 80 and 460).

How Can I Tell What I Think Till I See What I Say?

Page 575.

New Movements in the Study and Teaching of English was one of a series of books that included similar titles on geography and history. The editor, Nicholas Bagnall, was education correspondent of the *Sunday Telegraph*. The book was published in London by Temple Smith on 18 October 1973.

The Gift of Wonder

Page 579.

Auden's essay on Chesterton's poems was one of seven essays in a section of this collection titled "The Achievement"; the other sections were "The Man" and "The Relevance". The editor, John Sullivan, was a schoolmaster and inspector of schools who had compiled bibliographies of Chesterton.

Auden agreed to write the essay in a letter to Sullivan, 24 August 1972. On 25 November 1972, he sent the typescript with a cover letter: "Herewith my Chesterton piece. A bit on the short side, I fear, but I have tried to let the old boy speak for himself". Auden's letters to Sullivan and his corrected typescript of the essay are in the Berg Collection. I have corrected some paragraphing to match the typescript.

The book was published in London by Paul Elek on 25 April 1974; an American edition was released by Barnes & Noble later the same year. I have slightly regularized italicization.

Renderings

Page 585.

Auden had contributed a few poems in recent years to the *New Statesman* and the magazine had invited him to write book reviews, but on subjects on which he had nothing to say or was too busy to write about; this was his first prose contribution since 1958. It was probably commissioned by the magazine's literary editor, John Gross. Auden's quotations are slightly approximate.

An Odd Ball

Page 588.

Auden evidently persuaded the *New Yorker* to commission this piece, but the magazine never printed it, though perhaps it might have done so had Auden lived. He recorded in his pocket diary that he finished it on 13 February 1973. Auden's typescript and a more legible secretarial copy are in the magazine's archives in the New York Public Library; the secretarial copy is marked with the date 27 February 1973, perhaps the date it was typed. The text here is edited from Auden's original typescript. Before dropping the piece, the magazine made some editorial changes in the secretarial copy, which I have not followed.

George L. Kline, to whom I gave a copy of the typescript, edited it for posthumous publication in *Russian Review* (October 1983). Kline noted a few errors: in the third paragraph, Chaadayev did not meet Herzen in western Europe, and the quotation from Herzen at the end of the same paragraph was published after Chaadayev's death, not while he was abroad. In the paragraph that begins "He was, however" (p. 590) "Diplomatic Service" seems to be a slip for "civil service".

Auden's quotations vary slightly from the originals.

Veni, Vici, VD

Page 594.

See also the notes on Auden's foreword to Yanovsky's *No Man's Time* (*Prose V*, p. 551).

Larkin's Choice

Page 598.

"*Dura virum nutrix*" (stern nurse of men) was the motto of Sedbergh School and part of Auden's private mythology since he first heard it from his college friend Gabriel Carritt. A carbon-copy typescript of this review, in the Berg Collection, is titled "A Verse Panorama". The newspaper increased Auden's paragraphing, but the two-sentence paragraph that begins "But this is" seems to be authorial; it begins a new page of the typescript and is indented, and the preceding sentence does not fill out the last line on the preceding page.

In the paragraph that begins "I don't suppose" Auden muddled the logic that seems to require, in place of a title that begins *The Oxford Book*, something like *The Harvard* or *Yale Book.*

Rhyme and Reason

Page 600.

A carbon-copy typescript in the Berg Collection is titled "Necessary Instruction and Gratuitous Amusement". The typescript lacks the quotation from William Brighty Rands and the preceding "For example" and the following "And"; these may have been added on a lost added page, but they conceivably were added by an editor.

I have regularized Auden's erratic italicization of titles and have followed the typescript in italicizing "fairy".

Between Crossfires

Page 602.

Auden's typescript was dated by the *New Yorker* 14 December 1972, presumably the date it was received. The typescript is titled "Between Cross Fires" and the opening phrase reads, "This long and magnificently researched book (*Hammarskjöld*, by Brian Urquhart. Knopf. 597 pp.) is not", etc. (New York Public Library). Auden's typescript refers to "World War I" and "World War II", which the magazine, following its style sheet, altered to "the First" and "the Second World War".

Auden met Chou En-Lai in 1938, Teddy Kollek in 1970 (possibly earlier).

Indestructible

Page 609.

Auden replied on 17 February 1973 to a request from John Gross, sometime before the book was published, "Yes, I should like to do Peter Heyworth's book" (Sussex University Library). Auden sent his review on 16 April 1973. Peter Heyworth was Auden's friend and the dedicatee of *City without Walls* (1969).

A carbon-copy typescript is in the Berg Collection, titled "An Act of Homage and a Labour of Love". In the paragraph that begins "Much as he dislikes" the newspaper rewrote a few sentences that read in the typescript:

> [. . .] fault may be his. I have no space to discuss his experiences with the many [. . .] as they are. I can only mention two interesting facts. He says that the greatest success he ever had in his life as conducting *Lohengrin* in Hamburg in 1910, and that, in the early post-revolution years in Russia, there was no party line on music. In the last [. . .]

And after the sentence about Klemperer's own musical writings, the typescript has: "I myself, I am sorry to say, have never heard a note of them."

Progress Is the Mother of Problems

Page 611.

An incomplete carbon-copy typescript is in the Berg Collection; at the top, the title is in capitals, Chesterton's name in upper and lower case. The magazine, following its house style, severely reduced Auden's capitalization of abstractions such as "Art", "Science", "Nowness", "Permanence", and others.

Auden had reviewed his old friend E. R. Dodds's *Pagan and Christian in an Age of Anxiety* in 1966 (*Prose V*, p. 202).

Praiseworthy

Page 618.

John Gross invited Auden on 11 May 1973 to write this review for a supplement on religious books.

Responses to the Near East

Page 620.

The *New Yorker* marked Auden's typescript with the date 5 April 1973, presumably the date it was received (New York Public Library). In the first sentence, the magazine inserted "on *Flaubert in Egypt: A Sensibility on Tour*". A carbon copy of the same typescript is in the Berg collection.

In the paragraph that begins "But such contretemps" (p. 622) "squeezes" are impressions of inscriptions, made by squeezing wet paper into the surface; the magazine added quotation marks around the word.

Books Which Mean Much to Me

Page 624.

Printed in the magazine's regular section "Reading". Auden had been a occasional contributor to *Mademoiselle* since 1944.

Auden mistitles Henry Mayhew's *London Labour and the London Poor*, which he had reviewed in 1968 (*Prose V*, p. 374). I have corrected "Collet" to "Collett". Signet Books was an American paperback series.

A Russian with Common Sense

Page 626.

Auden's typescript was dated by the *New Yorker* 12 March 1973, presumably the date it was received (New York Public Library). In the typescript the third sentence ends "the author of these letters", expanded by the magazine to "the author of what Avrahm", etc. The passage that appears in the closing paragraph of the printed text, from "I myself disapprove" through "I had read them all", occurs in similar form in the typescript at the end of the paragraph that begins "As I read them" (p. 629), and refers to the book as "a complete edition" (not, as in the printed text, "what I at first assumed to be a complete edition". The final paragraph in the typescript reports, "I find I was wrong, by the way, in thinking he has translated the Complete Letters, so that he was not obliged to print all of the letters to Olga Knipper." The magazine rearranged this so that Auden seemed to be making an erroneous statement about a complete edition on one page, followed by his correct second thoughts on a later page.

"I have a ferocious bee in my bonnet"

Page 632.

When Auden's friend Leo Lerman became features editor at *Vogue*, he asked Auden to write a piece for a series titled "On My Mind". Auden replied on 4 June 1973: "I could do a piece about Liturgical Reform, to which I am fanatically opposed, but it doesn't seem quite a suitable subject for Vogue." Lerman replied that such a piece would be of interest to some readers and asked Auden to write it. Auden sent the piece on 5 July 1973 [cover letter misdated 5 June], asking: "Would the enclosed be of any interest to your *On My Mind* series?" (Columbia University Library).

An Odd Ball in an Odd Country at an Odd Time

Page 633.

Gerald Brenan's *The Literature of the Spanish People* (1951) had been Auden's source for verse forms and other models that he used in his poems. Auden's quotations are slightly approximate.

Where Are the Arts Going?

Page 638.

Auden's untitled contribution to the last part of a ten-week series "The Arts Today", published in the weekly color magazine of the *Observer*. An editorial note says: "This was among the last pieces written by the poet before his death in September." Typescripts of various versions of this piece are in the Berg Collection, with the title "Whither the Arts? I've No Idea". Auden's response to the question in the title was one of three; the others were by A. Alvarez and Martin Esslin.

Death at Random

Page 639.

Auden's last review for the *New York Review of Books*, apparently held over until more than a year after his death for use in a memorial section of the paper that also included two of his poems, together with reviews, essays, and poems about him.

Some Reflections on the Arts

Page 644.

This apparently unpublished piece seems to have been written in the summer of 1973. It survives as a carbon-copy typescript (Berg Collection) on A4-size paper; the lost top copy was presumably sent to the magazine editor or book editor who had commissioned it.

The text in this edition is very lightly edited from Auden's typescript. In the section that begins "By all means" Auden typed "raportage", which I have interpreted as "rapportage", not "reportage".

In the section that begins "I am thinking" the carbon copy evidently fails to reflect Auden's revisions. After "it may be different", an unfinished sentence begins "Neither under the Tsars nor the Communists has"; only the top half of this line is visible, as the carbon paper seems to have been folded or misaligned. Beneath this half-visible line is a narrow blank line that could perhaps have been the result of Auden's removing the top copy (with the carbon paper and carbon copy) from the typewriter, making a revision on the top copy in ink, then returning the pages to the typewriter. Beneath this narrow blank space, a new line has, at the left, some blank spaces, then the words "writer may have". The least obtrusive and least unlikely emendation that I can think of is to remove the unfinished sentence and add "[There the]" where the carbon copy has blank spaces and where Auden presumably wrote in some words on the top copy.

An Odd Fish

Page 645.

This piece is unfinished and hitherto unpublished. Auden was probably working on it shortly before he died on 29 September 1973. It could have been written for either the *New York Review of Books* or the *New Yorker*, but I have found no correspondence about it in the *New Yorker* archives, so the *New York Review* seems more likely.

The text has been lightly edited for this edition from a typescript in the Berg Collection. In the paragraph that begins "It's a great relief" I have restored "turned", which Auden mistyped and deleted but neglected to restore, and I have replaced "literature and the Middle Ages" with "literature of the Middle Ages". In the penulitmate paragraph I have added "what" after "Just".

Auden was mistaken about the publication of Hölderlin's poems; the first collection appeared in 1826.

Forewords and Afterwords

The phrase on the title page, "Selected by Edward Mendelson", is not entirely accurate, but Auden insisted on it. The story of this book is as follows.

In the late 1960s Auden began to tell friends that he wanted to compile a book of essays under this title but that he had forgotten what he had written; he said the same thing to his hosts at lectures and readings in colleges and universities. Perhaps around 1970, in a notebook now in the Berg Collection, he listed essays that he remembered, under the headings "Introductions" and "Reviews". On a visit to Yale in January 1971 he told me about his intentions for the book. I told him that I had copies of (I hoped) all his essays and reviews; he spent a few hours looking through them and said he would need to return for a longer stay.

Before he could do so, he made plans to return to Oxford and, at a farewell party given for him by Random House on 21 February 1972, told me that because he could not make a return visit to New Haven, he wanted to send me a list of the essays that he hoped to include, and asked if I could hire a graduate student to make copies for him. I agreed to this, but wrote him the next day to say that I hoped he could visit New Haven to look over my copies of his work, because he had written essays for which I was grateful that he might have forgotten. He replied on 24 February:

> I've come to the conclusion that you and not I should select my *Forewords and afterwords.* I enclose a list of some I remember. If you think there are some others worth reprinting, could you be a dear and pick them. I shall want three xeroxes, one for Random House, one for Fabers and one for myself. I enclose a cheque for $150.

His list, like the one in his notebook, was divided into "Reviews" and "Forewords", most of them written in the previous decade. I added some older essays and prepared a revised list that I brought to him in New York. He removed a few of my suggestions and accepted others. He asked why I had not included his introduction to *Romeo and Juliet* (*Prose IV*), but smiled broadly when I merely shook my head no (the essay struck me as less successful than his other essays on Shakespeare; evidently he was pleased that I had exercised judgement). He made further changes to the contents in letters to me from New York and Kirchstetten. On 31 March 1972 he added his introduction to *The Art of Eating.* On 3 April 1972, after receiving the set of photocopies that I sent him, he wrote (I have regularized his formatting):

> Going through them, I have decided to omit the following.
>
> *A Literary Transference* [on Thomas Hardy; *Prose II,* p. 42]. It opens with an awful lie, namely, that I was unhappy at school, which I wasn't. I can't understand how I could have written it.
>
> *A Knight of the Infinite* [on Gerard Manley Hopkins; *Prose II,* p. 218].
>
> *Through the Collar-bone of a Hare* [on George Santayana; *Prose III,* p. 364]. This violates my principle, as an occasional reviewer, of never reviewing a book which I don't basically like.

Some Notes on D. H. Lawrence [*Prose II*, p. 317]. I used this material in my Oxford lecture on D.H.L.

The Magician from Mississipi [on William Faulkner; *Prose IV*, p. 247].

Thinking what we are doing [on Hannah Arendt; *Prose IV*, p. 184]. This is just a Reader's Digest sort of summary of what H. A. says.

Query. In the xerox of *Calm Even in the Catastrophe*, the last page seems to be missing. Is this a sign from heaven that I should omit it?

Am making some revisions and will send you them as soon as they are all done.

On 8 April 1972 he sent a final list of contents together with a list of corrections and revisions (headed "Corrigenda" and described in the notes to the separate essays below). His contents list included (following "Shakespeare's Sonnets") "John Dryden (if I get the text from Faber's on time)"; this referred to his introduction to *A Choice of Dryden's Verse* (p. 567), not eventually included in *Forewords and Afterwords*. His list also included (following "Lewis Carroll"), "(Calm Even in the Catastrophe?)", which was in fact included, and "An Example (Stravinsky Obit. *The Observer*. April 11th, 1971", which appeared in the volume as "A Tribute", its text based on a typescript that he sent to me on 10 May 1972. All the other titles in the volume that differ from the titles of earlier versions of the same essays are the titles that Auden used in his list. On 28 April 1972 he asked me for a copy of his review of Chester Kallman's *A Voice of Importance*, saying he wanted to include it after his review of Lincoln Kirstein's poems.

On 15 May 1972 he wrote that he had decided to include "Calm Even in the Catastrophe" but with a revision described in the notes below.

With the exception of "A Tribute", the book was set from photocopies that I prepared of earlier texts, with Auden's corrections marked on the copies. Copyeditors and proofreaders at Random House regularized punctuation, italicization, and spelling (including the mistaken correction of "unchristian" to "un-Christian"); I have noted the more significant changes in the notes below.

Random House published the book on 19 March 1973; Faber & Faber published an identical British edition on 2 July 1973. An American paperback reprint published by Vintage Books in 1974 had some minor corrections; further corrections appeared in a second Vintage Books reprint in 1989. Faber & Faber published a British paperback edition in 1979.

The book ends with a "Note on the Text" in which I listed the original appearances of the essays (as described below). The note opens with this paragraph:

> For the present edition the author has made some minor corrections and changes. Otherwise the essays are reprinted from the original appearances listed below. The compiler is grateful to the author for advice in preparing the selection.

The final sentence was an attempt to suggest that Auden had had more to do with choosing the contents than the title page indicated.

The Greeks and Us

Page 657.

The introduction to *The Portable Greek Reader* (1948), including corrections that first appeared in a 1955 paperback edition. Auden had always planned to open *Forewords and Afterwords* with this essay, and he chose its new title. In the *Forewords and Afterwords* text, in Part IV of the essay, in the paragraph that begins "Even those of us" (*Prose II*, p. 364), a proofreader correctly changed "think of ourselves" to "think ourselves", but a compositor's eyeskip in the same paragraph caused the omission of "like the Pantheist god . . . or voluntarily" in the sentence that begins: "We may or may not believe that god exists, but the only kind of god in which we can think of believing is a god who suffers, either involuntarily like the Pantheist god because he is emergent, or voluntarily like the Christian god because he loves his creatures and suffers with them;". In the paragraph that begins "The secondary sins" (*Prose II*, p. 368) a proofreader moved a comma from after "initial sin" to after "its effects". For the earlier history of the text, see *Prose II*, p. 549.

Augustus to Augustine

Page 657.

A review of *Christianity and Classical Culture*, by Charles Norris Cochrane; from *New Republic*, 25 September 1944. For the earlier history of the text, see *Prose II*, p. 533.

Heresies

Page 657.

A review of *Pagan and Christian in an Age of Anxiety*, by E. R. Dodds; from *New York Review of Books*, 17 February 1966. The "Corrigenda" that Auden sent to me in 1972 specified that the sentence should be omitted which said that Auden would not spoil the reader's pleasure by quoting from Dodds' account of Perpetua's dreams. In preparing the text, I moved the title and author of the book to a footnote after "Alas, as these lectures" (*Prose V*, p. 202). For the earlier history of the text, see *Prose V*, p. 542.

The Protestant Mystics

Page 657.

Auden's introduction to the anthology with this title, edited by Anne Fremantle (1964). In preparing *Forewords and Afterwords*, I replaced the title "Introduction" with "The Protestant Mystics", a title that Auden accepted. A proofreader made minor changes to punctuation and italicization; in the paragraph that begins "How different" (*Prose V*, p. 56), in order to make room to restore a word accidentally omitted by the compositor in the first proofs, a proofreader deleted "that" after "a believing Christian". For the earlier history of the text, see *Prose V*, p. 523.

Greatness Finding Itself

Page 657.

A review of *Young Man Luther*, by Erik Erikson; from *Mid-Century*, June 1960. A proofreader made some unauthorized changes in *Forewords and Afterwords*: in the second paragraph (*Prose IV*, p. 283), the proofreader changed "their neurosis" to "their neuroses"; in the paragraph that begins "In the Identity crisis", in the phrase "Both the Identity and the Generativity crisis", the proofreader changed "crisis" to "crises";

and, in the paragraph that begins "Most modern books", the proofreader changed "because it is not" to "because he is not". For the earlier history of text, see *Prose IV*, p. 922.

Shakespeare's Sonnets

Page 657.

Auden's introduction to the Signet Classic edition of the *Sonnets* (1964). The "Corrigenda" that he sent to me in 1972 specifies two cuts to avoid repeating material in "The Protestant Mystics": in the paragraph fragment that begins "The beloved is always beautiful in the impersonal sense" (*Prose V*, p. 103) Auden cut everything from "It is unfortunate" through the end of the following paragraph ("of personal love."), and in the paragraph that begins "In the Vision of Eros" he cut the sentence that begins "The beloved is always beautiful in both". In preparing the book I replaced the title "Introduction" with "Shakespeare's Sonnets". For the earlier history of the text, see *Prose V*, p. 531.

A Civilized Voice

Page 658.

A review of *Alexander Pope: The Education of a Genius 1688-1728*, by Peter Quennell; from *New Yorker*, 22 February 1969. For the earlier history of the text, see p. 751.

Werther and *Novella*

Page 658.

Auden's foreword to the translation by Elizabeth Mayer and Louise Bogan of Goethe's *The Sorrows of Young Werther* and *Novella* (1971). In preparing the book, I replaced the title "Foreword" with "*Werther* and *Novella*". For the earlier history of the text, see p. 758.

Italian Journey

Page 658.

Auden's introduction to his translation (with Elizabeth Mayer) of Goethe's *Italian Journey* (1962), printed from the version printed in *Encounter*, November 1962, as "On Goethe: For a New Translation". In preparing the book, I replaced the title with "Italian Journey" and, in the paragraph that begins "We have tried" (*Prose IV*, pp. 332), after "We" I added a footnote: "*Italienische Reise* was translated with Elizabeth Mayer." For the earlier history of the text, see *Prose IV*, p. 924.

In the "Corrigenda" that Auden sent to me in 1972 he again revised his already-revised account of Goethe's departure from Weimar: at the end of the paragraph that begins "The first crisis" (*Prose IV*, pp. 327–28), he replaced "His father suggested a trip to Italy, but he did not go. At the beginning of November he was in Heidelberg; the young Duke of Weimar sent his coach and invited Goethe to join him; without a moment's hesitation, Goethe jumped in and was whisked away" with: "His father suggested a trip to Italy and he was making plans to go. At the beginning of November he was in Heidelberg; the young Duke of Weimar sent his coach and invited Goethe to join him. A day or two later Goethe did so."

Mr G

Page 658.

A review of *Goethe: Conversations and Encounters*, edited by David Luke and Robert Pick; from *New York Review of Books*, 9 February 1967. In preparing *Forewords and Afterwords* I moved the title and author to a footnote keyed to "This excellent compilation" (*Prose V*, p. 336). For the earlier history of the text, see *Prose V*, p. 551.

Portrait of a Whig

Page 658.

Auden's introduction to *Selected Writings of Sidney Smith* (1956). In preparing *Forewords and Afterwords*, I replaced the title "Introduction" with the title that Auden had used for an earlier version of the introduction published in 1952. For the earlier history of the text, see *Prose IV*, p. 904.

Søren Kierkegaard

Page 658.

Auden's introduction to *Living Thoughts of Kierkegaard* (1952). In preparing *Forewords and Afterwords*, I replaced the 1952 title "Presenting Kierkegaard" with "Søren Kierkegaard". For the earlier history of the text, see *Prose III*, p. 735.

A Knight of Doleful Countenance

Page 658.

A review of Kierkegaard's *Journals and Papers*, Vol. 1; from *New Yorker*, 25 May 1968. In the "Corrigenda" that he sent to me in 1972 Auden added the subtitle, in parentheses, "(Second Thoughts on Kierkegaard)". For the earlier history of the text, see *Prose V*, p. 554.

Grimm and Andersen

Page 659.

Auden's introduction to *Tales of Grimm and Andersen* (1952), written in 1947. In preparing *Forewords and Afterwords*, I replaced the title "Introduction" with "Grimm and Andersen"; when I sent the text of this essay to Auden I had given it the title of its separate appearance in *New World Writing* in 1952, "Some Notes on Grimm and Andersen", but Auden used the shorter title in his typed list of contents. In the "Corrigenda" that he sent to me in 1972, in the paragraph that begins "The hero is in the third or inferior position" (*Prose II*, p. 393), after the parenthetical sentence "(The youngest son inherits least"), Auden added a footnote: "I now think I was mistaken. In many peasant communities, where early marriages are the rule, it is the youngest son who inherits the farm." For the earlier history of the text, see *Prose II*, p. 550.

Edgar Allan Poe

Page 659.

Auden's introduction to *Selected Prose and Poetry*, by Edgar Allan Poe (1950). For the earlier history of the text, see *Prose III*, p. 724, which notes that the 1956 second edition of the original volume, followed by me in the text of *Forewords and Afterwords*, includes changes that Auden marked in a friend's copy of the original edition. In preparing the text, I replaced the title "Introduction" with Poe's name.

Tennyson

Page 659.

Auden's introduction to *A Selection from the Poems of Alfred, Lord Tennyson* (1944). In the list of "Corrigenda" that he sent me in 1972, in the paragraph that begins "He had a large, loose-limbed body" (*Prose II*, p. 204), after the phrases, "he had the finest ear, perhaps, of any English poet; he was also undoubtedly the stupidest", Auden added a footnote: "T. S. Eliot pointed out to me that he could think of two or three English poets who were stupider, and I had to agree." In preparing the text, I replaced the title "Introduction" with the poet's name. For the earlier history of the text, see *Prose II*, p. 531.

A Very Inquisitive Old Party

Page 659.

A review of a reissue of *London Labour and the London Poor*, by Henry Mayhew; from *New Yorker*, 24 February 1968. In the "Corrigenda" that he sent to me in 1972 Auden omitted the closing paragraph of the review (*Prose V*, p. 382), which recommended the book despite its high price. In preparing the text, I omitted the publisher's name and price that the magazine had added in a parenthesis after "The new reprint" (*Prose V*, p. 374) For the earlier history of the text, see *Prose V*, p. 554.

The Greatest of the Monsters

Page 659.

A review of *Richard Wagner, The Man, His Mind, and His Music*, by Robert Gutman; from *New Yorker*, 4 January 1969. In preparing the text, I omitted the publisher's name and price that the magazine had inserted in a parenthesis after the title of the book and the name of the publisher of *Aspects of Wagner*, also in a parenthesis (*Prose V*, pp. 389, 393). In the third paragraph (*Prose V*, p. 390) a proofreader mistakenly corrected "common-or-garden, though" to "common or garden-variety, though", and in the quotation that follows, mistakenly changed "autograph orchestral score" to "autographed orchestral score". For the earlier history of the text, see *Prose V*, p. 558.

A Genius and a Gentleman

Page 659.

A review of *Letters of Giuseppe Verdi,* edited by Charles Osborne; from *New York Review of Books,* 9 March 1972. In preparing the text I removed the publication details from the heading of the essay. For the earlier history of the text, see p. 764.

A Poet of the Actual

Page 659.

A review of *Anthony Trollope,* by James Pope Hennessy; from *New Yorker,* 1 April 1972. In preparing the text I removed the parenthetical reference to the publisher that the magazine inserted after the author's name. For the earlier history of the text, see p. 765.

George Macdonald

Page 660.

Auden's introduction to *The Visionary Novels of George Macdonald* (1954). In preparing the text I replaced "Introduction" with the author's name. For the earlier history of the text, see *Prose III,* p. 763.

A Russian Aesthete

Page 660.

A review of *Against the Current,* by Konstantin Leontiev; from *New Yorker,* 4 April 1970. In preparing the text I removed the parenthetical listing of the publishers of the two books named in the first paragraph (p. 406). For the earlier history of the text, see p. 758.

Lewis Carroll

Page 660.

First published as "Today's 'Wonder-World' Needs Alice", *New York Times Magazine,* 1 July 1962. For convenience, I copied the text from a reprint in *Aspects of Alice,* edited by Robert Phelps (1971), but without the arbitrary breaks introduced by the newspaper in order to break up the page. In preparing the text I replaced the newspaper's title with Carroll's name. For the earlier history of the text, see *Prose IV,* p. 934.

Calm Even in the Catastrophe

Page 660.

A review of *The Complete Letters of Vincent Van Gogh*; from *Encounter,* April 1959. In the list of contents that Auden sent to me on 8 April 1972, this item is enclosed in parentheses and preceded by a question mark. On 15 May 1972 he wrote to me that he wanted to include the piece, omitting the first three paragraphs in the original review (*Prose IV,* p. 209), which merely described the book. For the earlier history of the text, see *Prose IV,* p. 918.

An Improbable Life

Page 660.

A review of *The Letters of Oscar Wilde*, edited by Rupert Hart-Davis; from *New Yorker*, 9 March 1963. For consistency with other essays in *Forewords and Afterwords* I omitted the name of the publisher in the third paragraph. For the earlier history of the text, see *Prose V*, p. 522.

A Worcestershire Lad

Page 660.

A review of *The Letters of A. E. Housman*, edited by Henry Maas; from *New Yorker*, 19 February 1972. In preparing the text, I omitted, following "edited by Mr Maas", "and published by the Harvard University Press" (p. 495). In the paragraph that begins "In these letters" (p. 499) a proof correction (apparently made by Auden) moved the parenthesis "(not the later)" after "early poems" instead of after "Bridges". For the earlier history of the text, see p. 763.

C. P. Cavafy

Page 660.

Auden's introduction to *The Complete Poems of Cavafy*, edited by Rae Dalven (1961). In preparing the text I replaced the title "Introduction" with the poet's name. For the earlier history of the text, see *Prose IV*, p. 922.

A Marriage of True Minds

Page 661.

A review of *The Correspondence between Richard Strauss and Hugo von Hofmannsthal*, published in America as *A Working Friendship*; from *TLS*, 10 November 1961, and *Mid-Century*, March 1962. In preparing *Forewords and Afterwords* I chose the *Mid-Century* version of this review solely because it was more legible in a photocopy than was the *TLS* version. At that time, I had not noticed that the *Mid-Century* version was shorter than the *TLS* version, or I would have used the *TLS* version instead; however, the *Mid-Century* version includes changes that may have been made by Auden, so the shorter text may, at least in part, more accurately reflect his latest intentions. For the differences between the two versions and other details of the earlier history of the text, see *Prose IV*, p. 926. In the "Corrigenda" that he sent to me in 1972 Auden cut the closing paragraph about the quality of the translation (*Prose IV*, p. 354).

The Poet of the Encirclement

Page 661.

A review of *A Choice of Kipling's Verse*, made by T. S. Eliot; from *New Republic*, 24 October 1943. For the earlier history of the text, including a note on an emendation that I made for *Forewords and Afterwords*, see *Prose II*, p. 529.

Un Homme d'Esprit

Page 661.

Auden's introduction to *Analects*, by Paul Valéry (1970), written in 1955. Auden's typescript was titled "L'Homme d'Esprit", and the text placed in *Hudson Review*, Autumn 1969, by the general editor of the Bollingen Edition of Valéry was titled "Valéry: L'Homme d'Esprit". The title in *Forewords and Afterwords*, with the indefinite article, derives from Auden's 1972 list of contents. For the earlier history of the text, see *Prose III*, p. 773.

One of the Family

Page 661.

A review of *Max*, by David Cecil; from *New Yorker*, 23 October 1965. In preparing the text I removed the names of the publishers of three books. For the earlier history of the text, see *Prose V*, p. 539.

Walter de la Mare

Page 661.

Auden's introduction to *A Choice of de la Mare's Verse* (1963). In preparing the text I replaced the title "Introduction" with the poet's name. For the earlier history of the text, see *Prose IV*, p. 931.

G. K. Chesterton's Non-Fictional Prose

Page 661.

Auden's introduction to *G. K. Chesterton: A Selection from His Non-Fictional Prose* (1970). For the earlier history of the text, see p. 756. For *Forewords and Afterwords* I copied the text from the version in *Prose*, Autumn 1970, and used its title.

Lame Shadows

Page 661.

A review of *Tonio Kröger and Other Stories*, by Thomas Mann; from *New York Review of Books*, 3 September 1970. In the list of "Corrigenda" that he sent to me in 1972 Auden cut the final sentence, "What a pleasant surprise" (p. 351). For the earlier history of the text, see p. 759.

A Consciousness of Reality

Page 662.

A review of *A Writer's Diary*, by Virginia Woolf; from *New Yorker*, 6 March 1954. In preparing the text, I omitted the magazine's parenthetical identification of the publisher. For the earlier history of the text, see *Prose III*, p. 759.

Private Poet

Page 662.

A review of *Rhymes of a Pfc,* by Lincoln Kirstein; from *New York Review of Books,* 5 November 1964. For the earlier history of the text, see *Prose V,* p. 533.

A Voice of Importance

Page 662.

A review of *The Sense of Occasion,* by Chester Kallman; from *Harper's Magazine,* March 1972. Auden chose the title, reduced from the magazine's "Chester Kallman: A Voice of Importance." For the earlier history of the text, see p. 763.

A Tribute

Page 662.

First published as "Craftsman, Artist, Genius", *Observer,* 11 April 1971. Auden typed a revised version of the text, which he sent to me on 10 May 1972. The text in this edition is newly edited from that typescript, and corrects a typing error I made in 1972 when I omitted, from the paragraph that begins "When I contemplate" (p. 664), the words "or poetry". For the *Observer* text, see p. 472, and the textual notes, p. 762.

Markings

Page 665.

Auden's introduction to *Markings,* by Dag Hammaskjöld (1964), omitting the "Postscript" in the original text (*Prose V,* p. 91). In preparing the text, I replaced the title "Introduction" with the title of the book and omitted Auden's initials from the only footnote. For the earlier history of the text, see *Prose V,* p. 527.

Papa Was a Wise Old Sly-Boots

Page 665.

A review of *My Father and Myself,* by J. R. Ackerley; from *New York Review of Books,* 27 March 1969. In the list of "Corrigenda" that he sent to me in 1972 Auden cut "If I may be forgiven for quoting myself" and his haiku (p. 362). I moved the title and author of the book from the head of the review to a footnote after "this book" in the opening sentence (p. 360). For the earlier history of the text, see p. 752.

The Justice of Dame Kind

Page 665.

A review of *The Senses of Animals and Men,* by Loris J. and Margery Milne; from *Mid-Century,* Midsummer 1962. For the earlier history of the text, see *Prose IV,* p. 934.

Concerning the Unpredictable

Page 665.

A review of *The Unexpected Universe*, by Loren Eiseley; from *New Yorker*, 21 February 1970. In the magazine text, in the first paragraph (p. 397), the magazine had "his latest book (*The Unexpected Universe*, Harcourt, Brace & World)"; I removed the parentheses and omitted the name of the publisher. For the earlier history of the text, see p. 757.

The Megrims

Page 665.

A review of *Migraine*, by Oliver Sacks; from *New York Review of Books*, 3 June 1971. In preparing the text, I moved the title and author of the book to a footnote after "writing this book" (p. 478). In correcting proofs, in the paragraph that begins "The first part" (p. 479), I clarified the punctuation to read: "types of migraine: common migraine, popularly called 'a sick headache'; classical [. . .] visual field; and". For the earlier history of the text, including Auden's correction of a printer's error in the original text (also corrected in the "Corrigenda" that he sent to me in 1972), see p. 762.

Deborah

Page 666.

A review of *Deborah*, by David Roberts; from *New York Times Book Review*, 7 February 1971. In his 1972 "Corrigenda" Auden cut the last sentence ("A most fascinating book."). For the earlier history of the text, see p. 761.

The Kitchen of Life

Page 666.

Auden's introduction to the British edition of *The Art of Eating*, by M. F. K. Fisher (1963). In preparing the text I replaced the title "Introduction" with the title of Auden's review of the American edition in *Griffin*, June 1958. In the list of "Corrigenda" that he sent to me in 1972 Auden revised the second paragraph (*Prose V*, p. 37) by changing "She chose" to "He chose," perhaps in order to clarify that it was not Mrs Fisher who had made the choice he was writing about. For the earlier history of the text, see *Prose V*, p. 522.

As It Seemed to Us

Page 666.

A review of *A Little Learning*, by Evelyn Waugh, and *Beginning Again*, by Leonard Woolf; from *New Yorker*, 3 April 1965. In the list of "Corrigenda" that he sent to me in 1972 Auden cut a paragraph about prayer that begins "Though few persons" (*Prose V*, p. 157); he had used the same material in *A Certain World* (p. 235). In preparing the text I cut the magazine's parenthetical identifications of the publishers of the two books and, in the paragraph that begins "I said earlier" (*Prose V*, p. 151), the parenthetical "(Trades Union Congress)" after the initials "T.U.C.". In the paragraph that begins "Ethnically" (*Prose V*, p. 137), Auden, while correcting proof, changed "pure limey" to "pure Nordic". For the earlier history of the text, see *Prose V*, p. 537.

INDEX OF TITLES AND BOOKS REVIEWED

This index includes titles of each of the works printed or described in this edition and the titles and authors of the books Auden reviewed.

Titles of Auden's works that were originally published (or intended to be published) as separate books or pamphlets are printed in LARGE AND SMALL CAPITALS. Titles of books and other works that Auden edited or reviewed are in *italics.* Titles of Auden's essays and reviews are all printed in roman type, as are the names of authors of books reviewed, the names of persons who were the subjects of his essays, and the names of his coauthors.